A Practical Guide to the

UK Listing Regime

HERBERT
SMITH
FREEHILLS

London
Stock Exchange

A Practical Guide to the UK Listing Regime

Herbert Smith Freehills LLP

Fourth edition

icsa
The Governance
Institute

Published by ICSA Publishing Limited
Saffron House
6–10 Kirby Street
London EC1N 8TS

© ICSA Publishing Ltd

First edition published 2008
This edition published 2017

All rights reserved. No part of this publication may be reproduced, stored in a retrieval system, or transmitted, in any form, or by any means, electronic, mechanical, photocopying, recording or otherwise, without prior permission, in writing, from the publisher.

The right of Herbert Smith Freehills LLP to be identified as author of this work has been asserted in accordance with sections 77 and 78 of the Copyright, Designs and Patents Act 1988.

The Publishers thank the FCA for permission to reproduce extracts of FCA material in this work. FCA material is acknowledged at the point of inclusion. Use of FCA material does not indicate any endorsement by the FCA of this publication, or the material or views contained within it.

While every effort has been made to ensure the accuracy of the content of this book, neither the author, the editors, the contributors, the publisher nor any other person accepts any responsibility for any loss arising to anyone relying on the information contained within it. Advice should be sought in relation to specific facts and circumstances.

Typeset by Paul Barrett Book Production, Cambridge
Printed in Great Britain by Lightning Source, Milton Keynes, Buckinghamshire

British Library Cataloguing in Publication Data
A catalogue record for this book is available from the British Library

ISBN 978-1-86072-714-6

Contents

Editors and contributors	xii
Glossary and abbreviations	xiv
Quick reference table – The UKLA Guidance Notes	xxvi
Proposed new guidance notes and proposed revisions to existing notes	xlvii
Foreword	l
Preface	lii

Introduction — 1
1. Why does a company decide to list? — 2
2. The IPO advisory team — 3
   - 2.1 Investment bank — 3
   - 2.2 The company's lawyers — 3
   - 2.3 The investment bank's lawyers — 4
   - 2.4 The reporting accountants — 4
3. Key steps in the IPO process — 5
4. Preparing to float and suitability for listing — 7
5. Due diligence, drafting the prospectus and verification — 8
   - 5.1 Due diligence — 8
   - 5.2 The prospectus — 9
   - 5.3 Verification — 10
6. Marketing the IPO, the application process and pricing — 10
7. Continuing obligations as a listed company — 12
8. Accuracy of market disclosure — 13
9. Control and disclosure of inside information — 14
10. Notification of share dealings and interests in voting rights — 14
11. Financial reporting and corporate governance — 15
12. Market announcements and shareholder communications — 16
13. Significant and related party transactions, further share issues and share buy-backs — 17

1. Regulatory framework — 21
Carol Shutkever and Karen Anderson

Overview — 21
1. The Financial Services Action Plan — 22
   - 1.1 Strategic objectives of the FSAP — 22
   - 1.2 The European legislative process for financial services legislation — 23
   - 1.3 The Market Abuse Directive and the Market Abuse Regulation — 24
   - 1.4 The Prospectus Directive and the PD Regulation — 24
   - 1.5 The Transparency Directive — 26
   - 1.6 The IAS Regulation — 26
   - 1.7 Home and host member states – prospectuses — 27
2. Implementation of the FSAP Directives and Regulations in the UK — 28
   - 2.1 Part 6 of the FSMA — 29
   - 2.2 Revisions to the FSMA in 2013 – the new regulatory structure — 29
   - 2.3 The FCA Handbook — 30
   - 2.4 Guidance on the FSAP Directives, MAR and Part 6 Rules in practice — 32
3. The role of the FCA and the UKLA — 35
4. The role of the LSE — 36
5. Compliance with and enforcement of the UK listing regime — 37
   - 5.1 A company's responsibility for compliance with the LPDT Rules and MAR — 37
   - 5.2 Directors' responsibilities for compliance with the LPDT Rules and MAR — 37

5.3	The FCA's powers	38	
5.4	Criminal offences	39	
5.5	FCA enforcement actions for breach of the listing regime and market abuse findings relevant to listed companies	41	

2. Admission to the Official List — 51
Mike Flockhart and Antonia Kirkby

Overview — 51

1. Listing segments and categories of the Official List — 52
   1.1 The premium and standard segments — 52
   1.2 The listing categories — 53
   1.3 Alternative securities markets in the UK — 55
2. Admission to listing and to trading — 59
   2.1 Admission to listing on the Official List of the UKLA — 59
   2.2 Admission to trading on the main market of the LSE — 68
3. Procedural requirements for admission to listing and to trading — 69
   3.1 Procedure for an application for listing of shares — 70
   3.2 Requirements for a block listing — 72
   3.3 Procedure for an application for admission to trading — 73
4. Transfer between listing segments — 73
   4.1 Notification of transfer — 74
   4.2 Additional requirements if migrating from premium to standard — 74
   4.3 Additional requirements if migrating from standard to premium — 75
   4.4 A company's application to transfer — 75
5. Suspension, cancellation and restoration of listing — 76
   5.1 Suspension of listing — 76
   5.2 Cancellation of listing — 77
   5.3 Procedure for a company to request suspension or cancellation of a listing — 77
   5.4 Restoration of listing — 81

3. Role and responsibilities of a sponsor — 82
Mike Flockhart and Karen Anderson

Overview — 82

1. Regulatory framework for the sponsor regime — 83
   1.1 Section 88 of the FSMA and Listing Rule 8 — 83
   1.2 Criteria and process for approval as a sponsor — 83
   1.3 Competence of a sponsor — 84
   1.4 Appropriate systems and controls — 86
   1.5 Record keeping — 87
   1.6 Supervision and censure of sponsors — 89
2. Appointment and consultation of a sponsor — 91
   2.1 Circumstances in which a sponsor must be appointed or consulted — 91
   2.2 Notifications required on appointment and dismissal of a sponsor — 93
   2.3 Joint sponsors and agents — 93
3. General duties and obligations of a sponsor — 95
   3.1 Principles — 95
   3.2 Identifying and managing conflicts — 97
   3.3 Maintenance of records — 99
4. Transaction-specific duties and the obligations of a sponsor — 100
   4.1 Application for admission of a new applicant — 101
   4.2 Application for admission of further shares by a listed company — 104
   4.3 Publication of a circular by a listed company — 105
   4.4 Application for transfer of listing category — 107
   4.5 Disclosure announcement on a reverse takeover — 109
5. Sponsor's comfort package — 110
   5.1 Sponsor's agreement, reports and comfort letters — 111
   5.2 Directors' responsibilities and understanding of obligations — 115
   5.3 Admission detrimental to investors' interests — 116

CONTENTS

5.4	Working capital	117
5.5	Significant change	118
5.6	Historical financial information and pro forma financial information	118
5.7	Compliance with the Listing Rules and the Prospectus Rules	119
5.8	Continuing obligations and financial reporting procedures	119

4. Preparing and publishing a prospectus — 137
Charles Howarth

Overview — 137

1. **Requirement to prepare and publish a prospectus** — 138
   - 1.1 Transferable securities — 139
   - 1.2 Offer to the public — 140
   - 1.3 Admission to trading — 142
   - 1.4 Scope of the exemptions — 143
   - 1.5 Exempt offers to the public — 144
   - 1.6 Exempt admissions to trading — 153
2. **Format and content of a prospectus** — 157
   - 2.1 Single and tri-partite documents — 157
   - 2.2 Order of contents — 158
   - 2.3 Summary and risk factors — 159
   - 2.4 General duty of disclosure — 162
   - 2.5 Specific disclosure requirements — 163
   - 2.6 ESMA guidance — 163
   - 2.7 Financial disclosure — 164
   - 2.8 Incorporation by reference — 170
   - 2.9 Omission of information — 171
   - 2.10 Equivalent documents — 171
   - 2.11 Proportionate disclosure regime — 172
3. **Approval, publication and 'passporting'** — 181
   - 3.1 Review and approval procedure — 181
   - 3.2 Methods of publication — 182
   - 3.3 Passporting within the EEA — 185
4. **Supplementary prospectuses** — 186
   - 4.1 Obligation to prepare and publish a supplementary prospectus — 186
   - 4.2 Application of the Prospectus Rules — 188
   - 4.3 Impact on the summary — 188
   - 4.4 Timing of supplementary prospectuses — 189
   - 4.5 Method of publication — 189
   - 4.6 Impact of a supplementary prospectus on an offer – withdrawal rights — 189
5. **Liability regime** — 191
   - 5.1 Minimum requirements of the PD — 191
   - 5.2 Responsible persons under Prospectus Rule 5.5 — 192
   - 5.3 Section 90(1) of the FSMA – the statutory liability regime — 193
   - 5.4 Section 90(2) of the FSMA – the due diligence defence — 194
   - 5.5 Other potential heads of liability — 195
6. **Advertisement regime** — 196
7. **The New Prospectus Regulation** — 198

5. Control and disclosure of inside information — 199
Carol Shutkever, Antonia Kirkby and Karen Anderson

Overview — 199

1. **Obligations in relation to inside information** — 200
   - 1.1 The regulatory framework — 200
   - 1.2 Disclosure obligation of a listed company — 201
   - 1.3 Decision-making process — 201
2. **Defining 'inside information'** — 202
   - 2.1 Meaning of 'inside information' — 202
   - 2.2 When is information 'precise'? — 202
   - 2.3 When is information deemed to be public? — 205
   - 2.4 Meaning of 'financial instruments' and 'related investments' — 205
   - 2.5 Meaning of 'significant effect on price' — 206
3. **Identifying Inside Information** — 207
   - 3.1 Monitoring and gathering information — 207
   - 3.2 Implementing and documenting procedures — 208

4.	Delaying disclosure	**213**
	4.1 Entitlement to delay disclosure	213
	4.2 Meaning of 'legitimate interests'	214
	4.3 Meaning of 'misleading the public'	214
	4.4 Ensuring confidentiality	215
	4.5 Record-keeping requirement when disclosure is delayed	215
	4.6 Holding announcements	215
	4.7 Monitoring continued ability to delay	216
	4.8 Notification to the FCA of the delay	216
	4.9 Decision tree	217
5.	Selective disclosure of inside information	**217**
	5.1 Conditions for selective disclosure	218
	5.2 Persons to whom selective disclosure may be made	218
	5.3 Market soundings	220
6	Dealing with market rumour and speculation, the media and analysts	220
	6.1 Market rumours and leaks	221
	6.2 Media enquiries	222
	6.3 Analysts' briefings	222
	6.4 Analysts' research	223
7.	Control of inside information	**224**
8.	Insider lists	**225**
	8.1 Form and content of the Insider List	225
	8.2 Procedures for creating and maintaining insider lists within a company	226
	8.3 Company's advisers, agents and other third parties	228
	8.4 Notification to insiders and acknowledgement of duties by insiders	228
9.	Method and content of disclosure of inside information	**229**
	9.1 Approval process for announcements – disclosure committee	229
	9.2 Misleading statements	230
	9.3 Verification of announcements	232
	9.4 Contents requirements for announcements of inside information	233

	9.5 Methods of disclosing inside information: RIS and websites	233
10.	Breach of MAR and related offences	**234**
	10.1 Breach of obligation to announce inside information	234
	10.2 Enforcement actions for breach of requirement to announce inside information pre-MAR	235
	10.3 Market abuse offences	242
	10.4 Misleading statements and conduct	249
	10.5 Insider dealing criminal offences	250
	10.6 Fraud	250

6.	**Financial reporting and corporate governance**	**252**
	Carol Shutkever	
	Overview	**252**
1.	Financial reporting and listed companies	**253**
	1.1 The key rules that apply to financial reporting	253
	1.2 The DTR 4 regime	254
2.	Preliminary statements of annual results and statements of dividends	**255**
	2.1 Preliminary statements	255
	2.2 Statements of dividends	256
3.	Annual Financial Reports	**256**
	3.1 Publication requirements	257
	3.2 Audited financial statements	258
	3.3 The management report	259
	3.4 Responsibility statements	260
	3.5 The use of Alternative Performance Measures (APMs)	261
	3.6 Governance disclosures under DTR 7	262
	3.7 Additional Listing Rule requirements for premium listed companies' Annual Financial Reports	262
4.	Half-yearly Financial Reports	**268**
	4.1 Publication requirements	268
	4.2 Condensed financial statements	268
	4.3 The interim management report	269
	4.4 Responsibility statements	270

5.	Audit requirements	271
	5.1 The auditors' report	272
	5.2 Audit tender and rotation of auditors	272
	5.3 Composition and role of the audit committee	273
6.	Third country issuers with a premium listing	273
	6.1 Equivalence of relevant laws	274
	6.2 Equivalence of accounting standards with IFRS	275
	6.3 Audit and auditor requirements for third country issuers	276
7	Stakeholder reporting requirements	276
8	Corporate governance	277
	8.1 Background to the Governance Code	277
	8.2 The DTR 7 regime – audit committees and governance statement	278
	8.3 Application of the Governance Code	280
	8.4 Key provisions of the Governance Code	281
	8.5 Guidance relating to the Corporate Governance Code	291
9.	Enforcement by the Financial Reporting Council's Conduct Committee	296

7. Share dealings and interests in voting rights 298
Greg Mulley

Overview 298

1.	Disclosure of dealings by PDMRs and persons closely associated with them	299
	1.1 The regulatory framework	299
	1.2 The disclosure obligation	300
	1.3 Identifying PDMRs and their PCAs	300
	1.4 Maintaining a list of PDMRs and PCAs	303
	1.5 Notifications to PDMRs and PCAs of their obligations	303
	1.6 Transactions to be disclosed by PDMRs and PCAs	303
	1.7 Content, method and timing of notification	307
	1.8 Disclosure of PDMR and PCA interests in annual report	312
	1.9 Practical recommendations for compliance	313
2.	Prohibition on PDMR dealings during closed periods	314
	2.1 The prohibition	314
	2.2 Definition of a closed period	314
	2.3 Types of transactions falling within the dealing prohibition	315
	2.4 Exceptions to the prohibition on dealing during a closed period	316
	2.5 Restrictions on dealings at other times	318
3.	Share dealing policy	318
	3.1 Adopting a share dealing code	318
	3.2 The requirement to obtain clearance to deal	319
	3.3 Notification of dealings by PDMRs and PCAs	321
	3.4 Dealings by PCAs	321
	3.5 Penalties for breach of the dealing code	321
	3.6 Procedures for ensuring compliance	322
4.	Breach of dealing notification requirements and restrictions	322
5.	Disclosure of interests in voting rights	323
	5.1 Meaning of 'issuer' for the purposes of DTR 5	324
	5.2 What interests are relevant for DTR 5 purposes?	325
	5.3 Treatment of indirect holders of shares	327
	5.4 Voting rights to be notified and aggregated	332
	5.5 Exemptions to general notification requirements	337
	5.6 Procedural requirements for vote holder	339
	5.7 Procedural requirements in relation to proxies	342
	5.8 Procedural requirements for issuers	343
	5.9 Enforcement and penalties for breach	346
	5.10 Summary of notification obligations	347

8. Market announcements and shareholder communications — 348
Antonia Kirkby and Mike Flockhart

Overview — 348

1. Matters required to be announced to the market — 349
   1.1 Disclosure of information relating to directors — 351
   1.2 Information about general meetings — 352
   1.3 Changes to a company's name and accounting reference date — 352
   1.4 Information about changes in share rights — 352
   1.5 Information about dividends and issues of new shares — 353
   1.6 Announcements about information filed at the NSM — 353
   1.7 Notifications regarding lock-up arrangements — 353
2. Ensuring shareholders receive adequate information about their rights — 353
   2.1 Equality of treatment — 354
   2.2 Electronic communications — 354
   2.3 Financial agent — 355
   2.4 General meetings — 355
3. Adoption of employee share schemes — 356
4. Making information available to shareholders — 356
   4.1 Dissemination of regulated information — 356
   4.2 Circulars to shareholders — 360
   4.3 National Storage Mechanism — 362
5. Electronic communication — 363
   5.1 DTR 6 and the Companies Act 2006 — 364
   5.2 Interaction with Listing Rule 13 — 365
6. Issuer liability regime — 369
   6.1 Introduction — 369
   6.2 Scope of the regime — 369
   6.3 When will an issuer be liable? — 370
   6.4 To whom is the issuer liable? — 370
   6.5 Safe harbour from liability — 371
   6.6 Position of directors — 372
   6.7 Sanctions for issuing misleading statements — 372

9. Significant transactions, reverse takeovers, related party transactions and companies with controlling shareholders — 373
Antonia Kirkby and Mike Flockhart

Overview — 373

1. Significant transactions — 374
   1.1 Types of transaction — 375
   1.2 Classification tests — 376
   1.3 Abolition of Class 3 transactions — 387
   1.4 Class 2 requirements — 387
   1.5 Class 1 requirements — 389
   1.6 Exemptions for companies in severe financial difficulty — 401
   1.7 Acquisitions out of administration — 403
   1.8 Joint ventures — 404
2. Reverse takeovers — 413
   2.1 Application of rules to a premium listed company — 413
   2.2 Suspension of listing — 414
   2.3 Cancellation of listing — 417
3. Related party transactions — 418
   3.1 Defining 'related party transactions' — 418
   3.2 Transactions that are not subject to the requirements of Listing Rule 11 — 422
   3.3 Requirements for a related party transaction — 425
   3.4 Aggregation of transactions — 430
   3.5 Modified requirements for smaller related party transactions — 431
4. Companies with controlling shareholders — 437
   4.1 Who is a controlling shareholder? — 437
   4.2 Requirement for a relationship agreement — 438
   4.3 Independent business — 439
   4.4 Statement on compliance with the relationship agreement to be included in the annual report — 440
   4.5 Election/re-election of independent directors — 440

	4.6	Circulars in relation to election or re-election of independent directors	441
	4.7	Cancellation of listing	442

10. Further share issues and share buy-backs — 443
Antonia Kirkby and Greg Mulley

Overview			443
1.	**Further share issues**		**444**
	1.1	Rights issues, open offers and placings	445
	1.2	Authority to allot, pre-emption rights and other share capital considerations	448
	1.3	Other relevant Listing Rule and LSE requirements	454
	1.4	Requirement to publish a prospectus	455
	1.5	Notification and documentation requirements under the Listing Rules and Transparency Rules	460
	1.6	The Market Abuse Regulation	463
2.	**Share buy-backs**		**468**
	2.1	General requirements for a share repurchase	469
	2.2	Buy-backs within a listed company's annual authority	476
	2.3	Buy-backs not within a listed company's annual authority	479
	2.4	Restrictions on when a listed company may conduct a share buy-back	481
	2.5	Notifications and filings	483
	2.6	Purchase of own securities other than equity shares	484
	2.7	Treasury shares	485

Further guidance for UK listed companies	**488**
About Herbert Smith Freehills LLP	**493**
Index	**494**

Editors and contributors

Mike Flockhart (Co-editor)

Mike is a corporate partner at Herbert Smith Freehills and advises on a wide range of corporate finance transactions, mergers and acquisitions and corporate governance issues, specialising in equity capital markets transactions and domestic and cross-border public and private M&A. He advises leading corporates and investment banks and has particular expertise in advising principals and financial advisers on listed company transactions.

Antonia Kirkby (Co-editor)

Antonia practiced as a transaction lawyer specialising in corporate finance and M&A before becoming a professional support lawyer at Herbert Smith Freehills. Her focus is providing the firm's lawyers with technical advice on company and corporate finance law issues and analysing law and regulation. Antonia was secretary to the City of London Law Society's Company Law Sub-Committee and the Sub-Committee's Joint Working Party on Takeovers for a number of years, which involved considering and lobbying on a wide range of corporate law issues including changes to the Takeover Code and to the Listing Rules. She has written a number of articles and contributes to a number of books on these topics.

Karen Anderson

Karen is a partner in the financial services regulatory practice at Herbert Smith Freehills. She advises financial institutions, professionals and financial services providers in relation to regulatory matters and disputes in the UK and internationally. She also served a secondment with FSA enforcement. Through her participation in a range of working groups including the BBA Market Abuse working group, the CLLS Regulatory Committee and the Law Society Banking Reform working group, Karen remains actively involved in discussions with regulators and HM Treasury regarding the regulation of financial services.

Charles Howarth

Charles is a corporate partner at Herbert Smith Freehills who advises investment banks and major corporations in relation to securities offerings in the UK, the rest of Europe and worldwide. His expertise includes initial public offerings, rights issues and secondary market offerings, share placings, convertible bonds, global depositary receipts and stock exchange listings.

Greg Mulley

Greg is a corporate partner at Herbert Smith Freehills and advises companies and investment banks on corporate finance and capital markets transactions, public and private mergers and acquisitions, corporate governance issues and other aspects of corporate law. He has particular experience in advising listed corporate clients on complex, cross-border transactions and capital raisings, the leading banks in their roles as sponsor, underwriters, bookrunners and financial advisers on major transactions and issuers on IPOs, and has been closely involved in a range of securities and corporate law regulatory issues.

Carol Shutkever

Carol is a corporate partner at Herbert Smith Freehills and a member of the firm's Corporate Governance Advisory Team. She has extensive experience of corporate and corporate finance transactions and has particular technical expertise in corporate law, corporate governance and listed company regulation. Carol's expertise includes advising on company meetings, corporate reporting, continuing obligations under the Listing and Transparency Rules, the Market Abuse Regulation, directors' duties and board and committee procedures. Her role includes analysing new law and regulation and ensuring that the firm is at the forefront of corporate law and practice.

Additional Contributors

Special thanks also to the following for their valuable and considerable contributions:

Isla Dentice-Wood, Heidi Gallagher, Maisie Havelock-Smith, Rachel Hayward, Ellie Horrocks, Prakash Kakkad, Ben Parish, Sarah Ries-Coward, Patrick Skinner, Laura Stuckey, Shaun Williamson, Tom Vaughan, Imogen White and Paul Cruise.

Glossary and abbreviations

ABI	The Association of British Insurers now part of **The Investment Association**
Accounting Directive	The EU Accounting Directive (2013/34/EU)
AGM	Annual General Meeting
AIM	Formerly known as Alternative Investment Market, a market for smaller growing companies (see www.londonstockexchange.com/companies-and-advisors/aim/aim/aim.htm)
APB	The Auditing Practices Board, the body at the **FRC** that used to be responsible for setting auditing standards in the UK. Work on audit and assurance is now carried out by the FRC's Audit and Assurance Council.
APM	alternative performance measure, a financial measure that is not required as part of an issuer's financial reporting obligations but which it may voluntarily present to aid understanding of its performance
applicant	A company applying to list its shares for the first time
ASB	The Accounting Standards Board, the body of the **FRC** that used to be responsible for issuing accounting standards in the UK. Work on accounting and reporting policy is now carried out by the Accounting Council
Audit Directive	Directive 2014/56/EU which, together with the Audit Regulation, sets out the audit regime for public interest entities including listed companies
Audit Regulation	Regulation 2014/537/EU which, together with the Audit Directive, sets out the audit regime for public interest entities including listed companies
BEIS	The Department for Business, Energy & Industrial Strategy (see www.gov.uk/government/organisations/department-for-business-energy-and-industrial-strategy)
Buy-Back and Stabilisation Regulation	Buy-Back and Stabilisation Regulation ((EU) 2016/1052)

GLOSSARY AND ABBREVIATIONS

CA 1985	The Companies Act 1985
CA 2006	The Companies Act 2006
CESR	The Committee of European Securities Regulators, the **EU** body that provided technical advice to the Commission on detailed implementing measures required for directives forming part of the **FSAP**, now superseded by **ESMA**
CfDs	Contracts for differences
CFO	Chief financial officer
City Code	City Code on Takeovers and Mergers
CJA	Criminal Justice Act 1993
Class 1 Transaction	A transaction which, under the class tests in Listing Rule 10, requires shareholder approval because its size equals or exceeds 25 per cent of the size of the listed company
Class tests	The tests that measure the size of transactions by listed companies set out in Listing Rule 10
CLLS/Law Society Q&A	a series of Q&A on MAR published by the City of London Law Society and Law Society Company Law Committees' Joint Working Parties on Market Abuse, Share Plans and Takeovers Code (see www.citysolicitors.org.uk)
closed period	30 day period before interim and year-end results under MAR
CMA	Competition and Markets Authority, the successor body to the Office of Fair Trading and Competition Commission
CMA Order	Statutory Audit Services for Large Companies Market Investigation (Mandatory Use of Competitive Tender Processes and Audit Committee Responsibilities) Order 2014
Commission	The European Commission (see ec.europa.eu/index_en.htm)
Companies Act	the **CA 2006**
continuing obligations	The obligations set out in the **LPDT** Rules and MAR to which a listed company is subject
controlling shareholder	a shareholder that exercise or controls 30% or more of the voting rights in a premium listed company, either on their own or together with other persons with whom they are acting in concert
Corporate Governance Code or Governance Code	The UK Corporate Governance Code (previously known as the Combined Code) issued and maintained by the **FRC**
Council	The Council of the European Union
CP	**FCA** consultation paper

CRD	The Company Reporting Directive (2006/46/EC)
CREST	The UK's securities settlement system operated by Euroclear
DEPP	The **FCA**'s Decision Procedure and Penalties Manual
Disclosure Guidance	the guidance on MAR contained in DTRs 1 to 3
disclosure requirements	the requirements in articles 17, 18 and 19 of MAR
DLC	Dual listed company
DMP	disclosing market participant on a market sounding under **MAR**
DP	An **FCA** discussion paper
DTRs	The Disclosure Guidance and Transparency Rules
EDGAR	The online storage facility for registration statements, periodic reports and other forms filed electronically with the **SEC** by US domestic and international listed companies (accessed at www.sec.gov/edgar.shtml)
EEA	European Economic Area, being the **EU Member States**, Iceland, Liechtenstein and Norway
EEAP	European Electronic Access Point
EFRAG	The European Financial Reporting Advisory Group (see www.efrag.org/front/home.aspx)
Eighth Commencement Order	Companies Act 2006 (Commencement No. 8, Transitional Provisions and Savings) Order 2008 (SI No. 2860)
EPS	Earnings per share
equivalent document	A disclosure document, prepared by a listed company that is issuing and listing new shares in connection with a merger, takeover or acquisition, that is regarded by the **FCA** as having equivalent content to a prospectus
ESA	A European Supervisory Authority
ESC	The European Securities Committee
ESEF	European single electronic format
ESFS	European System of Financial Supervisors
ESMA	The European Securities and Markets Authority, the European regulatory body established by Regulation EU No. 1095/2010, which replaced **CESR** with effect from 1 January 2011
ESMA Guidelines on APMs	Guidelines published by ESMA on the use of Alternative Performance Measures (**APMs**)
ESMA Guidelines on Delay	Guidelines published by ESMA on when a company may delay disclosing inside information under **MAR**
ESMA MAR Q&A	Responses to commonly asked questions regarding MAR, updated periodically by ESMA

ESMA PD Q&A	Responses to commonly asked questions regarding prospectuses drawn up in accordance with the **PD**, originally published by **CESR**, now updated periodically by **ESMA**
ESMA Recommendations	Recommendations for the consistent implementation of the **Prospectus Regulation**, originally published by **CESR** in February 2005, now updated periodically by **ESMA**
ESMA TD Q&A	Responses to commonly asked questions regarding the **TD**, originally published by **CESR** and now updated by **ESMA**
EU	The European Union (see europa.eu)
EU Audit Regime	the regime under the Audit Directive and the Audit Regulation
EU Benchmarks Regulation	Regulation 2016/1011 of the European Parliament and of the Council of 8 June 2016 on indices used as benchmarks in financial instruments and financial contracts or to measure the performance of investment funds
Euroclear	The world's largest provider of domestic and cross-border settlement and related services for bond, equity, fund and derivative transactions (see www.euroclear.com)
European Parliament	The Parliament of the European Union
FCA	The Financial Conduct Authority, one of the three regulatory bodies which regulates financial services in the UK in succession to the **FSA**
FCA Glossary	The **FCA**'s glossary of defined terms used in the **FCA** Handbook
FCA Handbook	The **FCA**'s handbook of rules and guidance
FCA MAR	The Market Abuse Chapter of the FCA's Market Conduct Sourcebook, part of the FCA Handbook
Fourth Company Law Directive	Fourth Company Law Directive (78/660/EEC) which used to govern the preparation and content of individual company accounts but has been repealed and replaced by the **Accounting Directive**
FPC	The Financial Policy Committee, one of the three regulatory bodies established to regulate financial services in the UK in succession to the **FSA**
FRC	The Financial Reporting Council, the independent regulator for corporate reporting and governance in the UK responsible among other things for the **Corporate Governance Code** (see www.frc.org.uk)
FRC Conduct Committee	The body of FRC that reviews the directors' reports and accounts of public and large private companies for

	compliance with the law. It also keeps under review interim reports of all listed issuers and annual reports of certain other non-corporate listed entities.
FSA	The Financial Services Authority, the predecessor to the **FCA**
FSA 2012	The Financial Services Act 2012
FSAP	The Commission's Financial Services Action Plan
FSAP Directives	The various Directives implementing the **FSAP**, including the Lamfalussy Directives
FSMA	The Financial Services and Markets Act 2000
GAAP	Generally Accepted Accounting Principles
GC100	The Association of General Counsel and Company Secretaries of the FTSE 100 (see www.practicallaw.com/groups/uk-gc100)
GDRs	Global depositary receipts, certificates representing ownership of a given number of a company's shares which can be listed and traded independently from the underlying shares
General MAR Delegated Regulation	Regulation (EU) 2016/522, which contains, among other things, a non-exhaustive list of types of transactions that should be notified by PDMRs and their PCAs, and also details on when trading can take place during a MAR closed period
Guidance Note	A guidance note issued by the FCA to provide formal guidance on technical or procedural issues arising in connection with the LPDT Rules
High Growth Segment or HGS	Part of the LSE's main market but outside the UK's listing regime
HMRC	Her Majesty's Revenue and Customs (see www.gov.uk/government/organisations/hm-revenue-customs)
HMT	Her Majesty's Treasury (see www.gov.uk/government/organisations/hm-treasury)
home Member State	The **EEA** state which is an issuer's Home Member State for the purposes of the **PD**
host Member State	The **EEA** state where an offer to the public is made or an admission to trading is sought, when different to the Home Member State
IAS	International Accounting Standards, global accounting standards issued before April 2001; they are to be replaced by **IFRS**

IAS Regulation	The International Accounting Standards Regulation (EC No. 1606/2002)
IASB	The International Accounting Standards Board, an independent accounting standards setter based in the UK and responsible for **IFRS** (see www.iasb.co.uk)
IFRS	International Financial Reporting Standards, global accounting standards issued by the **IASB** from April 2001 onwards
IIC	Institutional Investor Committee
IMS	**interim management statements**
Inside Information	
Implementing Regulation	Regulation (EU) 2016/1055 which sets out the detailed requirements for announcements of inside information under MAR
insider dealing	The criminal offence of insider dealing under Part V of the CJA or the civil market abuse offence of insider dealing under MAR
insider list	a list required under **MAR** recording those people working for or on behalf of a company who have access to inside information
Insider List Implementing Regulation	Regulation (EU) 2016/347 which sets out the detailed requirements in relation to insider lists under **MAR**
Investment Association	A body that represents institutional investors, formed following the merger of the Investment Management Association and Investment Affairs division of the **ABI**
IPO	An initial public offering
issuer	A company seeking to issue and list shares
Issuer Liability Regulations	The Financial Services and Markets Act 2000 (Liability of Issuers) Regulations 2010 (SI No. 1192)
ITF	Announcement of intention to float
IVIS	Institutional Voting Information Service (see www.ivis.co.uk)
Lamfalussy Directives	**MiFID**, **MAD**, **PD** and **TD**, four 'level 1' Directives forming part of the **FSAP**
LEI	legal entity identifier
List!	The newsletter on the **LPDT** Rules which was produced periodically by the **FSA**
listed company	A company with listed shares
listing category	The eight categories of listing specified in LR 1.6.1

listing particulars	A disclosure document prepared by an issuer in connection with an admission of securities to listing on the **PSM** and that complies with the form, content and other requirements of Listing Rule 4
Listing Principles	The Listing Principles and Premium Listing Principles set out in Listing Rule 7
Listing Rules (LR)	The Listing Rules, the rules governing, among other things, the listing of shares, the sponsor regime and the continuing obligations of a listed company
listing segment	The two segments of the Official List, namely premium and standard
LPDT Rules	The Listing Rules, Prospectus Rules, Disclosure Guidance and Transparency Rules
LSE	London Stock Exchange plc (see www.londonstockexchange.com)
LSE Admission and Disclosure Standards	The rules issued by the **LSE** governing admission to trading on the **LSE**'s markets and the continuing obligations of companies once admitted to trading, the most recent version of which was published in May 2017
MAD	The Market Abuse Directive (2003/6/EC) which contained the market abuse regime prior to 3 July 2016
Main Market	The **LSE**'s main market for listed securities (see www.londonstockexchange.com/companies-and-advisors/main-market/main-market/home.htm)
Major Shareholding Regulation	Commission Delegated Regulation (EU) 2015/761 which provides regulatory technical standards on certain aspects of the regime for notifying major shareholdings
MAR	The EU Market Abuse Regulation ((EU) 596/2014)
MAR closed period	the 30-day period prior to publication of a company's interim and year-end results during which a company's PDMRs are restricted from dealing in the shares of the company
market abuse	The civil offence of market abuse under **MAR**
market sounding	a sounding out of investors for which a safe harbour is available under MAR
Market Watch	The newsletter on market conduct and supervision produced periodically by the **FCA**
Member State	An **EU** Member State
MiFID	The Markets in Financial Instruments Directive (2004/39/EC)

Model Code	A code which, prior to MAR, governed dealings by directors, **PDMR**s and their connected persons and was set out in the annex to Listing Rule 9
MSR	market sounding recipient, that is a person who is sounded out on a market sounding
MTF	Multilateral trading facility
National Storage Mechanism (NSM)	The online storage facility for regulated information published by UK listed companies accessed at www.morningstar.co.uk/uk/NSM
NEDs	Non-executive directors
New Prospectus Regulation	The new EU regulation ((EU) 2017/1129)) which will replace the Prospectus Directive
NEX Exchange	An independent UK exchange, with three markets, aimed at small to medium sized growth companies, which was previously known as ISDX
Non-Financial Reporting Directive	Directive (EU/2014/95) which amends the Accounting Directive and requires certain companies to disclose in their annual report information about policies, risks and outcomes as regards environmental, social and employee matters, respect for human rights, anti-corruption and anti-bribery matters and board diversity policies
Official List	The list maintained by the **FCA** pursuant to section 74 of the **FSMA**
OFR	The operating and financial review, the section of a prospectus that contains a narrative description of an issuer's historical financial statements and results of operations
Omnibus II Directive	Directive (2014/51/EU) which made changes to, among other things, the Prospectus Directive (2003/71/EC)
PAL	Provisional allotment letter
Panel	The Panel on Takeovers and Mergers
passporting	The ability to use a prospectus approved by the competent authority in one **EEA** state in other **EEA** states without the issuer having to publish further information or seek additional approvals
PCA	a person closely associated with a PDMR
PD	The Prospectus Directive (2003/71/EC)
PD Amending Directive	Directive (2010/73/EU) amending certain provisions of the **PD** adopted by the European Parliament on 17 June 2010 and published in the Official Journal on 11 December 2010

PD Amending Regulation	Regulation (EC No. 211/2007) amending the **PD Regulation** in relation to the disclosure of financial information in a prospectus where a company has a complex financial history or has made a significant financial commitment
PD Regulation or **Prospectus Regulation**	The Prospectus Directive Regulation (EC No. 809/2004)
PDMR	A person discharging managerial responsibility
PDMR Transaction Notification Implementing Regulation	Regulation (EU) 2016/523) which contains the requirements regarding the format and template for notification and public disclosure of transactions
PIE	public interest entities
PIEs	public interest entities, including listed companies, credit undertakings and insurers
PIP	A primary information provider, a provider of an **RIS**
PLSA	Pensions and Lifetime Savings Association, formerly known as the NAPF (see www.plsa.co.uk)
PRA	The Prudential Regulatory Authority, one of the three new regulatory bodies which regulates financial services in the UK in succession to the **FSA**
Pre-emption Group	A group representing listed companies, institutional investors and intermediaries that publishes guidance on the disapplication of pre-emption rights and monitors and reports on how this guidance is applied (see www.pre-emptiongroup.org.uk)
Pre-emption Group Statement of Principles	The guidance published from time to time by the Pre-emption Group on the disapplication of pre-emption rights
premium listed company	A company with a premium listing
premium listing	A listing on the premium segment of the Official List by virtue of which an issuer is subject to the full requirements of the Listing Rules relating to eligibility to listing and continuing obligations
Principles for sponsors	The principles for sponsors set out in LR 8.3.3 to LR 8.3.14 inclusive
Prospectus	A disclosure document prepared by an issuer in connection with an offer of shares to the public and/or an admission of shares to listing on a regulated market and that complies with the form, content and other requirements of the **PD** and **PD Regulation**

Prospectus Regulations	Prospectus Regulations 2011 (SI 2011 No. 1668)
Prospectus RTS Regulations	Regulation No 382/2014 supplementing the Prospectus Directive with regard to certain regulatory technical standards for publication of supplements to the prospectus; and Regulation 2016/301 supplementing the Prospectus Directive with regard to regulatory technical standards for approval and publication of the prospectus and dissemination of advertisements and amending the PD Amending Regulation
Prospectus Rules (PR)	The Prospectus Rules, rules governing the preparation and publication of, and responsibility for, a prospectus
PS	An **FCA** policy statement
PSM	The Professional Securities Market, the **LSE**'s market for issuers of specialist debt securities (see www.londonstockexchange.com/companies-and-advisors/psm/home/psm.htm)
QCA	The Quoted Companies Alliance, a not-for-profit organisation that works for small and mid-cap quoted companies in the UK and Europe (see www.theqca.com)
regulated market	A multilateral system operated and/or managed by a market operator (e.g. a stock exchange) which brings together or facilitates the buying and selling of financial instruments (e.g. shares), as more particularly defined in **MiFID**
related party	A person who is a related party as defined in LR 11.1.4, including a company's directors, shadow directors and substantial shareholders
related party transaction	Any transaction between a listed company and a related party that is subject to the provisions of Listing Rule 11
RIS	A regulatory information service
risk factors	The section of a prospectus, required to be included by the **PD** and the **PD Regulation**, that contains details of the principal risks relating to an issuer, its business, the industry in which it operates and its securities
RNS	The Regulatory News Service, an **RIS** operated by the **LSE**
SEC	The US Securities and Exchange Commission (see www.sec.gov)
Second Company Law Directive	The Second Company Law Directive (77/91/EEC)
Seventh Company Law Directive	The Seventh Company Law Directive (83/349/EEC) which has been repealed and replaced by the **Accounting Directive**

Shareholder Rights Directive	The Shareholders' Rights Directive (2007/36/EC)
Shareholder Rights Regulations	Companies (Shareholders' Rights) Regulations 2009 (SI 2009 No. 1632)
sponsor	A person approved by the **FCA** under section 88 of the **FSMA** to act as a sponsor for the purposes of the **Listing Rules**
sponsor service	A service that a sponsor provides or is requested or appointed to provide under LR 8.2, including any preparatory work relating to the same
standard listed company	A company with a standard listing
standard listing	A listing on the standard segment of the **Official List** by virtue of which an issuer is subject to the basic requirements of the Listing Rules relating to eligibility to listing and continuing obligations
Standards for Investment Reporting (SIRs)	Investment reporting standards published by the **APB** that apply to a reporting accountant when engaged in connection with the preparation and publication of a prospectus or circular
Statutory Audit Directive	The Statutory Audit Directive (2006/43/EC)
Statutory Audit Regulations	The Statutory Auditors and Third Country Auditors Regulations 2016 (SI 2016/649)
summary	The section of a prospectus, required under the **PD** and the **PD Regulation**, which conveys in non-technical language the essential characteristics of, and risks associated with, an issuer and the shares to which the prospectus relates
TD	The Transparency Directive (2004/109/EC)
TD Amending Directive or TDAD	Directive 2013/50/EU which amends the **TD** and was published in the Official Journal in November 2013
Transparency Rules	The rules governing, among other things, the disclosure of interests in voting rights and financial reporting by a listed company
TVR	Total Voting Rights
UK GAAP	UK Generally Accepted Accounting Policies
UKI Proxy Voting Guidelines	UK and Ireland Proxy Voting Guidelines and Benchmark Policy Recommendations for 2017 published by Institutional Shareholder Services Inc (ISS)

UKLA	The United Kingdom Listing Authority, the **FCA** when exercising its powers under Part VI of **FSMA**
unlawful disclosure	the civil market abuse offence under MAR of disclosure of inside information other than in the normal exercise of an employment, profession or duties
Upper Tribunal	Where disagreements arise between the FCA and firms or individuals about the FCA's regulatory decisions, the matter can be referred to the Upper Tribunal, an independent judicial body established by the Tribunals, Courts and Enforcement Act 2007.

Notes:

1 *Throughout this text, rule references prefixed by 'LR' are to paragraphs of the Listing Rules, rule references prefixed by 'PR' are to paragraphs of the Prospectus Rules and rule references prefixed by 'DTR' are to paragraphs of the Disclosure Guidance and Transparency Rules. The term 'LPDT Rules' is used to refer to the Listing Rules, Prospectus Rules, Disclosure Guidance and Transparency Rules in their entirety.*

2 *In addition, rule references ending with 'R' denote that the paragraph is a rule, whereas a suffix 'G' represents guidance to the LPDT Rules. In practice, there is little difference between rules and guidance because if an applicant or listed company does not comply with the guidance, then the FCA may consider that it has not complied with the corresponding rule.*

Quick reference table – The UKLA Guidance Notes

The FCA has published the following Guidance Notes on the LPDT Rules and disclosure requirements. They constitute formal guidance on the Rules.

No.	Title	Reference number	Matters covered	Relevant Rules
A. Procedural notes				
1.	Eligibility process	UKLA/ PN/901.3	Applicants must submit an eligibility letter before submitting a draft prospectus.	LR 2 LR 3 LR 6 LR 18.2 PR 1.2.3 (8)
2.	Listing securities via final terms	UKLA/ PN/902.2	How to list securities that are the subject of final terms and how to help avoid situations where securities that are the subject of final terms do not get listed.	LR 2.1.5 LR 2.2.3 LR 2.2.9 LR 3.2.7 LR 3.4.8
3.	Review and approval of documents	UKLA/ PN/903.3	The mechanics and timeline for the review and approval of documents under the LRs or PRs by the UKLA. Details on necessary supporting documents.	LR 3.1 LR 4.3 LR 13.2
4.	Public offer prospectus – drafting and approval	UKLA/ PN/904.3	How, and in what format, a prospectus should be submitted for approval to the UKLA. Guidance on prospectus contents, including historic financial information, security rights, responsibility statements, working capital and indebtedness.	PR 2 PR 3

No.	Title	Reference number	Matters covered	Relevant Rules
5.	Passporting	UKLA/PN/905.2	The key steps in the passporting process, including documents required time frames and the confirmation process. A list of EU Member States not requiring translations of prospectus summaries.	PR 4.1.6 PR 5.3
6.	Guidance on UKLA standard comments	UKLA/PN/906.1	Standard comments should be properly addressed in UKLA comments sheets.	n/a
7.	Block listings	UKLA/PN/907.2	How and when an issuer can use a block listing.	LR 3.5
8.	UKLA decision making and review process	UKLA/PN/908.1	The UKLA's internal decision-making and escalation procedure. The process for requesting a review of individual guidance and for appeals to the Listing Advisory Review Committee. *[Note: the FCA is consulting on amendments to this Guidance Note – see p. xlvii to xlix for details.]*	SUP 9.5.1–9.5.7
9.	Sponsor firms – ongoing requirements during reorganisations	UKLA/PN/909.2	The UKLA's expectations where one sponsor acquires another or on a change of control.	LR 8
10.	Additional powers to supervise sponsors	UKLA/PN/910.2	This note provides guidance to sponsors on the procedural aspects of the FCA's statutory powers to suspend, limit or restrict sponsors under sections 88 and 88E FSMA. It covers: ■ sponsors applying to the FCA for a suspension of approval (or a withdrawal thereof); ■ the imposition by the FCA of a limitation or restriction on the services a sponsor can provide; and	FSMA s. 88; FSMA s. 88E; LR 8 DEPP 2.5 DEPP 2 Annex 1G; Depp 2 Annex 2G DEPP 4

No.	Title	Reference number	Matters covered	Relevant Rules
			■ the suspension of a sponsor's approval or the limitation or restriction on the services a sponsor can provide by the FCA in order to advance one or more of the FCA's operational objectives.	
B. Eligibility for listing				
11.	Restrictions on transferability	UKLA/ TN/101.2	The UKLA's approach to provisions in articles of association that restrict the transfer of shares. Examples of the limited situations where restrictions have been permitted.	LR 2.2.4 LR 7.2.1A LR 16
C. Governance and conduct				
12.	Share buy-backs with mix and match facilities	UKLA/ TN/202.1	The UKLA applies a 'look-through' analysis to tender offers made through an intermediary, including those with mix and match facilities. *[Note: the FCA is consulting on amendments to this Guidance Note – see p. xlvii to xlix for details.]*	LR 9.5.10 LR 12.6 LR 15.4.11
13.	Compliance with the Listing Principles and Premium Listing Principles	UKLA/ TN/203.3	Reminder of the importance of the Listing Principles. Enforcement action can be taken for breach of LR 7 alone. Any compulsory acquisition procedures should not breach the equality of treatment principle.	LR 7 LR 2.2.4
14.	Ratification circulars	UKLA/ TN/204.2	Ratification resolutions will not normally fall to be treated as related party transactions. In assessing whether the potential benefit to directors is only an ancillary or unintended effect of the circular (which would mean that the transaction is not a related	LR 11.1.5

QUICK REFERENCE TABLE – THE UKLA GUIDANCE NOTES   xxix

No.	Title	Reference number	Matters covered	Relevant Rules
			party transaction), the FCA is of the opinion that it is difficult to come to this conclusion where a specific resolution (or part of a resolution) is included in the circular that has the effect of expressly releasing the directors from liability.	
15.	Circulation and publication of unapproved documents	UKLA/ TN/205.1	No changes can be made to a prospectus or circular once approved by the UKLA.	LR 13.2.1 PR 3.1.10
16.	Equality of treatment – Premium Listing Principle 5	UKLA/ TN/207.2	Application of PLP 5, in particular in relation to the treatment of small shareholders in share capital reorganisations.	LR 7.2.1A Premium Listing Principle 5
17.	Long-term incentive schemes	UKLA/ TN/208.1	Exemption from the requirement to obtain shareholder approval for a long-term incentive scheme is limited.	LR 9.4.2
18.	Dealing with the FCA in an open and co-operative manner	UKLA/ TN/209.2	Considerations for issuers when deciding whether to contact the FCA in relation to a proposed significant transaction. [Note: the FCA is consulting on amendments to this Guidance Note – see p. xlvii to xlix for details].	LR 1.2.5G LP 2
19.	Cancellation of listing or transfer between listing categories – requests to waive the 20 business day notice period	UKLA/ TN/210.1	The FCA is generally very reluctant to allow a reduction of the 20 business day notice period.	LR 1.2.1 LR 5
D. Transactions				
20.	Refinancing and reconstructions	UKLA/ TN/301.1	What constitutes a refinancing or reconstruction for the purpose of LR 9.5.12.	LR 9.5.12

No.	Title	Reference number	Matters covered	Relevant Rules
			What must be contained in the relevant circular, including a working capital statement on the basis that the reconstruction or refinancing has taken place.	
21.	Classification tests	UKLA/ TN/302.1	How the class tests apply to joint venture arrangements. How they apply to buying a company/asset out of administration. Profit adjustments for exceptional items and adjustments for post balance sheet events. The UKLA is reluctant to allow enterprise value to be used in place of the market capitalisation test. [Note: the FCA is consulting on amendments to this Guidance Note – see p. xlvii to xlix for details].	LR 10.1.3 LR 10 Annex I
22.	Amendments to the terms of a transaction	UKLA/ TN/304.1	Material amendments cannot be made to the terms of transaction without fresh shareholder approval. In a takeover offer situation, conditions may be waived (if permitted by the relevant shareholder resolution) without triggering the requirement for fresh shareholder approval.	LR 10.5.2 LR 10.5.4
23.	Hostile takeovers	UKLA/ TN/305.2	Where a listed offeror cannot access the relevant offeree information to prepare its shareholder circular, the offeror should find and publish the best information available to it.	LR 10.5.2 LR 13.4.1 LR 13.4.3 LR 13 Annex I PR 5.5.3

No.	Title	Reference number	Matters covered	Relevant Rules
			Modifications to the circular/prospectus content requirements may be permitted in relation to the responsibility statement, working capital, material contracts, litigation and significant change statements, and the pro forma financial information requirements.	PR Appendix 3 Annexes
			If due diligence access is granted while the offer is still open, a supplementary prospectus may be required.	
24.	Reverse takeovers	UKLA/ TN/306.3	When a reverse takeover is sufficiently advanced that a leak may trigger the suspension requirements.	LR 5.1.2
25.	Aggregating transactions	UKLA/ TN/307.1	The UKLA has the scope to require aggregation in wider circumstances than are specified in the rules.	LR 10.2.10
			Historic class tests need not be rerun when aggregating transactions.	
26.	Related party transactions – Modified requirements for smaller related party transactions	UKLA/ TN/308.3	Confirmations that the terms of a transaction are fair and reasonable should be clean, not seek to limit the UKLA's use of the confirmation nor contain disclaimers.	LR 11.1.10
27.	Related party transactions – content of RIS announcement	UKLA/ TN/309.2	Companies should take reasonable care to ensure, when disclosing details of a smaller related party transaction in an RIS announcement, that the disclosure is not misleading or confusing and that the transaction is easily identifiable as a related party transaction.	LR 11.1.10

No.	Title	Reference number	Matters covered	Relevant Rules
28.	Share buy-backs – novel/complex approaches and Premium Listing Principle 5	UKLA/ TN/310.1	The FCA's approach when different structures that replicate a buy-back are used is to interpret the rules purposively. The note includes specific examples that the FCA considers as potentially offending Premium Listing Principle 5, which states that all shareholders that are in the same position must be treated equally.	LR 12.4 LR 2.2.4 LR 7.2.1A
29.	Discounted share issues and standard of disclosure in circular	UKLA/ TN/311.1	Guidance on the disclosure required in the circular where shareholder approval is being sought for an issue of shares at a discount of more than 10%.	LR 13.3.1(3) LR 9.5.10(3)(a)
30.	Shareholder votes in relation to hypothetical transactions	UKLA/ TN/312.1	FCA's views on premium-listed issuers producing circulars for voting purposes at a particularly early stage of a transaction.	LR 13
31.	Reverse takeovers and uncapped consideration	UKLA/ TN/314.1	How uncapped consideration is treated when calculating whether a transaction should be classified as a reverse takeover.	LR 5.6 LR 10
E. Working capital				
32.	Working capital statements – basis of preparation	UKLA/ TN/320.1	Assumptions underlying a clean working capital statement cannot be included in a prospectus but the basis on which the statement is made can. Interaction between the Prospectus Directive requirements and the Listing Rule requirements on a Class 1 acquisition and a reverse takeover. When the proceeds of an issue can be taken into account in a clean working capital statement.	LR 13.4.1 LR 13 Annex 1 PR Appendix 3 Annexes

No.	Title	Reference number	Matters covered	Relevant Rules
33.	Working capital statements and risk factors	UKLA/ TN/321.1	Risk factors that cannot be reconciled with a clean working capital statement should not be included in a prospectus. High impact, low probability risks may be permitted. Disclaimers that a risk factor is not intended to qualify the issuer's working capital statement are not permitted.	PR Appendix 3 Annexes
F. Profit forecasts and estimates				
34.	Profit forecasts and estimates	UKLA/ TN/340.1	The definition of a profit forecast. Ensuring statements about future performance are not profit forecasts. The basis on which profit forecasts should be prepared and what they should reflect.	LR 13.5.32 LR 13.5.33 PR Appendix 3 Annexes
G. Closed-ended investment funds				
35.	Acquiring assets during investment trust rollovers	UKLA/ TN/401.1	When a rollover of an investment trust into a premium listed closed-ended investment fund, which would be a class 1 transaction for the fund, will be exempt under LR 15.5.2.	LR 15.5.2
36.	Co-investments between closed-ended funds and their investment managers' employees	UKLA/ TN/402.1	Matters to consider when employees of an investment manager co-invest in the equity of an investee company, alongside the listed fund.	LR 11 LR 15
37.	Alterations to investment management fees	UKLA/ TN/403.1	How to classify changes to investments manager's annual and performance fees for the purposes of LR 11.	LR 11 LR 15

No.	Title	Reference number	Matters covered	Relevant Rules
38.	Related party transactions by closed-ended investment funds – amendment of an existing investment management agreement to cover new money	UKLA/ TN/404.1	Guidance for issuers and their sponsors on what the FCA considers to be the correct treatment under the related party transactions rules in LR 11of revisions to an investment management agreement to cover new money.	LR 11 LR 15
39.	Closed-ended investment funds: investment management agreements and independence of the board	UKLA/ TN/405.1	Provides commentary on new developments that have been observed in fund management agreements, and how they may interact with LR 15.2.19.	LR 15.2.19 LR 15.4.7A
40.	Application of related party rules to funds investing in highly illiquid asset classes	UKLA/ TN/406.1	When the FCA might accept that acquisitions from a related party (such as its fund manager) should be considered to be in the ordinary course of business for a closed-ended investment fund.	LR 11.1.4 LR 15.5.4
41.	Closed-ended investment funds with multiple share classes	UKLA/ TN/407.1	Clarifies how funds listed under LR 15 that have multiple classes of shares should be reflected in the fund's investment policy.	LR 15.2.7 LR 15.4.1A LR 15.4.2 LR 15.4.8
42.	Closed-ended investment funds: eligibility of closed-ended investment funds	UKLA/ TN/408.1	Clarifies how the eligibility of applicants that seek a listing under LR 15, but have features that could suggest they are actually commercial companies, or investment entities that fail to spread investment risk, are assessed.	LR 15.2
43.	Closed-ended investment funds: master-feeder structures	UKLA/ TN/409.1	Sets out the FCA's views on more innovative fund structures.	LR 15.2.6 LR 15.4.6

No.	Title	Reference number	Matters covered	Relevant Rules
44.	Closed-ended investment funds: definition of 'investment manager'	UKLA/ TN/410.1	Clarifies the FCA's interpretation of the definition of 'investment manager' for the purpose of LR 15.	LR 11 LR 15
H. Specialist companies				
45.	Special purpose acquisition companies (SPACs)	UKLA/ TN/420.1	Definition of and guidance on SPACs. [Note: the FCA is consulting on amendments to this Guidance Note – see p. xlvii to xlix for details].	LR 5 LR 6 LR 14
46.	Real Estate Investment Trusts (REITs)	UKLA/ TN/421.1	Which listing categories are available to a REIT. Matters to consider when a property company is converting to a REIT status. How a REIT can comply with the 10% substantial shareholder restriction and other legislative provisions.	LR 2.2.4 LR 7.2.1 LR 14 LR 15
47.	Scientific research-based companies	UKLA/ TN/422.2	Guidance on the concession for scientific research-based companies who do not have a three year track record on admission. [Note: the guidance in LR 6.1.7 referred to in the note has been moved to LR 6.1.3E and LR 6.1.7G has now been deleted.] [Note: the FCA is consulting on amendments to this Guidance Note – see p. xlvii to xlix for details.]	LR 6.1.11 LR 6.1.12 LR 6.1.3EG
48.	Open-ended investment companies	UKLA/ TN/423.1	Which companies the listing category is available to and the key differences in the listing process for companies in this category.	LR 4.2.3 LR 16

No.	Title	Reference number	Matters covered	Relevant Rules
49.	Removal from the Official List of listed equity shares of individual funds (individual sub-funds) of Open-ended Investment Companies (OEICs)	UKLA/TN/424.1	Guidance on the position of OEICs and removing listed equity shares of individual sub-funds from the Official List.	LR 5.2 DEPP 2.5.11G
50.	Open-ended investment companies and transfer restrictions	UKLA/TN/425.1	Guidance on when an issuer may not be able to meet Listing Rule requirements.	LR 2.2.4R, LR 16.1.1R (1) LR 16.2.1R
I. Periodic financial information				
51.	Half-yearly and annual reports	UKLA/TN/501.1	Responsibility for annual and half-yearly reports. The requirement to disclose principal risks and uncertainties.	DTR 4.1.12 DTR 4.1.13 DTR 4.2.7 DTR 4.2.10 DTR 4.2.11
52.	Preliminary statement of annual results	UKLA/TN/502.2	Requirements for issuers choosing to issue a preliminary results announcement.	LR 9.7A.1
53.	Equivalence arrangements for third country issuers	UKLA/TN/503.2	Which third country (i.e. non-EEA) issuers are exempt from certain periodic financial reporting requirements.	DTR 4.4.8
54.	Exemptions from the periodic reporting requirements	UKLA/TN/504.2	When the exemption from periodic reporting requirements for a state, a regional or local authority or a public international body may cover issues of debt securities by an agency on behalf of such an entity.	DTR 4.4.1 DTR 4.4.4

QUICK REFERENCE TABLE – THE UKLA GUIDANCE NOTES

No.	Title	Reference number	Matters covered	Relevant Rules
55.	Periodic financial information and inside information	UKLA/TN/506.1	Disclosure of inside information, including information about financial performance, cannot be delayed to coincide with a scheduled announcement of a periodic financial report. [Note: the FCA is consulting on amendments to this Guidance Note – see p. xlvii to xlix for details.]	LR 7.2.1 LR 7.2.3 DTR 2.2.1 DTR 2.2.2
J. Regulatory announcements including inside information					
56.	Delaying disclosure / Dealing with leaks and rumours	UKLA/TN/520.2	The UKLA's expectations when there is a leak or rumour after disclosure of inside information has been delayed. The ability to delay public disclosure generally under the Market Abuse Regulation.	LR 5.1.3 Article 7 MAR Article 11 MAR Article 17 MAR
57.	Assessing and handling inside information	UKLA/TN/521.3	Who should have responsibility for determining what is inside information and for releasing it. Balancing positive and negative news. Materiality thresholds for disclosure of inside information. The interaction between disclosure under the DTRs and the Takeover Code. Announcements by regulators.	LR 7 LR 9.2.18R Articles 7 MAR Article 17 MAR DTR 2
58.	Disclosure of 'lock-up' agreements	UKLA/TN/522.2	The disclosure that is required in relation to lock up agreements, in particular the circumstances in which the shareholder is able to dispose of some or all of its holding before the lock-up term expires.	LR 1.3.3R PR Appendix 3 Annex 3 item 7.3 Article 12(1)(c) MAR

No.	Title	Reference number	Matters covered	Relevant Rules
K. Disclosure of positions held by issuers, investors and management					
59.	Scope and application of vote holder and issuer notification rules	UKLA/ TN/541.1	The scope of DTR 5 and which issuers it applies to, and in particular how it applies to issuers of GDRs. [Note: the FCA is consulting on amendments to this Guidance Note – see p. xlvii to xlix for details.]	DTR 5
60.	Issuer's obligations	UKLA/ TN/542.2	An issuer's disclosure obligations under DTR 5 and LR 12 on a purchase of own shares. The disclosure requirements in respect of treasury shares. Monthly total voting rights announcements. Table summarising the notification deadlines for the various disclosure requirements for an issuer.	LR 12.4.6 DTR 5.5.1 DTR 5.6 DTR 5.8.12
61.	Shareholder obligations	UKLA/ TN/543.2	Shareholders' notification obligations under DTR 5. Disclosure of interests in financial instruments. The position of indirect shareholders. The notifications required where shareholders have combined holdings. How and when notifications should be made. Notification of proxy holdings. [Note: the FCA is consulting on amendments to this Guidance Note – see p. xlvii to xlix for details.]	DTR 5.1.4 (2) DTR 5.2.1 DTR 5.3.3 DTR 5.8.4 DTR 5.10.1

No.	Title	Reference number	Matters covered	Relevant Rules
62.	Third country equivalent obligations	UKLA/TN/544.2	The application of the DTRs to non-EEA issuers. When non-EEA issuers might be exempt from certain disclosure and transparency obligations.	DTR 5.11 DTR 6
63.	Changes in holdings	UKLA/TN/545.2	Shareholders may have to notify under DTR 5, even if their shareholding (or interest in other disclosable instruments) has not increased/decreased, where there is a change in the total voting rights in the company.	DTR 5
64.	Voting rights that are disregarded for notification purposes	UKLA/TN/546.2	When voting rights can be disregarded for DTR 5 purposes. The treatment of investment managers and managers of lawfully managed investments, assets of a collective undertaking and open-ended investment companies. Disclosure obligations for a manager acting on a discretionary basis and for stock lending/borrowing. Exemptions for clearing and settlement houses, custodians and nominees, market makers, credit institutions or investment firms and collateral takers.	DTR 5.1.3 DTR 5.1.4 DTR 5.1.5 DTR 5.2.1
65.	Aggregation of managed holdings	UKLA/TN/547.2	When a parent and controlled undertakings must aggregate their holdings for DTR 5 purposes. The position of management and investment firms and how a parent can get an exemption from aggregation.	DTR 5.4

No.	Title	Reference number	Matters covered	Relevant Rules
66.	Market makers	UKLA/ TN/548.2	The DTR 5 exemption for market makers.	DTR 5.1.3 (3)
67.	Asset managers	UKLA/ TN/549.2	Holdings of certain interests held by asset and investment managers, and shares in open-ended investment companies, can be disregarded under DTR 5. How requirements interact where an entity also has non-exempt holdings.	DTR 5.1.5 (1)
68.	Trading book exemption	UKLA/ TN/550.2	The partial notification exemption for voting rights held in a firm's trading book and how to benefit from it.	DTR 5.1.3 (4)
69.	Aggregation of holdings	UKLA/ TN/551.2	When direct and indirect holdings must be aggregated and notifications required for changes in composition of holdings.	DTR 5.7.1
L. Public offers, admission to trading and the marketing of securities					
70.	Public offers	UKLA/ TN/601.1	Definition of a 'public offer' of securities requiring the issue of a prospectus.	PR 1.2.1
71.	Exemptions from the requirement to produce a prospectus	UKLA/ TN/602.1	Exemptions from the requirement to produce a prospectus: ■ up to 10% of shares of class already traded ■ employee share schemes ■ offers of under €5 million ■ takeovers and mergers (and vetting of equivalent documents) ■ convertible securities ■ redenomination of share capital.	PR 1.2.2 PR 1.2.3
72.	Public offers – the Six-day rule	UKLA/ TN/603.1	Six-day minimum period for availability of prospectus before end of offer. Application to pathfinders and pre-marketing documents.	PR 3.2.3

QUICK REFERENCE TABLE – THE UKLA GUIDANCE NOTES xli

No.	Title	Reference number	Matters covered	Relevant Rules
73.	PD advertisement regime	UKLA/TN/604.1	Types of communications that constitute an advert. Application to pathfinders' and analysts' reports. Requirement for warning wording on advertisements. [Note: the FCA is consulting on amendments to this Guidance Note – see p. xlvii to xlix for details.]	PR 3.3
74.	Supplementary prospectus	UKLA/TN/605.2	When a supplementary prospectus is required/permitted. Suspension of offer.	PR 3.4
M. Prospectus content				
75.	Incorporation by reference	UKLA/TN/620.1	Documents can be incorporated by reference if approved or filed with the Home Competent Authority.	PR 2.4.1
76.	Risk factors	UKLA/TN/621.3	Risk factors should be specific and relevant. Circumstances in which the UKLA will challenge proposed risk factors. Ordering of risk factors and disclosure in a prospectus summary.	PR Appendix 3 Annexes
77.	Collective investment undertaking prospectuses – portfolio disclosure	UKLA/TN/622.1	Disclosure must be as at the date of prospectus. The valuation date can be the balance sheet date.	PR Appendix 3 Annexes
78.	Documents on display	UKLA/TN/623.1	Requirements for display of valuations and statements by an expert and of material contacts.	PR Appendix 3 Annexes
79.	Operating and financial reviews (OFR)	UKLA/TN/624.1	Disclosure requirements for OFR. Drawing comparisons between periods within three-year track record.	PR Appendix 3 Annexes

No.	Title	Reference number	Matters covered	Relevant Rules
80.	Current trading and trend information	UKLA/ TN/625.1	Nature of requirement for backward and forward looking disclosures. Risk of unintended profit forecasts when disclosing expectations for current year.	PR Appendix 3 Annexes
81.	Directors' and management disclosures in share prospectuses	UKLA/ TN/626.1	Need for disclosures to cover senior managers who are not directors. Details of the disclosures that are required.	PR Appendix 3 Annexes
82.	Prospectus content – financial information	UKLA/ TN/627.1	If an issuer must audit a period of less than one year, the information should be prepared to the same standard as the annual financial statements.	PR Appendix 3 Annexes
83.	Significant change statements	UKLA/ TN/628.2	The expectations of the UKLA in relation to significant change disclosure (including in a prospectus summary).	PR Appendix 3 Annexes
84.	Final terms	UKLA/ TN/629.3	What information can be included in the final terms. How final terms should be filed in relation to a passported base prospectus. Programme issues and incorporation of terms from an expired base prospectus.	PD Regulations Article 22, 24, 26 PR 2.2.9R PR Appendix 3 Annex XX, XXI; ESMA Questions and Answers on Prospectuses
85.	Choice of home Member State under the PD	UKLA/ TN/630.1	Choice of home Member State for issuers of convertible securities and global depositary receipts. Definition of non-equity securities and application to GDRs.	PR 1.1.1

No.	Title	Reference number	Matters covered	Relevant Rules
86.	Zero-coupon notes	UKLA/ TN/631.1	Zero coupon notes are not securities which fall within the disclosure requirements set out in Annex XII or Annex XX (12) of the Prospectus Directive.	PR 2.2.9 PR Appendix 3, Annex XX
87.	Non-equity retail prospectuses	UKLA/ TN/632.1	Making a retail prospectus easily analysable and comprehensible.	PR 2.1.1
88.	Pro forma financial information	UKLA/ TN/633.1	Addresses changes in the way that pro forma financial information is typically presented as a result of the European Securities and Markets Authority (ESMA) revised Q&A (Q 51).	PR Appendix 3 PR 2.3.1 LR 13.4.1(5)
89.	Financial information on guarantors in debt prospectuses and requests for omission	UKLA/ TN/634.1	Clarifies the FCA's approach to requests to omit guarantor financial information from a debt prospectus and provides an indication of the circumstances in which it considers it may be appropriate to grant an omission request.	PR Appendix 3 PR 2.5.2UK
N. Sponsors				
90.	Sponsors: conflicts of interest	UKLA/ TN/701.2	Procedures for identifying and managing conflicts. Examples of circumstances which may mean that a firm cannot act as a sponsor. Issues when acting as an agent. Factors to consider when sponsor is a provider of loan finance. Requirements to liaise with UKLA and provide information. [Note: the FCA is consulting on amendments to this Guidance Note – see p. xlvii to xlix for details.]	LR 8.3 LR 8.6

No.	Title	Reference number	Matters covered	Relevant Rules
91.	The sponsor's role on working capital confirmations	UKLA/ TN/704.3	Requirement to apply judgement and to review and challenge issuer and accountants. Reliance on third parties not sufficient. The records management rules in LR 8.	LR 8
92.	Sponsors: uncertain market conditions	UKLA/ TN/705.2	Review of procedures during uncertain market conditions, including impact on assessment of working capital. Need for increased due diligence and risk assessment for new business.	LR 8
93.	Sponsors: innovative structures and schemes	UKLA/ TN/706.1	Sponsors should only approach the UKLA about new proposals from issuers if satisfied that they are bona fide and do not breach the rules.	LR 8.3
94.	Sponsors who are part of an investment management group	UKLA/ TN/707.1	Transaction with sponsor will be related party transaction if sponsor forms part of same group as issuer's investment manager.	LR 8 LR 11 LR 15.5.3 LR 15.5.4
95.	Sponsor's obligations on financial position and prospectus procedures	UKLA/ TN/708.2	Confirmation that issuer has established procedures to make proper judgements about financial position and prospects. Meaning of 'established'. Role of sponsor in reviewing and challenging work of issuer and accountants. Requirement for systematic process and documentation.	LR 8 LR 7.2.1
96.	Sponsors transactions – adequacy of resourcing	UKLA/ TN/709.2	Sponsor must ensure adequate resourcing to staff and supervise the transaction, including in particular taking into account relevant experience.	LR 8.3 LR 8.6

QUICK REFERENCE TABLE – THE UKLA GUIDANCE NOTES   xlv

No.	Title	Reference number	Matters covered	Relevant Rules
97.	Sponsor services: principles for sponsors	UKLA/TN/710.1	The meaning of 'sponsor services'. When a sponsor service ceases. Role of the sponsor in relation to listings, circulars and submissions. Communications with the FCA.	LR 3.3.3 LR 5.6.17 LR 8 LR 10.8.3(2) LR 11.1.10 LR 13.6.1(5)
98.	Sponsor notifications	UKLA/TN/711.1	Practical considerations for sponsors when complying with the notifications to be sent by a sponsor to the FCA.	LR 8.7.7 LR 8.7.8
99.	Additional powers to supervise and discipline sponsors	UKLA/TN/712.2	When the FCA may consider restricting or limiting the services a sponsor may provide. Circumstances when a sponsor may choose to request a suspension of its approval. When the FCA may suspend a sponsor's approval or impose restrictions or limitations on the services a sponsor can provide. What disciplinary powers the FCA has over sponsors.	LR 8.6 LR 8.7 DEPP 2.5 DEPP 2 Annex 1G DEPP 2 Annex 2G FSMA s. 88 FSMA s. 88A
100.	Sponsors: application of principle to deal with the FCA in an open and co-operative manner	UKLA/TN/713.1	Impact of this regulatory obligation on a sponsor's contractual arrangements with third parties, such as non-disclosure agreements.	R 8.3.5R LR 8.3.12G LR 8.6.12G–13BG
101.	Guidance on competence requirements set out under LR 8.6.7R(2)	UKLA/TN/714.2	A description of the types of skills, knowledge and expertise the FCA expects sponsors to consider when assessing whether they understand each of the 'competency sets'.	LR 8.6.7R LR 8.6.7R(2)(b)

No.	Title	Reference number	Matters covered	Relevant Rules
102.	Sponsors: practical implications of competence requirements for sponsors and applicants	UKLA/TN/715.1	Practical guidance on the provisions relating to sponsor competence.	LR 8
103.	Joint sponsors: communications with the FCA	UKLA/TN/716.1	Guidance in relation to non-administrative communications between joint sponsors and the FCA.	LR 8.3.5
104.	Sponsors: record keeping requirements	UKLA/TN/717.1	Guidance on the record-keeping requirements in LR 8.6.16AR, in particular on materiality.	LR 8

Proposed new guidance notes and proposed revisions to existing notes

The following new guidance notes and revisions to existing guidance notes have been issued for consultation but not yet finalised:

Title	Reference number	Matters covered	Relevant primary market bulletin
Proposed new notes			
Eligibility for premium listing – financial information and the track record requirements	UKLA/ TN/102.1	Details of changes to the way applicants for a premium listing calculate whether their audited accounts cover 75% of the business.	CP 17/4 (February 2017)
The independent business requirements for companies applying for premium listing – interpretation of LR 6.4, LR 6.5 and LR 6.6	UKLA/ TN/103.1	This Technical Note is intended to provide a non-exhaustive guide to cases where the FCA is required to consider an applicant's ability to meet the requirement for an independent business.	CP 17/4 (February 2017)
Property companies	UKLA/ TN/426.1	Guidance on the concession for certain property companies from the revenue earning track record requirements which is meant to allow property companies to demonstrate maturity in other ways than through three years of revenue generation.	CP 17/4 (February 2017)

Title	Reference number	Matters covered	Relevant primary market bulletin
Mineral companies	UKLA/TN/427.1	Guidance on the concessionary route to premium listing for mineral companies that would not otherwise be eligible for premium listing under LR 6.	CP 17/4 (February 2017)
Substitution of issuer of debt securities	UKLA/PN/911.1	Guidance on the procedural mechanics of replacing an issuer of debt securities on the Official List, through a substitution of an issuer.	PMB No. 17 (April 2017)
Proposed revisions to existing notes			
Share buy-backs with mix and match facilities	UKLA/TN/202.2	Minor changes, to reflect rule changes following the Market Abuse Regulation.	PMB No. 16 (June 2016)
Listing Principle 2 Dealing with the FCA in an open and cooperative manner	UKLA/TN/209.3	Minor amendments to guidance on Listing Principle 2.	CP 17/4 (February 2017)
Classification tests	UKLA/TN/302.2	Amendments to the profits test and the figures used to classify assets and profits for the purpose of the class tests in Annex 1 of LR 10.	CP 17/4 (February 2017)
Cash shells and special purpose acquisition companies (SPACs)	UKLA/TN/420.2	Guidance on definitions, listing eligibility and reverse takeovers.	CP 17/4 (February 2017)
Scientific research-based companies	UKLA/TN/422.3	Guidance on the concessionary route to premium listing for scientific research-based companies (SRBCs) that would not otherwise be eligible for premium listing under LR 6 without a three year track record.	CP 17/4 (February 2017)

PROPOSED NEW GUIDANCE NOTES

Title	Reference number	Matters covered	Relevant primary market bulletin
Periodic financial information and inside information	UKLA/ TN/506.2	Minor changes, to reflect rule changes following the Market Abuse Regulation.	PMB No. 16 (June 2016)
Scope and application of vote holder and issuer notification rules	UKLA/ TN/541.2	Amendments for Transparency Directive.	PMB No. 12 (November 2015) PMB No. 16 (June 2016)
Shareholder obligations	UKLA/ TN/543.3	Amendments to reflect ESMA's new TR-1 form that will come into force on 30 June 2017.	PMB No. 17 (April 2017)
PD advertisement regime	UKLA/ TN/604.2	Amendments to reflect Omnibus 2 Directive.	PMB No. 13 (March 2016)
Sponsors: conflicts of interest	UKLA/ TN/701.3	Amendments in response to the FCA's consultation on the effectiveness on the sponsors' conflicts regime.	PMB No. 17 (April 2017)
UKLA decision making and individual guidance processes	UKLA/ PN/908.2	The proposed amendments would reflect the fact that the Listing Authority Review Committee (LARC), which people could ask to review individual guidance they received, was abolished in January 2014. The FCA is also proposing to expand the note to explain the procedure for UKLA decision making more generally and to reflect the new strategic approach and structural changes that were announced on 8 December 2014.	PMB No. 8 (August 2014)

Foreword

In the early 1600s, the coffeehouses of the City of London served as a new focal point for merchants and adventurers, seeking to make their fortune and investors keen to explore new, global markets for silver and gold to spices and oil. Over the course of the last 400 years London and its stock exchange has remained one of the world's leading financial centres, with by far the most diverse and international offering of any market in the world.

A key part of that success has been our continual ability, as a market, to innovate within the context of balancing the evolving needs of investors and issuers. There are obvious examples like the development of AIM in the mid-1990s which from an initial coterie of just a few dozen companies, has passed a significant milestone this year of raising over £100bn for growth companies and has become, by some distance, the world's most successful growth market.

Less remarkable perhaps, but equally innovative has been the genesis of new segments like the Specialist Fund Segment, the High Growth Segment and our recently launched International Securities Market. Each built in response to demand from specialist investors and issuers and in concert with a regulator that understands that if London and the UK are to continue a play a global role – particularly as we negotiate our exit from Europe – our markets and rules need to be adaptable.

Today, our equity and fixed income capital markets provide a broad range of financing options to draw upon depending on your company's specific needs and we hope they will help fund the continued development of your business through changing economic times.

The latter point is important and often overlooked: equity is the ultimate form of long term financing. It provides a company not just with the initial boost of capital at IPO, but ongoing funding to back M&A, employee retention and even balance sheet support in more difficult times when credit markets seize up.

The diversity of issuers we have seen IPO in London over recent years reflects both increased investor appetite for new equity stories and the important tax and regulatory changes we have been working hard to push through. For example, the ability for retail investors to place AIM shares in ISAs and the removal of stamp duty on the trading of those shares has seen a huge boost to trading and liquidity in smaller companies' securities. Together with the wider financial community, we continue to work with government and regulators to ensure that our capital markets remain as deep and liquid as possible.

We are passionate about the success of our capital markets and strive to ensure they continue to meet your capital raising requirements, whatever the health of the economy. Recent initiatives such as our 1000 Companies to Inspire Britain report, now in its fourth year, the strong development of our ELITE programme to support private high growth businesses and ongoing dialogue with policy makers are some examples of how we have worked together with our clients to ensure that our markets retain their global reputation.

I am delighted to have been asked to write the foreword for this Guide by Herbert Smith Freehills and ICSA: The Governance Institute. With regulation playing such an important role, the practical interpretation and application of rules is key. This guide is a very helpful tool to anyone involved with the Main Market, combining essential practical theory with a commercial outlook, not to mention bringing together the various rule books and legislation into one place. Should any questions remain though, do come to see my team, who can talk you through any element of the market or regulation that's at issue.

Marcus Stuttard
Head of UK Primary Markets, London Stock Exchange

Preface

This Guide is aimed at company secretaries, directors, in-house lawyers, investment bankers and other market participants seeking a guide to the process in connection with the admission of a company's shares to listing on the premium segment of the Official List of the UKLA and to trading on the Main Market of the London Stock Exchange, and the range of continuing obligations that applies to such listed companies. It focuses on commercial companies rather than investment companies and the application of the rules and related company law to UK incorporated companies.

This Guide has been updated and revised to take account of all of the changes to the law and regulation governing listed companies, and all new guidance issued, since the third edition was published in 2015. The most significant of these changes was the implementation of the Market Abuse Regulation, which took effect in July 2016. It also reflects the latest FCA enforcement decisions and the latest developments in corporate reporting. This Guide also discusses possible forthcoming changes to the regulatory regime, including the proposals in the new draft Prospectus Regulation and the IPO process in the UK.

Readers will no doubt be aware that a considerable body of the law and regulation applicable to UK listed companies is derived – directly or indirectly – from European law. The decision by the UK Government to serve notice under Article 50 of the Treaty of the European Union of its intention to leave the European Union raises the question as to how, if at all, the legal and regulatory environment for UK listed companies will change following 'Brexit'. At the time of writing, neither the UK Government nor the FCA has published specific proposals in this regard. In the meantime, this Guide sets out the law and regulation as it currently applies.

This Guide maintains the focus of previous editions and does not attempt to cover – other than by way of passing reference – the specific provisions of the LPDT Rules that govern the Professional Securities Market, investment companies, issuers of certificates representing securities (e.g. GDRs) or the issuers of debt securities. Instead, this Guide covers the following topics:

- The UK listing regime and the rules applicable to companies seeking a premium listing.

- The role and responsibilities of a company's sponsor, both in the context of a company seeking a premium listing as a new applicant and in the context of a premium listed company considering certain types of corporate action, including a significant transaction or share issuance.
- The rules applicable to the preparation and publication of a prospectus.
- The continuing obligations applicable to premium listed companies, including those in relation to the control and disclosure of inside information, financial reporting and governance, disclosure of share dealings and interests in voting rights, market announcements and shareholder communications and certain transactions, including significant and related party transactions, further share issues and share buy-backs.

Throughout this book, references to paragraphs prefixed by 'LR' are to paragraphs of the Listing Rules, paragraphs prefixed by 'DTR' are to paragraphs of the Disclosure Guidance and Transparency Rules and paragraphs prefixed by 'PR' are to paragraphs of the Prospectus Rules. In addition, paragraph numbers that end in 'R' denote that the paragraph is a rule, whereas paragraph numbers that end in 'G' denote guidance. In practice there is very little difference between the two, because if an applicant or listed company has not complied with guidance the FCA may consider that it has not complied with the corresponding rule.

Although this book summarises the key provisions of the LPDT Rules, the Market Abuse Regulation and other current sources of law, regulation and guidance, reference should always be made to the full, current text of the relevant underlying rule or guidance and advice sought in relation to specific facts and circumstances. While every effort has been made to ensure the accuracy and completeness of this book, neither the author, the editors, the contributors nor the publisher accept any responsibility for any loss arising to anyone as a consequence of relying on it or the information contained herein.

Producing a book of this nature is a significant undertaking and I would like to convey my gratitude to my colleagues who have assisted in the effort. Their names appear on pages xii and xiii and much of the credit for this book is theirs. I would also like to acknowledge the contributions of Will Pearce and Chris Haynes, former partners of Herbert Smith Freehills and editors of earlier editions of this Guide, on which this latest edition builds.

The references to UK and EU law and guidance are as stated as at 30 June 2017.

Mike Flockhart
Partner, Herbert Smith Freehills LLP

Introduction

This Introduction gives an overview of the process involved when a company decides to float on the London Stock Exchange. As well as seeking admission to listing on the Official List and to trading on the London Stock Exchange's main market, companies will typically also offer shares to investors through an initial public offering (IPO). Once it is listed, it will have to be aware of and comply with the continuing obligations imposed by the rules.

The key rules that apply to a company seeking a listing and, following admission to listing, to a listed company are set out in the Financial Services and Markets Act 2000 (the FSMA), the Market Abuse Regulation (MAR) and the Listing Rules, Prospectus Rules, Disclosure Guidance and Transparency Rules (the LPDT Rules) that are made by the Financial Conduct Authority (the FCA), the securities and financial markets regulator in the UK, pursuant to powers granted to it by Part VI of the FSMA. The rules are mostly derived from and implement European Union law and apply across the EU to all listed companies, but there are some 'super equivalent' UK rules that only apply to companies with a premium listing in the UK.

Figure 3, included at the end of this Introduction, sets out a comparison of the key listing conditions and continuing obligations that apply to a company with shares admitted to the premium segment of the Official List (a 'premium listed company') and a company with shares admitted to the standard segment of the Official List (a 'standard listed company'), the two alternative listing options open to a commercial company seeking admission to the Official List and to trading on the London Stock Exchange's main market for listed securities.

In addition to the LPDT Rules, there are formal guidance notes issued by the FCA, as well as guidance published by the European Securities and Markets Authority (ESMA) and other market and industry bodies that influences the operation of the UK Listing Regime in practice.

Figure 1 below illustrates the relationship between EU law, and related guidance issued by ESMA, and UK securities law and regulation and related guidance issued by the FCA.

Figure 1: Relationship between EU and UK securities law and regulation

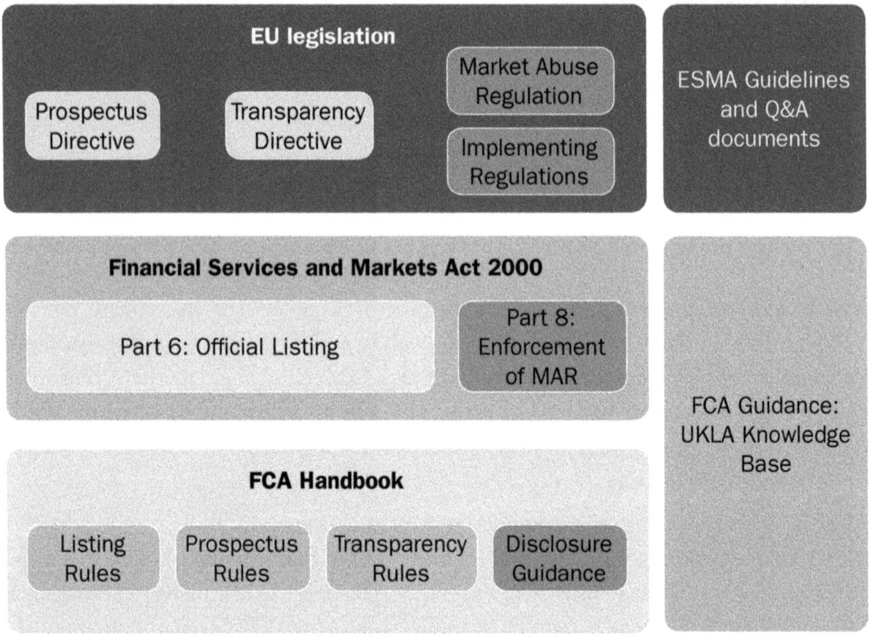

- **EU legislation**
  - Prospectus Directive
  - Transparency Directive
  - Market Abuse Regulation
  - Implementing Regulations
- ESMA Guidelines and Q&A documents

- **Financial Services and Markets Act 2000**
  - Part 6: Official Listing
  - Part 8: Enforcement of MAR
- FCA Guidance: UKLA Knowledge Base

- **FCA Handbook**
  - Listing Rules
  - Prospectus Rules
  - Transparency Rules
  - Disclosure Guidance

1. Why does a company decide to list?

A company may decide to carry out an IPO for a number of reasons. The most likely is to raise money, either for the company itself or for its shareholders (who may sell shares as part of the IPO process), or both. An IPO and listing also raises the company's profile.

Once it is listed, a further issue of shares can provide an additional source of money for the company, either to provide working capital, to reduce debt or to fund acquisitions. Shares can also be used to incentivise employees.

When it decides to list, a company and its shareholders need to be aware that the directors will be accountable to the new shareholders in the company. The existing shareholders will no longer have the same level of control and the company will be much more open to public scrutiny. The company will also be subject to a regulatory regime with which it must comply both on admission and on an ongoing basis.

The company will need to consider these factors when deciding to list and on which market. The key markets in the UK are discussed in Chapter 2.

2. The IPO advisory team

A company preparing for an IPO and life as a listed company will need the assistance of a team of professional advisers. This will include one or more investment banks, a firm of lawyers, accountants and a registrar. In addition, the investment banks will have their own legal advisers including an external law firm and their in-house legal and compliance team. Other advisers may be required for particular types of companies (e.g. a mineral experts report may be required for the IPO of a mining company).

2.1 The investment bank

When a company is carrying out an IPO in the UK, its principal investment bank (or banks) usually has the most important part to play in the process. Where the company is seeking a premium listing, the investment bank acts as the intermediary between the company and the UK Listing Authority and 'sponsors' the company's admission to the Official List (it is referred to in this capacity as the 'sponsor' to the IPO). The sponsor must formally declare to the UK Listing Authority that, among other things, the company has satisfied all requirements of the Listing Rules and Prospectus Rules relevant to an application for admission to the Official List. It will also review and comment on the prospectus about the company and the securities to be listed, which is typically drafted by the company's lawyers. The investment bank will enter into an agreement with the company – known as the sponsor's agreement – which governs its responsibilities and obligations in relation to admission.

The investment bank will generally also act as an 'underwriter' to the offering – often alongside a group of other underwriters acting as a syndicate. In simple terms, underwriting on an institutional IPO works as follows: if the selling shareholder and the company offer a certain number of shares to investors in the IPO to raise a certain amount of money and the investors default in their obligation to buy the shares that they have committed to buy, the underwriters undertake to buy those defaulted shares, thus guaranteeing that the selling shareholder and/or the company will sell the agreed number of shares and raise the intended amount of money. The underwriters enter into an agreement with the selling shareholder and the company, called the 'underwriting agreement' (generally combined with the sponsor's agreement), setting out their undertaking to buy any defaulted shares and the percentage commission charged for doing so. In addition, the underwriting agreement will contain a number of representations and warranties about the company, its business and the securities being offered.

2.2 The company's lawyers

The company's lawyers help the company to prepare for the IPO. A company may need to reorganise its corporate group structure or carry out a share capital reorganisation to make sure that the company is suitable for life as a public listed company (see section 4 below). As well as assisting with this, the company's lawyers will carry out a 'due diligence' exercise on the company. This will involve seeking to identify any legal issues that may need to be considered in the context of the IPO, for example, litigation, contracts or commercial arrangements that could be terminated by a third party as a result of the IPO or which are material to investors' understanding of the company. These issues will need to be addressed as part of the IPO process. The information gathered by the company's lawyers during the due diligence process helps them to draft the prospectus in collaboration with the company and the investment banks, to identify issues that will have to be disclosed in the prospectus and to verify that the contents of the prospectus are correct and not misleading.

2.3 The investment bank's lawyers

The investment bank's lawyers have a dual role. First, they shadow the work of the company's lawyers in preparing the company for IPO, carrying out due diligence and drafting the prospectus. Second, where a company is seeking a premium listing, they advise the investment bank on its role as sponsor under Listing Rule 8 and as underwriter of the offering. They will advise on the contents and requirements of, and the obligations imposed by, the LPDT Rules and MAR and on legal issues relating to the marketing of the offering. They will also draft the sponsor's agreement and underwriting agreement and negotiate it with the company and its lawyers.

2.4 The reporting accountants

The reporting accountants are the final core members of a company's advisory team. The terms of the reporting accountants' role will be set out in a detailed engagement letter agreed with both the company and the investment banks involved in the IPO. The reporting accountants will prepare a number of private and public reports and comfort letters for the benefit of the company and the investment banks in connection with the publication of the prospectus and the requirements of the LPDT Rules.

The reporting accountants will carry out a detailed review of the company and its business and prepare a private financial due diligence report on the company, known as the 'long form report'. The exact scope of the accountant's review is a matter of agreement between the company, the accountant and the investment banks but generally includes an overview of the business and a review of: the market in which the company operates; historical trading figures and historical balance sheets; cash flow; management information systems, accounting policies and controls; taxation; management and employees; contingent liabilities and litigation; compliance with legislation; insurance arrangements; real estate and intellectual property rights; and related party transactions.

The reporting accountants also prepare a report known as a 'working capital report'. This is to support the statement that is required to be included in the prospectus confirming that the company has enough money (or working capital) to fund its business over the 12-month period following the IPO. They will also carry out certain agreed procedures to support the 'no significant change' statement, likewise required to be included in the prospectus.

They will also review and provide comfort on the company's financial position and prospects procedures and systems and controls; one of the key confirmations that the sponsor is required to provide to the FCA is that the directors have established procedures to enable them to monitor the ongoing financial position of the company.

They will assist with the preparation, review and verification of all of the financial information that the company is required by the Prospectus Rules to include in the prospectus. Notably, they are required to prepare a public report for inclusion in the prospectus (known as a 'short form report') in relation to the company's historical financial statements (normally in respect of the last three financial years). The report will contain an opinion as to whether or not, for the purposes of the prospectus, the report gives a true and fair view of the financial matters set out in it. They will also prepare a report in relation to any pro forma financial information.

Finally, they will prepare a suite of comfort letters, including ones which support the 'no significant change' statement that is required to be included in the prospectus.

3. Key steps in the IPO process

The IPO process typically involves the following key steps:

- pre-IPO reorganisation;
- due diligence;
- drafting the prospectus and verifying its contents;
- announcing the company's intention to float;
- negotiating and finalising the transaction documents and underwriting arrangements;
- publishing a prospectus and marketing the IPO;
- pricing and allocating the shares; and
- admission to listing and closing.

Depending on the nature of the company, the complexity of its business, its financial reporting calendar and state of readiness, the process usually takes at least four months to complete. Figure 2 sets out an illustrative outline timetable for an institutional only offer (see section 6 below) and London listing, assuming that any substantive corporate pre-IPO reorganisation is completed at the outset of the timetable.

Figure 2: Illustrative outline IPO timetable for an institutional offer and London listing

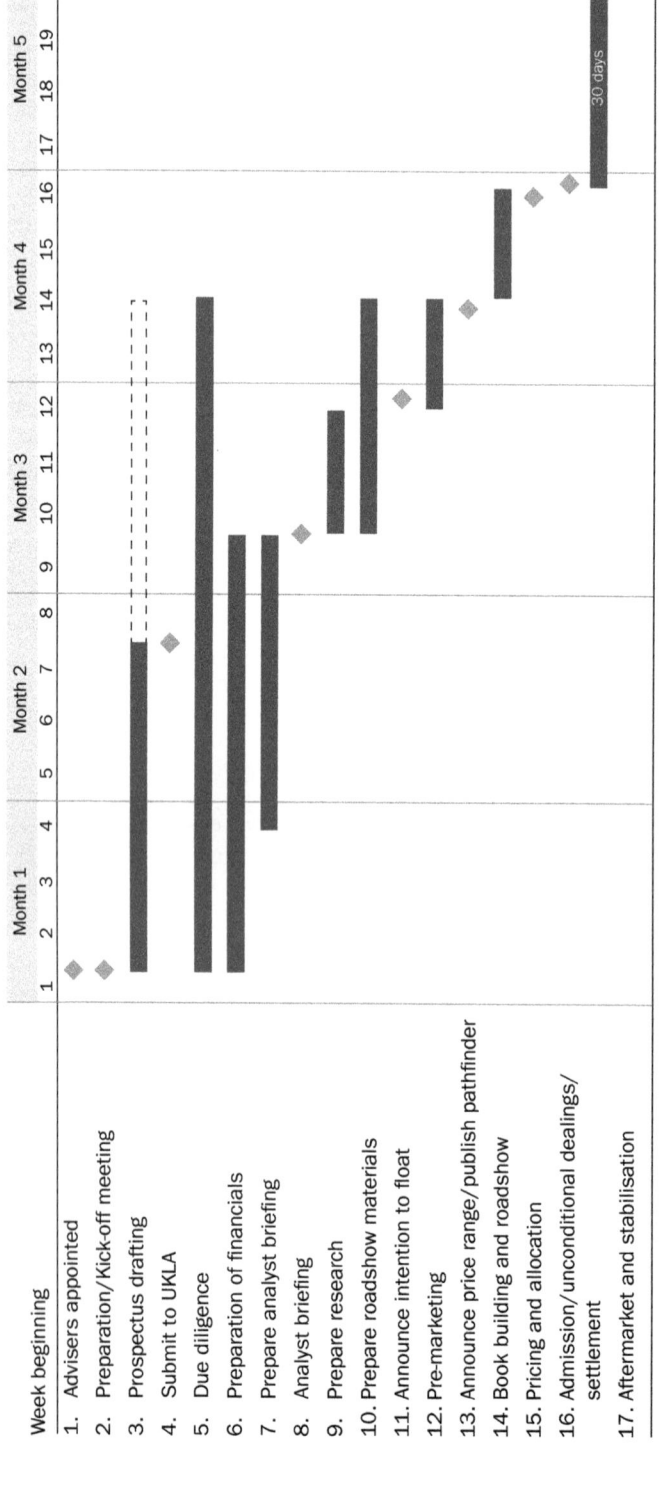

IPO: Indicative execution timetable

Week beginning	Month 1	Month 2	Month 3	Month 4	Month 5
	1 2 3 4	5 6 7 8	9 10 11 12	13 14 15 16	17 18 19 20

1. Advisers appointed
2. Preparation/Kick-off meeting
3. Prospectus drafting
4. Submit to UKLA
5. Due diligence
6. Preparation of financials
7. Prepare analyst briefing
8. Analyst briefing
9. Prepare research
10. Prepare roadshow materials
11. Announce intention to float
12. Pre-marketing
13. Announce price range/publish pathfinder
14. Book building and roadshow
15. Pricing and allocation
16. Admission/unconditional dealings/settlement
17. Aftermarket and stabilisation

30 days

[----] UKLA process

Note that the FCA is consulting (in CP 17/5) on proposals to amend the rules around the timing of the publication of the prospectus and analysts' research on an IPO. Any rule changes are expected in the second half of 2017.

4. Preparing to float and suitability for listing

In conjunction with the company's other advisers, the company's lawyers will usually co-ordinate any pre-IPO restructuring that is required, for example, the re-registration of the company as a public company (in order to offer shares to the public, a company must be a public limited company or 'plc', which will typically require either re-registration of an existing holding company as a plc or the insertion of a new plc holding company), reorganisation of its share capital, termination of any shareholder agreements put in place during private funding rounds and potentially putting in place a relationship agreement designed to ensure that the company's business is independent of any controlling shareholder.

As well as making the necessary amendments to the company's share capital, the company's existing shareholders will need to authorise the directors of the company to allot new shares, disapply pre-emption rights in connection with the issue of new shares as part of the IPO, approve the reregistration as a public company and adopt new articles of association in a form suitable for a public listed company. It is also usually necessary to ensure that any agreements and arrangements resulting from the company's debt and equity financing arrangements, which will commonly include restrictions and prohibitions on the actions of the company and its directors, are formally terminated or are amended to make them suitable for a listed company. A company must also satisfy certain criteria (known as 'eligibility criteria') under the Listing Rules in order to be admitted to listing. These may also require some form of share reorganisation, among other things, to ensure that its share voting structure complies with the Listing Rule requirements.

The Board will need to review and approve a raft of further 'public company' corporate documentation prior to the IPO to make its Board, employee and corporate governance arrangements suitable for a listed company.

Listed companies are expected to comply with high standards of corporate governance. As part of the preparatory steps for an IPO, and with a view to complying with market practice and accepted standards of corporate governance, as set out in the Corporate Governance Code, a company will generally need to appoint additional independent non-executive directors (NEDs), introduce new service contracts for its executive directors and new letters of appointment for its NEDs, adopt or revise terms of reference for nomination, remuneration and audit committees of the Board and adopt or revise a list of matters reserved for decisions of the full Board, rather than a Board committee.

The Board will also need to consider adopting employee share option schemes and long-term incentive plans for management and the company's employees as a whole. The 'incentivisation' of employees and management is a key area for a listed company; while one of the advantages of going public is that a company can use its share capital to remunerate its employees, it must make sure that it respects accepted market practice and institutional investor guidance. As a matter of company law, the company will be required to adopt a remuneration policy, which sets out the company's forward-looking policy on remuneration and is subject to a binding shareholder vote at least every three years.

In its role as sponsor, the investment bank must come to the reasonable opinion that the directors of the company have established procedures which enable the company to comply with the continuing obligations under the Listing Rules, the disclosure requirements under MAR and the Transparency Rules following its IPO. To do so, the company will need to show that it has considered and implemented policies on, among other things, the identification and disclosure of its inside information to the market and the control of that information while it is kept out of the public domain. These policies are commonly contained in a compliance manual, which will also cover other matters such as disclosure of share dealings, conflicts of interests and dealing with the press and analysts.

If the company is applying for a premium listing and will have a controlling shareholder after admission (one with 30% or more of the company), it will have to put in place a relationship agreement with any controlling shareholder(s) containing, among other things, an undertaking from the controlling shareholder(s) that transactions and arrangements between the company and the controlling shareholder (and/or any of its associates) will be conducted at arm's length and on normal commercial terms.

5. Due diligence, drafting the prospectus and verification

5.1 Due diligence

The key reasons for carrying out due diligence, as described above, are to ensure that all information relevant for disclosure in the prospectus is identified, that the company is suitable for listing and meets the conditions for listing and that the company and its directors and advisers are able to rely on the due diligence defence to a claim for compensation in circumstances where the prospectus is defective (see below).

In addition to the detailed contents requirements of the Prospectus Rules, FSMA contains an overriding general disclosure requirement which requires a prospectus to contain all such information as is necessary to enable investors to make an informed assessment of the assets and liabilities, financial position, profits and losses, and prospects of the company and the rights attaching to the shares. If the prospectus contains any information that is incorrect or misleading, or if any required information is omitted, then the people responsible for the prospectus, including the company and its directors, may be liable under FSMA to pay compensation to persons who have suffered loss. The people responsible could also face fines, censure or other penalties imposed by the Financial Conduct Authority and be subject to contractual, tortious and criminal liability. FSMA contains a defence to any compensation claims made pursuant to the FSMA (known as the due diligence defence); in order to rely on the defence the person must be able to show that they made reasonable enquiries and believed that the information in the prospectus was true and correct and not misleading at the date it was published and that no required information was omitted.

In addition, as described above, under the Listing Rules an additional standard of investigation applies and the financial adviser who is sponsor to the IPO must satisfy itself and give a declaration to the FCA that, to the best of its knowledge and belief, having made due and careful enquiry, the company has satisfied all applicable conditions for listing, the requirements of the Prospectus Rules in relation to the prospectus and all other relevant requirements and the directors have established procedures which enable the company to comply with the Listing Rules and the disclosure requirements under MAR and the Transparency Rules on an ongoing basis and which enable the directors to monitor the ongoing financial position and prospects of the company.

While what constitutes sufficient due diligence enquiries will always depend on the particular circumstances of each transaction, due diligence in relation to a UK IPO tends to include management due diligence meetings, a legal due diligence exercise, a long form financial due diligence report and a working capital report by the reporting accountants (as described above).

5.2 The prospectus

The prospectus is typically drafted by the company's lawyers and reviewed and commented on by other deal team members.

As described above, the prospectus must contain all material information on the company and all information that is necessary for investors to make an informed assessment about the position of the company and the rights attaching to the shares. The Prospectus Rules set out the detailed content requirements for prospectuses, including the requirement to include information on the directors, shareholders, details of the risks associated with the company, a section giving details on the company's business, important contracts and customers, its finances and business plan for the future, employees, litigation and premises. Further specific disclosure requirements apply if the company is a specialist issuer, for example, an investment, mining or real estate company. Under the Prospectus Directive, the prospectus must follow a prescribed format: it will start with a summary of the prospectus and a section giving details of the risks associated with the company. The other information required by the Prospectus Directive will follow, including a section giving details on the company's business, a section containing financial information, a section describing the shares to be issued and the terms of the offering and a section that contains additional information required to be included by the Prospectus Rules.

5.3 Verification

Having drafted the prospectus, the company's lawyers will assist the company in 'verifying' its contents. Typically, they will prepare a set of verification notes in relation to the prospectus and any other public documents to be issued. These consist of a set of questions and answers that verify and provide evidence to support the accuracy of the key statements in the prospectus.

After the prospectus has been drafted, it is submitted for review to the UK Listing Authority. The UK Listing Authority checks that the contents of the prospectus meet the requirements set out in the Prospectus Rules and gives its comments to the sponsor of the company's listing. When all of the UK Listing Authority's comments have been dealt with, the prospectus is 'stamped' as approved by the UK Listing Authority and it may then be published in accordance with the Prospectus Rules.

6. Marketing the IPO, the application process and pricing

The first public step in the IPO process is the announcement by the company of its intention to float, sometimes referred to as the 'ITF'. This raises the profile of the company and gives the market an indication of when a prospectus will be published and when the marketing of the offering by the investment banks will begin. If the company is planning on giving the general public – known as 'retail investors' – an opportunity to apply for shares in the IPO, the company will begin a publicity campaign to raise the public's awareness of the offering and how to apply. There are certain legal limits on how, when and where the company can market its IPO; the company's lawyers will provide publicity guidelines and details of applicable restrictions at an early stage.

If there is to be a retail offering, the prospectus will typically be published containing a price range to give an indication of the price at which the shares will be offered to the public, rather than a fixed price. In the case of an offer to institutional investors only, the prospectus will be published once the price has been fixed; the deal will be marketed using a draft prospectus that has not been formally approved by the UK Listing Authority.

The prospectus must be made available in electronic form but may also be made available in hard copy.

The investment banks will organise a 'roadshow' of presentations by the directors to interested institutional investors in the United Kingdom, Europe, the United States and potentially elsewhere (depending on the type of offering and targeted investors). During the roadshow, the investment bank will build a book of interest in the shares to be offered, noting how many shares institutional investors would be prepared to acquire and at what price. Retail investors complete an application form and return it to the company's registrars, stating the maximum sum they are prepared to invest. Alternatively, a company may elect to do an 'intermediaries' offer, in which retail shareholders can participate indirectly via intermediaries such as banks and stockbrokers.

When the 'bookbuilding' process has finished, and in the case of the retail or intermediaries offer the deadline for return of applications has passed, the company and the investment banks hold a 'pricing' meeting at which the exact price of the shares to be sold is determined. This final price is usually within the range published in the prospectus, but can, in exceptional circumstances, be outside it (this would trigger investor 'withdrawal rights' in the event the final price is outside the price range). The company and the investment banks then allocate the shares between the investors that have applied according to the maximum amount they said they were prepared to invest. Investors do not always receive as many shares as they have applied for in the IPO. If there is a high demand for shares in the offering, and investors have applied for more shares than are available in total, then the offer is described as 'oversubscribed'. If this happens, investors' applications may be 'scaled back'.

In the case of a retail offering, when the price is determined, the company must publish a pricing statement giving details of the final price – if there have been any other material developments since the date of the approved prospectus the company may also need to publish a 'supplementary prospectus'. In the case of an offer to institutional investors only, when the price is determined, the company will publish the approved prospectus including the final price as described above.

The final step in the IPO process is admission of the company's shares to the premium or standard segment of the Official List of the UK Listing Authority and to trading on the London Stock Exchange's main market. Admission to listing and to trading usually occurs approximately three business days following the announcement of the price.

The FCA is consulting, in its consultation paper CP 17/5, on measures to improve the range and quality of information made available to investors during the IPO process.

The consultation follows a Discussion Paper (DP 16/3) published by the FCA in April 2016. In that paper, the FCA considered the extent to which market participants have access to the right information at the right time during the IPO process. It noted that current market practice for IPOs in the UK is for banks to impose a blackout period before the circulation of the pathfinder prospectus so that no research is published by syndicate banks (known as 'connected research') in the 14 days prior to publication of the prospectus. The Discussion Paper suggested that this 14-day blackout period means that connected research is published well ahead of the prospectus and that investors do not have access to prospectuses early enough in the IPO process. They are therefore forced to rely on connected research. The FCA said that feedback on the Discussion Paper indicated strong support for reforming the availability and quality of information in the UK IPO process. The key proposals being consulted on by the FCA, which would be implemented by amendments to the Conduct of Business Sourcebook (COBS), focus on the timing of the publication of the prospectus and any connected research, and the interaction between the issuer and analysts. Any changes are expected in the second half of 2017.

7. Continuing obligations as a listed company

Once listed, a company must comply with various 'continuing obligations' set out in the LPDT Rules and MAR. The scope of a listed company's continuing obligations will depend on whether or not it has a 'premium listing' or a 'standard listing' – more onerous continuing obligations apply to companies with a premium listing (see Figure 3 for a comparison of the key requirements). Other specific continuing obligations apply if the company is a specialist issuer, for example, an investment, mining or real estate company.

Premium listed companies are subject to a set of general principles, which have continuing effect and guide how a listed company and its directors should behave, and a large number of continuing obligations some of which are 'super-equivalent' to the obligations common to companies listed elsewhere in the EU. Standard listed companies are subject to a more limited number of continuing obligations that are common to companies listed elsewhere in the EU and are derived solely from EU directives and regulations. If a listed company or its directors fail to comply with these rules, the 'Listing Principles' (see below) or the additional super-equivalent obligations, they may be subject to a number of civil and criminal sanctions, censures and fines.

The Listing Principles and Premium Listing Principles which are contained in LR 7 set out high-level standards with which a listed company must comply.

The Listing Principles, which apply to premium and standard listed companies, are as follows:

- *Listing Principle 1*: a listed company must take reasonable steps to establish and maintain adequate procedures, systems and controls to enable it to comply with its obligations.
- *Listing Principle 2*: a listed company must deal with the FCA in an open and co-operative manner.

The Premium Listing Principles, which apply only to premium listed companies, are as follows:

- *Premium Listing Principle 1*: a company must take reasonable steps to enable its directors to understand their responsibilities and obligations as directors.

- *Premium Listing Principle 2:* a company must act with integrity towards the holders and potential holders of its premium listed shares.
- *Premium Listing Principle 3:* all equity shares in a class that has been admitted to premium listing must carry an equal number of votes on any shareholder vote.
- *Premium Listing Principle 4:* where an issuer has more than one class of equity shares admitted to premium listing, the aggregate voting rights of the shares in each class should be broadly proportionate to the relative interests of those classes in the equity of the listed company.
- *Premium Listing Principle 5:* a company must ensure that it treats all holders of the same class of its listed equity shares that are in the same position equally in respect of the rights attaching to those listed equity shares.
- *Premium Listing Principle 6:* a company must communicate information to holders and potential holders of its listed equity shares in such a way as to avoid the creation of a false market in those listed equity shares.

The guidance to Listing Principle 1 in LR 7.2 makes it clear that it is aimed at ensuring timely and accurate disclosure of information to the market and a company's systems and controls should enable it properly to identify inside information in a timely manner. This means that a listed company needs adequate reporting lines and a flow of management information to the Board to ensure that relevant information is escalated within the organisation and to allow the directors to consider whether any information needs to be disclosed to the market. In addition, a premium listed company should have procedures, systems and controls which are sufficient to enable it to determine whether any obligations have arisen under Listing Rule 10 (Significant transactions) and Listing Rule 11 (Related party transactions) among others (see section 13).

A listed company's continuing obligations fall into a number of different categories relating broadly to:

- market reporting and continuous disclosure;
- financial reporting and corporate governance;
- the publication of 'regulated information' and market announcements;
- communication with shareholders;
- significant and related party transactions; and
- further share issues and share buy-backs.

8. Accuracy of market disclosure

Arguably one of the most important continuing obligations of a listed company, as set out in LR 1, is the requirement to ensure the accuracy of announcements made to the market. Information must be released by the listed company to the market via a

Regulatory Information Service (RIS). The FCA has approved a number of Primary Information Providers to provide RISs for the purposes of the LPDT Rules, a list of which is available on the FCA's website. A listed company must ensure that it has arrangements in place with one of these providers to ensure that it can comply with its disclosure requirements.

Listed companies must take all reasonable care to ensure that any information notified to an RIS is not misleading, false or deceptive and does not omit anything likely to affect the import of the information. In deciding whether an announcement is accurate and not misleading the directors should ensure that they seek appropriate advice from advisers, particularly the company's brokers.

9. Control and disclosure of inside information

A listed company's primary disclosure obligation, set out in Article 17 of MAR, is to notify an RIS as soon as possible of any 'inside information' which directly concerns the company, subject to certain exceptions relating to delaying disclosure and selective disclosure. MAR applies to both premium and standard listed companies.

'Inside information' is, broadly, information relating to a listed company that is precise, has not been made public and, if made public, would be likely to have a significant effect on the company's share price. A company's brokers and lawyers will have a key role to play in assisting the directors' analysis of whether or not disclosure is required.

A listed company must establish effective arrangements to deny access to inside information to persons other than those who require it for the exercise of their functions within the company. A listed company must draw up and maintain a list of those persons working for it, under a contract of employment or otherwise, who have access to inside information relating directly or indirectly to the company.

10. Notification of share dealings and interests in voting rights

Article 19 of MAR requires directors and other persons discharging managerial responsibilities (known as PDMRs) and persons closely associated with them to notify the company in writing of the occurrence of all transactions conducted on their own account in the company's shares, derivatives or any other financial instruments relating to those shares within three business days of the day on which the transaction occurred. A listed company must in turn notify the market of any PDMR or PCA dealing notifications it receives (again with three business days of the transaction). MAR also imposes some restrictions on when PDMRs may deal. These requirements apply to both premium and standard listed companies.

DTR 5 requires the disclosure by shareholders, and in some instances financial instrument holders, of the level of voting rights held directly and indirectly by them in listed companies. DTR 5 applies to premium and standard listed companies.

Under DTR 5, investors in a listed company are required to make a notification on a prescribed form when their interests in the voting rights in the capital of the listed company reaches, exceeds or falls below 3% (in the case of a UK company) or 5% (in the case of a non-UK company) or any whole percentage thereafter. When the company receives a notification from an investor, it must announce details to the market via an RIS as soon as possible, and in any event by the end of the trading day following the day of notification.

In order to enable investors to calculate the percentage of the voting rights they hold (and to establish whether or not they need to make a notification), a listed company must announce details of any share capital changes; at the end of each calendar month in which there has been an increase or decrease of capital, or changes in connection with any further share issue, it must announce the total number of voting rights in respect of each class of voting shares in issue, and how many of such shares are held in treasury. In addition, any material share capital change must be announced as soon as possible (and in any case no later than the following business day). The FCA gives guidance in the rules that states that an increase or decrease of 1% or more is likely to be material (DTR 5.6.1BG).

The listed company's secretariat will have a key role to play in managing the receipt of notifications under MAR and DTR 5.

11. Financial reporting and corporate governance

DTR 4 sets out the key financial reporting requirements for listed companies. It applies to both premium and standard listed companies.

Under DTR 4, a listed company is required to publish:

- *an annual financial report* – within four months of its year end, comprising consolidated audited accounts, a management report and responsibility statements; and
- *a half-yearly financial report* – as soon as possible and in any event no later than three months after the half-year end, comprising a condensed set of financial statements, an interim management report and responsibility statements.

The company's finance team, led by the CFO, will have primary responsibility for financial reporting obligations, working closely with the company's auditors.

DTR 7 requires both premium and standard listed companies to appoint an audit committee and to include a corporate governance statement in their report and accounts.

The corporate governance statement must describe the corporate governance code that the listed company is required to comply with and explain whether or not the company complies with such requirements in practice. In the UK, corporate governance requirements for premium listed companies are set out in the Corporate Governance Code. While a premium listed company is not obliged to follow the Corporate Governance Code's recommendations, in addition to its obligations under DTR 7 it must also include a 'comply or explain' compliance statement in its annual financial report in accordance with LR 9.8.6R. In practice, there is a high level of compliance with the Corporate Governance Code, particularly among larger listed companies.

12. Market announcements and shareholder communications

A listed company must ensure equality of treatment for holders of shares that are in the same position. The company must disseminate 'regulated information', which includes information required to be disclosed under the Listing Rules, the TD, the DTRs and Articles 17 to 19 of MAR, in a manner that ensures such information is capable of being disseminated to as wide a public as possible and, to the extent possible, simultaneously in the home Member State and in other EEA States.

Regulated information must be filed with the National Storage Mechanism (NSM) operated by Morningstar. A listed company is liable to compensate an investor in securities who has suffered a loss as a result of an untrue or misleading statement in an omission from, or a dishonest delay in releasing any regulated information.

DTR 6 and Listing Rule 9 contain a number of provisions aimed at ensuring that security holders receive adequate information about shareholder meetings and how to exercise their rights at them, together with a proxy form.

Other than by announcements via an RIS, a listed company communicates annually with its shareholders through the publication of its annual report and notice of AGM. If a listed company wishes to obtain the approval of its shareholders for matters at other times, it must send them a circular. Listing Rule 13, which applies only to premium listed companies, sets out the general requirements that apply to all 'circulars' sent by a company to holders of its listed securities. It also sets out specific requirements for circulars that relate to specific types of transaction and which circulars require the approval of the FCA before they can be published.

The use of electronic communications by a listed company is permitted under DTR 6 but must be approved by the shareholders in general meeting. The requirement to have individual shareholder consent to electronic communications does not apply to UK incorporated companies because they are subject to the separate Companies Act 2006 regime for approval of electronic communications.

13. Significant and related party transactions, further share issues and share buy-backs

Certain corporate transactions by premium listed companies are subject to the rules set out in Listing Rules 5, 9, 10, 11 and 12. These are designed to protect shareholders in the listed company, either by requiring disclosure on the part of the listed company of certain prescribed information or by requiring the listed company to seek shareholder approval for certain types of transaction.

Listing Rule 5 sets out rules for listed companies making a very large acquisition, called a reverse takeover. On completion of a reverse takeover, the company's listing will generally be cancelled and it will have to reapply for admission to listing. A premium listed company undertaking a reverse takeover will also have to comply with the requirements for significant transactions in LR 10.

Listing Rule 9 contains a set of obligations on premium listed companies relating to further share issues and, in particular, it sets out requirements relating to rights issues, placings and other offers of securities. It provides safeguards for existing shareholders by enshrining pre-emption rights on a further share issue, prescribing key aspects of the timetable for rights issues and open offers and requiring shareholder approval for non-pre-emptive further share issues at a discount in excess of certain thresholds.

Listing Rule 10 provides certain protections for shareholders (through the involvement of the company's sponsor, prescribed public disclosure and/or the requirement to obtain shareholder approval) where a premium listed company is contemplating a significant transaction, principally a large acquisition or disposal. Significant transactions include any transaction by any subsidiary undertaking of the listed company, but exclude those in the ordinary course of business.

Listing Rule 11 provides certain safeguards for shareholders against certain related parties of the listed company or its subsidiaries (including directors and holders of 10% or more of the voting share capital) taking advantage of their position. Unless an exemption applies or the transaction is *de minimis* in size, a related party transaction may require independent shareholder approval. A related party transaction also requires the involvement of the company's sponsor.

Listing Rule 12 sets out the rules that will apply to a premium listed company that wishes to purchase its own securities, whether as a market purchase or an off-market purchase. It also sets out the rules that apply to a premium listed company which (following a purchase of its own securities) holds a proportion of its shares as treasury shares which it wishes to sell, cancel or transfer.

A significant acquisition or a further share issue by a premium listed company will broadly require it to assemble the same advisory team as for its IPO. While the timetable for the transactions will differ from that for an IPO, certain key elements will be very similar.

Under Listing Rule 8, an investment bank may once again be required to fulfil the role of sponsor to the premium listed company in connection with the significant acquisition or further share issue, although the declaration that it will be required to give to the FCA will be less extensive than on an IPO.

The company's lawyers will be responsible for preparing and negotiating transaction documents and, in the case of a capital raising, assisting with the structure of the offer and the share issue. Due diligence and verification will be as important in relation to the preparation and publication of a shareholder circular, a prospectus or an equivalent document for a merger, takeover or acquisition or a prospectus for a further share issue as they were in connection with the preparation and publication of a prospectus for an IPO.

A premium listed company's auditors usually adopt the role of reporting accountants and will be involved in any financial or tax due diligence and in the preparation and review of any shareholder circular and prospectus, although the nature of their work and reports prepared will again be less extensive than on an IPO.

Figure 3: Comparison of key listing conditions and continuing obligations of a premium listed company and a standard listed company

	Requirement applicable to a 'premium listed' company?	Requirement applicable to a 'standard listed' company?
Listing		
Basic conditions for listing	Yes (LR 2.2)	Yes (LR 2.2)
Admission to trading on a regulated market	Yes (LR 2.2.3R)	Yes (LR 2.2.3R)
Cancellation of listing	Yes (with shareholder consent) (LR 5.2.5R)	Yes (must notify the FCA) (LR 5.2.8R)
Transfer to different listing category	Yes (with shareholder consent) (LR 5.4A.4R)	Yes (must notify intention via RIS) (LR 5.4A.5R)
Conditions for a premium listing (commercial company) (LR 6)	Yes (LR 6)	No
Listing Principles (LR 7)	Yes, Listing Principles and Premium Listing Principles (LR 7.1.1R (1) and (2))	Listing Principles only (LR 7.1.1R(1))
Sponsor regime (LR 8)	Yes (LR 8.1.2R)	No
Inside information		
Disclosure of inside information (MAR Art. 17)	Yes (MAR)	Yes (MAR)

INTRODUCTION

	Requirement applicable to a 'premium listed' company?	Requirement applicable to a 'standard listed' company?
Maintain insider lists (MAR Art. 18)	Yes (MAR)	Yes (MAR)
Share dealings and disclosure of interests		
Disclosure of dealings by directors and PDMRs (MAR Art. 19)	Yes (MAR)	Yes (MAR)
Restrictions on PDMR dealings (MAR Art. 19(11))	Yes (MAR)	Yes (MAR)
Disclosure of interests in voting rights (DTR 5)	Yes (DTR 5.1.2R)	Yes (DTR 5.1.2R)
Financial reporting and corporate governance		
Periodic financial reporting (DTR 4)	Yes (DTR 4.1.1R and 4.2.1R)	Yes (DTR 4.1.1R and 4.2.1R)
Preliminary statements (LR 9.7A) and contents of annual financial reports (LR 9.8)	Yes (LR 9.1.1R)	No
Audit committee (DTR 7.1)	Yes (DTR 1B.1.2R)	Yes (DTR 1B.1.2R)
Corporate governance statement (DTR 7.2)	Yes (DTR 1B.1.5R)	Yes (DTR 1B.1.5R)
Corporate governance 'comply or explain' statement (LR 9.8.6R(5) and (6))	Yes (LR 9.1.1R)	No
Relationship agreement with controlling shareholder (LR 6.1.4BR)	Yes (LR 6.1.4BR and LR 9.2.2AR)	No
Market announcements and shareholder communications		
Provision and dissemination of information (DTR 6)	Yes (DTR 6.1.1R)	Yes (DTR 6.1.1R)

	Requirement applicable to a 'premium listed' company?	Requirement applicable to a 'standard listed' company?
Disclosure of information on directors (LR 9.6 and LR 9.8)	Yes (LR 9.1.1R)	No
Shareholder circulars (LR 13)	Yes (LR 13.1.1R)	No
Significant and related party transactions		
Significant transactions (LR 10)	Yes (LR 10.1.1R)	No
Related party transactions (LR 11)	Yes (LR 11.1.1R)	No
Reverse takeovers (LR 5.6)	Yes (LR 5.6.1R)	Yes (LR 5.6.1R)
Further share issues and buy-backs		
Pre-emption rights (LR 9.3.11R)	Yes (LR 9.1.1R)	No
Rights issues, placings and open offers (LR 9.5)	Yes (LR 9.1.1R)	No
Share buy-backs (LR 12)	Yes (LR 12.1.1R)	No

Note:

References to 'LR' are to paragraphs of the Listing Rules, 'PR' are to paragraphs of the Prospectus Rules and 'DTR' are to paragraphs of the Disclosure Guidance and Transparency Rules.

CHAPTER 1

Regulatory framework

OVERVIEW

- The current UK listing regime has been heavily influenced and shaped by EU legislation originally enacted as part of the Commission's Financial Services Action Plan (FSAP). The FSAP, published in 1999, sought progress towards a single EU financial services market with no obstacles to cross-border activity and a sound supervisory structure.

- The key FSAP Directives that are still in force are the Prospectus Directive (PD) and the Transparency Directive (TD). These Directives were implemented in the UK primarily through Part 6 of the Financial Services and Markets Act 2000 (FSMA), which empowered the FSA (the predecessor to the FCA and the competent authority at the time) to make the Listing, Prospectus, Disclosure and Transparency Rules.

- The Market Abuse Directive (MAD) also formed a key part of the FSAP and was implemented in the UK primarily through Parts 6 and 8 of the FSMA. MAD was completely replaced by the Market Abuse Regulation (MAR) with effect from 3 July 2016. MAR is directly applicable across member states and therefore did not need to be implemented through UK legislation. However, the UK government and the FCA amended the parts of the FSMA and the LPDT Rules which implemented the previous market abuse regime under MAD, to remove overlapping and inconsistencies and to reflect the creation of the new directly applicable rules. In particular, the provisions in FSMA relating to market abuse have been repealed and the Disclosure Rules have become the 'Disclosure Guidance', with signposts to a number of MAR provisions.

- In some cases, the FSAP Directives have attempted to break down barriers and create a single market by using 'maximum harmonisation', meaning that Member States cannot impose more stringent requirements. This is the case with the Prospectus Directive. At other times the FSAP Directives have sought to achieve the same objective through common minimum standards, leaving Member States free to impose more onerous requirements. This is the case with certain aspects of the Transparency Directive.

- Both the PD and the TD have already been reviewed and amended. The PD is being replaced by a directly applicable new Prospectus Regulation, which was published in the Official Journal in June 2017 and will be fully in force from July 2019, to improve and simplify the prospectus regime in the EU. Upon implementation, the new regulation would repeal and replace entirely the PD and its implementing measures, including the PD Regulation.

- Following the reform of the structure of financial services regulation in the UK in 2013, the FSA was abolished and replaced by the FCA which now supervises the listing regime and takes enforcement action for breaches of the LPDT Rules and MAR.

1. The Financial Services Action Plan

It is important to appreciate how much of the current UK regulatory environment is (and has been over recent years) driven by European goals for a single market in financial services. Historically, the EU's various financial markets remained relatively segmented, with business and retail consumers being deprived of direct access to cross-border financial institutions. This was largely due to the ambiguities and inflexibilities caused by the range of different European regulatory structures, legal systems, trade barriers, taxation and cultural approaches. While steps had been taken to create a single market for financial services, in practice these tended to set 'minimum standards' so a wide variety of practices developed in different member states with little or no consistency across the EU. Increasingly, however, the EU is changing its approach by implementing legislation which is based on 'maximum harmonisation', including directly applicable Regulations, to create more consistency across the EU.

With the introduction of the Euro, and the increase in the financial products available to the enhanced numbers of participants entering the European money markets, there was a renewed impetus to create a single market for financial services and to ensure a more level playing field for all market participants.

The Financial Services Action Plan (FSAP) was a set of proposals put forward by the European Commission in May 1999, at the request of the Council of Ministers. The FSAP set out key objectives in creating a single market for financial services, which included the creation of a single EU wholesale market, open and secure retail markets and state-of-the-art prudential rules and supervision.

1.1 Strategic objectives of the FSAP

The Commission set out in the FSAP a programme for rapid progress towards a single financial services market. The FSAP contained strategic objectives and the actions that the Commission believed needed to be taken to achieve those objectives.

The Commission identified three key strategic objectives:

- *A single EU wholesale market* – to make it easier to issue and trade securities across the EU;
- *Open and secure retail markets* – to create open and secure retail markets by removing obstacles which hamper cross-border activity; and
- *State-of-the-art prudential rules and supervision* – to create sound supervisory structures.

1.2 The European legislative process for financial services legislation

There is a four-level approach to financial services legislation. The European Commission, Parliament and Council are responsible for 'Level 1' legislative acts (i.e. a directive or regulation). Directives then have to be implemented by individual member states, whereas regulations are directly applicable in member states.

The European Securities and Markets Authority (ESMA) is then asked to produce detailed implementing measures and technical standards, covering aspects of the Level 1 legislation where more detail is required. The European Commission then adopts these 'Level 2' measures, usually in the form of regulations.

ESMA is also responsible for publishing 'Level 3' guidance on the legislation (such as the ESMA Guidelines on Delay). While not directly legally binding, issuers are required to make every effort to comply with ESMA guidelines. ESMA also produces guidance in the form of Q&As on each of the regimes.

ESMA is also responsible for facilitating the exchange of information and agreement between national supervisory authorities, and where necessary, settling any disagreements, to ensure that securities regulators at a national level take a more coordinated approach.

Details of ESMA's role, powers, decision-making process and standing committees are available on its website (www.esma.europa.eu).

Figure 1.1: The Legislative Process

Level 1	▪ Commission adopts formal proposal for Directive or Regulation ▪ Council and European Parliament adopt legislative act
Level 2	▪ Commission requests ESMA advice on delegated and implementing acts ▪ ESMA drafts technical standards and Commission adopts
Level 3	ESMA: ▪ adopts guidelines and recommendations ▪ carries out peer review ▪ mediates and settles disagreements ▪ takes action in emergency situations ▪ facilitates delegation of tasks and responsibilities ▪ cooperates with European Systemic Risk Board (ESRB) ▪ monitors and assesses market developments ▪ undertakes economic analyses ▪ fosters investor protection

1.3 The Market Abuse Directive and the Market Abuse Regulation

MAD (Directive 2003/6/EC) covered both market manipulation and insider dealing and, prior to 3 July 2016, applied to all financial instruments admitted to trading on a regulated market in the EU. MAD required each member state to designate a single administrative regulatory and supervisory authority to ensure its provisions were applied, with the aim of harmonising each member state's approach to tackling insider trading and market manipulation using a common set of minimum responsibilities. MAD required price-sensitive information to be disseminated as soon as possible and prescribed the circumstances in which selective disclosure of such information could be made.

In 2009, the European Commission launched a full review of MAD and, in 2014, published a new regulation on insider dealing and market manipulation (the EU Market Abuse Regulation (596/2014) (MAR)) to completely replace MAD and also a new directive on criminal sanctions for insider dealing and market manipulation, the Criminal Sanctions for Market Abuse Directive (2014/57/EU) (CSMAD). The provisions of MAR and the detailed implementing and delegated regulations under it came into force on 3 July 2016 and have direct effect in member states so did not need to be implemented through the enactment of domestic legislation. However, member states did need to amend and repeal the provisions in their national legislation which applied the previous market abuse regime under the MAD. In the UK, the Disclosure Rules for listed companies were repealed in this area and the provisions of MAR have, in effect, taken their place. The Disclosure Rules have become the 'Disclosure Guidance' with signposts to some (but not all) MAR provisions and some of the guidance previously contained in the rules has been retained. Since the UK already has a separate criminal regime for insider dealing and misstatements, which goes beyond that in CSMAD, it has opted out of CSMAD.

The provisions in MAR include an extension of the market abuse regime to a wider range of trading platforms and financial instruments, express prohibition of the manipulation of benchmarks, such as LIBOR, greater harmonisation of sanctions and significant new procedural requirements in a number of areas.

MAR is discussed in more detail in Chapter 5.

1.4 The Prospectus Directive and the PD Regulation

The PD (Directive 2003/71/EC) regulates the prospectus to be published when a company's securities are to be offered to the public or admitted to trading on a regulated market in the EEA. The PD harmonises the requirements to draw up, scrutinise and distribute prospectuses across the EU and removes cross-border barriers on raising capital, by creating a single 'passport' for issuers.

All prospectuses must meet specific disclosure standards and be approved by the competent authority in the issuer's home member state. Once the relevant competent authority has approved the prospectus it is then available for use throughout the EEA without, in theory, the issuer having to publish any further information or seek additional approval from the competent authority in any other member state. The concepts of home member state and host member state are discussed in section 1.7.

The PD Regulation (EC) No. 809/2004, published on 29 April 2004, prescribes the detailed content requirements of a prospectus through a number of different 'building blocks' of disclosure. The regulation has direct impact in each member state with effect from July 2005.

The Prospectus Directive was the subject of a review (required by the terms of the original directive) and the PD Amending Directive (Directive 2010/73/EU) came into force on 31 December 2010 with member states having until 1 July 2012 to implement the required changes.

In 2014, EU Regulation 382/2014 supplemented the Prospectus Directive with regard to the publication of supplementary prospectuses and specifies situations when a supplementary prospectus must be published. The Prospectus RTS Regulation came into force on 5 May 2014 and is directly applicable in all member states.

Further changes were made to the Prospectus Directive via the 'Omnibus II' Directive which was published in 2014 (2014/51/EU). This includes detailed amendments in relation to the approval and publication process for prospectuses, and certain issues relating to content and the dissemination of advertisements. It required ESMA to develop regulatory technical standards (RTS) to be approved by the Commission in relation to these. The Omnibus II Implementing Regulation supplementing the Directive entered into force on 24 March 2016 and has direct effect in all member states.

The European Commission, Council and Parliament have agreed a new regulation to implement the findings of a review of the prospectus regime in Europe, which was undertaken as part of its initiative to accomplish a capital markets union. The changes are designed to simplify the prospectus regime to facilitate capital raising in the EU, while maintaining consumer and investor protection. The New Prospectus Regulation was published in the Official Journal on 30 June 2017. The new regulation will repeal and replace entirely the Prospectus Directive and its implementing measures, including the PD Regulation. Most of the new Regulation will only come into force two years later (i.e. in July 2019). However, certain aspects will come into force sooner. See Chapter 4 for further detail.

1.5 The Transparency Directive

The TD (Directive 2004/109/EC) harmonises transparency requirements (i.e. the core requirements for dissemination of information to the market) for issuers whose securities are admitted to trading on a regulated market, with the aim of improving the information available to investors. It also covers financial reporting and disclosure of interests in shares, as well as the mechanism for disseminating information. The TD was published in the Official Journal in December 2004 and was required to be implemented by member states by January 2007.

Minor amendments were made to the TD by Directive 2010/73/EU which were required to be implemented by member states by 1 July 2012. Additionally, the Commission published a consultation paper in relation to further modernising the TD in May 2010, resulting in an Amending Directive (2013/50/EU) which came into force on 26 November 2013. Member states were required to implement the provisions into national law within two years of that date.

1.6 The IAS Regulation

The EU decided that, in order to create a pan-European framework for listed companies, it would be necessary for them all to use the same accounting language in their annual reports and other periodic financial reports. Historically, there were no common European accounting standards: each member state had its own approach, with the more developed markets, such as the UK, France and Germany, having their own accounting standard-setter. However, there had been some movement towards international accounting standards (known generally now as International Financial Reporting Standards (IFRS)), so the Commission decided to use these as the basis for financial reporting in Europe. As international accounting standards were in the process of gaining greater international acceptance by non-EU regulators, particularly those in North America, there was a perception that this approach might assist EU companies seeking to raise capital from North American investors.

The mechanism chosen to bring international standards into EU law was not a Directive – this would have required each member state to adopt each standard into its own law – but rather a regulation that had direct legislative effect in each member state and therefore required no implementation action to be taken by member states. The IAS Regulation (EC No. 2002/1606), adopted by the council in June 2002, states that, for accounting periods beginning on or after 1 January 2005, EU companies with securities traded on a regulated market and which are required to produce consolidated accounts should follow international accounting standards as adopted in the EU. An adoption method was required for legal reasons as the international accounting standards were (and still are) developed and issued by a private sector body (the International Accounting Standards Board).

1.7 Home and host member states

The PD introduced the concept of a single 'passport' for issuers, whereby a prospectus approved by one competent authority is available for use throughout the EEA, without any other member states being able to impose any additional significant administrative requirements. This means that, once the competent authority in the relevant member state has approved the prospectus, it must then be accepted elsewhere in the EEA.

The identity of an issuer's home member state will determine the competent authority responsible for approving the prospectus: it is therefore very important to understand the concept and how the home member state is determined. As a general rule, the FCA will only approve a PD prospectus where the issuer's home member state is the UK (FSMA s. 87A(1)(a)). However, if the competent authority in the issuer's home member state decides that it would be more appropriate for the FCA to approve the issuer's prospectus, there are provisions allowing it to transfer the approval role to the FCA (FSMA s. 87F).

The TD also uses the concept of home and host member states and MAR uses the concept of home member state. The tests and exceptions are different under each regime.

1.7.1 Home member states for EEA issuers

The general rule is that the home member state for an EEA issuer is the EEA State in which the issuer has its registered office (Art. 2(1)(m)(i) PD).

There are certain exceptions to this general rule. These apply to (i) non-equity securities (as defined in the PD) with a minimum denomination per unit of at least €1,000 (or equivalent) and (ii) certain convertible or exchangeable non-equity securities ((i) and (ii) are together known as 'Qualifying Debt Securities').

1.7.2 Home member states for non-EEA issuers

The general rule is that the home member state for a non-EEA issuer is – at the choice of the issuer, the offeror or the person asking for admission – the member state in which the issuer's securities are first intended to be offered to the public or where the first application for admission to trading on a regulated market is made (Art. 2(1)(m)(iii) PD). There are, however, certain exceptions (e.g. for some securities).

1.7.3 Home member states for different issuers in the same group

The home member state is determined for each issuer separately, so if there are a number of different issuers in the same group of companies – for example, a listed holding company and a separate group-financing subsidiary – the home member state for each issuer may differ.

1.7.4 Host member states for issuers

The rules governing which competent authority must approve a prospectus do not restrict the choice of market on which an issuer may make an application for admission to trading nor the member states in which a public offer of securities can take place. While the competent authority of an issuer's home member state will approve the prospectus, it will be valid for use in any other EEA State (known as the 'host member state') provided that such host member states are notified.

Under the terms of the PD, the host member state is not allowed to impose any additional approval or administrative arrangements relating to the prospectus, other than a requirement that the 'Summary' be translated into its official language (see section 3.3 of Chapter 4). In practice however it appears that certain host member states do impose additional administrative requirements (e.g. the publication of a formal notice). It is therefore important, where the host and home member state differ, that local advice is sought in the host member state(s).

Where there is also an admission to listing, the host member state is able to impose eligibility for listing and continuing obligation requirements. This is the case in the UK and is explained in more detail in Chapter 2. For example, an issuer that has its registered office in France, but wishes to list its shares on the premium segment of the Official List, will have its prospectus approved by the competent authority in France. The FCA, as the competent authority in the host member state, will, subject to certain conditions, have to accept that prospectus as approved. The FCA will, however, still be able to require that the French issuer meets the eligibility requirements and complies with the continuing obligation requirements for premium listed companies contained in the Listing Rules.

2. Implementation of the FSAP Directives and Regulations in the UK

EU legislation in the form of directives must be implemented through national member state legislation (in contrast to other forms of EU legislation, such as regulations, that have direct legislative effect). Directives may be classified as 'minimum harmonisation' or 'maximum harmonisation'. Member states may add to or tighten the rules specified in a 'minimum harmonisation' directive, but may not do so with a 'maximum harmonisation' directive.

The PD and TD (and, prior to its replacement by MAR, the MAD) have been brought into UK law and regulation by a variety of routes, but the primary legislative sources are the FSMA and the Companies Act 2006. For the purpose of the UK listing regime, Part 6 of the FSMA is the most relevant. However, other parts of the FSMA are relevant, for example, Part 8 which has become the location for the enforcement powers of the FCA for breach of MAR.

2.1 Part 6 of the FSMA

Part 6 of the FSMA, as amended, establishes the FCA as the listing authority in the UK and lays out its general duties. It imposes on the FCA the responsibility to maintain the Official List, the admission of securities to listing, the discontinuance and suspension of listings and the approval of listing particulars, prospectuses and sponsors.

Most importantly, section 73A of the FSMA allows the FCA to make rules (known as 'Part 6 Rules') of various types, namely:

- *Listing Rules* – those relating to admission to the Official List;
- *Prospectus Rules* – those relating to the implementation of the PD and the PD Regulation; and
- *Transparency and Corporate Governance Rules* – those relating to the implementation of the TD, the Company Reporting Directive (CRD) and the Statutory Audit Directive.

Prior to MAR coming into effect, section 73A of the FSMA also allowed the FCA to make the Disclosure Rules; however, this provision was deleted by the FSMA Statutory Instrument SI 2016/680 with effect from 3 July 2016.

Part 6 of the FSMA deals in some detail with how these 'Part 6 Rules' are to be established, including setting certain criteria that the FCA must follow, for example, in relation to making decisions on applications for, or suspensions from, listing and the matters that may be included in a prospectus. It broadly lays out how the FCA is to exert its powers.

This reflects the overall approach of EU legislation, which is to set out the broad principles in primary legislation, but then to provide greater flexibility by allowing more detailed measures to be developed by a regulator through rules (in the UK, by the FCA), thus allowing it to change the rules easily and quickly, without having to resort, in most cases, to primary legislation.

2.2 Revisions to the FSMA in 2013 – the new regulatory structure

The reform of the structure of financial services regulation in the UK took effect on 1 April 2013. The Financial Services Act 2012 (FSA 2012) made amendments to the FSMA to create the new financial services regulatory architecture.

The FSA was abolished and the following institutions were established:

- a Bank of England Financial Policy Committee (FPC), responsible for macro-prudential regulation;
- the Prudential Regulation Authority (PRA), responsible for prudential regulation of financial institutions; and

- the Financial Conduct Authority (FCA), responsible for conduct issues across the entire spectrum of financial services. The UK Listing Authority (UKLA) functions under Part 6 of the FSMA fall within the remit of the FCA.

Overall, the changes to the FSMA, associated secondary legislation and the FSA Handbook (including the LPDT Rules) to implement the new financial services regime were only of limited significance to listed companies.

The FCA has the same powers as the FSA had to enforce any breaches of the LPDT Rules by listed companies. The FSA 2012 made two significant changes to these powers:

- the FCA has powers to fine sponsors and limit/restrict a sponsor's services (for a maximum of 12 months); and
- the FCA may publicise details of any enforcement action at an early stage in the enforcement process, by publishing summaries of 'warning notices' (whereas the FSA could only publish at the final notice stage).

The FCA also had the same powers of enforcement as the FSA for market abuse offences. However, these powers have since been updated to give the FCA a range of enforcement powers in Part 8 of the FSMA to investigate and impose sanctions for breaches of MAR and its implementing regulations.

There were some substantive changes made to the criminal market manipulation offences. Section 397 of the FSMA was repealed and replaced by ss 89, 90 and 91 of the FSA 2012 (see section 5.4.2 below).

2.3 The FCA Handbook

The FCA exercises its statutory rights and duties to set rules by promulgating the FCA Handbook.

The FCA Handbook contains all of the FCA's rules, including those on prudential standards and the authorisation of firms, as well as the 'Part 6 Rules' referred to above. The Handbook can be accessed online on the FCA's website and the electronic version is updated on a daily basis. There are also tailored and focused versions of the FCA Handbook that are available for different market participants and advisers. The contents of the FCA Handbook are divided into smaller 'Sourcebooks', 'Manuals' and 'Guides'.

The FCA Handbook applies to both FCA-authorised and PRA-authorised firms. There is also a PRA Handbook, which applies to PRA-authorised firms only (which, broadly, includes banks, building societies, insurers and certain systemically important investment firms that the UK Government considers should be subject to significant prudential regulation).

The Listing Rules, Prospectus Rules, and the Disclosure Guidance and Transparency Rules Sourcebook (commonly referred to as the 'LPDT Rules') consists of:

- *Listing Rules* – The Listing Rules contain the rules relating to the eligibility of companies to have their securities listed on the premium or standard segments of the Official List. They also contain the overarching Listing Principles and certain continuing obligations imposed on listed companies after their securities are admitted to listing on the Official List. These obligations vary according to whether a company has a premium or standard listing (see Figure 3 in the Introduction and Chapter 2 for a description of the key differences). For a company with a premium listing, the continuing obligations under the Listing Rules include requirements to notify the market of certain events or information and to produce a circular and/or seek shareholder approval in relation to certain types of corporate transaction. The Listing Rules also set out the obligations and responsibilities of a 'sponsor' (see Chapter 3). They impose a requirement on a company with, or applying for, a premium listing of its shares to appoint a sponsor when it applies for new securities to be listed on the Official List, when it is applying to transfer its listing of shares from a standard to a premium listing (or changing its listing from a commercial company to an investment company or vice versa), when it is required to produce a circular in connection with certain corporate transactions or when it is required by the FCA to appoint a sponsor because it appears to the FCA that there is, or may be, a breach of the Listing Rules, the disclosure requirements and/or the Transparency Rules. Companies with a premium listing are required to comply with all of the 'super-equivalent' provisions in the Listing Rules (which are higher than the EU minimum requirements) – these relate to eligibility criteria, the Premium Listing Principles, the requirement to appoint or consult a sponsor and corporate governance related provisions designed to protect shareholders through disclosure requirements and decision-making rights. By contrast, companies with a standard listing only have to comply with the minimum standards imposed by the FSAP Directives and the Listing Principles.
- *Prospectus Rules* – The Prospectus Rules contain the obligation to prepare and publish an approved prospectus and the process and requirements for doing so. A prospectus is required to be published and approved by the FCA where, subject to certain exemptions, there is an offer of securities to the public in the UK or an admission of securities to trading on a UK regulated market as required by the PD. The Prospectus Rules will apply to a company in the event that it raises new capital or seeks an admission of new securities to trading. Where the UK is the home member state of a company for PD purposes, the FCA will be responsible for approving the prospectus for any offer to the public or admission to trading anywhere in the EEA by such a company without additional significant administrative requirements from any other member states, regardless of whether the offering is made in the UK. The Prospectus Rules prescribe the form and content of a prospectus and include in an appendix the disclosure 'building blocks' from the PD Regulation (discussed in detail in Chapter 4) that prescribe the specific disclosures required to be included

in a prospectus. Parts of the Prospectus Rules are copy outs of the relevant EU Prospectus Directive implementing regulations.

- *Disclosure Guidance* – MAR contains the obligations on listed companies relating to the disclosure and control of inside information and disclosure of dealings in shares by directors, other senior managers and persons closely associated with them. These are among the most important continuing obligations of a listed company and its directors. MAR replaced the Disclosure Rules (which had implemented the MAD in the UK), with effect from 3 July 2016. Where the provisions of MAR have directly replaced provisions in the Disclosure Rules, the FCA has deleted those provisions and replaced them with references to the relevant MAR provisions. Additional guidance which was in the DTRs and which is not set out in, and does not conflict with the provisions of, MAR has also been retained. These sections are no longer referred to as 'rules' and instead are referred to as guidance. The Disclosure Rules have been renamed Disclosure Guidance.

- *Transparency Rules* – The Transparency Rules contain the obligations on listed companies relating to periodic financial reporting (including a requirement to produce annual reports and half-yearly reports), the disclosure of interests in voting rights attached to a company's shares, the provision of information to security holders and corporate governance. They also include an obligation on listed companies to disseminate 'regulated information' to as wide a public, and as close to simultaneously, as possible throughout the EEA. The Transparency Rules implement the TD, the CRD and certain parts of the the Non-Financial Reporting Directive and the Statutory Audit Directive in the UK and are aimed at improving the quality and quantity of the disclosure of information to investors on a pan-European basis. Parts of the Transparency Rules are a copy out of the Transparency Directive implementing regulations. The Statutory Audit Directive was amended by a new Amending Directive (2014/43/EC) and supplemented by a new Audit Regulation (537/2014) with effect from 17 June 2016, in relation to audits for financial years commencing on or after that date. In particular, the Audit Regulation applies more onerous rules directly to Public Interest Entities or PIEs (which includes listed companies), including mandatory rotation of auditors (see Chapter 6).

The general approach taken by the FCA in the LPDT Rules is to indicate which elements of the rules are mandatory (designated 'R'), and which are guidance only (designated 'G').

2.4 Guidance on the FSAP Directives, MAR and Part 6 Rules in practice

2.4.1 Guidance issued by ESMA

As referred to above, ESMA and its predecessor CESR played a crucial role in ensuring the transposition of the FSAP Directives into law in each of the member states. As part of this process, CESR and then ESMA issued Level 3 guidance on the transposition and operation of the FSAP Directives.

Notably, CESR issued the CESR recommendations (now adopted by ESMA) on the consistent implementation of Commission Regulation (EC) No. 809/2004 implementing the Prospectus Directive in January 2005. The recommendations provide an explanation of the disclosure required to comply with the requirements of the PD Regulation. In the UK, an issuer is obliged to comply with the requirements of these recommendations in order to determine its obligations under the PD and the PD Regulation (PR 1.1.6). Following the switch from CESR to ESMA in January 2011, ESMA has reviewed and periodically updates the Recommendations on the consistent implementation of the Prospectus Regulation.

In addition to these recommendations, ESMA publishes (and regularly updates) a set of questions and answers on the operation of the PD and the TD in practice.

ESMA has also played a crucial role in the implementation of MAR. The directly applicable MAR is supplemented by detailed EU implementing measures. ESMA published drafts of these during the course of 2015 which were then approved and adopted by the European Commission, Council and Parliament to become directly effective Level 2 implementing regulations. ESMA has also produced Level 3 guidelines in relation to some areas of MAR and has published and periodically updates a questions and answers document on MAR.

2.4.2 Guidance issued by the UKLA

Following implementation of the FSAP Directives in the UK in July 2005, the UKLA had a practice of issuing 'informal guidance' for market participants through different channels, notably through editions of the newsletters List! and Market Watch. The UKLA made it clear that this informal guidance did not constitute guidance (an important distinction in the context of the FCA's enforcement regime as regards the level of reliance that can be placed on informal guidance). In October 2010, the UKLA consolidated the informal guidance that it had given issuers, sponsors, advisers and other market participants in List! into a series of ten Technical Notes and six Procedural Notes.

In December 2012, the FSA (the predecessor to the FCA) published Primary Market Bulletin No. 4 announcing the launch of new UKLA Guidance Notes, split between Procedural Notes and Technical Notes, which constitute formal guidance on the Part 6 Rules. The guidance notes replaced the UKLA Factsheets and the 2010 UKLA Technical and Procedural Notes. They are updated from time to time by the FCA following consultation via its Primary Market Bulletins.

The UKLA Guidance Notes, which are available on the UKLA Knowledge Base, constitute binding FCA guidance. The Knowledge Base is intended to be a single repository of technical guidance in relation to the Part 6 Rules, and also contains links to useful resources such as forms and checklists on the website.

The UKLA notes that if market participants require additional guidance, they can submit written requests for individual guidance or, in 'live market' situations they can request guidance through the UKLA's emergency telephone line or seek assistance from their sponsor. However, it is not possible to do this on a 'no-names' basis.

The current Procedural Notes available on the UKLA Knowledge Base focus on:

- eligibility process;
- final terms;
- review and approval of documents;
- public offer prospectus – drafting and approval;
- passporting;
- UKLA standard comments;
- block listings;
- the UKLA decision making and review process;
- sponsor firms – ongoing requirements during reorganisations; and
- additional powers to supervise sponsors.

The current Technical Notes available on the UKLA Knowledge Base are divided into categories including:

- eligibility for listing;
- governance and conduct;
- transactions;
- working capital;
- profit forecasts and estimates;
- close-ended investment funds;
- specialist companies;
- periodic financial information;
- regulatory announcements including inside information;
- disclosure of positions held by issuers, investors and management;
- public offers, admission to trading and the marketing of securities;
- prospectus content; and
- sponsors.

A table listing each of the current notes and giving a brief description of their contents can be found on page xxvi.

Some material from the 2010 Technical and Procedural Notes and a significant amount of material from List! and other one-off updates issued by the UKLA have not been replicated in the guidance notes. (The 2010 Technical and Procedural Notes and

List! remain available on the National Archives version of the old FSA website.) In response to questions received during the consultation process about relying on material not carried forward from List! and the 2010 Technical and Procedural Notes, the FSA (the predecessor to the FCA) stated that those documents had never constituted formal guidance. The reason it was not repeated in the guidance notes was because either the rules have changed, the commentary now appears as formal guidance in the rules themselves or it did not think that the matter was suitable for formal guidance. It did not say that it is because the views are no longer held. Some of the old commentary from List! and the 2010 Technical and Procedural Notes remains useful for reference. Caution should, however, be exercised in seeking to rely on commentary which has not been included in the guidance notes; if there is any doubt, individual guidance should be sought from the FCA.

3. The role of the FCA and the UKLA

The FCA (which replaced the FSA in April 2013) is an independent, non-governmental body, given statutory powers by the FSMA (as amended by FSA 2012).

The FCA has a strategic objective and three operational objectives:

- The strategic objective is to ensure that the relevant markets function well.
- The operational objectives are:
  - to secure an appropriate degree of protection for consumers (the consumer protection objective);
  - to protect and enhance the integrity of the UK financial systems (the integrity objective); and
  - to promote effective competition in the interests of consumers in the markets for regulated financial services and services provided by recognised investment exchanges (RIEs) (the competition objective).

The FCA adopted the legal corporate entity of the FSA and is a company limited by guarantee and financed by the financial services industry. The Treasury appoints the FCA Board, consisting of a chairman, a chief executive officer, managing directors and non-executive directors. This Board sets the FCA's overall policy, but day-to-day decisions and management of the staff are the responsibility of the Executive.

The FCA, acting through one of its divisions, the UKLA, is the UK's competent authority for the regulation of the admission of securities to the premium and standard segments of the Official List. In several other European jurisdictions, stock exchanges fulfil this role. It is important to understand what the term 'listing' means in the UK. In most jurisdictions it is synonymous with admission to trading on an exchange, whereas in the UK, admission to the premium or standard segment of the Official List and admission to trading are different (although linked) concepts. While historically associated with the London Stock Exchange's Main Market, the Official List is, in fact, no longer linked to any single trading platform or venue. This is discussed further in Chapter 2.

4. The role of the LSE

While the responsibility for listing securities rests with the FCA, listed securities also need to be admitted to trading on a market, for example, the London Stock Exchange, and are therefore subject to that market's rules.

The LSE Admission and Disclosure Standards contain the admission requirements for companies seeking an admission to trading of their securities, and the continuing obligation requirements for companies that have securities admitted to trading on the main market of the London Stock Exchange. The LSE Admission and Disclosure Standards are updated periodically by the London Stock Exchange and can be downloaded from the LSE's website.

The LSE Admission and Disclosure Standards require listed companies to comply with the rules made by the FCA (Rule 4.1) and with certain rules relating to communication with the LSE and the market and the timetable and conduct of certain corporate actions (including the payment of dividends and further shares issues).

In particular, a listed company is required to:

- have a contact at the company who is responsible for ongoing communications with the LSE and to notify any change in this person (Rule 2.8);
- ensure all information provided in connection with an application for admission to trading is accurate, complete and not misleading (Rule 2.9);
- notify the LSE of the timetable for any proposed action affecting the rights of holders of securities such as dividends, open offers or bonus issues (Rules 4.7 and 4.8);
- include certain details in dividend announcements and agree a timetable with the LSE where a dividend timetable does not follow the LSE's Dividend and Procedure Timetable (Schedule 3, paragraph 6); and
- keep an open offer available for at least ten business days and ensure that valid claims through the market can be promptly satisfied (Schedule 3, paragraph 7).

A company must provide the LSE with any information or explanation which it may reasonably require for the purpose of verifying whether the LSE Admission and Disclosure Standards are being and have been complied with, or which relates to the integrity or orderly operation of the LSE's markets (Rule 4.4). If a company has contravened the LSE Admission and Disclosure Standards, the LSE has the power to privately censure the company, publish the fact that the company has been censured, fine the company and cancel the company's right to trade its securities on the LSE (Rule 4.21).

Trading in securities on the LSE will be suspended if the securities are suspended from listing by the FCA (see section 5 of Chapter 2) or if the LSE's ability to ensure the orderly operation of its markets is, or may be, jeopardised, even if only temporarily (Rules 4.12 and 4.13).

5. Compliance with and enforcement of the UK listing regime

5.1 A company's responsibility for compliance with the LPDT Rules and MAR

A listed company must provide to the FCA without delay:

- any information that the FCA considers appropriate to protect investors or ensure the smooth operation of the market (LR 1.3.1R(2));
- any other information or explanations which the FCA may reasonably require for the purpose of verifying whether the Listing Rules are being and have been complied with (LR 1.3.1R(3));
- any information and explanations that the FCA may reasonably require to decide whether to grant an application for admission to listing (LR 1.3.1R(1)); and
- when seeking approval for a prospectus, any information that the FCA considers necessary on reasonable grounds (PR 3.1.-1(EU)).

5.2 Directors' responsibilities for compliance with the LPDT Rules and MAR

Under the LPDT Rules, disclosure requirements and MAR, a number of direct personal obligations are imposed on directors, certain other senior executives and persons closely associated with them, including:

- under the Prospectus Rules (PR 5.5), directors are personally responsible, together with the company, for the contents of all prospectuses issued by the company in relation to equity securities if they were directors when the prospectus was published or they have authorised themselves to be named, and are named, in the prospectus as a director or as someone who has agreed to become a director either immediately or at a future time (see section 5 of Chapter 4);
- under Article 19(1) of MAR, directors and certain other senior executives (PDMRs) and persons closely associated with them are personally obliged to notify the company and the FCA of their dealings in the company's shares, derivatives or other financial instruments related to those shares (see section 1 of Chapter 7); and
- under the Transparency Rules (DTR 5), directors may, in their capacity as holders of securities in, or relating to, the company, be required to disclose details of their holdings of shares and certain financial instruments in the company (see section 5 of Chapter 7).

5.3 The FCA's powers

The FCA has administrative powers under Part 8 of the FSMA to investigate a breach of MAR. This includes the power to require companies (as well as directors, other PDMRs and persons closely associated with them) to provide the FCA with any information the FCA reasonably requires to protect investors or the orderly operation of the market, and to verify whether the requirements in MAR are being, or have been, complied with.

The FCA may suspend a company's securities from trading where the FCA considers it necessary for the purpose of exercising its functions under MAR or any of the MAR implementing regulations (FSMA s. 122I). The FCA has the power to censure a company or impose an unlimited fine upon it for breaches of MAR and its implementing regulations (FSMA s. 123). It also has power (FSMA s. 384) to require any person committing market abuse to compensate anyone who suffers a loss or is otherwise adversely affected as a result of the market abuse.

If the FCA considers that a listed company has contravened the LPDT Rules it may privately or publicly censure the company, or impose a financial penalty upon the company (FSMA s. 91).

The FCA may impose a fine on or censure a director, or former director, of the company if it considers that they were at the material time a director of the company and was 'knowingly concerned in the contravention' of the LPDT Rules or disclosure requirements and for breach of their direct personal obligations in the disclosure requirements contained in MAR or under the Transparency Rules.

The FCA may consider it appropriate to take action against a director even if it decides not to impose a disciplinary sanction on a company.

If the FCA has reasonable grounds to suspect non-compliance with the Prospectus Rules, the FSMA or any other provision relating to the Prospectus Directive, it may require a company to suspend or withdraw its offer to the public, suspend its request for admission to trading of securities or prohibit trading in securities if they have already been admitted to trading (FSMA ss 87K and 87L).

In addition, where the smooth operation of the market is, or may be, temporarily jeopardised or if the protection of investors so requires it, the FCA may suspend the listing of any securities at any time (LR 5.1.1R(1)) (see section 5 of Chapter 2). It may also cancel a listing under the Listing Rules if regular dealings in the securities are precluded, including where suspension of the securities lasts for more than six months (LR 5.2.1R and LR 5.2.2G(3)).

REGULATORY FRAMEWORK

In certain areas, the FSMA expressly requires the FCA to prepare and publish statements of policy or procedure on the exercise of its enforcement and investigation powers and in relation to the giving of statutory notices. These policies are set out in the Decision Procedure and Penalties Manual (DEPP), a module of the FCA Handbook.

The FCA's main enforcement powers are summarised in Figure 1.2.

Figure 1.2: The FCA's enforcement powers

Sections of FSMA	FCA's enforcement powers
87K	Power to suspend or prohibit offer to the public
87L, 89L	Power to suspend or prohibit admission to trading on a regulated market/trading of securities
87M, 89K	Public censure of issuer
87N, 89N	Rights to refer matters to the Tribunal
87P	Exercise of powers at request of competent authority of another EEA state
88A–88F	Disciplinary powers (in relation to sponsors)
89H, 89I, 89J	Power to call for information
91–94	Power to impose penalties for breach of the 'Part 6 Rules'
97	Power to appoint a person to carry out an investigation if apparent contravention of Part 6 of the FSMA or of the 'Part 6 Rules'
100A	Exercise of powers where UK is host member state
122A–122I	Administrative powers to investigate and deal with a breach of MAR
123–123C	Power to impose administrative sanctions relating to market abuse
380–384	Power to seek an injunction or restitution order

5.4 Criminal offences

5.4.1 Breach of FSMA section 85

It is a criminal offence to offer transferable securities to the public in the UK, or request admission of transferable securities to trading on a regulated market in the UK (which includes the main market of the LSE), unless an approved prospectus has been made available to the public before the offer or request has been made (FSMA s. 85(1) and (2)). This criminal offence may be committed by the directors of the company if they contravene these provisions of the FSMA.

If the company does not issue an approved prospectus when required to do so under the FSMA and the Prospectus Rules, the offence is punishable on summary conviction by imprisonment for up to three months or on indictment by imprisonment for up to two years, and/or a fine (FSMA s. 85(3)).

5.4.2 Misleading statements or conduct

It is a criminal offence under section 89 of the FSA 2012 for a person:

- to make a statement which they know to be materially false or misleading;
- to dishonestly conceal any material facts; or
- to recklessly make a statement which is materially false or misleading, for the purpose of inducing (or being reckless as to whether it may induce) a person to make an investment decision or exercise any rights relating to investments.

It is also a criminal offence under section 90 of the FSA 2012 if a person intends to create a false or misleading impression and intends by creating that impression to:

- induce another person to make an investment decision or exercise any rights conferred by those investments; or
- produce a gain, or create a loss to another, or is aware that creating the impression is likely to produce those results (where the person knows the impression is false or misleading or is reckless as to whether it is).

Under section 401 of the FSMA, the FCA has the power to prosecute the criminal offences under Part 7 of the FSA 2012 (offences relating to financial services).

The civil regime for misleading statements is in the FSMA itself. Section 90A and Schedule 10A of the FSMA contains the civil regime for misleading statements in relation to regulatory information (see section 6 of Chapter 8) and section 90 of the FSMA contains the regime for civil liability in relation to prospectuses (see section 5 of Chapter 4).

5.4.3 Insider dealing

Directors of a company should also be aware of the criminal offence of insider dealing contained in Part V of the Criminal Justice Act 1993. In particular, a director may be guilty of the criminal offence of insider dealing if he or she discloses the information otherwise than in the proper performance of his employment, office or profession or if he or she deals in the company's securities, or encourages another person to deal, at a time when he or she is in possession of price sensitive information. This is a separate regime to the civil offence of market abuse contained in MAR.

5.4.4 Fraud

Directors and employees of a company should also be aware of the criminal offence of fraud contained in the Fraud Act 2006. Fraud can be committed in three different ways. In each case the relevant behaviour must be dishonest and intended to secure either a gain for the defendant or a loss or risk of loss to another of money or any other property. No gain or loss, however, need actually be suffered for the offence to be committed. A corporate body may commit the offences and any director, manager, secretary or other similar officer of the company (or any person purporting to act in such a capacity) will also commit the relevant offence if the company's offence is proved to have been committed with the consent or connivance of that individual.

The three relevant offences under the Fraud Act are:

- to make a false representation (by words or conduct as to any fact, law or state of mind of any person) whether express or implied, either knowing that the representation is false or misleading, or being aware that it might be. The victim of the representation need not actually rely upon it;
- to fail to disclose information where there is a legal duty to do so (e.g. a contractual duty, or a duty arising from a fiduciary relationship). Those who fail to make full disclosure pursuant to legal obligations will therefore be at risk of prosecution. This could catch the company and its directors if they fail to make disclosures, for example, in an announcement, in breach of the disclosure requirements; and
- where a person who occupies a privileged position, such that he would be expected to safeguard the victim's financial interest, abuses that position. The types of relationship which may lead to the expectation are the relationship between a director and the company. Such an abuse is capable of being committed by omission. A director of the company who covertly fails to act in the best financial interests of the company, its staff or its clients could therefore fall foul of this provision, if the other requisite elements are present.

5.5 FCA enforcement actions for breach of the listing regime and market abuse findings relevant to listed companies

A summary of the key enforcement actions taken by the FCA (and previously, the FSA) for breach of the LPDT Rules and/or related sections of the FSMA since 2008 is set out in Figure 1.3.

Figure 1.3: Key FCA enforcement actions

Issuer	Date	Sanction	Summary
Tesco plc	March 2017	Public censure; order to pay £85 million to compensate investors	*Market abuse for publishing misleading trading update* The FCA publicly censured Tesco and ordered it to pay compensation to certain shareholders and bondholders following the FCA's finding that it and a subsidiary had committed market abuse in relation to a trading update published in August 2014. The FCA found that the trading update gave a false or misleading impression as to the value of Tesco plc's shares and publicly traded bonds issued by other Tesco group companies. As such, Tesco had engaged in market abuse contrary to section 118(7) of the Financial Services and Markets Act 2000 (FSMA) (now Articles 12 and 15 of the Market Abuse Regulation (MAR)). The FCA did not suggest that the Tesco plc board knew that the information was false or misleading.
Co-operative Bank plc	August 2015	Public censure	*Breach of the Listing Rules for publishing misleading information* The FCA censured the Co-operative Bank plc for including misleading statements about its capital position in its 2012 annual report and accounts in breach of the obligation under LR 1.3.3 to take reasonable care to ensure that any information notified to a regulatory information service or made available through the FCA is not misleading, false or deceptive.

REGULATORY FRAMEWORK 43

Issuer	Date	Sanction	Summary
			The FCA found that the Co-operative Bank also breached Principle 11 of the regulators' Principles of Business, the requirement for an authorised firm to deal with its regulators in an open and cooperative way, by failing to notify the regulators of two intended personnel changes in senior positions. The PRA also censured the Co-operative Bank for breach of Principle 11 and Principle 3, the requirement for an authorised firm to have adequate control frameworks and risk management systems in place. The FCA and PRA would have fined the Co-operative Bank for the breaches but given the exceptional circumstances, in particular the Co-operative Bank's turnaround plan and changes in its board of directors and senior management, decided that a censure was more appropriate.
Asia Resource Minerals plc	June 2015	Fined £4,651,200	*Breaches of LP 2 (now LP 1), LR 8.2.3, LR 11 and DTR 4.1.3* The company failed to identify three transactions entered into by a key Indonesian subsidiary as related party transactions and failed to aggregate the transactions as required by LR 11.1.11. The company was also unable to confirm that all other previously unknown related party transactions had been identified and failed to publish its annual report within four months of the end of the financial year in breach of DTR 4.1.13. The FCA fined the company approximately £4.65 million principally for failing in its systems and controls to identify related party transactions.

Issuer	Date	Sanction	Summary
Reckitt Benckiser Group plc	January 2015	Fined £539,800	*Breaches of LR 9.2.8, LP 1 (now PLP 1), LP 2 (now LP 1) and DTRs 3.1.4 and 3.1.5 relating to share dealings by PDMRs (now in Art. 19 MAR)* The company discovered in late 2012 that there had been breaches of its share dealing requirements by two PDMRs in prior years and dealings were not announced to the market under DTR 3. There was no suggestion that the PDMRs traded on the basis of inside information or deliberately breached the requirements. The FCA focused on the company's systems and controls and fined the company for failing to take reasonable steps to: ■ secure compliance by PDMRs with the Model Code (LR 9.2.8); ■ enable the directors to understand their responsibilities, and obligations under the Model Code (then LP 1, now PLP 1); ■ maintain adequate systems, procedures and controls to enable the company to comply with its obligations (LP 2, now LP 1); and ■ notify the market of the PDMR share dealings (DTRs 3.1.4 and 3.1.5).
Execution Noble & Company Limited	December 2014	Fined £231,000	*Breach of the Listing Rules relating to sponsors* The FCA fined the sponsor £231,000 for failing to inform the UKLA that two-thirds of the firm's sponsor team had left the firm. The sponsor did notify the FCA's authorisation department; however, there is a need for sponsors to make appropriate notifications to the UKLA (in its sponsor supervision capacity) as distinct from other arms of the FCA.

REGULATORY FRAMEWORK 45

Issuer	Date	Sanction	Summary
			The FCA emphasised the need for sponsor firms to have an open and co-operative relationship with the UKLA, on an ongoing basis, as required by LR 8.3.5R(1) and the guidance in LR 8.7.1G.
Prudential plc	March 2013	Fined £14 million	*Breach of Listing Principle 6 (now LP 2)* The company failed to deal with the FSA in an open and cooperative way in relation to its proposed reverse takeover of AIA in breach of LP 6. On the same date, the FSA published a final notice imposing a £16 million fine on the Prudential Assurance Company Limited (PAC) for breach of Principle 11 of the FSA's Principles for Business (PRIN). PAC is the Prudential group entity through which the FSA supervised the Prudential group. The FSA also published a final notice censuring Prudential's Chief Executive for being knowingly concerned in PAC's contravention of Principle 11.
Lamprell plc	March 2013	Fined £2.4 million	*Breaches of DTR 1.3.4R, DTR 2.2.1R, paragraph 8 of the Model Code and LP 2 (now LP 1)* The FSA fined Lamprell for breaches of the Listing and Disclosure Rules, in particular a failure to disclose inside information and a failure in its systems and controls which meant that it was not able to adequately monitor its financial performance. The FSA also found that the company breached paragraph 8 of the Model Code by giving clearance to PDMRs to deal in the company's shares during a prohibited period.

Issuer	Date	Sanction	Summary
Nestor Healthcare Group Limited	February 2013	Fined £175,000	*Breaches of LR 9.2.8R and LP 1 and 2 (now PLP 1 and LP 1)* The company failed to take: - all proper and reasonable steps to secure the compliance of its persons discharging managerial responsibility with paragraphs 3 to 7 of the Model Code, in breach of LR 9.2.8R (this was the first substantive enforcement action taken by the FSA in respect of a failure to take reasonable steps to ensure compliance with the Model Code); - reasonable steps to enable its directors to understand their responsibilities and obligations as directors under the Model Code, in breach of Listing Principle 1 (now Premium Listing Principle 1); - reasonable steps to maintain adequate procedures, systems and controls to enable it to comply with its obligations under LR 9.2.8R, in breach of Listing Principle 2 (now Listing Principle 1); and - reasonable steps to ensure adherence to its share dealing policy, or to review and update it where necessary.
Cattles Limited	March 2012	Public censure (The FSA stated that it would have imposed a 'substantial financial penalty' were it not for Cattles' financial circumstances.)	*Breaches of LR 1.3.3R, LP 3 (now PLP 2) and LP 4 (now PLP 6)* The FSA censured Cattles Limited, formerly a listed PLC, for market abuse and breaches of the Listing Rules. The FSA ruled that Cattles was in breach of LR 1.3.3R, Listing Principle 3 (now Premium Listing Principle 2) and Listing Principle 4 (now Premium Listing Principle 6). The company's annual report and prospectus were misleading as loan impairments were not being properly accounted for.

Issuer	Date	Sanction	Summary
Exillon Energy	April 2012	Fined £292,950	*Breaches of LR 11 and LP 2 (now LP 1)* The company failed to identify certain payments made to its chairman as related party transactions and breached LR 11.1.10R(2) and LR 11.1.11(3) as a result. The company breached Listing Principle 2 (now Listing Principle 1) in failing to take reasonable steps to establish and maintain adequate procedures, systems and controls to enable it to comply with its related party transaction obligations.
Andrew Osborne	February 2012	Fined £350,000	*Market abuse* The FSA fined corporate broker Andrew Osborne for improperly disclosing inside information during a call with a shareholder in Punch Taverns plc ahead of a proposed equity issue by the company in June 2009, even though he had not provided definitive information on the terms or actual timing of the transaction.
Ian Hannam	February 2012	Fined £450,000	*Market abuse* The FSA fined Ian Hannam, a senior investment banker, £450,000 for committing market abuse through the improper disclosure of inside information in September and October 2008. This decision was confirmed by the Upper Tribunal in May 2014.
David Einhorn and Greenlight Capital Inc	January 2011	Fined £7.2 million	*Market abuse* The FSA fined David Einhorn and Greenlight Capital Inc a total of £7.2 million for engaging in market abuse by dealing on the basis of inside information in relation to a proposed equity fundraising by Punch Taverns in June 2009.

Issuer	Date	Sanction	Summary
Sir Ken Morrison	August 2011	Fined £210,000	*Breach of DTR 5.8.3R* The FSA fined Sir Ken Morrison, the ex-Chairman of Wm Morrison Supermarkets plc for breach of DTR 5.8.3R for failure to notify the company until 1 March 2011 that, between 16 September 2009 and 21 June 2010, his voting rights had fallen below 6%, 5%, 4% and 3%. The company was not in a position to update the market in accordance with DTR 5.8.12R(1) and his level of shareholding was incorrectly stated in the company's annual report of 31 January 2010. The FSA considered the failings were serious due to his prominent position and the significant delay in his eventually making the required notification. This was the first time that the FSA had imposed a fine for breach of DTR 5.
BDO LLP (Sponsor)	May 2011	Public censure of sponsor	*Contravention of LR 8.3.3R and LR 8.3.5R* Contravention of LR 8.3.3R for failure to act with due care and skill in relation to a sponsor service and contravention of LR 8.3.5R by not dealing with the FSA in an open and co-operative way when acting as a sponsor on a proposed merger. The sponsor agreed it would delay contact with the UKLA until after announcement of the transaction (there were clear indications it might constitute a reverse takeover). The sponsor's position that the transaction was a Class 1 transaction indicated a lack of objective oversight, required of a sponsor.

REGULATORY FRAMEWORK **49**

Issuer	Date	Sanction	Summary
BDO LLP (Sponsor)	May 2011	Public censure of sponsor	There was a further lack of objective oversight through the sponsor's focus on the company's desire to expedite the process and to avoid a suspension of its shares.
JJB Sports plc	January 2011	Company fined £455,000	*Breach of DTR 2.2.1R (now Art. 17 of MAR) and LP 4 (now PLP 6)* Breach of DTR 2.2.1R for failure to disclose certain liabilities in connection with acquisitions. Continued breach of DTR 2.2.1R for an extensive period of time as the company failed to disclose the liabilities until publication of interim results. During these periods there was a false market in the company's shares.
Photo-Me International plc	June 2010	Company fined £500,000	*Breach of DTR 2.2.1R (now Art. 17 of MAR) and LP 4 (now PLP 6)* Breach of DTR 2.2.1R due to delay of 44 days in making an announcement of inside information from 17 January 2007 to 2 March 2007. The question of whether information is likely to have a significant effect on price must be assessed in accordance with the test in section 118C(6) of FSMA.
Entertainment Rights plc	January 2009	Company fined £245,000	*Breach of DTR 2.2.1R (now Art. 17 of MAR) and LP 4 (now PLP 6)* Breach of DTR 2.2.1R due to delay of 78 days in making an announcement of inside information (July–September 2008). The delay led to the creation of a false market in Entertainment Rights' shares during this period, breaching LP 4 (now PLP 6).

Issuer	Date	Sanction	Summary
Wolfson Micro-electronics plc	January 2009	Company fined £140,000	*Breach of DTR 2.2.1R (now Art. 17 of MAR) and LP 4 (now PLP 6)* Breach of DTR 2.2.1R due to delay of 16 days in making an announcement of inside information (March 2008). The delay led to the creation of a false market in Wolfson's shares during this period, breaching LP 4 (now PLP 6).
Woolworths Group plc	June 2008	Company fined £350,000	*Breach of DTR 2.2.1R (now Art. 17 of MAR, DR 2.2.1R at the time of breach) and LP 4 (now PLP 6)* Breach of DR 2.2.1 due to delayed announcement of inside information from 20 December 2005 until 18 January 2006. The delay led to the creation of a false market in Woolworths' shares during this period, breaching LP 4 (now PLP 6).

CHAPTER 2

Admission to the Official List

OVERVIEW

- There are a number of different routes to market in the UK. The route that is generally taken by a UK incorporated company is admission to the Official List of the UK Listing Authority (UKLA) and to trading on the main market for listed securities of the London Stock Exchange (LSE).
- Commercial companies seeking to admit securities to the Official List can apply for either a 'premium listing' or a 'standard listing'.
- Listing Rule 2 sets out the minimum requirements for all applicants for admission of securities to listing, including due incorporation, validly issued and freely transferable securities, a minimum market capitalisation and the publication of a PD-compliant prospectus.
- Listing Rule 6 sets out the additional requirements that must be satisfied if a commercial company wishes to apply for a 'premium listing' of its shares, including a three-year track record, an independent business, sufficient working capital, minimum free-float requirements and shares that are capable of electronic settlement.
- Listing Rule 14 sets out the additional requirements that must be satisfied if a company wishes to apply for a 'standard listing' of its shares.
- The procedure for applying to the FCA for admission to listing is set out in Listing Rule 3. The listing timetable will largely be driven by the time taken to obtain the FCA's approval of the prospectus required to be prepared and published.
- A company seeking a premium listing must appoint a sponsor who will liaise with the FCA in connection with the company's application for listing.
- In addition to applying to the FCA for admission to listing, if a company wishes to have its shares traded on the LSE an application must also be made to the LSE for admission to trading. The requirements and application procedure for admission to trading are set out in the LSE Admission and Disclosure Standards.
- Listing Rule 5 sets out how a company moves from a premium listing to a standard listing and vice versa.
- Listing Rule 5 also sets out when the FCA may, either of its own volition or at the request of a listed company, suspend or cancel a listing, and when such a listing may then be restored at a subsequent date. Rules 4.12 to 4.19 of the LSE Admission and Disclosure Standards set out when the LSE may likewise suspend or cancel trading.

1. Listing segments and categories of the Official List

1.1 The premium and standard segments

There are two segments of the Official List of the UKLA to which securities are admitted: the premium segment (formerly known as primary) and the standard segment (formerly known as secondary).

The segment to which the securities are admitted will determine the standards with which the company must comply under the Listing Rules. Where securities are admitted to the standard segment, the company must comply with the minimum requirements derived from the FSAP Directives (known as 'Directive-minimum' standards). Where securities are admitted to the premium segment, the company must comply with both the FSAP 'Directive-minimum' requirements and the more stringent 'super-equivalent' listing requirements of the Listing Rules.

A premium listing of shares is the 'gold standard' of the Official List to which additional requirements, otherwise known as 'super-equivalent' requirements, apply. All the other listing categories for commercial companies are based on 'Directive-minimum' standards only (i.e. the minimum standards which EU legislation imposes on all securities trading on a regulated market and/or offered to the public). The FSA (the predecessor to the FCA) put this structure in place in July 2005, following consultation with the market as to whether they should retain London's 'super-equivalent' standards following the implementation of the FSAP Directives (see Chapter 1). In April 2010, the FSA concluded a review of the listing regime and retained broadly the same structure, albeit with different labels for the listing segments. In particular, it retained the super-equivalent requirements for all companies with a premium listing.

A company with a standard listing of shares only has to comply with the 'Directive-minimum' standards and not the 'super-equivalent' standards imposed by the FCA on companies with a premium listing. A company with a standard listing must not hold itself out in any way as having a premium listing or make any representation which suggests, or may be taken to suggest, that it has a premium listing or that it complies with the requirements that apply to a premium listing (LR 1.5.2R).

A commercial company may alternatively apply for a listing of global depositary receipts (GDRs), although they are more typically issued by overseas companies.

In its Discussion Paper 'Review of the Effectiveness of Primary Markets: The UK Primary Markets Landscape' (SP 17/2), the FCA looks at how the UK primary capital markets can most effectively meet the needs of issuers and investors, and whether the current structures should change. The Discussion Paper considers whether the current boundary between the standard and premium listing categories is appropriate and whether the regime should be redrawn to improve effectiveness for issuers and investors. The FCA sought views on a number of aspects of the regime, including whether standard listing is sufficiently understood and valued by investors and issuers and whether there should be an 'international segment' for overseas companies, with higher standards of conduct than apply to a standard listing, such as an obligation to appoint a sponsor in specific situations, but without being subject to the full suite of premium listing requirements. The Discussion Paper closed for comments on 14 May 2017. If the FCA decides to take any specific proposals forward, it will publish a detailed consultation paper on its proposed rule changes.

This Guide is focused on UK incorporated commercial companies (i.e. companies that are not investments entities) with or seeking a premium listing for shares. Listings of debt, GDRs and securitised derivatives are not therefore considered further.

The Listing Rules have separate chapters for investment entities. The rules for premium listed closed-ended investment funds are set out in LR 15 and the rules for premium listed open-ended investment companies are set out in LR 16. Again, the requirements for these companies are not considered further in this Guide.

1.2 The listing categories

The two listing segments are broken down into eight listing categories, with three of these being in the premium segment and five in the standard segment. The listing category reflects the characteristics of the issuer (in the case of the premium segment) and of the securities to be listed (in the case of the standard segment). Figure 2.1 gives an overview of the structure of the regime and the key chapter of the Listing Rules applicable to each category.

Figure 2.1: The UK listing regime: segments and categories

Listing Segment	Premium			Standard				
Listing category	Equity shares: commercial company	Equity shares: closed ended investment funds	Equity shares: open-ended investment companies	Shares	Certificates representing certain securities	Debt and debt-like securities	Securitised derivatives	Misc securities
Examples of type of security	–	–	–	Equity shares (see Note (1)) Non-equity shares	GDRs	Debt securities ABS Convertible securities Preference shares		Warrants Options

Listing Segment	Premium					Standard			
Listing Rules	LR 2, LR 6 and LR 7 to LR 13	LR 2 and LR 15 (see Notes (1) and (2))	LR 2 and LR 16 (see Notes (1) and (2))	LR 2 and LR 14 (see Note (3))	LR 18 (see Note (3))	LR 17 (see Note (3))	LR 19 (see Note (3))	LR 20 (see Note (3))
Standards	Super-equivalent standards	Super-equivalent standards	Super-equivalent standards	Directive-minimum standards	Directive-minimum standards	Directive-minimum standards	Directive-minimum standards	Directive-minimum standards

Notes:

1. An investment entity will only be able to obtain a standard listing for equity shares if it already has a class of equity shares admitted to a premium listing.
2. Further obligations in LR 7 to LR 13 also apply.
3. Further obligations in LR 7 also apply.

Despite there being eight listing categories, in practice only in limited circumstances will an issuer have a choice as to which category its securities should be admitted to listing. For example, only equity shares are eligible for a premium listing (LR 1.5.1G(3)). For these purposes, equity shares are shares that confer an unlimited right to participate in any dividend or capital distribution. In addition, the Listing Rules contemplate that shares that have a premium listing will be voting shares (see Premium Listing Principles 3 and 4, in LR 7.2.1AR, and LR 9.2.21R). As a result, non-voting shares are not able to have a premium listing. An investment company may only have a standard listing for equity shares if it already has a class of equity shares with a premium listing (LR 14.1.1R(1)).

The only securities in relation to which there is an unrestricted choice as to whether they should be premium or standard listed are equity shares issued by a commercial company.

Broadly, the same listing standards apply and the same choices are available for issuers irrespective of the country of incorporation of the issuer. Figure 2.2 sets out the choice of listing segment and category by security open to an issuer.

Figure 2.2: Choice of listing segment by securities to be listed

Securities	Possible listing segment	Available to which issuer?
Equity shares	Premium listing or standard listing	UK and overseas companies (see notes 1 and 2)
Non-equity shares	Standard listing	UK and overseas companies
Global Depository Receipts (GDRs)	Standard listing	UK and overseas companies
Debt	Standard listing	UK and overseas companies

Securities	Possible listing segment	Available to which issuer?
Securitised Derivatives (SDs)	Standard listing	UK and overseas companies
Miscellaneous securities	Standard listing	UK and overseas companies

Notes:
1. Investment companies may only have a standard listing of equity shares if they have, and retain, a premium listing for at least one class of equity shares (LR 14.1.1R(1)).
2. Where the shares of a company incorporated outside the EEA are not listed in the company's jurisdiction of incorporation or in the country in which a majority of its shares are held, the FCA will not admit the shares to listing unless it is satisfied that the absence of listing is not due to the need to protect investors (LR 6.1.21R and LR 14.2.4R).

While the focus of this chapter (and this Guide) is on the admission of equity shares of a commercial company to listing, it is worth nothing that in the UK equities market there are a number of other ways in which a company may raise equity capital, not all of which involve listing on the Official List.

1.3 Alternative securities markets in the UK

As well as the 'super-equivalent' standard of a premium listing or the 'Directive-minimum' standard of a standard listing of equity shares, a company may raise equity capital by obtaining a standard listing of GDRs on the Official List when seeking admission to the LSE's main market. The NEX Exchange Main Board provides another option for trading securities for a company that is seeking or has obtained a listing of its securities on the Official List.

It is also possible for securities to be admitted to a regulated market segment which operates to 'Directive-minimum' standards, but not listed on the Official List. The Specialist Fund Segment (which the LSE opened as the Specialist Fund Market in March 2008) and the High Growth Segment (opened by the LSE in March 2013) are examples of such a segment (see section 1.3.1 below for further information on the High Growth Segment).

There are also successful 'junior' non-listed markets, such as AIM and the NEX Exchange Growth Market, which operate outside the scope of many of the provisions of the FSAP Directives that apply to markets operating under 'Directive-minimum' standards.

The NEX Exchange Main Board and the NEX Exchange Growth Market were formerly known as the ISDX Exchange Main Board and the ISDX Exchange Growth Market, respectively, and were operated by the ICAP Securities & Derivatives Exchange before it was renamed the NEX Exchange in December 2016, alongside other former ICAP businesses, within the NEX Group.

Figure 2.3 sets out the choices available for a commercial company wishing to raise public equity capital in London.

Figure 2.3: Choice of securities markets in the UK

Market	Are securities admitted to the Official List?	Are securities admitted to a regulated market?	Standards that apply
Premium listing and admission to the LSE's main market	✓	✓	'Directive-minimum' plus additional 'super-equivalent' standards.
Standard listing and admission to the LSE's main market	✓	✓	'Directive-minimum' standards.
Specialist Fund Segment for specialised investment entities targeting institutional, knowledgeable investors as a segment of the LSE's main market	✗	✓	'Directive-minimum' standards.
High Growth Segment for fast-growing companies as a segment of the LSE's main market	✗	✓	'Directive-minimum' standards. Issuers must comply with the High Growth Segment Rulebook.
AIM for smaller growing companies: an 'Exchange-regulated market' (i.e. regulated by LSE)	✗	✗	Issuers are not subject to 'Directive-minimum' standards. Issuers must comply with the AIM Rules for Companies.
Professional Securities Market for wholesale debt securities: an 'Exchange-regulated market' (i.e. regulated by LSE)	✓	✗	Issuers are not subject to 'Directive-minimum' standards. Issuers must comply with the relevant provisions of the Listing Rules.
NEX Exchange Main Board operated by NEX Exchange	✓	✓	'Directive-minimum' standards.
NEX Exchange Growth Market operated by NEX Exchange	✗	✗	Issuers are not subject to 'Directive-minimum' standards.

1.3.1 High Growth Segment (HGS)

The HGS of the main market of the LSE opened in March 2013. The aim of the HGS is to attract fast-growing UK and European companies, particularly in the technology sector, to list on the main market.

The HGS is part of the LSE's main market, but sits outside the UK's listing regime. When companies are seeking admission to the main market, they are required to publish a PD-compliant prospectus approved by the FCA, even if no public offer of securities is made, as they will be seeking admission to a regulated market. Securities of companies on the HGS are not admitted to the Official List and therefore the Listing Rules (including the eligibility criteria set out in LR 2, LR 6 and LR 14) do not apply. Instead, companies applying for admission to the HGS must satisfy the eligibility criteria set out in the HGS Rulebook (Schedule 5 of the LSE Admission and Disclosure Standards) as well as the existing conditions for admission to trading on the main market of the LSE (discussed in section 2.2 below), and appoint a Key Adviser (who must be approved as a sponsor under the Listing Rules and as a Key Adviser by the LSE).

The key eligibility requirements for companies seeking to be traded on the HGS include a requirement that 10% of the securities to be admitted to trading must be in public hands and the value of securities in public hands must be at least £30 million, the majority of which must be raised at admission by the issue of new securities or the sale of existing securities from the same class as that to be admitted.

An applicant must include a (non-binding) statement in its prospectus on admission (and in any notification to an RIS on admission) saying that it intends to apply for admission to the Official List in the future and setting out how it intends to satisfy the eligibility criteria for admission to the Official List.

The HGS Rulebook contains certain continuing obligations for companies on the HGS, including satisfying continuing eligibility requirements, obtaining advice from its Key Adviser, making disclosures of notifiable transactions and related party transactions, making notifications to an RIS and continuing website disclosures, making certain corporate governance disclosures and obtaining shareholder consent for a reverse takeover or cancellation of admission. As the HGS is part of a UK regulated market, companies on it also have to comply with the Market Abuse Regulation, the relevant Prospectus Rules and the FCA's Disclosure Guidance and Transparency Rules (although if they are not UK incorporated and their shares are listed elsewhere in the EEA, other rules may take precedence). They must, for example, disclose inside information to an RIS in accordance with Article 17 of MAR.

1.3.2 Specialist Fund Segment

The Specialist Fund Segment (formerly the Specialist Fund Market) is a segment of the main market of the LSE designed for highly specialised investment entities that wish to target institutional, highly knowledgeable investors or professionally advised investors only. The Specialist Fund Segment is not open to trading companies or for investment entities intending to make a wide public offer of securities to less sophisticated investors.

Investment entities seeking admission to the Specialist Fund Segment are required to publish a PD-compliant prospectus approved by the FCA as they are applying for admission to a regulated market and must comply with the eligibility criteria for the Specialist Fund Segment (Schedule 4 of the LSE Admission and Disclosure Standards), but do not need to comply with LR 15 for closed-ended investment funds.

1.3.3 AIM

AIM is the LSE's market for smaller growing companies, catering for a wide range of businesses ranging from early stage, venture capital-backed start-ups to more established companies seeking access to capital.

Launched in 1995, AIM has been joined by over 3,600 companies, raising capital through initial public offerings and further capital raisings. Some companies have migrated from AIM to the main market and a premium listing as they have grown. They also have the choice of migrating to a standard listing, but to date, AIM companies have not favoured this option.

AIM was designed to be a flexible public market. To join AIM, companies do not need a particular financial track record or trading history. There is no minimum requirement in terms of size or number of shareholders. This more flexible approach reflects the fact that AIM was designed specifically for smaller growing companies.

Specialist advisers are an important element of the way AIM operates. In particular, dedicated Nominated Advisers (Nomads) play a central role in the life of an AIM company.

As AIM is not a regulated market, no PD-compliant prospectus is required for admission to trading. An 'AIM admission document' complying with the requirements of the AIM Rules for Companies is all that is generally required. Offers by companies seeking an AIM listing are generally structured as offers to institutional investors only, in order to avoid having to prepare and publish a PD-compliant prospectus in connection with an offer to the public (there being no admission to trading on a regulated market to trigger the requirement to produce a prospectus). However, if an offer were to involve an offer to the public, a PD-compliant prospectus would be required (see Chapter 4 for guidance on when a PD-compliant prospectus is required).

Companies on AIM are subject to MAR.

AIM also looks to attract non-UK companies. AIM requires companies to publish accounts prepared under IFRS or equivalent standards.

1.3.4 Professional Securities Market (PSM)

The PSM is primarily a market for debt securities and provides a more flexible alternative to the regime under the FSAP Directives. It is aimed at issuers targeting professional investors.

Securities admitted to the PSM are listed on the Official List but the market is not a regulated market (it is an exchange-regulated market). The PSM is a 'recognised stock exchange' within the meaning of section 1005 of the Income Tax Act 2007. As a result, payments of interest on notes listed on the PSM may be made without withholding or deduction for or on account of UK income tax provided that the notes are and continue to be listed.

On the PSM, debt securities, regardless of the denomination, can be admitted under a wholesale regime. By following the PSM route to listing, companies are able to admit any type of debt security.

As the PSM is not a regulated market, no PD-compliant prospectus is required for admission. Instead, the issuer is required to prepare 'listing particulars' that comply with the requirements of Listing Rule 4. In addition, PSM issuers do not need to submit accounts in accordance with IFRS as local GAAP suffices (see Chapter 6 for information on financial reporting).

2. Admission to listing and to trading

Obtaining a standard or premium listing is a two-step process that involves admission of a company's shares to the Official List of the UKLA (referred to as 'admission to listing') and admission of the company's shares to trading on the LSE's main market for listed securities (referred to as 'admission to trading').

Admission to listing is governed by the Listing Rules. Admission to trading is governed by the LSE Admission and Disclosure Standards and is broadly a procedural step.

2.1 Admission to listing on the Official List of the UKLA

Listing Rule 2 sets out the requirements that apply to all new applicants for admission to listing and Listing Rule 3 sets out the requirements and process for applications for admission to listing. In the case of admission to a premium listing, Listing Rule 6 imposes additional requirements or, in the case of admission to a standard listing, Listing Rule 14 contains (more limited) additional requirements with which issuers must comply.

The eligibility requirements apply to new applicants, but through Listing Rule 9 (in the case of a premium listed company) and Listing Rule 14 (in the case of a standard listed company) listed companies are required to satisfy many of the requirements on a continuing basis after admission to listing. The FCA has published a procedural note setting out how the eligibility review process works (see the UKLA Guidance Note *Eligibility process (UKLA/PN/901.3)*).

The FCA will not grant an application for admission to listing unless it is satisfied that all requirements of the Listing Rules have been complied with and the applicant has met any special requirement that it considers appropriate to protect investors (LR 2.1.2G and LR 2.1.4R). The FCA may also refuse an application for admission to listing if it considers that admission of the securities would be detrimental to investors' interests (LR 2.1.3G(1)).

In earlier commentary on the rules (which has not been repeated in the formal Guidance Notes published by the FCA), the FSA stated that this test may become relevant if there is a risk that a company is engaging in activity as part of its business model that is illegal, or that any of its management or founders have criminal associations. It might also be relevant if there is a risk that a significant part of the company's assets might be confiscated or become worthless after admission. In such circumstances, the FCA may make enquiries of a company and its advisers that it would not normally make, reflecting the increased risk and particular challenges of such companies. In the past, the FSA has required sight of reports or opinions upon which the company's sponsor has relied when giving its confirmations (see section 5.3 of Chapter 3). This commentary, which was set out in List! Issue No. 18 and the old 2010 UKLA Technical Note on the Listing Rules, has not been repeated in the current UKLA Guidance Notes. There is therefore no formal UKLA guidance on the point.

Admission to listing cannot be conditional on any event (LR 2.1.5G).

2.1.1 Requirements for all admissions to listing

The key requirements for admission to listing are as follows:

- *Incorporation of issuer* – The applicant must be duly incorporated under the laws of its place of incorporation and operating in accordance with its constitution (LR 2.2.1R).
- *Validity of shares* – The shares to be listed must conform with the law of the applicant's place of incorporation, be duly authorised in accordance with its constitution and have any necessary statutory or other consents (LR 2.2.2R).
- *Free transferability of shares* – The shares to be listed must be freely transferable, free from any restriction on right of transfer, fully paid and free from liens (LR 2.2.4R). The UKLA Guidance Note *Restrictions on transferability (UKLA/TN/101.2)* sets out the very limited circumstances when the FCA will accept restrictions on transfer (e.g. if they are necessary to avoid falling within onerous legislative requirements).

- *Listing of whole class of shares* – Where no shares are already listed, an application for listing must relate to all shares of the same class that are issued or proposed to be issued (LR 2.2.9R).
- *Admission to trading* – The shares to be listed must be admitted to trading on a regulated market (LR 2.2.3R).
- *Minimum market capitalisation* – Where the class of shares is not already listed, the expected aggregate market value of all the securities to be listed must be at least £700,000 (LR 2.2.7R).
- *Publication of a prospectus* – A prospectus must have been approved by the FCA and published; or the competent authority of another EEA state must have supplied the FCA with a certificate of approval and a copy of the prospectus as approved (LR 2.2.10R).

2.1.2 Additional requirements for a premium listing of shares

Where a new commercial company applicant is applying for admission of shares to a premium listing, it must satisfy the additional 'super-equivalent' requirements of Listing Rule 6 (LR 6.1.1R and LR 6.1.2G). These additional listing requirements include the following:

Three-year financial track record

A new applicant must have published consolidated accounts covering at least three years, with the last balance sheet dated not more than six months before the date of the prospectus and not more than nine months before the date the shares are admitted to listing. The accounts must have been independently audited in accordance with IFRS or equivalent and have been reported on without modification (LR 6.1.3R(1)). In addition, a new applicant must take all reasonable steps to ensure its auditors are independent and obtain written confirmation from the auditors that they comply with guidelines on independence issued by their national accountancy or auditing bodies (LR 6.1.3R(2)).

The historical financial information required must represent at least 75% of the applicant's business for the full period covered by the accounts (LR 6.1.3BR(1)) and put prospective investors in a position to make an informed assessment of the company's business (LR 6.1.3BR(2)). In determining what amounts to 75% of the business, the FCA will consider any acquisitions made in the three-year period covered by the financial information and the size of those acquisitions relative to the size of the (enlarged) applicant. In assessing the size of the transactions, the FCA will look at factors such as assets and profitability (LR 6.1.3CG).

Where the new applicant has made an acquisition or series of acquisitions such that its own consolidated financial information is insufficient to meet the 75% requirement in LR 6.1.3BR, there must be historical financial information relating to the acquired entity or entities that, among other things, covers the period starting from at least three years prior to the date of the applicant's latest balance sheet, up to the earlier of the applicant's latest balance sheet or the date of acquisition by the applicant. The financial information relating to the acquired entity or entities must be presented in a form that is consistent with the accounting policies adopted in the applicant's financial information and, in aggregate with the applicant's own historical financial information, represent at least 75% of the enlarged new applicant's business for the full three-year period (LR 6.1.3DR).

The FCA may consider that a new applicant does not have representative historical financial information and that its equity shares are not eligible for a premium listing if a significant part or all of the new applicant's business has one or more specified characteristics:

- a business strategy that places significant emphasis on the development or marketing of products or services which have not formed a significant part of the new applicant's historical financial information;
- the value of the business on admission will be determined, to a significant degree, by reference to future developments rather than past performance;
- the relationship between the value of the business and its revenue or profit-earning record is significantly different from those of similar companies in the same sector;
- there is no record of consistent revenue, cash flow or profit growth throughout the period of the historical financial information;
- the applicant's business has undergone a significant change in its scale of operations during the period of the historical financial information or is due to do so before or after admission; and
- it has significant levels of research and development expenditure or significant levels of capital expenditure (LR 6.1.3EG).

Separate requirements apply in relation to mineral companies (LR 6.1.8R to LR 6.1.10R) and scientific research-based businesses (LR 6.1.11R and LR 6.1.12R) that do not have the requisite historical financial information because they have been operating for a shorter period.

The FCA can modify or dispense with the requirements in relation to historic financial information in LR 6.1.3R(1)(a) or in LR 6.1.3BR provided that (i) there is an overriding reason for the company to seek a premium listing, rather than seeking admission to another market; (ii) the FCA is satisfied that it is in the interests of investors; and (iii) investors have the necessary information available to arrive at an informed judgment regarding the company and the securities to be listed (LR 6.1.13G and LR 6.1.14G). The factors that the FCA will consider in determining this include whether the company (i) is attracting funds from sophisticated investors; (ii) is undertaking a significant marketing of the shares in connection with admission and has demonstrated that having listed status will be a significant factor in its ability to raise funds; and (iii) has demonstrated that it is likely to have a significant market capitalisation on admission (LR 6.1.15G).

In its consultation paper 'Review of the Effectiveness of Primary Markets: Enhancements to the Listing Regime' (CP 17/4), published in February 2017, the FCA sought views on proposals to clarify the drafting of the requirements in LR 6 and make it clearer that only a company that has been generating revenues in its declared line of business for the past three financial years can demonstrate that it is eligible for premium listing. It is also proposing to delete the guidance which explains where the FCA might waive the requirement for financial information and a track record, on the basis that it does not normally waive these requirements. Any rule changes are expected to be published in the second half of 2017.

Independent business

A new applicant must also be able to demonstrate that it will be carrying on an independent business as its main activity (LR 6.1.4R). There is guidance in LR 6.1.4AG on factors that may indicate a company will not satisfy this requirement. Most of the factors relate to companies with controlling shareholders and these are discussed in the section on companies with controlling shareholders below and in section 4 of Chapter 9. The factors that are relevant to all applicants for premium listing are:

- where it does not have strategic control over commercialisation of its product, strategic control over its ability to earn revenue and/or freedom to implement its business strategy; or
- except in relation to a mineral company, where its business consists principally of holdings of shares in entities that it does not control, including entities where:
  - the applicant is only able to exercise negative control; and/or
  - the applicant's control is subject to contractual arrangements which could be altered without its agreement or could result in a temporary or permanent loss of control.

In its consultation paper 'Review of the Effectiveness of Primary Markets: Enhancements to the Listing Regime' (CP 17/4), published in February 2017, the FCA proposed to clarify the independence requirements by splitting the rule into three separate limbs and clarifying which factors (indicating whether or not a company meets the independence requirement) apply to which of the three limbs. Any rule changes are expected to be published in the second half of 2017.

Sufficient working capital

An applicant must have sufficient working capital available for the group's requirements for at least the next 12 months from the date of publication of the prospectus (LR 6.1.16R).

The FCA may waive this requirement if:

- a company already has equity shares listed and the FCA is satisfied that the prospectus contains satisfactory proposals for providing the additional working capital that the company believes to be necessary (LR 6.1.17G); or
- the company's business is substantially in the provision of banking, insurance or other financial services, its solvency and capital adequacy is regulated by the FCA or similar authority and it is meeting and is expected to meet, for the next 12 months, its solvency and capital adequacy requirements without having to raise further capital (LR 6.1.18G).

While the FCA can waive this requirement, it is worth noting that if the company is preparing a PD-compliant prospectus it is required to include a working capital statement in the prospectus and regard should be had to paragraphs 107 to 126 of the ESMA Recommendations before making such statement. In addition, in its consultation paper 'Review of the Effectiveness of Primary Markets: Enhancements to the Listing Regime' (CP 17/4), published in February 2017, the FCA proposed to delete the guidance which states that it can waive these requirements. Any rule changes are expected to be published in the second half of 2017.

Minimum numbers of shares in public hands

Where an application is made for the admission of a class of shares, a sufficient number of shares of that class must be distributed to the public no later than admission (known as the 'free float') (LR 6.1.19R(1)). A sufficient number of shares will be taken to have been distributed to the public when 25% of the shares are in public hands in one or more EEA states (LR 6.1.19R(3)). Account may also be taken of holders in one or more non-EEA states if the shares are listed in such state or states (LR 6.1.19R(2)). Shares are not treated as being in public hands if they are subject to a lock-up period of more than 180 calendar days or are held directly or indirectly by:

- directors of the applicant or its subsidiaries or any connected persons;
- trustees of the group's employee share schemes or pension funds;
- any person who has a right under an agreement to nominate a director to the Board of the applicant; or
- any person or persons in the same group or persons acting in concert who have an interest in 5% or more of the shares of that class (LR 6.1.19R(4)).

Shares held by investment managers in one organisation, which in aggregate, amount to more than 5% may still be treated as being in public hands provided that the investment decisions are made independently by the individual fund manager and the decisions are unfettered by the organisation to which the investment manager belongs (LR 6.1.20BG).

The FCA may accept a free float below 25% for a particular company if it considers the market will operate properly with a lower percentage because of the large number of shares of the same class and the extent of their distribution to the public (LR 6.1.20AG(1)). The Listing Rules set out the factors that the FCA may take into account when deciding whether to accept a lower free float. These factors are:

- shares of the same class that are held (even though they are not listed) in states that are not EEA states;
- the number and nature of the public shareholders; and
- in relation to premium listing (commercial companies), whether the expected market value of the shares in public hands at admission exceeds £100 million (LR 6.1.20AG(2)).

Practical experience suggests that the FCA is unlikely to accept a free float below 20%.

Other eligibility requirements for a premium listing

- *Pre-emption rights* – Where an overseas company is applying for a premium listing and the laws of the country of incorporation do not confer on shareholders pre-emption rights, the company must ensure its constitution provides for pre-emption rights for its shareholders. The pre-emption rights must provide that when the company proposes to issue equity securities for cash (or to sell treasury shares that are equity shares for cash), it must first offer those securities to existing holders of that class of shares (and to holders of any other equity shares of the listed company who are entitled to be offered them) in proportion to their existing holdings. As with a UK-incorporated company, an overseas company can then disapply the pre-emption rights with the consent of its shareholders (LR 9.3.12R(4)). The company must also be satisfied that conferring such rights would not be incompatible with the law of the country of its incorporation (LR 6.1.25R).
- *Shares of a non-EEA company* – In the case of a company which is not incorporated in an EEA state and does not have its shares listed in either its country of incorporation or the country where the majority of its shares are held, the FCA will only admit the shares of the company to listing if it is satisfied that the absence of the listing is not due to the need to protect investors (LR 6.1.21R).
- *Warrants* – The total of all issued warrants or options to subscribe for equity shares must not exceed 20% of the issued equity share capital (excluding treasury shares) of the applicant as at the time of issue of the warrants or options (this does not include rights under employees' share schemes) (LR 6.1.22R).
- *Voting on matters relevant to premium listing* – Where a shareholder vote is required under the Listing Rules due to a company's premium listing (e.g. under LR 10 to approve a Class 1 transaction or LR 11 to approve a related party transaction), the applicant's constitution must allow that vote to be decided by a resolution of the

holders of the company's premium listed shares only and, where required under the Listing Rules, that resolution must in addition be approved by independent shareholders of the company's premium listed shares only (LR 6.1.28R).

Companies with a controlling shareholder

Where the company will have one or more controlling shareholders upon admission, it must put in place a legally binding agreement with each such controlling shareholder (LR 6.1.4BR(1)). A controlling shareholder is a person who exercises or controls 30% or more of the voting rights in a premium listed company, either on their own or together with persons acting in concert with them (LR 6.1.2AR). This agreement must contain undertakings, known as 'independence provisions', that:

- transactions and arrangements with the controlling shareholder (and/or any of its associates) will be conducted at arm's length and on normal commercial terms;
- neither the controlling shareholder nor any of its associates will take any action that would have the effect of preventing the company from complying with its obligations under the Listing Rules; and
- neither the controlling shareholder nor any of its associates will propose or procure the proposal of a shareholder resolution which is intended or appears to be intended to circumvent the proper application of the Listing Rules (LR 6.1.4DR).

Where there is more than one controlling shareholder in a company, it may not be necessary to have separate agreements in place with each controlling shareholder if the company considers that one controlling shareholder is able to procure compliance of another controlling shareholder (and its associates) with the independence provisions. Where a controlling shareholder agrees to this, the relationship agreement must contain: (i) a provision in which the controlling shareholder that is signing up to the agreement agrees to procure the compliance of the non-signing controlling shareholders (and their associates) with the independence provisions; and (ii) the names of such non-signing controlling shareholders (LR 6.1.4CR).

As discussed above, the Listing Rules contain guidance (in LR 6.1.4AG) on when a company with a controlling shareholder is unlikely to satisfy the requirement in LR 6.1.4R to have an independent business. The factors which may indicate that a company with a controlling shareholder does not have an independent business are where:

- a majority of the revenue generated by the company's business is attributable to business conducted directly or indirectly with a controlling shareholder (or any of its associates);
- the company cannot demonstrate that it has access to financing other than from a controlling shareholder (or its associates);
- the company has granted or may be required to grant security over its business in connection with the funding of a controlling shareholder or a member of a controlling shareholder's group; and

- a controlling shareholder (or its associates) appears to be able to influence the operations of the company outside its normal governance structures or via material shareholdings in one or more significant subsidiary undertakings.

The company's constitution must also allow for the procedure for electing independent directors under LR 6.1.4BR(2); this is discussed in Chapter 9.

As discussed above, in its consultation paper 'Review of the Effectiveness of Primary Markets: Enhancements to the Listing Regime' (CP 17/4), published in February 2017, the FCA published proposals to clarify the independence requirements by splitting the rule into three separate limbs and clarifying which factors (indicating whether or not a company meets the independence requirement) apply to which of the three limbs. Its proposals also include additional guidance on factors which indicate that a company with a controlling shareholder may not meet the independence requirement. These would include where the shareholder appears to be able to exercise improper influence over the applicant. Any rule changes are expected to be published in the second half of 2017.

Externally managed companies

Commercial companies that are externally managed (i.e. where significant management functions are outsourced to an advisory firm) will not be able to obtain a premium listing. A company applying for the admission of equity shares to premium listing must satisfy the FCA that the discretion of its Board to make strategic decisions on behalf of the company has not been limited or transferred to a person outside the company's group, and that the Board has the capability to act on key strategic matters in the absence of a recommendation from a person outside the company's group (LR 6.1.26R).

In considering whether a company applying for the admission of equity shares to premium listing has satisfied LR 6.1.26R, the FCA will consider, among other things, whether the Board of the company consists solely of non-executive directors and whether significant elements of the strategic decision-making of or planning for the company take place outside the company's group (e.g. with an external management company) (LR 6.1.27G).

2.1.3 Additional requirements for a standard listing of shares

Where a new applicant is applying for admission of shares to a standard listing, as well as complying with LR 2, it must also meet the requirements set out in LR 14.2. These include a requirement that a sufficient number of shares are or will be in public hands no later than admission (LR 14.2.2R(1)). As with an application for a premium listing, this will be satisfied if 25% of the class of shares to be admitted to listing is held by the public in one or more EEA states (LR 14.2.2R(3)) and account may be taken of holders in non-EEA states if the shares are also listed in such states (LR 14.2.2R(2)) (in practice the UKLA is often willing to take into account shares held by institutional investors in certain other non-EEA states, e.g. the United States, irrespective of whether or not such shares are listed in that country). Again, shares are not treated as being in public hands if they are subject to a lock-up period of more than 180 calendar days or are held directly or indirectly by:

- directors of the applicant or its subsidiaries or any connected persons;
- trustees of the group's employee share schemes or pension funds;
- any person who has a right under an agreement to nominate a director to the Board of the applicant; or
- any person or persons in the same group or persons acting in concert who have an interest in 5% or more of the shares of that class (LR 14.2.2R(4)).

Shares held by investment managers in one organisation, which in aggregate amount to more than 5%, may still be treated as being in public hands provided that the investment decisions are made independently by the individual fund manager and the decisions are unfettered by the organisation to which the investment manager belongs (LR 14.2.3AG).

The FCA may accept a free float below 25% for a particular company if it considers the market will operate properly with a lower percentage because of the large number of shares of the same class and the extent of their distribution to the public (LR 14.2.3G).

In the case of a company not incorporated in an EEA state which does not have its shares listed in either its country of incorporation or the country where the majority of its shares are held, the FCA will only admit it to listing if it is satisfied that the absence of a listing is not due to the need to protect investors (LR 14.2.4R).

2.2 Admission to trading on the main market of the LSE

Rules 2.1 to 2.9 of the LSE Admission and Disclosure Standards set out the requirements that an applicant for admission to trading must meet.

The key requirements for admission to trading are as follows:

- An application for admission to trading of any class of securities must relate to all securities of that class or, where a listed company is listing further securities of the same class, to all further securities of that class (Rule 2.1).
- The company applying for admission to trading must be in compliance with the requirements of its securities regulator and of any stock exchange where its securities are traded (Rule 2.2).
- All transferable securities must be 'freely negotiable' (i.e. they can be traded between the parties to a transaction, transferred without restriction and are fully fungible with other securities in the same class) (Rule 2.3).

- All securities admitted to trading must be capable of being traded in a fair, orderly and efficient manner (Rule 2.4).
- All securities must also be eligible for electronic settlement (Rule 2.7).
- The company must ensure that all information provided in connection with the application for admission to trading is in all respects accurate, complete and not misleading and must be open, honest and co-operative in all dealings with the LSE (Rule 2.9).

The LSE may refuse an application for admission to trading if it considers that either the applicant's situation is such that admission would be detrimental to the orderly operation or integrity of the LSE's markets or the applicant does not or will not comply with the LSE Admission and Disclosure Standards or any special condition imposed on it by the LSE (Rule 2.5).

3. Procedural requirements for admission to listing and to trading

For a listing of equity shares, the FCA will require submission of all of the relevant documents (as set out below), submission of any additional documents it requests and the payment of the fees required (LR 3.2.2R). The FCA's document vetting fees payable for an application for listing are set out in FEES (The Fees Manual) which forms part of the FCA Handbook. The fees must be paid by the date that the relevant document (i.e. the prospectus) is first submitted to the FCA (FEES 3.2.7R).

Prior to its application, a company should establish contact with the FCA and book a date for a listing hearing at which the FCA will first consider the application (LR 3.2.3G). All relevant documents should be submitted to the Issuer Management team at the FCA's address (LR 3.2.4R).

Provided that all of the documents are in order and the requirements of the Listing Rules are satisfied, the FCA will announce its decision to admit the securities on an RIS; it is at this point that admission becomes effective (LR 3.2.7G). When considering an application for admission to listing, the FCA may carry out further enquiries, either independently (including consulting with other regulators or exchanges) or through discussions with company representatives, regarding the company and its suitability for listing and may request verification of information provided by the company and/or impose any additional conditions to listing which it deems appropriate (LR 3.2.6G).

In practice, where the company is required to appoint a sponsor in connection with the listing (see Chapter 3 in relation to the requirement to appoint a sponsor) the sponsor will liaise with the FCA on the company's behalf. In addition to the FCA's procedural requirements for the admission to listing, the company will also need to comply with the LSE's procedural requirements for admission to trading (discussed further in section 3.3 below). The sponsor will, likewise, liaise with the LSE about the application for admission to trading.

In practice, the key driver of the listing timetable is likely to be not the application for admission, but rather the approval of the prospectus by the FCA (see Chapter 4).

3.1 Procedure for an application for listing of shares

There are a number of procedural requirements that apply to any application for admission of shares to listing. Broadly the same requirements apply to a premium listing and a standard listing.

3.1.1 Submission of 48-hour documents

The following documents should be provided to the FCA by 12.00pm (midday) two business days before it is due to consider the application for listing:

- a completed Application for Admission of Securities to the Official List (in the form provided on the UKLA section of the FCA's website);
- a prospectus approved by the FCA or, if another EEA state is the home member state, a copy of the prospectus, a certificate of approval and, if applicable, an English version of the prospectus summary. If no prospectus is required, the Application for Admission must confirm that no prospectus is required and explain why (LR 3.3.2AR);
- any circular published in connection with the application;
- any supplementary prospectus;
- written confirmation of the number of securities to be allotted (pursuant to a board resolution allotting the shares); and
- if a prospectus is not produced, a copy of the RIS announcement detailing the number and type of shares that are the subject of application for admission, and the circumstances of their issue (LR 3.3.2R).

3.1.2 Submission of application day documents

The following documents should be signed by the sponsor (where one is required), or a duly authorised officer of the company, and submitted to the FCA before 9.00am on the day it is to consider the application for listing of shares:

- a completed Shareholder Statement (in the form provided on the UKLA section of the FCA's website), if the application is for the listing of a class of shares for the first time; or
- a completed Pricing Statement (in the form provided on the UKLA section of the FCA's website), in the case of a placing, open offer, vendor consideration placing, offer for subscription or an issue out of treasury of shares already listed (LR 3.3.3R).

3.1.3 Alterations in the number of shares to be listed

If written confirmation of the number of shares to be allotted cannot be provided two business days before the application is considered, or the number of shares to be admitted is lower than that applied for, the FCA requires written confirmation of the number of shares to be allotted or admitted to be provided no later than one hour before the admission to listing will become effective (LR 3.3.4R).

If the FCA has considered an application for listing and the shares the subject of the application are not all allotted and admitted following the initial allotment (e.g. under an offer for subscription) further allotments of shares may be admitted if, before 4.00pm on the day before admission, the FCA is provided with:

- written confirmation of the number of shares allotted pursuant to a Board resolution; and
- a copy of the RIS announcement detailing the number and type of shares, and the circumstances of their issue (LR 3.3.4AR).

If the number of shares allotted is lower than that announced as being admitted to listing, the FCA requires written confirmation of the number allotted to be submitted as soon as is practicable after admission (LR 3.3.5R).

3.1.4 Retention of documents related to the application

The FCA requires the company which makes the application to retain copies of the following documents for six years after admission to listing (LR 3.3.6R) and copies must be provided to the FCA if requested (LR 3.3.7R):

- any acquisition agreement pursuant to which the company's shares were issued as consideration;
- any document referred to in the prospectus;
- the memorandum and articles of association of the company on admission;
- the annual report and accounts of the company and of any guarantor covering the period of the applicant's financial record contained in the prospectus;
- any interim accounts drawn up between the last annual report and admission;
- any temporary and definitive documents of title;
- the scheme document relating to any issue of shares under an employee share scheme;
- any court order and certificate of registration where listing particulars or another document are published in connection with a scheme requiring court approval; and
- copies of the Board resolutions allotting or issuing the shares.

3.2 Requirements for a block listing

When a company makes frequent or irregular allotments of shares (e.g. when share options are exercised and new shares are issued), the process of applying for listing may prove to be very onerous. In those circumstances, and provided no prospectus is required in connection with the issue or admission to trading of new shares under PR 1.2.2R or PR 1.2.3R, the company may apply for admission of those securities using a block listing, which allows it to apply for admission of a specified number of securities (LR 3.5.2G). The securities can then be allotted as and when required over time. The grant of a block listing constitutes admission to listing for the shares that are the subject of the block (LR 3.5.3G).

The FCA has published a procedural note setting out how and when a company can use a block listing (see the UKLA Guidance Note *Block listings* (UKLA/PN/907.2)). In particular, it notes that, in practice, the reference in the rules to block listing being available where the process of applying for listing would be 'very onerous due to the frequent or irregular nature of allotments' makes it unlikely that a company that is, for example, contemplating infrequent allotments, seeking flexibility for procedural convenience, seeking to limit fees or acting speculatively (e.g. anticipating future events/demand) would be able to meet this condition and therefore justify a block listing.

Block listings are predominantly used for routine employee share schemes.

3.2.1 Submission of 48-hour documents

A completed Application for Admission of Securities to the Official List must be submitted in final form two business days before the application is considered by the FCA (LR 3.5.4R). Multiple schemes can be applied for using the same form, provided that each scheme is separately identifiable.

3.2.2 Submission of application day documents

By 9.00am on the day the application is to be considered by the FCA, the company must notify an RIS of the number and type of shares which are the subject of the block listing, and the circumstances of their issue (LR 3.5.5R).

3.2.3 Six-monthly block listing return

The company should notify an RIS of the details of the shares covered by the block listing which have been allotted in the last six months, using the Block Listing Six Monthly Return (in the form provided on the UKLA section of the FCA's website) (LR 3.5.6R).

3.3 Procedure for an application for admission to trading

Rules 2.14 to 2.16 and 3.1 to 3.5 of the LSE Admission and Disclosure Standards set out the procedural requirements for an application for admission to trading of shares. The key points to note are that a company should agree the timetable in advance with the LSE (Rule 2.14), contacting the LSE no later than ten business days before the application is to be considered (Rule 2.15).

An applicant must complete and submit to the LSE a Form 1 – Application for Admission of Securities to Trading (in the form provided on the LSE's website) confirming that it meets the criteria and requirements of the market to which it is applying (Rules 2.6 and 3.1).

In the case of a new applicant, a provisional Form 1 together with a draft copy of the prospectus must be submitted by 12.00pm (midday) at least ten business days before the day on which the LSE is requested to consider the application (Rule 3.1). An application is only deemed to have been made when the prospectus relating to the admission of the securities to trading has been approved.

The final Form 1 must submitted by 12.00pm (midday) at least two business days before the day on which the LSE is requested to consider the application, along with an electronic copy of any prospectus and a copy of the RIS announcement relating to admission (Rule 3.3). The written confirmation of the number of securities to be allotted must be submitted no later than 4.00pm on the day before admission (Rule 3.3).

In the case of a listed company applying to list further shares, an application for admission to trading must be submitted at the same time as the application for admission to listing, but no later than 48 hours before the application is to be considered (Rule 3.6).

As is the case for admissions to listing, the LSE also operates a simplified block admission procedure where a company issues securities on a regular basis (Rule 3.12).

4. Transfer between listing segments

Listing Rule 5.4A prescribes how a company can transfer its equity shares between the premium and standard segments of the Official List.

A company can transfer from a premium to a standard listing or vice versa, without cancelling its listing. Where a company's business has changed over a period of time so that it no longer meets the requirements of its relevant listing category, as an alternative to cancelling the company's listing, the FCA may suggest that the company applies for a transfer of its listing category (LR 5.4A.16G).

The company applying for a transfer must comply with all the eligibility requirements for the category of listing to which it wishes to transfer (LR 5.4A.11R).

4.1 Notification of transfer

A commercial company wishing to transfer from one listing category to another must notify the FCA as early as possible and in any event not less than 20 business days before it sends the requisite circular to shareholders or makes the RIS announcement (see below) (LR 5.4A.3R).

The notification to the FCA must include:

- an explanation of why the company is seeking the transfer;
- if a sponsor's letter is not required under Listing Rule 8 (e.g. in the case of a commercial company proposing to transfer from a premium to a standard listing), an eligibility letter setting out how the company satisfies each listing rule requirement relevant to the category of listing to which it wishes to transfer;
- a proposed timetable for the transfer; and
- if relevant, a draft RIS announcement.

In addition, a company wishing to transfer between listing segments must notify the LSE of its intention to transfer not later than three business days before the transfer is due to take place (Rule 4.2A of the LSE Admission and Disclosure Standards). The notification should include: details of the listed company, the relevant security and the change in listing category sought; an explanation of why the listed company is seeking to transfer; the date on which the listed company wishes the transfer to take effect; and contact details of the person the LSE should liaise with in relation to the transfer.

4.2 Additional requirements if migrating from premium to standard

A premium listed commercial company wishing to transfer to the standard segment is required to send a circular to its shareholders (LR 5.4A.4R) and obtain shareholder approval for the transfer. The circular must comply with the requirements of LR 13 (LR 5.4A.6R(1)) and, to satisfy LR 13.3.1R(1) (Contents of all circulars), should include an explanation of:

- the background and reasons for the proposed transfer;
- any changes to the company's business that have been made or are proposed to be made in connection with the proposal;
- the effect of the transfer on the company's obligations under the Listing Rules;
- how the company will meet any new eligibility requirements, for example, working capital requirements, that the FCA must be satisfied of under LR 5.4A.12R(3); and
- any other matter that the FCA may reasonably require (LR 5.4A.9G).

The circular must also contain a notice of general meeting to pass a resolution to approve the transfer and give the anticipated date of transfer (which must be not less than 20 business days after the passing of the resolution) (LR 5.4A.6R(3)). The circular must be approved by the FCA prior to its publication (LR 5.4A.6R(2)).

The company must also notify an RIS of the intended transfer and of the notice period and meeting date at the same time as the circular is dispatched (LR 5.4A.4R(2)).

At the general meeting, the company must obtain the approval of at least 75% of shareholders voting at that meeting (LR 5.4A.4R(3)(a)). Where the company has a controlling shareholder (i.e. a person who exercises or controls 30% or more of the voting rights in the company, either on their own or together with persons acting in concert with them) the resolution must also be approved by a majority of the votes attaching to the shares of the independent shareholders voting on the resolution (i.e. the shareholders in the company who are entitled to vote excluding the controlling shareholder) (LR 5.4A.4R(3)(b)). Once the company has obtained the requisite shareholder approval it must notify an RIS of the passing of the resolution (LR 5.4A.4R(2)(d)).

4.3 Additional requirements if migrating from standard to premium

A standard listed company wishing to move to a premium listing must release an RIS announcement giving notice of its intention to transfer its listing category (LR 5.4A.5R). The RIS announcement must include the anticipated date of transfer (which must be not less than 20 business days after the date of announcement) and contain the same substantive information as would be required in the circular when transferring from a premium to a standard listing. However, no shareholder approval is required for the transfer and the RIS announcement must make that clear (LR 5.4A.7R). The announcement must be approved by the FCA prior to its publication (LR 5.4A.8R).

The company will also be required to appoint a sponsor (LR 8.2.1AR).

4.4 A company's application to transfer

Following the initial notification, the company must make a formal application to the FCA to transfer between segments. The application should include:

- the company's name;
- details of the shares to be transferred;
- the date on which the company wishes the transfer to take effect;
- a copy of any relevant circular, resolution and announcements; and
- the name and contact details of an appropriate person at the company for the FCA to liaise with (LR 5.4A.10R).

Provided the company has complied with the relevant procedural requirements described in sections 4.1 to 4.3 above, the notice period has elapsed and the company will comply with all eligibility requirements that would apply if the company was seeking admission to listing to the category of listing to which it wishes to transfer, the FCA may approve the transfer (LR 5.4A.12R). It will announce its decision via an RIS; the transfer takes effect at that point (LR 5.4A.14R).

5. Suspension, cancellation and restoration of listing

Listing Rule 5 sets out when the FCA may, either of its own volition or at the request of a company, suspend or cancel a listing and when such a listing may then be restored. The decision-making process followed by the FCA in such circumstances is set out in DEPP (The Decision Procedure and Penalties Manual), which forms part of the FCA Handbook (LR 5.5.1G). Rules 4.12 to 4.19 of the LSE Admission and Disclosure Standards set out when the LSE may likewise suspend or cancel trading of a company's shares. While the LSE's rules are not considered in any further detail in this Guide, they should be considered in the context of planning the procedural requirements of a suspension or cancellation of listing.

If a company is listed in more than one country, it is the company's responsibility to inform the FCA if its listing is suspended, cancelled or restored by any overseas authority (LR 5.5.2R). It does not follow automatically that the FCA will also suspend, cancel or restore the listing, even if the overseas authority has asked the FCA to do so; instead, the FCA's initial reaction, wherever practical, will be to contact the company in question or its sponsor. It is prudent, therefore, for a company to contact the FCA directly in the event of any suspension, cancellation or restoration of its listing overseas and discuss the matter with them (LR 5.5.3G).

5.1 Suspension of listing

The FCA may suspend a listing at any time if the smooth operation of the market either is, or may be, temporarily jeopardised or if it is necessary to protect investors (LR 5.1.1R(1)). The FCA may impose such conditions as it considers appropriate on the procedure for lifting such a suspension (LR 5.1.1R(3)). During the period of suspension, the company must continue to comply with the Listing Rules (LR 5.1.1R(2)).

Examples of when the FCA may suspend listing include:

- a company failing to meet its continuing obligations for listing;
- a company failing to publish financial information in accordance with the listing rules or being unable to assess accurately its financial position and inform the market accordingly;
- where there is insufficient information in the market regarding a proposed transaction;
- when the company's securities have been suspended on an overseas exchange;

- if the company appoints administrators or receivers; or
- in the case of a security which relates to an underlying instrument, where the underlying instrument is suspended (LR 5.1.2G).

A company may request that the FCA suspends its listing, in accordance with Listing Rule 5.3 (see section 5.3 below). However, the FCA is under no obligation to grant this request unless the circumstances are justified (LR 5.1.4G).

5.2 Cancellation of listing

The FCA may cancel the listing of securities if it is satisfied that there are special circumstances that preclude normal dealings in them (LR 5.2.1R).

Examples of when the FCA may cancel a listing include:

- where the securities are no longer admitted to trading;
- when the company no longer complies with its continuing obligations for listing;
- when a listing has been suspended for more than six months; or
- on completion of a reverse takeover (LR 5.2.2.G and LR 5.2.3G).

A company may request cancellation of the listing of its securities provided it complies with the applicable requirements (see section 5.3 below) (LR 5.2.4R). These requirements will still apply even if the securities have been suspended (LR 5.2.4AG).

5.3 Procedure for a company to request suspension or cancellation of a listing

A listed company may request the suspension of its listing or, having complied with certain requirements, the cancellation of its listing. Listing Rule 5 prescribes the information required to be submitted to the FCA when the company makes its formal request for suspension or cancellation and the timing of any such request.

The LSE will ordinarily cancel the admission to and trading of any securities on its markets if a listing of such securities is delisted by the FCA or other relevant competent authority (Rule 4.17). In addition to complying with the FCA's procedures for cancellation of listing, a listed company that wishes to cancel the admission of its securities to trading must advise the LSE, in writing, of the proposed cancellation not later than 20 business days before the date it intends trading in its securities to be discontinued. The LSE requires a listed company to also announce the intended cancellation of trading of any of its securities through an RIS; upon cancellation, the LSE will announce the cancellation through the Datasync email service and through an RIS (Rule 4.18). Cancellation of admission to trading will only be effective if the listed company has complied with any legal or regulatory obligations (i.e. the FCA's procedures) and provided the LSE with appropriate confirmation of this (Rule 4.19).

5.3.1 Requirements for cancellation of a premium listing

General requirements for a cancellation

In order to request the cancellation of the premium listing of its shares, a company must, in accordance with LR 5.2.5R:

- send a circular to the holders of the shares, which must comply with the content requirements contained in LR 13.3.1R and LR 13.3.2R, be submitted to the FCA for approval prior to its publication and state the intended date of cancellation (being not less than 20 business days following the passing of the shareholder resolution referred to below);
- obtain shareholder approval for the cancellation from at least 75% of the shareholders of the company at a general meeting (and, where the company has a controlling shareholder, also from a majority of the votes attaching to the shares of the independent shareholders voting on the resolution);
- notify an RIS, on dispatch of the circular, of the intended cancellation, notice period and general meeting; and
- notify an RIS of the passing of the resolution by the shareholders, in accordance with LR 9.6.18R.

Cancellation in connection with a restructuring or insolvency

The requirements of LR 5.2.5R will not apply where a company notifies an RIS:

- that there is a restructuring proposal or transaction of the company or its group that is necessary to ensure its survival and which will be jeopardised by a continued listing;
- that its financial position is so precarious that, but for the restructuring proposal or transaction, there is no reasonable prospect that the company would avoid going into formal insolvency proceedings;
- explaining why the cancellation is in the best interests of the company, its shareholders and creditors, and why the approval of the shareholders will not be sought prior to the cancellation; and
- giving at least 20 business days' notice of the intended cancellation (LR 5.2.7R).

Cancellation in connection with a takeover offer

The requirements of LR 5.2.5R do not apply to the cancellation of equity shares following a takeover offer. The requirements that apply instead are set out in LR 5.2.10R to LR 5.2.11CR. Rather than obtaining shareholder approval for the cancellation of listing, the offeror must acquire (whether through market purchases or through acceptances of the offer) a specified percentage of shares in the company. The level of shareholding required in order to be able to delist the company varies according to the size of the offeror's interest in the company's shares before it announces its firm intention to make its takeover offer.

- If there is no controlling shareholder or the offeror is a controlling shareholder who is interested in 50% or less of voting rights of a company before it announces its offer, the offeror must acquire or agree to acquire shares carrying at least 75% of the voting rights of the company (LR 5.2.10R(2)).
- If the offeror is a controlling shareholder and is interested in more than 50% of the voting rights of the listed company before it announces its offer, the offeror must, in addition to reaching that 75% threshold referred to above, obtain acceptances or acquire shares from independent shareholders that represent a majority of the voting rights held by all independent shareholders on the date its firm intention to make a takeover offer was announced (LR 5.2.11AR(2)–(3)).

The offeror must state in the offer document or a subsequent circular, that a notice period of 20 business days for the cancellation will commence either on the date on which the offeror acquires the requisite percentage of shares in the company or on the first date of issue of 'squeeze out' notices under section 979 of CA 2006 (LR 5.2.10R(3) and LR 5.2.11AR(4)). The circular must also make clear that the notice period only begins when the offeror announces that it has reached the requisite percentage (LR 5.2.10AG and LR 5.2.11BR).

The company must itself then notify the shareholders that the requisite threshold has been reached, that the notice period has commenced and of the anticipated date of cancellation; or the explanatory letter or other material accompanying the section 979 notice must state that the notice period has commenced and the anticipated date of cancellation (LR 5.2.11R and LR 5.2.11CR).

Cancellation in connection with a scheme of arrangement

The requirements for cancellation set out in LR 5.2.5R and LR 5.2.8R will not apply to a cancellation of equity shares with a premium listing as a result of either a takeover or restructuring effected by a scheme of arrangement, administration or liquidation of the company pursuant to a court order under the Insolvency Act 1986 or equivalent insolvency procedure (LR 5.2.12R).

Note, however, that even where the requirements of LR 5.2.5R do not apply, the company must still comply with the procedure for requesting a cancellation or suspension in LR 5.3 (as set out in section 5.3.3 below).

5.3.2 Requirements for cancellation of a standard listing

A company wishing to have a standard listing cancelled must notify an RIS, giving at least 20 business days' notice of the intended cancellation. It does not, however, need to obtain shareholder approval for the cancellation (LR 5.2.8R).

Where an investment entity no longer has a premium listing of equity shares under LR 15, it must apply for the cancellation of the listing of any other class of equity shares it has listed (LR 5.2.7AR). Under LR 14.1.1R, an investment entity can only have equity shares admitted to a standard listing if it has another class of equity shares admitted to a premium listing.

5.3.3 Company's application for suspension or cancellation

The request from a company for a suspension or cancellation of its listing of securities must be in writing and include:

- the name of the company, details of the securities to which the request relates and the recognised investment exchange(s) on which they are traded;
- an explanation of the background to and reasons for the request;
- the date and, for a suspension, the time for the request to take effect;
- if relevant, a copy of any related circular or announcement and any resolution under LR 5.2.5R;
- the name and contact details of an appropriate person to liaise with at the company;
- if the request is conditional, a clear statement of the conditions; and
- a copy of any RIS announcements that the company proposes to make relating to the suspension or cancellation (LR 5.3.1R).

If the request relates to a cancellation following a takeover or scheme of arrangement, the relevant approval documentation required for each (such as 'squeeze out' notices to dissenting shareholders in the case of a takeover offer or a copy of a certificate from the Registrar of Companies that the scheme has become effective) should also be submitted (LR 5.3.2R).

5.3.4 Timing of the company's request

A written request for a suspension should be provided as soon as is practicable, if possible before the markets open and with sufficient time to allow the FCA to suspend trading before opening (LR 5.3.4G).

A written request for cancellation should be made not less than 24 hours before the cancellation is to take effect (LR 5.3.5R). The guidance in LR 5.3.6G says that cancellations will only take effect when the markets open and a company should ensure that all accompanying information should be provided to the FCA well before the date on which the company wishes the cancellation to take effect, and at the very latest by 3.00pm on the business day preceding the day of intended cancellation.

A request may be withdrawn at any time before a suspension or cancellation takes effect. The initial request for withdrawal should be made by telephone and then confirmed in writing as soon as possible, with an explanation of the reasons for the withdrawal (LR 5.3.7G(1)). However, if the FCA considers that the securities in question should still be suspended or cancelled, this may occur regardless of the withdrawal of the request (LR 5.3.7G(2)). If a company has published a circular or other statement regarding the intended suspension or cancellation and it no longer intends to proceed with it, an RIS should be notified as soon as possible of the withdrawal of the request (LR 5.3.7G(3)).

5.4 Restoration of listing

5.4.1 Restoration following suspension

The FCA can restore the listing of suspended securities at any time, provided that it is satisfied that the smooth operation of the market is no longer jeopardised or if the suspension is no longer required to protect investors, whether or not the company requests such restoration (LR 5.4.2R). If the FCA is not so satisfied, it will refuse any request to restore the listing (LR 5.4.4R).

A company can request that the FCA restores its suspended listing of securities, provided that such a request is made sufficiently in advance of the time and date it wishes the securities to be restored to allow the FCA time to consider it. The request can be oral, but the FCA may require documentary evidence to be submitted in support. Once the listing has been restored, the FCA will issue a dealing notice confirming this on an RIS (LR 5.4.3G).

A request for restoration can be withdrawn at any time while the securities are still suspended. However, if the FCA believes that the circumstances are justified it may restore the listing regardless (LR 5.4.5G).

Where the listing of a securitised derivative has been suspended because of a problem with its underlying security, once the underlying security is restored, the listed securitised derivative will normally also be restored to listing. Where such a security relates to a basket of underlying securities, the securitised derivative's listing may be restored regardless of the status of the underlying securities if the FCA is satisfied that the restoration is not inconsistent with either the protection of investors or the smooth operation of the market and the company confirms to the FCA that a market in the securitised derivative will continue to be made (LR 5.4.6G).

5.4.2 Restoration following cancellation

Once a company has the listing of its securities cancelled, it can only have them readmitted by reapplying for listing on the Official List (LR 5.4.1G).

CHAPTER 3

Role and responsibilities of a sponsor

OVERVIEW

- The FCA requires a company to appoint a sponsor in a range of circumstances, for example, where it is publishing a prospectus in connection with an application for admission of shares to the premium segment of the Official List or applying to transfer its category of equity shares from a standard to a premium listing. In addition, a premium listed company must consult a sponsor where it is contemplating a transaction that could be classified as a Class 1 transaction, reverse takeover or related party transaction and must appoint a sponsor where it is publishing certain types of circular including a Class 1 circular.

- In addition to the obligation on a company to appoint a sponsor in these transaction-specific circumstances, the FCA can require the appointment of a sponsor if it appears that there may have been a breach of the Listing Rules, the disclosure requirements under MAR or the Transparency Rules by a company with or applying for a premium listing.

- A person must be approved to act as a sponsor by the FCA. Approval will only be granted once an applicant has met certain criteria, including that the FCA is satisfied that the applicant is competent to provide sponsor services and that it has appropriate systems and controls in place to carry out its role.

- While a company remains responsible for its own compliance with the Listing Rules, a sponsor provides advice and guidance on the company's obligations.

- A sponsor has a general obligation under Listing Rule 8.3 to deal with the FCA in an open and co-operative way and to deal with all enquiries raised by the FCA promptly. In addition, when providing a 'sponsor service', it must act in accordance with certain principles, including to guide the company in understanding and meeting its responsibilities under the Listing Rules, the disclosure requirements and the Transparency Rules, to take reasonable steps to ensure that the directors understand their responsibilities, to provide its services as sponsor with due care and skill, to act with honesty and integrity and to identify and manage conflicts.

- A sponsor also has certain transaction-specific obligations under Listing Rule 8.4, – including to make a 'sponsor declaration' to the FCA, using one of four forms (application for listing, production of a circular, transfer of listing category and reverse takeover announcement) regarding, among other things, the company's compliance with the Listing Rules and the Prospectus Rules.

- In order to assist a sponsor in complying with its general obligations under Listing Rule 8.3, including the principles for sponsors, and its transaction-specific obligations under Listing Rule 8.4, a sponsor will look to the company and its advisers to provide certain comfort letters, reports and opinions to the sponsor, referred to as the 'sponsor's comfort package', to support its declaration to the FCA.
- The relationship between a company and its sponsor is often set out in a 'sponsor's agreement' providing a framework for the delivery of the sponsor's comfort package, the provision of warranties and an indemnity from the company in favour of the sponsor.

1. Regulatory framework for the sponsor regime

1.1 Section 88 of the FSMA and Listing Rule 8

Section 88(1) of the FSMA sets out the statutory basis for the sponsor regime, providing that the Listing Rules may require a person (e.g. a new applicant or a listed company) to make arrangements with a 'sponsor' for the performance of such services as may be specified by the Listing Rules. The sponsor regime is one of the super-equivalent aspects retained in the UK listing regime following the implementation of the FSAP directives. The FCA considers the sponsor regime to be crucial to ensuring an appropriate level of consumer protection and market integrity.

A 'sponsor' means a person approved by the FCA for the purposes of the Listing Rules (FSMA s. 88(2)). The Listing Rules may also provide for the FCA to maintain a list of sponsors, specify the services which must be performed by sponsors, impose requirements on sponsors in relation to the provision of such services, specify when a person is qualified for being approved as a sponsor, provide for limitations or other restrictions to be imposed on the services to which an approval relates and provide for the approval of a sponsor to be suspended on the application of the sponsor (FSMA s. 88(3)). These matters are dealt with in Chapter 8 of the Listing Rules.

The FCA undertakes periodic reviews of the sponsor regime, with reform proposals published in consultation papers (see e.g. CP 08/5 *Sponsor regime – a targeted review*; CP 12/02 *Amendments to the Listing Rules, Prospectus Rules, Disclosure Rules and Transparency Rules*; CP 12/25 *Amendments to the Listing Rules, Prospectus Rules, Disclosure Rules and Transparency Rules*; and CP 14/2 *Proposed amendments to the Listing Rules in relation to sponsor competence and other amendments to the Listing Rules and Prospectus Rules*).

1.2 Criteria and process for approval as a sponsor

A person who wants to provide services as a sponsor – and consequently to be included on the list of sponsors that the FCA maintains on its website – must submit an application in the prescribed form to the FCA's Sponsor Supervision Team and provide such information as may be required by the FCA (LR 8.6.2R and LR 8.6.3R). The application form can be found on the UKLA section of the FCA website.

LR 8.6.5R provides that the FCA will only approve a person as a sponsor if it is satisfied that the person is FCA authorised or a member of a designated professional body, is competent to provide sponsor services (see section 1.3) and has appropriate systems and controls in place to carry out its role as a sponsor (see section 1.4). A sponsor must comply with these requirements at all times (LR 8.6.6R). The FCA may impose restrictions or limitations on the services a sponsor can provide at the time of granting a sponsor approval (or any time thereafter) (LR 8.6.5AR to LR 8.6.5CG and LR 8.7.2AR). The FCA has published a UKLA Guidance Note *Additional powers to supervise and discipline sponsors (UKLA/TN/712.2)*. This gives the FCA the flexibility to approve a new applicant, or maintain a sponsor's approval, where the sponsor approval criteria under LR 8.6 may not have been fully met (e.g. if the applicant has insufficient relevant experience or appropriate systems and controls to provide the complete range of sponsor services). The FCA explains that this provision allows sponsors to specialise in providing certain services (e.g. providing sponsor services only in connection with premium listed investment companies).

Sections 88(4), (5), (6) and (7) of the FSMA set out a person's right to receive a warning notice and make representations prior to the FCA deciding not to approve a person as a sponsor or to limit, restrict or cancel an approval and, ultimately, the right to refer a decision of the FCA to the Upper Tribunal.

1.3 Competence of a sponsor

In order to be competent to provide sponsor services, a sponsor is required to:

(a) have submitted a sponsor declaration to the FCA within the last three years; and

(b) have a sufficient number of employees with the skills, knowledge and expertise necessary for a sponsor to provide sponsor services (in accordance with LR 8.3) and who meet five 'key competencies' (including an understanding of the rules, guidance and ESMA publications directly relevant to sponsor services and the responsibilities and obligations of a sponsor set out in LR 8) (LR 8.6.7R).

When assessing whether a sponsor satisfies LR 8.6.7R the FCA will consider factors such as: (i) the nature, scale and complexity of its business; (ii) the diversity of its operations; (iii) the volume and size of transactions it undertakes and anticipates undertaking in the following year; and (iv) the degree of uncertainty associated with the transactions it undertakes or anticipates undertaking in the following year (LR 8.6.7CG). The FCA may also take into account, where relevant, the guidance or advice on the Listing Rules or disclosure requirements and Transparency Rules the sponsor has given in other circumstances other than producing sponsor services (LR 8.6.9BG).

Accompanying Guidance Notes were introduced in UKLA/TN/714.2 and UKLA TN/715.1. UKLA Guidance Note *Sponsors: Guidance on the competence requirements set out under LR 8.6.7R(2)(b) (UKLA/TN/714.2)* sets out a description of the types of knowledge and expertise that the FCA expects sponsors to consider when assessing whether they understand each of the 'competency sets'. In particular, the FCA expects sponsors to have a detailed working knowledge of aspects of the rulebooks and guidance that are pertinent to their role, as well as being proficient in those procedures and processes of the UKLA that a sponsor would undertake. UKLA Guidance Note *Sponsors: Practical implications of competence requirements for sponsors and applicants (UKLA/TN/715.1)* sets out some FAQs to assist sponsors and new applicants in considering the practical application of the provisions relating to sponsor competence.

The definition of 'sponsor services' is very broad. It includes the services (relating to a matter referred to in LR 8.2) that a sponsor must provide or is requested or appointed to provide. It also includes preparatory work that a sponsor may undertake before it decides whether or not it will act as sponsor for a listed company or applicant or in relation to a particular transaction. The definition also includes all of the sponsor's communications with the FCA in connection with the service. However, nothing in the definition is to be taken as requiring a sponsor, when requested, to agree to act for a company or in relation to a transaction.

The UKLA Guidance Note *Sponsor services: Principles for sponsors (UKLA/TN/710.1)* provides further guidance on the application of the definition. It states that if a sponsor is in discussion with the FCA concerning a matter that is a sponsor service, it will still be carrying out a 'sponsor service' notwithstanding any lack of formal confirmation of appointment. It also says that the sponsor service continues (in the case of a listing) until admission to listing (or transfer of listing) becomes effective or (in the case of a class 1 transaction) until the class 1 transaction completes. It also notes that if a sponsor voluntarily provides guidance on the Listing Rules or the Disclosure Guidance and Transparency Rules, or enters into communications with the FCA in relation to an event which requires a listed company to appoint or obtain guidance from a sponsor, this falls within the definition of 'sponsor services'.

In order to be competent to provide sponsor services, a sponsor must also have at least two employees who can satisfy the key contact requirements set out in LR 8.6.19R, but the FCA expects that active sponsors will require considerably more (see section 1.4 for further information on key contacts).

1.4 Appropriate systems and controls

In accordance with LR 8.6.12R, a sponsor will not satisfy the requirement to have appropriate systems and controls in place unless it has clear and effective reporting lines and effective systems and controls:

- which require employees with management responsibilities for the provision of sponsor services to understand and apply the requirements of LR 8;
- for the appropriate supervision of employees performing sponsor services;
- for compliance with applicable Listing Rules at all times, including when performing sponsor services;
- which require appropriate staffing arrangements for providing each sponsor service in line with the sponsor principles in LR 8.3;
- for employees performing sponsor services to receive appropriate guidance and training to provide each sponsor service in line with the sponsor principles in LR 8.3;
- to identify and manage conflicts of interest;
- for compliance with the requirements in relation to the competence of the sponsor in accordance with LR 8.6.7R(2)(b); and
- which comply with the requirements in relation to record keeping and management.

When considering a sponsor's ability to comply with LR 8.6.12R, the FCA will consider a variety of factors including the nature, scale and complexity of its business, the diversity of its operations, the volume and size of the transactions it undertakes and anticipates undertaking in the following year and the degree of risk associated with the transactions it undertakes or anticipates undertaking in the following year (LR 8.6.13G).

In accordance with LR 8.6.13AG, a sponsor will generally be regarded as having appropriate systems and controls for identifying and managing conflicts of interest if it has in place effective policies and procedures:

- to ensure that decisions taken on managing conflicts of interest are taken by appropriately senior staff and on a timely basis;
- to monitor whether arrangements put in place to manage conflicts are effective; and
- to ensure that individuals within the sponsor are appropriately trained to enable them to identify, escalate and manage conflicts of interest.

Such policies and procedures are distinct from the actual organisational and administrative arrangements that a sponsor is required to put in place and maintain under LR 8.3.9R to manage specific conflicts. See section 3.2 for further discussion.

The UKLA Guidance Note *Sponsor transactions – Adequacy of resourcing* (UKLA/TN/709.2) provides guidance on the nature and extent of systems and controls which a sponsor will need; it encourages sponsors to assess carefully whether or not they have the relevant experience and the appropriate systems and controls to carry out the sponsor services in accordance with LR 8.6.7R, 8.6.12G and 8.6.13G.

For each sponsor service requiring the submission of a document to the FCA or contact with the FCA, a sponsor must notify the FCA of the key contact for the matter when it first makes contact with the FCA (the 'key contact' regime). As well as having sufficient knowledge about the company and the transaction and being available to answer queries from the FCA between 7.00am and 6.00pm on any business day, the key contact must be authorised to make representations to the FCA on behalf of the sponsor, possess technical knowledge of the rules, guidance and ESMA publications directly relevant to the sponsor service and understand the responsibilities and obligations of the sponsor under LR 8 in relation to the sponsor service (LR 8.6.19R). The FCA also expects a key contact will have provided a sponsor service in the previous three years (LR 8.6.20G).

1.5 Record keeping

In accordance with LR 8.6.16AR, a sponsor must have effective arrangements to create and retain for six years accessible records which are capable of demonstrating that it has provided sponsor services and otherwise complied with its obligations under LR 8 in accordance with the Listing Rules, including:

- where a sponsor's declaration is to be submitted to the FCA, the basis of each declaration given;
- where any opinion, assurance or confirmation is provided to the FCA or a company with or applying for a premium listing in relation to a sponsor service, the basis of that opinion, assurance or confirmation;
- where a sponsor provides guidance to a listed company or applicant for a premium listing, the basis upon which the guidance is given and upon which any judgments or opinions underlying the guidance have been made or given; and
- the steps taken to comply with its conflicts obligations and its competency obligation to meet the sponsor-approved criteria.

In relation to record keeping, LR 8.6.16BG goes on to state that records should:

- be capable of timely retrieval; and
- include material communications which relate to the provision of sponsor services, including advice or guidance given to a company with or applying for a premium listing in relation to their responsibilities under the Listing Rules and disclosure requirements and Transparency Rules.

In considering whether a sponsor has satisfied the record-keeping requirements, the FCA will consider whether the records would enable a person with general knowledge of the sponsor regime, but no specific knowledge of the actual sponsor service undertaken, to understand and verify the basis upon which material judgments have been made throughout the provision of sponsor services (LR 8.6.16CG).

The UKLA Guidance Note *Sponsors: record keeping requirements (UKLA/TN/717.1)* provides additional guidance on the application of the record-keeping requirements in LR 8.6.16AR as follows:

- *Recording material judgements* – The FCA will generally expect to be able to ascertain from a sponsor's records the nature of the issue being considered, the facts and circumstances taken into account by the sponsor and the due and careful enquiry undertaken to establish the facts and circumstances, the sponsor's analysis of the issue and the judgment reached. The FCA is likely to regard a judgement as being material if the outcome of the matter could affect the sponsor's ability to reach one of the opinions it is required to provide in a sponsor declaration.

- *E-mails* – The FCA expect sponsors to keep all e-mails that contain substantive points, including those that share information between the parties and advisers involved in the transaction, provide advice or guidance by the sponsor, concern discussions or decisions about material judgements or opinions, or discussions about timing or progress on significant steps in the transaction. The FCA also expects the records to include material emails between deal team members, e-mails to or from any committee member, senior manager, peer reviewer or compliance staff relating to the transaction, and e-mails discussing potential conflicts of interest in relation to the sponsor service.

- *Records of meetings/calls* – The FCA expects records of meetings, calls or other discussions to be prepared on a near contemporaneous basis. The FCA also expects sponsors to keep records showing appropriate supervision of the staff who are providing the sponsor services (including e.g. keeping records of information provided to any committee).

- *Use of control schedules* – Sponsors are not required to use control schedules as part of their record keeping but the FCA notes that, where they are designed and used effectively, control schedules can assist with navigation of a deal file. If using a control schedule, the FCA notes that (i) this does not remove or reduce the need to retain underlying records, such as material e-mails, file notes of material discussions, records evidencing review and challenge of information and opinions provided by the client, other advisers or third parties, and records of the basis upon which key decisions or judgements are made; and (ii) sponsors need to determine how their control schedule fits into their record-keeping procedures and controls structures, and the FCA expect sponsors to have processes in place to ensure that the control schedule is updated within appropriate timeframes.

The note acknowledges that the application of the record-keeping requirements is fact specific; sponsors will need to exercise professional judgement about the nature, type and extent of records they keep in relation to a particular sponsor service.

1.6 Supervision and censure of sponsors

Once approved by the FCA, a sponsor must pay an annual fee to remain on the FCA list of sponsors (LR 8.7.6R). In accordance with LR 8.7.7R, the sponsor must provide annual written confirmation that it continues to meet the criteria for approval as a sponsor set out in LR 8.6.5R and, for each of the criteria in that rule, evidence of the basis upon which it considers that it meets the criteria. This written confirmation is provided by submitting a completed Sponsor Annual Notification Form to the FCA on or after the first business day in January each year, but no later than the last business day in January.

In addition to this annual confirmation, a sponsor must notify the FCA of certain other events on an ad hoc basis in accordance with LR 8.7.8R, for example, where:

- it ceases to satisfy the criteria for approval as a sponsor set out in LR 8.6.5R, or becomes aware of any matter which, in its reasonable opinion, would be relevant to the FCA in considering whether the sponsor continues to comply with LR 8.6.6R;
- it becomes aware of any fact or circumstance relating to it, or any of its employees engaged in the provision of sponsor services, which in its reasonable opinion would be likely to adversely affect market confidence in sponsors;
- it (or any of its employees engaged in the provision of sponsor services) are convicted of any offence involving fraud, theft or other dishonesty or are the subject of a bankruptcy proceeding, a receiving order or an administration order; are subject to any public criticism, regulatory intervention or disciplinary action by the FCA, by any designated professional body, by any body comparable to the FCA (or a designated professional body) or under any comparable legislation in any jurisdiction outside the United Kingdom;
- any of its employees engaged in the provision of sponsor is disqualified by a court from acting as a director of a company or from acting in a management capacity or conducting the affairs of any company;
- it changes its name;
- it identifies or otherwise becomes aware of any material deficiency in its systems and controls;
- there is intended to be a change of control of the sponsor, or any restructuring of the sponsor's group or a re-organisation of or a substantial change to the directors, partners or employees engaged in the provision of sponsor services by the sponsor;
- there is expected to be a change in the financial position of the sponsor or any of its group companies that would be likely to adversely affect the sponsor's ability to perform the sponsor services or otherwise comply with LR 8;
- it resigns or is dismissed by a listed company or applicant (details of any relevant facts or circumstances must be given – see also section 2.2); or

- a listed company or applicant denies it access to documents or information that have been the subject of a reasonable request by the sponsor.

In the UKLA Guidance Note *Sponsor notifications (UKLA/TN/711.1)*, the FCA says that certain of these circumstances are purposefully broad and that a high degree of self-monitoring is required by the sponsor. A firm's operating and reporting structures need to ensure that the relevant information is disseminated to those individuals responsible for making such notifications.

These ad hoc notifications should be made as soon as possible to the Sponsor Supervision Team at the FCA. They may be made in the first instance by telephone, but must always be confirmed promptly in writing to the Sponsor Supervision Team (LR 8.7.9G). Where a sponsor is of the opinion that notwithstanding the circumstances giving rise to a notification obligation under LR 8.7.8R, it continues to satisfy the ongoing criteria for approval as a sponsor in accordance with LR 8.6.6R, it must include in its notification to the FCA a statement to that effect and the basis for its opinion (LR 8.7.8AR).

The FCA uses a combination of the annual confirmation and these general notifications – together with its own assessment of a sponsor's performance 'on the transaction' – to monitor a sponsor's performance and its continued ability to satisfy the requirements of LR 8.6.5R.

The FCA was given additional statutory powers regarding the supervision and discipline of sponsors through amendments to the FSMA 2000, effected by FSA 2012. Section 88A of the FSMA 2000 gives the FCA the power to impose a wide range of disciplinary sanctions on sponsors in the event of a breach of the Listing Rules including:

- imposing a financial penalty on the sponsor of such an amount as it considers appropriate;
- suspending the sponsor's approval for up to a maximum of 12 months;
- imposing limitations or restrictions on a sponsor's approval for up to a maximum of 12 months; and
- publicly censuring the sponsor.

The FCA has set out its policy on when and how it will use such disciplinary powers in the UKLA Guidance Note *Additional powers to supervise and discipline sponsors (UKLA/TN/712.2)* and the UKLA Procedural Note *Additional powers to supervise sponsors (UKLA/PN/910.2)*.

Section 88B of FSMA 2000 set out a sponsor's right to receive a warning notice and make representations prior to any FCA decision to impose any sanction on a sponsor and, ultimately, the right to refer the FCA's decision to its Upper Tribunal for a de novo (full merits) hearing.

While the regulator has since 1 July 2005, censured and fined a number of listed companies for breaches of the LPDT Rules (see Figure 1.3 in Chapter 1) the first public censure of a sponsor was in May 2011. In that case, the FSA publicly censured BDO LLP for contraventions of LR 8.3.3R (failure to act with due care and skill in relation to a sponsor service) and LR 8.3.5(1)R (failure to deal with the FSA in an open and cooperative way). The FSA criticised BDO for failing to act with the necessary objectivity as sponsor, by having agreed not to liaise with the FSA until after the announcement (and not having reviewed that decision), even though it was aware that the transaction might be treated as a reverse takeover, which would have required a suspension of the company's shares unless the FSA agreed otherwise (see section 2 of Chapter 9). By not liaising with the FSA before the announcement, the FSA was denied the opportunity of deciding whether suspension was appropriate.

In January 2015, the FCA issued its first fine of a sponsor. Execution Noble & Company Limited was fined £330,000 (subsequently reduced to £231,000 as a result of an early settlement discount) for breach of the Listing Rules. The key facts were that two-thirds of the firm's sponsor team had departed over a period of months (including all of the key individuals responsible for leading and executing sponsor services) and the firm had failed to advise the UKLA. The FCA was concerned about the potential impairment of the sponsor's ability to meet the criteria for approval as a sponsor and discharge the sponsor function.

Although the sponsor failed to inform the UKLA that a number of individuals had left the firm, it did notify the FCA's Authorisations department. Sponsors must therefore make appropriate notifications to the UKLA (in its sponsor supervision capacity) as distinct from other arms of FCA. The FCA emphasises the need for sponsor firms to have an open and co-operative relationship with the UKLA, on an ongoing basis, as required by LR 8.3.5R(1) and the guidance in LR 8.7.1G. The FCA also emphasised that sponsors are critical to the integrity of the premium listing segment when it fined Cenkos Securities £530,500 for breaches of LR 8 in 2016.

2. Appointment and consultation of a sponsor

2.1 Circumstances in which a sponsor must be appointed or consulted

2.1.1 Premium listing of shares

A company with (or applying for) a premium listing of its shares is required to appoint a sponsor where it makes an application for admission of shares requiring the production of a prospectus (or of an equivalent document) (LR 8.2.1R(1)). A company must also appoint a sponsor when it is required under LR 8.4.3R(4) to submit to the FCA a letter in relation to its eligibility.

The preparation and publication of a prospectus is considered in detail in Chapter 4 and further share issues are considered in detail in Chapter 10.

2.1.2 Transfer of listing category

A listed company is required to appoint a sponsor where it applies to transfer its listing category from:

- a standard listing (shares) to a premium listing (commercial company) (and a standard listing (shares) to a premium listing (investment company);
- a premium listing (investment company) to a premium listing (commercial company); or
- a premium listing (commercial company) to a premium listing (investment company) (LR 8.2.1AR).

The transfer of listing categories is considered in detail in Chapter 2.

2.1.3 Corporate transactions by premium listed companies

A premium listed company must obtain the guidance of a sponsor:

- to assess the application of Listing Rule 10, if it is proposing to enter into a transaction which, due to its size or nature, could amount to a Class 1 transaction or a reverse takeover (LR 8.2.2R); and
- to assess the application of Listing Rule 11, if it is proposing to enter into a transaction which is, or may be, a related party transaction (LR 8.2.3R).

A premium listed company is required to appoint a sponsor where it is required to:

- produce a Class 1 circular (LR 8.2.1R(2));
- produce a circular that proposes a reconstruction or refinancing which is required by LR 9.5.12R to include a working capital statement (LR 8.2.1R(3));
- produce a circular for the proposed purchase of its own shares which is required by LR 13.7.1R(2) to include a working capital statement (LR 8.2.1R(4));
- obtain from a sponsor confirmation that the terms of a proposed smaller related party transaction are fair and reasonable or to submit to the FCA a related party circular which is required by LR 13.6.1R(5) to include a statement by the Board that the transaction or arrangement is fair and reasonable and that it has been so advised by a sponsor;
- make an announcement or request a suspension in connection with a reverse takeover under LR 5.6.6R, provide a disclosure regime confirmation in connection with a reverse takeover under LR 5.6.12G(1), make a disclosure announcement in connection with a reverse takeover under LR 5.6.15G that contains a declaration described in LR 5.6.15G(3) or (4), or submit to the FCA a letter in relation to the company's eligibility in connection with a reverse takeover under LR 5.6.23G(2);
- provide the FCA with a confirmation of severe financial difficulty for the purposes of LR 10.8.3G(2); or
- provide an assessment of the appropriateness of an investment exchange or multilateral trading facility under LR 13.5.27BR.

Class 1 transactions, reverse takeovers and related party transactions are considered in detail in Chapter 9; share buy-backs are considered in detail in Chapter 10.

2.1.4 Apparent breach of the Listing Rules

The FCA can also require a company with (or applying for) a premium listing of its shares to appoint a sponsor if it appears that there may have been a breach of the Listing Rules, the disclosure requirements or the Transparency Rules (LR 8.2.1R(5)).

2.2 Notifications required on appointment and dismissal of a sponsor

Where an applicant or a listed company appoints a sponsor in accordance with LR 8.2.1R or LR 8.2.1AR, it must promptly inform the FCA of the name and contact details of the sponsor (LR 8.5.1R).

Any notification made by an applicant or listed company will usually take the form of a short letter, an illustrative form of which is set out in Figure 3.1.

In addition to the notification from the applicant or listed company, for each sponsor service requiring the submission of a document to the FCA or contact with the FCA, a sponsor must notify the FCA at the time of submission or on first making contact with the FCA the name and contact details of a key contact in the sponsor for that matter (LR 8.6.19R(1)). The sponsor must ensure that the key contact has sufficient knowledge about the applicant or listed company and proposed transaction to be able to answer questions from the FCA and that they are available to answer any questions on any business day from 7.00am to 6.00pm (LR 8.6.19R(2)). The 'key contact' must also be technically competent and understand a sponsor's regulatory obligations under LR 8. They should also be authorised to make representations to the FCA for and on behalf of the sponsor. See also section 1.4 above.

If a sponsor resigns or is dismissed, the applicant or listed company must immediately notify the FCA in writing, copied to the sponsor (LR 8.5.2R). Where the sponsor has been dismissed, the notification to the FCA must include the reasons for the dismissal (there is a corresponding obligation on the sponsor under LR 8.7.8R(5) as described in section 1.6).

2.3 Joint sponsors and agents

It is relatively common for companies to appoint two investment banks as joint sponsors, especially on larger, more complex, transactions.

The appointment of more than one sponsor by an applicant or listed company does not relieve any sponsor of their obligations (LR 8.3.14R). Each sponsor must comply with the provisions of LR 8.

Figure 3.1: Illustrative form of sponsor appointment letter

[PRINT LETTER ON COMPANY'S LETTERHEAD]

UK Listing Authority
Financial Conduct Authority
25 The North Colonnade
Canary Wharf
London E14 5HS

[DATE]

Dear Sirs

[NAME OF COMPANY] (the 'Company')

Pursuant to Listing Rule 8.5.1R [and Listing Rule 8.5.3R], we are writing to inform you of the appointment of [NAME OF SPONSOR[S]] as [sponsor/joint sponsors] to the Company in connection with [DESCRIPTION OF TRANSACTION] (the 'Transaction').

The contact details of the [sponsor/joint sponsors] are as follows:

[NAME AND ADDRESS OF SPONSOR(S)]

[In addition, [NAME OF SPONSOR] has assumed responsibility for contact with the Financial Conduct Authority for administrative arrangements under LR 8.5.3R(1).]

Yours faithfully

Director/Company Secretary

for and on behalf of [INSERT NAME OF COMPANY]

A joint sponsor arrangement can have advantages for a listed company or applicant, including bringing sector or other relevant experience to a transaction or benefiting from multiple experienced advisers on a complex transaction.

In early 2015, the FCA issued a policy statement setting out minor changes to Listing Rule 8 in response to its consultation on joint sponsors (see CP 14/21 *Feedback and*

Policy Statement on CP 14/02, Consultation on joint sponsors and call for views on sponsor conflicts). LR 8.5.3R was amended so that the requirement for only one sponsor to take responsibility for contact with the FCA in respect of sponsor services applies in respect of administrative arrangements only. The applicant or listed company must inform the FCA in writing of the name and contact details of the sponsor that has agreed to take such responsibility (LR 8.5.3R(2)). New guidance was introduced in LR 8.3.15G which sets out the FCA's expectation that joint sponsors co-operate with each other in relation to the provisions of sponsor services.

3. General duties and obligations of a sponsor

3.1 Principles

3.1.1 Summary of the principles

A sponsor has a number of general duties and obligations – described as 'principles' – which apply at all times (whether or not the sponsor is carrying out a sponsor service), namely to:

- deal with the FCA in an open and co-operative way; and
- deal with all enquiries raised by the FCA promptly (LR 8.3.5R).

Other principles only apply when a sponsor is providing a sponsor service. A sponsor is obliged to:

- provide assurance to the FCA, when required, that the responsibilities of the listed company or applicant under the Listing Rules have been met (LR 8.3.1R(1));
- provide to the FCA any explanation or confirmation it reasonably requires for the purposes of ensuring that the Listing Rules are being complied with by the premium listed company or applicant (LR 8.3.1R(1A));
- guide the premium listed company or applicant in understanding and meeting its responsibilities under the Listing Rules, disclosure requirements and Transparency Rules (LR 8.3.1R(2));
- take such reasonable steps as are sufficient to ensure that any communication or information it provides to the FCA is, to the best of its knowledge and belief, accurate and complete in all materials respects and, as soon as possible, provide to the FCA any information of which the sponsor becomes aware that materially affects the accuracy or completeness of information it has previously provided (LR 8.3.1AR);
- act with due care and skill (LR 8.3.3R);
- when giving guidance or advice on the application or interpretation of the Listing Rules, the disclosure requirements or the Transparency Rules, take reasonable steps to satisfy itself that the directors of the listed company understand their

responsibilities and obligations under the Listing Rules, disclosure requirements and Transparency Rules *(LR 8.3.4R)*;
- act with honesty and integrity (LR 8.3.5BR);
- take all reasonable steps to identify conflicts of interest that could adversely affect its ability to perform its functions under Listing Rule 8 (LR 8.3.7BR); and
- notify the FCA promptly if it becomes aware that the listed company or applicant is failing to, or has failed to, comply with its obligations under the Listing Rules or the disclosure requirements or the Transparency Rules (LR 8.3.5AR).

Reference will often be made to these duties in an investment bank's terms of engagement (and Sponsor's Agreement discussed at section 5.1.3) and the bank will often require the company to agree to certain terms to facilitate compliance with its obligations.

The UKLA Guidance Note *Sponsors: Innovative structures and scheme (UKLA/ TN/706.1)* discusses the obligation to act with due care and skill in the context of unusual transactions. Where a listed company proposes a novel structure or scheme, the FCA considers that the obligation to act with due care and skill requires the sponsor to consider carefully whether the proposed scheme or structure is appropriate having regard to the Listing Rules and other relevant legislation, before contacting the FCA.

3.1.2 Assurance that responsibilities have been met

LR 8.3.1R(1) requires a sponsor to provide assurance to the FCA, when required, that the responsibilities of the premium listed company or applicant under the Listing Rules have been met. In addition, LR 8.3.1R(1A) requires a sponsor to provide to the FCA any explanation or confirmation in such form and within such time limits as it may reasonably require for the purposes of ensuring that the Listing Rules are being complied with by a premium listed company or applicant. See also section 3.1.4 below.

3.1.3 Guidance on understanding and meeting responsibilities

LR 8.3.1R(2) requires a sponsor to guide the listed company or applicant in understanding and meeting its responsibilities under the Listing Rules, disclosure requirements and Transparency Rules. Where a sponsor gives such guidance or advice in relation to the application or interpretation of the Listing Rules, disclosure requirements or Transparency Rules, it must take reasonable steps to ensure that the directors of the company understand their responsibilities (LR 8.3.4R). The FCA looks to sponsors to act as gatekeepers for the regime and to consider whether the company or the transaction in question is one which they should be 'sponsoring'.

To assist a sponsor in meeting its obligations under LR 8.3.4R, the sponsor will generally (depending on the nature of the sponsor service) require the company's lawyers to circulate a memorandum to the directors and (in the context of an IPO) give a presentation to the directors summarising their responsibilities – both generally and in connection with the transaction in question – and will typically seek confirmation that the directors have had explained to them and have understood the nature of their responsibilities in the Company's Listing Rule 8 letter (discussed in section 5.1.1 and Figure 3.10).

3.1.4 Disclosure of non-compliance

LR 8.3.5AR requires a sponsor, when providing a sponsor service, to promptly notify the FCA if it becomes aware that a premium listed company or applicant is failing or has failed to comply with its obligations under the Listing Rules, disclosure requirements or Transparency Rules. This obligation effectively amounts to a whistle-blowing obligation of a sponsor in respect of its own client. It is common for sponsors' terms of engagement to specifically recognise the sponsor's obligation in this regard and expressly permit the sponsor to bring to the FCA's attention any relevant matter.

3.2 Identifying and managing conflicts

Sponsors must take reasonable steps to identify conflicts of interest that could adversely affect their ability to perform their functions properly under Listing Rule 8 (LR 8.3.7BR). The purpose behind this principle is to ensure that conflicts of interest do not adversely affect the ability of a sponsor to perform its functions or market confidence in sponsors (LR 8.3.7AG).

Sponsors are required to identify and manage conflicts on an ongoing basis as long as they provide a sponsor service (LR 8.3.12AG) and to decline instructions or cease to act if necessary. In addition to the guidance for sponsors in LR 8.3.8G(1) that, in identifying conflicts of interest, the sponsor should take into account circumstances that could create a perception in the market that a sponsor may not be able to perform its functions properly, there is also guidance expressly acknowledging the potential for 'regulatory conflicts' (those that may compromise the ability of a sponsor to fulfil its obligations to the FCA in relation to a sponsor service) (LR 8.3.8G(2)).

In the UKLA Guidance Note *Sponsors: Conflicts of interest (UKLA/TN/701.2)*, the FCA provides further guidance as regards the conflicts of interest regime whereby the FCA recognises that a sponsor may have more than one interest in a transaction and that it should be possible, in most cases, to manage conflicts between those interests. The FCA says that the steps a sponsor puts in place to manage conflicts may include establishing 'Chinese Walls' between the sponsor team and other areas of the business with an interest in the company. The Guidance Note also encourages sponsors to create a comprehensive conflicts policy that reflects the unique role of the sponsor and the nature and diversity of that firm's operations and which identifies and manages conflicts on a case-by case-basis.

In March 2017, the FCA announced in its Primary Market Bulletin No. 17 that it is consulting on revisions to this Guidance Note to address concerns raised in the feedback to CP 14/21. Proposed amendments include asking sponsors to consider whether there could be a perception of conflict from the point of view of a theoretical reasonable market user and to consider the amount and terms of the sponsor fee.

If, however, a sponsor cannot manage a particular conflict, then it must not act (LR 8.3.11R) as providing sponsor services in such a case could adversely affect both a sponsor's ability to perform its functions and market confidence in the sponsor regime (LR 8.3.12G). The sponsor must be 'reasonably satisfied' that the organisational and administrative arrangements it has in place will ensure that the conflict will not adversely affect its ability to perform its functions under Listing Rule 8; if not satisfied, it must decline to act.

The UKLA Guidance Note *Sponsors: Conflicts of interest (UKLA/TN/701.2)* sets out some examples as to when a sponsor may be unable to carry out its role in a proper manner:

- listings, capital raisings or disposals which may be perceived as facilitating an exit for the sponsor's group;
- unusual, synthetic or high-risk investment structures developed or promoted by the sponsor for listing; or
- previous involvement of the sponsor's group in the management or corporate governance of an applicant where the sponsor has either Board representation or private equity style holdings and the subsequent listing provides a full or partial exit for the group.

The Guidance Note also provides guidance on the situation where the sponsor or the sponsor's group has an interest in the company (e.g. through a loan facility) and the company is in financial distress and is either seeking a rescue capital fund raising or is taking pre-emptive action as regards its financial structure. The FCA sets out a number of non-exhaustive factors to be considered by the sponsor to assess the extent of the conflict. The FCA notes that, while the sponsor team will need to have certain information regarding the existence of a loan facility being provided by its group so as to ensure that it has carried out due and careful enquiry and that there has been appropriate disclosure, it would not expect the sponsor team to know the significance of the loan to the group nor to be in contact with colleagues that are accountable for the loan. The FCA Sponsor Supervision Team would expect to hold detailed discussions with the sponsor's compliance or legal department as to the significance of the loan to the sponsor group.

The UKLA Guidance Note also notes that there are no defined criteria for when a sponsor should discuss its conflicts assessment with the FCA, but it provides some examples as to when that might be appropriate. The FCA also lists certain confirmations that it may require from a sponsor when considering LR 8.3.7AG onwards.

As noted in section 1.4 above, a sponsor must have appropriate systems and controls in place for identifying and managing conflicts of interest. A sponsor will generally be regarded as having appropriate systems and controls in place if it has policies and procedures to:

- ensure that decisions taken on managing conflicts are taken by appropriately senior staff and on a timely basis;
- monitor whether arrangements put in place are effective; and
- ensure that individuals within the sponsor are appropriately trained to enable them to identify, escalate and manage conflicts of interest (LR 8.6.13AG).

The UKLA Guidance Note *Sponsors: Conflicts of interest (UKLA/TN/701.2)* states that sponsors should be able to demonstrate the basis on which they have reached a conclusion on conflicts and should maintain accessible records for these purposes.

The sponsor must also notify the FCA immediately if it becomes aware that it is no longer able to comply with LR 8.3.9R to LR 8.3.11R.

It is common for sponsors' terms of engagement to include a provision to allow the sponsor to cease to act if it concludes that it is required to do so as a result of a conflict of interest emerging.

3.3 Maintenance of records

The prescribed forms of a sponsor's declaration contain a confirmation from the sponsor that it has maintained accessible records which are sufficient to demonstrate that the sponsor has complied with its obligations under LR 8, including the basis of the matters confirmed elsewhere in the declaration.

LR 8.6.16AR provides that a sponsor must have in place effective arrangements to create, and retain for six years, accessible records which are sufficient to be capable of demonstrating that, in accordance with the Listing Rules, it has provided sponsor services and has otherwise complied with its obligations under Listing Rule 8. A sponsor must have a document retention system in place. The guidance in LR 8.6.16BG goes on to state that records should be capable of timely retrieval and should include material communications which relate to the provision of sponsor services, including any advice or guidance given to a premium listed company concerning their responsibilities under the Listing Rules, the disclosure requirements and the Transparency Rules. In considering whether a sponsor has satisfied the requirements regarding the sufficiency of records, the test that the FCA will apply is whether the records would enable a person with general knowledge of the sponsor regime, but no specific knowledge of the sponsor service actually being undertaken, to understand and verify the basis upon which material judgments have been made throughout the provision of the sponsor service (LR 8.6.16CG). The records should, therefore, cover not only the fact of a decision/judgment, but also provide some basis for it.

The maintenance of adequate and appropriate records remains a key area of focus for the FCA when it is conducting transaction reviews.

4. Transaction-specific duties and the obligations of a sponsor

In addition to its general obligations under LR 8.3, LR 8.4 sets out certain transaction-specific obligations for sponsors, summarised in Figure 3.2 below, for transactions that involve:

- an application for admission by a new applicant (LR 8.4.1R to LR 8.4.4G);
- an application for admission of further shares by a company that already has listed shares (LR 8.4.7R to LR 8.4.10G);
- the production of a Class 1 circular or a circular in connection with a reconstruction or refinancing or a buy-back of shares (LR 8.4.11R to LR 8.4.13R);
- an application to transfer between listing categories (LR 8.4.14R to LR 8.4.16R); or
- a company making an announcement under LR 5.6.15G on disclosure of information on the target in connection with a reverse takeover (LR 8.4.17R).

Where a transaction by a listed company involves both an application for admission of further shares and the production of a circular (e.g. where the company intends to make a Class 1 acquisition and issue new shares as consideration) the sponsor must comply with both sets of transaction-specific duties and give two distinct declarations to the FCA.

Figure 3.2: Summary of a sponsor's additional responsibilities in relation to certain transactions

Listing Rule requirement	Type of corporate transaction						
	IPO	Further share issue	Class 1 transaction	Transfer of listing category	Related party transaction	Reverse takeover
Consult or appoint sponsor	Appoint	Appoint	Consult and, if circular required, appoint	Appoint	Consult, and, if fair and reasonable opinion required, appoint	Consult and appoint
Confirmation LR and/or PR satisfied	LR and PR	LR and PR	LR	LR	–	LR and PR

ROLE AND RESPONSIBILITIES OF A SPONSOR 101

Listing Rule requirement	Type of corporate transaction					
	IPO	Further share issue	Class 1 transaction	Transfer of listing category	Related party transaction	Reverse takeover
Established procedures to comply with obligations	Yes	–	–	Yes (if standard to premium)	–	Yes
No adverse impact on ability to comply with rules	–	–	Yes	–	–	Yes
Established financial position and prospects procedures	Yes	–	–	Yes (if standard to premium)	–	Yes
Reasonable basis for working capital statement	Yes	Yes	Yes	Yes (if standard to premium)	–	Yes
Disclosed relevant matters to FCA	Yes	Yes	Yes	Yes	–	Yes
Eligibility letter	Yes	–	–	Yes	–	Yes
Sponsor's declaration	Listing	Listing	Circular	Transfer	–	Reverse Takeover Announcement and Listing

Although the sponsor must submit the relevant sponsor declaration to the FCA on publication of the prospectus or circular (as applicable), a sponsor will still be providing a sponsor service up to the date of admission (in relation to an admission of shares) or date of completion of the transaction (in relation to a class 1 or other transaction) (see UKLA Guidance Note *Sponsor services: Principles for sponsors (UKLA/ TN/710.1)*). Sponsors must, therefore, be mindful of their ongoing obligations, as well as the transaction-specific duties set out below, through the whole process of a transaction.

4.1 Application for admission of a new applicant

Under LR 8.4.3R, in connection with an application for admission by a new applicant, a sponsor must:

- submit a letter to the FCA setting out how the applicant satisfies the eligibility criteria for listing set out in Listing Rules 2 and 6 (commonly referred to as an eligibility letter) no later than when the first draft of the prospectus is submitted for review. The UKLA Guidance Note *Eligibility process (UKLA/PN/901.3)* sets out further guidance on the timing of submission of the eligibility letter;
- submit a Sponsor's Declaration on Application for Listing to the FCA prior to approval of the prospectus;
- ensure that all matters known to it which, in its reasonable opinion, should be taken into account by the FCA in considering (i) the application for listing, and (ii) whether the admission of the shares would be detrimental to investors' interests have been disclosed with sufficient prominence in the prospectus or otherwise in writing to the FCA; and
- submit a completed Shareholder Statement or Pricing Statement, as applicable, to the FCA by 9.00am on the day the FCA is to consider the application for listing.

LR 8.4.2R provides that the sponsor must not submit an application for admission in accordance with Listing Rule 3, unless it has come to a reasonable opinion, after having made due and careful enquiry, that:

- the applicant has satisfied all requirements of the Listing Rules relevant to an application for admission to listing;
- the applicant has satisfied all applicable requirements set out in the Prospectus Rules;
- the directors of the applicant have established procedures which enable the applicant to comply with the Listing Rules, the disclosure requirements and the Transparency Rules on an ongoing basis;
- the directors of the applicant have established procedures which provide a reasonable basis for them to make proper judgments on an ongoing basis as to the financial position and prospects of the applicant and its group; and
- the directors of the applicant have a reasonable basis on which to make the working capital statement required to be made by LR 6.1.16R.

The Sponsor's Declaration on an Application for Listing, the Shareholder Statement and the Pricing Statement must each be submitted to the FCA in the prescribed form, which can be found on the FCA's website.

Figure 3.3 summarises the key confirmations that a sponsor must give to the FCA in connection with an application for admission of a new applicant.

Figure 3.3: Application for admission of a new applicant – key sponsor confirmations

Key confirmations to be provided by the sponsor to the FCA	Listing Rules
Eligibility Letter setting out how the applicant satisfies the criteria in LR 2 (Requirements for listing) and LR 6 (Additional requirements for premium listing of equity securities) and, if applicable, LR 15 and 16.	LR 8.4.3R(4)
Sponsor's Declaration on Application for Listing confirming that:	LR 8.4.3R(1)
▪ the sponsor has acted with due care and skill in relation to the provision of sponsor services	LR 8.3.3R
▪ the sponsor has taken reasonable steps to satisfy itself that the directors of the applicant understand their responsibilities and obligations under the Listing Rules, the disclosure requirements and the Transparency Rules	LR 8.3.4R
▪ having made due and careful enquiry, the sponsor has come to a reasonable opinion that the applicant has satisfied all requirements of the Listing Rules relevant to an application to listing	LR 8.4.2R(1)
▪ having made due and careful enquiry, the sponsor has come to a reasonable opinion that the applicant has satisfied all applicable requirements set out in the Prospectus Rules	LR 8.4.2R(2)
▪ having made due and careful enquiry, the sponsor has come to a reasonable opinion that the directors of the applicant have established procedures which enable it to comply with the Listing Rules, the disclosure requirements and the Transparency Rules on an ongoing basis	LR 8.4.2R(3)
▪ having made due and careful enquiry, the sponsor has come to a reasonable opinion that the directors of the applicant have established procedures which provide a reasonable basis for them to make proper judgments on an ongoing basis as to the financial position and prospects of the applicant and its group	LR 8.4.2R(4)
▪ having made due and careful enquiry, the sponsor has come to a reasonable opinion that the directors of the applicant have a reasonable basis on which to make the working capital statement required to be made by LR 6.1.16R	LR 8.4.2R(5)
▪ the sponsor has maintained accessible records which are sufficient to be capable of demonstrating that the sponsor has complied with its obligations under the Listing Rules including the basis of each confirmation set out above	LR 8.6.16A
▪ all matters known to the sponsor which, in its opinion, should be taken into account by the FCA in considering (i) the application for listing and (ii) whether the admission of the shares would be detrimental to the investors' interests, have been disclosed with sufficient prominence in the prospectus or otherwise in writing to the FCA.	LR 8.4.3R(3)

4.2 Application for admission of further shares by a listed company

Under LR 8.4.9R, in connection with an application for admission of further shares by a listed company, a sponsor must:

- submit a Sponsor's Declaration on Application for Listing to the FCA prior to approval of the prospectus (or at a time agreed with the FCA if the FCA is not approving the prospectus);
- ensure that all matters known to it which, in its reasonable opinion, should be taken into account by the FCA in considering the application for listing have been disclosed with sufficient prominence in the prospectus or otherwise in writing to the FCA; and
- submit a completed Shareholder Statement or Pricing Statement, as applicable, to the FCA by 9.00am on the day on which the FCA is to consider the application for listing.

Under LR 8.4.8R, the sponsor must not submit an application for admission in accordance with Listing Rule 3, unless it has come to a reasonable opinion, after having made due and careful enquiry, that:

- the applicant has satisfied all requirements of the Listing Rules relevant to an application for admission to listing;
- the applicant has satisfied all applicable requirements set out in the Prospectus Rules; and
- the directors of the applicant have a reasonable basis on which to make the working capital statement required to be made by LR 6.1.16R (or, if applicable, a qualified working capital statement in accordance with LR 6.1.17G).

Prescribed forms of the Sponsor's Declaration on an Application for Listing, the Shareholder Statement and the Pricing Statement are the same as for an application for admission of a new applicant, save that certain confirmations required by the FCA on an application for admission by a new applicant are not required where a listed company is applying to list further shares and may be manually deleted.

Figure 3.4 summarises the key confirmations that the sponsor must give to the FCA in connection with an application for admission of further shares by a listed company.

Figure 3.4: Application for admission of further shares by a listed company – key sponsor confirmations

Key confirmations to be provided by the sponsor to the FCA	Listing Rules
Sponsor's Declaration on Application for Listing confirming that:	LR 8.4.9R(1)
■ the sponsor has acted with due care and skill in relation to the provision of sponsor services	LR 8.3.3R

Key confirmations to be provided by the sponsor to the FCA	Listing Rules
■ the sponsor has taken reasonable steps to satisfy itself that the directors of the applicant understand their responsibilities and obligations under the Listing Rules, the disclosure requirements and the Transparency Rules	LR 8.3.4R
■ having made due and careful enquiry, the sponsor has come to a reasonable opinion that the applicant has satisfied all requirements of the Listing Rules relevant to an application to listing	LR 8.4.8R(1)
■ having made due and careful enquiry, the sponsor has come to a reasonable opinion that the applicant has satisfied all applicable requirements set out in the Prospectus Rules	LR 8.4.8R(2)
■ having made due and careful enquiry, the sponsor has come to a reasonable opinion that the directors of the applicant have a reasonable basis on which to make the working capital statement required to be made by LR 6.1.16R or a qualified working capital statement in accordance with LR 6.1.17R (as the case may be)	LR 8.4.8R(3)
■ the sponsor has maintained accessible records which are sufficient to be capable of demonstrating that the sponsor has complied with its obligations under the Listing Rules, including the basis of each confirmation set out above	LR 8.6.16A
■ all matters known to the sponsor which, in its opinion, should be taken into account by the FCA in considering the application for listing have been disclosed with sufficient prominence in the prospectus or otherwise in writing to the FCA.	LR 8.4.9R(3)

4.3 Publication of a circular by a listed company

Under LR 8.4.13R, in connection with the publication of a circular for a Class 1 transaction, a reconstruction or a buy-back which requires a working capital statement, a sponsor must:

- submit a Sponsor's Declaration for the Production of a Circular to the FCA;
- ensure that all matters known to it which, in its reasonable opinion, should be taken into account by the FCA in considering the transaction have been disclosed with sufficient prominence in the documentation or otherwise in writing to the FCA; and
- where relevant, submit a completed Pricing Statement to the FCA by 9.00am on the day on which it is to consider the application.

Under LR 8.4.12R, the sponsor must not submit an application for approval of a circular regarding a transaction set out in LR 8.4.11R unless it has come to a reasonable opinion, after having made due and careful enquiry, that:

- the listed company has satisfied all requirements of the Listing Rules relevant to the production of a Class 1 circular or other circular;

- the transaction will not have an adverse impact on the listed company's ability to comply with the Listing Rules or the disclosure requirements and Transparency Rules; and
- the directors of the listed company have a reasonable basis on which to make the working capital statement required to be made by LR 9.5.12R, LR 13.4.1R or LR 13.7.1R, as the case may be.

Prescribed forms of the Sponsor's Declaration for the Production of a Circular and the Pricing Statement can be found on the FCA's website.

Figure 3.5 summarises the key confirmations that the sponsor must give to the FCA in connection with the production of a circular by a listed company.

Figure 3.5: Publication of a circular by a listed company – key sponsor confirmations

Key confirmations to be provided by the sponsor to the FCA	Listing Rules
Sponsor's Declaration for the Production of a Circular confirming that:	LR 8.4.13R(1) LR 13.2.4R(1)
■ the sponsor has acted with due care and skill in relation to the provision of sponsor services	LR 8.3.3R
■ the sponsor has taken reasonable steps to satisfy itself that the directors of the applicant understand their responsibilities and obligations under the Listing Rules, the disclosure requirements and the Transparency Rules	LR 8.3.4R
■ having made due and careful enquiry, the sponsor has come to a reasonable opinion that the applicant has satisfied all requirements of the Listing Rules relevant to the production of a Class 1 circular or other circular	LR 8.4.12R(1)
■ having made due and careful enquiry, the sponsor has come to a reasonable opinion that the transaction will not have an adverse impact on the listed company's ability to comply with the Listing Rules or the disclosure requirements and Transparency Rules	LR 8.4.12R(2)
■ having made due and careful enquiry, the sponsor has come to a reasonable opinion that the directors of the applicant have a reasonable basis on which to make the working capital statement required to be made by LR 9.5.12R, LR 13.4.1R or LR 13.7.1R	LR 8.4.12R(3)
■ the sponsor has maintained accessible records which are sufficient to be capable of demonstrating that the sponsor has complied with its obligations under the Listing Rules, including the basis of each confirmation set out above	LR 8.6.16A
■ all matters known to the sponsor which, in its opinion, should be taken into account by the FCA in considering the transaction have been disclosed with sufficient prominence in the documentation or otherwise in writing to the FCA.	LR 8.4.13R(3)

4.4 Application for transfer of listing category

Under LR 8.4.14R, in connection with a proposed transfer of listing category by a listed company under LR 5.4A (e.g. where a commercial company is transferring from a standard to a premium listing), a sponsor must:

- submit a letter to the FCA setting out how the company satisfies each Listing Rule requirement relevant to the category of listing to which it wishes to transfer no later than when the first draft of the circular or announcement required under LR 5.4A is submitted for review;
- submit a Sponsor's Declaration for a Transfer of Listing Category to the FCA; and
- ensure that all matters known to it which, in its reasonable opinion, should be taken into account by the FCA in considering the transfer of listing have been disclosed with sufficient prominence in the circular or announcement referred to in LR 5.4A or otherwise in writing to the FCA.

Under LR 8.4.15R, the sponsor must not submit a final circular or announcement for approval or the sponsor's declaration unless it has come to a reasonable opinion, after having made due and careful enquiry, that:

- the company satisfies all eligibility requirements of the Listing Rules that are relevant to the new category of listing to which it wishes to transfer. The UKLA Procedural Note *Eligibility process (UKLA/PN/901.3)* sets out further guidance on the timing of submission of the eligibility letter;
- the company has satisfied all requirements relevant to the production of the circular required under LR 5.4A.4R or the announcement required under LR 5.4A.5R (whichever is relevant);
- the directors of the company have established procedures which enable the applicant to comply with the Listing Rules, the disclosure requirements and the Transparency Rules on an ongoing basis;
- the directors of the company have established procedures which provide a reasonable basis for them to make proper judgments on an ongoing basis as to the financial position and prospects of the company and its group; and
- the directors of the company have a reasonable basis on which to make the working capital statement (if any) required in connection with the transfer.

A sponsor is not required to reach an opinion on the final three points above (LR 8.4.15R(3), (4) and (5)) if the company was already required to meet such requirements under its existing listing category (LR 8.4.16R).

The prescribed form of the Sponsor's Declaration on a Transfer of Listing Category can be found on the FCA's website.

Figure 3.6 summarises the key confirmations that the sponsor must give to the FCA in connection with the transfer of listing category.

Figure 3.6: Application for transfer of listing category – key sponsor confirmations

Key confirmations to be provided by the sponsor to the FCA	Listing Rules
Eligibility Letter setting out how the company satisfies each Listing Rule requirement relevant to the category of listing to which it wishes to transfer.	LR 8.4.14R(1)
Sponsor's Declaration for a Transfer of Listing Category confirming that:	LR 8.4.14R(2)
■ the sponsor has acted with due care and skill in relation to the provision of sponsor services	LR 8.3.3R
■ the sponsor has taken reasonable steps to satisfy itself that the directors of the company understand their responsibilities and obligations under the Listing Rules, the disclosure requirements and the Transparency Rules	LR 8.3.4R
■ having made due and careful enquiry, the sponsor has come to a reasonable opinion that the company satisfies all eligibility requirements of the Listing Rules that are relevant to the new listing category to which it is seeking to transfer	LR 8.4.15R(1)
■ having made due and careful enquiry, the sponsor has come to a reasonable opinion that the company has satisfied all requirements relevant to the production of the circular required under LR 5.4A.4R or the announcement required under LR 5.4A.5R (whichever is relevant)	LR 8.4.15R(2)
■ (to the extent that the company was not required to meet the requirement under its existing listing category) having made due and careful enquiry, the sponsor has come to a reasonable opinion that the directors of the company have established procedures which enable it to comply with the Listing Rules, the disclosure requirements and the Transparency Rules on an ongoing basis	LR 8.4.15R(3)
■ (to the extent that the company was not required to meet the requirement under its existing listing category) having made due and careful enquiry, the sponsor has come to a reasonable opinion that the directors of the company have established procedures which provide a reasonable basis for them to make proper judgments on an ongoing basis as to the financial position and prospects of the company and its group	LR 8.4.15R(4)
■ (to the extent that the company was not required to meet the requirement under its existing listing category) having made due and careful enquiry, the sponsor has come to a reasonable opinion that the directors of the company have a reasonable basis on which to make the working capital statement (if any) required in connection with the transfer	LR 8.4.15R(5)

ROLE AND RESPONSIBILITIES OF A SPONSOR

Key confirmations to be provided by the sponsor to the FCA	Listing Rules
▪ the sponsor has maintained accessible records which are sufficient to be capable of demonstrating that the sponsor has complied with its obligations under the Listing Rules, including the basis of each confirmation set out above	LR 8.6.16AR
▪ all matters known to the sponsor which, in its opinion, should be taken into account by the FCA in considering the transfer between listing categories have been disclosed with sufficient prominence in the circular or announcement referred to in LR 5.4A or otherwise in writing to the FCA.	LR 8.4.14R(3)

4.5 Disclosure announcement on a reverse takeover

Under LR 8.4.17R, where a company decides to make a disclosure announcement under LR 5.6.15G to avoid suspension of a listing on a reverse takeover (discussed in more detail in section 2.2.1 of Chapter 9), a sponsor must:

- submit a Sponsor's Declaration for a Reverse Takeover Announcement to the FCA; and
- ensure that all matters known to it which, in its reasonable opinion, should be taken into account by the FCA in considering the proposed disclosure announcement have been disclosed with sufficient prominence in the announcement or otherwise in writing to the FCA.

Under LR 8.4.17R(2), the sponsor must not submit the Sponsor's Declaration for a Reverse Takeover Announcement unless it has come to a reasonable opinion, having made due and careful enquiry, that it is reasonable for the company to provide the declarations described in LR 5.6.15G(3) and LR 5.6.15G(4).

A prescribed form of the Sponsor's Declaration for a Reverse Takeover Announcement can be found on the FCA's website.

Figure 3.7 summarises the key confirmations that the sponsor must give to the FCA in connection with the Reverse Takeover Announcement. As the company will generally be required to reapply for admission to listing, the confirmations given in connection with an application for listing are also likely to be relevant.

Figure 3.7: Reverse Takeover Announcement – key sponsor confirmations

Key confirmations to be provided by the sponsor to the FCA	Listing Rules
Sponsor's Declaration for a Reverse Takeover Announcement confirming that:	LR 8.4.17R(1)
▪ the sponsor has acted with due care and skill in relation to the provision of sponsor services	LR 8.3.3R

Key confirmations to be provided by the sponsor to the FCA	Listing Rules
■ the sponsor has taken reasonable steps to satisfy itself that the directors of the company understand their responsibilities under the Listing Rules, the disclosure requirements and the Transparency Rules	LR 8.3.4R
■ having made due and careful enquiry, the sponsor has come to a reasonable opinion that the company has satisfied all requirements of LR 5.6.15G(3) and (4) in relation to the announcement of the proposed reverse takeover and it is reasonable for the company to provide the declaration described in those rules	LR 8.4.17R(2)
■ the sponsor has maintained accessible records which are sufficient to be capable of demonstrating that the sponsor has complied with its obligations under the Listing Rules, including the basis of each confirmation set out above	LR 8.6.16A
■ all matters known to the sponsor which, in its opinion, should be taken into account by the FCA in considering the announcement have been disclosed with sufficient prominence in the announcement or otherwise in writing to the FCA.	LR 8.4.17R(3)

5. Sponsor's comfort package

Given the broad nature of the duties and obligations that follow the appointment of an investment bank as sponsor, it will seek to carefully document the terms of its appointment by the company in its engagement letter and, depending on the nature of the transaction, potentially also a sponsor's agreement or an underwriting agreement. In particular, the sponsor will ask the company for certain contractual protections (e.g. warranties and an indemnity) to minimise, as far as possible, the risk of incurring a loss as a result of the provision of its services.

To assist in discharging its regulatory responsibilities under Listing Rule 8.4, as well as providing a potential 'shield' to any claims that may be brought against it, the sponsor will seek a package of comfort letters, reports and opinions from the company, its directors and professional advisers, including lawyers and reporting accountants. This collection of comfort letters, reports and opinions, illustrated in Figure 3.9, is commonly referred to as the 'sponsor's comfort package'. While no substitute for its own enquiry and due diligence (and LR 8.3.1BG expressly requires the sponsor to use its own knowledge, judgment and expertise to review and challenge the information provided to it by third parties), receipt of the 'sponsor's comfort package' from the company and its advisers provides a degree of comfort to the sponsor in giving its declaration to the FCA. In turn, receipt of the declaration from the sponsor helps the FCA to determine that all relevant requirements of the LPDT Rules have been satisfied in connection with the transaction.

5.1 Sponsor's agreement, reports and comfort letters

The scope of the 'sponsor's comfort package' will depend on the type of transaction and the scope of the sponsor's obligations under Listing Rule 8.4, as well as particular facts or circumstances relating to the company, its business and the industry and jurisdictions in which it operates. The level and scope of comfort provided will be a matter for negotiation between the sponsor and its advisers and the company and its advisers.

The larger investment banks have developed standard sponsor comfort packages for different types of transactions.

Generally speaking, a greater degree of comfort is required by a sponsor from the company and its advisers on an IPO than on a further share issue; on a further share issue than on a Class 1 transaction; and on a Class 1 acquisition than on a Class 1 disposal.

Figures 3.10, 3.12, 3.14 and 3.16, respectively, set out the key items of comfort that will be required to be provided to a sponsor on, as the case may be, an application for admission of shares by a new applicant (e.g. an IPO), an application for admission of further shares by a listed company (e.g. a rights issue, a placing or an issue of shares as consideration on a large acquisition), on production of a circular by a listed company (e.g. in connection with a Class 1 acquisition or disposal or a large share buy-back) or on a transfer between listing categories. This comfort largely mirrors the confirmations required to be given by the sponsor to the FCA (as set out in Figures 3.3, 3.4, 3.5, 3.6 and 3.7 respectively).

5.1.1 Listing Rule 8 comfort letters

One of the key items of comfort is a comfort letter from the applicant or listed company to the sponsor confirming – on a back-to-back basis – the specific elements of the enquiries that the sponsor is obliged to make prior to giving its declaration to the FCA and of the declaration itself. This letter is commonly referred to as a 'Listing Rule 8 comfort letter'. Figures 3.11, 3.13, 3.15 and 3.17 set out illustrative forms of the Listing Rule 8 comfort letter that will be required to be given by the applicant or listed company to the sponsor in connection with, as the case may be, an application for admission of shares by a new applicant, an application for admission of further shares by a listed company, the production of a circular by a listed company or a transfer between listing categories.

Where a transaction by a listed company involves both an application for admission of further shares and the production of a circular (e.g. where the listed company intends to make a Class 1 acquisition and issue new shares as consideration) it is usual for the company to combine the confirmations to be given to the sponsor in one Listing Rule 8 comfort letter.

Figure 3.8: Relationship between the company, its advisers, its sponsor and the FCA

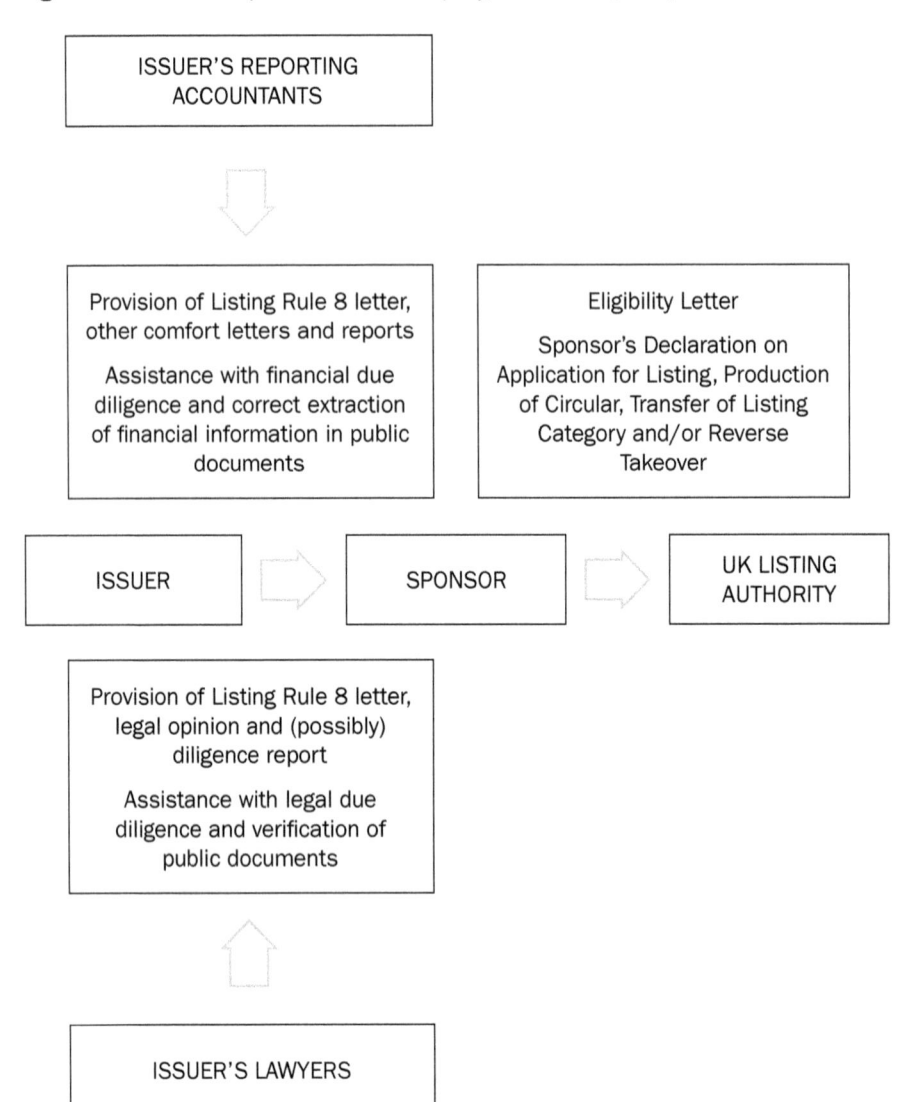

```
        ISSUER'S REPORTING
           ACCOUNTANTS
                  ⇩

Provision of Listing Rule 8 letter,         Eligibility Letter
other comfort letters and reports
                                       Sponsor's Declaration on
  Assistance with financial due        Application for Listing, Production
  diligence and correct extraction     of Circular, Transfer of Listing
  of financial information in public   Category and/or Reverse
           documents                           Takeover


                                                          UK LISTING
    ISSUER    ⇨    SPONSOR    ⇨                           AUTHORITY


Provision of Listing Rule 8 letter,
   legal opinion and (possibly)
          diligence report

   Assistance with legal due
  diligence and verification of
       public documents
                  ⇧
         ISSUER'S LAWYERS
```

5.1.2 Comfort from the company's reporting accountants

In order to obtain any comfort direct from the applicant's or listed company's reporting accountants, the sponsor will enter into an engagement letter with the applicant or listed company and their reporting accountants (an accountant's engagement letter) setting out, among other things:

- the scope of the reporting accountants' work;
- the form in which the reporting accountants will issue the results of their work (i.e. a report, a comfort letter or an opinion);
- to whom the results of their work will be addressed and by whom they may be relied upon (usually the company and the investment banks); and
- any limitations on the liability of the reporting accountants in providing their services (the limitations could take the form of a limited period in which to bring a claim or a restriction on the ability of the company or the investment banks to rely on their work in certain jurisdictions or for certain purposes or both, but typically would not include a cap on the accountants' liability).

Helpful guidance on the scope of reporting accountants' work and the professional standards that they are obliged to follow is set out in the FRC's *Standards for Investment Reporting* (SIRs). These were originally published by the Auditing Practices Board (part of the FRC) and copies are available on the FRC's website.

In summary, the SIRs cover the following areas:

- SIR 1000 – investment reporting standards applicable to all engagements in connection with an investment circular (published July 2005);
- SIR 2000 *(revised)* – investment reporting standards applicable to public reporting engagements on historical financial information (published March 2011);
- SIR 3000 – investment reporting standards applicable to public reporting engagements on profit forecasts (published January 2006);
- SIR 4000 – investment reporting standards applicable to public reporting engagements on pro forma financial information (published January 2006); and
- SIR 5000 – investment reporting standards applicable to public reporting engagements on financial information reconciliations under the Listing Rules (published February 2008).

5.1.3 Sponsor's agreement

As referred to above, depending on the nature of the transaction, the sponsor may require the applicant or listed company to enter into a sponsor's agreement. This may be a stand-alone agreement or, where the transaction also involves an underwritten equity offering, the relevant provisions may be combined with those provisions typically found in an underwriting agreement, in a sponsor's and underwriting agreement.

The principal purpose of a sponsor's agreement is to:

- confirm the appointment of a sponsor by the company (although the sponsor will typically be providing a sponsor service prior to entering into the sponsor's agreement due to the wide definition of 'sponsor service' in the Listing Rules, which includes, for example, preparatory work);

- set out the respective duties and responsibilities of the company and the sponsor in relation to the transaction, and in particular any applications for admission to listing and to trading; and
- provide the sponsor with warranties and indemnities in relation to any liabilities arising as a result of its role as sponsor.

The agreement also provides a useful framework for the delivery of the various comfort letters, reports and opinions, a full list of which is usually set out in a schedule to the agreement.

Figure 3.9 sets out the illustrative contents of a sponsor's agreement.

Figure 3.9: Illustrative contents of a sponsor's agreement

Key clause	Purpose of the provision
Parties	The parties to the agreement will be the sponsor and the company. They may also include the directors of the company and selling shareholders in the case of an IPO.
Recitals	These set out the background to and overview of the transaction and the purpose of the agreement.
Appointment of sponsor	The agreement will formally appoint the sponsor – generally the company's broker or proposed broker – as sponsor and give the sponsor the necessary discretion and authority to carry out its role. This clause will also deal with the role of joint sponsors and the duties of the sponsor to the FCA.
Publication of announcements and documents	The company will give certain undertakings to the sponsor in relation to the publication of announcements and public documents in connection with the transaction.
Delivery of comfort letters to sponsor	The agreement provides the framework for the delivery of the various comfort letters and reports that are given to the sponsor by the company and their respective advisers. These documents will assist in providing a potential defence to any legal or regulatory actions or claims in connection with the public documents or the transaction and assist the sponsor in giving its relevant declaration to the FCA.
Conduct of business	A sponsor's duties continue to apply through to admission or completion of the transaction and therefore the sponsor may seek undertakings from the company in relation to the period following publication of the relevant document and admission or completion (as applicable) (see UKLA Guidance Note *Sponsor services: Principles for sponsors* (UKLA/TN/710.1)).

Key clause	Purpose of the provision
Warranties	Warranties are generally required to be given by the company (and, on an IPO or introduction to listing, may also be required to be given by the directors of the company and selling shareholders) to the sponsor on the initial date of publication of the document and on the date of publication of any supplementary announcement or document. Where there is an admission of securities, the sponsor will also request repetition of warranties at admission.
	The scope of the warranties will vary depending on the transaction and the person giving them. Where the agreement is entered into in connection with an IPO or introduction to listing, the sponsor will require a full set of warranties covering the prospectus, the company, its management, its business and assets, its financial results etc. If the agreement is entered into in connection with a Class 1 transaction or on a further listing of shares, the warranties will be more limited in scope and focus on the contents of the public document, the impact of the transaction on the listed company and the key warranties.
Indemnity	A key requirement for the investment bank acting as sponsor will be for the company to grant an indemnity pursuant to which the sponsor is indemnified against any liabilities arising in connection with the public document and the transaction.
Termination	The sponsor will generally require the right to terminate the agreement in circumstances where the company or other parties fail to comply with their obligations, there is a breach of warranty, or the sponsor ceases to be able to act as sponsor pursuant to the Listing Rules (e.g. due to a conflict of interest) among other things.
Assignment and variation	Generally no party will have the right to assign or vary the agreement without the consent of the other.
Governing law and jurisdiction	This will invariably be English law and the English courts. The sponsor may retain the right to bring an action against the company, or join the company to proceedings, in another jurisdiction, particularly if the transaction also involves a capital raising.

5.2 Directors' responsibilities and understanding of obligations

A prospectus must contain a responsibility statement from at least, the company and the company's directors (PR 5.5.3R and item 1 of Annex I of PR Appendix 3). Similarly, Class 1 circulars must also include a responsibility statement (LR 13.4.1R(4)). In support of this, the company will usually require the directors to confirm in writing that they understand the requirements for a prospectus or a circular, as the case may be, and accept responsibility in the terms required.

This confirmation is ordinarily obtained in the form of a responsibility statement or letter which each director will be required to sign having reviewed the prospectus or circular and a memorandum prepared by the company's lawyers which summarises the directors' responsibilities and obligations in connection with the transaction under the LPDT Rules and MAR.

The sponsor will usually request that the directors' responsibility letters are also addressed to it, even if on a limited or no reliance basis, in order to provide some comfort in its role as sponsor that the directors understand and accept their responsibilities and obligations. It also assists in evidencing compliance by the sponsor with its obligations under Listing Rule 8.3 (see sections 3 and 4).

5.3 Admission detrimental to investors' interests

In relation to an application for admission for a new applicant (see section 2.1 of Chapter 2), LR 8.4.3R(3) requires a sponsor to ensure that all matters known to it which, in its reasonable opinion, should be taken into account by the FCA in considering (among other things) *'whether the admission of the shares would be detrimental to investors' interests'* have been disclosed with sufficient prominence in the prospectus, or otherwise in writing to the FCA. This is backed up in the form of the declaration that a sponsor is required to give to the FCA in connection with an application for admission on behalf of a new applicant (see Figure 3.3).

The uncertainty of the meaning and possible breadth of the test of 'detrimental to investors' interests', combined with the difficulty in determining how compliance would be assessed (especially with the benefit of hindsight), clearly poses a problem for sponsors. The FSA, as it then was, previously stated that exercise of its discretion to refuse an application for admission on the basis that it would be detrimental to investors' interests has always carried a high materiality threshold and that it had never interpreted this to apply, for example, simply to a risk that the share price could go down after admission.

While no substitute for its own due diligence and enquiries, to assist its enquiries a sponsor will seek comfort from the company, its legal advisers and reporting accountants that all material information has been included in the prospectus or disclosed in writing to the FCA.

The sponsor should bear in mind that if the FCA thinks that there may be a high risk that admission of the applicant's securities may be detrimental to investors' interests for a reason relating to the applicant, it may ask to see the applicant or sponsor's due diligence and may also commission its own (UKLA Guidance Note *Eligibility process (UKLA/PN/901.3)*).

5.4 Working capital

One of the disclosure items required to be included in prospectuses and certain circulars is a statement by the applicant or listed company that it has sufficient working capital for its present purposes, being at least 12 months from the date of the public document.

In the context of an application for admission to listing (new applicants and further issues), the production of a Class 1 circular (or certain other circulars) and an application to transfer between listing categories (save where the company was required to meet such requirements under its existing listing category (LR 8.4.16 R)), the sponsor cannot give its relevant declaration to the FCA unless it has come to a reasonable opinion, after due and careful enquiry, that 'the directors of the company have a reasonable basis upon which to make the working capital statement'.

The sponsor will require the management of the company to prepare working capital and cash-flow projections that are approved by the directors. It is customary for the company's reporting accountants to review these projections and prepare a detailed working capital report for review by and discussion with the company and its sponsor and other investment banks involved in the transaction.

In addition, both the company and its reporting accountants will be required to provide a comfort letter on the working capital statement to the sponsor in connection with its transaction specific obligations under LR 8.4.

In the UKLA Guidance Note *The sponsor's role on working capital confirmations (UKLA/TN/704.3)*, the FCA gives guidance on a sponsor's role in relation to the working capital confirmation. It states that a sponsor should apply its judgement, experience, knowledge and expertise on the Listing Rules, the disclosure requirements and Transparency Rules when deciding if a company has a reasonable basis to make the working capital statement, having regard to the company's circumstances and the context of the transaction (see also LR 8.3.1BG). It states that a sponsor's role is in addition to the work done by third parties (i.e. the company and its reporting accountants) and that reliance on third-party work alone will not be sufficient evidence that a sponsor has discharged its obligations. Specifically, a sponsor should review and challenge the work of the company and reporting accountant, using its own knowledge of the company and its business and industry, to ensure that the conclusions reached are the right ones under the circumstances.

The sponsor should have regard to the guidance relating to working capital statements given to companies in paragraphs 107 to 126 of the ESMA Recommendations and in particular the principles for preparing such statements set out in paragraphs 124 to 126 of the ESMA Recommendations.

Where there are uncertain market conditions or a transaction involves a 'rescue' element, particular attention should be paid to the working capital statement and sponsors should consider carefully how to assess working capital in these situations. The

FCA, in the UKLA Guidance Note *Sponsors: Uncertain market conditions (UKLA/ TN/705.2)*, states that it is important for sponsors to carry out sufficient due diligence, notes a number of issues that may arise and makes suggestions for approaching the due diligence in these circumstances.

It is important that the sponsor keeps clear records showing the work that it has done and procedures it has been through to reach an opinion on the working capital statement, in addition to receiving and keeping copies of the documents prepared by the company and its reporting accountants during the process.

5.5 Significant change

Another of the specific disclosure items required to be included in both a prospectus and certain circulars is a statement by the company of any significant change in its financial or trading position or that of its group since the end of the last financial period for which either audited financial information or interim financial information has been published.

As well as making its own enquiries of the directors and management team of the company, the sponsor will require the company's reporting accountants to make enquiries of management and to review management accounts and any other financial information that may be available for the period since the end of the company's last financial period and compare it with corresponding information from the prior year in order to identify any items that could constitute a significant change in the financial or trading position of the company or its group.

In addition, and given the importance of the disclosure, the company is often required to give a direct confirmation of any significant change to the sponsor either as part of the company's Listing Rule 8 comfort letter or in a separate comfort letter addressed to the sponsor.

A significant change statement in relation to the target group will also be required in a Class 1 acquisition circular and similar steps will be taken in relation to the target as set out above in relation to the company.

5.6 Historical financial information and pro forma financial information

The reporting accountants will be required to provide an opinion in connection with the historical financial information included in a prospectus or circular, to review and opine upon the basis of preparation of any pro forma financial information included in a prospectus or circular and to provide comfort that any numbers referred to in the body of a prospectus or circular have been correctly extracted from the company's audited annual financial statements, unaudited interim financial statements or other underlying accounting records (this is referred to as 'correct extraction' comfort).

5.7 Compliance with the Listing Rules and the Prospectus Rules

In the context of an application for admission to listing, an application for transfer between listing categories and the production of a Class 1 circular, the sponsor is required to confirm to the FCA that having made due and careful enquiry, it has come to a reasonable opinion that the relevant provisions of the Listing Rules and the Prospectus Rules have been complied with and that all material information and facts relevant to the listing or the transaction have been disclosed with sufficient prominence in the document or otherwise in writing to the FCA.

To assist in giving these confirmations to the FCA, the sponsor will seek comfort from each of the company, the company's lawyer and the reporting accountants. The confirmation from the company will be included in its Listing Rule 8 comfort letter (see Figures 3.11, 3.13, 3.15 and 3.17).

5.8 Continuing obligations and financial reporting procedures

5.8.1 Procedures to enable compliance with the LPDT Rules and obligations under MAR

In relation to an application for admission for a new applicant (e.g. on an IPO), LR 8.4.2R(3) states that a sponsor must not submit the application to the FCA 'unless it has come to a reasonable opinion, having made due and careful enquiry, that the directors of the applicant have established procedures which enable the applicant to comply with the Listing Rules and the disclosure requirements and Transparency Rules on an ongoing basis'.

During the consultation process in relation to the implementation of the PD in the UK, the FSA (the predecessor to the FCA) clarified that this assessment by the sponsor only has to be made once on admission.

The requirement in LR 8.4.2R(3) is in addition to the requirement in LR 8.4.2R(4) for the sponsor to give comfort in relation to the directors having 'established procedures which enable them to make proper judgments on an ongoing basis as to the financial position and prospects of the applicant and its group'.

The sponsor's obligation under LR 8.4.2R(3) is borne out by Listing Principle 1, which requires a listed company to take reasonable steps to establish and maintain adequate procedures, systems and controls to enable it to comply with its obligations. In its guidance on Listing Principle 1, the FCA states that listed companies should place particular emphasis on adequate procedures, systems and controls in relation to compliance with Listing Rule 10 (Significant Transactions) and Listing Rule 11 (Related Party Transactions) and the timely and accurate disclosure of information (both financial and non-financial) to the market (LR 7.2.2G). The FCA further states that listed companies should have adequate systems and controls to ensure that they can properly identify information which requires disclosure under the Listing Rules, disclosure requirements, Transparency Rules or Corporate Governance Rules in a timely manner and ensure it is properly considered by directors and that such consideration should encompass whether the information should be disclosed (LR 7.2.3G).

Accordingly, on an IPO, in addition to making enquiries of management on both financial and non-financial reporting systems, procedures and controls, a sponsor will typically seek a report on financial position and prospects procedures (and a related comfort letter) from the reporting accountants and a comfort letter from the company in relation to its ability to comply with its continuing obligations as a listed company under the LPDT Rules and under MAR together with a copy of the relevant company manuals.

Save where the company was required to meet such requirement under its existing listing category (LR 8.4.16R), a sponsor is also required to reach similar opinions to those set out in LR 8.4.2R(3) and LR 8.4.2R(4) in the context of an application for transfer between listing categories in accordance with LR 8.4.15R(3) and LR 8.4.15R(4).

The UKLA Guidance Note *Sponsor's obligations on financial position and prospects procedures (UKLA/TN/708.2)* provides helpful guidance on the sponsor's obligations in relation to financial position and prospects procedures (FPPP). As with the sponsor's role in relation to the working capital confirmation, the FCA emphasises that the sponsor's role is in addition to the role of the company and the reporting accountants and that review and challenge of their work is required. The guidance suggests that a sponsor may wish to carry out an analysis in the context of the directors' regulatory obligations, which identifies the necessary procedures that should be in place at admission to generate the information required to make proper judgements on FPPP, the quality and extent of the procedures in place and the extent to which there are any gaps. The guidance also emphasises that receipt of a comfort letter from the reporting accountants without appropriate enquiry and challenge will not be sufficient evidence to show that the sponsor has reached its opinion having made due and careful enquiry. Finally, the guidance states the importance of record keeping in relation to FPPP due diligence, in particular when defining the scope of the reporting accountant's work and reviewing the reporting accountant's recommendations and observations.

In relation to 'established procedures' as used in LR 8.4.2R(3), the FCA acknowledges that at the time the sponsor's declaration is given, not all of the procedures will have operated, but the FCA's expectation is that the procedures should have been designed, approved and communicated to those responsible for implementation and use following admission.

5.8.2 Impact of a transaction on ability to comply with continuing obligations

In relation to listed companies undertaking a Class 1 transaction, LR 8.4.12R(2) states that a sponsor must not submit an application for approval of a Class 1 circular to the FCA 'unless it has come to a reasonable opinion, having made due and careful enquiry, that the transaction will not have an adverse impact on the listed company's ability to comply with the Listing Rules or the disclosure requirements and Transparency Rules'.

The FCA has stated that this does not require the sponsor to provide assurance on an ongoing basis (i.e. it is a one-off assessment). However, the sponsor will nonetheless have to decide what enquiries to make to assess the impact of a particular transaction on the listed company and its compliance and reporting procedures, systems and controls. Given the breadth of the listed company's obligations under the Listing Rules and the disclosure requirements and Transparency Rules in relation to having in place systems, procedures and controls to enable compliance on an ongoing basis, the sponsor will need to make various enquiries in relation to the impact of the transaction.

For example, a disposal of part of the listed company's business or of a key subsidiary may result in the loss of key staff or those key to the company's systems, procedures and controls and might well have an adverse impact on the company's ability to comply with the Listing Rules or the disclosure requirements and Transparency Rules; so too might the acquisition of a private company which does not have in place adequate systems, procedures and controls to enable compliance with the Listing Rules or the disclosure requirements and Transparency Rules or which has a large number of employees who have inadequate familiarity with the requirements of the Listing Rules or the disclosure requirements and Transparency Rules. See, for example, the FCA enforcement decision in the case of Lamprell plc, summarised in Figure 1.3 in Chapter 1.

To get comfort on this, the sponsor will make enquiries of management on the impact of the transaction on the company's financial and non-financial reporting systems, procedures and controls. A sponsor often seeks a report on the impact of the transaction on the listed company's financial reporting systems, procedures and controls (and a related comfort letter) from the reporting accountants and an accompanying Board memorandum (and a related comfort letter) from the company on the impact of the transaction on the company's ability to comply with its continuing obligations as a listed company.

Figure 3.10: Application for admission of shares by a new applicant – key sponsor comfort

Key confirmations to be provided to the sponsor by the applicant and its advisers	Applicable LPDT Rules
LR 8 *Comfort letter from the applicant* confirming that:	
■ the directors of the applicant have been advised on and understand their responsibilities and obligations under the Listing Rules and the disclosure requirements and Transparency Rules	LR 8.3.4R

Key confirmations to be provided to the sponsor by the applicant and its advisers	Applicable LPDT Rules
■ the applicant has satisfied all requirements of the Listing Rules relevant to an application for admission to listing	LR 8.4.2R(1)
■ the applicant has satisfied all applicable requirements set out in the Prospectus Rules	LR 8.4.2R(2)
■ the directors of the applicant have established procedures which enable the applicant to comply with the Listing Rules and the disclosure requirements and Transparency Rules on an ongoing basis	LR 8.4.2R(3)
■ the directors of the applicant have established procedures which provide a reasonable basis for them to make proper judgments on an ongoing basis as to the financial position and prospects of the applicant and its group	LR 8.4.2R(4)
■ the directors of the applicant have a reasonable basis on which to make the working capital statement required to be made by LR 6.1.16R	LR 8.4.2R(5)
■ all matters known to the applicant which, in its reasonable opinion, should be taken into account by the FCA in considering (i) the application for listing and (ii) whether the admission of the equity shares would be detrimental to the investors' interests, have been disclosed with sufficient prominence in the prospectus or otherwise in writing to the FCA.	LR 8.4.3R(3)
Directors' responsibility statements	Item 1.2, Ann I PR App 3
LR 8 *Comfort letter from the applicant's lawyers* confirming that:	
■ the directors of the applicant have been provided with advice on their responsibilities and obligations under the Listing Rules and the disclosure requirements and Transparency Rules	LR 8.3.1R(2) and LR 8.3.4R
■ as a result of their role in connection with the application for admission to listing, they are not aware of any matter that is not disclosed in the prospectus which they consider is required to be brought to the sponsor's attention in the context of its obligations, other than matters of which they believe the sponsor is aware.	LR 8.4.2R(1) and (2)
Comfort letter, report or opinion from the reporting accountants confirming:	
■ that they have reported to the applicant and the sponsor all matters material to the transaction	LR 8.4.2R(1) and LR 8.4.3R(3)

ROLE AND RESPONSIBILITIES OF A SPONSOR

Key confirmations to be provided to the sponsor by the applicant and its advisers	Applicable LPDT Rules
■ that the directors of the applicant have established procedures which provide a reasonable basis for them to make proper judgments on an ongoing basis as to the financial position and prospects of the applicant and its group	LR 8.4.2R(4)
■ that the directors of the applicant have a reasonable basis on which to make the working capital statement required to be made by LR 6.1.16R	LR 8.4.2R(5)
■ that the historical financial information included in the prospectus gives a true and fair view	Item 20.1, Ann I PR App 3
■ a report in relation to any pro forma financial information and any profit estimate or forecast	Item 7, Ann II and Item 13.2, Ann I PR App 3
■ any significant change in the financial or trading position of the applicant and its group since the end of the last audited financial period	Item 20.9, Ann I PR App 3
■ that financial information in the prospectus has been properly extracted from the underlying source.	

Figure 3.11: Application for admission of shares by a new applicant – illustrative form of company's comfort letter

[PRINT LETTER ON COMPANY'S LETTERHEAD]

[INSERT NAME AND ADDRESS OF SPONSOR]

[DATE]

Dear Sirs

[NAME OF COMPANY] (the 'Company')

1. We refer to the submission to the Financial Conduct Authority (the 'FCA') for the approval of a prospectus (the 'Prospectus') and application for admission to listing on the premium segment of the Official List of [DESCRIPTION OF THE SHARES] (the 'shares') in connection with the Company's proposed [DESCRIPTION OF THE TRANSACTION] (the 'Transaction').

2. For the purposes of this letter, the 'Listing Rules', the 'Transparency Rules' and the 'Prospectus Rules' shall mean those rules made under Part VI of the Financial Services and Markets Act 2000, as set out in the FCA Handbook and 'disclosure requirements' shall mean Articles 17 to 19 of EU Regulation 596/2014 on market abuse.

3. We understand that:
    (i) under Listing Rule 8.3.1R, a sponsor to the Company must provide assurance to the FCA, when required, that the responsibilities of the applicant under the Listing Rules have been met, and must guide the applicant in understanding and meeting its responsibilities under the Listing Rules and the disclosure requirements and Transparency Rules;

    (ii) under Listing Rule 8.3.4R, where a sponsor gives any guidance or advice to an applicant in relation to the application or interpretation of the Listing Rules or the disclosure requirements and Transparency Rules, the sponsor must take reasonable steps to satisfy itself that the directors of the applicant understand their responsibilities and obligations under the Listing Rules and the disclosure requirements and Transparency Rules;

    (iii) as sponsor to the Company, prior to submitting a Sponsor's Declaration on an Application for Listing to the FCA, you are obliged to have come to a reasonable opinion, having made due and careful enquiry, that the Company complies with the requirements set out in Listing Rule 8.4.2R; and

    (iv) under Listing Rule 8.4.3R(3), in relation to submitting a Sponsor's Declaration on an Application for Listing, as sponsor you must, inter alia, ensure that all matters known to you which, in your reasonable opinion, should be taken into account by the FCA in considering the Transaction have been disclosed with sufficient prominence in the Prospectus or otherwise in writing to the FCA.

4. Having made due and careful enquiry, we confirm that, to the best of our knowledge and belief:
    (i) we have satisfied all the requirements of the Listing Rules relevant to the application for admission to listing of the Shares;

    (ii) we have satisfied all applicable requirements set out in the Prospectus Rules;

    (iii) we have established procedures which enable the Company to comply with the Listing Rules and the disclosure requirements and Transparency Rules on an ongoing basis;

    (iv) we have established procedures which provide a reasonable basis for the directors of the Company to make proper judgements on an ongoing basis as to the financial position and prospects of the Company and its group;

    (v) the directors of the Company have a reasonable basis on which to make the working capital statement required to be made by Listing Rule 6.1.16R; and

    (vi) all matters known to us which should be taken into account by the FCA in considering the Transaction have been disclosed with sufficient prominence in the Prospectus or otherwise in writing to the FCA.

5. We also confirm that the Company's solicitors, [NAME OF COMPANY's LAWYERS], have explained to the directors of the Company by way of a memorandum dated [DATE], a copy of which has been received by you, and in person at the meeting of the Board of directors of the Company held on [DATE] the nature and extent of their responsibilities and obligations as directors of a listed company under the Listing Rules and the disclosure requirements and Transparency Rules and the directors have confirmed that they have read and understood the memorandum and understand their responsibilities and obligations as directors of a listed company.

6. We undertake to inform you immediately, in writing, if we become aware at any time before admission of the Shares of any matter which may, in any way, affect the confirmations referred to in this letter.

7. This letter has been considered and approved at a meeting of the Board of the directors of the Company. We acknowledge that you will be relying on this letter when making your declarations to the FCA under Listing Rule 8.4.3R(1), in making the assessments you are required to make as sponsor pursuant to Listing Rule 8.4.2R and in relation to your responsibility under Listing Rule 8.4.3R(3).

8. This letter is provided to you solely for this purpose and, save for disclosure to the FCA, may not be disclosed to any person or referred to or quoted in any other context without our prior written consent.

Yours faithfully

Director/Company Secretary
for and on behalf of [NAME OF COMPANY]

Figure 3.12: Application for admission of further shares by a listed company – key sponsor comfort

Key confirmations to be provided to the sponsor by the listed company and its advisers	Applicable LPDT Rules
LR 8 *Comfort letter from the listed company* confirming that:	
▪ the directors of the listed company have been advised on and understand their responsibilities and obligations under the Listing Rules and the disclosure requirements and Transparency Rules	LR 8.3.1R(2) LR 8.3.4R
▪ the listed company has satisfied all requirements of the Listing Rules relevant to an application for admission to listing	LR 8.4.8R(1)
▪ the listed company has satisfied all applicable requirements set out in the Prospectus Rules	LR 8.4.8R(2)
▪ the directors of the applicant have a reasonable basis on which to make the working capital statement required to be made by LR 6.1.16R (or the qualified working capital statement in accordance with LR 6.1.17G)	LR 8.4.8R(3)

Key confirmations to be provided to the sponsor by the listed company and its advisers	Applicable LPDT Rules
■ all matters known to the listed company which, in its reasonable opinion, should be taken into account by the FCA in considering the application for listing have been disclosed with sufficient prominence in the prospectus or otherwise in writing to the FCA.	LR 8.4.9R(3)
Directors' responsibility statements	Item 1.2, Ann I PR App 3
LR 8 Comfort letter from the listed company's lawyers confirming that:	
■ the directors of the listed company have been provided with advice on their responsibilities and obligations under the Listing Rules and the disclosure requirements and Transparency Rules	LR 8.3.1R(2) and LR 8.3.4R
■ as a result of their role in connection with the application for admission of further shares to listing, they are not aware of any matter that is not disclosed in the prospectus which they consider is required to be brought to the sponsor's attention in the context of its obligations, other than matters of which it believes the sponsor is aware.	LR 8.4.8R(1) and (2)
Comfort letter, report or opinion from the reporting accountants confirming:	
■ that they have reported to the applicant and the sponsor all matters material to the transaction	LR 8.4.8R(1) and (2) LR 8.4.9R(3)
■ that the directors of the applicant have a reasonable basis on which to make the working capital statement required to be made by LR 6.1.16R (or, as the case may be, the qualified working capital statement required by LR 6.1.17G)	LR 8.4.8R(3)
■ that the historical financial information included in the prospectus gives a true and fair view	Item 20.1, Ann I PR App 3
■ a report in relation to any pro forma financial information and any profit forecast or estimate	Item 1, Ann II and item 13.2, Ann I PR App 3.
■ any significant change in the financial or trading position of the listed company and its group since the end of the last audited financial period	Item 20.9, Ann I PR App 3
■ that financial information in the prospectus has been properly extracted from the underlying source.	LR 13.5.7G

Figure 3.13: Application for admission of further shares by a listed company – illustrative form of company's comfort letter

---

[PRINT LETTER ON COMPANY'S LETTERHEAD]

[INSERT NAME AND ADDRESS OF SPONSOR]

[DATE]

Dear Sirs

[NAME OF COMPANY] (the 'Company')

1. We refer to the submission to the Financial Conduct Authority (the 'FCA') for the approval of a prospectus (the 'Prospectus) and application for admission to listing on premium segment of the Official List of [DESCRIPTION OF THE SHARES] (the 'shares') in connection with the Company's proposed [DESCRIPTION OF THE TRANSACTION] (the 'Transaction').

2. For the purposes of this letter, the 'Listing Rules', the 'Transparency Rules' and the 'Prospectus Rules' shall mean those rules made under Part 6 of the Financial Services and Markets Act 2000, as set out in the FCA Handbook and 'disclosure requirements' shall mean Articles 17 to 19 of EU Regulation 596/2014 on market abuse.

3. We understand that:

    (i) under Listing Rule 8.3.1R, a sponsor to the Company must provide assurance to the FCA, when required, that the responsibilities of the listed company under the Listing Rules have been met, and must guide the listed company in understanding and meeting its responsibilities under the Listing Rules, the disclosure requirements and Transparency Rules;

    (ii) under Listing Rule 8.3.4R, where a sponsor gives any guidance or advice to a listed company in relation to the application or interpretation of the Listing Rules or the disclosure requirements and Transparency Rules, the sponsor must take reasonable steps to satisfy itself that the directors of the listed company understand their responsibilities and obligations under the Listing Rules and the disclosure requirements and Transparency Rules;

    (iii) as sponsor to the Company, prior to submitting a Sponsor's Declaration on an Application for Listing to the FCA, you are obliged to have come to a reasonable opinion, having made due and careful enquiry, that the Company complies with the requirements set out in Listing Rule 8.4.8R; and

    (iv) under Listing Rule 8.4.9R(3), in relation to submitting a Sponsor's Declaration on an Application for Listing, as sponsor you must, inter alia, ensure that all matters known to you which, in your reasonable opinion, should be taken into account by the FCA in considering the Transaction have been disclosed with sufficient prominence in the Prospectus or otherwise in writing to the FCA.

4. Having made due and careful enquiry, we confirm that, to the best of our knowledge and belief:
   (i) we have satisfied all the requirements of the Listing Rules relevant to the application for admission to listing of the Shares;
   (ii) we have satisfied all applicable requirements set out in the Prospectus Rules;
   (iii) the directors of the Company have a reasonable basis on which to make the working capital statement required to be made by Listing Rule 6.1.16R; and
   (iv) all matters known to us which should be taken into account by the FCA in considering the Transaction have been disclosed with sufficient prominence in the Prospectus or otherwise in writing to the FCA.
5. We also confirm that the Company's solicitors, [NAME OF COMPANY's LAWYERS], have explained to the directors of the Company by way of a memorandum dated [DATE], a copy of which has been received by you, and in person at the meeting of the Board of directors of the Company held on [DATE] their responsibilities and obligations as directors of a listed company under the Listing Rules and the disclosure requirements and Transparency Rules and the directors have confirmed that they have read and understood the memorandum and understand their responsibilities and obligations as directors of a listed company.
6. We undertake to inform you immediately, in writing, if we become aware at any time before admission of the Shares of any matter which may, in any way, affect the confirmations referred to in this letter.
7. This letter has been considered and approved at a meeting of the Board of the directors of the Company. We acknowledge that you will be relying on this letter when making your declarations to the FCA under Listing Rule 8.4.9R(1), in making the assessments you are required to make as sponsor pursuant to Listing Rule 8.4.8R and in relation to your responsibility under Listing Rule 8.4.9R(3).
8. This letter is provided to you solely for this purpose and, save for disclosure to the FCA, may not be disclosed to any person or referred to or quoted in any other context without our prior written consent.

Yours faithfully

Director/Company Secretary
for and on behalf of [NAME OF COMPANY]

Figure 3.14: Production of a circular by a listed company – key sponsor comfort

Key confirmations to be provided to the sponsor by the listed company and its advisers	Applicable LPDT Rules
LR 8 *Comfort letter from the listed company* confirming that:	
■ the directors of the listed company have been advised on and understand their responsibilities under the Listing Rules and the disclosure requirements and Transparency Rules	LR 8.3.1R(2) LR 8.3.4R

Key confirmations to be provided to the sponsor by the listed company and its advisers	Applicable LPDT Rules
■ the listed company has satisfied all requirements of the Listing Rules relevant to the production of a Class 1 circular or other circular	LR 8.4.12R(1)
■ the transaction will not have an adverse impact on the listed company's ability to comply with the Listing Rules or the disclosure requirements and Transparency Rules	LR 8.4.12R(2)
■ the directors of the listed company have a reasonable basis on which to make the working capital statement required to be made by LR 9.5.12R, LR 13.4.1R or LR 13.7.1R	LR 8.4.12R(3)
■ all matters known to the listed company which, in their reasonable opinion, should be taken into account by the FCA in considering the transaction have been disclosed with sufficient prominence in the documentation or otherwise in writing to the FCA.	LR 8.4.13R(3)
Directors' responsibility statements	Item 1.2, Ann I PR App 3
LR 8 Comfort letter from the listed company's lawyers confirming that:	
■ the directors of the listed company have been provided with advice on their responsibilities under the Listing Rules and the disclosure requirements and Transparency Rules	LR 8.3.1R(2) and LR 8.3.4R
■ as a result of their role in connection with the application for admission to listing, they are not aware of any matter that is not disclosed in the circular which they consider is required to be brought to the sponsor's attention in the context of its obligations, other than matters of which they believe the sponsor is aware.	LR 8.4.12R(1)
Comfort letter, report or opinion from the reporting accountants confirming:	
■ that they have reported to the listed company and the sponsor all matters material to the transaction	LR 8.4.12R(1) and (2) LR 8.4.13R(3)
■ that the directors of the listed company have a reasonable basis on which to make the working capital statement required to be made by LR 9.5.12R, LR 13.4.1R or LR 13.7.1R	LR 8.4.12R(3)
■ any significant change in the financial or trading position of the listed company and its group (and in the case of a Class 1 acquisition, of the target group) since the end of the last audited financial period	LR 13 Annex 1R (Item 20.9, Ann I PR App 3)

Key confirmations to be provided to the sponsor by the listed company and its advisers	Applicable LPDT Rules
■ where a circular contains a modified accountants' report, whether the modification is significant to the shareholders and, if so, the reason why	LR 13.4.2R
■ where a circular contains a financial information table that must be accompanied by an accountants' report, whether: (i) for the purposes of the circular, the financial information table gives a true and fair view of the financial matters set out in it; and (ii) the financial information table has been prepared in a form that is consistent with the accounting policies adopted in the listed company's latest annual accounts	LR 13.5.21R and LR 13.5.22R
■ where a circular contains a reconciliation of a target's historical financial information on the basis of the listed company's accounting policies, whether: (i) the reconciliation has been has been properly compiled on the basis stated; and (ii) the adjustments are appropriate for the purpose of presenting the target's historical financial information on a basis consistent in all material respects with the company's accounting policies	LR 13.5.27R(2)
■ a report in relation to any pro forma financial information and any profit estimate or forecast	Item 7, Ann II and Item 13.2, Ann I PR App 3
■ that financial information in the prospectus has been properly extracted from the underlying source.	LR 13.5.7G

Figure 3.15: Production of a circular by a listed company – illustrative form of company's comfort letter

---

[PRINT LETTER ON COMPANY'S LETTERHEAD]

[INSERT NAME AND ADDRESS OF SPONSOR]

[DATE]

Dear Sirs
[NAME OF COMPANY] (the 'Company')

1. We refer to the submission to the Financial Conduct Authority (the 'FCA') for the approval of a circular (the 'Circular') in connection with the Company's proposed [DESCRIPTION OF THE TRANSACTION] (the 'Transaction').
2. For the purposes of this letter, the 'Listing Rules', the 'Transparency Rules' and the 'Prospectus Rules' shall mean those rules made under Part VI of the Financial Services and Markets Act 2000, as set out in the FCA Handbook and 'disclosure requirements' shall mean Articles 17 to 19 of EU Regulation 596/2014 on market abuse.
3. We understand that:
   (i) under Listing Rule 8.3.1R, a sponsor to the Company must provide assurance to the FCA, when required, that the responsibilities of the listed company under the Listing Rules have been met, and must guide the listed company in understanding and meeting its responsibilities under the Listing Rules, the disclosure requirements and Transparency Rules;
   (ii) under Listing Rule 8.3.4R, where a sponsor gives any guidance or advice to a listed company in relation to the application or interpretation of the Listing Rules or the disclosure requirements and Transparency Rules, the sponsor must take reasonable steps to satisfy itself that the directors of the listed company understand their responsibilities and obligations under the Listing Rules and the disclosure requirements and Transparency Rules;
   (iii) as sponsor to the Company, prior to submitting a Sponsor's Declaration on the Production of a Circular to the FCA, you are obliged to have come to a reasonable opinion, having made due and careful enquiry, that the Company complies with the requirements set out in Listing Rule 8.4.12R; and
   (iv) under Listing Rule 8.4.13R(3), in relation to submitting a Sponsor's Declaration on the Production of a Circular, as sponsor you must, inter alia, ensure that all matters known to you which, in your reasonable opinion, should be taken into account by the FCA in considering the Transaction have been disclosed with sufficient prominence in the Circular or otherwise in writing to the FCA.
4. Having made due and careful enquiry, we confirm that, to the best of our knowledge and belief:
   (i) we have satisfied all the requirements of the Listing Rules relevant to the production of the Circular;
   (ii) the Transaction will not have an adverse impact on the Company's ability to comply with the Listing Rules or the disclosure requirements and Transparency Rules;
   (iii) the directors of the Company have a reasonable basis on which to make the working capital statement required to be made by Listing Rule 13.4.1R and Annex 1 to Listing Rule 13; and
   (iv) all matters known to us which should be taken into account by the FCA in considering the Transaction have been disclosed with sufficient prominence in the Circular or otherwise in writing to the FCA.

5. We also confirm that the Company's solicitors, [NAME OF COMPANY'S LAWYERS], have explained to the directors of the Company by way of a memorandum dated [DATE], a copy of which you have received, and in person at the meeting of the Board of directors of the Company held on [DATE] their responsibilities and obligations as directors of a listed company under the Listing Rules, the disclosure requirements and Transparency Rules and the directors have confirmed that they have read and understood the memorandum and understand their responsibilities and obligations as directors of a listed company.

6. We undertake to inform you immediately, in writing, if we become aware at any time before the publication of the Circular of any matter which may, in any way, affect the confirmations referred to in this letter.

7. This letter has been considered and approved at a meeting of the Board of the directors of the Company. We acknowledge that you will be relying on this letter when making your declarations to the FCA under Listing Rule 8.4.13R(1), in making the assessments you are required to make as sponsor pursuant to Listing Rule 8.4.12R and in relation to your responsibility under Listing Rule 8.4.13R(3).

8. This letter is provided to you solely for this purpose and, save for disclosure to the FCA, may not be disclosed to any person or referred to or quoted in any other context without our prior written consent.

Yours faithfully

Director/Company Secretary
for and on behalf of [NAME OF COMPANY]

Figure 3.16: Application for transfer of listing category – key sponsor comfort

Key confirmations to be provided to the sponsor by the applicant and its advisers	Applicable LPDT Rules
LR 8 *Comfort letter from the applicant* confirming that:	
■ the directors of the applicant have been advised on and understand their responsibilities under the Listing Rules, the disclosure requirements and Transparency Rules	LR 8.3.1R(2) LR 8.3.4R
■ the applicant satisfies all eligibility requirements of the Listing Rules that are relevant to the new category to which it is seeking to transfer	LR 8.4.15R(1)
■ the applicant has satisfied all requirements relevant to the production of the circular (required under LR 5.4A.4R) or announcement (required under LR 5.4A.5R), as the case may be	LR 8.4.15R(2)

ROLE AND RESPONSIBILITIES OF A SPONSOR

Key confirmations to be provided to the sponsor by the applicant and its advisers	Applicable LPDT Rules
■ (to the extent that the applicant was not required to meet the requirement under its existing listing category) the directors of the applicant have established procedures which enable the applicant to comply with the Listing Rules and the disclosure requirements and Transparency Rules on an ongoing basis	LR 8.4.15R(3)
■ (to the extent that the applicant was not required to meet the requirement under its existing listing category) the directors of the applicant have established procedures which provide a reasonable basis for them to make proper judgments on an ongoing basis as to the financial position and prospects of the applicant and its group	LR 8.4.15R(4)
■ (to the extent that the applicant was not required to meet the requirement under its existing listing category) the directors of the applicant have a reasonable basis on which to make the working capital statement (if any) required in connection with the transfer	LR 8.4.15R(5)
■ all matters known to the applicant which, in its reasonable opinion, should be taken into account by the FCA in considering the transfer between listing categories have been disclosed with sufficient prominence in the circular or announcement (as the case may be) or otherwise in writing to the FCA.	LR 8.4.14R(3)
Directors' responsibility statements	Item 1.2, Ann I PR App 3
LR 8 Comfort letter from the applicant's lawyers confirming that:	
■ the directors of the applicant have been provided with advice on the their responsibilities under the Listing Rules and the disclosure requirements and Transparency Rules	LR 8.3.1R(2) and LR 8.3.4R
■ as a result of their role in connection with the application for admission to listing, they are not aware of any matter that is not disclosed in the circular or announcement which they consider is required to be brought to the sponsor's attention in the context of its obligations, other than matters of which they believe the sponsor is aware.	LR 8.4.15R(2)
Comfort letter, report or opinion from the reporting accountants confirming:	
■ that they have reported to the applicant and the sponsor all matters material to the transaction	LR 8.4.15R(1) and (2) LR 8.4.14R(3)

Key confirmations to be provided to the sponsor by the applicant and its advisers	Applicable LPDT Rules
■ (to the extent that the applicant was not required to meet the requirement under its existing listing category) that the directors of the applicant have established procedures which provide a reasonable basis for them to make proper judgments on an ongoing basis as to the financial position and prospects of the applicant and its group	LR 8.4.15R(4)
■ (to the extent that the applicant was not required to meet the requirement under its existing listing category) that the directors of the applicant have a reasonable basis on which to make the working capital statement required to be made (if any) required in connection with the transfer.	LR 8.4.15R(5)

Figure 3.17: Application for transfer of listing category – illustrative form of company's comfort letter

---

[PRINT LETTER ON COMPANY'S LETTERHEAD]

[INSERT NAME AND ADDRESS OF SPONSOR]

[DATE]

Dear Sirs

[NAME OF COMPANY] (the 'Company')

1. We refer to the submission to the Financial Conduct Authority (the 'FCA') for the approval of the Company's application to transfer its listing category from [DESCRIPTION OF THE TRANSACTION] (the 'Transaction') and the application for admission to listing on the premium segment of the Official List of [DESCRIPTION OF THE SHARES] (the 'shares') in connection with the Transaction.

2. For the purposes of this letter, the 'Listing Rules', the 'Transparency Rules' and the 'Prospectus Rules' shall mean those rules made under Part VI of the Financial Services and Markets Act 2000, as set out in the FCA Handbook and 'disclosure requirements' shall mean Articles 17 to 19 of EU Regulation 596/2014 on market abuse

3. We understand that:
    (i) under Listing Rule 8.3.1R, a sponsor to the Company must provide assurance to the FCA, when required, that the responsibilities of the applicant under the Listing Rules have been met, and must guide the applicant in understanding and meeting its responsibilities under the Listing Rules and the disclosure requirements and Transparency Rules;

(ii) under Listing Rule 8.3.4R, where a sponsor gives any guidance or advice to an applicant in relation to the application or interpretation of the Listing Rules or the disclosure requirements and Transparency Rules, the sponsor must take reasonable steps to satisfy itself that the directors of the applicant understand their responsibilities and obligations under the Listing Rules and the disclosure requirements and Transparency Rules;

(iii) as sponsor to the Company, prior to submitting a Sponsor's Declaration on Transfer of a Listing Category to the FCA, you are obliged to have come to a reasonable opinion, having made due and careful enquiry, that the Company complies with the requirements set out in Listing Rule 8.4.15R; and

(iv) under Listing Rule 8.4.14R(3), in relation to submitting a Sponsor's Declaration on Transfer of a Listing Category, as sponsor you must, inter alia, ensure that all matters known to you which, in your reasonable opinion, should be taken into account by the FCA in considering the Transaction have been disclosed with sufficient prominence in the circular or announcement (as the case may be) or otherwise in writing to the FCA.

4. Having made due and careful enquiry, we confirm that, to the best of our knowledge and belief:

   (i) we satisfy all eligibility requirements of the Listing Rules that are relevant to the new category to which we are seeking to transfer;

   (ii) we have satisfied all requirements relevant to the production of the circular required under LR 5.4A.4R/announcement required under LR 5.4A.5R;

   (iii) we have established procedures which enable the Company to comply with the Listing Rules and the disclosure requirements and Transparency Rules on an ongoing basis;

   (iv) we have established procedures which provide a reasonable basis for the directors of the Company to make proper judgements on an ongoing basis as to the financial position and prospects of the Company and its group;

   (v) the directors of the Company have a reasonable basis on which to make the working capital statement required in connection with the transfer; and

   (vi) all matters known to us which, on the basis of advice from yourselves and the Company's other advisers, should be taken into account by the FCA in considering the Transaction have been disclosed with sufficient prominence in the circular required under LR 5.4A.4R / announcement required under LR 5.4A.5R or otherwise in writing to the FCA.

5. We also confirm that the Company's solicitors, [NAME OF COMPANY's LAWYERS], have explained to the directors of the Company by way of a memorandum dated [DATE], a copy of which you have received, and in person at the meeting of the Board of directors of the Company held on [DATE] their responsibilities and obligations as directors of a listed company under the Listing Rules and the disclosure requirements and Transparency Rules and the directors have confirmed that they have read and understood the memorandum and understand their responsibilities and obligations as directors of a listed company.

6. We undertake to inform you immediately, in writing, if we become aware at any time before admission of the Shares of any matter which may, in any way, affect the confirmations referred to in this letter.

7. This letter has been considered and approved at a meeting of the Board of the directors of the Company. We acknowledge that you will be relying on this letter when making your declarations to the FCA under Listing Rule 8.4.14R(1), in making the assessments you are required to make as sponsor pursuant to Listing Rule 8.4.15R and in relation to your responsibility under Listing Rule 8.4.14R(3).

8. This letter is provided to you solely for this purpose and, save for disclosure to the FCA, may not be disclosed to any person or referred to or quoted in any other context without our prior written consent.

Yours faithfully

Director/Company Secretary
for and on behalf of [NAME OF COMPANY]

CHAPTER 4

Preparing and publishing a prospectus

OVERVIEW

- The Prospectus Directive (PD) and PD Regulation harmonised across Europe the circumstances in which a prospectus is required, as well as setting a common European standard for the format and content of a prospectus. Various amendments were made to the PD through the PD Amending Directive, which member states were required to implement by 1 July 2012, and through the Omnibus II Directive in 2016.
- Save where an exemption applies, a prospectus is required to be prepared and published in connection with an offer of transferable securities to the public (a public offer) or an admission to trading on a regulated market of transferable securities (admission to trading).
- A prospectus can comprise a single document or be 'tri-partite' comprising a summary, registration document and securities note. A prospectus must include a table of contents in a prescribed format, a summary and risk factors relating to the company, its business and its shares.
- Section 87A of the FSMA sets out the general duty of disclosure that applies to prospectuses and the PD Regulation prescribes specific disclosure that is required. The ESMA Recommendations provide guidance on disclosure required to satisfy the requirements of the PD Regulation.
- In the UK, a prospectus must be approved by the FCA before it can be published. The review period takes up to ten days for a new applicant and at least five days for a listed company. Once approved by the FCA, a prospectus must be made available to the public in accordance with the Prospectus Rules. The review process is iterative and therefore the approval process takes longer in practice.
- An approved prospectus can be 'passported' and used to offer shares to investors in any other member state. While the host member state may require a translation of the summary into a local language, it cannot impose any other substantive conditions and has no approval right.
- If a significant new matter arises following publication of a prospectus, the issuer may be required to prepare and publish a 'supplementary prospectus' in accordance with section 87G of the FSMA. The publication of a supplementary prospectus triggers a right for investors to withdraw their participation in the offer or other acceptance of securities.

- Under PR 5.5, a company and its directors are generally required to take responsibility for the contents of a prospectus. Section 90(1) of the FSMA provides a statutory right of action against those responsible for the prospectus to an investor who has suffered a loss as a result of untrue or misleading statements in the prospectus. Section 90(2), section 90(5) and Schedule 10 of the FSMA provide a number of defences for those responsible for the prospectus to actions based on section 90(1) of the FSMA.

1. Requirement to prepare and publish a prospectus

Figure 4.1 sets out the main points that should be considered when establishing whether or not a prospectus is required in the UK.

Figure 4.1: Is a prospectus required by the Prospectus Rules?

Is a prospectus required by the Prospectus Rules?

1. Are the securities 'transferable securities'?
For more details on the meaning of 'transferable securities', please see section 1.1 below.
No: then the PD, and therefore the Prospectus Rules, do not apply and no prospectus will be required.
Yes: go to Question 2.

2. Is there an offer to the public of the transferable securities?
For more details on the meaning of 'offer to the public', see section 1.2 below.
No: no prospectus will be required in respect of an offer but, if there is an admission to trading on a regulated market, then a prospectus may still be required. Go to Question 4.
Yes: go to Question 3.

3. Is it an exempt offer to the public?
For more details on relevant exemptions, see sections 1.4 and 1.5 below.
No: a prospectus will be required for the offer to the public.
Yes: no prospectus will be required for the offer to the public. Go to Question 4

4. Is there an admission to trading on a regulated market?
For more details on the meaning of 'admission to trading on a regulated market', see section 1.3 below.
No: no prospectus will be required in respect of the admission to trading.
Yes: go to Question 5.

5. Is it an exempt admission to trading?
For more details on the relevant exemptions, see sections 1.4 and 1.6 below.
No: a prospectus will be required for the admission to trading.
Yes: no prospectus will be required for the admission to trading.

1.1 Transferable securities

In establishing whether the Prospectus Rules apply to a particular public offer or admission to trading in the UK, the first question to consider is whether the security which is the subject of such public offer or admission to trading is a 'transferable security' within the meaning of the Prospectus Rules.

Where a security is not a 'transferable security' within the meaning of the Prospectus Rules, a PD-compliant prospectus is not required. 'Transferable securities' for the purpose of the Prospectus Rules means transferable securities excluding money-market instruments with a maturity of less than 12 months (FSMA s. 102A(3)). 'Transferable securities' are defined by reference to Article 4.1(18) of MiFID, which provides:

> Transferable securities means those classes of securities which are negotiable on the capital market, with the exception of instruments of payment, such as:
>
> (a) shares in companies and other securities equivalent to shares in companies, partnerships or other entities, and depositary receipts in respect of shares;
>
> (b) bonds or other forms of securitised debt, including depositary receipts in respect of such securities; or
>
> (c) any other securities giving the right to acquire or sell any such transferable securities or giving rise to a cash settlement determined by reference to transferable securities, currencies, interest rates or yields, commodities or other indices or measures.

See also Question 67 of the ESMA PD Q&A.

'Money-market instruments' are defined in Article 4.1(19) MiFID, which provides:

> 'Money-market instrument' means those classes of instruments which are normally dealt in on the money market, such as treasury bills, certificates of deposit and commercial papers and excluding instruments of payment.

In broad terms, 'money-market instruments' are transferable, marketable instruments creating or evidencing debt and are issued by a borrower. One of the key areas of debate on the scope of the definition of 'transferable securities' has been whether non-transferable options over transferable securities (e.g. employee stock options) should be classified as non-transferable securities and thus fall outside the scope of the Prospectus Rules.

In List! Issue No. 10 (issued in June 2005) the FSA (the predecessor to the FCA) said that whether the PD applies to a share option scheme depends on whether the option is transferable within the meaning of 'transferable securities'. The FSA said that it would not expect the grant of an option under an employee share option scheme to involve a security that is negotiable on the capital market and hence would not expect it to be subject to the provisions of the PD. In that publication, the FSA also confirmed its view that it is unlikely that the exercise of an employee share option would amount to a public offer. Although this commentary was not repeated in the

UKLA Guidance Note *Exemptions from the requirement to prepare a prospectus* (*UKLA/TN/602.1*) so there is no FCA formal guidance on the point, the Commission and ESMA agree with this analysis (see Question 5 of the ESMA PD Q&A). The FCA states that it is up to the issuer and its advisers to consider, for any particular scheme, whether an offer of transferable securities has been made to the public and whether they are exempt from producing a prospectus. (See *UKLA/TN/602.1*; see further section 1.2.2. below.)

ESMA has also noted (see Question 67 of the ESMA PD Q&A) that the transferability of securities may be restricted or reduced on a contractual basis, such as via a shareholders' agreement or lock-up agreement between the company and existing shareholders. ESMA considers that, generally, such securities will remain transferable securities falling within the scope of the PD but that some restrictions may be so broad that they result in transforming transferable securities into non-transferable securities, no longer falling within the scope of the PD. ESMA will analyse whether any such restrictions make securities non-transferable on a case-by-case basis.

In a rare case considering the Prospectus Directive, *Almer Beheer and Daedalus Holding v Van den Dungen Vastgoed BV and Oosterhout II BVBA (2014 EUECJ C-441/12)*, the Advocate-General concluded that the Prospectus Directive does not apply to an enforced sale of securities 'that have been ordered by a court to be seized from their holder and sold in order to satisfy a debt'. The opinion noted that, on the face of it, the directive would appear to cover an enforced sale but 'such sales do not belong to the sphere that the Prospectus Directive was intended to regulate'. This decision may also offer hope to issuers trying to demonstrate that they have not made an offer to the public, if the reason for their transaction differs substantially from that contemplated in the PD. In addition, the comments of the CJEU acknowledge the difficulty of a third party compiling a PD prospectus for securities which it is not the issuer of where it has no access to the management of the issuer.

1.2 Offer to the public

1.2.1 Definition of offer to the public

Having established that the securities are 'transferable securities' for the purpose of the Prospectus Rules, the next question to consider is whether or not there is a public offer of those securities in the UK. The Prospectus Rules require, subject to the availability of an exemption, an approved prospectus to be published whenever there is a public offer of transferable securities in the UK.

During EU Level 1 discussions it proved challenging to obtain a satisfactory pan-European definition of a public offer of securities. As a result, the definition of a public offer of securities in the PD was drafted very broadly to accommodate different models of public offer and differing opinions across the EEA.

A person is treated, for the purposes of Part VI of the FSMA and the Prospectus Rules, as offering transferable securities to the public where he communicates sufficient information on the terms of an offer and the securities that are the subject of the offer so as to enable an investor to decide to buy or subscribe for the securities (s. 102B(1)).

Section 102B(2) of the FSMA makes it clear that, to the extent that an offer of transferable securities is made to a person in the UK, it is an offer of transferable securities to the public in the UK.

The communication may be made in any form and by any means (FSMA s. 102B(3)). However, to ensure that normal secondary market communications, such as the posting of prices by traders on electronic dealing systems, would not amount to an offer of transferable securities to the public, section 102B(5) of the FSMA provides that a communication in connection with trading on:

(a) a regulated market;

(b) a multilateral trading facility; or

(c) a market prescribed by an order under s. 130A(3) of the FSMA

will not amount to a public offer.

See also Question 74 of the ESMA PD Q&A.

1.2.2 FCA, Commission and ESMA guidance

In the UKLA Guidance Note *Public offers (UKLA/TN/601.1)*, the FCA makes it clear that, while it is happy to discuss particular circumstances about what amounts to a public offer, it will not provide formal binding guidance on whether a particular set of circumstances amounts to a public offer which requires the publication of a prospectus. It has made it clear that where a person may be subject to the legislation concerning public offers, that person should take legal advice on applying the legislation to their own particular circumstances.

However, the FCA, the Commission and ESMA have given various pieces of guidance on the likely treatment of certain securities and instruments or certain circumstances:

- *Share schemes* – As discussed above, in List! Issue No. 10, the FSA said that, in its view, it is unlikely that the exercise of an employee share option would amount to a public offer. The rationale behind this is that the exercise simply involves the option holder choosing to exercise or not to exercise, a right which they have already acquired (see Question 5 of the ESMA PD Q&A). By contrast it is generally thought that the offer of shares by way of direct investment employee share schemes, rather than share option schemes, may amount to an offer of transferable securities to the public. This guidance is, however, not repeated in the UKLA Guidance Notes and there is therefore no formal FCA guidance on the point. See Question 71 of the ESMA PD Q&A that sets out a short-form disclosure regime applicable to employee share scheme prospectuses where the issuer already has securities admitted to trading.

- *Schemes of arrangement* – The view that has been taken generally in the UK since July 2005 is that a scheme of arrangement (under Part 26 of the CA 2006) is not a public offer under the Prospectus Rules. This is because there is no offer that enables investors to buy or subscribe for securities: instead, there is a court-approved procedure under which members and creditors, as appropriate, are asked to vote on and approve an arrangement. Once the scheme is approved, it is binding on all members or creditors, as the case may be. In List! Issue No. 10, the FSA was not willing to give an absolute view on this and said that this was a matter of law for the courts to decide, but that it was inclined to agree that the view that a scheme is not a public offer was correct. However, in List! Issue No. 23, the FSA subsequently stated that if a mix-and-match facility is made available to shareholders on a scheme of arrangement (allowing them the chance to elect the proportions of cash and shares they receive) a prospectus is required as the shareholder is making an investment decision whether to elect to receive shares. The guidance given in List! Issue Nos 10 and 23 is not repeated in the UKLA Guidance Notes and there is, therefore, no formal guidance on the point.
- *Free shares* – The treatment of free shares is considered in Question 6 of the ESMA PD Q&A. ESMA's view is that in the case of allocations of securities (almost invariably free of charge) where there is no element of choice on the part of the recipient, including no right to repudiate the allocation, there is no 'offer to the public' of transferable securities. This is because the definition in the PD refers to a communication containing sufficient information 'to enable an investor to decide to' purchase or subscribe for the securities. Where no decision is made by the recipient of the securities, there is no offer for the purposes of the PD and so such allocations fall outside the scope of the PD. It is worth noting that even in the case of offers of free shares where the recipient decides whether to accept the offer, no prospectus will be required because the consideration will be zero and so the minimum consideration exemption will apply (see further sections 1.5.1 and 1.5.2 below).
- *Rights issues and other pre-emptive offers* – Question 42 of the ESMA PD Q&A confirms that where a custodian tells its clients in one member state about a rights issue in another member state (normally under its contractual duty to inform them) that will not constitute an offer to the public requiring the prospectus to be passported into the member state where the clients are, unless the custodian provides them with the terms of the offer and the shares and it acts on behalf of the issuer when doing so.

1.3 Admission to trading

Having established that the securities are 'transferable securities' for the purpose of the Prospectus Rules, and whether there is a public offer of those securities in the UK, it is necessary to consider whether there is an admission to trading on a regulated market in the UK. Subject to the availability of an exemption, the FSMA and the Prospectus Rules require an approved prospectus to be issued whenever there is an admission to trading of transferable securities on a regulated market in the UK, regardless of whether or not there is also a public offer.

The definition of 'admission to trading' covers all regulated markets in the UK. 'Regulated market' is defined in the Prospectus Rules (using the definition in Article 4 of MiFID) as:

> a multilateral system operated and/or managed by a market operator, which brings together or facilitates the bringing together of multiple third-party buying and selling interests in financial instruments – in the system and in accordance with its non-discretionary rules – in a way that results in a contract, in respect of the financial instruments admitted to trading under its rules and/or systems, and which is authorised and functions regularly and in accordance with the provisions of Title III of MiFID.

In the UK, the LSE's main market for listed securities (the Main Market) is a regulated market. AIM is not a regulated market for these purposes. See Chapter 2 for a discussion of the status of other markets in the UK.

1.4 Scope of the exemptions

Having established that the securities are transferable securities for the purpose of the Prospectus Rules, whether there is a public offer of those securities in the UK and/or an admission to trading of those securities on a regulated market in the UK, the next step is to consider whether any exemptions to the requirement to publish an approved prospectus are available for the public offer and/or the admission to trading, as the case may be.

The exemptions from the requirement to publish an approved prospectus vary depending on whether there is an offer of transferable securities to the public or an admission to trading on a regulated market.

Where a transaction involves both a public offer and an admission to trading on a regulated market, both the public offer and the admission must be exempt to avoid the approved prospectus requirement. The exemptions for public offers are generally wider than those for admissions to trading on a regulated market.

The exemptions to the approved prospectus requirement are contained in Part VI and Schedule 11A of the FSMA and Prospectus Rules 1.2.2 and 1.2.3. Part VI of the FSMA includes a wide number of exemptions to the requirement to publish an approved prospectus. Prospectus Rules 1.2.2 and 1.2.3 contain further exemptions from the requirement to produce a prospectus: Prospectus Rule 1.2.2 provides exemptions from the approved prospectus requirement for offers to the public of transferable securities, while Prospectus Rule 1.2.3 covers those for admissions to trading on a regulated market.

It is important to remember that even where no prospectus is required, the issuer, offeror or applicant, as the case may be, must make sure that any material information they provide to qualified investors or special categories of investors, including information disclosed in marketing meetings and road shows, is disclosed to all such qualified investors or special categories of investor to whom the offer is exclusively addressed (PR 5.6.1R). This general principle applies, irrespective of whether the offer is addressed to qualified investors, or to fewer than 150 persons in one member state, or any other category of persons to whom securities can be offered without the publication of a prospectus. The principle is that material information which is disclosed to some persons in that category must be disclosed to all such persons.

1.5 Exempt offers to the public

The exemptions from the requirement to publish an approved prospectus in respect of an offer of transferable securities to the public are contained in Schedule 11A to the FSMA, Part VI of the FSMA and Prospectus Rule 1.2.2R. As mentioned above, if the public offer is accompanied by an admission to trading on a regulated market, in order to avoid having to produce an approved prospectus both the public offer and the admission to trading must fall within applicable exemptions.

The New Prospectus Regulation will result in changes to these exemptions and these are described in the relevant sections below. The New Prospectus Regulation, which came into force in July 2017, is discussed more generally in section 7 below.

1.5.1 Schedule 11A exemptions for public offers

Exempt transferable securities

The public offer of certain transferable securities (albeit that they technically fall within the definition of 'transferable securities') are entirely outside the scope of the PD (Article 1(2)) and, therefore, the Prospectus Rules. Section 85(5) of the FSMA therefore provides that those securities specified in Schedule 11A of the FSMA fall outside the requirement to produce a prospectus in connection with an offer. They include, among others:

- as further described below, securities included in an offer with a total consideration of less than €5 million, calculated over 12 months (FSMA paragraph 9, Part 2, Schedule 11A);
- units issued by an open-ended collective investment scheme (FSMA paragraph 1, Part 1, Schedule 11A);
- shares in the share capital of the central bank of an EEA State (FSMA paragraph 3, Part 1, Schedule 11A);
- non-equity transferable securities which are issued by the government of an EEA State, a regional or local authority of an EEA State, a public international body of

which an EEA State is a member, the European Central Bank or the central bank of an EEA State (FSMA paragraph 2, Part 1 of Schedule 11A); and
- non-equity transferable securities which are issued by credit institutions in a continuous or repeated manner and meet certain conditions (FSMA paragraph 5, Part 2 of Schedule 11A).

It is, therefore, important to check whether the type of transferable security which is the subject of the public offer falls within any of the exemptions contained in Schedule 11A of the FSMA. Note that the exemptions contained in Part 1 of Schedule 11A also apply to admissions.

€5 million exemption

The exemption for securities included in an offer with a total consideration of less than €5 million, calculated over 12 months, is one of the main exemptions for offers under Schedule 11A (FSMA paragraph 9, Part 2, Schedule 11A). However, any offers that are covered by this exemption fall outside of the scope of the PD altogether; individual member states are therefore free to regulate them as they see fit. Before relying on this exemption in any member state it is worth checking whether such offer would be regulated in any way by the member state. It should also be noted that, prior to the Amending Directive, the threshold for this exemption was €2.5 million rather than €5 million.

The €5 million limit has to be calculated over a 12-month period (FSMA paragraph 9(2), Part 2, Schedule 11A).

In 2005, the Commission held a meeting where this exemption was discussed. It stated that, in general, the 12-month period should be calculated from the opening of the offer (in the case of an offering programme, from the beginning to the end). The Commission also made it clear that this exemption does not prevent a competent authority from assessing retrospectively whether a series of offers, each having a total consideration of less than €2.5 million (the limit at the time this meeting was held, being prior to the Amending Directive – it is assumed that the same view will still apply in light of the increase to €5 million) should properly be regarded as a single offer (with a total consideration of more than that sum) requiring a prospectus. The Commission has also confirmed that this exemption applies separately to offers of different kinds of securities within a 12-month period. Accordingly, if in the same 12-month period an issuer offers shares with a total consideration of €5 million and debt with a total consideration of €5 million, both offers would fall within the exemption because they must be considered separately. Therefore, an issuer or offeror is not required to aggregate the total consideration of different types of securities offered for the purposes of this provision (this view is reflected by ESMA in Question 26 of the ESMA PD Q&A). The limit should be calculated on an EEA-wide basis rather than a country-by-country basis. The Commission has not issued any updated guidance or published the minutes of any meeting which considers this exemption in light of the increase in the limit to €5 million pursuant to the amending directive. However, it is not expected that this increase would cause the Commission to change their view.

Under the New Prospectus Regulation, Member States will have discretion to exempt others below €8 million. See section 7 for further details.

As the exemption has been included in Part 2 of Schedule 11A of the FSMA, it only applies to a public offer. It does not apply in the context of an admission to trading on a regulated market.

1.5.2 Part VI of the FSMA exemptions for public offers

Qualified investors

An offer of securities addressed only to 'qualified investors' is exempt (FSMA s. 86(1)(a)). Section 86(7) of the FSMA defines a qualified investor as:

(a) a person falling within (1) to (4) of Section I of Annex II to MiFID, other than a person who, before the making of the offer, has agreed in writing with the relevant firm (or each of the relevant firms) to be treated as a non-professional client in accordance with the final paragraph of Section I of Annex II to that directive;

(b) a person who has made a request to one or more relevant firms to be treated as a professional client in accordance with Section II of Annex II of MiFID and has not subsequently, but before the making of the offer, agreed in writing with that relevant firm (or each of those relevant firms) to be treated as a non-professional client in accordance with the final paragraph of Section I of Annex II of MiFID;

(c) a person who is an eligible counterparty in accordance with Article 24 of MiFID and has not, before the making of the offer, agreed in writing with the relevant firm (or each of the relevant firms) to be treated as a non-professional client in accordance with the final paragraph of Section I of Annex II of MiFID (see further 'Persons who will be considered eligible counterparties' below); or

(d) a person whom any relevant firm is authorised to continue to treat as a professional client in accordance with Article 71(6) of MiFID.

Each of these is discussed below.

Persons who will always be considered to be 'qualified investors' (unless agreement to the contrary is reached with the relevant firm)

People falling within (1) to (4) of Section I of Annex II of MiFID will always be considered to be qualified investors, unless they have agreed to be treated as non-professional clients before the offer is made. The persons in this category are as follows:

(a) Entities which are required to be authorised or regulated to operate in the financial markets. The list below should be understood as including all authorised entities carrying out the characteristic activities of the entities mentioned:

that is, entities authorised by a member state under a directive, entities authorised or regulated by a member state without reference to a directive, and entities authorised or regulated by a non-member state:
- credit institutions
- investment firms
- other authorised or regulated financial institutions
- insurance companies
- collective investment schemes and management companies of such schemes
- pension funds and management companies of such funds
- commodity and commodity derivatives dealers
- locals
- other institutional investors.

(b) Large undertakings meeting two of the following size requirements on a company basis:
- balance sheet total: €20 million
- net turnover: €40 million
- own funds: €2 million.

(c) National and regional governments, public bodies that manage public debt, Central Banks, international and supranational institutions such as the World Bank, the IMF, the ECB, the EIB and other similar international organisations.

(d) Other institutional investors whose main activity is to invest in financial instruments, including entities dedicated to the securitisation of assets or other financing transactions.

Persons who may be considered to be 'qualified investors'

Other persons may be allowed to be considered 'qualified investors' and waive some of their protection provided certain criteria and procedures are fulfilled pursuant to Section II of Annex II of MiFID.

Any such waiver of the protection afforded by the standard conduct of business regime can only be valid if an adequate assessment of the expertise, experience and knowledge of the client, undertaken by the investment firm, gives reasonable assurance, in light of the nature of the transactions or services envisaged, that the client is capable of making his own investment decisions and understanding the risks involved. MiFID states that the fitness test applied to managers and directors of entities licensed under Directives in the financial field could be regarded as an example of the assessment of expertise and knowledge; in the case of small entities, the person subject to the above assessment should be the person authorised to carry out transactions on behalf of the entity.

MiFID also states that in the course of the above assessment, as a minimum, two of the following criteria should be satisfied:
   (a) The client has carried out transactions, in significant size, on the relevant market at an average frequency of ten per quarter over the previous four quarters.
   (b) The size of the client's financial instrument portfolio, defined as including cash deposits and financial instruments exceeds €500,000.
   (c) The client works, or has worked, in the financial sector for at least one year in a professional position, which requires knowledge of the transactions or services envisaged.

The clients may waive the benefit of the detailed rules of conduct only where the following procedure is followed:
   (a) They must state in writing to the investment firm that they wish to be treated as a professional client, either generally or in respect of a particular investment service or transaction, type of transaction or product.
   (b) The investment firm must give them a clear written warning of the protections and investor compensation rights they may lose.
   (c) They must state, in writing, in a separate document from the contract, that they are aware of the consequences of losing such protections.

Before deciding to accept any request for waiver, investment firms, as regulated entities, are required to take all reasonable steps to ensure that the client requesting to be treated as a professional client meets the relevant requirements stated above.

Persons who will be considered to be 'eligible counterparties'

Eligible counterparties for the purposes of the definition of 'qualified investor' include:
   (a) investment firms, credit institutions, insurance companies, UCITS and their management companies, pension funds and their management companies, other financial institutions authorised or regulated under Community legislation or the national law of a member state, certain undertakings exempted from the application of MiFID (persons whose main business consists of dealing on own account in commodities and/or commodity derivatives (Art. 2(1)(k)) and investment firms exclusively dealing on own account on markets in financial futures or options or other derivatives and on cash markets for the sole purpose of hedging positions (MiFID Art. 2(1)(l)) national governments and their corresponding offices including public bodies that deal with public debt, central banks and supranational organisations;
   (b) other undertakings recognised by the member state as meeting pre-determined proportionate requirements, including quantitative thresholds; and
   (c) third-country entities equivalent to those categories of entities mentioned above as recognised by the member state (Art 24 MiFID).

Use of the 'professional client' exemption under the transitional provisions of MiFID

Article 71(6) was a transitional provision of MiFID which allowed investment firms to continue to treat clients as professional clients, provided that this categorisation had been granted by the investment firm on the basis of an adequate assessment of the expertise, experience and knowledge of the client which gave a reasonable assurance, in light of the nature of the transactions or services envisaged, that the client was capable of making his own investment decisions and understood the risks involved. These clients also fell under the definition of 'qualified investor'.

One issue that arises is that if an offer of securities is made to a person acting on behalf of clients whose terms of engagement allow him to make the decision to purchase securities without reference to those clients, the offer should nonetheless be treated as being made to those underlying clients for the purpose of determining whether the qualified investor exemption applies. In List! Issue No. 10, the FSA confirmed that this would not be treated as an offer to the underlying client. This guidance is not, however, repeated in the UKLA Guidance Notes, so there is no formal guidance on the point. Section 86(2) of the FSMA makes it clear that, in considering whether the qualified investor or less than 150 persons per member state exemption applies to such a situation, the offer is not treated as being made to the discretionary broker's underlying clients.

Where an issuer sells securities to a stockbroker which it knows has non-discretionary private clients, there is the possibility that, while the financial intermediary will fall within the exemption for qualified investors, if the intermediary on-sells the shares to retail investors, it may trigger the need to produce an approved prospectus. Issuers may seek to tackle this by seeking a representation from those financial intermediaries who acquire shares that the securities acquired by them are not acquired on a non-discretionary basis on behalf of, nor acquired with a view to their offer or resale to, persons in circumstances which may give rise to an offer of securities to the public (other than their offer or resale to qualified investors or with prior consent).

150 persons per member state

An offer of securities addressed to fewer than 150 natural or legal persons, other than qualified investors, per member state is exempt (FSMA s. 86(1)(b)). The making of an offer of transferable securities to trustees of a trust, members of a partnership in their capacity as such, or two or more persons jointly, is treated as the making of an offer to a single person (FSMA s. 86(3)). In addition, as outlined in the paragraph above, the making of an offer to a discretionary broker is treated as an offer to that one person and not to his underlying clients.

€100,000 minimum consideration and €100,000 minimum denomination

An offer where the minimum consideration which may be paid by any person for the securities acquired by him pursuant to the offer is at least €100,000 (or an equivalent amount) is exempt (FSMA s. 86(1)(c)).

An offer where the securities being offered are denominated in amounts of at least €100,000 (or an equivalent amount) is exempt (FSMA s. 86(1)(d)).

€100,000 total consideration

An offer of securities where the total consideration payable for the securities being offered cannot exceed €100,000 (calculated over a period of 12 months) is exempt (FSMA s. 86(1)(e) and 86(4)). However, as described above, any offer where the total consideration is less than €5 million will also be exempt (FSMA paragraph 9, Schedule 11A and s. 85(5)(a)). Free share awards will come within this exemption (see Question 6 of the ESMA PD Q&A).

Retail cascades

Where the retail cascade exemption is available, intermediaries are able to offer securities in the company without being required to produce a separate prospectus. Section 86(1A) of the FSMA states that a prospectus is not required where transferable securities are being sold or placed through a financial intermediary where:

(a) the transferable securities have previously been the subject of one or more offers to the public;

(b) in respect of one or more of those offers to the public:
  (i) the offer was made to or directed at qualified investors only,
  (ii) the offer was made to or directed at fewer than 150 persons other than qualified investors per EEA State,
  (iii) the minimum consideration paid by any person for the transferable securities was at least €100,000,
  (iv) the minimum denomination of the transferable securities was at least €100,000, or
  (v) the total consideration for the offer did not exceed €100,000;

(c) a prospectus is available for the securities which has been approved by a competent authority no earlier than 12 months before the date of the current offer is made; and

(d) the issuer or other person who was responsible for drawing up the prospectus has given written consent to the use of the prospectus for the purpose of the current offer.

The Prospectus Regulation (as amended by Regulation (EU) 862/2012) sets out detailed requirements in relation to the issuer's written consent. The written consent may either be in the form of a consent for one or more specified financial intermediary or be a general consent for any financial intermediary. The consent must be included in the prospectus together with an acknowledgement by the issuer that it accepts responsibility for the contents of the prospectus for resales by intermediaries.

Certain additional information is also required to be included in the relevant prospectus with respect to such consent, including:

(a) the period for which the consent is valid;
(b) the offer period upon which subsequent resale or final placement of securities by financial intermediaries can be made;
(c) an indication of the member states where financial intermediaries may use the prospectus;
(d) any clear and objective conditions attached to the consent; and
(e) a bold warning notice that the financial intermediary will provide information to investors on the terms and conditions of the offer at the time the offer is made.

If the issuer is not able to identify all financial intermediaries in the prospectus, and so a general consent is given, any financial intermediary using the prospectus must state on its website that it is using the prospectus in accordance with the conditions attached. Alternatively, if consent is restricted to individual financial intermediaries, these should be named in the prospectus together with an indication of how any new information relating to the intermediaries will be published.

1.5.3 Prospectus Rules – exemptions for public offers

Shares issued in substitution for shares of the same class

A public offer is exempt where the shares are issued in substitution for shares of the same class already issued, if the issue of shares does not involve any increase in issued share capital (PR 1.2.2R(1)).

Takeovers where there is an equivalent document

A public offer is exempt where the securities are offered in connection with a takeover by means of an exchange offer, if a document (an 'equivalent document') is available containing information which the FCA regards as equivalent to that of the prospectus taking into account the requirements of EU legislation (PR 1.2.2R(2)). This can include a private acquisition as well as a public acquisition. It is worth noting that the passporting regime within the PD will not apply to an equivalent document and that the competent authority of any EEA member state can therefore challenge such a document's equivalence (UKLA Guidance Note *Exemptions from the requirement to* produce a prospectus (UKLA/TN/602.1)). The FCA requires the equivalent document to be identical in content to a PD-compliant prospectus (see section 2.10 below for further detail).

Mergers or divisions where there is an equivalent document

A public offer is exempt where the securities are offered, allotted or to be allotted in connection with a merger or division, if a document (an 'equivalent document') is available containing information which the FCA regards as equivalent to that of the prospectus taking into account the requirements of EU legislation (PR 1.2.2R(3)). The FCA requires the equivalent document to be identical in content to a PD-compliant prospectus (see section 2.10 below for further detail).

Scrip dividends

A public offer is exempt where dividends are paid out to existing shareholders in the form of shares of the same class as the shares in respect of which dividends are paid, if a document is made available containing information on the number and nature of the shares and the reasons for and details of the offer (PR 1.2.2R(4)). This exemption only applies to shares of the same class and not to other securities.

Employee share schemes

A public offer is exempt where the securities are offered, allotted or to be allotted to existing or former directors or employees by their employer or by an affiliated undertaking, if a document is made available containing information on the number and nature of the securities and the reasons for and details of the offer (PR 1.2.2R(5)).

As discussed in section 1.1, the FSA (as it then was) stated that it would not expect the grant of an option under an employee share scheme to involve the issue of transferable securities (see List! Issue No. 10, issued in June 2005). Consequently, normal share option schemes, in contrast to other types of employee share schemes, should fall outside the scope of the Prospectus Rules. However, this commentary has not been repeated in the UKLA Guidance Notes, so there is no formal guidance on this point.

For the purposes of this exemption, where the securities are offered or allotted to employees through the device of a trustee who holds the securities on trust for the employees, the Commission has said that it would be consistent with the objectives of the exemption to treat the securities as issued to the employees if that is the effect of the trust (see the minutes of the fourth informal meeting on the transposition of the PD held in March 2005).

This exemption only applies where the issuer or an affiliated undertaking either:

(a) has a head office or registered office in the EU;

(b) is a company established outside the EU but whose securities are admitted to trading on an EEA regulated market; or

(c) is established outside the EU and has its securities admitted to trading on a third country market which the Commission has deemed equivalent for the purposes of the PD.

As of the date of publication no such equivalence decision has been made.

If a non-EEA issuer is listed on a regulated market, such as the LSE's main market, it will be able to use this exemption. However, as a consequence of (b) and (c) many non-EEA issuers listed on non-regulated markets (e.g. AIM) and unlisted non-EEA issuers cannot rely on this exemption. Unless their offers are for less than €5 million or addressed to fewer than 150 persons per member state, their employee share schemes will not be exempt. This has resulted in a number of issuers who are only listed in the US having to publish prospectuses for employee share schemes operating in the EEA.

Where a prospectus is required for an employee share scheme, a short form disclosure regime is available where the issuer already has securities admitted to trading. See Question 71 of the ESMA PD Q&A on the short-form disclosure regime applicable to employee share scheme prospectuses.

1.6 Exempt admissions to trading

The exemptions from the requirement to publish an approved prospectus in respect of the admission to trading on a regulated market are contained in Part 1 of Schedule 11A of the FSMA, Part VI of the FSMA and the Prospectus Rules. As mentioned above, if the admission to trading is accompanied by a public offer, in order to avoid having to produce an approved prospectus both the admission to trading and the public offer must fall within applicable exemptions.

The New Prospectus Regulation will result in changes to these exemptions, which are discussed below. The New Prospectus Regulation, which came into force in July 2017, is discussed more generally in section 7 below.

1.6.1 Part 1 of Schedule 11A of the FSMA – exemptions for admissions to trading

The admission to trading on a regulated market of certain securities (albeit that they technically fall within the definition of transferable securities) is entirely outside the scope of Article 1(2) of the PD and therefore the Prospectus Rules and the FSMA. Section 85(6) of the FSMA, therefore, provides that those securities specified in Part 1 of Schedule 11A to the FSMA fall outside the requirement to produce a prospectus on admission. They include, for example:

- units in an open-ended collective investment scheme;
- non-equity transferable securities issued by the government of an EEA state, a local or regional authority of an EEA state, a public international body of which an EEA state is a member, the European Central Bank or the central bank of an EEA state; and

- shares in the share capital of the central bank of an EEA state.

It is worth noting that the exemption for offers with a total consideration of less than €5 million does not apply to admissions to trading.

1.6.2 Prospectus rules – exemptions for admissions to trading

Less than 10% of the issued share capital

The admission to trading of shares is exempt where those shares represent, over a period of 12 months, less than 10% of the number of shares of the same class already admitted to trading on the same regulated market (PR 1.2.3R(1)).

This exemption is calculated on an aggregated basis calculated over a 12-month period ending with the date on which the relevant admission is to take place. New share issues increase the denominator for the purposes of the calculation (see the UKLA Guidance Note *Exemptions from the requirement to produce a prospectus (UKLA/TN/602.1)* for more discussion of the calculation).

Under the New Prospectus Regulation, which came into force in July 2017, the threshold for this exemption will increase to 20% and the exemption will be available for all securities not just shares. While most of the New Prospectus Regulation will only apply 24 months after the Regulation came into force, this provision came into force with immediate effect (see the FCA's Quarterly Consultation Paper CP 17/6 for further information).

Shares issued in substitution for shares of the same class

The admission to trading of shares is exempt where those shares are issued in substitution for shares of the same class already admitted to trading on the same regulated market, if the issue of the shares does not involve any increase in the issued capital (PR 1.2.3R(2)).

Takeovers where there is an equivalent document

The admission of securities is exempt where those securities are offered in connection with a takeover by means of an exchange offer, if an equivalent document is available, that is a document containing information which is regarded by the FCA as being equivalent to that of the prospectus, taking into account the requirements of EU legislation (PR 1.2.3R(3)). The FCA requires the equivalent document to be identical in content to a PD-compliant prospectus. See section 1.5.3 above for more detail regarding this exemption.

Mergers or divisions where there is an equivalent document

The admission to trading of securities is exempt where those securities are offered, allotted or to be allotted in connection with a merger or division, if an equivalent document is available, which contains information regarded by the FCA as being equivalent to that of the prospectus, taking into account the requirements of EU legislation (PR 1.2.3R(4)). The FCA requires the equivalent document to be identical in content to a PD-compliant prospectus. (See section 1.5.3 above for more detail regarding this exemption.)

Bonus issues

The admission to trading of shares is exempt where shares are offered, allotted or to be allotted free of charge to existing shareholders, and where dividends are paid out in the form of shares, provided they are of the same class as those in respect of which the dividends are paid. The shares must be the same class as the shares already admitted to trading on the same regulated market and a document must be made available containing information on the number and nature of the shares and the reasons for and details of the offer (PR 1.2.3R(5)). This exemption cannot be relied on for the admission to trading, for example, of a new B-share issue as the new B-shares will not be in the same class as the shares in the issuer that are already listed.

Employee share schemes

The admission to trading of securities is exempt where those securities are offered, allotted or are to be allotted to existing or former directors or employees by their employer or an affiliated undertaking, if (a) the securities are of the same class as the securities already admitted to trading on the same regulated market; and (b) if a document is made available containing information on the number and nature of the securities and the reason for and details of the offer (PR 1.2.3R(6)). Please also see the additional discussion on offers of shares to employees at sections 1.2 and 1.5.3 above.

Convertibles and exchangeables

The admission to trading of shares is exempt where those shares result from the conversion or exchange of other transferable securities or from the exercise of the rights conferred by other securities, if the shares are of the same class as the shares already admitted to trading on the same regulated market (PR 1.2.3R(7)).

There is no requirement that the convertible security must have been admitted to trading or the subject of a prospectus for the exemption to apply. However, competent authorities may consider taking enforcement action against those issuers who exploit this loophole (Question 27 of the ESMA PD Q&A) which has been confirmed by the FCA in UKLA Guidance Note *Exemptions from the requirement to produce a prospectus (UKLA/TN/602.1)*. The view that has been taken generally in the UK since July 2005 (principally as a result of the views expressed by the FSA in relation to the exercise of options granted under an employee share scheme – see sections 1.1 and 1.5.3 above) is that the exercise of options to convert or exchange by holders of convertible or exchangeable securities will not ordinarily amount to a public offer.

Under the New Prospectus Regulation, this exemption will be limited to an increase of less than 20% of the shares of the same class already admitted to trading on the same regulated market over a period of 12 months. That 20% limit will be disapplied in certain situations, including where (i) a prospectus was drawn up for the original securities which convert or exchange into the shares to be admitted; or (ii) the original securities were issued before the New Prospectus Regulation. This provision came into force with immediate effect with the New Prospectus Regulation in July 2017 (see the FCA's Quarterly Consultation Paper CP 17/6 for further information).

Securities already admitted to trading on another regulated market

The admission to trading of securities is exempt where those securities are already admitted to trading on another regulated market (PR 1.2.3R(8)) provided the following conditions are satisfied:

(a) that those securities, or securities of the same class, have been admitted to trading on that other regulated market for more than 18 months;

(b) that, for securities first admitted to trading after 31 December 2003, the admission to trading on that other regulated market was associated with an approved prospectus made available to the public in accordance with Article 14 of the PD;

(c) that, except where (b) applies, for securities first admitted to listing after 30 June 1983, listing particulars were approved in accordance with the requirements of Directive 80/390/EEC or Directive 2001/34/EC;

(d) that the ongoing obligations for trading on that other regulated market have been fulfilled;

(e) that the person seeking the admission to trading under this exemption makes a summary document available to the public in a language accepted by the competent authority of the EEA state of the regulated market where admission is sought;

(f) that the summary document referred to in (e) is made available to the public in the EEA state of the regulated market where admission to trading is sought in the manner set out in Article 14 of the PD; and

(g) that the contents of the summary document comply with Article 5(2) of the PD. The document must also state where the most recent prospectus can be obtained and where the financial information published by the issuer pursuant to its ongoing disclosure obligations is available.

PR 1.2.4G makes it clear that the summary document should at least contain the information that would be required in a summary of a prospectus if one were being produced.

2. Format and content of a prospectus

The format and content requirements for a prospectus are governed and guidance is provided by:

- Part VI of FSMA;
- the Prospectus Rules;
- the PD Regulation (as amended);
- the ESMA Recommendations, the ESMA PD Q&A and the ESMA Guidelines on the use of Alternative Performance Measures; and
- the Omnibus II Directive (2014/51/EU).

The PD Regulation sets out the order and contents requirements for a prospectus, while the ESMA Recommendations and the ESMA PD Q&A provide guidance on how a number of those content requirements should be implemented. Issuers, offerors or any other person requesting admission to trading are entitled to include additional information in a prospectus over and above the items required to be included by the PD Regulation. However, any such information should be appropriate to the type of securities or nature of the issuer involved (PD Regulation Recital 9).

Although member states are not allowed to require additional disclosure in a prospectus to that contained in the PD, the PD Regulation, the ESMA Recommendations and the ESMA PD Q&A, certain regulators and exchanges have used other means of strengthening disclosure (e.g. by using eligibility requirements). The FCA has taken advantage of this by retaining eligibility criteria and 'super-equivalent' measures in the Listing Rules for issuers seeking admission to the Official List (see Chapter 2).

2.1 Single and tri-partite documents

Under the Prospectus Rules, the issuer has a choice of format for the prospectus which can be drawn up either as a single or tri-partite document (PR 2.2.1R). Under PR 2.2.2R, a prospectus comprised of separate documents (a 'tri-partite prospectus') must comprise:

- a registration document, containing information relating to the issuer;
- a securities note, containing details of the securities to be offered or admitted to trading; and
- a summary.

Where a company chooses to produce a tri-partite document, there will be no approved prospectus unless all three of the necessary components have been published.

Companies contemplating an issue of securities may file a registration document with the FCA which will then be valid for a period of 12 months (PR 5.1.4R). The advantage of taking the tri-partite prospectus route is that, when securities are subsequently offered to the public or admitted to trading, the issuer is only required to prepare and submit for the approval of the FCA the summary (PR 2.2.4R) and the securities note (which should also contain any information that would normally be in the registration document where there has been a material change or development since the registration document was approved) if this could affect the investors' assessment of the securities (unless such information is provided in a supplementary prospectus (PR 2.2.5R)).

Having a tri-partite prospectus may enable an issuer to be in a position to issue securities more quickly once the registration document is published because the work involved in putting together a securities note and summary for each subsequent offer or issue will be considerably less than having to prepare an entirely new prospectus. Question 34 of the ESMA PD Q&A states that a single document prospectus can be used for multiple offers, but only if no circumstance has occurred which would require a supplementary prospectus to be published. ESMA has also noted that if multiple offers are to be made pursuant to a single document prospectus, the issuer would need to consider whether the prospectus contains all the information required by the PD Regulation in relation to any subsequent offer. If an issuer were required to publish a subsequent prospectus it could incorporate by reference all the information contained in the first prospectus.

If an issuer or offeror wishes to circulate a part of a prospectus (e.g. if the summary is to be distributed in hard copy to retail investors as a self-standing marketing document) the UKLA requires the issuer to produce a tri-partite prospectus. Once approved and published, each of the constituent parts can be circulated separately (a number of issuers have used this route on IPOs).

2.2 Order of contents

2.2.1 Single document

Where the applicant chooses to draw up a prospectus as a single document it must consist of the following parts in the following order (PR 2.2.10 and PD Regulation Art. 25(1)):

- a clear and detailed table of contents;
- the summary;
- risk factors; and
- the other information items required by the PD Regulation.

Question 9 of the ESMA PD Q&A states that this order is mandatory, but this does not mean that the issuer may not include a cover note containing general information about the issuer before these items.

2.2.2 Tri-partite document

Where the applicant chooses to draw up a tri-partite prospectus both the securities note and registration document must consist of the following parts in the following order (PR 2.2.10 and PD Regulation Art. 25(2)):

- a clear and detailed table of contents;
- risk factors; and
- the other information items required by the PD Regulation.

Question 10 of the ESMA PD Q&A states that, while there should not be any duplication of information between the securities note and the registration document, where there is, cross-references can be made between the two documents.

2.2.3 Order of other required information

The issuer is free, subject to complying with the requirements discussed in sections 2.2.1 and 2.2.2 above (and the common modular basis required for the summary described at 2.3.1 below) to present the other information items required to be disclosed in any order (PR 2.2.10 and PD Regulation Art. 25(3)). However, where this differs from the order as set out in the PD Regulation, the FCA may require that the applicant provides a cross-reference list for the purpose of checking the prospectus before its approval (PR 2.2.10 and PD Regulation Art. 25(4)). The checklists, prescribed forms of which are available on the FCA website, must identify the pages where each disclosure item can be found in the prospectus.

2.3 Summary and risk factors

2.3.1 Summary

All prospectuses, whether prepared as a single or tri-partite prospectus, will need to include a summary (PR 2.1.2 and FSMA s. 87A(5) and (6)) with the exception of those relating to non-equity securities having a denomination of €100,000 or more where the prospectus relates to admission to trading (PR 2.1.3R).

The summary must convey concisely, in non-technical language and in an appropriate structure, the key information relevant to the securities which are the subject of the prospectus and, when read with the rest of the prospectus, must be an aid to investors considering whether to invest in the securities. (PR 2.1.2 and FSMA s. 87A(6)). The summary must also be drafted in clear language, presenting the key information in an easily accessible and understandable way (PR 2.1.4 and Art. 24.1 of the PD Regulation).

'Key information' equates to that defined in section 87A of the FSMA as 'information which is essential to enable investors to understand the transferable securities to which the prospectus relates and to decide whether to consider the offer further'. Under Prospectus Rules 2.1.2 and section 87A(10) of the FSMA it must include:

(a) the essential characteristics of, and risks associated with, the issuer and any guarantor, including their assets, liabilities and financial position;
(b) the essential characteristics of, and risks associated with, the investment in the transferable securities, including any rights attaching to the securities;
(c) general terms of the offer, including estimated expenses charged to the investor by the issuer or the person offering the securities to the public, if not the issuer;
(d) details of the admission to trading; and
(e) the reasons for the offer and proposed use of proceeds.

Article 24 of the PD Regulation requires (a) that the summary contains the key information as prescribed in Annex XXII, and (b) that summaries are produced in a common modular basis, made up of five tables (one for each of the five sections set out below).

The elements to be included in the summary are built up in accordance with the annexes in the PD Regulation on which the prospectus itself is based. The tables state which annexes each particular element relates to (e.g. for a share prospectus, the elements indicated as applying to Annexes I and III must be considered). The order of the sections and the elements within each section set out in Annex XXII is mandatory. The five sections for the summary are:

- introduction and warnings;
- issuer and any guarantor;
- securities;
- risks (the requirement here is only to disclose key risk factors); and
- the offer.

If any of the items is not applicable, then it must still appear in the summary, with the reference 'not applicable'.

The length of the summary should take into account the complexity of the issuer and of the securities offered, but should not generally exceed 7% of the length of a prospectus or 15 pages, whichever is the longer. It must not contain cross-references to other parts of the prospectus (Article 24.1 of the PD Regulation and PR 2.1.4).

The summary must be in the language in which the prospectus was originally drawn up (PR 2.1.6R) and, pursuant to PR 2.1.7R and Article 5(2) of the PD, it must contain a warning to the effect that:

- it should be read as an introduction to the prospectus;
- any decision to invest in the securities should be based on consideration of the prospectus as a whole by the investor;
- where a claim relating to the information contained in the prospectus is brought before the court, the plaintiff might, under the national legislation of the EEA

states, have to bear the costs of translating the prospectus before legal proceedings are initiated; and
- civil liability attaches to those persons who are responsible for the summary, but only if the summary is misleading, inaccurate or inconsistent when read together with the other parts of the prospectus.

Question 80 of the ESMA PD Q&A provides further detail on the format of the summary, including prescribed introductory wording.

Civil liability does attach to those persons who are responsible for the summary, but only if it is misleading, inaccurate or inconsistent when read together with the other parts of the prospectus or it does not provide key information help investors (Article 6(2) of the PD Regulation and PR 2.1.7R(4)).

2.3.2 Risk factors

All prospectuses, whether prepared as a single or a tri-partite prospectus must include risk factors that are 'specific to the issuer or its industry' (PD Regulation, item 4 of Annex I) and that are 'material to the securities being offered and/or admitted to trading in order to assess the market risk associated with these securities' (PD regulation, item 2 of Annex III).

For a single prospectus, the risk factors section will need to cover both of these requirements. In the case of a tri-partite prospectus, the registration document will cover the first of these requirements and the securities note will cover the second.

The FCA has issued a UKLA Guidance Note providing guidance on risk factors (UKLA Guidance Note *Risk factors (UKLA/TN/621.3)*). In this guidance, the FCA acknowledges that the requirements in the PD Regulation are broadly drafted and are not prescriptive, but reminds issuers that the risk factors should be specific to the company and its industry and should be relevant to the type of securities being offered. The FCA also states that it will not generally challenge risk factors, but will do so if it considers that key risks are not adequately described. The FCA continues by stating that it will challenge risk factors where:

- they conflict with or undermine other rule requirements (e.g. by qualifying the working capital statement – see further below);
- they conflict with an issuer's eligibility or continuing obligations (e.g. detriment to investors, shares in public hands);
- they contradict the Listing Principles;
- sufficient prominence is not given to material risks;
- disclosure elsewhere in the prospectus clearly seems to present a risk that is not disclosed in the risk factor section; or
- they are simply statements of fact with no actual explanation of the risk in the context of the issuer's business or industry.

The FCA has also published a UKLA Guidance Note on the interaction between working capital statements and risk factors (UKLA Guidance Note *Working capital statements and risk factors (UKLA/TN/321.1)*) in which it notes the potential for a significant degree of overlap between the risk factors section of a prospectus and the issuer's working capital. The ESMA Recommendations say that the addition of assumptions in a clean working capital statement will detract from its value; in making a clean working capital statement, there should be no reference to, among other things, risk factors.

In its Guidance Note, the FCA clarifies its approach and sets out the principles it will have regard to when applying the ESMA Recommendations in this area:

- some risk factors are fundamentally inconsistent with a clean working capital statement: the FCA gives as an example the inclusion of a risk factor stating that the issuer may not be able to meet a significant scheduled repayment if its business does not generate sufficient cash over the next 12 months;
- the document as a whole should be consistent and the risk factors, business strategy and working capital statement should present a consistent picture;
- high impact but low probability risks may be consistent with a clean working capital statement, but these risks should be tightly and clearly drafted;
- the risk factor section should be particular to the issuer: the risk factors should not be generic or just follow the factors included in documents put out by other issuers or by the same issuer in an earlier document;
- risks should only be expressed to operate 'in the longer term' if this is genuinely the case; and
- risk factors cannot be made consistent with a clean working capital statement merely through the use of disclaimers or a preamble stating that the risk factors are not intended to qualify the working capital statement: the FCA will ignore disclaimers of this nature when considering the interaction between the working capital statement and the risk factors.

2.4 General duty of disclosure

Section 87A(2) of the FSMA sets out the general duty of disclosure for a prospectus, stating that it must contain the information necessary to enable investors to make an informed assessment of:

(a) the assets and liabilities, financial position, profit and losses, and prospects of the issuer of the transferable securities and of any guarantor; and

(b) the rights attaching to the transferable securities.

PR 3.1.2AR and 3.1.2BR make it an explicit requirement that an issuer must take all reasonable care to ensure that a prospectus contains the required information and is, to the best of its knowledge, in accordance with the facts and contains no omission likely to affect its import. The FCA says this clarifies its ability to take enforcement action for defective prospectuses.

The information must 'be presented in a form which is comprehensible and easy to analyse' (FSMA s. 87A(3)) and 'be prepared having regard to the particular nature of the transferable securities and their issuer' (FSMA s. 87A(4)).

2.5 Specific disclosure requirements

In addition to satisfying the general duty of disclosure, a prospectus must include the specific disclosure required by the PD Regulation. These disclosure requirements are reproduced in full in Appendix 3 to the Prospectus Rules.

The PD Regulation adopts a 'building-block' approach towards the specific content of a prospectus (PD Regulation Art. 3). Accordingly, the level of disclosure is determined by the type of security involved and, in certain cases, the identity of the issuer.

The specific disclosure items to be included in a prospectus are determined based on a combination of:

- *schedules* – these contain the minimum disclosure requirements for the registration document and the securities note for different categories of securities and issuers; and
- *building blocks* – these contain specific additional disclosure requirements, for example, for pro forma information, guarantees and asset-backed securities.

Annex XVIII to the PD Regulation sets out how the schedules and building blocks should be combined. The information required by the relevant schedules and building blocks is then combined to create the prospectus.

Figure 4.2 sets out the illustrative contents of a prospectus to be published in connection with an offer to the public (or admission to trading) of shares.

The then FSA indicated that where disclosure is required to be provided at 'the latest practicable date', this means the latest date before publication that disclosure can be prepared; this would normally be within 48 hours of the publication date (List! Issue No. 22). However, this guidance has not been repeated in the UKLA Guidance Notes.

2.6 ESMA guidance

CESR (the predecessor to ESMA) played a crucial role in ensuring the timely and consistent transposition of the FSAP Directives across the EU.

As part of its Level 3 work, CESR issued Recommendations on the consistent implementation of the PD Regulation in February 2005. The recommendations provide an explanation of some of the disclosure required to comply with the requirements of the PD Regulation. In addition to these Recommendations, CESR also published a set of frequently asked questions (Q&A) regarding prospectuses, providing market participants with quick responses to practical issues arising in connection with the operation of the PD and the PD Regulation. In January 2011, ESMA took over these roles from CESR. To determine its obligations under the PD in the UK, an issuer is obliged by PR 1.1.6G to consider the ESMA Recommendations, the ESMA Q&A and the ESMA Opinions (in addition to the relevant sections of Part VI of the FSMA, the Prospectus Rules, the PD Regulation and the Prospectus RTS Regulations).

The latest set of ESMA Recommendations was published on 20 March 2013; the latest version of the ESMA PD Q&A were published in December 2016, but they are updated from time to time, so the latest version on the ESMA website should always be used. ESMA Opinions are published on an ad hoc basis on matters of relevance to the prospectus regime, including on ESMA's assessment of third country prospectuses.

ESMA has also published Guidelines on the use of Alternative Performance Measures (APMs) (ESMA/2015/1415). An APM is a financial measure that is not required as part of an issuer's financial reporting obligations but which is presented voluntarily by an issuer as an aid to understanding the performance of its business. Examples include net debt, operating earnings and EBITDA (earnings before interest, tax, depreciation and amortisation). Measures specified in the applicable financial reporting framework (such as revenue, profit and earnings per share) and physical or non-financial measures (e.g. customer numbers) are not within the scope of the Guidelines. The ESMA Guidelines on the use of APMs are aimed at promoting the usefulness and transparency of APMs in prospectuses or regulated information and are effective for all documents issued on or after 3 July 2016. Issuers are required (under Regulation (EU) 1095/2010, which gives ESMA the power to issue guidelines in this area) to make 'every effort' to comply with the Guidelines. The Guidelines apply to issuers (other than member states and their regional or local authorities) whose securities are traded on a regulated market (therefore including listed companies, but not AIM companies in the UK) and to persons responsible for a prospectus. Further guidance in relation to APMs can be found in the Q&A published by ESMA on Alternative Performance Measures (ESMA 32-51-370) which provide guidance on how the ESMA Guidelines on the use of APMs should be interpreted.

2.7 Financial disclosure

The PD Regulation has a number of key requirements in terms of financial disclosure in a prospectus:

- historical financial information relating to an issuer and its group;
- an 'operating and financial review' (OFR) explaining the key drivers of an issuer's financial statements, condition and performance, and information on the company's capital resources;

- a working capital statement; and
- a significant change statement.

2.7.1 Historical financial information

Three-year track record

Issuers must include in a prospectus audited consolidated financial information covering the latest three financial years (or such shorter period that the issuer has been in operation) (Item 20.1 of Annex I of PR Appendix 3).

For issuers incorporated in the EEA, this must be prepared according to the IAS Regulation (EC No. 1606/2002) or if the issuer is incorporated in an EU member state in which the IAS Regulation is not applicable, then it can present the information in accordance with its domestic GAAP.

For non-EEA issuers, the financial information must be prepared according to IAS/IFRS or national accounting standards 'equivalent' to these standards in the country in which the issuer is established. The Commission determines which GAAP are 'equivalent' for these purposes. To date, it has said third-country issuers may present their historical financial information in accordance with the accounting standards of the following countries: the United States, Japan, Canada, South Korea and Canada. Third-country issuers may present their historical information in accordance with Indian GAAP for a transitional period, pending further work with the aim of achieving equivalence for Indian GAAP. The Commission has stated that it will continue to monitor the ongoing status of equivalence.

Complex financial history or significant financial commitment

The view of many commentators was that the original PD Regulation did not adequately deal with the disclosure of historical financial information by issuers that had either been through a significant change in the preceding three financial years or had undertaken a significant financial commitment. This was because the PD Regulation only applied to the issuer of the shares in question (i.e. only financial information regarding the issuer was required to be disclosed) which could mean that other relevant information was omitted (e.g. in the context of a new shelf company, or an issuer acquiring other underlying businesses in the IPO track record period). The PD Regulation was therefore amended (by Regulation (EC) 211/2007) to deal with situations where issuers have a 'complex financial history' or a significant financial commitment.

Broadly, a 'complex financial history' arises when the existing financial statements of an issuer preparing a prospectus fail to provide a comprehensive overview to investors as to its financial history over the preceding three years. For example, in the context of a special purpose acquisition structure, it is common for the new company to have been formed specifically for the purpose of the admission/offer, but that company will either have acquired, or have agreed to acquire, certain underlying entities that carry out trading activities which, in essence, the investors are indirectly being asked to invest in.

It would be reasonable for investors to expect to see financial information regarding these underlying entities, so that they can make an informed assessment, and so additional disclosure may be required in that situation.

An issuer will be treated as having a complex financial history if:

- its entire business undertaking at the time the prospectus is drawn up is not accurately represented in the historical financial information required under item 20.1 of Annex 1;
- that inaccuracy will affect the ability of an investor to make an informed assessment; and
- information relating to its business undertaking that is necessary for an investor to make such an assessment is included in financial information relating to another entity.

Additional disclosure may also be required where an issuer has agreed to acquire another business and requires the disclosure of the financial track record of the business if the issuer has incurred a 'significant financial commitment', meaning that it has 'entered into a binding agreement to undertake a transaction which, on completion, is likely to give rise to a significant gross change'. The transaction being subject to conditions does not, in itself, prevent it from being treated as binding provided that it is reasonably certain that such conditions will be fulfilled.

For these purposes, 'significance' is determined in the same way as for pro forma financial information (see below) being a variation of more than 25% relative to one or more indicators of the size of the entities' business (e.g. this would include turnover, revenue or profit and loss).

The Prospectus Regulation does not prescribe what additional disclosure is required where an issuer is found to have a complex financial history or has undertaken a significant financial commitment. Article 4A provides that the competent authority will determine what additional information is required. It may include additional financial information relating to the acquired entities, possibly including pro forma information, based on the requirements of item 20.1 of Annex I. The nature and extent of this disclosure will be driven by the specific facts, including the availability of such additional information and the relative cost of acquiring it (see Article 4A of the PD Regulation, PR 2.3.1 and UKLA Guidance Note *Public offer prospectus – Drafting and approval (UKLA/PN/904.3)*).

Audit requirements

It is necessary to include in a prospectus a statement that the historical financial information has been audited (Item 20.4.1 of Annex I of PR Appendix 3). If these audit reports have been refused by the statutory auditors or if they contain qualifications or disclaimers, these must be reproduced in full and the reasons given.

Where financial data in the prospectus has not been extracted from the issuer's audited financial statements, the source of the data must be stated together with the fact that the data is unaudited.

Age of latest audited annual financial information

The last set of audited annual financial statements may not be older than (a) 18 months before the date of the prospectus if the issuer includes audited interim financial statements, or (b) 15 months before the date of the prospectus if the issuer includes unaudited interim financial statements (Item 20.5 of Annex I of PR Appendix 3).

Interim and other financial information

If the issuer has published quarterly or half-yearly financial information since the date of its last audited financial statements, this must be included in the prospectus (Item 20.6.1 of Annex I of PR Appendix 3). If the quarterly or half-yearly financial information has been reviewed or audited, the audit or review report must also be included. If the quarterly or half-yearly financial information is unaudited, or has not been reviewed, then the prospectus will need to state that fact.

If the prospectus is dated more than nine months after the end of the last audited financial year it must contain interim financial information, which may be unaudited (which must be stated), covering at least the first six months of the financial year.

The interim financial information must include comparative statements for the same period in the prior financial year; the requirement for comparative balance sheet information may be satisfied by presenting the year-end balance sheet.

Even if not technically required by the PD Regulation, there may be other important reasons why an issuer may choose to include interim financial information in a prospectus (e.g. there are additional considerations if it is being prepared in connection with a capital raising that involves a US Rule 144A offering to institutional investors). If the underwriters request a SAS 72 negative assurance comfort letter as to subsequent changes in specified financial statement items as of a date more than 135 days or more subsequent to the end of the most recent period for which the accountants have performed an audit or review, the accountants may not provide such negative assurance. The practical effect of this is that the audited or reviewed financial statements to be included in the prospectus must not be more than 135 days old (sometimes referred to as the '135 day' rule). If this information is not available and the accountants are unable to issue a standard SAS 72 negative assurance comfort letter, the underwriters may not be prepared to proceed with a Rule 144A offering to institutional investors.

Pro forma financial information

Pro forma financial information is required in the case of a 'significant gross change' (i.e. a variation of more than 25% of the size of the issuer's business, due to a particular transaction) with the exception of those situations where merger accounting is required (item 20.2 of PR Appendix 3). The size of the issuer's business for these purposes is generally measured against a non-exhaustive list of indicators, including total assets, revenue and profits or loss. The specific content and presentation requirements are set out in Annex II of PR Appendix 3. The UKLA has clarified (in UKLA Guidance Note *Pro forma financial information (UKLA/TN/633.1)*) that the contents requirements of Annex II should not be regarded as mandating the production of any or all of these items of pro forma financial information, but rather as describing the way in which it should be presented and the information which must be included. An issuer may also include 'voluntary' pro forma financial information – the UKLA states in UKLA Guidance Note *Pro forma financial information (UKLA/TN/633.1)* that, if voluntary financial information is included in a prospectus, it should be subject to the requirements of Annex II (a view also iterated in Question 54 of the ESMA PD Q&A).

An auditor's report is required to be published in the prospectus in respect of the pro forma financial information; this must include the exact wording set out in item 7 of Annex II of PR Appendix 3. This is not an audit opinion, but a report on methodology. See Question 55 of the ESMA PD Q&A.

2.7.2 Operating and financial review

An issuer is required to include in a prospectus an operating and financial review (OFR) which explains the key drivers of the financial statements (Item 9 of Annex I of PR Appendix 3). The OFR will comprise a description of the issuer's financial condition, changes in its financial condition and results of operations for each year and interim period for which historical information is required, including the causes of material change to the financial information to the extent necessary for an understanding of the issuer's business. A year-on-year comparison prepared on the basis of the same accounting principles should be considered (see further paragraphs 27 to 32 and 60 of the ESMA Recommendations).

In addition, the issuer is required to provide a narrative discussion of the reasons for any material change in the income statement. An issuer must also provide information regarding any governmental, economic, fiscal, monetary or political policies which could materially affect its operations.

The FCA has published guidance on OFRs in its UKLA Guidance Note *Operating and financial reviews (UKLA/TN/624.1)*.

2.7.3 Capital resources and statement of capitalisation and indebtedness

An issuer needs to supply information concerning the issuer's capital resources (both short and long term) and a statement of capitalisation and indebtedness no earlier than 90 days prior to the date of the prospectus (Item 3.2 of Annex III of PR Appendix 3). The practical effect of this is that the issuer needs to prepare additional financial information if the last audited or reviewed financial statements included in the prospectus are more than 90 days old at the date of the approval of the prospectus. Paragraph 127 of the ESMA Recommendations sets out the prescriptive format which the statement of capitalisation and indebtedness should follow.

There will also need to be an explanation of the sources and amounts of the issuer's cash flow along with a narrative description (Item 10.2 of Annex I of PR Appendix 3). Information must be disclosed on the borrowing requirements and funding structure of the issuer, together with information on its anticipated sources of funds (Item 10.3 of Annex I of PR Appendix 3). Details of any restrictions on the use of capital resources that have either materially affected or could materially affect, directly or indirectly, the issuer's operations, must also be included in the prospectus (Item 10.4 of Annex I of PR Appendix 3).

2.7.4 Working capital statement

An issuer is required to include in a prospectus a statement that, in its opinion, the working capital (i.e. the issuer's ability to access cash and other available liquid resources to meet its liabilities as they fall due) is sufficient for present requirements (being 12 months from the date of the prospectus) or, if not, how the issuer proposes to provide the additional working capital needed (Item 3.1 of Annex III of PR Appendix 3).

A distinction is to be drawn between a 'clean' working capital statement and a qualified working capital statement (where an issuer has insufficient working capital for the 12-month post-prospectus period). See further paragraphs 107 to 126 of the ESMA Recommendations.

Where an issuer is aware of working capital difficulties beyond its present 12-month requirements, it should consider whether supplementary disclosure in the prospectus is required (paragraph 110 of the ESMA Recommendations). For an issuer with subsidiaries, the working capital statement should relate to the issuer's group.

In UKLA Guidance Note *Working capital statements and risks factors (UKLA/ TN/321.1)*, the FCA considers the interaction between a clean working capital statement and the requirement to include risk factors in the prospectus. See section 2.3.2 above.

See Chapter 3 on the role of the sponsor in respect of working capital.

2.7.5 Significant change statement

An issuer is also required to include details of any significant change in the financial or trading position of the group which has occurred since the end of the last financial year for which either audited financial information or interim financial information has been published, or a statement that there is no such information (Item 20.9 of Annex I of PR Appendix 3).

2.8 Incorporation by reference

Incorporation by reference (the inclusion of a cross-reference to a previously published document rather than the inclusion of the full text in the prospectus) is permitted in certain limited circumstances on the basis that it will facilitate the drawing up of a prospectus and make it less costly. These cross-references are allowed in a prospectus to refer to information contained in one or more previously or simultaneously published documents that have either been approved by (or filed with) the FCA or which have been provided to the FCA in accordance with the PD or the TD (PR 2.4.1R) including annual accounts and half-yearly reports (PR 2.4.2G).

In UKLA Guidance Note *Incorporation by reference (UKLA/TN/620.1)*, the FCA says it also permits documents to be incorporated by reference where they have been approved or filed with another competent authority that was the home competent authority for the issuer at the time of approval or filing.

In Question 8 of the ESMA PD Q&A, ESMA states that information from a previous base prospectus that is no longer valid could be incorporated by reference into a new base prospectus.

Question 7 of the ESMA PD Q&A considers whether it is possible to incorporate information by reference to the translation of a document that has been approved or filed with the competent authority in a different language and concludes that a translation may be incorporated by reference as long as it complies with Article 11 (Incorporation by reference) and Article 19 (Use of languages) of the PD.

The summary must not incorporate information by reference (PR 2.4.4R). Information which is to be incorporated by reference must be the latest available to the issuer (PR 2.4.3R) and a cross-reference list of the information incorporated by reference must be included in the prospectus to enable investors to identify easily specific items of information (PR 2.4.5R). The cross-reference list must specify where the information can be accessed by investors.

'Daisy chaining' – whereby an issuer seeks to incorporate information by reference to documents which themselves incorporate that information by reference to other documents – is not permitted. Each document must be incorporated by reference separately.

2.9 Omission of information

Without prejudice to the general duty of disclosure set out in section 87A(2) of the FSMA, if information required to be disclosed by the PD Regulation is inappropriate to the issuer's activity or to the legal form of the issuer or to the transferable securities to which the prospectus relates, the prospectus must contain information equivalent to the required information (unless there is no such information) (PR 2.5.1R).

In addition, the FCA can, in very limited circumstances, authorise information to be omitted from the prospectus (PR 2.5.2 and FSMA s. 87B(1)).

In summary, the FCA may authorise the omission of information from a prospectus where:

- disclosure would be contrary to the public interest;
- disclosure would be seriously detrimental to the issuer and omission would be unlikely to mislead investors as to any facts and circumstances which are essential to make an informed assessment of the kind mentioned in section 87A(2) of the FSMA (the general duty of disclosure discussed in section 2.4 above); or
- the information is only of minor importance for the specific offer to the public or admission to trading on a regulated market and unlikely to influence an informed assessment of the kind mentioned in section 87A(2) of the FSMA.

In practice, the FCA will not readily permit an issuer to omit information under these provisions. Any request to omit information must be in writing, include specific details about the information for which the derogation is sought and explain why, in the opinion of the issuer, one or more of the grounds in section 87B(1) of the FSMA applies (PR 2.5.3G).

2.10 Equivalent documents

The Prospectus Rules (PR 1.2.2(2) and (3) and PR 1.2.3(3) and (4)) provide that if the securities are offered, allotted or are to be allotted in connection with a merger or takeover, a prospectus is not required if a document is available containing information that is regarded by the FCA as being equivalent to that contained in a prospectus (an 'equivalent document') (see also sections 1.5.2 and 1.5.3 above). In practice, the FCA requires the content of an equivalent document to be identical to that of a prospectus (see the UKLA Guidance Note *Exemptions from the requirement to produce a prospectus (UKLA/TN/602.1)*).

An equivalent document offers the key advantage over a prospectus that the issuer and its directors will not have statutory liability under section 90(1) of the FSMA for its contents.

In the UKLA Guidance Note on the exemptions, the FCA makes it clear that there is no obligation to publish a supplementary prospectus for an equivalent document.

This means that withdrawal rights under section 87G of the FSMA would not apply in relation to the offer or admission being made. However, an equivalent document cannot be 'passported' into any other EEA states and where an offer is to be made in other EEA member states, any 'host' competent authority may challenge such a document as not being equivalent.

2.11 Proportionate disclosure regime

The PD provides for a proportionate disclosure regime, which imposes fewer disclosure requirements, in the case of:

- companies with a reduced market capitalisation and small and medium sized enterprises (SMEs); and
- pre-emptive offers of shares by companies whose shares of the same class are admitted to trading on an EEA regulated market or MTF (in the latter case provided that the MTF has appropriate ongoing disclosure requirements).

This regime is discussed in further detail in the context of rights issues in Chapter 10.

Figure 4.2: Illustrative contents of a prospectus published in connection with a public offer or admission to trading of shares

Heading	Disclosure required
Front sheet	Details of the issuer, including its name, place of incorporation and registration and legislation under which it operates (see Items 5.1.1, 5.1.2 and 5.1.4 of Annex I of PR Appendix 3) and details of the securities offered, the currency of the securities, an indication of pricing and where such securities will be admitted to trading (Items 4.1, 6.1 and 6.2 of Annex III of PR Appendix 3).
Contents	The prospectus must include a clear and detailed table of contents (see Art. 25(1) of the PD Regulation and PR 2.2.10).
Summary	The prospectus must include a summary (see PR 2.1.2 and FSMA s. 87A(5)). This should not generally exceed 7% of the length of a prospectus or 15 pages, whichever is the longer, should concisely convey in non-technical language and in an appropriate structure, the key information relevant to the securities associated with the issuer, any guarantor and the securities to which the prospectus relates (see PR 2.1.2 and FSMA s. 87A(6)). The summary must be produced on a common modular basis and should contain the key information items set out in the five tables Annex XXII of the PD Regulation.

Heading	Disclosure required
Risk factors	Detailed description of the principal risks relating to the issuer, including risks relating to its business, the industry in which it operates and the securities being offered and/or admitted to trading (see item 4 of Annex I of PR Appendix 3 and item 2 of Annex III of PR Appendix 3). This section should come after the table of contents and summary (see Art. 25(1) of the PD Regulation and PR 2.2.10). See also UKLA Guidance Note *Risk factors* (UKLA/TN/621.3).
Directors, company secretary, registered office and advisers	A list of the directors, company secretary, registered office and advisers (see Items 2.1, 5.1, 14.1 of Annex I of PR Appendix 3 and Item 10.1 of Annex III of PR Appendix 3).
Share capital statistics and expected timetable	A table setting out the issuer's share capital and details of the shares to be issued as part of the offer (see Item 21 of Annex I of PR Appendix 3 and Items 4.1 to 4.5 of Annex III of PR Appendix 3) and details of the key transaction dates including the offer period and the expected date of issue and listing of the shares (see Items 4.7 and 5.1 of Annex III of PR Appendix 3).
Part I – Business overview	A description of the issuer and its business and details of its products, assets, investments, services, activities, business strengths and strategy and the industry and markets in which it operates (see Items 5, 6, 7, 8 and 11 of Annex I of PR Appendix 3).
Overview, group structure and history	(See Items 5.1.5, 6.1.1 and 7 of Annex I of PR Appendix 3.)
Industry, competitive strengths and strategy	(See Items 6.2 and 6.5 of Annex I of PR Appendix 3.)
Products and services	(See Item 6.1 of Annex I of PR Appendix 3.)
Research & development and intellectual property	(See Items 6.4 and 11 of Annex I of PR Appendix 3.)
Part II – Management and employees	Details of the directors and senior managers and their compensation arrangements, the Board and committee structure, compliance with corporate governance requirements and summary details of employees (see Items 14, 15, 16 and 17 of Annex I of PR Appendix 3).

Heading	Disclosure required
Directors	Information on each of the directors including, in each case, their name, position, length of time in office, short biographical details and information regarding their entitlement to benefits on termination of employment (see Items 14.1 and 16.2 of Annex I of PR Appendix 3).
Senior managers	Information on each of the senior managers who are relevant to establishing that the issuer has the appropriate expertise and experience for the management of its business, including, in each case, their name, position and short biographical details (see item 14.1 of Annex I of PR Appendix 3).
Compensation	Details of the remuneration paid (including contingent or deferred compensation) and benefits-in-kind granted to the directors and senior managers (see Item 15 of Annex I of PR Appendix 3). Where this information is not otherwise required by applicable law to be disclosed on an individual basis, an aggregate amount for compensation and benefits may be disclosed. In the UK, while directors' remuneration is required to be disclosed in a listed company's Annual Financial Report on an individual basis, there is no corresponding requirement for senior managers' remuneration to be disclosed on the same basis.
Board and committees	Details of the members and terms of reference of the Board and any committees of the Board including audit and remuneration committees (see Items 14 and 16.3 of Annex I of PR Appendix 3).
Corporate governance	A description of the issuer's corporate governance practices and an assessment of its compliance with the Corporate Governance Code (see Item 16.4 of Annex I of PR Appendix 3).
Employees	Details of the average number of group employees at the end of the last three financial periods and, if possible, a breakdown of the average number of persons employed by the group, broken down by business activity and geographic location for the last three financial periods (see Item 17.1 of Annex I of PR Appendix 3).
Part III – Selected financial information	The prospectus is required to include selected historical financial information for the issuer, presented for each financial year for the period covered by the historical financial information, and any subsequent interim financial period, in the same currency as the financial information. This must provide the key figures that summarise the financial condition of the issuer (see Item 3.1 of Annex I of PR Appendix 3). If selected financial information for interim periods is provided, comparative data for the same period in the prior financial year must also be provided. For comparative balance sheet information, this is satisfied by presenting the year-end balance sheet information (see Item 3.2 of Annex I of PR Appendix 3). Refer to the guidance given in paragraphs 20 to 26 of the ESMA Recommendations.

Heading	Disclosure required
Part IV – Operating and financial review	Details of the factors that affect the issuer's results of operations, a breakdown of results of operation by sector, product or geography, a comparative review of results of operations for the last three financial years, details of capital resources and current trading, trends and prospects (see Items 9, 10 and 12 of Annex I of PR Appendix 3).
Overview	A summary of the issuer's business and key performance indicators.
Significant factors affecting results of operations	A summary of significant factors, including unusual or infrequent events or new developments, materially affecting the issuer's income from operations and the extent to which income was affected. This includes information as to any governmental, economic, fiscal, monetary or political policies or factors that have materially affected or could materially affect, directly or indirectly, operations, e.g. acquisitions and disposals, production costs, exchange rates, seasonality and pension issues (see Item 9.2 of Annex I of PR Appendix 3). Refer to the guidance given in paragraphs 27 to 32 of the ESMA Recommendations.
Results of operations, by sector, product and geography	This typically comprises a table setting out a breakdown of the issuer's turnover by sector, product market and/or geographic region, depending on the financial information available and how the issuer is accustomed to reporting its results, for each year for which historical financial information is required to be included in the prospectus (see Items 6.1.1 and 6.2 of Annex I of PR Appendix 3).
Comparative review of results of operations	A description of the issuer's financial condition, changes in financial condition and results of operations for each year and interim period for which historical financial information is required to be included in the prospectus, including the causes of material changes from year to year in the financial information to the extent necessary for an understanding of the issuer's business as a whole (see Item 9.1 of Annex I of PR Appendix 3). This customarily includes a comparative year-on-year review of key line items including turnover, net operating costs, profit on ordinary activities before interest and taxation, net interest, taxation on profit on ordinary activities, retained profit/loss and dividends.
Liquidity and capital resources	A description of cash flow, capital expenditure, resources (both short and long term) existing and new facilities and working capital requirements (see Items 10.1 to 10.5 of Annex I of PR Appendix 3). Refer to the guidance in paragraphs 33 to 37 of the ESMA Recommendations.

Heading	Disclosure required
Capitalisation and indebtedness	The prospectus must include a statement of capitalisation and indebtedness (distinguishing between guaranteed and non-guaranteed, and secured and unsecured indebtedness) as of a date no earlier than 90 days prior to the date of the prospectus (see Item 3.2 of Annex III of PR Appendix 3). For these purposes, indebtedness also includes indirect and contingent indebtedness. Refer to the guidance and prescribed form of capitalisation and indebtedness table in paragraph 127 of the ESMA Recommendations and Question 62 of the ESMA PD Q&A.
Dividends and dividend policy	A description of the issuer's policy on dividend distributions and any restrictions thereon and the amount of the dividend per share for each financial year for the period covered by the historical financial information, adjusted where the number of shares in the company has changed to make it comparable (see Item 20.7 of Annex I of PR Appendix 3).
Current trading, trends and prospects	Details of the most significant recent trends in production, sales and inventory, and costs and selling prices since the end of the last financial year, together with information on any known trends, uncertainties, demands, commitments or events that are reasonably likely to have a material effect on the issuer's prospects for at least the current financial year (see Item 12 of Annex I of PR Appendix 3). See the UKLA Guidance Note *Current trading and trend information (UKLA/TN/625.1)*.
Part V – Historical financial information	Financial information for the last three financial years and the audit report for each such year (see Items 20.1 and 20.4 of Annex I and Item 10.2 of Annex III of PR Appendix 3). Refer to the guidance in paragraphs 51 to 86 of the ESMA Recommendations.
Part VI – Pro forma financial information	If pro forma financial information is included, it must, among others (i) clearly state the purpose for which it has been prepared and that it is for illustrative purposes only and may not reflect the issuer's actual financial position or results; (ii) be prepared in a manner consistent with the accounting policies adopted in its last or next financial statements; (iii) ensure that adjustments are clear, directly attributable to the transaction and factually supportable; and (iv) include an accountant's report stating that the pro forma has been properly compiled on the basis stated and that the basis is consistent with the issuer's accounting policies (see Annex II of PR Appendix 3). Refer to the guidance in paragraphs 87 to 94 of the ESMA Recommendations and Questions 54 and 55 of the ESMA PD Q&A.
Part VII – The offer	Details of the offer and the securities being offered (see Item 5 of Annex III of PR Appendix 3).

Heading	Disclosure required
The offer	A description of the type and the class of the securities being offered, the legislation under which they have been created, the rights attached to the securities, currency, whether the securities are in registered form or bearer form and whether the securities are in certificated or book-entry form (see Item 4 Annex III of PR Appendix 3).
Use of proceeds	The reasons for the offer and use of proceeds. Where applicable, and among other details, the issuer should indicate when the proceeds will be used to acquire assets other than in the ordinary course of business, to finance acquisitions of other business or to discharge, reduce or retire indebtedness (see Item 3.4 of Annex III of PR Appendix 3).
Terms and conditions of the offer	This includes conditions to the offer, the time period during which the offer will be open and a plan of distribution and allotment (see Item 5 of Annex III of PR Appendix 3).
Over-allotment and stabilisation	Details of any over-allotment facility. This includes, where applicable, that the issue may be stabilised, the period during which this may occur, the identity of the stabilisation manager and the fact that such transactions may result in a higher market price (see Items 5.2.5 and 6.5 of Annex III of PR Appendix 3).
Settlement and dealing arrangements	A description of any restrictions on the free transferability of the securities (see Item 4.8 of Annex III of PR Appendix 3).
Selling shareholders	The name and address of each person or entity selling the securities (if any) including, the number and class of securities being offered by each of the selling shareholder and the nature of any position, office or material relationship the selling shareholder has had within the past three years with the issuer or any of its predecessors or affiliates (see Items 7.1 and 7.2 of Annex III of PR Appendix 3).
Underwriting arrangements	Names and addresses of the co-ordinators, paying agents, depository agents, underwriters, and the material features of the underwriting agreement including the portion of the issue to which it relates and the overall amount of the underwriting commission (see Item 5.4 of Annex III of PR Appendix 3).
Lock-up arrangements	Details of any restrictions on disposals of shares, including the parties involved, the lock-up period and the content and exceptions of the lock-up agreement (see Item 7.3 of Annex III of PR Appendix 3).
Securities laws	Legislation under which the securities have been created (Item 4.2 of Annex III of PR Appendix 3).

Heading	Disclosure required
Part VIII – Taxation	Information on tax on the income from the securities withheld at source and whether the issuer assumes responsibility for the withholding of such taxes (see item 4.11 of Annex III of PR Appendix 3).
Part IX – Additional information	This section will include all of the additional information that is required to be included in the prospectus by the Prospectus Rules.
Responsibility statement	A declaration from the issuer and its directors that they accept responsibility for the contents of the document and that to the best of their knowledge and belief they have taken all reasonable care to ensure the same the document is in accordance with the facts and does not omit any information likely to affect the import of the information in the document (see Items 1.1 and 1.2 of Annex I and Items 1.1 and 1.2 of Annex III of PR Appendix 3).
The company	The issuer's name and details of its registration and incorporation (see Items 5.1.1 to 5.1.4 of Annex I of PR Appendix 3).
Share capital	The amount of issued capital, and for each class of share capital: the number of shares authorised, the number of shares issued and fully paid and issued but not fully paid, the par value per share or a statement that the shares have no par value and a reconciliation of the number of shares outstanding at the beginning and end of the year. If more than 10% of capital has been paid for with assets other than cash within the period covered by the historical financial information, state that fact (see Item 21.1 of Annex I of PR Appendix 3).
Memorandum and articles of association	A description of the issuer's objects and a summary of its articles of association (see Item 21.2 Annex I of PR Appendix 3).
Major shareholdings	Names and details of those shareholders that are required to notify their interests in capital or voting rights, whether or not any such shareholders have special voting arrangements or rights, whether or not the listed company is controlled or owned by a party and a description of any arrangements in place to ensure that such control is not abused (see Item 18 of Annex I of PR Appendix 3).
Directors' and senior managers' interests	Details of directors' and senior managers' interests in shares and options over shares of the issuer (see Item 17.2 of Annex I of PR Appendix 3). See UKLA Guidance Note *Directors' and management disclosures in share prospectuses* (UKLA/TN/626.1).

Heading	Disclosure required
Directors' and senior managers' remuneration and service agreements	Details of the remuneration paid and benefits in kind granted to each of the directors and senior managers of the issuer, dates of expiration of the current term of office and summary terms of service contracts (see Items 15.1, 16.1 and 16.2 of Annex I of PR Appendix 3).
Directors' and senior managers' conflicts of interest and confirmations	Potential conflicts of interest between duties to the issuer and the private interests of directors and senior managers. Other duties must be clearly stated, together with details of any arrangements or understandings by which that person was appointed to their position within the company (see Item 14.2 of Annex I and Item 3.3 of Annex III of PR Appendix 3). Details of any bankruptcies, convictions for fraud etc. for each director and senior manager or a statement that there are none (see Item 14.1 of Annex I of PR Appendix 3). A statement to the effect that none of the directors or senior managers has during at least the previous five years breached the requirements set out in Item 14.1 of Annex I of PR Appendix 3. See also see UKLA Guidance Note *Directors' and management disclosures in share prospectuses (UKLA/TN/626.1)* and Question 69 of the ESMA PD Q&A.
Pension schemes	Details of employee and, if different, director/executive pension schemes (see Item 15.2 of Annex I of PR Appendix 3).
Share schemes	Details of the employee share schemes (see Items 17.3 and 21.1.6 of Annex I of PR Appendix 3).
Subsidiaries	A list of the issuer's significant subsidiaries and undertakings (see Items 7.1, 7.2 and 25 of Annex I of PR Appendix 3).
Principal investments	A description of the issuer's principal investments for each of the previous financial years covered by the historical financial information and information on the status of pending investments and future investments on which the issuer has made a firm commitment (see Item 5.2 of Annex I of PR Appendix 3).
Property	Details of property, plant and equipment in tabular format (see Item 8 Annex I of PR Appendix 3).
Material contracts	A summary, for the issuer and any group company of the (i) material contracts entered into other than in the ordinary course of business to which the issuer or any member of its group is a party in the two years prior to the publication of the prospectus, and (ii) any other contracts not entered into in the ordinary course of business which contain any provision under which any member of the group has an obligation or entitlement which is material as at the date of the prospectus (see Item 22 of Annex I of PR Appendix 3). See Question 73 of the ESMA PD Q&A and List! Issue No. 23.

Heading	Disclosure required
Related party transactions	Details of related party transactions (under IFRS) that the issuer has entered into during the period covered by the historical financial information and up to the date of the prospectus must be disclosed in accordance with IFRS (see Item 19 of Annex I of PR Appendix 3).
Litigation	Details of any governmental, legal or arbitration proceedings (including any such proceedings which are pending or threatened) for at least the previous 12 months which may have, or have had in the recent past, significant effects on the issuer and/or the group's financial position or profitability or a statement that there are no such claims (see Item 20.8 of Annex I of PR Appendix 3).
Significant change	Details of any significant change in the financial or trading position of the group which has occurred since the end of the last financial period for which either audited financial information or interim financial information has been published or a statement that there is no such information to disclose (see Item 20.9 of Annex I of PR Appendix 3). See Question 65 of the ESMA PD Q&A and the UKLA Guidance Note *Significant change statements (UKLA/TN/628.2)*.
Working capital	A statement by the issuer that, in its opinion, the working capital is sufficient for its present requirements or, if not, how it proposes to provide the additional working capital needed (see Item 3.1 of Annex III of PR Appendix 3). Refer to guidance paragraphs 107 to 126 of the ESMA Recommendations and UKLA Guidance Note *Working capital statements – Basis of preparation (UKLA/TN/320.1)* and UKLA Guidance Note *Working capital statements and risk factors (UKLA/TN/321.1)*.
Costs and expenses	A statement of the total net proceeds and estimated expenses of the issue/offer (see Item 8 of Annex III of PR Appendix 3).
Auditors	Details of the auditors, including their professional qualifications. If the auditors have resigned, been removed or not been re-appointed during the period covered by the historical financial information this should be indicated if material (see Items 2.1 and 2.2 of Annex I of PR Appendix 3).
Consents	Confirmation that auditors, financial advisers or any other third party from whom information has been sourced have given and not withdrawn written consent to the inclusion of their names in the prospectus (see Item 23 of Annex I and Items 10.3 and 10.4 of Annex III of PR Appendix 3).

Heading	Disclosure required
Documents available for inspection	Documents that are available for inspection in connection with the publication of the prospectus, for example, the issuer's memorandum and articles of association, annual report and accounts and any accountants' reports included in the prospectus (see Item 24 of Annex I of PR Appendix 3). See Question 72 of the ESMA PD Q&As and UKLA Guidance Note *Documents on display (UKLA/TN/623.1)*.
Definitions	This includes defined terms used in the prospectus. Where it is helpful to assist investors' understanding, the issuer may also choose to include a glossary of technical terms.

3. Approval, publication and 'passporting'

3.1 Review and approval procedure

3.1.1 Requirement for approval

A prospectus must be approved before any offer can be made to the public or admission to trading can take effect. It is the competent authority of the home member state of an issuer that must approve a prospectus for an issuer (unless the competent authority agrees it is more appropriately dealt with by another competent authority) irrespective of where in the EEA the offering or admission is being made – in the United Kingdom this is the FCA in its role as the UK Listing Authority.

3.1.2 Applying for approval

Prospectus Rule 3.1 sets out the review and approval process for a prospectus and details, for example, which documents in addition to the prospectus itself should be submitted to the FCA. The following documents must be submitted to the FCA (for a premium listing the sponsor will submit these to the FCA on behalf of the issuer):

- a completed Form A;
- the prospectus;
- if the order of items in the prospectus does not coincide with the order in the schedules and building blocks in the PD Regulation, a cross-reference list identifying the pages where each item can be found in the prospectus;
- a letter identifying any items from the schedules and building blocks that have not been included because they are not applicable;
- if information is incorporated in the prospectus by reference to another document, a copy of the document (annotated to indicate which item of the schedules and building blocks in the PD Regulation it relates to);

- if the applicant is requesting the FCA to authorise the omission of information from the prospectus, the information required by PR 2.5.3R;
- contact details of individuals who are (a) sufficiently knowledgeable about the documentation to be able to answer queries from the FCA; and (b) available to answer queries between the hours of 7.00am and 6.00pm; and
- any other information that the FCA may require.

The FCA will then aim to review and give comments on the first draft within ten business days (in the case of a new application/issuer making an offer for the first time) and within five business days for subsequent drafts.

The FCA has published a number of procedural notes providing practical details of the document approval process. The UKLA Guidance Note *Review and approval of documents (UKLA/PN/903.3)* covers the submission of documents to the FCA for review and approval and contains a useful checklist of information which should be included with the initial submission, guidance on how subsequent drafts are dealt with and information on how long the document review process will take.

The issuer's and sponsors' legal advisers will check the document for compliance with the Prospectus Rules and Listing Rules before it is sent to the FCA for approval. This check will also involve putting in the paragraph references for the Prospectus Rules and the Listing Rules against the corresponding disclosure in the prospectus (referred to as 'annotating the prospectus'); this demonstrates to the FCA compliance with the Prospectus Rules and the Listing Rules. Separate lists of variations and non-applicability will also be provided to the FCA. The approval process is iterative. The FCA will perform its own compliance check on the prospectus and will send back a comment sheet to the sponsor. The issuer's advisers will respond to the FCA's comments, usually through a combination of revising the documents to address the comments and providing confirmations or explanations where sought. The process continues on successive drafts of the prospectus. The FCA will not approve the prospectus until all of its comments have been addressed to its satisfaction.

3.2 Methods of publication

3.2.1 Publication requirement

Once a prospectus has been approved it must be filed with the FCA (through the National Storage Mechanism – PR 3.2.1.AR) and made available to the public at the same time (PR 3.2.1R). A prospectus is deemed to be made available to the public when it has been published in one of the following ways:
- inserted in one or more newspapers, circulated throughout or widely circulated in, the member states in which the securities are to be offered or admitted to trading (PR 3.2.4R(1)). Recital 32 of the PD Regulation states that where a newspaper is used for the publication of a prospectus it should have a wide area of distribution

and circulation. Article 30(1) of the PD Regulation and PR 3.2.6A state that publication must be made in a general or financial information newspaper having national or supra-regional scope. PR 3.2.6A also states that if the competent authority does not believe that a nominated newspaper complies with this scope that it shall determine a newspaper which it considers to be appropriate taking into account the geographic area, number of inhabitants and reading habits in each member state;

- in printed form, free of charge to the public, at the offices of the regulated market on which the securities are being admitted to trading, or at the registered office of the issuer and at the offices of the financial intermediaries placing or selling the securities, including paying agents (PR 3.2.4R(2));
- in electronic form on the issuer's website or, if applicable, on the website of the financial intermediaries placing or selling the securities, including paying agents (PR 3.2.4R(3)); or
- in electronic form on the website of the regulated market where admission to trading is sought (PR 3.2.4R(4)).

If the prospectus is made available by insertion in a newspaper or by making hard copies available at the offices of the regulated market or the issuer's office, it must also be published electronically on the issuer's website or on the website of the financial intermediaries placing or selling the securities. This means that publication of prospectuses (and documents incorporated by reference) in electronic form via the specified websites is now effectively always required.

A prospectus published in electronic form must adhere to the requirements of PR 3.2.6A and Commission Delegated Regulation 2016/301 and must:

- be easily accessible when entering the website;
- be in a searchable electronic format that cannot be modified;
- not contain hyperlinks with the exception of links to the electronic addresses where information incorporated by reference is available, and
- be downloadable and printable, and access to a prospectus published in electronic form shall not be subject to completion of a registration process, the acceptance of a disclaimer limiting legal liability or the payment of a fee (see PR 3.2.6A).

Also, where a prospectus containing information incorporated by reference is published in electronic form, it must include hyperlinks to each document containing information incorporated by reference or to each webpage on which the document containing information incorporated by reference is published (PR 3.2.6A). If a prospectus is available on the website of an issuer than it must also take measures to avoid targeting residents in Member States or third countries where the offer of securities to the public does not take place, such as the insertion of a disclaimer as to who are the addressees of the offer.

Following the European Court of Justice's decision in *Michael Timmel v Aviso Zeta AG [2014] CJEU C-359/12*, if a 'click-through' webpage is used, and access to the prospectus is restricted unless, for example, an investor provides an e-mail address, this would breach electronic prospectus publication requirements in PR 3.2.6A. Issuers using such methods should therefore consider additional methods of publication, such as a hard copy being made available at the issuer's registered office.

3.2.2 Circulation of hard copies

There are no specific provisions in the Prospectus Rules or the Listing Rules which require a prospectus to be sent to shareholders: an issuer only has to comply with the provisions of PR 3.2.4R (described above). A listed company may, of course, wish to send copies of any prospectuses they produce to their shareholders, but the FCA has made it clear that this decision lies with issuers and is not an FCA requirement.

It is important to remember, however, that if a prospectus is made available by publication in electronic form, a hard copy must nonetheless be delivered to the investor, upon request and free of charge, by the issuer, the offeror, the person requesting admission or the financial intermediaries placing or selling the securities (PR 3.2.6R).

3.2.3 Timing of publication

Generally, a prospectus must be filed with the FCA and made available to the public as soon as is practicable and, in any case at a reasonable time in advance of, and at the latest, at the beginning of, the offer or admission (PR 3.2.2R).

In the case of an initial public offering, the prospectus must be made available to the public at least six working days before the end of the offer (PR 3.2.3R). However, in the UKLA Guidance Note *Public offers – The six day rule (UKLA/TN/603.1)* the FCA said that where there is an institutional placing of new shares to be admitted to trading on a regulated market, this requirement in PR 3.2.3R does not apply because there is no public offer which requires the production of a prospectus (the offer is exempt as it is made to qualified investors) only the admission to trading does. To market to institutions, the issuer can produce an unapproved pre-marketing document under the advertisements regime in PR 3.3 (see further section 6 below).

3.2.4 Publication on FCA website

The FCA has the option under the PD (Art. 14(4) PD) of publishing prospectuses on its website. The FCA does not do this. However, under PR 3.2.7G, the FCA is obliged to publish on its website a list of prospectuses it has approved over the previous 12 months. The list must specify how a prospectus was made available to the public and where it can be obtained, including, if applicable, a hyperlink to the website of the issuer or relevant regulated market. The FCA has this list on its website together with a list of prospectuses which have been passported into the UK.

3.2.5 National storage mechanism

All prospectuses approved by the FCA (and all other information required to be disclosed under the LPDT Rules) are required to be published on the national storage mechanism (NSM) (which replaced the document viewing facility in 2010). The issuer must forward the document to Morningstar, which operates the NSM. The document is then published on www.morningstar.co.uk/uk/NSM. Issuers must bear in mind that the prospectus will be freely accessible when drafting the disclaimers for the prospectus.

3.2.6 Validity of the prospectus once approved

A prospectus is valid for 12 months from the date it is approved.

Where an issuer produces a single prospectus, the document is only valid for the offer or admission to trading described in the document.

As further described in section 2.1, where an issuer produces a tri-partite prospectus, once the registration document has been approved, it will remain valid for 12 months and can be combined with a new or updated securities note and summary note for future issues of securities during that period (see Question 75 of the ESMA PD Q&A). The securities note can, in those circumstances, contain information that would otherwise be in the registration document.

3.3 Passporting within the EEA

Articles 17 and 18 of the PD introduced the concept of a 'single passport' for issuers where a prospectus approved by one competent authority is available for use throughout the EEA, without additional significant administrative requirements from any other member states. The host member state may require the summary of an English language prospectus to be translated into the language customarily spoken and used in the relevant host member state.

In the UKLA Guidance Note *Passporting (UKLA/PN/905.2)* the FCA provides guidance on the 'passporting' process and sets out those jurisdictions that do not require a translation of the summary. In addition, the ESMA PD Q&A consider a number of issues which arise when passporting a prospectus (see, in particular, Question 33) including where member states take a different approach (e.g. whether an issuer is required to publish a notice that a prospectus has been passported in a host member state) (see Question 2).

The mechanics for passporting a prospectus out of the UK are relatively straightforward. An issuer wishing to take advantage of the option to passport must, where the UK is its home member state, ask the FCA to provide the relevant host member state with a copy of the prospectus that has been approved by the FCA, a certificate of approval and, where requested by the competent authority in the host member state, a translation of the summary of the prospectus (FSMA s. 87I(1)).

The request should be made by sending a request letter to the FCA. A suggested form is available on the FCA's website. Most importantly, the letter must include details of the name and date of the document to be passported and the jurisdictions into which the document should be sent (see the UKLA Guidance Note *Passporting (UKLA/PN/905.2)*).

The issuer can make this request either with the application for approval of its prospectus or after it has been approved. In the former case, the certificate and documents will be issued within one working day of the approval of the relevant prospectus; in the latter, it will be issued within three working days of the request being made beginning with the date of the request (FSMA s. 87I(5)). The FSA (the predecessor to the FCA) stated that, technically, it should be possible for it to approve and passport a prospectus on the same day, but there are practical issues for them. If it is important that passporting and approval happen on the same day, this should be discussed with the FCA at an early stage and there should be ongoing liaison with them about their and any host member state requirements.

If a prospectus is passported into the UK, the same process applies in reverse. See the UKLA Guidance Note *Passporting (UKLA/PN/905.2)*.

One further point to note is in relation to responsibility for an approved prospectus that is passported outside the UK. While the PD provides that responsibility must attach to certain minimum categories of person, it does not provide for a single system of who may be responsible for a prospectus in any EEA state. Consequently, if a prospectus is passported, the issuer (and possibly other parties to the transaction including the issuer's directors and the underwriters) may find that the responsibility regime in the host member states into which the prospectus is being passported is different to the UK.

4. Supplementary prospectuses

4.1 Obligation to prepare and publish a supplementary prospectus

If at any time after a prospectus is approved, and before the later of (i) the final closing of the offer and (ii) admission to trading, there arises a significant new factor, material mistake or inaccuracy relating to the information included in a prospectus, a supplementary prospectus must be submitted to the FCA for its approval and then (if approved) published (PR 3.4.1 and FSMA s. 87G).

The Prospectus Rules were amended in 2014 to set out the circumstances in which a supplementary prospectus must be published to reflect an EU Regulation (382/2014).

PR 3.4.4 provides that the situations in which an issuer of equity securities must publish a supplementary prospectus include:

- publication of new annual audited financial statements;
- publication of any modification to a profit forecast or profit estimate contained in the initial prospectus;
- a change of control of the issuer;
- if the issuer's working capital becomes insufficient for its requirements (or conversely, if a qualified working capital statement was included in the initial prospectus, the issuer's working capital becomes sufficient for its present purposes); and
- if the prospectus is used to make a public offer into an additional EU member state or to seek admission to trading on an additional EU regulated market, which is not contemplated in it.

This list is not comprehensive but simply prescribes situations where a supplementary prospectus must be published. In situations outside the scope of the list, it remains the issuer's responsibility to determine the significance of an event, taking into account the issuer and the securities in question, and to decide whether publication of a supplementary prospectus is required.

Both ESMA and the FCA have considered when a supplementary prospectus will be required. Question 19 of the ESMA PD Q&A considers the impact of the publication of interim financial information while the prospectus is still 'live'. It states that whether or not a supplementary prospectus is required when interim financial statements are produced will depend on the circumstances of the case, for example, if there is a significant deviation in relation to previous financial information.

Question 20 of the ESMA PD Q&A states that there would be a presumption that the publication of a profit forecast before the final closing of an offer would be material, triggering the requirement for the preparation and publication of a supplementary prospectus.

The UKLA Guidance Note *Supplementary prospectuses (UKLA/TN/605.2)* also considers other situations where a supplementary prospectus may be required (e.g. to describe external events, such as a factory burning down, or to inform investors of an increase in the number of shares to be admitted for the acquisition of a target).

The FSA considered whether a supplementary prospectus would be required if an offer was priced above or below a price range in an approved prospectus. Its guidance states that a supplementary prospectus may be required in these circumstances, even where the prospectus contains the usual language about the price range being indicative only, states that the offer price may be set above the price range, and gives the usual factors for determining the final offer price, namely level and nature of demand for the shares, prevailing market conditions and the objective of establishing an orderly after-market in the shares.

Supplementary prospectuses are commonly published, among other reasons, for interim results, to provide details of new threatened litigation and to amend an offer price range.

If new information arises after the publication of a prospectus which is not significant (and so does not require the publication of a supplementary prospectus) but could be useful for investors (e.g. where the prospectus contains mistakes or inaccuracies which are not material) Question 23 of the ESMA PD Q&A states that the issuer should be entitled to make an announcement to the market explaining the mistake or inaccuracy but cannot amend the prospectus. It is necessary to undertake an assessment of whether new information does, in fact, trigger the requirement for a supplementary prospectus to be published. In the UKLA Guidance Note *Supplementary prospectuses (UKLA/TN/605.2)*, the FCA states that it would challenge the use of a supplementary prospectus where it was aware that any matter presented was not factually accurate or could not be credibly considered to be a significant factor. It is not appropriate to publish a supplementary prospectus simply to clarify or revise drafting nor should drafting changes be made as part of a supplementary prospectus.

In the UKLA Guidance Note *Exemptions from the requirement to prepare a prospectus (UKLA/TN/602.1)*, the FCA has made it clear that there is no obligation to publish a supplementary prospectus for an equivalent document produced on a takeover or merger pursuant to PR 1.2.2R(2) PR 1.2.2R(3) PR 1.2.3R(3) and/or PR 1.2.3R(4). This means that withdrawal rights under section 87Q of the FSMA would not arise.

A premium listed company must appoint a sponsor when submitting a supplementary prospectus to the FCA (LR 8.2.1R(1)(a)). Additionally, an amending advertisement must also be disseminated if any earlier advertisement is rendered inaccurate or misleading by a significant new factor or material mistake or inaccuracy disclosed in, or corrected by, a supplementary prospectus (see PR 3.3.3A) (see section 6 below for more detail).

4.2 Application of the Prospectus Rules

Pursuant to PR 1.1.9R, unless the context requires otherwise, a reference in the Prospectus Rules to a 'prospectus' includes a reference to a 'supplementary prospectus'. For example, this means that the rules on responsibility for prospectuses also apply to supplementary prospectuses, as do the rules on the publication. If a prospectus has been passported out of the UK, this will be required for any supplementary prospectus.

4.3 Impact on the summary

When preparing a supplementary prospectus, it is also necessary to consider the summary that was included in the original approved prospectus. The supplementary prospectus will need to include any amendment or supplement to the summary to take account of the new information (PR 3.4.2R).

4.4 Timing of supplementary prospectuses

On an offer of transferable securities to the public, the obligation to produce a supplementary prospectus expires on the closure of the offer of the transferable securities. On the admission of the securities to trading, the relevant period will end when trading in those securities on a regulated market begins (s. 87G(3) FSMA). Section 87G(3A) confirms that the obligation to publish ends on the later of the closing of the offer and admission to trading. In relation to an offeror whose securities are not admitted to a regulated market (e.g. an AIM issuer) the FSA stated in List! Issue No. 11 that it expected that the relevant period would run until the date on which the offer closes.

Where a prospectus has been produced in respect of an application for an admission to trading and subsequently a supplementary prospectus needs to be published, the FCA has said that it will not admit the relevant securities to trading until the supplementary prospectus has been published.

Section 87G(2) of the FSMA does not provide an express time limit for the submission of draft supplementary prospectuses to the UKLA for approval. This led the FCA to introduce PR 3.4.3R; this requires supplementary prospectuses to be submitted as soon as is practicable after the new factor, mistake or inaccuracy arose or was noted.

In the UKLA Guidance Note *Supplementary prospectuses (UKLA/TN/605.2)*, the FCA also notes that, even though no express time limit is stipulated, failure to produce a supplementary prospectus in a timely manner may expose an issuer to the compensation provisions of section 90 of FSMA in relation to any loss suffered as a result of such a failure. See also Question 22 of the ESMA PD Q&A.

4.5 Method of publication

A supplementary prospectus must be published in accordance with PR 3.2.4R in the same way as a prospectus (see section 3.2 above). While there is no requirement under the Prospectus Rules or the Listing Rules to provide a copy of the supplementary prospectus to all potential investors who requested a copy of the original prospectus, it is often advisable to send a copy to those persons who have already applied for shares under the offer.

4.6 Impact of a supplementary prospectus on an offer – withdrawal rights

The FCA states in UKLA Guidance Note *Supplementary prospectus (UKLA/TN/605.2)* that, in offer situations, it considers it to be best practice for the offer to be suspended between an event triggering the requirement to prepare and publish a supplementary prospectus and the date of its publication. This ensures that investors are not unconditionally allotted shares based on incomplete disclosure.

The PD provides for withdrawal rights on the publication of a supplementary prospectus:

Where the prospectus relates to an offer of securities to the public, investors who have already agreed to purchase or subscribe for the securities before the supplement is published, shall have the right, exercisable within two working days after the publication of the supplement, to withdraw their acceptance provided that the new factor, mistake or inaccuracy which triggered the requirement to publish the supplement arose before the final closing of the offer to the public and the delivery of the securities.

This is implemented in the UK in section 87Q(4) of FSMA, pursuant to which a person may withdraw their acceptance of an offer of transferable securities to the public before a specified deadline if certain conditions are met. The conditions are set out in section 87Q(5) and are:

- a prospectus which relates to an offer of transferable securities to the public has been published;
- a supplementary prospectus has been published;
- prior to the publication of the supplementary prospectus, the person agreed to buy or subscribe for transferable securities to which the offer relates; and
- the significant new factor, material mistake or inaccuracy which caused the supplementary prospectus to be published arose before delivery of the securities.

The withdrawal rights must be exercised before the end of the second working day after the day on which the supplementary prospectus was published, or such later time as may be specified in the supplementary prospectus (s. 87Q(6)).

The first edition of the UKLA Guidance Note *Supplementary prospectuses (UKLA/TN/605.1)* stated that withdrawal rights do not apply in relation to any investor whose agreement to buy or subscribe securities is not subject to any condition. This was not repeated in the second edition of this Guidance Note: UKLA/TN/605.2. It is thought, however, that if withdrawal rights are triggered, issuers should not seek to complete allotments during the 48-hour withdrawal rights period to try to prevent investors from exercising their rights. The significance of statutory withdrawal rights will depend on the transaction in question.

On an IPO, withdrawal rights may extend the period of risk for underwriters and consideration will need to be given as to who should assume the risk and how this will then feed into the overall process including settlement.

If an approved prospectus is produced for a takeover and the need for a supplementary prospectus arises, target shareholders will have the chance to withdraw their acceptance.

In relation to a rights issue, a subscriber who has submitted a PAL but whose cheque has not yet been processed and who has not yet been allotted the fully paid share could withdraw if a supplementary prospectus is issued.

Investors will also have withdrawal rights if the prospectus does not contain the final offer price and the amount of securities to be offered. Clearly, in the case of a price range prospectus, these details are not included so withdrawal rights will, *prima facie*, be exercisable until those details have been notified to the FCA (FSMA s. 87Q(2)(b)). However, withdrawal rights will not arise (FSMA s. 87Q(3)) if the price-range prospectus includes the criteria and/or conditions according to which the number of securities to be offered will be determined and the criteria and/or conditions according to which the final offer price will be determined (or the maximum price). The FCA has confirmed that the notification of the final offer price and the number of securities to be offered will not (assuming the price is within the price range) require a supplementary prospectus (so no withdrawal rights arise). Instead, there is an obligation on the applicant to notify the FCA in writing of that information once it is finalised (FSMA s. 87A(7)), usually by way of a pricing statement. If publication of a supplementary prospectus is required because the disclosed criteria for determining the price (or size) was not certain enough, withdrawal rights will arise and extend the period of risk for underwriters.

5. Liability regime

5.1 Minimum requirements of the PD

The PD requires member states to ensure that responsibility for the information given in a prospectus attaches at least to the issuer or its administrative, management or supervisory bodies, the offeror, the person asking for the admission to trading on a regulated market or the guarantor, as the case may be. The persons responsible must be clearly identified in the prospectus by their names and functions or, in the case of legal persons, their names and registered offices. The prospectus must also contain declarations by them that, to the best of their knowledge, the information contained in the prospectus is in accordance with the facts and that the prospectus makes no omission likely to affect its import.

The PD also requires member states to ensure that their laws, regulations and administrative provisions on civil liability apply to those persons responsible for the information given in a prospectus.

However, under the PD, no civil liability will attach to any person solely on the basis of the summary (including any translation), unless it is misleading, inaccurate or inconsistent when read together with the other parts of the prospectus or it does not provide, when read together with the other parts of the prospectus, key information to help investors when considering whether to invest in such securities. The summary must contain a clear warning to that effect (PR 2.1.7R).

5.2 Responsible persons under Prospectus Rule 5.5

5.2.1 Definition of 'responsible persons'

The categories of person who are responsible for a prospectus prepared in respect of equity securities are set out in PR 5.5. They include:

- the issuer of the relevant securities;
- the directors of the issuer at the time the prospectus is published;
- each person who has authorised himself to be named in, and is named in, the prospectus as a director, or as having agreed to become a director, of the issuer either immediately or at a future time;
- each person who is a senior executive of any external management company of the issuer;
- each person who accepts, and is stated in the prospectus as accepting, responsibility for the prospectus; and
- any other person who has authorised the contents of the prospectus.

If the offer is of existing as well as new shares and the offeror is not the issuer, unless PR 5.5.7R(3) (i.e. where the offeror is making the offer in association with the issuer) is being relied on in relation to the offer of existing securities, then the offeror of those securities (and each person who is a director of that offeror when the prospectus is published) will also have statutory responsibility.

In relation to a request for the admission to trading of transferable securities, if the person requesting the admission to trading is not the issuer, then the person requesting admission (and each person who is a director of such applicant when the prospectus is published) will also have statutory responsibility.

Prospectus Rule 5.5 only applies if the UK is the home member state for the issuer in relation to the transferable securities to which the prospectus relates (PR 5.5.2R). If the home member state of the issuer is not the UK, advice should be sought on the law governing responsibility in the relevant member state.

5.2.2 Responsibility statement

A prospectus must contain a responsibility statement from, at least, the issuer and the issuer's directors (PR 5.5.3R, item 1 of Annex I of PR Appendix 3 and item 1 of Annex III of PR Appendix 3).

In support of that responsibility statement the issuer and the issuer's sponsor will usually require directors to confirm, in writing, that they understand the requirements for a prospectus and accept responsibility in the terms required. This confirmation is ordinarily obtained in the form of a responsibility letter which the directors will sign after they have reviewed the prospectus and a memorandum of their responsibilities as directors of a listed company (see Chapter 3 for more detail).

It will typically be the case that the reporting accountant will include a responsibility statement in respect of any reports prepared for the purposes of inclusion in the prospectus.

5.3 Section 90(1) of the FSMA – the statutory liability regime

5.3.1 Right to compensation

Section 90 of the FSMA provides a right of action to an investor who has acquired securities which are the subject of the prospectus and has suffered loss (a) as a result of any untrue or misleading statements in the prospectus, or (b) as a result of the omission of any matter required to be included in it. This right of action is in addition to any other available statutory or common law remedy.

The persons liable to pay compensation are 'any person responsible' for the prospectus (see section 5.2).

It should be noted that there is no need for the injured party to show that he actually relied on the statement or omission in question. Although the position has not been tested in the courts, it would appear that section 90 of the FSMA could provide a remedy to any shareholder who can show a loss as a result of the statement or omission in question (i.e. they would not have to show that they would not have acquired the shares, or that they would have acquired them at a lower price, had the error or omission been generally known). They simply have to have acquired the shares and suffered a loss as a result of the statement or omission.

The measure of compensation will be the loss suffered by an investor calculated by comparing the actual value of the shares and their value had the prospectus been correct.

5.3.2 Duration of liability

Neither the FSMA nor the Prospectus Rules give any guidance as to the duration of liability under section 90 of the FSMA. It is clear that it may continue after admission of the relevant securities to the Official List and to trading on a regulated market, and therefore extends a right of action to those who purchased shares in the after-market, as well as those who acquired shares in the initial public offering. However, it is not clear how long this period of reliance would last. Certain information (such as that relating to current trading) will become out-of-date very quickly, whereas other information, such as that relating to future prospects, will have a longer 'shelf-life'.

As a rough guide, the prospectus will certainly form the primary source of information about the company, at least until the publication of its first significant financial report following its initial public offering. It would be progressively more difficult to found a claim arising out of the prospectus in relation to an investment made after that date.

5.3.3 Position in relation to the summary

Statutory liability does attach to those persons who are responsible for the summary, but only if it is misleading, inaccurate or inconsistent or it does not provide, when read together with the other parts of the prospectus, key information to help investors when considering whether to consider an offer (PR 2.1.7R(4)).

5.3.4 Position in relation to supplementary prospectuses

Pursuant to PR 1.1.9R, unless the context requires otherwise, a reference in the Prospectus Rules to a prospectus includes a reference to a supplementary prospectus. This means that the rules on responsibility for prospectuses also apply to supplementary prospectuses.

5.4 Section 90(2) of the FSMA – the due diligence defence

Section 90(2) and Schedule 10 of the FSMA provide a number of defences to actions based on section 90(1) of the FSMA.

A person responsible will not be liable to pay compensation if, broadly speaking, they can satisfy the court that when the prospectus was submitted to the FCA, they reasonably believed, having made all reasonable enquiries, that the relevant statement was true and not misleading or that the omitted matter was properly omitted and:

- they continued in that belief until the securities were acquired by the aggrieved investor; or
- the securities were acquired by the aggrieved investor before it was reasonably practicable to bring a correction to the attention of likely investors; or
- before the securities were acquired by the aggrieved investor, the person responsible had taken all reasonable steps to ensure that a correction was brought to the attention of investors; or
- the person responsible continued in that belief until after the commencement of dealings in the securities following their admission to the Official List, and the securities were acquired after such a lapse of time that he ought in the circumstances to be reasonably excused (paragraphs 1(2) and 1(3) of Schedule 10 FSMA).

Where the loss is caused by an expert's statement included in the prospectus, a person responsible for the prospectus will not be liable to pay compensation if, broadly speaking, they can satisfy the court that:

- they reasonably believed that the expert was competent to make or authorise the statement; and
- the expert had consented to its inclusion in the prospectus in the form and context in which it was included,

provided at least one of the following requirements is also satisfied:

- they continued in that belief until the securities were acquired by the aggrieved investor;
- the securities were acquired by the aggrieved investor before it was reasonably practicable to bring a correction to the attention of likely investors;
- before the securities were acquired by the aggrieved investor, the person responsible had taken all reasonable steps to ensure that a correction was brought to the attention of investors; or
- the person responsible continued in that belief until after the commencement of dealings in the securities following their admission to the Official List, and the securities were acquired after such a lapse of time that he ought in the circumstances to be reasonably excused (paragraphs 2(2) and 2(3) of Schedule 10 FSMA).

A person responsible for a prospectus will also have a defence if:

- before the securities were acquired a correction, or the fact that an expert was not competent or had not consented to the inclusion of his statement, is published in a manner likely to bring it to the attention of likely investors (paragraphs 3(2) and 4(2) of Schedule 10 FSMA); or
- the person responsible took all reasonable steps to secure the publication of such correction and reasonably believes that it took place before the securities were acquired (paragraphs 3(2) and 4(2) of Schedule 10 FSMA).

Where the loss results from a statement made by an official person or is contained in an official public document, the person responsible will not be liable to pay compensation if the statement was accurately and fairly reproduced in the prospectus (paragraph 5 of Schedule 10 FSMA).

Whether the belief of a person responsible is 'reasonable' will depend on the circumstances. A non-executive director cannot be expected to know as much about the company's business as an executive director and can, to an extent, rely on the executive directors. Similarly, an executive director may not be expected to have the same detailed knowledge and exercise the same judgment in pursuing enquiries about areas of the company's activities outside his immediate responsibility, as he would for areas within his responsibility. He can rely, to an extent, on the other executive directors. However, in each case, a robust process of diligence, drafting and verification will be important to establish that a person acted reasonably and each director will be accountable to a certain extent for that process.

5.5 Other potential heads of liability

It should be noted that the issuer will give certain customary representations and warranties in relation to the content of the prospectus to the sponsor and other corporate finance institutions advising it or underwriting the issue and sale through the underwriting agreement. In turn, the sponsor has an obligation to the FCA under the

Listing Rules to ensure that the issuer has complied with the applicable parts of the Prospectus Rules (see Chapter 3).

6. Advertisement regime

If an issuer wishes to advertise the offer or admission, it may do so in printed or electronic form or other form of electronic communication.

'Advertisement' is defined as an announcement relating to a specific offer to the public of securities or to an admission to trading on a regulated market and aiming to specifically promote the potential subscription or acquisition of securities.

It should be considered carefully whether any communication issued might constitute an advertisement. Article 34 of the PD Regulation previously contained a non-exhaustive list of the types of document or event that could amount to an advertisement. The list was very long and included standard letters, newspaper advertising (with or without an order form), seminars and presentations, posters, brochures and faxes.

In the UKLA Guidance Note *PD Advertisement regime (UKLA/TN/604.1)*, the FCA states that the following types of oral and written communication are likely to fall within the advertisement regime, where they are aiming to specifically promote the subscription or acquisition of securities:

- investor or analyst roadshow presentations;
- television interviews;
- pathfinders;
- key features brochures;
- discussions or comments made at a general meeting;
- discussions with potential placees or subscribers for securities;
- discussions with existing or potential shareholders;
- discussions with underwriters or potential underwriters of securities; and
- discussions between brokers/sales staff in an investment bank.

Any advertisement must not be issued unless:

- it states that a prospectus has been or will be published and indicates where investors are, or will be, able to obtain it;
- it is clearly recognisable as an advertisement;
- information in the advertisement is not inaccurate, or misleading; and
- information in the advertisement is consistent with the information contained in the prospectus, if already published, or with the information required to be in the prospectus, if the prospectus is published afterwards (PR 3.3.2R).

Advertisements (and indeed any other information in oral or written form in relation to an offer to the public or admission to trading) may not (i) contradict information contained in the prospectus, (ii) refer to information which contradicts that contained in the prospectus, (iii) present a materially unbalanced view of the information contained in the prospectus or (iv) contain alternative performance measures concerning the issuer unless these are also included in the prospectus (PR 3.3.7).

Under PR 3.3.3G, written advertisements are also required to contain a bold and prominent statement to the effect that the advertisement is not a prospectus but an advertisement and that investors should not subscribe for any securities referred to in the advertisement except on the basis of the information provided in the relevant approved prospectus. In the UKLA Guidance Note *PD Advertisement regime (UKLA/ TN/604.1)*, the FCA said that, in practice, a broad and prominent statement would mean a heading inserted on the front page of the document titled 'Advertisement' followed closely by the requisite warnings. An example of a possible advertisement rubric is set out in Figure 4.3 below.

Figure 4.3: Advertisement rubric

> This announcement is an advertisement and not a prospectus and investors should not subscribe for or purchase any shares referred to in this announcement except on the basis of information in the prospectus (the 'Prospectus') to be published by [INSERT THE NAME OF THE COMPANY] (the 'Company') in due course in connection with the [offer and] admission of the ordinary shares in the capital of the Company to the Official List of the UK Listing Authority and to trading on the London Stock Exchange's main market for listed securities. Copies of the Prospectus will, following publication, be available from [INSERT DETAILS OF THE COMPANY'S REGISTERED OFFICE].

If no prospectus is required to be published, then an advertisement must include a warning to that effect unless the issuer, offeror or person asking for admission to trading chooses to publish a prospectus (PR 3.3.3A).

Under PR 3.3.3A, an amended advertisement must be disseminated if a supplementary prospectus is published and such supplementary prospectus and the significant new factor which has arisen or material mistake or inaccuracy in the original prospectus would render the content of any previously disseminated advertisement inaccurate or misleading. Such amended advertisement must make reference to the previous advertisement and be disseminated without undue delay following the publication of the supplementary prospectus. The obligation to publish an amended advertisement ceases on the later of a public offer closing or when trading on a regulated market begins. Question 99 of the ESMA PD Q&A also states that an amended advertisement, which specifies that the previous advertisement has been amended and details the difference between the two advertisements, must be disseminated 'through the same means as the original advertisement'. ESMA has clarified in Question 99 of the

ESMA PD Q&A that this requirement does not apply to advertisements disseminated orally. In particular, a new roadshow does not have to be organised in order to deliver an amended version of the information provided in the original roadshow. However, the information should still be disseminated to the participants of the original roadshow, via another suitable method.

7. The New Prospectus Regulation

The text of a new regulation which replaces the PD was published in the Official Journal. It entered into force 20 days later (in July 2017).

The aim of the New Prospectus Regulation is to reduce the cost of raising capital (in particular for SMEs), improve the availability of financing and help reduce the current dependency on bank funding. The proposed reforms include:

- an 'alleviated disclosure regime' for secondary equity capital raises;
- proposed amendments to the exemptions from producing a prospectus; and
- new requirements about the summary and risk factors in a prospectus.

Most aspects of the New Prospectus Regulation, which will be directly applicable in member states, will apply 24 months after it came into force. However, some measures, relating to the exemptions for an issuer from the obligation to publish a prospectus when securities are admitted to trading on a regulated market, will have immediate effect. The measures that come into force earlier relate to the exemptions for the admission to trading of shares representing less than 10% of a class already admitted and the admission to trading of shares resulting from the conversion or exchange of other securities. These are discussed in section 1.6.2 of this chapter. The FCA is consulting on changes to the Prospectus Rules to implement these provisions (see its Quarterly Consultation Paper CP 17/6).

Another measure will apply 12 months after the New Prospectus Regulation came into force. As referred to in section 1.5, the New Prospectus Regulation will not apply to offers of securities with a total consideration of less than €1 million, calculated over a 12-month period, but will allow Member States to decide to exempt offers of securities from the obligation to publish a prospectus where the total consideration over a period of 12 months is not more than €8 million. (Currently an offer of securities does not require a prospectus if the total consideration is below €5 million over a 12-month period.) This change will have to be reflected in the FSMA.

CHAPTER 5

Control and disclosure of inside information

OVERVIEW

- Under Article 17 of MAR, premium and standard-listed companies are required to announce 'inside information' (i.e. precise, price-sensitive information which concerns the company that is not generally available) as soon as possible to a Regulatory Information Service (RIS).
- Disclosure of inside information can only be delayed by a listed company to protect its legitimate interests (e.g. because it may affect the outcome of negotiations) and only then if the delay in disclosure will not mislead the public and the confidentiality of the information can be ensured.
- If a company delays disclosing inside information, it must follow prescribed procedures, including creating a record of delay and notifying the FCA, when the information is subsequently announced, that disclosure was delayed.
- Where a listed company has decided that it is entitled to delay disclosure, it may selectively disclose inside information to certain third parties provided the disclosure is made in the normal exercise of employment, profession or duties. The person receiving the information must also owe a duty of confidentiality. Where information is being disclosed as part of a 'market sounding', a safe harbour from the market abuse offence of unlawful disclosure is available where prescribed procedures are followed.
- Listed companies and their advisers must compile and maintain insider lists, in a prescribed form, recording those people working for them who have access to inside information before it is announced to the market.
- Under Listing Principle 1, a listed company must take reasonable steps to ensure that its procedures, systems and controls enable it to comply with its obligations, including its obligations in relation to inside information under MAR.
- A listed company needs to be able to analyse and respond quickly to developments in its business, which may require disclosure to the market. Policies safeguarding inside information from inadvertent disclosure must be implemented, including the imposition of controls on those with access to inside information.

- A listed company must ensure that all relevant officers and employees understand and adhere to its internal controls on inside information and that their directors understand their responsibilities under MAR. Directors are responsible for monitoring whether an announcement obligation has arisen.
- If a listed company fails to comply with its obligations under MAR, it risks becoming the subject of an FCA investigation and ultimately an enforcement action for breach of MAR and Listing Principle 1.
- A listed company that breaches the requirements in MAR in relation to inside information may commit a range of offences including market abuse, the related criminal offences of misleading the market under sections 89 or 90 of the FSA 2012, insider dealing under the CJA and fraud under the Fraud Act 2006.

1. Obligations in relation to inside information

1.1 The regulatory framework

The key obligations on listed companies in relation to inside information are the requirement to identify the existence of and disclose inside information as soon as possible (MAR, Art. 17) and the requirement to create and maintain an insider list, that is a list of those people working for it who have access to inside information (MAR, Art. 18).

The provisions of MAR are supplemented by a series of EU Implementing Regulations which provide further detail on the procedures with which a company must comply. The key regulations for the inside information regime under MAR are the Inside Information Implementing Regulation (EU/2016/1055) and the Insider Lists Implementing Regulation (EU/2016/347).

ESMA has also published guidelines on delaying disclosure of inside information (ESMA/2016/1478).

The FCA Handbook provides guidance on the MAR regime for companies with securities admitted to trading in the UK. The FCA guidance relating to disclosure of inside information can be found in the Disclosure Guidance and Transparency Rules (DTR 2). Further guidance is also set out in the UKLA Guidance Notes on the UKLA Knowledge Base pages of the FCA website. The Market Conduct section of the FCA Handbook (MAR 1) also contains guidance on the market abuse offences, including the definition of inside information.

The FCA Handbook refers to the inside information requirements for companies under Articles 17 and 18 of MAR, together with the rules in Article 19 relating to dealings by directors and other senior managers, as the 'disclosure requirements'.

1.2 Disclosure obligation of a listed company

The primary disclosure obligation in Article 17 of MAR is that a listed company must notify an RIS (and hence the market) as soon as possible of any inside information that directly concerns it. This is subject to some exceptions relating to delaying disclosure and selective disclosure discussed in sections 4 and 5 below.

The key to understanding the primary disclosure obligation in MAR is the definition of inside information which is considered in section 2 below.

The process for announcing inside information is discussed in section 9.

1.3 Decision-making process

Ultimate responsibility for the disclosure of inside information falls upon the Board of the listed company. DTR 2.2.8G provides that the directors must carefully and continuously monitor whether changes in circumstances are such that an announcement obligation arises.

The guidance to Listing Principle 1, which requires a listed company to take reasonable steps to establish and maintain adequate procedures, systems and controls to enable it to comply with its obligations, states that a listed company must ensure that it has adequate systems and controls to ensure that it can properly identify inside information and that any such information is properly considered by the directors, including as to whether an announcement should be made (LR 7.2.3G). In the context of Premium Listing Principle 1, which requires that premium listed companies take reasonable steps to enable their directors to understand their responsibilities and obligations, this means that the Board needs to be well briefed as to what constitutes inside information and have the right information to decide what needs to be disclosed.

The FCA recognises that responsibility for the identification, control and dissemination of inside information may be delegated to a small number of directors who can react quickly (see the UKLA Guidance Note *Assessing and handling inside information (UKLA/TN/521.3)*. Consequently, the use of a disclosure committee to analyse whether inside information has arisen and whether an immediate announcement is required can be helpful (see section 9.1).

Listed companies should also involve their external advisers in any decision as to whether information needs to be disclosed and the content of any announcement (DTR 2.2.7G). In particular, whenever there is any doubt, the company's brokers should always be asked to advise on whether information is likely to have a significant effect on price if made public.

Procedures for identifying inside information are discussed in section 3 below.

Figure 5.1 sets out a decision tree designed to provide assistance in understanding whether a listed company is in possession of inside information and, if it is, how it should be handled. The subsequent sections of this chapter provide more detailed guidance on each element.

2. Defining 'inside information'

2.1 Meaning of 'inside information'

The definition of 'inside information' for the purposes of MAR is set out in Article 7(1)(a).

Inside information is information which:

- is of a precise nature;
- relates, directly or indirectly, to the company or one or more of its financial instruments;
- has not been made public; and
- if it were made public, would be likely to have a significant effect on the price of those instruments or on the price of related derivative financial instruments.

Each element of this definition must be satisfied for the information to be inside information. The definition under MAR is essentially the same as it was under the pre-MAR regime. There are some changes in the detailed language but these reflect the interpretation that has been applied to the definition in case law under MAD.

2.2 When is information 'precise'?

Article 7(2) of MAR states that information will be considered of a precise nature if it satisfies the following two tests:

- it indicates a set of circumstances which exists or which may reasonably be expected to come into existence or an event which has occurred or which may reasonably be expected to occur; and
- it is specific enough to enable a conclusion to be drawn as to the possible effect of that set of circumstances or event on the prices of the financial instruments or the related derivatives.

The more specific the information, the more likely it is to be inside information. However, a company does not need to know all of the facts before having to make an announcement. Information is capable of being sufficiently precise to be inside information if the relevant circumstances may be reasonably expected to come into existence, or an event may be reasonably expected to occur.

There must be a realistic prospect that the event or circumstance will occur (MAR Recital (16)), meaning that the prospect must be more than merely fanciful. However, it does not need to be more probable than not that this event or circumstance will

Figure 5.1: Inside information disclosure decision tree

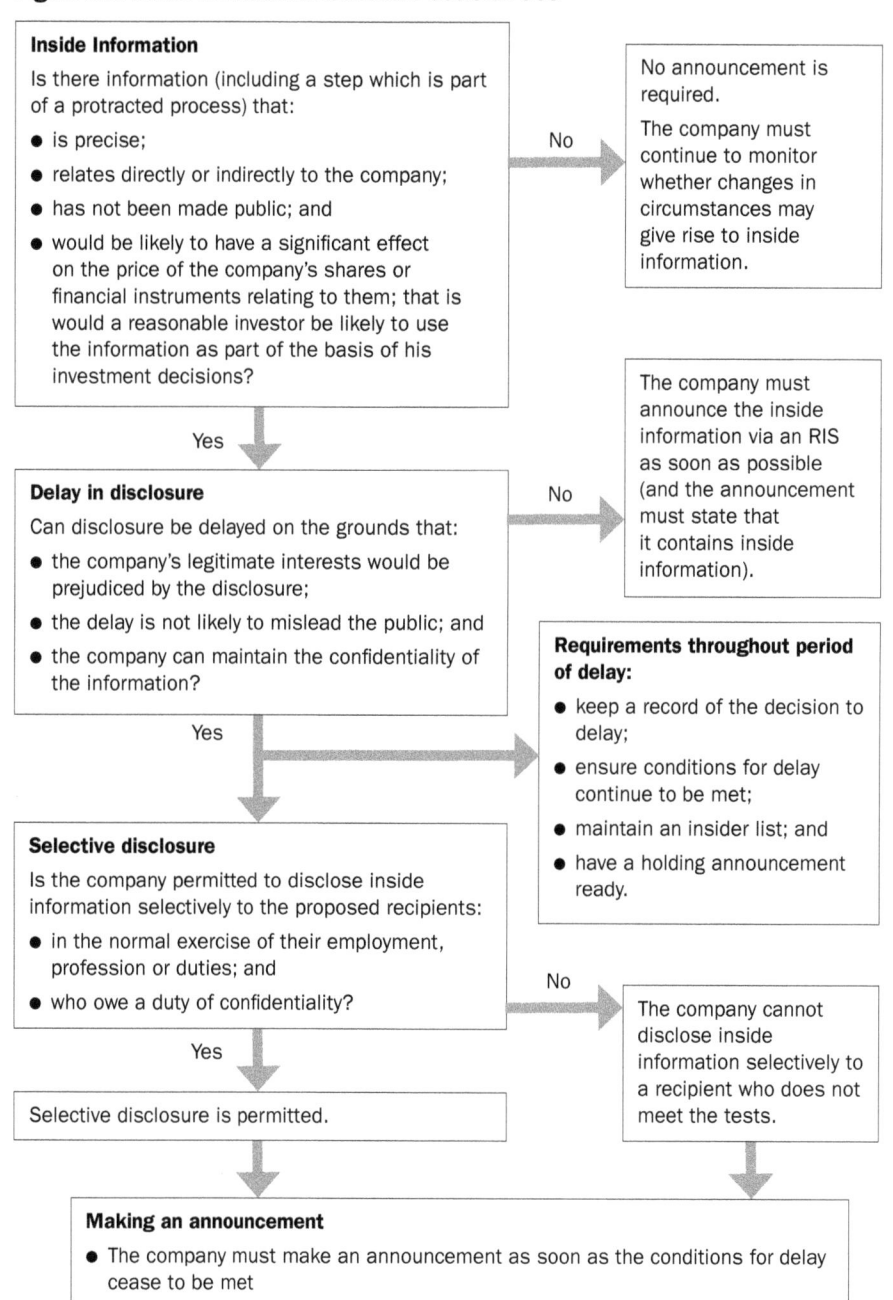

Inside Information

Is there information (including a step which is part of a protracted process) that:
- is precise;
- relates directly or indirectly to the company;
- has not been made public; and
- would be likely to have a significant effect on the price of the company's shares or financial instruments relating to them; that is would a reasonable investor be likely to use the information as part of the basis of his investment decisions?

→ No → No announcement is required. The company must continue to monitor whether changes in circumstances may give rise to inside information.

↓ Yes

Delay in disclosure

Can disclosure be delayed on the grounds that:
- the company's legitimate interests would be prejudiced by the disclosure;
- the delay is not likely to mislead the public; and
- the company can maintain the confidentiality of the information?

→ No → The company must announce the inside information via an RIS as soon as possible (and the announcement must state that it contains inside information).

↓ Yes

Requirements throughout period of delay:
- keep a record of the decision to delay;
- ensure conditions for delay continue to be met;
- maintain an insider list; and
- have a holding announcement ready.

Selective disclosure

Is the company permitted to disclose inside information selectively to the proposed recipients:
- in the normal exercise of their employment, profession or duties; and
- who owe a duty of confidentiality?

→ No → The company cannot disclose inside information selectively to a recipient who does not meet the tests.

↓ Yes

Selective disclosure is permitted.

↓

Making an announcement
- The company must make an announcement as soon as the conditions for delay cease to be met
- The company must make an announcement via an RIS (and the announcement must state that it contains inside information).
- The company must notify the FCA of any delay immediately after announcement.

occur. A company should not therefore wait for a likely future event to become highly probable or actually happen before announcing the information (unless there is an ability to delay disclosure, as discussed in section 4 below).

If the elements of the inside information definition are all met, a company cannot delay making the announcement just because a transaction has not been formally concluded or a matter has not been fully investigated. In that situation, unless the criteria for delaying disclosure of inside information in Article 17(4) of MAR are met, a holding announcement should be issued until the company has established more detail (see section 4.6 below).

Article 7(2) of MAR explains that, in the case of a protracted process that is intended to bring about, or that results in, particular circumstances or a particular event, both those future circumstances or that future event, and the intermediate steps of that process, may be deemed to be precise information.

Article 7(3) of MAR then expressly states that an intermediate stage leading up to a particular event can be inside information if 'by itself' it satisfies the criteria for inside information in Article 7 of MAR.

This means that even the early stages of a protracted process can constitute information of a precise nature, which could amount to inside information. For example, Recital 17 of MAR specifically contemplates that information relating to the state of contract negotiations, the terms provisionally agreed in such negotiations or a proposal for a placing of securities, can be deemed precise enough and amount to inside information requiring an announcement to be made (unless the company is able to delay disclosure of the information as described in section 4 below).

In order for the second limb of the precise test to be met, the information must enable an investor to know that the price of a financial instrument might move if the information were to be made public. The prospect of such movement in price must be real, and not merely fanciful, but need not be more probable than not.

The potential price movement does not need to be substantial. Recital 16 of MAR states that the magnitude of the effect of the set of circumstances or event on the price of the financial instruments should not be taken into consideration. Furthermore, in order to be precise, the information does not need to indicate the direction of the movement in price.

The more specific the information, the more likely it is to be inside information. At an early stage, information may not be inside information because it is not sufficiently precise. For example, if a company receives one report of potential illegality within its organisation as a result of a whistle-blowing procedure, there may not be sufficient detail or any material corroboration of the truth of the report for the information to constitute inside information. Consequently, no announcement may be required at that stage because the 'realistic prospect' test has not been met. If, at a later stage, there is corroboration, the information may become sufficiently precise and an announcement may then be required. Caution is needed because, as explained above, a company does not need to know all of the facts before having to make an announcement. Companies should, therefore, monitor how the information evolves and be ready, if the information becomes inside information, to announce the information immediately, unless a delay in announcement is permitted.

2.3 When is information deemed to be public?

In order to constitute inside information, MAR requires that the information concerned 'has not been made public'. MAR does not provide any further detail to assist with the interpretation of 'not been made public'.

MAR 1 of the FCA Handbook (FCA MAR) gives guidance on when information has been made public. Factors to consider include whether the information is contained in records which are open to inspection by the public and whether the information is otherwise generally available, including via the internet (even if it is only available on payment of a fee).

However, even if information is publicly available, a company should consider whether the company's own knowledge or understanding of the impact which that information will have on the company constitutes inside information. For example, an announcement by the Bank of England that interest rates are to rise does not constitute inside information, but if the effect of the rate rise on the company is significant (e.g. because it affects its ability to cover its debt repayments) then the information about the impact may constitute inside information.

It is also important to note that, if the company provides unpublished information to third parties, such as analysts and credit rating agencies, the fact that the information is unpublished does not make it inside information (DTR 2.2.10G). It is only if the information is inside information (i.e. if the other three tests of inside information are met) that the obligations relating to inside information arise.

However, if inside information becomes generally available as a result of a leak, that does not mean that the company no longer needs to make an RIS announcement. Only an RIS announcement can satisfy the company's obligation to announce inside information.

2.4 Meaning of 'financial instruments' and 'related investments'

For the purposes of the definition of inside information, 'financial instruments' means:

- any transferable securities, including shares and bonds, which are admitted to trading on any regulated market, multi-lateral trading facility (MTF) or, from January 2018, any organised trading facility (OTF) in the EEA; and
- any financial instrument whose price or value depends on, or has an effect on, the price or value of such financial instruments.

A wider range of instruments are caught by MAR than were covered by MAD (which only applied to financial instruments on a regulated market in the EEA and did not have the second category of financial instruments whose price or value depends on or has an effect on the price or value of traded financial instruments).

2.5 Meaning of 'significant effect on price'

Article 7(4) of MAR explains that, for the purposes of the inside information test in Article 7(1), information which would be likely to have a significant effect on price means information that a reasonable investor would be likely to use as part of the basis of his or her investment decisions.

The 'significant effect on price' test must therefore be viewed by reference to whether the information is of a type that a reasonable investor would be likely to use as part of his or her investment decisions.

It should be noted in particular that MAR does not set out a specific percentage price movement or materiality threshold for assessing whether the information is of a type that a reasonable investor would be likely to use as part of his investment decision. This is also confirmed in the FCA Guidance in DTR 2.2.4G(2).

For this purpose, the FCA Upper Tribunal decision in the *Hannam* case suggests that a reasonable investor would only be expected to take into account information that may have a non-trivial effect on price, and would not be expected to take into account information which would have no, or only a trivial effect on price (i.e. the reasonable investor's decision is 'economically motivated', which is also confirmed in DTR 2.2.5G as discussed below).

The FCA Upper Tribunal decision in the *Hannam* case also suggests that information will be regarded as 'likely' to have a significant effect on price for this purpose if there is a real prospect of it having that effect, which is more than fanciful, although it does not need to be more likely than not.

The assessment of whether information is of a type that a reasonable investor would use as part of his investment decisions must be made on a case-by-case basis, in light of the company's activities, the reliability of the source of information and any other market variables likely to affect the financial instruments (MAR Recital (14)).

Market expectation will, in part, be based on public profit or earnings forecasts but may also be based on historic information such as past trading performance, public statements on developing strategy and previous market announcements by the company. Note that it is the general expectation of the market which is relevant and this may differ from the company's own expectations as to its performance.

DTR 2.2 provides the following guidance on the matters that companies should consider when determining whether information meets the 'reasonable investor' test:

- the significance of the information to the company will depend on a variety of factors, such as the size of the company, recent developments and market sentiment in relation to the company and the sector in which it operates (DTR 2.2.5G(1)); and
- information that affects one or more of the following is likely to be relevant to a reasonable investor's decision (DTR 2.2.6G):
    - the assets and liabilities of the company;
    - the performance, or the expectation of the performance, of the company's business;
    - the financial condition of the company;
    - the course of the company's business;
    - major new developments in the business of the company; or
    - information previously disclosed to the market.

Companies must assess each piece of information individually and decide whether it constitutes inside information on its own.

A company cannot set off good news against bad when assessing price sensitivity. For example, where a company has made an unexpected loss in one area of its business but has realised gains in another part of its activities which have not previously been announced or accounted for, it will need to assess whether the losses and the gains are each inside information separately, even where the figures net off against each other so as to leave the overall financial forecast unchanged.

3. Identifying inside information

3.1 Monitoring and gathering information

The guidance in DTR 2.2.8G says that the directors should carefully and continuously monitor whether changes in circumstances are such that an announcement obligation arises under Article 17 of MAR.

In addition, Listing Principle 1 requires listed companies to ensure that they have taken reasonable steps to establish and maintain adequate procedures, systems and controls to enable them to comply with their obligations under the Listing Rules and Transparency Rules and the disclosure requirements under MAR. This means that directors will need to ensure that procedures are implemented, and adhered to, in order to ensure that relevant information flows up to those responsible for assessing and disclosing inside information.

Listed companies should implement procedures to ensure a regular, reliable flow of management information on key performance indicators (KPIs) and forecasts, particularly to show actual performance against any forecast provided to the market. They should also ensure that all relevant information is made available to the Board and the disclosure committee. This will enable the Board to assess whether further announcements are required to update publicly available information. This is vital if the management information indicates a worsening financial performance because delay in the disclosure of this information is not permitted.

Listed companies should also have in place procedures for monitoring movements in share price, market rumours and market expectations. In a number of these areas, the company's brokers and public relations advisers will be able to assist. The need for such a system to be in place is likely to be most keenly felt when a major transaction or product development is in the offing.

A person or team should also be given the responsibility for assessing new legal, governmental and regulatory developments and their potential impact on the company. A listed company will need to consider making an announcement if the effect of the development is significant for the company specifically, rather than for companies in its sector or the market as a whole.

As soon as it is decided that inside information exists, a company must announce it (as described in section 9 below) unless it concludes it is able to delay disclosure as described in section 4 below.

3.2 Implementing and documenting procedures

Listing Principle 1 requires listed companies to take reasonable steps to establish and maintain adequate procedures, systems and controls to enable them to comply with their obligations. The guidance in LR 7.2.3G refers specifically to having adequate systems and controls in relation to inside information. Reasonable steps are likely to include establishing and implementing clear written procedures, systems and controls, and providing adequate information and training to relevant officers and employees. It is therefore important that listed companies not only implement procedures for dealing with inside information, but also ensure that they are adhered to in order to avoid breaching Listing Principle 1. Consequently, listed companies should prepare written policies to apply to all relevant staff members; these should be simply stated and easy to follow.

The reporting lines within a listed company's group should be documented, as should minutes of meetings convened to discuss significant information relating to the company's business and whether the information should be announced to the market (including whether other relevant persons were consulted, such as the company's advisers). Evidence of procedures in place to monitor the business and its information would assist in defending any claim for breach of a listed company's obligations under MAR or the LPDT Rules. If a company concludes that there is inside information but that disclosure can be delayed, MAR imposes specific record-keeping requirements (see section 4 below for further information).

3.2.1 Documenting disclosure procedures

Figure 5.2 provides an illustrative introduction and checklist of policies and related documents that a listed company may wish to put in place to assist in complying with its obligations under MAR and Listing Principle 1.

Figure 5.2: Illustrative introduction and contents for a disclosure manual

[Name of listed company] (the 'Company') Disclosure policies and documentation	
Introduction	
Below is a list of policies and documentation to enable the Company to comply with (and evidence its compliance with) the obligations that it has under MAR relating to the control and disclosure of inside information. [The Company is a [premium] listed company and, as a result, it also needs to comply with the Listing Principles [and Premium Listing Principles] notably Listing Principle 1, set out in Chapter 7 of the Listing Rules.]	
The policies and documents below can only ever cover basic procedural issues; the Company also relies on many other internal systems and controls (in particular in relation to financial information) to comply with its MAR obligations.	
Contents	

Document	LPDT Rules/ MAR	
Contact details		
Contact details of first point of contact with the FCA, (as provided to the FCA on [insert date])	LR 9.2.11R	
Name and contact details of sponsor (as provided to the FCA on [insert date])	LR 8.5 LR 9.2.13G	
Insider lists		
Guidance note in relation to preparing and maintaining insider lists to be provided to the disclosure committee members and anyone responsible for compiling and maintaining insider lists	MAR Art. 18	
Pro forma permanent insider list (if any), recording details required under MAR and Implementing Regulation	MAR Art. 18(3)	
Pro forma project insider list, recording details required under MAR and Implementing Regulation	MAR Art. 18(3)	

Document	LPDT Rules/ MAR	
Pro forma notification to persons on insider lists	MAR Art. 18(2)	
Pro forma acknowledgement from individuals on insider list	MAR Art. 18(2)	
Pro forma notification to persons when they cease to be on the insider list		
Insider lists, to be kept for five years from the date on which drawn up or updated	MAR Art. 18(5)	
Pro forma letter to advisers in relation to maintaining insider lists and acknowledging legal and regulatory duties	MAR Art. 18(5)	
Acknowledgements received from advisers in response to the above-mentioned letters	MAR Art. 18(5)	
Inside information policy		
Guidance on inside information: what it is and the consequences of misuse		
Procedures for controlling access to inside information		
Training session on compliance for directors, senior managers and other staff		
External communications policy when dealing with rumours		
Protocol for selective disclosure of inside information		
Memorandum explaining inside information to managers in the reporting chain to ensure inside information filters up to disclosure committee	Listing Principle 1	
Procedure for making RIS announcements of inside information		
Confidentiality agreements for recipients of selective disclosures (or written record of terms and nature of confidentiality obligations)		
Disclosure committee		
Terms of reference for the disclosure committee		

Document	LPDT Rules/ MAR	
Minutes of meetings of the disclosure committee		
Pro forma record of delay in disclosure of inside information		
Website disclosure arrangements for inside information		
Procedure for uploading RIS announcements containing inside information on the company's website and maintaining them for at least five years	MAR Art 17(1)	
Monitoring developments		
Financial position and prospects procedures memorandum	Listing Principle 1 LR 7.2.2G LR 7.2.3G	
Procedure for monitoring share price		
Procedure for monitoring legal, governmental, regulatory and other developments affecting the company		

3.2.2 Documenting the identification of inside information and decision making

Identifying whether or not a piece of information is inside information can often be difficult. Figure 5.3 below sets out a checklist for identifying potential inside information that may require disclosure. Listed companies should ensure that the broader management team are aware of how to assess inside information and the need to escalate any potential inside information to the disclosure committee or the Board.

Listed companies should ensure that they keep a written record of their decisions as to whether information is inside information and the justification for the decision. If there is any uncertainty, the listed company should consult its brokers and/or lawyers, ensuring that they are made aware of all relevant information when they are asked to advise. Advice received from the company's brokers and lawyers should also be documented. In the event of an FCA investigation (which can occur some time after the information came to light) a record of the time line of events and written summaries of the directors' views and advice received from third parties will enable the company to respond to FCA queries and may help in justifying the company's actions. Companies will also need to keep a record of any decision to delay disclosure of inside information, as discussed in section 4 below.

Figure 5.3: Checklist for identifying inside information

[Name of listed company] (the 'company')
Checklist for identifying inside information

It is not possible to provide definitive guidance on what types of information will and will not be inside information because the analysis will vary between pieces of information and between listed companies.

However, the following matters ought to be considered when analysing whether information must be disclosed:

- Consider the impact of the particular piece of information on the company in the context of a series of factors, such as: the size of the company and its group; developments in its recent past; previous announcements to the market; and activity and market sentiment in relation to the company and its business sector.
- Assume that a reasonable investor will make investment decisions relating to the company's securities to maximise his economic self-interest (DTR 2.2.5G (2)).
- Consider those factors which are likely to be considered relevant to a reasonable investor's decision (DTR 2.2.6G) which is likely to include information that affects:
  - the assets and liabilities of the company;
  - the performance or the expectation of the performance of the business;
  - the financial condition of the company;
  - the course of the company's business;
  - major new developments in the business of the company; or
  - information previously disclosed to the market.
- Consider in particular whether or not an event or information would have a significant effect on: future reported earnings per share; pre-tax profits; borrowings; market expectation of performance; and/or any other factors which are commonly used to determine the company's share price.
- In relation to market expectations, these will in part be based on public profit or earnings forecasts, but may also include historic information such as past trading performance for a particular part of the year and public statements on developing strategy. Note that it is the general expectation of the market which is relevant here; this may differ from the company's own expectations as to its performance.
- Consensus analyst forecasts can be a useful measure of current market expectations but they can be influenced by out-of-date estimates. Appropriate weighting should be given to published forecasts, internal expectations and specific individual circumstances when determining current market expectations.
- Consider whether any factors exist which may affect the way in which the company's financial performance will be achieved, even where the overall financial performance will be in line with the market's expectations. For example, regardless of whether the company will make the year-end profit it has previously projected, it will need

to consider carefully whether a reasonable investor would expect any change in the source, composition or timing of that profit to be announced. If any such change may be relevant to a reasonable investor's investment decision then this is likely to be price sensitive and require announcement pursuant to MAR Art. 17. Conversely, new monthly trading figures that are following the pattern forecast by the company in a recent announcement are unlikely to be inside information, if the market has no expectation that the figures will differ from the forecast.

- The more specific the information the greater the risk that the information is inside information.
- Assess each piece of information individually as to whether it constitutes inside information, even if more than one piece of information can be announced simultaneously and the likely net effect on the company's share price is not significant. The company cannot set off good news against bad when assessing price sensitivity (see the UKLA's Guidance Note *Assessing and handling inside information* (UKLA/TN/521.3)). For example, if the company has negative trading results to announce and positive information relating to a substantial contract win, it should still disclose both pieces of information to the market if they are individually capable of being inside information. Equally, if it has made an unexpected loss in one area of its business but has realised gains in another part of its activities which have not previously been announced or accounted for, the requirement to announce the losses and the gains needs to be assessed separately, even where the figures net off against each other so as to leave the overall financial forecast unchanged.
- Seek advice from the company's advisers, and in particular its brokers, if there is any uncertainty as to whether particular information amounts to inside information (DTR 2.2.7G).
- If information is inside information, consider whether disclosure can be delayed and, if appropriate, start a record of delay.

4. Delaying disclosure

4.1 Entitlement to delay disclosure

Once it has been established that the information is inside information, then an immediate announcement is required, unless disclosure may be delayed under Article 17(4) of MAR.

Under Article 17(4), a listed company may delay the public disclosure of inside information, provided that the following conditions are met:

- immediate disclosure is likely to prejudice the company's legitimate interests;
- the delay in disclosure is not likely to mislead the public; and
- the company is able to ensure the confidentiality of that information.

ESMA has published guidelines on delaying disclosure of inside information. The guidelines emphasise that both the legitimate interests test and the test that the delay will not mislead the public must be met in order for a company to be able to delay disclosure.

4.2 Meaning of 'legitimate interests'

The ESMA Guidelines on Delay provide a non-exhaustive list of situations in which the legitimate interests of a company are likely to be prejudiced by immediate disclosure of inside information. These include when the company plans to buy or sell a major holding in another entity where disclosure would be likely to jeopardise implementation of the plan.

DTR 2.5.1B cross-refers to the ESMA Guidelines. The FCA has deleted its previous guidance in DTR 2.5.3G which gave examples of where a company's legitimate interests may be prejudiced (including ongoing negotiations where the outcome would be likely to be affected by public disclosure). It emphasised in its consultation paper on this change (CP 16/38) that the changes were not intended to extend a company's ability to delay the disclosure of inside information but to ensure that the guidance in DTR 2 is consistent with the ESMA Guidelines on Delay.

Where a company is in financial difficulty, the FCA says that, in its view, the ESMA Guidelines do not envisage that a company can delay disclosure of the fact that it is in financial difficulty or of its worsening financial condition; the company's ability to delay disclosure in that situation is limited to the fact or substance of the negotiations to deal with such a situation (DTR 2.5.4G). MAR only has a very limited provision which permits a credit or financial institution to delay disclosure of information relating to a temporary liquidity problem (for example, the need to receive temporary liquidity assistance from a central bank) provided certain criteria are met, including that the disclosure would entail a risk of undermining the stability of the company and of the financial system (MAR Art. 17(5)).

A company should not delay announcing inside information to coincide with a scheduled results announcement (UKLA Guidance Note *Periodic financial information and inside information (UKLA/TN/506.1)*) or to allow time for preparation for a results announcement such as organising analyst presentations or webcasts (though such preparations can legitimately occur alongside efforts to release the results quickly).

4.3 Meaning of 'misleading the public'

The ESMA Guidelines on Delay also set out examples of situations where a delay in disclosure will be regarded as likely to mislead the public. The examples given include where the inside information that a company intends to delay disclosing is materially different from the last public announcement of the company on the matter to which the inside information relates or is in contrast with the market's expectations, where those expectations are based on signals that the company has previously sent to the market through, for example, interviews or roadshows.

4.4 Ensuring confidentiality

It is a pre-requisite for any decision to delay an announcement of inside information that the company is able to ensure the confidentiality of that information.

Where disclosure has been delayed and the confidentiality of the inside information can no longer be ensured, the information must be announced via an RIS as soon as possible (MAR Art. 17(7)). This includes situations where a rumour is sufficiently accurate to indicate that the confidentiality of the information is no longer ensured (see section 6 below for dealing with rumour and speculation).

4.5 Record-keeping requirement when disclosure is delayed

As soon as a company decides it has inside information, it must decide whether it meets the conditions to enable it to delay disclosure of the information.

If it concludes it can delay disclosure, the decision to delay must be recorded, together with the reasons for reaching the conclusion that the conditions for delay are met.

The Inside Information Implementing Regulation sets out the specific information which must be recorded when a decision to delay disclosure is made, including:

- a description of the inside information;
- the date and time when inside information first existed;
- who was responsible for the decision to delay; and
- how the conditions for delay were met.

Companies should have a pro forma record for these purposes.

The company should also create an insider list at the same time, as discussed in section 8 below.

4.6 Holding announcements

If a listed company delays disclosure of inside information, DTR 2.6.3G states that the company should prepare a holding announcement in advance to enable it to react to an actual or likely breach as soon as possible.

A short delay in the release of more detailed information may be acceptable for a listed company to clarify the situation, provided that a holding announcement is released in the event of a leak.

Any holding announcement should be 'meaningful' and reflect the extent to which a leak or rumour is truthful (see the UKLA Guidance Note *Delaying disclosure/dealing with leaks and rumours (UKLA/TN/520.2)*). A holding announcement should also contain as much detail about the subject matter as possible, set out the reasons why a full announcement cannot be made and include an undertaking to announce further details as soon as possible (DTR 2.2.9G(2)). The immediate issue of an appropriate holding announcement will protect against allegations that there was a delay in disclosure which was not permitted under MAR. If there is any doubt about the timing of announcements, a listed company should contact the FCA at the earliest opportunity (DTR 2.2.9G(4)). Listed companies should remember that any announcement must not be misleading, false or deceptive, even if released at short notice (see section 9.2).

If the company is unable or unwilling to make a holding announcement, it may be appropriate for trading in its securities to be suspended until the company can make an announcement (DTR 2.2.9G). See Chapter 2 for a summary of the circumstances in which (a) the FCA may suspend a listed company's shares from admission to listing and (b) the LSE may suspend a listed company's shares from admission to trading.

The FCA's policy and approach to leaks of inside information and the requirement to release a holding announcement – together with circumstances where the FCA may consider it appropriate to contact a listed company for further information – is set out in the UKLA Guidance Note *Delaying disclosure/dealing with leaks and rumours (UKLA/TN/520.2)*.

Listed companies should ensure that a person is given responsibility for preparing a holding announcement and updating it where necessary, when working on a transaction that may ultimately result in an RIS announcement.

4.7 Monitoring continued ability to delay

Throughout the period of delay, the company must ensure that the conditions for delay continue to be met, particularly the condition relating to confidentiality and should amend the internal record of delay if there is any change in the fulfilment of the conditions.

When significant new inside information arises, even if it relates to an existing project or matter, there should be a reassessment of whether the conditions for delay are still satisfied; if necessary, the internal record of delay should be updated or a new record created, to reflect the new information.

4.8 Notification to the FCA of the delay

If the company has delayed the disclosure of inside information, it is required to send a written notification of the delay to the FCA if and when the inside information is announced (MAR Art. 17(4)). The notification must be made immediately after the announcement.

Under Article 4(3) of the Inside Information Implementing Regulation, the following information should be included in the notification to the FCA:

- the identity of the company including its full name;
- the identity of the person within the company making the notification (name, surname, position, contact details including professional email address and phone number);
- identification of the inside information that was delayed (giving the title of the announcement and the reference number assigned by the RIS);
- the date and time of the announcement of the inside information;
- the date and time of the decision to delay the disclosure of the inside information; and
- the identity of all persons with responsibilities for the decision to delay the public disclosure of inside information.

A form for notifying the FCA ('Notification of Delayed Disclosure of Inside Information') is available on the FCA's website for this purpose.

The FCA may also require the company to provide a written explanation as to how the delay conditions were met. This explanation only needs to be submitted if specifically requested by the FCA.

As a result of this notification obligation, it is important for a company to consider carefully whether it is entitled to delay disclosure (and to monitor on an ongoing basis whether it continues to meet the grounds for delay) and to record its decision (including the grounds on which it has decided it can delay) as discussed in section 4.5 above.

4.9 Decision tree

See Figure 5.1 for a decision tree in relation to the identification, announcement and ability to delay disclosure of inside information.

5. Selective disclosure of inside information

Unlawful disclosure of inside information, where a person who possesses inside information discloses that information to any person other than in the normal exercise of an employment, profession or duties, is an offence under Article 10 of MAR.

Consequently, where a listed company has decided to delay disclosure of inside information, that information can only be selectively disclosed to third parties if the specific criteria contained in MAR are met.

5.1 Conditions for selective disclosure

Under Articles 10 and 17(8) of MAR, where the disclosure of inside information has been delayed, the company may selectively disclose that information to third parties provided that:

- the disclosure is made in the normal exercise of an employment, profession or duties; and
- the recipient owes a duty of confidentiality, regardless of whether such duty is based on law, regulation or contract.

If the person receiving the selectively disclosed inside information is an adviser or is otherwise acting for the company, they must maintain their own insider list of those who have access to the information, as described in section 8 below.

Selective disclosure cannot be made to any person merely on the basis that they owe the company a duty of confidentiality. There must be a reason for the selective disclosure of inside information to such persons in advance of its disclosure to the market (DTR 2.5.7G).

Prior to the selective disclosure of inside information to third parties, the company must therefore ensure that:

- there is a justifiable purpose for the disclosure to the relevant recipients;
- the recipient is aware that the information is or may be inside information and that disclosure or misuse of inside information may result in them committing the market abuse offences of insider dealing or unlawful disclosure of inside information under MAR;
- the recipient has consented to disclosure of such nature; and
- the recipient has entered into a confidentiality undertaking with the company in relation to the inside information (unless it is clear that a duty of confidentiality exists).

In addition, further requirements must be met if the selective disclosure constitutes a market sounding and the company wishes to avail itself of the market sounding safe harbour, as discussed in section 5.3 and Chapter 10 below.

A leak announcement should be prepared in advance of any such disclosure and, in the event of a leak of inside information, an announcement should be made immediately. See section 4.6 above for further detail.

5.2 Persons to whom selective disclosure may be made

The guidance in DTR 2.5.7G(2) states that the categories of people to whom a company may selectively disclose inside information may include, but are not limited to, the following:

- the company's advisers and the advisers of any other person involved in the matter;
- persons with whom the company is negotiating, or intends to negotiate, any commercial, financial or investment transaction (including prospective underwriters or places on an new issue of shares by the company);
- employee representatives or trade unions acting on their behalf;
- any government department, the Bank of England, the Competition and Markets Authority or any other statutory or regulatory body or authority;
- major shareholders of the company;
- the company's lenders; and
- credit rating agencies.

There must, however, always be a substantive and legitimate reason why the information needs to be disclosed to the recipient. Simply falling within one of the above categories is not sufficient (DTR 2.5.8G). The other conditions for selective disclosure, discussed above, must also be met. A company may, for example, disclose information to a major shareholder about a forthcoming acquisition or disposal if it is a Class 1 transaction requiring shareholder approval and the company wants to assess the shareholder's support. The shareholder must be subject to confidentiality restrictions and should be warned about the risk of committing market abuse if it deals in the company's shares or unlawfully discloses the information, for as long as it remains inside information. In practice it is common for companies' financial advisers to conduct wall-crossings on their client's behalf to manage the risk of unlawful disclosure.

The list of people set out in DTR 2.5.7G to whom information may be selectively disclosed is not exclusive. Selective disclosure may therefore be made to other third parties provided they owe an express duty of confidentiality and disclosure is made for a proper purpose.

The company also needs to take into account the fact that the wider the group of recipients, the greater the risk of the information leaking out; this would, in turn, trigger an obligation to make the information public (DTR 2.5.9G).

When the company has selectively disclosed inside information about a matter (e.g. information about a proposed transaction) which does not then proceed, and so is not announced to the market, the company will need to consider whether there is any residual inside information in relation to that matter. If there is, the company should make a 'cleansing' announcement to the market (to cleanse any residual inside information relating to the transaction). Otherwise, the recipient of the inside information would continue to be restricted from dealing. The question of whether there is residual inside information, and so whether an announcement is required and the contents of such an announcement, should be discussed with the company's external advisers.

Listed companies should have procedures for selectively disclosing inside information to third parties to ensure that inside information is only given to such third parties where delay in the disclosure of the information is permitted under MAR, there is a legitimate purpose for the listed company to disclose that information to that third party before making the information generally known to the market (that is the person will receive the information in the normal course of the exercise of his employment, profession or duties) and the recipient owes a duty of confidentiality.

When selectively disclosing inside information, other relevant law or regulation (such as the City Code) should also be complied with. This is also important for compliance with MAR. For example, where the disclosure is permitted by the City Code that will indicate it was made in the proper course of a person's employment, profession or duties (FCA MAR 1.4.5G).

5.3 Market soundings

Article 11 of MAR provides a safe harbour from the market abuse offence of unlawful disclosure of inside information where the communication of inside information is selectively made in the course of a 'market sounding' which complies with the detailed conditions set out in MAR.

A market sounding is defined, for this purpose, to mean:

- communications prior to the announcement of a transaction in order to gauge the interest of potential investors in a possible transaction and the conditions relating to it, such as size or pricing (Article 11(1) of MAR); or
- disclosure of inside information by a potential bidder to target shareholders, to assess their willingness to accept the offer (Article 11(2) of MAR).

Prescriptive requirements apply to market soundings, including, for example, regarding the use of recorded phone lines where available. These requirements are discussed in Chapter 10.

In light of the complexities and prescriptive nature of the requirements, market soundings should generally only be carried out by listed companies with the assistance and participation of the company's financial advisers, who will often lead the market sounding on the company's behalf.

6. Dealing with market rumour and speculation, the media and analysts

Article 17(7) of MAR says that where the disclosure of inside information has been delayed and its confidentiality is no longer ensured, the information must be disclosed as soon as possible.

Where there is press speculation or market rumour, a listed company will have to assess whether it has a disclosure obligation under MAR.

The decision as to whether a listed company is obliged to make an announcement in response to market rumour can require careful assessment of the speculation or rumour and finely balanced judgment.

DTR 2.7 contains guidance for listed companies in this area and the FCA has also given guidance on dealing with rumour and speculation in its Guidance Note *Delaying disclosure/dealing with leaks and rumours (UKLA/TN/520.2)*.

6.1 Market rumours and leaks

Where the rumour or speculation is sufficiently accurate and the information underlying the rumour is inside information, then it is likely that there has been a breach of confidence and an immediate announcement of the inside information to the market will be required (Article 17(7) of MAR).

In these circumstances, the company should disclose the inside information via an RIS as soon as possible, using a holding announcement if the company is unable to produce a detailed announcement (see section 4.6 above).

It is for companies to assess, with their advisers, whether the rumour is largely accurate and, therefore, likely to have been based on a leak of information by or on behalf of the company. The FSA previously gave, in commentary on DTR 2, an example of a large multinational company which is known to have been in talks with a number of potential US partners in the past. If a rumour emerges that it has resumed talks with a US entity, the listed company may not need to respond to this speculation, even if it is true, because the rumour may have resulted from guesswork rather than a breach of confidence. This will be matter of judgment for the company and its advisers.

However, if the rumour contains more concrete information, such as the names of the parties or details of the proposed consideration, this would suggest a leak has occurred and an announcement must be made as soon as possible. Inaccuracies in some aspects of a story may not, in themselves, be justification for non-disclosure. The FCA gives the example of a capital raising: inaccuracies in a rumour as to the size or pricing of a capital raising may not, of themselves, negate the obligation to announce the existence of a planned capital raising (see the UKLA Guidance Note *Delaying disclosure/ dealing with leaks and rumours (UKLA/TN/520.2)*).

If the market rumour is false, DTR 2.7.3G states that the knowledge that press speculation or market rumour is false may not be inside information. Furthermore, even if the knowledge that the rumour is false does constitute inside information, a company may be able to delay disclosure. The FCA has previously indicated that Premium Listing Principle 6 (which requires companies with a premium listing to communicate information to holders and potential holders of their listed equity securities in such a way as to avoid the creation or continuation of a false market in such securities) does not require a company to respond to false market rumours.

Consequently, companies will generally only be expected to make an announcement in the event of a rumour if it is founded on a leak from an inside source. It is unlikely to need to respond to a false rumour.

Where market rumours or speculation are unfounded, or where there has been no response by the market to such rumours or speculation, companies can, in general, issue a 'no comment' response to any enquiries.

As discussed in section 4.6 above, whenever a company delays disclosure, it should prepare a holding announcement (DTR 2.6.3G) so that, if there is a leak from an inside source (i.e. there is a breach of confidentiality) and the company is not able to make a full announcement, it is able to release a holding announcement. Any holding announcement should contain as much detail as possible, set out the reasons why a full announcement cannot be made and include an undertaking to announce further details as soon as possible (DTR 2.2.9G(2)). The announcement should be meaningful and, at a minimum, reflect the extent to which a leak or rumour is truthful (see the UKLA Guidance Note *Delaying disclosure/dealing with leaks and rumours (UKLA/TN/520.2)*).

6.2 Media enquiries

In relation to dealing with media enquiries, listed companies should consider implementing a 'no comment' policy when journalists are pressing for unannounced inside information. If a listed company comments to the press about significant rumours which involve inside information, it will no longer meet the criteria for delaying disclosure and so will have to issue an announcement.

However, in order to be effective, a 'no comment' policy needs to be used consistently (i.e. both when there is no obligation to announce because the matter is still being negotiated (and therefore an announcement can be delayed under MAR) and also when the company is not in possession of any inside information or the matter being inquired about is untrue).

If disclosure is required, the company should make a formal announcement via an RIS, rather than making a comment to journalists.

Companies should not give inside information to journalists or others under an embargo, to prevent them using the information until it has been released to an RIS (see the UKLA Guidance Note *Delaying disclosure/dealing with leaks and rumours (UKLA/TN/520.2)*).

6.3 Analysts' briefings

Meetings and telephone calls with analysts will periodically be arranged by a listed company to enable the company to give presentations relating to the company and to engage with analysts in more in-depth discussions.

If and to the extent that inside information is to be disclosed to analysts then, unless the disclosure is a permissible selective disclosure and the requirements for delaying disclosure are fulfilled, an announcement detailing the inside information must be made to the market via an RIS prior to the event. In practice it is common for listed companies to selectively disclose inside information to analysts employed by the company's main corporate brokers shortly before announcement to receive feedback on the relevant matter and prepare management for likely investor questions.

It is important for the company to consider what constitutes inside information in advance of the briefing, both to avoid inadvertent disclosure and to enable a swift response if any inside information is disclosed. It is therefore advisable to use a script and have Q&As prepared in advance of any meeting or a telephone call with analysts.

It is helpful to have more than one representative of the company participate in meetings and telephone calls with analysts, shareholders and the media, regardless of whether such meetings and calls are of an ongoing or discrete nature. It also helpful to record or take notes of what is said. It is important to refuse to answer questions that would result in the company releasing inside information, unless the criteria for selective disclosure are met. Analysts and the press are generally aware of what the rules are and should understand why no response is given.

Following any analysts' meeting or telephone call, a copy of the presentation should be published on the company's website.

6.4 Analysts' research

There is no obligation on a listed company to review and comment on analysts' research, but if the company chooses to do so, it may find that it is forced into announcing inside information. In particular, listed companies should avoid correcting any conclusions that the analysts may have reached. Incorrect facts or assumptions contained in the draft of an analyst's research report should only be corrected if, in doing so, no inside information is disclosed. If a listed company needs to make comments to avoid the impression of accepting errors in the report, it should only correct the underlying factual information (not the opinions or conclusions reached) by disclosing information which is already in the public domain or is otherwise not inside information or which relates to the markets generally.

Companies should not authorise or otherwise endorse analysts' commentary, earnings or other estimates (whether specific or otherwise) or conclusions contained in any commentary.

The FCA has said that a listed company should consider making an RIS announcement to correct any significant errors in analysts' research that has come to its attention and which, in its view, has led to a widespread and serious misapprehension in the market. This comment does not detract from the general view that a listed company is not generally obliged to correct errors.

7. Control of inside information

DTR 2.6.1G says that a listed company should establish effective arrangements to deny access to inside information to persons other than those who require it for the exercise of their functions within the company. Companies should, therefore, put in place systems to ensure that only the employees that need to have access to inside information for the exercise of their functions can access it.

This is part of the requirement in Listing Principle 1 for a listed company to take reasonable steps to establish and maintain adequate procedures, systems and controls to enable it to comply with its obligations, including its obligations under MAR. This will include ensuring that inside information is not selectively disclosed other than in compliance with MAR (see section 5 above on when inside information may be selectively disclosed).

Methods for controlling access to inside information include:

- only disclosing inside information to members of management, employees and external advisers or other permitted third parties on a strict 'need to know' basis;
- when someone is being made an insider, making it clear that the company is providing inside information and that it must be kept confidential and asking them to acknowledge that they understand this and that they may not deal in the company's securities while on the insider list; and
- limiting the inside information provided to what the individual needs to know (rather than giving access to all information).

Figure 5.4 sets out an illustrative checklist of controls that a listed company may wish to put in place in order to limit access to inside information.

Figure 5.4: Illustrative checklist of access controls

Checklist of access controls

- Use appropriate code names in all documents, correspondence, e-mails and discussions (including at internal meetings) that relate to individual projects and which constitute inside information.
- Limit attendance at calls and meetings for a project to the core team.
- Do not discuss relevant information in public areas (even within the office).
- Ensure that documents containing inside information are not read or worked on where they can be read by others and are only taken off-site when absolutely necessary.
- Mark relevant documents as confidential.
- Report loss or theft of sensitive documents to a line manager and, if significant, to the disclosure committee immediately.
- Use password-controlled access to electronic documents to restrict access to inside information within the listed company to a specific group of persons.
- Ensure that IT systems facilitate the possibility of separating documents likely to be accessed by those with inside information from other documents.

8. Insider lists

A listed company must draw up a list of those persons working for them (under a contract of employment or otherwise) who have access to inside information relating directly or indirectly to the company, whether on a regular or occasional basis (MAR, Art. 18). Each time a company delays disclosure of inside information, it must compile an insider list. Companies are also permitted to have a list of permanent insiders.

Companies must also ensure that advisers and other persons acting on its behalf compile a list of persons with access to inside information relating to the company.

There is no guidance on the degree of access required for someone to be included on the list. However, it should be assumed that any person who clearly has access to documents which may contain inside information is covered. In contrast, those employees who do not have access to inside information as part of their duties, but could gain access if they acted improperly or exceeded their authority (e.g. cleaning staff) would not be covered.

The FCA can ask for a copy of the insider list in the format, and containing all of the personal details, required by MAR at any time and so it is essential that a company (and its advisers) keep their insider lists, and the information contained in it, complete and up to date at all times.

8.1 Form and content of the Insider List

The detailed requirements for insider lists are set out in the Insider List Implementing Regulation.

The insider list must be divided into separate sections for different pieces of inside information, referred to as project insider lists.

Companies can also opt, under Article 2 of the Insider List Implementing Regulation, to have a list including all persons (if any) having access to all inside information at all times (a 'permanent insider list'). A person can only be added to a permanent insider list if they have access at all times to all inside information that exists in the company (i.e. they will always have access to all inside information immediately). Any person whose name is included on the permanent insider list must not be included on any project insider list.

Templates for both a permanent insider list and a project insider list can be found in the Annexes to the Insider List Implementing Regulation. Figure 5.5 below sets out the prescribed template for a project insider list.

A company may also decide to maintain confidential project lists, setting out persons with knowledge of information about a project or matter that is not yet inside information but which has the potential of becoming inside information in the near future.

Article 18(3) of MAR and the Insider List Implementing Regulation prescribe the information required to be included about each person on the Insider List:

- their role or function and reason for being included in the list;
- the date and time at which that person obtained access to the inside information and then ceased to have access to the inside information;
- first name(s) and surnames, plus birth surname if different;
- date of birth;
- national identification number (if applicable);
- work and home address; and
- all work, home and mobile telephone numbers.

Insider lists must be kept in electronic format and companies are required (under Article 2(4) of the Insider List Implementing Regulation) to ensure the confidentiality of the information contained in the insider list, by restricting access to clearly identified persons, as well as the accuracy of the information on the list.

MAR requires that an insider list is kept for a period of five years from the date it was drawn up or updated. To comply with this obligation, each time the list is updated, a new version of the list should be created and dated. Procedures will also be needed to safeguard the old versions for the required period.

8.2 Procedures for creating and maintaining insider lists within a company

Listed companies need to establish a key person or team responsible for the creation and updating of their insider lists and monitoring which persons within the company should be included on such lists.

When the disclosure committee, or other team or person responsible for identifying inside information, identifies that there is inside information relating to the company, disclosure of which is being delayed, the team responsible for the insider lists should be notified and they should create a new section of the insider list and add to it the names of the person(s) with knowledge of the relevant information.

If a new person is given access to existing inside information, they must be added to the existing insider list. As noted in section 8.1 above, each time a new person is added to an insider list, a new version of the list should be created (and the previous version kept for the requisite five-year period).

As discussed above, where a listed company is working on specific projects which involve information which may become inside information, it may want to create a separate confidential project list which can then become a MAR-compliant list as necessary when the information becomes inside information.

If an employee leaves the listed company's employment, then that individual can be removed from the list. However, if a person moves department and no longer has

CONTROL AND DISCLOSURE OF INSIDE INFORMATION   227

Figure 5.5: Illustrative form of project insider list

Project [insert name] Insider List

Date and time (of creation of this section of the insider list, i.e. when this inside information was identified): [yyyy-mm-dd; hh:mm UTC (Coordinated Universal Time)]

Date and time (last update): [yyyy-mm-dd, hh:mm UTC (Coordinated Universal Time)]

Date of transmission to the competent authority: [yyyy-mm-dd]

First name(s) of the insider	Surname(s) of the insider	Birth surname(s) of the insider (if different)	Professional telephone number(s) (work direct telephone line and work mobile numbers)	Company name and address	Function and reason for being insider	Obtained (the date and time at which a person obtained access to inside information)	Ceased (the date and time at which a person ceased to have access to inside information)	Date of birth	National identification number (if applicable)	Personal telephone numbers (home and personal mobile telephone numbers)	Personal full home address (street name; street number; city; post/zip code; country)
[Text]	[Text]	[Text]	[Numbers (no space)]	[Address of issuer/emission allowance market participant/auction platform/auctioneer/auction monitor or third party of insider]	[Text describing role, function and reason for being on this list]	[yyyy-mm-dd, hh:mm UTC]	[yyyy-mm-dd, hh:mm UTC]	[yyyy-mm-dd]	[Number and/or text]	[Numbers (no space)]	[Text: detailed personal address of the insider – Street name and street number – City – Post/zip code – Country]

access to inside information as part of their new role, they should remain on the insider list until any inside information of which they have knowledge is announced to the market (or otherwise ceases to be inside information). The team responsible for the insider list should also ensure that the human resources (HR) department is aware of the need to maintain the list. The HR department should ensure that the identity of relevant new joiners, leavers and those seconded to key business areas are highlighted and that the personal details required to be recorded on an insider list are kept up to date on their records for each individual.

Each time a person is added to an insider list, he or she should be sent the requisite notification (see section 8.4 below).

8.3 Company's advisers, agents and other third parties

A person acting on behalf of or on account of a listed company who has access to inside information must also be recorded on an insider list. Even though the adviser may maintain their own insider lists, the company remains responsible for compliance with MAR and must retain a right of access to the lists (MAR, Art. 18(2)). The company's advisers and agents must therefore be required by the company to keep their own insider lists of their employees and other persons working for them who have access to inside information relating directly or indirectly to the company or its financial instruments.

It is standard practice for certain advisers (e.g. law firms, financial advisers and brokers) to include clauses in their terms and conditions stating that they will comply with the requirements of MAR in this way. If it is not a standard term in the adviser's contract, the listed company may wish to consider sending a standard form letter to its main contact at the adviser asking for confirmation that it will comply with the insider list obligations in the MAR. A listed company should also consider including in its contracts with advisers and agents a requirement that such advisers and agents take necessary measures to ensure that those employees who have access to the listed company's inside information acknowledge the legal and regulatory duties entailed and the sanctions involved for misuse or improper disclosure.

8.4 Notification to insiders and acknowledgement of duties by insiders

A listed company is obliged to take all reasonable steps to ensure that any person on the insider list acknowledges in writing the legal and regulatory duties entailed and is aware of the sanctions for insider dealing and unlawful disclosure of inside information (MAR, Art. 18(2)). Listed companies should ensure that their directors and employees are fully aware of the market abuse regime and related offences (further details of which are set out in section 10 below) and the sanctions for breach.

All those on the insider list should be prohibited from dealing in the company's securities and any other securities to which the inside information relates. They also need to be aware of the restrictions on control and disclosure of the information (see section 7 above).

In practice, therefore, listed companies may wish to include a provision in their standard form employment contracts requiring employees to read and comply with the company's policy on inside information and share dealing. Companies should also have a pro forma notification to send to insiders and a standard form of acknowledgement of duties and sanctions to be returned by them.

Listed companies should also have effective communications, training and compliance procedures in place to ensure that confidentiality and dealing restrictions are understood by those with access to inside information. For example, companies should consider whether new members of staff should attend a training course on inside information or whether an internal memorandum should be provided containing the key legal and regulatory obligations imposed on staff as a reference guide.

Listed companies must also ensure that their advisers and agents also take the necessary measures to ensure that every person on their insider lists has acknowledged the legal and regulatory duties entailed and is aware of the sanctions.

9. Method and content of disclosure of inside information

9.1 Approval process for announcements – disclosure committee

If information emerges which may be inside information, the obligation is to disclose it to the market as soon as possible (subject to the ability to delay disclosure under MAR, Art 17(4) as discussed in section 4 above).

Consequently, listed companies should ensure that their approval processes for announcements are able to cope with unexpected developments and the need to disclose quickly in that circumstance. If a full Board meeting is required to make an announcement, this could impact on the listed company's ability to respond in a timely way. Therefore, use of a disclosure committee (comprising selected Board members, internal legal counsel and supported by external advisers, such as the principal contacts at the company's brokers and lawyers) will help companies to respond more quickly.

The membership, quorum and procedures for a disclosure committee need to be sufficiently flexible to allow for quick decisions and action. Illustrative terms of reference for a disclosure committee are set out in Figure 5.6.

The logistics for convening a quorate Board meeting or disclosure committee meeting should be such that disclosure is not delayed for more than a few hours by those procedures. It is up to companies to have the necessary procedures and delegated authorities in place. A company will not have legitimate reasons for delaying announcement of material information where a decision regarding that information has been clearly made but no formal approval has been given by the Board of directors.

Figure 5.6: Illustrative terms of reference for a disclosure committee

Disclosure Committee – Terms of Reference

1. *Formation:* The committee has been established by the Board (the **Board**) of directors of [*name of listed company*] (the **Company**) at the Board meeting held at [*place*] on [*date*] and is a properly constituted committee of the Board. The committee is to be known as the 'Disclosure Committee'.
2. *Membership:* The members of the Disclosure Committee shall include [*all*] [*executive directors*] of the Company from time to time, [*the Company Secretary*], [*the General Counsel*] and [*add any other non-executive directors or senior personnel*].
3. *Quorum:* The quorum for a meeting of the Disclosure Committee shall be two members, [*at least one of whom must be an executive director of the Company*] and one of whom must be [*one of the Company Secretary or the General Counsel*] or [*add any non-executive directors/other senior personnel*]. A duly convened meeting of the Disclosure Committee at which a quorum is present shall be competent to exercise all of the authorities, powers and discretions vested in or exercisable by the Disclosure Committee.
4. *Frequency of meetings:* Meetings shall be held at such times as any member of the Disclosure Committee deems appropriate.
5. *Proceedings:* There shall be no notice requirement for the convening of meetings of the Disclosure Committee and a quorum of members of the Disclosure Committee may reach a decision in any reasonable manner without notice to other members. The members of the Disclosure Committee shall otherwise regulate their proceedings as they see fit.
6. *Authority:* The Disclosure Committee is authorised at the expense of the Company to carry out any steps within its remit. It is authorised (i) to seek any information it requires from any employee in order to perform its duties, and all employees are directed to co-operate with any requests made by the Disclosure Committee, and (ii) to obtain external professional advice at the expense of the Company and to secure the attendance of third parties with relevant experience and expertise at meetings of the Disclosure Committee if considered necessary. It may also delegate the implementation of its decisions to any relevant officers or employees of the Company or its advisers as it considers necessary. This remit may be amended from time to time, subject to the approval of the Board.
7. *Duties:* The Disclosure Committee's primary duty shall be to assist the Board in identifying inside information under the Market Abuse Regulation (**MAR**) and making recommendations as to how and when the Company should disclose that information in accordance with MAR. In its fulfilment of this role, it shall have the following duties:
    - to assess whether information which directly concerns the Company is 'inside information' as defined in MAR, Art. 7;
    - to monitor market rumour and press speculation;
    - to procure the announcement of inside information via an RIS as soon as possible, unless delay is permitted;

- to assess whether it is permissible to delay disclosure of inside information in accordance with MAR;
- if delay is permitted, to arrange for an internal record of delay to be prepared and maintained;
- to monitor whether disclosure can continue to be delayed;
- to prepare a holding announcement when disclosure of inside information is delayed;
- to assess whether inside information may be disclosed selectively to third parties in accordance with MAR;
- to prepare and verify announcements for notification of inside information to an RIS and arrange for the posting of inside information announced to an RIS on the Company's website (and ensure it is kept on the website for a period of at least five years);
- if disclosure of inside information has been delayed, to notify the FCA when the information is subsequently announced;
- to arrange for a Project Insider List to be prepared, in the prescribed format, whenever required by MAR and update when details change;
- to determine whether the Company should maintain a Permanent Insider List;
- to ensure that the Company's procedures, systems and controls relating to the disclosure of inside information are adequate to enable effective dissemination to the Disclosure Committee;
- to monitor any changes in the Company's circumstances and assess whether they trigger an obligation to make an announcement via an RIS;
- to take any other action it sees fit to ensure that the Company complies with the MAR;
- to ensure that a record is kept of all decisions of the Disclosure Committee and any procedures put in place to ensure the effective dissemination of information to the Disclosure Committee; and
- to review and, where necessary, propose the amendment of this remit of the Disclosure Committee.

9.2 Misleading statements

A listed company must take all reasonable care to ensure that any information that it notifies to an RIS is not misleading, false or deceptive and does not omit anything likely to affect the import of such statement, forecast or information (LR 1.3.3R and DTR 1A.3.2R). This is the case irrespective of whether the information being disclosed is inside information.

For example, a listed company may breach LR 1.3.3R and DTR 1A.3.2R by a failure to announce a piece of information (which is not price sensitive) but where the failure to make the announcement causes prior statements made by the company to be misleading or inaccurate.

In addition, a listed company must not combine the disclosure of inside information with the marketing of its activities (MAR, Art. 17(1)). This means that a company must be careful that the overall context of the announcement is not misleading and that, despite being in the interests of a company to present facts in the best possible way, the primary responsibility of the company is to ensure its accuracy and that it fairly presents the situation.

As discussed above, premium listed companies also need to be aware of Premium Listing Principle 6, which requires a listed company to communicate information to shareholders (and potential shareholders) in such a way as to avoid the creation or continuation of a false market in its equity shares.

9.3 Verification of announcements

It is very important when issuing public announcements to make sure they are checked carefully. Listed companies need to ensure that their announcements are accurate and tell the whole story fairly, having regard to the information in question and the content of the announcement, on its own and when taken in conjunction with previous announcements.

As well as being a breach of LR 1.3.3R and DTR 1A.3.2R, issuing an inaccurate or misleading announcement through the RIS may constitute a breach of Premium Listing Principle 6 (avoiding a false market) for companies with a premium listing. It may also result in liability under section 90A of the FSMA (see Chapter 8 on market announcements) or amount to the civil offence of market abuse or a criminal offence under section 89 or section 90 of the FSA 2012 (see section 10 below).

It is advisable to step back from the announcement before issuing it and ask whether the announcement is complete and accurate and whether there is anything else which might be material for disclosure at the same time or which is currently pending but which might need to be announced in the near future. It is not relevant that information omitted from an announcement is not price sensitive and therefore not inside information. If the overall impression given to the market is misleading, then this is sufficient to constitute a breach of LR 1.3.3R and DTR 1A.3.2R.

The announcement should not be made misleading by the inclusion of other statements designed to market the listed company's activities in the same announcement or by reading them in the context of statements made previously by the company.

In considering whether or not an announcement is misleading by omission or otherwise, listed companies should review their past comments regarding particular matters in previous announcements and public statements, such as in their annual accounts, to assess whether the announcement is made misleading by such comments. They should not base their views on what they believe market sentiment to be as a result of those statements.

Listed companies should involve their brokers and external lawyers as necessary in reviewing announcements and deciding whether any information needs to be disclosed. It is particularly important that the advisers consider what is not included in the announcement as well as the accuracy of the information which is contained within it.

The guidance to Listing Principle 1 makes clear that the listed company's procedures, systems and controls must be adequate to ensure accurate as well as timely disclosure.

RIS announcements should be written so that the key content of the message is given due prominence. Information should be clearly visible, readily understandable by the reasonable investor and not relegated to the final paragraphs of the announcement. The announcement headline should reflect the information that has the greatest significance.

9.4 Contents requirements for announcements of inside information

Any RIS announcement containing inside information must, under Article 1(b) of the Inside Information Implementing Regulation, clearly identify:

- that the information communicated is inside information;
- the identity of the company;
- the identity of the person making the notification and their position in the company;
- the subject matter of the inside information; and
- the date and time at which it is taking place.

The CLLS Q&A on MAR give guidance on these requirements. For example, in relation to the requirement to include the identity of the person making the notification, the CLLS Q&A say that the individual who manages the release of the announcement (e.g. the company secretary) should be named. In addition, the CLLS Q&A say that where an announcement includes some items that are inside information, even if it includes other information that is not, it is sufficient to include a general reference such as 'This announcement contains inside information'. Where the announcement covers a number of clearly different matters that could have been the subject of separate announcements it would be appropriate to distinguish between those matters that include inside information and those that do not. However, it is important that inside information within the announcement is not concealed (i.e. buried in with large amounts of non-inside information).

9.5 Methods of disclosing inside information: RIS and websites

Inside information must be published via an RIS as soon as possible. The company must also post the information on its website (MAR Art 17(1)).

Under DTR 1.3.6G, if a listed company is required to notify information to an RIS at a time when the RIS is not open for business, it may distribute the information as soon as possible to:

- not less than two national newspapers in the United Kingdom;
- two newswire services operating in the United Kingdom; and
- an RIS for release as soon it opens.

The release of announcements via an RIS is discussed in Chapter 8.

A listed company should not publish inside information on its website as an alternative to disclosure via an RIS.

Article 3 of the Inside Information Implementing Regulation requires that the website on which inside information is posted by a company should comply with the following features:

- access to the website should be non-discriminatory and free of charge;
- inside information should be located in an easily identifiable section of the website; and
- the date and time of disclosure should be indicated and the announcements should be organised in chronological order.

Listed companies should liaise with their website teams to ensure that inside information announcements are posted on their websites as required by Article 17(1) of MAR and kept there for a period of five years from the date of posting.

It is important to recognise that the announcement via an RIS remains the principal disclosure obligation: a listed company should not publish inside information on its website as an alternative to or in advance of its disclosure via an RIS.

10. Breach of MAR and related offences

As discussed above, it is important for a listed company and its directors to have an appreciation of the consequences of breaching MAR and of some of the related offences that can be committed by companies and individuals in connection with the control and disclosure of inside information. This has become even more important in light of the FCA's approach to enforcement in recent years. We have seen an increasing number of enforcement actions relating to the requirement to announce inside information, as well as an increase in the fines imposed and successful prosecutions for both market abuse and insider dealing.

10.1 Breach of obligation to announce inside information

Section 123 of FSMA gives the FCA power to impose penalties on any person who has either contravened or is knowingly concerned in the contravention of any provision of MAR, including any of the MAR Implementing Regulations.

If a person either contravenes or is knowingly concerned in the contravention of the requirements of MAR, the FCA may:

- privately censure the person;
- publish a statement censuring the person;
- impose a financial penalty (of an unlimited amount) on the person;
- prohibit an individual from dealing;
- suspend the company's securities from trading; and/or
- require the company to publish a new or corrective statement.

There is no requirement for fault or intention in relation to the contravention.

The FCA's Enforcement Manual sets out its approach to enforcement and its Decision Procedure and Penalties Manual sets out its approach to decision making and penalties.

10.2 Enforcement actions for breach of requirement to announce inside information pre-MAR

Before MAR came into force, one of the key areas of non-compliance with the LPDT Rules that the FSA and then the FCA focused on was breach of DTR 2 (which contained the obligation to disclose inside information prior to MAR) and related breaches of what is now Premium Listing Principle 6 (previously Listing Principle 4). This focus resulted in enforcement actions against a number of listed companies including notably:

- Woolworths Group (June 2008);
- Wolfson Microelectronics (January 2009);
- Entertainment Rights (January 2009);
- Photo-Me International (June 2010);
- JJB Sports (January 2011); and
- Lamprell (March 2013).

The key points of each of these enforcement actions are summarised in Figure 1.3 in Chapter 1 and are considered in further detail below. Enforcement actions for market abuse in relation to inside information are of equal relevance to companies when considering their obligations under MAR. These are discussed in section 10.3 below.

10.2.1 Woolworths Group

In June 2008, the FSA fined Woolworths £350,000 for breaching the requirement to announce inside information as soon as possible (at the time in DTR 2.2.1R) and what was at the time Listing Principle 4 (now Premium Listing Principle 6). This was the first fine imposed by the FSA under the Disclosure Rules and the Listing

Principles; it took two-and-a-half years for the FSA to conclude its investigation and issue its enforcement notice.

In August 2004, Woolworths entered into an agreement with Tesco for the supply of entertainment products. The agreement was varied in December 2005, creating a direct loss of profit for Woolworths estimated at £8 million in a year. This represented over 10% of Woolworth's anticipated profits for the following financial year. Woolworths did not announce the variation of the contract to the market until 18 January 2006, when it made its scheduled Christmas trading update. Following the announcement, Woolworths' share price fell by around 12%.

The FSA concluded that the variation of the contract was inside information and that Woolworths' failure to announce it promptly was a breach of DTR 2.2. The FSA also found that the delay in announcing the variation led to the creation of a false market in Woolworths' shares and this breached the then Listing Principle 4 (now Premium Listing Principle 6).

The key question that the FSA considered was whether the signing of the variation amounted to inside information. Under DTR 2, as under MAR, in order to constitute inside information, information must be likely to have a significant effect on the share price. Woolworths sought to argue that a significant effect on price required a share price fall of 10% or more which could be attributed to the information and that this had not been the case – Woolworths argued that the 12% fall following the announcement was attributable not only to the variation of the contract, but also to other factors. The FSA rejected this approach and concluded that the relevant test for the definition of inside information (which at the time was found in section 118(6) of the FSMA) was whether a reasonable investor would be likely to use the information when considering its investment decisions.

In considering the appropriate penalty, the FSA notice highlighted the following factors:

- the extensive delay in announcing the variation, leading to a period of 29 days during which there was a false market in Woolworths' shares;
- the failure by Woolworths to take professional advice on its disclosure obligations and, in particular, whether the variation would amount to inside information (it also did not fully brief its advisers on the consequences of varying the agreement); and
- the failure of Woolworths' internal processes to identify the variation to the agreement as inside information, even though the Board of directors was made aware of the potential impact of the variation before the agreement was signed.

10.2.2 Wolfson Microelectronics

In January 2009, the FSA fined Wolfson £140,000 for failing to reveal inside information to the market as soon as possible, in breach of the then Disclosure Rules and the Listing Principles.

On 10 March 2008, a major customer informed Wolfson that it would not be required to supply parts for future editions of two of its products. This represented a loss to Wolfson of $20 million or 8% of its forecast revenue for 2008. Two days later, Wolfson consulted its investor relations advisers about whether it should disclose this negative news and was advised that it was not necessary. One of the reasons for this advice – and for Wolfson's decision to not announce the information – was that Wolfson also expected, based on other more positive information, that notwithstanding the loss of the order, its 2008 forecast revenue would remain the same. Later, following a Board meeting, Wolfson decided to consult its legal advisers and corporate brokers on the point; they both advised that the information should be disclosed. Wolfson eventually announced the negative news on 27 March 2008, which resulted in its share price closing approximately 18% lower than on the previous day.

The FSA ruled that the negative news about the loss of the order was inside information. The obligation to disclose arose on 10 March 2008. Breach of this obligation led to the creation of a false market in Wolfson's shares, which constituted a breach of what was at the time Listing Principle 4 (now Premium Listing Principle 6).

The FSA notice in the Wolfson case contains a useful reminder of some of the issues that often arise in relation to the obligation to announce inside information:

- the company should seek advice from its legal advisers or corporate brokers when there may be inside information which is required to be announced – it is not appropriate to rely on advice from an investor relations adviser;
- a company cannot avoid the disclosure of negative news because it believes that positive news is likely to offset it;
- the fact that the company thought that the market would overreact to the bad news, so that the share price would not then represent the 'true' value of the company, was not relevant in deciding whether or not to disclose the negative information;
- companies cannot rely on confidentiality agreements with third parties as a justification for withholding price-sensitive information (this was one of the reasons that Wolfson gave for its concern that it would be unable to properly disclose the positive news at the same time as the negative news); and
- companies must act with urgency when they are considering whether information constitutes inside information which must be announced – leaving delays of a few days between each part in the process showed a lack of urgency.

10.2.3 Entertainment Rights

In January 2009, the FSA also fined Entertainment Rights £245,000 for failing to disclose inside information as soon as possible, in breach of the Disclosure Rules and the Listing Principles.

Entertainment Rights had an important distribution agreement with a US distributor. This agreement was varied on 10 July 2008. The effect of the variation was to significantly lower margins and future payments to Entertainment Rights, leading to a US$13.9 million reduction in profits for the year ending 2008. It was not until 26 September 2008 that Entertainment Rights issued an announcement about the variation; its shares fell 55% on that day.

The reason given for non-disclosure was that, at the time of negotiation of the variation and after it was executed, the Board considered that there would be opportunities over the course of the year to mitigate the negative impact of the variation. They concluded, incorrectly, that the existence of these opportunities permitted the delay of any announcement of the variation.

In its press release, the FSA summarised its approach: 'Listed companies must carefully assess what could be inside information and whether they need to disclose it. Putting off disclosure in the hope that future events may mitigate the impact is unacceptable.'

10.2.4 Photo-Me International

In June 2010, the FSA fined Photo-Me £500,000 for failing to disclose inside information to the market as soon as possible, in breach of the then Disclosure Rules and the Listing Principles.

In September, November and December 2006, Photo-Me made a series of announcements that created an expectation in the market that it would benefit from winning some large sales contracts and would have strong sales generally. On 17 January 2007, Photo-Me was informed that it was no longer engaged in exclusive negotiations for a major sales contract, but rather that the contract was being re-tendered. All previous announcements relating to the major contract had stated that it was 'under negotiation'. The FSA said that a reasonable investor would have concluded that there was a high degree of confidence that the contract would be won. The FSA found that, from 17 January 2007, the contract was no longer under negotiation; indeed, there was a significant risk that it might not be won at all. This was inside information that should have been disclosed as soon as possible under the then DTR 2.2.1R.

By 12 February 2007, one Photo-Me director had information that its January 2007 sales had been 40% behind target and that revised forecasts were predicting significantly lower sales up to the end of April 2007. The director did not consider whether a disclosure obligation had arisen or discuss the matter with the Board. The FSA found that this was also inside information and should have been disclosed as soon as possible.

Photo-Me's Board did not consider either the impact of the risk of losing the potential contract or of the January sales figures and revised forecasts until its next scheduled quarterly Board meeting on 1 March 2007. A profit warning was issued on 2 March 2007. Photo-Me's share price closed down 24% that day.

The FSA was not persuaded that the failure of a Board member to open an e-mail attachment containing the sales figures (due to his absence from the office and subsequent departure on leave) excused a delay of over two weeks in communicating the change in expectation to the market, particularly when the company was on notice from its auditors that close monitoring of trading performance was required. The FSA did not accept that, in those circumstances, disclosure was impossible. Failure to disclose the inside information was a breach of DTR 2.2.1R and led to the creation of a false market in Photo-Me's shares, which constituted a breach of what was at the time Listing Principle 4 (now Premium Listing Principle 6).

Key points to note from the FSA final notice against Photo-Me in relation to compliance with listed company disclosure obligations are:

- the question of whether information is likely to have a significant effect on price requires consideration of whether the information is of a kind which a reasonable investor would be likely to use as part of the basis of his investment decisions;
- there is no set percentage or other figure to determine whether an effect on price is significant and the application of the reasonable investor test will not necessarily be determined by calculating the potential profit impact;
- if a company is shown to have been in possession of inside information, a failure by the Board to consider or identify the inside information does not mean that there is no breach of the requirement to announce inside information as soon as possible; and
- previous announcements by a company will be a key consideration in determining what market expectation has been created, and therefore in determining whether there needs to be an announcement or a change in expectation.

10.2.5 JJB Sports

In January 2011, the FSA issued a final notice in connection with its decision to fine JJB for breach of the then DTR 2.2 and what was at the time Listing Principle 4 (now Premium Listing Principle 6). The fine of £455,000 was the second largest fine imposed by the FSA on a company for breach of the DTRs and Listing Rules (following the fine of £500,000 imposed on Photo-Me).

The breaches occurred in relation to two separate acquisitions made by JJB.

In December 2007, JJB announced that it had agreed to acquire the Original Shoe Company Limited (OSC) a shoe retail chain. Under the OSC acquisition agreement, JJB agreed to pay £5 million for OSC plus an additional amount which was to be calculated by reference to the cost price of the stock in the OSC stores. The amount payable for the stock was not subject to any cap. The amount eventually paid in respect of stock was approximately £10 million (inclusive of VAT).

In May 2008, JJB announced the acquisition of Qubefootwear Limited (Qube). Under the Qube acquisition agreement, the consideration payable was £1. JJB also agreed to settle Qube's bank overdraft on the day before completion of the acquisition. Again, the amount payable under the obligation to settle the overdraft was not subject to any cap. The final amount paid to settle the overdraft came to approximately £6.4 million.

The RIS announcements by the company in relation to the acquisitions contained details of the principal consideration payable (i.e. the £5 million and £1 respectively), but they did not mention the further uncapped liabilities to pay for the stock and settle the overdraft. These details were only announced to the market in the company's half-yearly results announcement on 26 September 2008. On the day those half-yearly results (which also contained other negative news and a going concern emphasis of matter) were released, JJB's share price fell by approximately 49.5%.

The FSA concluded that the costs of the OSC acquisition (including the liability to pay for the stock) amounted to inside information in relation to JJB's shares, as did the costs of the Qube acquisition (including the liability to settle the overdraft). The delay in disclosing the additional liabilities payable under the acquisitions meant that the company was found to have failed to disclose inside information, in breach of the then DTR 2.2.1R. The failure to disclose these additional liabilities also meant that JJB was found to be in breach of the then Listing Principle 4.

Mitigating factors which the FSA took into account in determining the financial penalty included the facts that:

- subsequent to the events, the entire executive Board and nearly all of JJB's non-executive directors had been replaced;
- the new Board had received training on compliance with the LPDT Rules and its continuing obligations under the LPDT Rules; and
- JJB had substantially improved its systems and controls for the approval of regulatory announcements.

Aggravating factors included the nine-month delay in the information being released to the market. The fine would have been £650,000 had JJB not agreed to settle with the FSA at an early stage.

JJB's fine for a failure to disclose the full details of the consideration payable on an acquisition was the first of its kind. The case reinforces the importance of having proper systems and controls in place for identifying inside information and ensuring that such information is properly released to the market and that any announcement that is made is complete and accurate. In JJB's case, the Board minute relating to the Qube acquisition did not record there ever having been a discussion with the full Board of the likely cost of the acquisition.

The FSA's decision also reinforces the need, where reliance is placed on the company's brokers in relation to disclosure issues, to ensure they are fully informed and have been specifically asked to advise on the relevant issues. In JJB's case, although the OSC acquisition was discussed with JJB's brokers and they were informed of the £5 million purchase price, they understood that no stock was being purchased. In the case of the

Qube acquisition they understood the purchase price to be £1; while an e-mail chain containing a reference to the Qube overdraft was forwarded to the brokers, the brokers did not read the full e-mail chain (instead only reading the two most recent e-mails) and were not otherwise made fully aware of the terms of the acquisitions.

10.2.6 Lamprell

In March 2013, the FSA fined Lamprell plc £2.4 million for breaches of the Listing Rules and Disclosure Rules, in particular for failure to disclose inside information and a failure in its systems and controls which meant that it was not able to adequately monitor its financial performance.

From early 2012, Lamprell's financial performance against its budget was deteriorating due to operational issues. At the end of April 2012, some preliminary figures indicating the deterioration were produced but senior managers were sceptical about the accuracy of the figures because a new model had been used. On 16 May, Lamprell released a trading update in which it said its profit margin was expected to be significantly below the Board's original expectation for the year. Following the announcement, its share price dropped by 57%.

The most significant aspect of the decision is the level of the fine. The fine was £2.4 million and would have been £3.4 million if the company had not settled with the FSA. It was far larger than other fines the FSA had previously imposed on listed companies for breaches of the Listing Rules and Disclosure Rules because there was a new regime for fines in relation to conduct taking place after March 2010 and so, for the first time for a decision relating to the failure to disclose inside information, the size of the fine was determined using a percentage of the company's market capitalisation as a starting point.

The FSA notice said that the decision sets a precedent for the method of calculating the fine for similar breaches in future. For larger listed companies, in particular, this method could result in very substantial fines, running into tens or even hundreds of millions of pounds. The FSA said it considers a scale of 0 to 0.5% of the market cap, applied according to the seriousness of the breach, is appropriate for this type of Listing or Disclosure Rules breach. On a scale of 1 to 5, according to the seriousness of the breach, the percentages it regards as appropriate are level 1 – 0%, level 2 – 0.125%, level 3 – 0.25%, level 4 – 0.375% and level 5 – 0.5%. In the Lamprell case, the FSA said that the breach was level 4, meaning that the starting point for the fine was 0.375% of the company's market cap. The market cap figure used in this case was an average over the period in which the company was in default (but before it released its profit warning).

The UKLA had sent Lamprell a letter in July 2011 (when it made a major acquisition) highlighting concerns around the company's systems and controls for dealing with the release of inside information. The fact that the company had received prior warning from the FSA regarding these issues was an aggravating factor when determining the fine, which cancelled out a reduction for the full co-operation given by the company to the FSA in its investigation.

The FSA concluded that Lamprell's systems and controls, in respect of financial oversight of the business, had not grown and developed in line with the company's operational growth or coped with the major acquisition.

The FSA therefore found that Lamprell:

- breached what was at the time Listing Principle 2 (now Listing Principle 1) by failing to take reasonable steps to establish and maintain adequate procedures, systems and controls to enable it to comply with certain of its obligations as a listed company;
- failed to take all reasonable care to ensure that information it notified to an RIS did not omit anything likely to affect the import of the information, because it released a number of RIS announcements during the first quarter of 2012 which did not give any indication of the company's deteriorating financial position; and
- failed to release inside information relating to its deteriorating financial position to the market as soon as possible, in breach of the then DTR 2.2.1R, because once the figures had been produced at the end of April, senior management questioned their accuracy and further work was carried out to verify the figures before an amount was issued in mid-May. The FSA said that the company should have released a holding announcement when the original figures were produced.

The FSA decision reinforces the need for companies to:

- review their procedures for the flow of management and financial information, with particular focus on reporting systems;
- ensure that their systems and procedures keep pace with the company's expansion;
- when acquiring another company, pre-plan the integration, with a particular focus on reporting systems;
- if necessary, for example, after expansion or acquisition, engage extra staff to make sure that the company is able to monitor its financial performance; and
- when asking for verification of unexpected results which are out of line with market expectations, companies should consider issuing a holding announcement immediately.

10.3 Market abuse offences

As well as containing the obligation to announce inside information, MAR sets out the market abuse offences. The offences apply in relation to financial instruments traded on an EEA market and financial instruments, the price or value of which depends on, or has an effect on, those financial instruments.

The market abuse offences in MAR are civil offences, not criminal offences. Both the company and individual directors, employees or other persons can be sanctioned for market abuse. As discussed in section 10.1 above, the FCA's possible sanctions for a breach of MAR, including, therefore, the market abuse offences, include potentially unlimited financial penalties and public censure. The FCA also has power under section 384 FSMA to require a listed company to pay compensation to persons suffering a loss, or who have otherwise been adversely affected as a result of the market abuse. The FCA used this power for the first time when it found that Tesco had committed market abuse in relation to a trading update published in August 2014.

There are three categories of market abuse in MAR. In summary, a person will commit market abuse if that person:

- commits insider dealing;
- unlawfully discloses inside information; or
- engages in market manipulation.

10.3.1 Basic offences of market abuse

Insider dealing

The offence of insider dealing (Articles 8 and 14 of MAR) is committed where a person:

- is in possession of inside information and uses that information by acquiring or disposing of (for its own account or for the account of a third party, directly or indirectly) financial instruments to which that information relates; or
- cancels or amends an order concerning a financial instrument to which the information relates, where the order was placed before the person concerned possessed the inside information.

The offence extends to attempting to insider deal as well as actual insider dealing. In addition, it is an offence to recommend or induce another person to engage in insider dealing (MAR, Art. 8(2)).

Any person who possesses inside information as a result of being an officer, shareholder, employee or other insider will be deemed to have known that the information was inside information for the purposes of the offence (MAR, Art. 8(4)). Persons who possess inside information otherwise than as an insider will only commit the offence if they knew or should have known that the information was inside information.

In the context of the insider dealing offence, MAR contains a rebuttable presumption (Recital 24) that a person in possession of inside information who carries out transactions in financial instruments to which the information relates will be deemed to have used that information.

Article 9 of MAR then sets out a list of circumstances in which that presumption can be rebutted because the dealing is for a legitimate purpose, for example, where:

- the dealing is to discharge a pre-existing legal commitment;
- a person uses their own knowledge that they have decided to acquire or dispose of financial instruments in the acquisition or disposal of those financial instruments; or
- a person deals while in possession of inside information obtained in the conduct of a takeover or merger and the inside information is used for the purpose of proceeding with the bid, provided the inside information has, at the point of approval of the merger or acceptance of the offer, been made public or otherwise ceased to be inside information (FCA MAR gives as examples of behaviour that will fall within this test seeking irrevocable undertakings and making arrangements for the consideration for the bid (FCA MAR 1.3.17G)).

Unlawful disclosure

The offence of unlawful disclosure (MAR, Arts 10 and 14) is committed where:

- a person possesses inside information; and
- discloses the information to another person otherwise than in the normal exercise of an employment, profession or duties (MAR, Art. 10(1)).

Again, a director, employee or other insider is deemed to know that the information is inside information for this purpose.

The onward disclosure of any recommendation or inducement that a person receives in breach of the insider dealing prohibition also amounts to unlawful disclosure of inside information where the person disclosing the recommendation or inducement knows or ought to know that it was based on inside information (MAR, Art.10(2)).

Market manipulation

It is an offence for a person to engage in (or to attempt to engage in) market manipulation (MAR, Arts 12 and 15). Market manipulation includes:

- entering into transactions, orders or other behaviour which give false or misleading signals of supply, demand or price of financial instruments, or which secure the price at an abnormal or artificial level; and
- disseminating information which gives false or misleading signals as to supply or demand or price, or which secure the price at an abnormal or artificial level.

The offence applies if the person carrying out the act or behaviour either knew or ought to have known that it was false or misleading. There are exceptions for specific types of legitimate behaviours which conform with an accepted market practice which has been confirmed by the competent authority in a member state and ESMA. There are currently no accepted market practices in the UK.

10.3.2 Importance of market abuse offences for listed companies

A listed company could commit market abuse if it deals while in possession of inside information, relating to itself or another issuer of securities which is subject to MAR.

A listed company can also be guilty of unlawful disclosure, if it discloses inside information unless:

- disclosure is in the normal exercise of an employment, a profession or duties (i.e. there is a legitimate purpose for the disclosure) (MAR, Art. 10(1)); and
- the recipient owes a duty of confidentiality (MAR, Art. 17(8)).

Directors, employees, agents and advisers of listed companies and employees of agents and advisers may commit market abuse if they deal while in possession of inside information or unlawfully disclose it. FCA MAR gives as specific examples of market abuse (unlawful disclosure) disclosure of inside information by a director in a social context and the selective briefing of analysts by directors and other PDMRs (FCA MAR 1.4.2G).

Companies may also commit market abuse if they publish an RIS announcement, or otherwise disseminate information, which give a false or misleading impression as to the value of the company's shares or other securities.

Listed companies should, therefore, ensure that their officers and employees are fully aware of the market abuse offences and the sanctions for breach. As discussed above, under MAR, listed companies are required to take the necessary measures to ensure that such persons acknowledge their legal and regulatory duties and the sanctions involved.

10.3.3 Safe harbours from market abuse

MAR provides certain safe harbours from the market abuse offences:

- *Unlawful disclosure and market soundings:* There is a safe harbour from the offence of unlawful disclosure where the market soundings procedures are followed (see section 5.3 above and Chapter 10 for further information).
- *Share buy-backs and stabilisation:* There is a safe harbour from the market abuse offences of insider dealing, unlawful disclosure and market manipulation for share buy-backs and stabilisation which comply with the provisions of the MAR and the Buy-back and Stabilisation Implementing Regulation. However, just because the provisions of MAR and the Buy-back and Stabilisation Implementing Regulation are not followed does not mean that a buy-back will constitute market abuse. It will be for a listed company and its advisers to consider that issue on a case-by-case basis (see Chapter 10 for further information).

10.3.4 Market abuse decisions relevant to listed companies

Market abuse decisions under the MAD regime are still relevant and informative in relation to the MAR regime and may provide some helpful background.

David Einhorn and Greenlight Capital

In January 2012, the FSA fined David Einhorn and Greenlight Capital Inc (the US investment management firm which he owned) a total of £7.2 million for engaging in market abuse in relation to a proposed equity fundraising by Punch Taverns in June 2009.

Shortly before the announcement of the fundraising, Mr Einhorn was told of the possibility of a significant equity fundraising by Punch and was invited to be wall-crossed (a process where a company provides inside information to a third party, who is then restricted from trading until the inside information is made public). Although Mr Einhorn declined to be wall-crossed, a 45-minute call took place between Mr Einhorn, Punch management and its broker, during which certain information was disclosed. Immediately after the call, Greenlight reduced its holding significantly, thereby avoiding losses when Punch shares fell following the announcement of the fundraising.

In imposing the fines, the FSA concluded, among other things, that:

- the information was price-sensitive (and therefore inside information) because a reasonable investor would be likely to use the information as part of the basis of his investment decisions;
- whilst there was no one piece of information on the call that, in isolation, amounted to inside information, taken as a whole, the call amounted to a disclosure of inside information because the size, purpose and (by indicating how long any wall-crossing would last) the timing of the deal was disclosed; and
- David Einhorn had dealt on the basis of inside information for market abuse purposes even though he did not believe the information he had received was inside information. The fact that he had declined to be wall-crossed was not an adequate defence.

Ian Hannam

In 2014, the Upper Tribunal confirmed the FSA decision that Mr Ian Hannam had committed market abuse under section 118(3) of the FSMA (now MAR, Arts 10 and 14) through the improper disclosure of inside information.

The basis of the market abuse decision against Mr Hannam was two e-mails sent by him in 2008 which were held to constitute a disclosure of inside information to another person otherwise than in the proper course of the exercise of his employment, profession or duties. Both e-mails related to Mr Hannam's UK-listed company client, Heritage Oil Plc. Both were sent to Dr Hawrami, a Minister of State in the Kurdish

Regional Government. The elements of the e-mails that were held to be improper disclosure were:

- In a September e-mail, a reference to a potential (unnamed) acquirer of Heritage's business with a potential offer price of £3.50–£4.00 per share.
- In an October e-mail, a postscript which said that Heritage 'has just found oil and it is looking good'.

The FSA accepted that Mr Hannam had not intended to commit market abuse, that his honesty and integrity were not in question, that he had not gained personally as a result of the disclosure and that there was no evidence that anyone had dealt in shares as a result of the disclosure.

The key issues that the Upper Tribunal considered in its judgment were whether the e-mails contained information which was inside information and whether the disclosures in the e-mails were made in the proper course of Mr Hannam's employment. The Tribunal analysed in great detail the definition of inside information in section 118C of FSMA (now MAR, Art. 7).

The key points made in the Tribunal decision were as follows:

- *Precise information* – In order to satisfy the first element of the test of whether the information is sufficiently 'precise' to be inside information, there must be a 'realistic prospect' (in accordance with the test in the European Court judgment of *Geltl v Daimler* [2012] 3 CMLR 262) that the circumstances or events will come into existence or occur. This does not mean that it must be more likely than not. In order to satisfy the second element of the 'precise' test (i.e. for the information to be 'specific' enough to enable a conclusion to be drawn as to the possible effect on price) the information must indicate the direction of movement in the price which would or might occur if the information were made public but does not need to indicate the extent to which the price would or might be effected.
- *Inaccurate information* – Even if the relevant statement or communication is to a certain extent inaccurate, the information which it contains is capable of being sufficiently precise to be inside information if, despite the inaccuracy, it nevertheless indicates that relevant circumstances exist or will come into existence or that an event has occurred or may reasonably be expected to occur. Furthermore, statements by an insider which indicate a genuinely held belief are capable of constituting inside information even if that belief subsequently turns out to be mistaken.
- *Significant effect on price* – A reasonable investor would not be expected to take into account information having no, or a 'trivial', effect on price. For the purposes of this test, information would be 'likely' to have a significant effect on price if there is a 'real prospect' of the information having a significant effect on price.
- *The information in the e-mails* – Applying these tests to the information in the September e-mail and the October e-mail, both met the test of being sufficiently precise and likely to have an effect on price. Although the postscript to the October

e-mail would not allow a reasonable investor to conclude that the reserves in the well would then be developed, there was a real possibility that it would, if made generally available, have had a significant effect on the price of Heritage shares.

- *Ability of Heritage to delay announcing inside information* – The Tribunal rejected Mr Hannam's argument that the FCA's stance in submitting that Heritage was not required to have announced the information about the oil find referred to in the October e-mail was inconsistent with the case made against him. Mr Hannam argued that this meant that there could not have been inside information until Heritage itself made an announcement (which was not until two weeks later). The Tribunal agreed with the FCA that Heritage was entitled to delay the announcement of the drilling results because otherwise a burden would have been placed on it to monitor, on a daily basis, whether the most recent drilling results would be likely to have a significant effect on Heritage share price; if announced, this could result in volatility as the results came in. Requiring this level of iterative disclosure would create uncertainty in the market about Heritage's share price and could lead to a disorderly market in the shares. It would therefore be reasonable for Heritage to take the view that an announcement should wait until completion of the drilling programme (or that phase of the drilling programme) unless some really significant results were obtained.

- *Proper purpose test* – In determining whether Mr Hannam had a proper purpose in disclosing the inside information in the two e-mails, the Tribunal referred to the tests for proper disclosure set out in the guidance in the FCA Handbook on Market Abuse (previously in the Code of Market Conduct, MAR 1.4.5, now in FCA MAR 1.4.5G). The Tribunal found that Mr Hannam did not disclose the information in the proper course of his employment because the tests set out in the guidance were not met. In particular:
    – in relation to the September e-mail, the disclosure was in breach of the City Code;
    – in relation to both e-mails, the disclosure was not reasonable; and
    – no express confidentiality restriction was imposed on Dr Hawrami.

Tesco

In 2017, the FCA publicly censured Tesco plc, and its subsidiary Tesco Stores Limited and ordered them to pay compensation to certain Tesco shareholders and bond holders under section 384 of the FSMA.

On 29 August 2014, Tesco plc published, via an RIS, a trading update which contained a statement as to its expected trading profit for the half-yearly period just ended (the August trading update). In producing that update, Tesco plc relied on information provided to it by its wholly owned subsidiary, Tesco Stores Limited, which was not correct. On 22 September 2014, Tesco plc published a further trading update in which it announced that it had 'identified an overstatement of its expected profit for the half year, principally due to the accelerated recognition of commercial income and delayed accrual of costs'.

The FCA found that the August trading update gave a false or misleading impression as to the value of Tesco plc's shares and publicly traded bonds issued by other Tesco group companies. As such, Tesco had engaged in market abuse contrary to section 118(7) of the Financial Services and Markets Act 2000 (FSMA) (now MAR, Arts 12 and 15). The FCA did not suggest that the Tesco plc Board knew that the information was false or misleading.

The FCA publicly censured Tesco for its conduct. In light of its agreement to pay compensation to investors under the FCA's compensation order, Tesco's high level of co-operation with the FCA and the Deferred Prosecution Agreement (DPA) with the Serious Fraud Office (SFO), discussed below, the FCA did not impose a financial penalty for the market abuse.

Separately, Tesco Stores Limited entered into a DPA with the SFO relating to false accounting, under which it agreed to pay a penalty of approximately £129 million. In the UK, DPAs provide a means of resolving offending by corporate entities. Under a DPA, a company agrees to certain conditions, which are likely to include a financial penalty; in return the company will not face prosecution. DPAs are public and must be approved by a court before coming into effect. The DPA concerned only the potential criminal liability of Tesco Stores Limited and did not address whether liability attached to Tesco plc or any employee/agent of Tesco plc or Tesco Stores Limited.

10.4 Misleading statements and conduct

Under section 89 of the FSA 2012, it is a criminal offence for a person to:

- make a statement which they know to be materially false or misleading;
- dishonestly conceal any material facts; or
- recklessly make a statement which is materially false or misleading,

for the purpose of inducing (or being reckless as to whether it may induce) a person to make an investment decision or exercise any rights relating to investments.

Under section 90 of the FSA 2012, it is also a criminal offence if a person intends to create a false or misleading impression and intends by creating that impression to:

- induce another person to make an investment decision or exercise any rights conferred by those investments; or
- produce a gain, or create a loss to another, or is aware that creating the impression is likely to produce those results (where the person knows the impression is false or misleading or is reckless as to whether it is).

The offence is punishable by up to seven years' imprisonment, an unlimited fine, or both. A body corporate can be convicted of the offence as well as an individual.

10.5 Insider dealing criminal offences

Listed companies and their employees with access to inside information should also be aware of the criminal offence of insider dealing contained in Part V of the CJA. This is a separate prohibition from the prohibition on insider dealing in MAR, which is a civil offence. Unlike the MAR prohibition, the criminal offence of insider dealing can only be committed by an individual.

An individual who has information as an insider is guilty of the criminal offence of insider dealing if he:

- deals in securities that are price-affected securities in relation to the information;
- encourages another person to deal in securities that are price-affected securities in relation to the information, whether or not that other person knows they are price-affected securities, knowing or having reasonable cause to believe that securities would be bought or sold on a regulated market; or
- discloses inside information, otherwise than in the proper performance of his employment, office or profession.

The offence may be committed merely by disclosing the inside information to another person. It is not necessary for an acquisition or disposal of securities to take place or for any encouragement to deal to be found. No offence will be committed if the person making the disclosure can show that he did not expect, because of the disclosure, any dealing to take place or that he did not expect the dealing to result in a profit (or the avoidance of a loss) attributable to the fact that the information was price-sensitive information in relation to the securities. However, these defences are difficult to establish.

The penalty for committing the criminal offence of insider dealing is imprisonment for up to a maximum of seven years and/or a fine.

10.6 Fraud

Finally, listed companies and their employees should also be aware of the offence of fraud contained in the Fraud Act 2006. The offence of fraud can be committed in three different ways. The two most relevant offences are outlined below.

Section 2 of the Fraud Act 2006 makes it an offence to make a false representation (by words or conduct as to any fact, law or state of mind of any person) whether express or implied either knowing that the representation is false or misleading, or being aware that it might be. The victim of the representation need not actually rely upon it. A false assertion made in an announcement could therefore lead to a criminal charge if accompanied by the appropriate guilty intent.

Section 3 of the Fraud Act 2006 makes it an offence to fail to disclose information where there is a legal duty to do so (e.g. statutory, contractual, custom from a trade or market or a fiduciary relationship). Those who fail to make full disclosure pursuant to legal obligations will therefore be at risk of prosecution. This could include a deliberate failure to make a disclosure in an announcement in breach of the MAR requirements.

In each case, the relevant behaviour must be dishonest and intended to secure either a gain for the defendant, or a loss or risk of loss to another, of money or any other property. However, no actual gain or loss is required for the offence to be committed.

The Fraud Act 2006 explicitly recognises that a corporate body may commit the offences and also provides that any director, manager, secretary or other similar officer of a company (or any person purporting to act in such a capacity) will also commit the relevant offence if the company's offence is proved to have been committed with the consent or connivance of that individual. This is important for directors as it leads to the risk of prosecution for those who merely acquiesce in, as opposed to positively promoting, dishonest conduct (of the type outlined above) by their company. The offence is punishable by up to ten years' imprisonment and/or an unlimited fine.

CHAPTER 6

Financial reporting and corporate governance

OVERVIEW

- Premium and standard listed companies must comply with the periodic financial reporting requirements of DTR 4 and the corporate governance-related requirements of DTR 7. Premium listed companies must also comply with the additional financial reporting and corporate governance requirements of Listing Rule 9.

- DTR 4 requires a listed company to publish an Annual Financial Report and a Half-yearly Financial Report. It prescribes the high-level content requirements, responsibility regime and timing of publication for these financial reports that must be considered alongside the requirements of IFRS and applicable company law.

- Listing Rule 9 prescribes additional financial reporting requirements for premium listed companies, including those that apply to the publication of preliminary statements of results and dividend statements.

- For a premium listed company, 'closed periods' apply under the Market Abuse Regulation in relation to dealings in shares by directors, PDMRs and persons closely associated with them prior to the publication of its Annual Financial Report (or, if earlier, preliminary statement of results) and Half-yearly Financial Report (see Chapter 7).

- DTR 7 requires a listed company to have an audit committee or other body (or bodies) responsible for financial reporting and audit-related matters and requires the inclusion of corporate governance, internal controls and risk-related disclosures in its Annual Financial Report.

- The EU audit regime sets out audit requirements for listed companies, including requirements regarding audit tender, mandatory rotation of auditors and audit committees.

- The Financial Reporting Council (FRC) publishes and maintains the UK Corporate Governance Code (Governance Code). This sets out standards of good practice in relation to Board leadership and effectiveness, remuneration, accountability and relations with shareholders to be observed by UK incorporated listed companies.

- Under Listing Rule 9, a premium listed company is required to explain in its Annual Financial Report how it seeks to comply with the Corporate Governance Code and, where it does not do so, the reasons for its non-compliance.
- The FRC also publishes and maintains the UK Stewardship Code. This aims to enhance the quality of engagement between institutional investors and listed companies to help improve long-term returns to shareholders and the efficient exercise of governance responsibilities.
- The FRC's Conduct Committee is responsible for reviewing listed and large company accounts. The FRC has the power to require the revision of Annual Financial Reports. It publishes an annual report summarising the results of its review of financial reports.

1. Financial reporting and listed companies

1.1 The key rules that apply to financial reporting

DTR 4 implements those parts of the Transparency Directive which relate to financial reporting by listed companies. The provisions of DTR 4 on periodic financial reporting, which apply to both premium and standard listed companies, are generally very high level, covering overall content, timing and the requirements for audit.

The detailed content requirements of a listed company's periodic financial reports are derived from company law and accounting standards. All UK incorporated listed companies are subject to the requirements of the CA 2006 in relation to other elements of their Annual Financial Report, in particular the requirements for a strategic report, a directors' report and a directors' remuneration report, as well as detailed rules on their content.

In the case of premium listed companies, the super-equivalent requirements of Listing Rule 9 must also be complied with, which include specific content requirements for annual reports. There are also specific corporate governance disclosures for listed companies required by DTR 7.

The vast majority of UK incorporated listed companies will prepare accounts under International Financial Reporting Standards (IFRS).

Accordingly, a premium listed company's Annual Financial Report will be governed by an amalgam of the requirements of DTR 4, DTR 7, the Listing Rules, CA 2006 and accounting standards (as well as the 'comply or explain' disclosure requirements in the Governance Code, as described in section 8.4.11). Where requirements overlap (e.g. in relation to producing a narrative report about the company's performance) separate reports are not required, but those produced will need to satisfy all of the different legal, regulatory and accounting requirements. The FRC has stated that it is an overarching principle of corporate reporting that it should be clear and concise; this should be taken into account when considering the overlapping reporting requirements.

The situation is more straightforward for Half-yearly Financial Reports as these are not required by CA 2006, and are just creatures of DTR 4.

This chapter only seeks to cover the periodic reporting requirements of the Listing Regime (i.e. the DTRs and Listing Rules). It does not attempt to summarise the detailed requirements of applicable UK company law, the separate regimes relating to stakeholder reporting or accounting standards; some indication of these issues is given where there are areas of significant overlap.

1.2 The DTR 4 regime

The main requirements of DTR 4 for premium and standard listed companies are to produce periodic financial information as follows:

- *Annual Financial Report* – within four months of the end of the full year (see section 3); and
- *Half-yearly Financial Report* – as soon as possible but no later than three months after the end of the first six months of the accounting period (see section 4).

However, where financial information is inside information because it is out of line with market expectations, it will need to be made public by immediate announcement ahead of publication of the full Annual or Half-yearly Financial Report, in accordance with the obligations under MAR (see Chapter 5).

Companies may also choose to produce preliminary statements of their full annual results on a voluntary basis. If a premium listed company does so, it must comply with the requirements of Listing Rule 9 (see section 2.1).

Under the original TD, listed companies had to produce Interim Management Statements (IMSs) in each of the first and second six months of its financial year. Following amendments to the TD removing this obligation, this requirement was abolished in the UK with effect from November 2014. Listed companies may continue to publish interim management statements on a voluntary basis.

A typical financial reporting calendar under the DTR 4 regime for a premium listed company with a 31 December year end and a premium listed company with a 31 March year end is set out in Figure 6.1.

It is worth noting that there are certain exemptions from the periodic disclosure requirements under DTR 4.4 for, among other specialist issuers, public sector issuers and debt issuers. As this *Guide* focuses on the rules that apply to premium listed commercial companies incorporated in the UK, these exemptions are not considered further in this chapter.

The requirements in respect of publishing periodic financial information refer to a listed company having to make the information public. The detailed requirements in relation to how information is made public under the DTRs is not set out in DTR 4, but rather in DTR 6.3 (see section 3.1 below and Chapter 8 for further detail).

2. Preliminary statements of annual results and statements of dividends

2.1 Preliminary statements

There is no concept of a preliminary announcement of results under the DTR 4 regime. Preliminary announcements are also not compulsory under Listing Rule 9, but under LR 9.7A.1R, if a premium listed company chooses to publish a preliminary results announcement, it must follow certain rules on content requirements. These include the requirement for preliminary announcements to be disseminated in full text and to be agreed by auditors (see the UKLA Guidance Note *Preliminary statement of annual results (UKLA/TN/502.2)*). Note that, while the approval of the auditors is needed, a preliminary statement must not include an audit opinion because a preliminary statement does not meet the requirements of statutory accounts.

Listing Rule 9.7A.1R states that if a premium listed company prepares a preliminary statement of annual results then:

- the statement must be published as soon as possible after it has been approved by the Board;
- the statement must be agreed with the company's auditors prior to publication;
- the statement must show the figures in the form of a table, including the items required for a Half-yearly Financial Report, consistent with the presentation to be adopted in the annual accounts for that financial year;
- the statement must give details of the nature of any likely modification that may be contained in the auditor's report required to be included with the Annual Financial Report (such as an emphasis of matter in relation to going concern); and
- the statement must include any significant additional information necessary for the purpose of assessing the results being announced.

The FCA has confirmed in the UKLA Guidance Note *Preliminary statement of annual results (UKLA/TN/502.2)* that, if preliminary results are prepared, they do not need to be prepared in accordance with IAS 34.

The requirement to get the approval of the auditors means that, in practice, a preliminary statement is unlikely to be issued until the audit work is substantially complete and the full financial statements are nearly finalised. This will reduce the risk that the final numbers change after the preliminary statement has been issued. Some companies do not release the preliminary announcement until the auditor's report has been signed off for the Annual Report.

Many issuers choose to publish preliminary statements because of market expectations and also to ensure that there is less of a risk of breaching the requirements in MAR to make inside information public as soon as possible and to end the closed period for PDMR dealings under MAR (see Chapter 7). MAR does not state that the announcement of preliminary results will end the closed period but the ESMA MAR Q&A clarify that the announcement of preliminary results will end a MAR closed period provided the preliminary financial results contain all the key information relating to the financial figures expected to be included in the Annual Financial Report. If the information announced in the preliminary statement changes after publication, this will not trigger another closed period but should be disclosed in accordance with Article 17 of MAR as soon as possible.

Where a listed company issues a preliminary results announcement, the information contained in it does not need to be repeated in the announcement of the Annual Financial Report required under DTR 6.3.5R (see section 3.1 below).

2.2 Statements of dividends

Listing Rule 9 also contains provisions governing statements of dividends by premium listed companies.

LR 9.7A.2R states that a premium listed company must notify an RIS as soon as possible after the Board has approved any decision to pay or make any dividend or other distribution on listed equity securities giving details of:

- the exact net amount payable per share;
- the payment date;
- the record date (where applicable); and
- any foreign income dividend election, together with any income tax treated as paid at the lower rate and not repayable.

In addition, a premium listed company must also notify an RIS if it decides to withhold any dividend or interest payment on listed securities (LR 9.7A.2R).

3. Annual Financial Reports

DTR 4.1 deals with the Annual Financial Report. In summary, this must consist of audited financial statements, a management report (equivalent to the strategic report and the directors' report under CA 2006), responsibility statements and an audit report (DTR 4.1.5R and DTR 4.1.7R(3)).

Guidance on preparing the Annual Financial Report can be found in guidance, reports, studies and statements published by the FRC and its Financial Reporting Lab. The FRC reviews corporate reporting on an annual basis, monitors compliance and reports on areas of current focus and areas with potential for improvements.

Companies should also consider the guidance note *Good practice for annual reports* (May 2015) and the checklist issued by ICSA for UK companies when preparing their Annual Financial Report. The guidance note, which is available on the ICSA's website, offers examples of good practice and general guidance in preparing the various parts of the Annual Financial Report, while the checklist sets out ICSA's summary contents for Annual Financial Reports of UK companies.

3.1 Publication requirements

The Annual Financial Report must be made public no later than four months after the year end (DTR 4.1.3R) and must remain publicly available on a website for at least ten years (DTR 4.1.4R and DTR 6.3.5R(3)). Under the TD, from 1 January 2020, issuers listed on regulated markets will be required to prepare their Annual Financial Report in a European Single Electronic Format (ESEF).

Under the TD, the Annual Financial Report is classed as 'regulated information'; this means it must be disseminated in the same way as all other regulated information and made available on a rapid, non-discriminatory, basis to the public in all EEA states (see Chapter 8 for more information).

Generally, under DTR 6.3.5R(1), all regulated information must be made public in unedited full text. Publication of the Annual Financial Report is, however, partially exempt from this general requirement because the length of the RIS announcement would make full dissemination impractical for many companies. Instead, a company is permitted, under DTR 6.3.5R(2), to limit the information included in the RIS announcement released at the time of publication of its Annual Financial Report to the type of information that would be included in its Half-yearly Financial Report (namely financial statements showing only those line items required in the Half-yearly Financial Report, the management report and the responsibility statement).

The Annual Financial Report must also be published via the NSM (see Chapter 8). Notwithstanding that NSM requirement, the information required by DTR 6.3.5R(2) must still be announced in unedited full text to the market.

The FSA (as it then was) issued a statement (FSA Update, March 2009) to confirm which practices were acceptable. In particular, it confirmed that an announcement containing a hyperlink to a company's Annual Financial Report or embedding an Annual Financial Report in a pdf format would not satisfy DTR 6.3.5R. Helpfully for companies who produce preliminary statements (see section 2), the FSA confirmed that it was acceptable not to repeat information from an earlier preliminary statement in an announcement or publication of the Annual Financial Report, although a company still has to ensure that that any information required under DTR 6.3.5R(2) that was not included in the preliminary statement is disclosed in the Annual Financial Report announcement.

Companies should also bear in mind their obligations under MAR to announce inside information to the market discussed in Chapter 5 (see also the UKLA Guidance Note *Periodic financial information and inside information (UKLA/TN/506.1)*). If companies discover that there is inside information when compiling their Annual Financial Reports, they must make an immediate announcement.

Another practical issue in respect of the announcement is that the condensed financial information included in the announcement would generally not constitute statutory accounts. The publication of an audit opinion with these non-statutory accounts is prohibited under section 435(2) of the CA 2006. The DTRs, however, would require inclusion of the audit report (DTR 4.1.7R(3)) and this is technically one of the items to be included in the announcement under DTR 6.3.5R. The FSA (as it then was) has, however, said that UK incorporated issuers are not expected to breach their statutory obligations. Therefore the announcement does not need to include the audit report, but the information contained in the announcement should be identified as either audited or unaudited.

The responsibility statement relates to the full financial statements and management report, not to the condensed information included in the announcement. However, it does still need to be included in the announcement. One accepted approach is to present an explanatory paragraph alongside the responsibility statement to clarify that it has been extracted from the Annual Financial Report to meet the requirements in DTR 6.3.5R(2) and that it does not refer to the content of the announcement itself.

Figure 6.1 (see p. 266) sets out a checklist of the key CA 2006 and DTR 4 disclosure requirements for an Annual Financial Report.

3.2 Audited financial statements

Under DTR 4.1.6R(1), issuers governed by EU law must prepare their consolidated group accounts in accordance with IFRS. Non-EEA issuers are permitted to use other accounting principles, but they must be equivalent to IFRS (see section 6.2 below).

UK incorporated issuers will apply IFRS through the operation of the IAS Regulation (see Chapter 1 for more detail). Under the IAS Regulation, issuers must follow IFRS as formally adopted by the EU, not simply IFRS as issued by the IASB. Current information on adopted standards can be found on the websites of both the Commission and the European Financial Reporting Advisory Group (EFRAG). Although companies preparing accounts in accordance with IFRS are not required to comply with the detailed content requirements of CA 2006, in relation to the financial statements there are a handful of disclosures that are still required, for example, information about:

- related undertakings (CA 2006 s. 409);
- off balance sheet arrangements (CA 2006 s. 410A);
- employee numbers and costs (CA 2006 s. 411); and
- directors' benefits (CA 2006 ss 412 and 413).

Parent company individual accounts must be included with the audited consolidated financial statements. These must be drawn up in accordance with national law in the member state where the issuer is incorporated. For a UK company, this will either be IFRS or UK GAAP (DTR 4.1.6R(1)). Unlike IFRS accounts, UK GAAP accounts are governed by the detailed content requirements of the CA 2006.

An issuer that is not required to prepare consolidated financial statements must prepare its single entity financial statements in accordance with the national law applicable in the EEA state where the issuer is incorporated (DTR 4.1.6R(2)). There are only a few issuers to which this is likely to apply (e.g. some investment companies do not form a group). UK incorporated companies can follow IFRS or UK GAAP in their accounts, as both are permitted by English law (CA 2006 s. 395).

3.3 The management report

The requirement to produce a narrative report to accompany the main financial statements is an EU requirement introduced with the TD. In the UK, the CA 2006 requires the narrative part of the annual report to be contained in the strategic report and directors' report, which therefore are where the requirements for the management report are covered.

Under DTR 4.1.8R, the management report must contain a fair review of the listed company's business and a description of the principal risks and uncertainties facing the company. The review must:

- be a balanced and comprehensive analysis of (i) the development and performance of the listed company's business during the financial year and (ii) the position of the listed company's business at the end of that year, consistent with the size and complexity of the business (DTR 4.1.9R(1));
- include, to the extent necessary for an understanding of the development, performance or position of the listed company's business, (i) analysis using financial key performance indicators (DTR 4.1.10G says that these are factors by reference to which the development, performance or position of the company's business can be measured effectively), and (ii), where appropriate, analysis using other key performance indicators, including information relating to environmental matters and employee matters (DTR 4.1.9R(2)); and
- include references to, and additional explanations of, amounts included in the listed company's annual financial statements, where appropriate (DTR 4.1.9R(3)).

Further, in accordance with DTR 4.1.11R, the management report must also give an indication of:

- any important events that have occurred since the end of the financial year;
- the company's likely future development;
- activities in the field of research and development;
- the information concerning acquisitions of own shares prescribed by Article 22(2) of the Second Company Law Directive;
- the existence of branches of the company; and
- in relation to the company's use of financial instruments and where material for the assessment of its assets, liabilities, financial position and profit or loss (i) the company's financial risk management objectives and policies, including its policy for hedging each major type of forecasted transaction for which hedge accounting is used, and (ii) the company's exposure to price risk, credit risk, liquidity risk and cash flow risk.

While the high-level requirements for a management report under the DTRs are similar to the combined requirements in UK company law for publication of strategic and directors' reports (CA 2006 ss 414C and 415–416) they are not identical, so listed companies should ensure they dovetail the requirements so that their narrative reporting encompasses the information required to be included in the reports required by CA 2006 and the management report specified in DTR 4.

Since 3 July 2016, listed companies must also make 'every effort' to comply with ESMA Guidelines on Alternative Performance Measures (APMs) when disclosing additional non-GAAP numbers in the narrative parts of the Annual and Half-yearly Financial Reports (see section 3.5).

3.4 Responsibility statements

Responsibility statements must be made by the persons responsible within the listed company for the Annual Financial Report and the name and function of any person who makes a responsibility statement must be clearly indicated in the responsibility statement (DTR 4.1.12R(1) and (3)).

Under DTR 4.1.12R(3), for each person making a responsibility statement, the statement must set out that to the best of his or her knowledge:

- the financial statements, prepared in accordance with the applicable set of accounting standards, give a true and fair view of the assets, liabilities, financial position and profit or loss of the issuer and the undertakings included in the consolidation taken as a whole; and
- the management report includes a fair review of the development and performance of the business and the position of the issuer and the undertakings included in the

consolidation taken as a whole, together with a description of the principal risks and uncertainties that they face.

The DTRs do not specify who are 'persons responsible within the issuer'. They specify only that the issuer is responsible as is required under the TD (DTR 4.1.13R). The FSA (as it then was) confirmed in List! Issue No. 14 (and in its 2010 Technical Note *Disclosure and Transparency Rules*) that the company has exclusive regulatory responsibility for the Annual Financial Report. It acknowledged the 'potential difference' between that position and DTR 4.1.12R(1), which requires identification of the persons making responsibility statements. The FSA said that the requirements in DTR 4.1.12R(1) were included only because they are in the TD (Article 4.2(c)) and that they 'should be considered as standalone provisions with no effect on the issuer's exclusive regulatory responsibility'.

In a UK context, the persons responsible within the issuer will be the directors. In its UKLA Guidance Note *Half-yearly and annual reports (UKLA/TN/501.1)*, the FCA says that while 'person' is not defined in the DTRs, issuers should identify those individuals responsible for the reports; in most cases it would expect this to be either the whole Board of directors or one or more directors on behalf of the whole Board. The company should explicitly state the name and function of those responsible in the responsibility statement. The liability of an individual signing the responsibility statement on behalf of the Board will not be increased beyond that of his or her fellow directors. Thus, the naming of one or two directors giving the responsibility statement on behalf of the Board is the acceptable and usual UK practice.

3.5 The use of Alternative Performance Measures (APMs)

Companies often disclose additional non-GAAP numbers in their periodic financial statements. For example, they may quote earnings or earnings per share excluding the impact of certain items (e.g. exceptional or unusual items or perhaps fair value changes).

ESMA has published Guidelines on the use of alternative performance measures (APMs) which came into force in July 2016. Listed companies must make 'every effort' to comply with the ESMA Guidelines on APMs when disclosing non-GAAP numbers in the narrative parts of the Annual and Half-yearly Financial Reports. The Guidelines do not apply to APMs in the financial statements themselves.

An APM is defined in the ESMA Guidelines as a financial measure that is not required as part of an issuer's financial reporting obligations but which it may voluntarily present to aid understanding of its performance (e.g. adjusted earnings, operating earnings and EBITDA).

Listed companies using APMs in the narrative sections of their Annual Financial Report or Half-yearly Report should, under the ESMA Guidelines:

- define the APMs they use;
- explain why and how the company uses these APMs;
- in the event that a company redefines an APM, explain why the alternative APM is more relevant;
- reconcile the APMs they use with the most relevant parts of the financial statements; and
- provide a comparison against the corresponding previous period.

The FRC, as competent authority (along with the FCA) for monitoring compliance with the APM Guidelines, issued an FAQ document (May 2016) to assist companies in complying with the ESMA Guidelines on APMs. ESMA has also published a Q&A document to assist in the consistent application of the ESMA Guidelines on APMs.

3.6 Governance disclosures under DTR 7

DTR 7 contains specific disclosure requirements relating to corporate governance matters. The scope and application of DTR 7 to different types of companies is set out in DTR 1B.

Under DTR 7.2, listed companies must produce an annual corporate governance statement, either as a specific section of the directors' report, as a separate corporate governance statement published together with the Annual Financial Report, or in a document publicly available on its website to which reference is made in the directors' report (DTR 7.2.9R). The corporate governance statement must set out prescribed information, including the governance code to which the company is subject (DTR 7.2.2R(1)). Under DTR 7.1, a company must publish a statement disclosing details about its audit committee. This statement can be included in the company's corporate governance statement (DTR 7.1.5R and DTR 7.1.6R).

The content requirements of a corporate governance statement prepared in accordance with DTR 7.2 overlap with the relevant disclosure provisions in the Governance Code and compliance with the relevant disclosure requirements in the Governance Code will ensure compliance with the corresponding provisions in DTR 7.2.

For further details see Section 8.2.

3.7 Additional Listing Rule requirements for premium listed companies' Annual Financial Reports

There are a number of additional obligations in Listing Rule 9.8 which apply to premium listed companies' Annual Financial Reports.

The key elements are summarised below.

3.7.1 Directors' remuneration disclosures

LR 9.8.8R previously required a premium listed company's Annual Financial Report to include a report by the Board to shareholders on the remuneration of the directors but this requirement was removed in December 2013 in light of the new disclosure requirements introduced by amendments to the Large and Medium-Sized Companies and Groups (Accounts and Reports) Regulations 2008 (Schedule I, Part 4). Under these Regulations, companies are required to produce implementation and policy reports on directors' remuneration and to put the reports to shareholder votes at the annual general meeting. As a result, LR 9.8.8R now only contains very limited disclosure obligations regarding the unexpired term of directors' service contracts.

3.7.2 Governance disclosures under LR 9

LR 9.8.6R(5) and (6) contain additional corporate governance disclosure requirements and require issuers to make a two-part statement on corporate governance. The first part is a report on how the company has applied the Main Principles of the Governance Code (LR 9.8.6R(5)). The second part is a confirmation of whether the company has complied, throughout the relevant accounting period, with the relevant provisions in the Governance Code and if not, an explanation of why not (LR 9.8.6R(6)).

The Governance Code itself also requires certain matters (such as each non-executive director it considers to be independent) to be included in the Annual Financial Report.

The provisions in the Governance Code are discussed in further detail in section 8 of this chapter.

3.7.3 Going concern disclosures

Going concern is a fundamental accounting concept that underlies the preparation of the Annual Financial Report. LR 9.8.6R(3) requires that the Annual Financial Report includes statements by the directors on the appropriateness of adopting the going concern basis of accounting and on their assessment of the prospects of the company. These requirements cross-refer to and align with provisions C.1.3 and C.2.2 of the UK Corporate Governance Code. The Listing Rules require these statements to be prepared in accordance with the FRC's Guidance on *Risk Management, Internal Control and Related Financial and Business Reporting*, which has been issued alongside the Governance Code.

The directors will need to make disclosures in the accounts to explain any doubts over the going concern of the business. Auditors will seek evidence from the directors that, despite the uncertainties, the business is a going concern. Should auditors not receive sufficient support and evidence they may have to qualify the audit opinion, but this will be very rare. Nevertheless, it is often the case that even after all available evidence is considered, significant doubt about the company's ability to continue as a going concern remains. As required by auditing standards, auditors will then include an additional paragraph in the audit opinion (known as an emphasis of matter paragraph) to highlight the going concern problems. The emphasis of matter paragraph in the audit opinion is a modification, not a qualification. It is important to distinguish a modification from a qualification because they may have different effects on the company. A modification, for example, would usually not result in default in relation to most standard debt agreements, while a qualification most likely would.

The Governance Code also requires the inclusion of a going concern statement in the Half-yearly Financial Report. This is, however, not a requirement of the Listing Rules. The FRC's Guidance on *Risk Management, Internal Control and Related Financial and Business Reporting* states that the same considerations should apply to the half-yearly statement as they do to the annual financial statements in relation to disclosures about the going concern basis on accounting and material uncertainties. Directors should build on their understanding since the full year accounts and revise their disclosures as necessary.

3.7.4 Publication of unaudited financial information

LR 9.2.18R applies to a premium listed company that has published any unaudited financial information in a Class 1 circular, a prospectus or any profit forecast or profit estimate.

The first time a premium listed company publishes its Annual Financial Report after the publication of such unaudited financial information, profit forecast or profit estimate, it must:

- reproduce that financial information, profit forecast or profit estimate in the annual report and accounts (LR 9.2.18R(2)(a));
- produce and disclose in the annual report and accounts the actual figures for the same period covered by that information (LR 9.2.18R(2)(b)); and
- if there is a difference of 10% or more between the two sets of figures, provide an explanation of the difference (LR 9.2.18R(2)(c)).

However, under LR 9.2.19G, these requirements do not apply to any pro forma financial information prepared in accordance with Annex I and Annex II of the PD Regulation or any preliminary statements of annual results or half-yearly or quarterly reports that are reproduced with the unaudited financial information.

3.7.5 Long-term incentive plans for directors

Generally a long-term incentive plan will require shareholder approval prior to adoption (LR 9.4.1R(2)). This is in addition to the company law requirements under the CA 2006 for shareholder approval.

There is an exemption where such a plan is established for a director of the company (and the director is the only participant) specifically to facilitate the recruitment or retention of that person in unusual circumstances. Where this exemption is used, the premium listed company must include certain information in its next Annual Financial Report (LR 9.4.3R). The information to be disclosed includes that required by LR 13.8.11R (information to be included in premium listed company circulars relating to approval employee share schemes and long-term incentive plans), the name of the sole participant, an explanation of why the circumstances were unusual, the conditions to be satisfied and the maximum awards under the terms of the arrangements. The FCA has published a UKLA Guidance Note *Long-term incentive schemes (UKLA/TN/208.1)* which says that the circumstances in which the exemption may be used will be rare in practice.

3.7.6 Statement of compliance about controlling shareholder rules

Where a premium listed company has a controlling shareholder (i.e. a person who exercises or controls 30% or more of the voting rights in the company, either on their own or together with persons acting in concert with them), certain additional rules apply, including a requirement for the company to have in place with the controlling shareholder an agreement containing certain undertakings (known as independence provisions) to ensure that the company is independent from the controlling shareholder. See Chapter 9 for more information. Under LR 9.8.4R(14), a company with a controlling shareholder must confirm each year in its Annual Financial Report that:

- it has entered into an agreement with its controlling shareholder containing the requisite independence provisions (LR 9.2.2A(2)(a));
- it has complied with the independence provisions in the agreement throughout the relevant period;
- so far as the listed company is aware, the independence provisions have been complied with by the controlling shareholder and its associates throughout the relevant period; and
- where the controlling shareholder has agreed to procure that another controlling shareholder and its associates will comply with the independence provisions, so far as the listed company is aware that procurement obligation has been complied with.

If the company is unable to confirm compliance with any of these, under LR 9.8.4R(14) the Annual Financial Report must contain a statement that the FCA has been notified and the reasons for the non-compliance. The enhanced oversight provisions discussed in Chapter 9 will also be triggered. If an independent director of the listed company declines to support the statements of compliance, the FCA must be notified and the statement must record that fact (and again the enhanced oversight provisions will be triggered).

3.7.7 Strategic report with supplementary information

Under LR 9.8.13R, any separate strategic report with accompanying supplementary information issued by a premium listed company as permitted under CA 2006 must disclose earnings per share, the information required for a strategic report under CA 2006 and the supplementary information required under section 426A of the CA 2006.

3.7.8 All information required by LR 9.8.4R to be in same place

Under LR 9.8.4CR, all information required by LR 9.8.4R to be disclosed in the Annual Financial Report must be in a single identifiable section or signposted in a cross-reference table.

Figure 6.1: Checklist of key CA 2006 and DTR 4 disclosure requirements for an Annual Financial Report

Key section in Annual Financial Report	Key disclosure requirements		Points to note
	CA 2006	DTR	
Chairman's statement and chief executive's review	n/a	n/a	These are not mandatory. To take advantage of the statutory safe harbour provision in CA 2006 s. 463 they should be cross-referred into the strategic report or directors' report.
Corporate Governance Report	s. 419A	DTR 7.2	LR 9.8.6R requires a comply or explain statement. Usually cross-referenced into the directors' report. CA 2006 s. 463 safe harbour applies (if the corporate governance statement is separated from the directors' report, it must be cross-referenced into the directors' report to take advantage of the safe harbour and comply with DTR 7.2).
Strategic report	ss. 414A–414D and 433	n/a	The purpose of the strategic report is to help shareholders assess how directors have performed their duty under CA 2006 s. 172.
Management report	n/a	DTR 4.1.8R	Management report is the equivalent to the combined strategic report and directors' report required by CA 2006. Most companies do not produce a separate management report, but include all information in the strategic or directors' report.

FINANCIAL REPORTING AND CORPORATE GOVERNANCE 267

Directors' report	ss 415–418 and s. 236	DTR 7.2	Further disclosures may be required by LR 9.8.4R and LR 9.8.6R. CA 2006 s. 463 (safe harbour) applies. Disclosures required by LR 9.8.4R must be in one place or cross-referenced in a table. See also the Large and Medium-sized Companies and Groups (Accounts and Reports) Regulations 2008 (SI 2008/410).
Directors' remuneration report	ss 420–422A	n/a	Additional disclosures may be required by LR 9.8.6R(1) and LR 9.8.6AG on directors' interests and LR 9.8.8R on the unexpired terms of directors' service contracts. The CA 2006 s. 463 safe harbour provision applies.
Auditors' report	ss 487 and 495–497	DTR 4.1.7R(3)	The content of this report derives predominantly from auditing standards but also CA 2006 to some extent. The content is entirely the responsibility of the auditors.
Directors' Responsibility Statement	n/a	DTR 4.1.12R	The Governance Code and auditing standards (ISA 700) also require the disclosure of directors' responsibilities in respect of the preparation of the reports. This is a separate and stand-alone requirement to DTR 4.1.12R.
Group consolidated accounts	ss 399, 403, and 404	DTR 4.1.5R(1)	The accounts of UK listed groups have to be prepared in accordance with IFRS (CA 2006 s. 403).
Parent company individual entity accounts	ss 394–397 and 408	DTR 4.1.6R(1)(b) and 4.1.6R(2)	The issuer has a choice to prepare the parent company accounts in accordance with either IFRS or UK GAAP (CA 2006 s. 395).
Notes to the accounts	ss 409–413, 494 and 538	n/a	The notes are an integral part of the accounts and are subject to full audit. IFRS and UK GAAP, as applicable to the accounts, contain additional requirements. Details of 'related undertakings' and registered offices must be disclosed (which are wider than just subsidiary undertakings).

4. Half-yearly Financial Reports

The requirements in relation to the Half-yearly Financial Report are contained in DTR 4.2. An issuer is required to publish a Half-yearly Financial Report covering the first six months of the year, which must include a condensed set of financial statements, an interim management report and a responsibility statement (DTR 4.2.3R).

4.1 Publication requirements

The Half-yearly Financial Report must be made public as soon as possible and no later than three months after the half-year end and must remain publicly available for at least ten years (DTR 4.2.2R).

Under the TD, the Half-yearly Financial Report is classed as 'regulated information', which means that it must be disseminated in the same way as all other regulated information. Under DTR 6.3.5R(1) all regulated information must be made public in unedited full text (see Chapter 8). The obligation to 'make public' for these purposes requires an RIS announcement and website publication of such results on the listed company's website.

The report does not have to be posted in hard copy to shareholders.

As the announcement will be released via an RIS, it will automatically be stored within the NSM and does not need to be uploaded separately by the company.

4.2 Condensed financial statements

The condensed set of financial statements in the Half-yearly Financial Report must be prepared in accordance with the applicable accounting framework (i.e. either IAS 34 *Interim financial statements* for issuers who prepare consolidated accounts or UK GAAP for others (DTR 4.2.4R and DTR 4.2.5R)).

Consistency of accounting policies is required by IAS 34 in any case, but under DTR 4.2.6R, the accounting policies and presentation applied to half-yearly figures must be consistent with those applied in the latest published annual accounts unless either the accounting policies and presentation are to be changed in the subsequent annual financial statements (in which case the new accounting policies and presentation should be followed and the changes and the reasons for the changes should be disclosed in the Half-yearly Financial Report) or the FCA otherwise agrees. In situations where a listed company is not required to prepare consolidated accounts (and hence is not caught by the IAS Regulation requirement to produce IFRS accounts), the condensed financial statements must at least include a condensed balance sheet, a condensed profit and loss account and explanatory notes on the accounts (DTR 4.2.4R(2)).

The ASB has issued a non-mandatory statement on interim reports that should be applied by UK incorporated issuers that prepare their financial statements in accordance with UK GAAP. The ASB's statement is notionally voluntary, but the DTRs make it effectively mandatory: under DTR 4.2.10R(4) an issuer who applies UK GAAP is required to confirm compliance with the ASB's statement in its responsibility statements (see section 4.4 below).

DTR 4.2.5R provides more detailed rules in relation to the content of the Half-yearly Financial Report for those listed companies that do not produce consolidated accounts.

There is no requirement for an audit or auditor review of a Half-yearly Financial Report, but any report or review carried out by the auditor under the APB's guidance on Review of Interim Financial Information must be disclosed (DTR 4.2.9R(1)). If the Half-yearly Financial Report has not been audited or reviewed pursuant to the APB's guidance, this fact must be disclosed (DTR 4.2.9R(2)).

As mentioned in section 3.7.3 above, while there is no requirement in the Listing Rules or DTRs in relation to going concern in the context of Half-yearly Financial Reports, the Governance Code does include a requirement for a statement about going concern in the Half-yearly Financial Report.

4.3 The interim management report

The interim management report required to be included in the Half-yearly Financial Report must include at least an indication of the important events in the first six months of the year, their impact on the financial statements and a description of the principal risks and uncertainties for the next six months (DTR 4.2.7R). As with the Annual Financial Report, if APMs are used in the narrative part of the Half-yearly Financial Report, additional disclosures are required (see section 3.5 of this chapter).

In its UKLA Guidance Note *Half-yearly and annual reports (UKLA/TN/501.1)*, the FCA gives guidance on the requirement to include a description of the principal risks and uncertainties. It notes that most companies give considerable thought to the subject of risks and uncertainties in their Annual Financial Reports. It says that as these are the principal risks and uncertainties the company faced at the time of its Annual Financial Report, they may remain valid for the purpose of the interim management report. Where this is the case, in the Half-yearly Financial Report it is acceptable for the company to:

- state that the principal risks and uncertainties have not changed;
- provide a summary of those principal risks and uncertainties; and
- include a cross-reference to where a detailed explanation of the principal risks and uncertainties can be found in the Annual Financial Report.

If the principal risks and uncertainties have changed since the Annual Financial Report, the company should describe the new principal risks and uncertainties in the interim management report.

In addition to the requirement set out in DTR 4.2.7R, a listed company must disclose the following information in the interim management report:

- any related parties transactions (for the purposes of IFRS, not the Listing Rules) that have taken place in the first six months of the current financial year and that have materially affected the financial position or the performance of the enterprise during that period; and

- any changes in the related parties transactions (for the purposes of IFRS, not the Listing Rules) described in the last Annual Financial Report that could have a material effect on the financial position or performance of the enterprise in the first six months of the current financial year (DTR 4.2.8R(1)).

If a company with listed shares is not required to prepare consolidated accounts, it must disclose, as a minimum, any transactions which have been entered into with related parties by the company, including the amount of such transactions, the nature of the related party relationship and other information about the transactions necessary for an understanding of the financial position of the company, if such transactions are material and have not been concluded under normal market conditions (DTR 4.2.8R(2)). Information about such transactions may be aggregated according to their nature except where separate information is necessary for an understanding of the effects of related party transactions on the financial position of the company (DTR 4.2.8R(3)).

4.4 Responsibility statements

As in the case of the Annual Financial Report, responsibility statements must be made by the persons responsible within the listed company and the name and function of any person who makes a responsibility statement must be clearly indicated in the responsibility statement (DTR 4.2.10R(1) and (2)).

As discussed in section 3.4 above, the FCA confirms in its UKLA Guidance Note *Half-yearly and annual reports (UKLA/TN/501.1)* that companies should identify those individuals responsible for the reports; in most cases it would expect this to be either the whole Board of directors or one or more directors on behalf of the whole Board. Companies should explicitly state the name and function of those responsible in the responsibility statement. The FCA would not expect this information to be cross-referenced to other documents.

For each person making a responsibility statement, the statement must confirm that to the best of his or her knowledge (DTR 4.2.10R(3)):

- the condensed set of financial statements, which has been prepared in accordance with the applicable set of accounting standards, gives a true and fair view of the assets, liabilities, financial position and profit or loss of the issuer, or the undertakings included in the consolidation as a whole as required by DTR 4.2.4R; and
- the interim management report includes a fair review of the information required by DTR 4.2.7R and, in the case of an issuer with listed shares, the information required by DTR 4.2.8R.

The requirement to confirm that the condensed financial statements give a true and fair view raised considerable concerns in the UK when DTR 4 was originally consulted on because the condensed set of financial statements is not prepared to the same level of detail as the full financial statements to which the 'gold standard' of true and fair applies. The FSA (as it then was) responded to these concerns and DTR 4.2.10R(4) provides that a statement saying that the condensed financial statements have been prepared in accordance with IAS 34 or (for UK issuers not using IFRS) the guidance on Half-yearly Financial Reports issued by the ASB will satisfy the requirement under DTR 4.2.10R(3)(a), provided always that the person making such a statement has reasonable grounds to be satisfied that the condensed set of financial statements prepared in accordance with such a standard is not misleading.

As with the Annual Financial Report, the issuer is responsible for all information drawn up and made public in accordance with DTR 4.2 (DTR 4.2.11R).

5. Audit requirements

Under DTR 4.1.7R the annual financial statements must be audited and the audit must be carried out under EU law.

For financial years beginning on or after 17 June 2016, public interest entities (being listed companies, credit undertakings and insurers) (PIEs) must comply with the requirements of the Audit Regulation (2014/537/EU) and Audit Directive (2014/56/EU) (the EU Audit Regime), as implemented in the UK by the Statutory Auditors and Third Country Auditors Regulations 2016 (SI 2016/649) (Statutory Audit Regulations) and by the FRC's Ethical Standards for Auditors and the provisions in DTR 7 on audit committees. There are separate requirements for companies regulated by the Prudential Regulatory Authority which are beyond the scope of this chapter.

The EU Audit Regime introduced a range of new requirements to the audit regime for PIEs. In particular, it introduced mandatory rotation of auditors, tighter restrictions on the provision of non-audit services and new requirements in relation to audit committees.

The FRC is the 'competent authority' for audit in the UK; it monitors the quality of audits and compliance with the audit regime and takes enforcement action where necessary.

This section discusses the audit requirements applicable to companies listed in the UK. Third country issuers should additionally refer to section 6.3 below.

5.1 The auditors' report

Under DTR 4.1.7R, a company's audit report, signed by the auditor, must be disclosed, in full, to the public with the Annual Financial Report. Although the audit report primarily relates to the financial statements within the Annual Financial Report, the auditors have a responsibility, under auditing standards, to read the accompanying information to ensure it is consistent with the audited financial statements. For financial years commencing on or after 1 January 2016, the auditor of a UK incorporated company must also state in the audit report whether, in its opinion, the strategic report and the directors' report have been prepared in accordance with applicable legal requirements and whether the auditor has identified any material misstatements in the reports in the course of the audit (CA 2006 s. 496).

The Listing Rules impose additional requirements on auditors in relation to the Annual Financial Report. A listed company must ensure that its auditors review each of the following before the Annual Financial Report is published (LR 9.8.10R):

- the statements required to be made by the directors in accordance with LR 9.8.6R(3) regarding the appropriateness of the going concern basis of accounting and the longer-term viability of the business (containing the information set out in provision C.2.2 of the Corporate Governance Code); and
- the parts of the statement required to be made by LR 9.8.6R(6) (on corporate governance) that relate to provisions C.1.1 (the Board's responsibility for the annual report and accounts), C.2.1 and C.2.3 (risk management and internal control systems) and C.3.1 to C.3.7 (the audit committee and auditors) of the Corporate Governance Code.

The requirements of the Corporate Governance Code are discussed in section 8 of this chapter.

5.2 Audit tender and rotation of auditors

The EU Audit Regulation requires PIEs to put their audit work out to tender at least every ten years and change their auditor at least every 20 years. The Governance Code recommendation for FTSE 350 companies to put their external audit contract out to tender every ten years was removed in the 2016 edition of the Governance Code because it had become a regulatory requirement under the EU Audit Regulation and so it is no longer a 'comply or explain' matter.

These requirements have been implemented in the UK by new provisions in Part 16 of the CA 2006, which operate alongside the directly applicable provisions of the EU Audit Regulation. When overseeing the external audit tender process, the audit committee must comply with detailed process requirements set out in Article 16 of the EU Audit Regulation.

In addition, the Competition and Markets Authority issued an order (with effect from financial years beginning on or after 1 January 2015) setting out requirements for FTSE 350, UK incorporated companies in relation to audit tenders and the role of the audit committee in the tender. The order is called the Statutory Audit Services for Large Companies Market Investigation (Mandatory Use of Competitive Tender Processes and Audit Committee Responsibilities) Order 2014 (the CMA Order). This requires companies to whom it applies to put their audit contract out to tender every ten years and, if there has been no tender after five years of an audit term, the company must explain why in its Annual Financial Report. The CMA Order remains in force alongside the requirements of the EU Audit Regime. Listed companies must include a statement each year in their Annual Reports that they have complied with the Order.

5.3 Composition and role of the audit committee

The provisions in the EU Audit Regime in relation to audit committees have been implemented in the UK via requirements in DTR 7; DTR 7.1 focuses on the composition and role of the audit committee.

UK incorporated standard or premium listed companies and certain other issuers are required to comply with DTR 7.1 (see DTR 1B.1.2R and DTR 1B.1.3R on the application of DTR 7.1). Although some of its provisions overlap with the requirements of the Corporate Governance Code, compliance with DTR 7.1 is mandatory. While listed companies therefore have the ability to 'comply or explain' against the requirements of the Governance Code, they must comply with the requirements contained in DTR 7.1 in relation to audit committees.

See section 8.2 of this chapter for a further discussion of the requirements in DTR 7.1 in relation to the audit committee.

In addition, the CMA Order requires the audit committee to be responsible for any audit tender, for agreeing the terms of appointment of an auditor (including remuneration) and for approving any provision by the auditor of non-audit services.

6. Third country issuers with a premium listing

The previous sections in this chapter focus on the ongoing reporting requirements of premium listed companies incorporated in the UK.

The financial reporting obligations set out in Listing Rule 9 (see section 2 above) also apply to overseas issuers with a premium listing in the UK, although some of the corporate governance disclosure provisions are not applicable to overseas companies (see LR 9.8.7R and LR 9.8.7AR for the corporate governance requirements for overseas companies with a premium listing).

The majority of the DTR 4 reporting requirements also apply to overseas issuers with a premium listing in the UK, but only apply where the UK is the company's home member state. Therefore, a company incorporated in another EU member state will normally be required to comply instead with the equivalent to DTR 4 in its home jurisdiction (subject to the detailed rules in the TD about determining the home member state for each issuer).

6.1 Equivalence of relevant laws

Generally, non-EEA issuers with a premium listing and with the UK as their home member state must comply with the DTR 4 requirements in the same way as UK incorporated companies with a premium listing. However, the FCA has the discretion (see the UKLA Guidance Note *Equivalence arrangements for third country issuers (UKLA/TN/503.2)*) to exempt third country issuers from certain aspects of its periodic financial reporting requirements, if it is satisfied that the domestic regulation of the home state of the third country issuer is equivalent to LPDT Rules. Where it deems the relevant legislation in a third country to be equivalent, companies from that jurisdiction do not have to comply with the corresponding provisions in LPDT Rules. The TD refers to non-EEA countries as 'third countries' and this terminology is used throughout the remainder of this section.

The FCA maintains a list of exempt third countries on its website. Companies that use this exemption must still meet the requirements in DTR 6 as regards filing language and dissemination of financial information with the FCA (DTR 4.4.9G). Further, an exempt third-party issuer must still meet the auditor requirements as set out in DTR 4.1.7R(4) (see section 6.3).

The FCA has determined Switzerland, the United States and Canada to have equivalent laws to DTR 4 in place:

- Issuers incorporated in Switzerland are exempt from most of the DTR 4 requirements, except for the financial statements requirements in DTR 4.1.6R (see section 6.2 for further details).
- Issuers with a registered office in the United States and which have securities registered with the US Securities Exchange Commission and comply with all the relevant US rules governing financial reporting are exempt from producing the Annual and Half-yearly Financial Reports. If, however, an issuer is exempt from any of the US periodic financial reporting requirements, it will not be exempt from DTR 4.

- Issuers whose registered office is in Canada and who are subject to specified Canadian periodic disclosure requirements are exempt from producing Annual Financial Reports and Half-yearly Financial Reports under DTR 4. However, the exemption does not apply to DTR 4.1.7R(4), which relates to the identity of the issuer's auditors. Further, if an issuer is exempt from any of the Canadian periodic financial reporting requirements, it will not be exempt from DTR 4.

The latest position should be checked on the FCA website.

6.2 Equivalence of accounting standards with IFRS

Third country issuers applying accounting standards determined by the Commission to be equivalent to IFRS are not obliged to produce financial statements applying IFRS as adopted by the Commission.

As required under the TD, the Commission has set up a mechanism to determine the equivalence of third country accounting standards with IFRS (Commission Regulation (EC) No. 1569/2007). The following accounting standards are the subject of equivalence decisions (Decision 2008/961/EC, as amended):

- IFRS as issued by the IASB;
- GAAP principles of Japan and the US;
- GAAP principles of the People's Republic of China, Canada and the Republic of Korea; and
- GAAP principles of the Republic of India for a transitional period.

The measures mean that foreign companies listed on EU markets continue to be able to file their financial statements prepared in accordance with those GAAPs.

As the Commission is in regular dialogue about convergence, the latest position should always be checked.

Third country issuers that follow GAAP deemed to be non-equivalent have to assess whether they are required to produce consolidated financial statements. If they are, the consolidated accounts must be prepared in accordance with IFRS as adopted by the Commission (DTR 4.1.6R(1)). The DTRs require EEA-state issuers to produce accounts for the parent company as well as group accounts, but whether this also applies to third country issuers is not clear. Similarly, if an issuer is not required to produce group accounts, the DTRs specify that its audited financial statements must comprise accounts prepared in accordance with the national law of the EEA states in which the issuer is incorporated (DTR 4.1.6R(2)). They do not address the preparation requirements for third country issuers. Issuers affected should if necessary seek advice on the application of the DTRs from the FCA.

6.3 Audit and auditor requirements for third country issuers

Third country issuers, as with EEA issuers, must have their annual financial statements audited; the signed audit report must be publicly disclosed with the Annual Financial Report (DTR 4.1.7R(3)). The audit of the consolidated financial statements must be conducted in accordance with the Seventh Company Law Directive (DTR 4.1.7R(1)). The same requirements apply to the audit of entity-only accounts, which have to be audited in accordance with the Fourth Company Law Directive (DTR 4.1.6R(2)). (Note that while the DTRs still refer to the Seventh Company Law Directive and the Fourth Company Law Directive, they have been repealed and replaced by the EU Accounting Directive but the DTRs have not yet been updated to reflect this. However, Article 52 of the EU Accounting Directive states that references to the repealed Directives shall be construed as references to the correlating provisions of the EU Accounting Directive.)

A third country issuer can engage as auditor any person or firm registered as an auditor in the UK or a person or firm approved by a competent authority in another EEA member state (DTR 4.1.7R(4)(b) and (c)).

Alternatively, the audit can be performed by a third country auditor, if they are registered with the FRC, which has responsibility for the registration and oversight of third country auditors in the UK.

An audit performed by a person or entity that does not comply with the registration conditions in DTR 4.1.7R(4) will have no legal effect in the UK. It is the responsibility of the auditor to ensure that all requirements are met and issuers must not engage an auditor that fails to comply.

7. Stakeholder reporting requirements

Companies incorporated or operating in the UK are increasingly subject to a variety of stakeholder reporting obligations. The details of these regimes are outside the scope of this Guide, as (with the exception of the government payments report for extractive industry companies required by DTR 4.3A) they are not required by the LPDT Rules nor do they apply by virtue of a company being listed.

The application of a reporting obligation may for example depend on the size of the company or the number of employees it has. Each reporting obligation focuses on a particular issue and requires publication outside of the Annual Financial Report, either on the company's website or on a government-sponsored website (or both). Examples include reporting on modern slavery, payment practices, gender pay gap and tax.

8. Corporate governance

Corporate governance may be defined as 'the system by which companies are directed and controlled'. The corporate governance obligations which apply to listed companies in the UK are derived from:

- the Corporate Governance Rules in DTR 7, which set out the requirements for listed companies in relation to audit committees and the inclusion of a corporate governance statement in their annual directors' report (see section 8.2); and
- the UK Corporate Governance Code (Governance Code) (see sections 8.3 and 8.4);
- the Listing Rules (LR 9.8.6R(5) and (6) and LR 9.8.7R) which require a comply or explain statement about the Corporate Governance Code as a continuing obligation for listed companies (see section 3.6); and
- guidance from the FRC and others on governance issues and the views of institutional shareholders, as set out in institutional voting policies and guidelines (see section 8.5).

8.1 Background to the Governance Code

The Governance Code includes good practice guidance on leadership (including the role of the Board and the division of responsibilities), the effectiveness of the Board (including its composition and appointments, Board evaluation and development), accountability (including financial reporting, risk management and internal controls and audit), Board remuneration and relations with shareholders.

The Governance Code is published, maintained and amended by the FRC. The code and all related FRC guidance is available on the FRC website (frc.org.uk/Our-Work/Corporate-Governance-Reporting). Its provisions are considered in more detail in section 8.4.

The Governance Code is now 25 years old. Its origins lie with the Financial Aspects of Corporate Governance Report produced in 1992 by a committee chaired by Sir Adrian Cadbury. The key recommendations of that Report, including the 'comply or explain' principle, remain in the UK Corporate Governance Code today. However, corporate governance guidance has evolved greatly since then, with several further committees and reports recommending significant changes and additional principles. The Higgs Review led to the publication of a radically revised and expanded Combined Code on Corporate Governance in July 2003. The financial crisis of 2008 prompted a further review and resulted in an updated code, renamed the 'UK Corporate Governance Code' published in June 2010. Further editions were published in 2012 and 2014 and the most recent edition was published in June 2016.

In September 2016, a Parliamentary Select Committee announced an inquiry into corporate governance focusing on directors' duties, executive pay and the composition of Boards. It published a Report on its findings in March 2017. Separately, the government published a Corporate Governance Green Paper in November 2016 setting out potential options for reform of UK corporate governance under three broad headings: executive pay; strengthening the employee, customer and wider stakeholder voice; and corporate governance in large privately held businesses.

The FRC announced in early 2017 that, in light of this review of governance, it was undertaking a fundamental review of the Corporate Governance Code and associated guidance for consultation during 2017, in particular to address the issue of the responsibilities of companies to a wider range of stakeholders and society.

The FRC also publishes and maintains the Stewardship Code which gives guidance to institutional shareholders on how they, as shareholders, should engage with listed companies (see section 8.5.9).

8.2 The DTR 7 regime – audit committees and governance statement

The corporate governance rules set out in DTR 7 were introduced to implement certain requirements of the Company Reporting Directive and of the Statutory Audit Directive and were amended with effect for financial reporting periods commencing on or after 17 June 2016 to reflect the EU Audit Regime.

8.2.1 DTR 7.1 on audit committees

DTR 7.1 focuses on the composition and responsibilities of audit committees.

Under DTR 1B.1.2R, DTR 7.1 applies to UK incorporated standard or premium listed companies but not to overseas premium or standard listed companies. Companies subject to DTR 7.1 are required to have an audit committee (or a body responsible for performing similar functions).

Under DTR 7.1, audit committees must:

- be composed of a majority of independent directors and have a chairman who is independent;
- be comprised of directors who as a whole are competent in the company's sector; and
- have at least one member who is competent in auditing, accounting or both.

DTR 7.1.2G advises that the requirements for independence and competence in accounting and/or auditing may be satisfied by the same or different members of the company.

DTR 7.1 sets out the minimum functions the audit committee must carry out, which include (DTR 7.1.3R):

- monitoring the financial reporting process and submitting recommendations or proposals to ensure its integrity;
- monitoring the effectiveness of the issuer's internal quality control and risk management systems and, where applicable, its internal audit;
- monitoring the statutory audit;
- reviewing and monitoring the independence of the auditor, and in particular the appropriateness of the provision of non-audit services to the company;
- informing the board of the outcome of the external audit; and
- being responsible for the procedure for the selection of auditor.

An issuer must make a statement available to the public disclosing the composition of its audit committee (DTR 7.1.5R). This statement may be included in its corporate governance statement required under DTR 7.2 (see below).

The Governance Code also contains overlapping provisions regarding the composition and responsibilities of audit committees (see section 8.4.7 below). Compliance with certain provisions of the Governance Code will satisfy the requirements of DTR 7.1 (DTR 7.1.7G).

In addition, the CMA Order contains certain provisions about the role of the audit committee in the appointment of auditors and fixing their appointment terms (see section 5.3 above).

8.2.2 DTR 7.2 on corporate governance statements

Under DTR 7.2, companies are required to include a corporate governance statement in their directors' report, setting out certain prescribed information including the governance code that applies to the company and an explanation of any departure from it.

The corporate governance statement must include a description of the main features of the group's internal control and risk management systems in relation to the financial reporting process for the undertakings included in the consolidation, taken as a whole (DTR 7.2.10R).

DTR 7.2.8AR also requires listed companies that have more than 500 employees (or group employees in the case of a parent company) to disclose the diversity policy in relation to the board (including age, gender, educational and professional backgrounds of directors), the objectives of that policy, how the policy has been implemented and the results in the reporting period. If no policy is applied, the statement must explain why.

DTR 7.2 applies to UK incorporated listed companies (see DTR 1B.1.5R). However, in addition, overseas premium listed companies (pursuant to LR 9.8.7AR) and overseas companies with a standard listing of shares (pursuant to LR 14.3.24R) or GDRs (pursuant to LR 18.4.3R), which are not required to comply with requirements imposed by another EEA member state that correspond to DTR 7.2 are also required to comply with DTR 7.2 (see DTR 1B.1.5AG).

Again, for premium listed companies there is quite a degree of overlap in DTR 7.2 with the Governance Code and the requirements of LR 9 in relation to making a statement of compliance with the Governance Code (see section 3.6 above). Compliance with certain provisions of the Governance Code will satisfy the requirements of parts of DTR 7.2 (see DTR 7.2.4G).

8.3 Application of the Governance Code

The UK Governance Code applies to all companies (wherever they are incorporated) with a premium listing of equity shares in the UK.

Although the Code does not actually form part of the Listing Rules, it is effectively embedded in the continuing obligations of premium listed companies incorporated in the UK by LR 9.8.6R(5) and (6) and, for standard listed companies, by the requirements of DTR 7.2 (see section 8.2 above).

LR 9.8.7R also requires overseas premium listed companies to comply with LR 9.8.6R(5) and (6) and LR 9.8.8R.

The Corporate Governance Code contains 18 main principles, supplemented by supporting principles and more detailed Code provisions. Companies are expected to either comply with the provisions of the Governance Code or explain why they do not (see section 8.3.1). The emphasis is on compliance with the spirit of the Governance Code rather than the letter.

The key provisions of the Governance Code are discussed in more detail in section 8.4 below.

8.3.1 Listing Rules requirements to comply or explain against the Governance Code

LR 9.8.6R(5) requires premium listed companies to state how they have applied the main principles of the Governance Code: there is no prescribed form for the statement, but it must be set out in a manner that would enable shareholders to evaluate how the principles have been applied. The statement must be included in the annual report and accounts.

LR 9.8.6R(6) requires premium listed companies to state whether or not they have complied throughout the accounting period with all relevant provisions set out in the Governance Code. Where a company has not complied with these provisions throughout the accounting period, it must set out the provisions it has not complied with, the period within which it did not comply and its reasons for such non-compliance. These requirements are referred to as 'comply or explain'. Guidance is set out in the introductory section of the Governance Code on drafting the 'comply or explain' statement required under LR 9.8.6R(6). Where a listed company complies with LR 9.8.6R(6), it will satisfy the requirements of DTR 7.2.2R and DTR 7.2.3R (discussed in section 8.2 above).

Under LR 9.8.10R in the case of UK incorporated companies, the auditors must review the statement of compliance before publication, insofar as it relates to certain specified Governance Code provisions relating to audit and accountability which are objectively verifiable (being C.1.1, C.2.1, C.2.3 and C.3.1 to C.3.8).

8.3.2 Application of the Governance Code to smaller listed companies

There are specific carve-outs from the Governance Code for smaller companies (i.e. those outside the FTSE 350). These relate to the number of independent non-executive directors (NEDs), the numbers of audit and remuneration committee members, external evaluation of the Board and annual election of all directors by the shareholders.

The Quoted Companies Alliance (QCA) publishes guidance for smaller listed companies on complying with the Corporate Governance Code. The QCA has also published a Remuneration Committee Guide for Smaller Quoted Companies. This covers the objectives of the remuneration committee, factors to consider when setting pay policy, membership and organisation of the committee and communicating with shareholders on remuneration issues.

8.4 Key provisions of the Governance Code

8.4.1 The Board

The first main principle is that every company should be headed by an effective Board which is collectively responsible for the long-term success of the company (main principle A.1). In support of this, there are two supporting principles on the role of the Board and the need for all directors to act in the best interests of the company. Governance Code provision A.1.1 requires the Board to meet regularly, to have a formal schedule of matters specifically reserved to it for decision and for the company's Annual Financial Report to include a statement of how the Board operates. The reserved matters will normally include matters such as material acquisitions or disposals of assets of the company or its subsidiaries, material investments and capital projects, treasury policies such as foreign currency and interest rate exposure, risk management policies, establishing the managerial authority limit for smaller transactions and the governance of company pension schemes.

The FRC *Guidance on Board Effectiveness* describes the Board's role as providing the entrepreneurial leadership of the company within a framework of prudent and effective controls and notes that challenge, as well as teamwork, is an essential feature of an effective Board.

8.4.2 Chairman and chief executive

Governance Code main principle A.2 states that there should be a clear division of responsibilities at the head of a company between the running of the Board and the executive responsibility for the running of the company's business. No one individual should have unfettered powers of decision. The FRC *Guidance on Board Effectiveness* highlights that the relationship between the chief executive and chairman is key to helping the Board be more effective. The roles of chairman and chief executive should not be exercised by the same individual (A.2.1). The division of responsibilities between the chairman and chief executive should be clearly established, set out in writing and agreed by the Board (A.2.1). A chief executive should not go on to become chairman of the same company (A.3.1). On appointment, the chairman should meet the independence criteria (A.3.1) (see below).

8.4.3 Board balance and independence

The Board should include an appropriate combination of executive and non-executive directors (and in particular independent non-executive directors) such that no individual or small group of individuals can dominate the Board's decision taking (supporting principles to main principle B.1).

For FTSE 350 companies, at least half the Board, excluding the chairman, should comprise non-executive directors determined by the Board to be independent (B.1.2). The chairman should therefore be excluded from the calculation on both sides of the equation unless the same person is both chairman and chief executive For smaller companies, the requirement is to have at least two independent non-executive directors (B.1.2).

The Governance Code contains guidance on the criteria for assessing independence. B.1.1 states:

> The Board should state its reasons if it determines that a director is independent notwithstanding the existence of relationships or circumstances which may appear relevant to its determination, including if the director:
>
> - has been an employee of the company or group within the last five years;
> - has, or has had within the last three years, a material business relationship with the company either directly, or as a partner, shareholder, director or senior employee of a body that has such a relationship with the company;
> - has received or receives additional remuneration from the company apart from a director's fee, participates in the company's share option or a performance-related pay scheme, or is a member of the company's pension scheme;
> - has close family ties with any of the company's advisers, directors or senior employees;

- holds cross-directorships or has significant links with other directors through involvement in other companies or bodies;
- represents a significant shareholder; or
- has served on the Board for more than nine years from the date of their first election.

However, the Governance Code makes it clear that none of the factors relevant to determining independence are in themselves a bar to a director being considered independent. Some of the instrumental shareholder groups have issued guidelines on their approach to a company treating a director as independent notwithstanding the existence of one of the factors.

The Board should identify in its Annual Financial Report each non-executive director it considers to be independent (B.1.1).

Governance Code provision A.3.1 states that the chairman should, on appointment, meet the independence criteria set out in B.1.1. However, he is not thereafter regarded as independent and should not be regarded as such for the purpose of Board balance or the minimum requirements for membership of committees. This is made clear by the footnote to B.1.1 which states that the independence test is not appropriate for the chairman after his appointment.

The Governance Code also states that Boards should not be so large as to become unwieldy (supporting principles to B.1).

The Board should appoint one of the independent non-executive directors to be the senior independent director (A.4.1). The senior independent director (who should be identified in the Annual Financial Report) has an important role under the Governance Code. The FRC *Guidance on Board Effectiveness* recommends that the role of the senior independent director should be set out in writing. He or she should be available to shareholders if they have concerns which contact through the normal channels of chairman, chief executive or other executive directors has failed to resolve or is inappropriate (A.4.1). The non-executive directors, led by the senior independent director, should meet without the chairman present at least once a year to appraise the chairman's performance and on such other occasions as are deemed appropriate (A.4.2). The senior independent director should attend sufficient meetings with a range of major shareholders to listen to their views to help develop a balanced understanding of the issues and concerns of major shareholders (E.1.1).

The role of the senior independent director becomes critically important during periods of stress and the FRC *Guidance on Board Effectiveness* sets out some examples of when the senior independent director may intervene to maintain Board and company stability.

8.4.4 Appointments to the Board

Before appointing a new director, the nomination committee should evaluate the balance of skills, experience, independence and knowledge of the directors already on the Board and, in light of this, prepare a description of the role and capabilities required for a particular appointment (Governance Code provision B.2.2) – see also section 8.4.7 below for information relating to the nomination committee.

The Governance Code requires the search for Board candidates to be conducted, and appointments to the Board to be made, on merit, against objective criteria with due regard for the benefits of Board diversity, including, specifically, gender (supporting principles to main principle B.2). The Board should explain to shareholders why they believe an individual proposed as a non-executive director should be elected (Governance Code provision B.7.2). In the case of a non-executive director, the question of whether or not the director can be treated as an independent director for the purposes of the Governance Code (see section 8.4.3 above) in particular as regards its provisions on Board balance and committee membership, will be an important issue to take into account on appointment.

A newly appointed non-executive director should undertake that they will have sufficient time to meet what is expected of them, taking into account their other commitments, which should be disclosed to the Board before appointment (Governance Code provision B.3.2). Provision B.2.4 states that a separate section of the annual report should describe the work of the nomination committee, including the process used in relation to Board appointments, the Board's diversity policy and details relating to external search consultancies used.

The Governance Code does not place any limit on the number of non-executive directorships that an individual may hold (although institutional investors have guidelines on 'overboarding' (i.e. how many directorships are acceptable)). However, the Governance Code states that the Board should not agree to a full-time executive director taking on more than one non-executive directorship, or becoming chairman, of a FTSE 100 company (B.3.3). The chairman and non-executive directors will need to disclose any other significant commitments to the Board before appointment and those of the chairman should be included in the annual report. Any changes should be reported to the Board as they arise and their impact explained in the next annual report (B.3.1). The FRC *Guidance on Board Effectiveness* recognises the benefits of executive directors taking up non-executive roles elsewhere, thereby broadening their understanding of their Board responsibilities.

The Governance Code says that non-executive directors' terms and conditions of appointment should be made available for inspection (provision B.3.2).

8.4.5 Re-election of directors

All directors of FTSE 350 companies should be subject to annual election by shareholders, as should all non-executive directors of non-FTSE 350 companies who have served longer than nine years (B.7.1). All other directors should be subject to (a) election by shareholders at the first annual general meeting after their appointment and (b) re-election afterwards at intervals of no more than three years. Shareholders should be given sufficient biographical detail and any other relevant information, including on the individual's performance (see below) to be able to make an informed decision about each director standing for election/re-election at the annual general meeting.

8.4.6 Information, professional development and performance evaluation

Governance Code main principle B.5 states that the Board should be supplied in a timely manner with information in a form and of a quality appropriate to enable it to discharge its duties. The FRC *Guidance on Board Effectiveness* states that non-executive directors should insist on receiving high-quality information sufficiently in advance to ensure thorough consideration and debate. It notes the company secretary's responsibility for ensuring the whole Board receives such information. All directors should receive induction training on joining the Board and should regularly update and refresh their skills and knowledge (main principle B.4). The chairman should ensure that new directors receive a full, formal and tailored induction on joining the Board (Governance Code provision B.4.1). He is also responsible for ensuring that the directors continually update their skills and knowledge and familiarity with the company required to fulfil their role. The Governance Code also requires the chairman to regularly review and agree with each director his/her training and development needs (B.4.2).

The company secretary also has various responsibilities in relation to the provision of information and facilitating training and development. These are referred to in the supporting principles to main principle B.5. The FRC *Guidance on Board Effectiveness* also provides guidance on the role of the company secretary.

It is a principle of the Governance Code that Boards should formally and rigorously evaluate their performance and that of their committees and individual directors on an annual basis (main principle B.6). This is supported by Governance Code provision B.6.1, which states that the Board should state in the annual report how performance evaluation of the Board, its committees and the individual directors has been conducted. The FRC *Guidance on Board Effectiveness* provides additional guidance on how performance should be evaluated and the areas which should be considered. It notes that the chairman has overall responsibility for both the evaluation process and acting on its outcome.

For FTSE 350 companies, the Governance Code requires that Board evaluation must be conducted externally at least every three years. Any connection between the external evaluator and the company should be disclosed in the annual report (Governance Code provision B.6.2).

8.4.7 Board committees

It is important that the Board sets out clearly the powers and responsibilities of any Committee to which it delegates functions. If there is any doubt about the scope of the Committee's powers, a court is likely to assume that important decisions were intended to be reserved to the full Board. The FRC *Guidance on Board Effectiveness* notes that, although the Board may use audit, risk and remuneration committees, it retains responsibility for and makes final decisions on these areas.

The Governance Code requirement is that a company should appoint three Committees: an audit committee (C.3.1), a remuneration committee (D.2.1) and a nomination committee (B.2.1). The terms of reference for these committees should be put on the company's website and should, according to the FRC *Guidance on Board Effectiveness*, be reviewed regularly. The chairmen of these committees should be available to answer questions at the annual general meeting (Governance Code provision E.2.3). The FRC *Guidance on Board Effectiveness* provides that the minutes of committee meetings should be circulated to the whole Board and the company secretary, unless it would be inappropriate to do so.

The Governance Code sets out the membership requirements for each of these three committees, all of which must include non-executive directors as members (see Figure 6.2 below for the exact membership requirements for each committee). Note that, as mentioned in section 8.4.3 above, the chairman does not count as independent for the purposes of the requirement for independent non-executives as committee members. The footnote to Governance Code provision B.1.1 makes it clear that that the independence test is not appropriate for the chairman after his appointment. Accordingly, even if the chairman fulfils the requirements set out in the test for independence, he will not count as an independent non-executive director for the purposes of committee membership.

The chart below summarises the membership requirements for each committee.

Figure 6.2: Board committees – Governance Code requirements

Governance Code requirements for committee membership				
Committee	Code Provision	FTSE 350 Company	Smaller Company
Nomination	B.2.1	Majority of members independent NEDs. Chairman can be a member. Chair of committee can be independent NED or chairman.	Majority of members independent NEDs. Chairman can be a member. Chair of committee can be independent NED or chairman.

FINANCIAL REPORTING AND CORPORATE GOVERNANCE 287

Committee	Code Provision	FTSE 350 Company	Smaller Company
Audit	C.3.1 (see also DTR 7.1)	All independent NEDs (at least three). At least one member with recent and relevant financial experience. Committee as a whole to have competence relevant to the company's sector. Note overlap with DTR 7.1 requirements, which are mandatory	At least two independent NEDs. Chairman can be additional member (but not chair) if independent on appointment. At least one member with recent and relevant financial experience. Committee as a whole to have competence relevant to the company's sector.
Remuneration	D.2.1	All independent NEDs (at least three). Chairman can be additional member (but not chair) if independent on appointment.	At least two independent NEDs. Chairman can be additional member (but not chair) if independent on appointment.

Audit committee

The audit committee should have written terms of reference (C.3.2). It should be made up of at least three, or in the case of smaller companies, two independent non-executive directors (C.3.1). The chairman of a FTSE 350 company should not be a member of the audit committee. The chairman of a company outside the FTSE 350 may be a member (but not chair) of the audit committee in addition to the independent non-executive directors, provided he or she was considered independent on appointment (C.3.1). At least one member of the audit committee should have recent and relevant financial experience and the audit committee as a whole should have competence relevant to the sector in which the company operates.

Complying with Governance Code provisions C.3.1 and C.3.2 will satisfy the overlapping, mandatory requirements for audit committees in DTR 7.1.1R to DTR 7.1.5R – see DTR 7.1.7G (with the only additional provision in DTR 7.2 as regards composition being the reference to one member having accounting or audit competence). The DTR 7.1 requirements in relation to audit committees are discussed in section 8.2.

In addition the EU Audit Regime and the CMA Order set out the responsibilities of the audit committee in relation to the tender process for appointment and remuneration of the auditor (see section 5.3):

The Governance Code sets out specific duties for the audit committee including:

- monitoring the integrity of the financial statements of the company and formal announcements relating to the company's financial performance;

- reviewing the company's internal financial controls and, unless expressly addressed by a separate Board risk committee or by the Board itself, the company's internal control and risk management systems;
- making recommendations to the Board in relation to the appointment, re-appointment and removal of the external auditor;
- approving the remuneration and terms of engagement of the external auditor; and
- reviewing and monitoring the external auditor's independence and objectivity and the effectiveness of the audit process.

Where the Board does not accept the audit committee's recommendations on the appointment, reappointment and removal of auditors, it must include in the annual report, and in any papers recommending appointment or reappointment, a statement from the audit committee explaining its recommendation and setting out reasons why the Board has taken a different position (C.3.7 and the EU Audit Regulation).

The audit committee should also review arrangements for staff of the company to raise concerns (i.e. to whistle-blow) in confidence (C.3.5).

Where requested to do so by the Board, the audit committee is also required to provide advice as to whether the annual report and accounts, taken as a whole, is fair, balanced and understandable, and provides the information necessary for shareholders to assess the company's performance, business model and strategy (C.3.4).

To assist audit committees, the FRC has issued *Guidance on Audit Committees* and *Guidance on Risk Management, Internal Control and Related and Business Reporting* which are available on the FRC's website and are discussed in section 8.5.

Remuneration committee

It is a Governance Code main principle (D.2) that there should be a formal and transparent procedure for developing policy on executive remuneration and for fixing the remuneration packages of individual directors. No director should be involved in deciding his or her own remuneration. In support of this principle, a listed company should establish a remuneration committee which should have delegated responsibility for setting remuneration for all executive directors and the chairman, including pension rights and any compensation payments (Governance Code provision D.2.2). The committee should also recommend and monitor the level and structure of remuneration for senior management and should make its terms of reference publicly available. The committee should be made up of at least three (or, in the case of companies outside the FTSE 350, two) independent non-executive directors. In addition, whatever the size of company the chairman may be a member, although not the chair, of the remuneration committee provided he or she was considered independent on appointment as chairman (D.2.1). However, it does not affect the number of independent non-executive directors required to be on the committee since, as noted above, the chairman is not regarded as an independent non-executive director after appointment. His or her presence on the remuneration committee must, therefore, be in addition to the minimum number of independent non-executive director members.

Nomination committee

It is a Governance Code main principle (B.2) that there should be a formal, rigorous and transparent process for the appointment of new directors to the Board. In support of this, the nomination committee's task is to lead the process for Board appointments and make recommendations to the Board. A majority of the members of the nomination committee should be independent non-executive directors (B.2.1). The chairman, or an independent non-executive director, may chair the committee (except that the chairman should not act as chair when it is dealing with the appointment of his or her successor). The FRC *Guidance on Board Effectiveness* states that the chairman will usually chair the nomination committee.

8.4.8 Directors' remuneration

It is a Governance Code main principle (D.1) that executive directors' remuneration should be designed to promote the long-term success of the company and that performance-related elements should be transparent, stretching and rigorously applied.

The principle is supported by a number of more detailed Governance Code provisions (D.1.1–D.1.5 and Schedule A), which should be observed by the remuneration committee.

For UK incorporated companies, the CA 2006 sets out detailed requirements in relation to reporting on, and approval of, directors' remuneration. Regulations made pursuant to section 421 of the CA 2006 require companies to publish a two-part directors' remuneration report:

- the report on remuneration, which contains a statement from the chair of the remuneration committee and a report setting out actual payments made to directors in the last financial year, including single total pay figures and is put to an annual advisory shareholder vote; and

- the directors' remuneration policy, which sets out the company's forward-looking policy on remuneration and potential payments (including the approach to exit payments) and is subject to a binding shareholder vote at least every three years.

See also section 8.5.5. below as regards guidance on executive remuneration.

8.4.9 Accountability

Governance Code main principle C.1 on financial and business reporting states that the Board should present a fair, balanced and understandable assessment of the company's position and prospects. There is a supporting principle which says that the principle applies to interim and other price-sensitive public reports, reports to regulators and statutory information. It is for the Board to establish arrangements which will enable it to ensure the information presented is fair, balanced and understandable (see below on the annual report and accounts).

Governance Code main principle C.2 states, among other things, that the Board should maintain sound risk management and internal control systems. Governance Code provision C.2.1 requires the Board to confirm in the annual report that they have carried out a robust assessment of the principal risks facing the company, including those that would threaten its business model, future performance, solvency or liquidity. The directors should describe those risks and explain how they are being managed or mitigated.

As described in section 3.7.3 above, the annual report and half yearly report are required by the Governance Code (and in the case of the annual report, the Listing Rules) to include a going concern statement covering 12 months from the date of the financial statements.

In addition under the Governance Code (C.2.2) the directors are required to explain how they have assessed the financial viability of the company, over what period they have done so and why they considered that period to be appropriate. The directors should state whether they have a reasonable expectation that the company will be able to continue in operation and meet its liabilities as they fall due during the period of that assessment, drawing attention to any qualifications or assumptions as necessary. This is known as a viability statement. It was introduced by the 2014 Governance Code. The FRC's guidance on *Risk Management, Internal Control and Related Financial and Business Reporting* and its *Report on Developments in Corporate Governance and Stewardship* 2016 explain that the period is expected to be significantly longer than 12 months and describe the processes the Board should go through to make this statement. Boards should include an explanation of qualifications and assumptions and explain the linkage to principal risks and uncertainties. The IA has published guidelines setting out the expectations of institutional investors in relation to viability statements and in particular recommends that the period should be longer than three to five years. The IA also recommends that when evaluating risks to a company's viability, it is the risks that threaten the company's day-to-day operations and existence that should be considered, rather than those that relate to a company's performance prospects.

In addition, the Board is required under the Governance Code (C.2.3) to monitor the company's risk management and internal control systems and carry out at least an annual review of their effectiveness and report on that review in the annual report.

Finally in relation to accounts and audits, Governance Code main principle C.3 relates to the audit committee and auditors. It requires the Board to establish formal and transparent arrangements for considering how it should apply the corporate reporting and risk management and internal control principles. The Board must also establish arrangements for maintaining an appropriate relationship with the company's auditors. The provisions relating to audit tendering which were formerly in the Governance Code have been deleted because they are now included (for EU incorporated companies at least) in the EU Audit Regime (see section 5 above).

8.4.10 Relations with shareholders

The main principles in Section E of the Governance Code are that companies should enter into a dialogue with shareholders based on the mutual understanding of objectives, and that Boards should use general meetings to communicate with investors and encourage their participation. These principles are supported by various supporting principles and best practice provisions on relationships with shareholders and on the conduct of general meetings. The FRC *Guidance on Board Effectiveness* also notes the importance of the annual report as a means of communicating with shareholders.

8.4.11 The annual report and accounts

The Governance Code sets out a number of disclosures which should be included in the annual report and accounts. The directors are required to explain in the annual report their responsibility for preparing the annual report and accounts. The directors must also state that they consider the annual report and accounts, taken as a whole, to be fair, balanced and understandable and that it provides the information necessary for shareholders to assess the company's performance, business model and strategy (C.1.1).

More detailed disclosures required to be set out in the annual report and accounts include:

- separate sections describing the work of the nomination committee and the audit committee;
- if an external search consultancy was used for Board appointments, the consultancy should be identified in the annual report and accounts and a statement should be included as to whether the consultancy has any other connection with the company;
- if the external auditors provides non-audit services to the company, an explanation of how auditor objectivity and independence are safeguarded; and
- where remuneration consultants are appointed, they should be identified in the annual report and a statement should be made as to whether the consultants have any other connection with the company.

8.5 Guidance relating to the Corporate Governance Code

As well as the Corporate Governance Code, there is a range of additional guidance which is designed to help companies comply with it and to give companies guidance on best practice in the corporate governance arena. Figure 6.3 below lists the main guidance on Corporate Governance issued by the FRC and ICSA. The FRC Guidance is available on the Governance Code section of its website.

In addition, there is a range of specific guidance on board diversity and executive remuneration and the institutional shareholder groups issue guidelines on a range of issues (see section 8.5.6 below).

The Institute of Directors also publishes an annual Good Governance Report, in which it ranks the 100 largest listed companies (excluding investment companies) by their quality of corporate governance. The report focuses on Board effectiveness, audit and risk, remuneration and reward, shareholder and stakeholder relations and business environment.

8.5.1 Risk management and internal control: Guidance to directors

The provisions relating to internal controls, risk and risk management and the disclosures in annual reports in relation to them were revised and expanded in the 2014 edition of the Corporate Governance Code. The FRC's *Guidance on Risk Management, Internal Control and Related Financial and Business Reporting* covers all aspects of the Governance Code provisions in relation to these areas, including the approach of the Board to their responsibilities and the approach to disclosure in the annual report. This guidance replaced the previous internal control guidance (known as the Turnbull guidance) and the 2009 guidance on risk and going concern.

8.5.2 Guidance on Board effectiveness and culture

The FRC *Guidance on Board Effectiveness* was published in 2011. As with other guidance issued by the FRC, the guidance has no formal status and companies are not required to follow it; they may find it provides helpful guidance on matters relating to the Governance Code such as the role of the Board and directors, the role of the company secretary and decision-making processes.

In July 2016, the FRC published a report on the results of its study exploring the relationship between corporate culture and long-term business success in the UK. The FRC has stated that it will update its *Guidance on Board Effectiveness* to reflect its findings from this report.

ICSA has also produced supporting guidance notes and terms of reference for audit, remuneration and nomination committees which are available on its website.

8.5.3 Guidance on audit committees

The FRC *Guidance on Audit Committees* is available on the FRC website. Boards of listed companies are not required to follow this, but it is intended to help them when implementing the provisions of the Corporate Governance Code on audit committees. The Guidance also assists directors on audit committees to carry out their role and was completely reworked in 2016 to reflect updated views on best practice and the EU Audit Regime (see section 5). The FRC has also updated its *Audit Tenders: Notes on best practice* (February 2017) on conducting an audit tender to help audit committees evaluate external auditor quality.

8.5.4 Guidance on Diversity

There is increasingly pressure for Boards to embrace diversity.

The Equality and Human Rights Commission has published a guide for FTSE 350 companies entitled *How to improve board diversity – a six step guide to good practice* (March 2016). The guide's recommendations include establishing clear Board accountability for diversity and widening diversity of the senior leadership talent pool.

Boards should be mindful of broad diversity objectives when considering Board appointments. Lord Davies of Abersoch was asked in July 2010 to review the obstacles to women reaching the Boardroom. The Davies Report on *Women on Boards* was published in February 2011. The report rejected mandatory quotas for female Board representation, but recommended that FTSE 350 companies announce targets for the percentage of women they aim to have and that FTSE 100 companies should aim for a minimum of 25% female representation by 2015.

In October 2015, the Davies Review published its five-year summary. This stated that representation of women on FTSE 100 Boards had more than doubled since 2011, that the target of 25% female representation on FTSE 100 Boards had been exceeded (reaching 26.1%). No all-male Boards remained in the FTSE 100 and only 15 remained in the FTSE 250, compared to 152 in the FTSE 350 in 2011. The summary made several recommendations, including increasing the voluntary target of female representation on FTSE 350 Boards to 33% by 2020 and increasing the number of women appointed to the roles of chair, senior independent director, executive director and other senior leadership roles, as well as to positions on executive committees.

The Hampton-Alexander Review, led by Sir Philip Hampton and Dame Helen Alexander, was established to follow on from the work of the Davies Review. The Hampton-Alexander Review builds on the recommendations of the Davies Review's five-year summary and extends gender diversity focus to include the representation of women in leadership positions of FTSE 350 companies. The review also recommends that FTSE 350 companies should voluntarily disclose in their annual reports and the reports of the executive committee the number of women on the executive committee and that the Governance Code be amended to require this.

The Equality and Human Rights Commission guidance referred to above confirms that the Equality and Human Rights Commission is of the view that, save for preferring the under-represented gender when choosing between candidates of equal merit, it is unlawful direct sex discrimination to make appointments to Boards based on gender (e.g. through the use of all-women shortlists). However, it is of the view that taking proportionate positive action (such as targeted networking opportunities and opportunities to shadow Board members) is permitted.

In November 2016 the Parker Review, led by Sir John Parker, published a consultation version of its report into the ethnic diversity of UK Boards. The report notes that the Boards of leading UK public companies do not reflect the ethnic diversity of the UK or the stakeholders that such companies seek to engage and represent. The draft report sets out the benefits of increasing such diversity (at the time of the report, 53 FTSE 100 companies had no directors of colour) and makes several recommendations, including that each FTSE 100 Board should have at least one director of colour by 2021 and each FTSE 250 Board should have one by 2024. Further, the report recommends that commentary on a company's efforts to increase ethnic diversity, including at Board level, should be included in the description of the company's diversity policy set out in the annual report. Final recommendations are expected to be published during 2017.

8.5.5 Guidance on executive remuneration

The Executive Remuneration Working Group, established as an independent panel by the IA in Autumn 2015, published its Final Report on how to improve trust in executive pay structures in the UK in July 2016. The Working Group recommended addressing five areas to help restore trust in the executive remuneration system, being:

- strengthening remuneration committees and their accountability;
- improving shareholder engagement;
- increasing transparency in target setting and use of discretion;
- addressing the level of executive pay; and
- setting parameters to illustrate how different structures may operate to gain market trust.

Its specific recommendations include greater disclosure of bonus arrangements and a requirement for Boards to disclose why their company's remuneration cap is appropriate based on comparisons such as the pay ratio between the CEO and median employees.

The IA updated its Principles of Remuneration in October 2016 and published an open letter to all FTSE 350 companies setting out its expectations on executive pay. The Principles state that a Board must justify levels of executive pay (both the maximum potential remuneration and the actual payments made) in the context of the company's performance. The IA also recommends disclosure of the pay ratio between the CEO and the executive team and suggests that Boards consider implementing post-employment shareholding requirements.

The GC100 and Investor Group published a revised version of their guidance for listed companies on the directors' remuneration reporting regime in August 2016.

A range of institutional shareholders, including Blackrock and Hermes, also issue separate guidelines on executive remuneration.

Figure 6.3: Main guidance on Corporate Governance issued by the FRC and ICSA

FRC	ICSA
■ Annual Report on Developments in Corporate Governance and Stewardship ■ Guidance on Board Effectiveness (March 2011) ■ Guidance on Audit Committees (April 2016) ■ Guidance on Risk Management and Internal Control and Related Financial and Business Reporting (September 2014) ■ Audit tenders – notes on best practice (February 2017)	■ Good practice for annual reports (May 2015) ■ Notice periods for general meetings (Code E.2.4) (April 2015) ■ Electronic communications with shareholders (February 2014) ■ Register of members access: the proper purpose test (January 2014) ■ Sample board committee terms of reference (July 2013 and March 2017) ■ Liability of NEDs: care, skill and diligence (January 2013) ■ Induction of directors (July 2012) ■ Sample non-executive director appointment letter (December 2011) ■ Due diligence for new directors (May 2011)

8.5.6 Institutional shareholder voting guidelines

Various institutional shareholders and other bodies issue voting guidelines, most of which are updated annually – see Figure 6.4 for the main policies and guidelines currently in issue, although the latest position should always be checked. Notable examples are the Investment Association (IA) (previously the Investment Management Association, which merged with the ABI Investment Affairs Division in 2014), the Pensions and Lifetime Savings Association (PSLA) (formerly the National Association of Pension Funds (NAPF)), Institutional Shareholder Services (ISS) and Pensions Investment Research Consultants Limited (PIRC). The PLSA, the IA (through the IVIS service), ISS and PIRC all run shareholder voting services, which analyse, for the benefit of their institutional shareholder subscribers, the resolutions which listed companies propose to put to shareholders and, where appropriate, either recommend to subscribers how they should vote or flag up issues of concern.

Institutional guidelines do not have the force of law and compliance is not required by the Listing Rules or any regulation, but investors may vote against particular shareholder resolutions or publicly criticise the company if the guidelines are not followed.

Figure 6.4: Main voting policies and guidelines of institutional shareholder groups

Investment Association	PLSA (formerly NAPF)	ISS	PIRC/ISS	Others
■ Principles of Remuneration ■ Share Capital Management Guidelines ■ Transaction Guidelines ■ Guidelines on Viability Statements	■ Report on AGM season ■ Corporate Governance Policy and Voting Guidelines ■ Guidelines on directors' remuneration	■ UK and Ireland Proxy Voting Guidelines	■ Shareholder Voting Guidelines	■ Pre-Emption Group Guidelines and Pro Forma Resolutions ■ LAPFF guidelines ■ Trade Union Share Owners Voting and Engagement Guidelines

8.5.9 Stewardship Code

The UK Stewardship Code, published by the FRC, is a code for institutional investors when engaging with the UK listed companies in which they invest. The Stewardship Code, which applies on a 'comply or explain' basis, is principally addressed to firms who manage assets on behalf of institutional shareholders (e.g. pension funds, insurance companies and investment trusts).

Under the Conduct of Business Sourcebook (COBs) which is part of the FCA Handbook, relevant authorised firms are required to disclose clearly on their websites the nature of their compliance with the Stewardship Code or their alternative investment strategy. This requirement only applies to UK authorised firms (other than venture capital firms) managing investments on behalf of professional clients that are not natural persons (see COBs 2.2.3R).

9. Enforcement by the Financial Reporting Council's Conduct Committee

It is not just the FCA that is involved in regulatory enforcement in relation to periodic financial reporting. The Conduct Committee of the FRC (formerly the Financial Reporting Review Panel (FRRP)) has statutory authority to review the accounts, strategic report and directors' reports of all UK companies that prepare accounts under the CA 2006 (under UK GAAP or IFRS) or the FCA's rules. In practice, the Conduct Committee normally exercises this authority only in relation to public and large private companies, including UK incorporated listed companies. The Conduct Committee is a committee of the FRC Board.

The Conduct Committee aims to reach agreement with the directors of a company under review by persuasion. However, if its concerns are not resolved via the voluntary process, at least in respect of the annual accounts or reports companies produce under CA 2006, it can apply to court for (a) a declaration that a set of financial statements or report is defective and (b) for an order requiring the directors of the company to prepare revised accounts or a revised report (CA 2006 s. 456). Where significant remedial action is required, a public announcement is made by the FRC by means of a press notice. The FRC can also require the company to refer to the involvement of the Conduct Committee in the report and accounts in which the agreed change is made. The Conduct Committee does not give guidance or pre-clearance to companies. It has not, to date, made use of its power to apply for a court order.

The Conduct Committee's selection criteria for review are risk based and will focus on companies and sectors where non-compliance could have significant consequences.

Recent decisions and findings of the Conduct Committee, as well as indications of areas of particular concern or focus, can be found on the FRC's website.

CHAPTER 7

Share dealings and interests in voting rights

OVERVIEW

- Article 19 of MAR applies to premium and standard listed companies. It sets out the disclosure regime that applies to the directors and senior managers of a listed company (and persons closely associated with them) when dealing in the listed company's securities. The disclosure regime applies to dealings in shares and debt instruments and to dealings in derivatives and other financial instruments linked to shares and debt instruments.

- Directors and senior managers (PDMRs) and persons closely associated with them (their PCAs) are obliged under Article 19(1) of MAR to notify the company and the FCA of any dealings within three business days of the day on which the dealing occurred. The listed company is then required to disclose to the market via an RIS announcement the information disclosed to it by PDMRs and PCAs, again within three business days of the transaction.

- PDMRs of listed companies are also subject to restrictions on dealing in the company's securities during a MAR closed period (i.e. for 30 days prior to the publication of the company's annual and half-yearly reports).

- A listed company must maintain a list of its PDMRs and their PCAs and notify its PDMRs in writing of their dealing disclosure obligations and the dealing restrictions under Article 19 of MAR. PDMRs must in turn notify each of their PCAs in writing of their disclosure obligations under Article 19 of MAR and keep a record of that notification.

- Any dealing, or attempted dealing, in shares, securities or any other financial instruments while in possession of inside information relating to them may constitute insider dealing.

- Companies may choose to impose a share dealing policy and share dealing code on their directors and other PDMRs to control their securities dealings and to ensure their compliance with MAR.

- DTR 5 applies to premium and standard listed companies. It requires a vote-holder to notify a listed company if the percentage of voting rights it holds directly or indirectly as a shareholder and/or through a holding of financial instruments reaches, exceeds or falls below a relevant threshold – namely 3% and every percentage point thereafter for shares in a UK incorporated listed company.

- A listed company must announce its total voting rights (TVR) at the end of each calendar month in which there has been an increase or decrease in total voting rights and notifications by vote-holders will then be made by reference to the month-end figures announced by the listed company.
- If the total number of voting rights in a listed company changes materially in the course of a month, the company must announce the new number of total voting rights.
- Vote-holders must notify a listed company of their interest in voting rights within two trading days (in the case of a UK issuer) or four trading days (in the case of a non-UK issuer) of the date upon which their interest reaches, exceeds or falls below a threshold, using the FCA's prescribed form (TR-1). Vote-holders must, if the notification relates to shares admitted to trading on a regulated market in the UK, make a separate private filing of the level of their interest with the FCA.

1. Disclosure of dealings by PDMRs and persons closely associated with them

1.1 The regulatory framework

MAR applies to premium and standard listed companies, as well as AIM and other traded companies. Article 19(1) of MAR requires the directors and other senior managers of a listed company (collectively known as 'persons discharging managerial responsibilities' or PDMRs) and persons closely associated with them (their PCAs) to disclose their dealings in the listed company's securities to the listed company and the FCA.

A listed company must, in turn, notify an RIS of any information notified to it by its PDMRs and their PCAs.

Article 19(11) of MAR contains restrictions on when the PDMRs of a company may deal in the company's securities.

The provisions of MAR are supplemented by a series of EU Implementing Regulations which provide further detail on the procedures with which a company (and in certain cases its PDMRs and their PCAs) must comply. The key regulations in relation to PDMR and PCA dealings are:

- the PDMR Transaction Notification Implementing Regulation ((EU) 2016/523) which contains requirements regarding the format and template for notification and public disclosure of transactions; and

- the General MAR Delegated Regulation ((EU) 2016/522), which contains, among other things, a non-exhaustive list of types of transactions that should be notified, as well as details on when trading can take place by PDMRs during a closed period.

ESMA has also published Questions and Answers on the Market Abuse Regulation (the ESMA MAR Q&A), which provides guidance in relation to the practical application of the MAR framework.

The FCA provides guidance in its Handbook on the MAR regime for companies with securities admitted to trading in the UK. The (fairly limited) FCA guidance relating to PDMR and PCA dealings can be found in Chapter 3 of the Disclosure Guidance and Transparency Rules (DTR 3). Further guidance is also set out in the UKLA Guidance Notes on the UKLA Knowledge Base pages of the FCA website.

The City of London Law Society and Law Society Company Law Committees' Joint Working Parties on Market Abuse, Share Plans and Takeovers Code has also published guidance on the regime, in particular Article 19 of MAR, in their CLLS/Law Society MAR Q&A, available on the citysolicitors.org.uk website.

1.2 The disclosure obligation

Article 19(1) of MAR requires PDMRs and their PCAs to notify the company and the FCA of every transaction conducted on their own account (subject to a *de minimis* exemption – see section 1.6.1 below) relating to the shares or debt instruments of that company or to derivatives or other financial instruments linked thereto. This notification must be made promptly and no later than three business days after the date of the transaction.

Following a notification under Article 19(1) of MAR, the company is required to make that information public promptly and no later than three business days after the transaction (Article 19(3) of MAR). Directors, other PDMRs and their PCAs are, like any other investor, also subject to the disclosure regime in DTR 5. This is discussed in detail in section 5 below.

1.3 Identifying PDMRs and their PCAs

1.3.1 PDMRs

Under Article 3(1)(25) of MAR, a PDMR of a company is defined as being a natural or legal person who is either:

(a) a member of the administrative, management or supervisory body of the company (i.e. a director); or

(b) a senior executive who is not a director, but who has regular access to inside information relating, directly or indirectly, to the listed company and power to take managerial decisions affecting the future developments and business prospects of the company.

Therefore, all the directors of a company, both executive and non-executive, will be PDMRs. In addition, certain other senior managers of the company may be PDMRs depending on their role and powers. The list of PDMRs of a company, other than the directors, is however much narrower than a list of all senior managers. Each company must consider for itself who its PDMRs are. There is not a single test which works for all companies.

Companies should consider senior executives (who are not directors) to be PDMRs only if their decision-making powers extend to matters which can affect the business of the company as a whole. However, those who offer analysis or information to enable others ultimately to make a managerial decision may not be PDMRs, even where they give informed recommendations. Likewise senior executives who only have decision-making powers which affect one limited aspect of the listed company's business may not be PDMRs (unless the one particular area in question is of considerable importance to the company or the decisions which that person could take may have long-term or significant consequences for the company).

It is not necessary for a PDMR to make decisions alone. Where a person is involved in a collective decision, it is important to consider the substance of their role when assessing if they are a PDMR. Any listed company with an executive management committee one level down from the Board of directors should carefully consider whether the members of this committee are PDMRs.

The key test is the substance of an individual's role: if the individual makes decisions which affect the future development and business prospects of the listed company (even if the decision is later ratified by the Board), he or she is likely to be a PDMR. However, where decisions are clearly made by the Board members and not senior management, a non-Board member is unlikely to be a PDMR.

In addition to having the requisite level of decision-making powers, the person must also have regular access to inside information in order to be treated as a PDMR.

DTR 3.1.2AG(2) states that an individual can be a 'senior executive' of the company irrespective of the nature of any contractual arrangements between him or her and the company and even without a contractual arrangement between the individual and the company, provided the individual has regular access to inside information relating, directly or indirectly, to the company and has the power to make managerial decisions affecting the future development and business prospects of the company.

1.3.2 PCAs

Article 3(1)(26) of MAR defines a person closely associated with a PDMR (a PCA) as follows:

- a spouse, or a partner considered to be equivalent to a spouse in accordance with national law;
- a dependent child, in accordance with national law;
- a relative who has shared the same household for at least one year on the date of the transaction concerned; or
- a legal person, trust or partnership:
  - the managerial responsibilities of which are discharged by a PDMR or by a person referred to in any of the above categories;
  - which is directly or indirectly controlled by such a person;
  - which is set up for the benefit of such a person; or
  - the economic interests of which are substantially equivalent to those of such a person.

Section 131AC of FSMA provides the following additional detail:

- a 'partner considered to be equivalent to a spouse' includes a civil partner;
- a 'dependent child' means a child who is under the age of 18 years, is unmarried and does not have a civil partner; and
- a 'child' includes a step-child.

Neither MAR nor FSMA gives any guidance on the meaning of 'relative', and so this could be interpreted widely to cover parents, grandparents and adult children, as well as other members of a family (e.g. siblings, aunts and uncles). In practice, however, even applying a broad definition of 'relative' should not significantly increase the number of dealing disclosures because a relative will only be a PCA if they have shared the same household as the PDMR for at least 12 months prior to the date of the transaction.

Neither MAR nor FSMA contains any provisions as to what 'control' of a company is. Under the previous Market Abuse Directive (2003/6/EC), this was described as meaning 20% of the voting powers or share capital of an entity. In the absence of guidance, a typical control test of 50% could be considered appropriate.

In relation to the 'legal person' limb of the PCA definition above, and its application where a PDMR is a director of another company, the currently accepted view in the UK is that, if an individual who is a PDMR of Company A is also a director of Company B, then Company B will only be treated as a PCA of the PDMR for the purposes of Company A if the PDMR:

- is the sole director of, or has the right to appoint a majority of the Board of directors of, Company B; or
- personally has control over the management decisions of Company B affecting Company B's future development and business prospects.

1.4 Maintaining a list of PDMRs and PCAs

A listed company is obliged under Article 19(5) of MAR to keep a list of its PDMRs and all of their PCAs. Companies must therefore identify their PDMRs and keep the list under review. They must also ask their PDMRs to provide the company with a list of their PCAs and require the PDMRs to inform the company promptly of any change to this list. When providing a list of their PCAs to the company, each PDMR will need to consider the definition carefully and should seek advice from the company secretary or legal personnel if there is any uncertainty.

Each new director joining the Board and any other new PDMR should also be asked by the company to provide details of all of their PCAs.

The company should seek an annual confirmation from its PDMRs that the list of PCAs is correct and up to date.

1.5 Notifications to PDMRs and PCAs of their obligations

Under Article 19(5) of MAR, a company is required to send each of its PDMRs a notification setting out the PDMR's obligations under Article 19 of MAR. The notification should be provided to each new director when joining the Board or a person otherwise becoming a PDMR.

PDMRs are then required, again by Article 19(5) of MAR, to notify each of their PCAs in writing of their dealing notification obligations and keep a record of this notification (see section 1.9.1 below). This applies even to infant children.

Again, each new director and other PDMR should make this notification to each of his or her PCAs on joining the Board or becoming a PDMR as the case may be, and should make a notification to each person who subsequently becomes a PCA (in each case keeping a record of this notification).

1.6 Transactions to be disclosed by PDMRs and PCAs

Subject to the *de minimis* threshold discussed below, PDMRs and PCAs must notify the listed company and the FCA of all transactions conducted on their own account in the shares or debt instruments of the company, or derivatives or any other financial instruments relating to those shares or debt instruments (Art. 19(1) of MAR). The types of security or investment caught are explored further in section 1.6.2 below.

Provided the transaction relates to a relevant financial instrument, the venue or place where the transaction is conducted is not relevant in assessing whether the transaction needs to be disclosed.

1.6.1 *De minimis* threshold

Article 19(8) of MAR provides for a *de minimis* threshold of €5,000, so that PDMRs and PCAs are only obliged to notify the company and the FCA of transactions once the aggregate gross value of their transactions in each calendar year has reached or exceeded €5,000. MAR contains a member state discretion to increase this threshold to €20,000 per calendar year (MAR Art. 19(9)) but the UK has not exercised this discretion and has retained the level at €5,000 (DTR 3.1.2BG).

Where transactions are carried out in a currency which is not the euro, the exchange rate to be used to determine if the *de minimis* threshold has been reached is the official daily spot foreign exchange rate which is applicable at the end of the business day when the transaction is conducted. Where available, the daily euro foreign exchange reference rate published by the European Central Bank on its website should be used (see the ESMA MAR Q&A).

Transactions carried out by a PDMR and by his or her PCAs should not be aggregated for the purposes of determining whether the *de minimis* threshold has been crossed. For example, if a CEO buys €4,000 of shares and his or her spouse buys another €2,000, no notification is required as neither of them has reached the €5,000 threshold (see ESMA MAR Q&A).

Companies may, in practice, choose to ignore the €5,000 threshold and in their internal policies require PDMRs and PCAs to notify all transactions in the company's securities. The company can then announce this information to the market on a voluntary basis. This may be an easier approach for PDMRs and PCAs, as it removes the need to monitor when the *de minimis* threshold has been reached. See section 3 below for discussion of why a company may want to put in place a share dealing policy and what it might cover.

1.6.2 Types of security or investment

The PDMRs of a listed company and their PCAs are required to disclose transactions in the shares and debt instruments of the company and in derivatives or other financial instruments linked to those shares or debt instruments.

The definition of 'financial instrument' for the purposes of MAR, dealings in which must therefore be disclosed, refers to the definition in MiFID (and will be replaced by the definition in MiFID II when it comes into force, expected to be January 2018). It includes, among other things:

- transferable securities (including shares in companies and other securities equivalent to shares in companies, depositary receipts in respect of shares, bonds and other forms of securitised debt and any other securities giving the right to acquire or sell any such transferable securities or giving rise to a cash settlement determined by reference to transferable securities, which in each case are negotiable on the capital market but excluding instruments of payment);
- units in collective investment undertakings;
- money-market instruments;
- options, futures, swaps, forward rate agreements and any other derivative contracts relating to securities, currencies, interest rates or yields, or other derivatives

instruments, financial indices or financial measures which may be settled physically or in cash; and
- financial contracts for difference.

The above will therefore catch, among other things, shares, share options, share warrants, bonds and equity swaps.

It is important to note that the financial instruments that are the subject of the dealing do not themselves need to be listed securities; however, they must relate to listed shares or debt instruments of the relevant company.

1.6.3 Types of transactions

The definition of 'transaction' for the purposes of the Article 19(1) disclosure obligation is very broad. The starting assumption should be that any activity undertaken or event occurring in relation to a PDMR's or PCA's holding of listed company shares or listed debt instruments (or derivatives or other financial instruments linked to such shares or debt instruments) is a 'transaction'.

Article 10 of the General MAR Delegated Regulation sets out a non-exhaustive list of transactions which must be disclosed. The list includes (among other things):

- an acquisition, disposal, short sale, subscription or exchange;
- acceptance or exercise of a stock option, including of a stock option granted to managers or employees as part of their remuneration package, and the disposal of shares stemming from the exercise of a stock option;
- transactions in or related to derivatives, including cash-settled transactions;
- entering into a contract for difference on a financial instrument of the company concerned;
- acquisition, disposal or exercise of rights, including put and call options, and warrants;
- transactions which are conditional upon the occurrence of the conditions and actual execution of the transactions;
- automatic or non-automatic conversion of a financial instrument into another financial instrument, including the exchange of convertible bonds to shares;
- gifts and donations made or received, and inheritance received;
- transactions executed in index-related products, baskets and derivatives, insofar as required by Article 19 of MAR; and
- transactions executed by a third party under an individual portfolio or asset management mandate on behalf or for the benefit of a PDMR or a PCA.

Article 19(7) of MAR also states that the types of transaction that must be notified include:

- the pledging or lending of financial instruments by or on behalf of a PDMR or PCA (except that a pledge, or a similar security interest, of financial instruments in connection with the depositing of the financial instruments in a custody account does not need to be notified unless and until such time that such pledge or other security interest is designated to secure a specific credit facility);
- transactions undertaken by persons professionally arranging or executing transactions or by another person on behalf of a PDMR or a PCA, including where discretion is exercised (see, however, the exception for collective investment undertakings discussed in section 1.6.4 below);
- transactions made under a life insurance policy, defined in accordance with the Solvency II Directive (2009/138/EC), where:
  - the policyholder is a PDMR or a PCA;
  - the investment risk is borne by the policyholder; and
  - the policyholder has the power or discretion to make investment decisions regarding specific instruments in that life insurance policy or to execute transactions regarding specific instruments for that life insurance policy.

The PDMRs of a company and their PCAs will therefore generally have to disclose any change of any sort to the size or nature of their holdings or interests in the company's securities or other financial instruments. This includes changes which are not triggered by an action on their part, such as a gift or grant of an employee share award. It is not relevant whether the PDMR's or PCA's interest is as registered holder or as beneficial owner. The notification requirement also includes dealing in a trustee capacity and dealings by an investment manager on behalf of that PDMR or PCA, even if that dealing is on a discretionary basis. PDMRs and PCAs should therefore notify any investment manager acting on their behalf of their Article 19 disclosure obligations under MAR.

Conditional transactions only need to be notified once the conditions are satisfied.

1.6.4 Collective investment undertakings and portfolios of assets

Article 19(1) of MAR, which contains the requirement to notify transactions, was amended by Article 56 of the EU Benchmarks Regulation (EU 2016/1011) so that a dealing by a PDMR or PCA in a financial instrument is not treated as a transaction under Article 19(1) of MAR if:

(a) the financial instrument is a unit or share in a collective investment undertaking (such as a UCITS or an Alternative Investment Fund) in which the exposure to the company's shares or debt instruments does not exceed 20% of the assets held by that collective investment undertaking;

(b) the financial instrument provides exposure to a portfolio of assets in which the exposure to the company's shares or debt instruments does not exceed 20% of the portfolio's assets; or

(c) the PDMR or PCA does not know, and could not know, whether or not the company's securities comprise more than 20% of the assets held by that collective investment undertaking or portfolio of assets, and there is no reason for that person to believe that the 20% threshold is exceeded.

If information regarding the investment composition of the collective investment undertaking or the portfolio of assets is available, then the PDMR or PCA must make all reasonable efforts to avail themselves of that information.

Article 56 of the EU Benchmarks Regulation also provides that transactions do not need to be notified under Article 19(7)(b) of MAR where the transactions are executed by managers of a collective investment undertaking in which the PDMR or PCA has invested and the manager of the collective investment undertaking operates with full discretion. This means that the manager must not receive any instructions or suggestions on portfolio composition directly or indirectly from investors in that collective investment undertaking.

1.7 Content, method and timing of notification

MAR and the PDMR Transaction Notification Implementing Regulation set out the detailed requirements for making a notification.

1.7.1 Content and template for notification

Under Article 19(6) of MAR, the notification of a transaction by a PDMR or PCA must contain the following information:

- the name of the PDMR or PCA making the notification;
- the reason for the notification;
- the name of the relevant listed company;
- a description and the identifier of the financial instrument;
- the nature of the transaction(s) (e.g. acquisition or disposal) indicating whether it is linked to the exercise of share option programmes or to the specific examples set out in Article 19(7) of MAR;
- the date and the place of the transaction(s); and
- the price and volume of the transaction (in the case of a pledge whose terms provide for its value to change, this should be disclosed together with its value at the date of the pledge).

The PDMR Transaction Notification Implementing Regulation contains a mandatory prescribed template for notification and public disclosure of transactions by PDMRs and PCAs. This mandatory template is set out in the Annex to the PDMR Transaction Notification Implementing Regulation and is replicated in Figure 7.1.

A PDMR or a PCA can use a single notification to cover multiple transactions provided the three-business day deadline is complied with (see ESMA final report

(ESMA/2015/1455)). In the case of multiple transactions, the mandatory prescribed form requires disclosure on an individual and aggregated basis (see section 1.7.2 below).

The prescribed template has also been replicated by the FCA in its PDMR Notification Form (available on the FCA website) (see section 1.7.3 below).

Figure 7.1: Form of template for notification and public disclosure of transactions by PDMRs and PCAs

1	Details of the person discharging managerial responsibilities/person closely associated	
(a)	Name	[For natural persons: the first and last name(s).]
		[For legal persons: full name including legal form as provided for in the register where it is incorporated, if applicable.]
2	Reason for the notification	
(a)	Position/ status	[For PDMRs: the position occupied within the issuer, e.g. CEO, CFO.]
		[For PCAs:
		■ An indication that the notification concerns a PCA;
		■ Name and position of the relevant PDMR.]
(b)	Initial notification/ Amendment	[Indication that this is an initial notification or an amendment to prior notifications. In case of amendment, explain the error that this notification is amending.]
3	Details of the issuer, emission allowance market participant, auction platform, auctioneer or auction monitor	
(a)	Name	[Full name of the entity.]
(b)	LEI	[Legal Entity Identifier code in accordance with ISO 17442 LEI code.]
4	Details of the transaction(s): section to be repeated for (i) each type of instrument; (ii) each type of transaction; (iii) each date; and (iv) each place where transactions have been conducted.	
(a)	Description of the financial instrument, type of instrument Identification code	[Indication as to the nature of the instrument:
		■ A share, a debt instrument, a derivative or a financial instrument linked to a share or a debt instrument;
		■ Instrument identification code as defined under Commission Delegated Regulation supplementing Regulation (EU) 600/2014 of the European Parliament and of the Council with regard to regulatory technical standards for the reporting of transactions to competent authorities adopted under Article 26 of Regulation (EU) No 600/2014].

(b)	Nature of the transaction	[Description of the transaction type using, where applicable, the type of transaction identified in Article 10 of the General MAR Delegated Regulation or a specific example set out in Article 19(7) of MAR. Pursuant to Article 19(6)(e) of MAR, it shall be indicated whether the transaction is linked to the exercise of a share option programme].
(c)	Price(s) and volume(s)	<table><tr><td>Price(s)</td><td>Volume(s)</td></tr><tr><td></td><td></td></tr></table> [Where more than one transaction of the same nature (purchases, sales, lendings, borrows, …) on the same financial instrument are executed on the same day and on the same place of transaction, prices and volumes of these transactions shall be reported in this filed, in a two columns form as presented above, inserting as many lines as needed. Using the data standards for price and quantity, including where applicable the price currency and the quantity currency, as defined under Commission Delegated Regulation supplementing Regulation (EU) No 600/2014 of the European Parliament and of the Council with regard to regulatory technical standards for the reporting of transactions to competent authorities adopted under Article 26 of Regulation (EU) No 600/2014.]
(d)	Aggregated information Aggregated volume Price	[The volumes of multiple transactions are aggregated when these transactions: - relate to the same financial instrument; - are of the same nature; - are executed on the same day; and - are executed on the same place of transaction. Using the data standard for quantity, including where applicable the quantity currency, as defined under Commission Delegated Regulation supplementing Regulation (EU) No. 600/2014 of the European Parliament and of the Council with regard to regulatory technical standards for the reporting of transactions to competent authorities adopted under Article 26 of Regulation (EU) No. 600/2014.] [Price information: - In case of a single transaction, the price of the single transaction; - In case the volumes of multiple transactions are aggregated: the weighted average price of the aggregated transactions.

(d)	Aggregated information Aggregated volume Price	Using the data standard for price, including where applicable the price currency, as defined under Commission Delegated Regulation supplementing Regulation (EU) No. 600/2014 of the European Parliament and of the Council with regard to regulatory technical standards for the reporting of transactions to competent authorities adopted under Article 26 of Regulation (EU) No. 600/2014].
(e)	Date of the transaction	[Date of the particular day of execution of the notified transaction. Using the ISO 8601 date format: YYYY-MM-DD; UTC time.]
(f)	Place of the transaction	[Name and code to identify the MiFID trading venue, the systematic internaliser or the organised trading platform outside of the EU where the transaction was executed as defined under Commission Delegated Regulation supplementing Regulation (EU) No. 600/2014 of the European Parliament and of the Council with regard to regulatory technical standards for the reporting of transactions to competent authorities adopted under Article 26 of Regulation (EU) No. 600/2014, or if the transaction was not executed on any of the above mentioned venues, please mention 'outside a trading venue'.]

1.7.2 Single transactions and aggregation

The prescribed template for PDMR and PCA transactions and the FCA's PDMR Notification Form (see section 1.7.3 below) require disclosure of information on each single transaction carried out.

In addition, for multiple transactions it is necessary to show aggregated information indicating the volume and the volume weighted average price of all the transactions meeting the following conditions:

(i) they are of the same nature;
(ii) they relate to the same financial instrument;
(iii) they have been carried out on the same trading day; and
(iv) they have been carried out on the same trading venue, or outside any trading venue.

The aggregated volume is a cumulative figure obtained by adding the volume of each of the transactions taken into account for the aggregation. Transactions of a different nature, such as purchases and sales, should never be aggregated nor should they be netted between themselves. The fact that transactions meeting the above conditions are reported in an aggregated form does not affect the requirement to report the information regarding the same transactions also in a separate transaction-by-transaction way within the same notification (see ESMA final report (ESMA/2015/1455)).

1.7.3 Method for notifying transactions

PDMRs and their PCAs are required under Article 19(1) of MAR to notify both the company and the FCA of transactions.

Article 2 of the PDMR Transaction Notification Implementing Regulation requires PDMRs and PCAs to notify transactions electronically. The electronic means used 'shall ensure that completeness, integrity and confidentiality of the information are maintained during the transmission and provide certainty as to the source of the information transmitted'.

For notifications to the company, PDMRs or PCAs will usually email a completed copy of the template notification document to the company. In order to ensure the confidentiality of the information, there should be a designated contact at the company who deals with PDMR and PCA notifications.

The company must then make public any notifications made to it by PDMRs and PCAs. It will do this by way of an RIS announcement.

For the notification to the FCA, MAR requires competent authorities to specify and publish on their website the relevant electronic means with respect to the transmission to them (Article 2 of the PDMR Transaction Notification Implementing Regulation). The FCA has made available on its website an electronic form (the PDMR Notification Form) for the submission of relevant information by PDMRs or PCAs to the FCA. The FCA has also published a practical guide to assist PDMRs and PCAs in completing the PDMR Notification Form (see 'Guide to submitting a Person Discharging Managerial Responsibilities and persons closely associated with them notification via the FCA website', available on the FCA website).

Listed companies may need to assist PDMRs and PCAs in submitting their notifications to the FCA. In some cases the listed company may choose to submit the notification forms to the FCA on behalf of their PDMRs and PCAs. PDMRs may also choose to notify dealings on behalf of their PCAs to the company. It is important to note, however, that the PDMR or PCA remain personally responsible for any failure to make a notification.

1.7.4 Timing of notifications

Under Article 19(1) of MAR, the notification to the company and to the FCA must be made promptly and no later than three business days after the date of the transaction. The company is then required under Article 19(3) of MAR to make a regulatory announcement of the same information to the market, again by no later than three business days after the date of the transaction.

This could create an issue in practice if the PDMR or PCA only notifies the company at the end of the three business day period, leaving no time for the company to comply with its own deadline to make the information public.

Companies may therefore choose to implement a share dealing policy which requires notifications to be made to it as soon as possible and by no later than one or two business days after the date of the transaction to give the company sufficient time to disclose the information publicly. See section 3 below for further information.

Where the dealing is also caught by DTR 5 (e.g. a director's direct or indirect holding of voting rights in a UK company (including by way of financial instruments) has increased to, or through a percentage point above, 3% of the issued share capital) the PDMR or PCA will also need to comply with the requirements of DTR 5 (see section 5 below).

1.7.5 Correcting a notification

If a notification has been made and needs to be corrected, the notifying PDMR or PCA should submit a new notification to the company and the FCA containing the correct information. The new notification should indicate in the relevant field that it is an amendment notification, and explain the error that such notification is amending (see ESMA final report (ESMA/2015/1455)).

1.7.6 Responsibility for disclosure

The responsibility for making the disclosures by the PDMR or PCA falls upon the relevant individual, who may be found to be liable for failure to make any necessary disclosures under MAR by the FCA.

PDMRs are not responsible for the disclosures required to be made by their PCAs. As noted in section 1.5 above, Article 19(5) of MAR only requires PDMRs to notify their PCAs of their disclosure obligations under MAR and to keep a copy of this notification.

1.8 Disclosure of PDMR and PCA interests in annual report

Chapter 9 of the Listing Rules (LR 9) applies to companies with a premium listing of equity shares. LR 9.8.6R(1) requires a listed company incorporated in the UK to include in its annual report a statement setting out all of the interests notified to it under Article 19 of MAR by each person who was a director of the company as at the end of the financial year and any changes in those interests that occurred between the end of the financial year and a date not more than one month before the date of notice of the company's annual general meeting. The interests of each director must also include the interests of their PCAs of which the company is, or ought upon reasonable enquiry to become, aware.

The annual report must also include a statement, on the same basis, of all information disclosed to the company in accordance with DTR 5 (see section 5.8.4 below).

1.9 Practical recommendations for compliance

1.9.1 Notifying individuals of their disclosure obligations

As discussed in section 1.5 above, Article 19(5) of MAR requires a listed company to notify a PDMR of their notification obligations and the dealing restrictions under Article 19 of MAR. Premium Listing Principle 1 also requires companies with a premium listing of shares to ensure that their directors understand their obligations, including under MAR. If any PDMR fails to disclose dealings to the company due to a lack of understanding of their duties, the company may be held responsible by the FCA for breach of Premium Listing Principle 1 (and Article 19(5) of MAR if the company did not provide the initial notification of obligations to the PDMR). In addition, the individual PDMR will be liable for failure to make the disclosure.

Companies should therefore:

- draw up a list of the company's PDMRs;
- ensure each PDMR provides the company with a list of their PCAs;
- maintain the list of the company's PDMRs and their PCAs; and
- create a template notification from the company to PDMRs about their obligations (as required by Article 19(5) of MAR) and keep a record of the notification to each PDMR.

Companies should also consider providing a training course on disclosure of dealings for all relevant personnel. These requirements could be addressed as part of the new director and new PDMR induction programme and as part of the regular training programme for existing directors and PDMRs.

As discussed in section 3 below, listed companies may wish to have a share dealing code for PDMRs to help ensure compliance with the MAR requirements. Companies may also put in place a formal share dealing policy, applicable to all employees, reminding them, for example, that they should not deal while in possession of inside information.

In relation to PCAs, companies should consider providing PDMRs with a form of notification which they can send to their PCAs (again, as required by Article 19(5) of MAR) and a pro forma record of notification that each PDMR can keep. The notification to PCAs should include information on their disclosure obligations and the sanctions that may be imposed on them for breach. If a company has a share dealing code, it may choose to send a copy of the code directly to the PCAs who are notified to the company by the PDMRs. Note that a company cannot require PCAs to comply with any code (as they are not directors or employees of the company). In particular, if a company chooses to require its PDMRs to notify all transactions (and so to ignore the €5,000 *de minimis* threshold discussed in section 1.6.1 above), it cannot impose a similar requirement on PCAs. The company could, however, suggest or recommend that PCAs notify all transactions.

1.9.2 Procedures for making disclosure

Listed companies should identify a key contact person or team to whom PDMRs and their PCAs should send their Article 19 disclosures. This contact person or team should understand the detailed obligations in relation to disclosure of dealings and be able to answer questions from all persons with a disclosure duty. The name of the relevant contacts should be included in the notification to PDMRs and in any share dealing code. The team should preferably involve at least one member of the company secretarial department if they are involved in the clearance procedure for dealings where required under MAR or the company's internal share dealing code.

PDMRs should be provided with the template for notification (see section 1.7.1 above and Figure 7.1) and be given information on how and when notifications should be made (see sections 1.7.2 and 1.7.3 above).

The relevant person or team responsible for disclosure of dealings should ensure that an RIS announcement is made of the dealing information before the end of the third business day following the transaction (Art. 19(3) of MAR).

Companies should ensure that they review their announcement procedures and that they are able to disclose dealing information to the market via an RIS announcement within the relevant time frame to ensure that they comply with MAR and Listing Principle 1 which requires all listed companies to take reasonable steps to have adequate systems and controls to enable them to comply with their continuing obligations.

2. Prohibition on PDMR dealings during closed periods

2.1 The prohibition

Under Article 19(11) of MAR, PDMRs are prohibited from conducting, directly or indirectly, any transaction on their own account or for the account of a third party which relates to the company's securities, or other financial instruments linked to them, during a MAR closed period.

This restriction only applies to PDMRs; it does not apply to their PCAs. It does, however, apply to a dealing by a PDMR on behalf of a PCA. Furthermore, if a company chooses to put in place a share dealing code (see section 3 below) the company could require PDMRs under that code to inform their PCAs that they should not deal during the closed periods specified in the dealing code.

2.2 Definition of a closed period under MAR

Closed periods are defined in Article 19(11) of MAR. A closed period is the 30-day period prior to the announcement of the company's half-year report and financial year-end report.

If the company issues a preliminary results announcement, then the closed period is the 30-day period before that preliminary announcement is made, provided the preliminary announcement contains all the key financial information expected to be included in the year-end report (see ESMA MAR Q&A).

If a company adopts a share dealing code, it could impose longer closed periods on its PDMRs during which they cannot deal. It could also extend the dealing restriction so that it applies to other employees as well as PDMRs (see section 3 below for further details).

2.3 Types of transactions falling within the dealing prohibition

The types of 'transaction' falling within the prohibition in Article 19(11) of MAR are the same as those that are required to be disclosed under Article 19(1) of MAR, which are set out in section 1.6 above. The exemption for dealings in collective investment undertakings described in section 1.6.4 above also applies to the closed period restrictions.

However, this does not mean that a transaction that has to be disclosed under Article 19(1) of MAR always falls within the Article 19(11) closed period restriction or vice versa. This is because Article 19(1) requires a PDMR to disclose 'every transaction conducted on their own account' whereas Article 19(11) states that during a MAR closed period a PDMR 'shall not conduct any transactions on its own account or for the account of a third party'. Therefore, Article 19(11) only applies where it is the PDMR itself conducting the transaction, whereas for the disclosure requirement in Article 19(1) it is not relevant who conducts the transaction, so long as it relates to the PDMR's interest. In addition, Article 19(11) applies to transactions conducted by a PDMR on behalf of a third party, whereas the disclosure requirement in Article 19(1) does not.

A PDMR may enter into a conditional transaction before a closed period which completes during the closed period, provided that satisfaction of the condition is outside the control of the PDMR and the only action taken by the PDMR occurs before the start of a closed period. This is because, in that situation, there is no 'conduct' by the PDMR during the closed period for the purposes of Article 19(11) of MAR. The decision to trade (i.e. the entry into the conditional transaction) is made outside the MAR closed period and the PDMR is not 'trading' during the MAR closed period (see CLLS/Law Society MAR Q&A).

Similarly, if a PDMR enters into a share savings scheme or a dividend reinvestment plan in relation to the company's shares outside a closed period, the PDMR can continue to acquire shares under the relevant scheme or election during the closed periods but must not cancel or amend his or her participation during a MAR closed period. Again, this is because the only action taken by a PDMR takes place before the start of a closed period and there is no 'conduct' by the PDMR during the closed period for the purposes of Article 19(11) of MAR.

Also, dealings by an investment manager with complete discretion will not be treated as a dealing conducted by the PDMR, even though it is required to be disclosed under Article 19(1).

Conversely, the prohibition in Article 19(11) of MAR applies to a conditional contract entered into, or other action taken, by a PDMR during a closed period even if the condition cannot be satisfied until after the end of the closed period and even though the transaction is not required to be disclosed under Article 19(1) until the condition is satisfied.

2.4 Exceptions to the prohibition on dealing during a closed period

There are very limited exceptions to the prohibition imposed on PDMRs for dealing during a closed period. These are set out in Article 19(12) of MAR, which provides that a company may permit a PDMR to deal during a closed period where:

- due to the existence of exceptional circumstances, such as severe financial difficulty, an immediate sale of shares is required; or
- the transactions are made under, or relate to, an employee share or saving scheme, qualification or entitlement of shares, or are transactions where the beneficial interest in the relevant security does not change.

The General MAR Delegated Regulation sets out (in Articles 7 to 9) a limited but non-exhaustive list of transactions falling within the above exceptions (and described in further detail in sections 2.4.1 and 2.4.2 below). Importantly, it also limits the exceptions by providing that they can only apply if the PDMR is able to demonstrate that the particular transaction could not have been executed at another moment in time, other than during the closed period (Article 7(1)(b) of the General MAR Delegated Regulation).

Even if an exception does apply, consideration must also be given to whether the PDMR has inside information at the time of any dealing. See section 2.5 below.

2.4.1 Exceptional circumstances

Article 8(2) of the General MAR Delegated Regulation provides that in order for circumstances to be exceptional, they must be extremely urgent, unforeseen and compelling and their cause must be external to the PDMR and the PDMR has no control over them.

If a PDMR wishes to seek permission to trade during a closed period based on exceptional circumstances, they must provide a reasoned written request to the company prior to any trading which describes the envisaged transaction and provides an explanation of why the sale of shares is the only reasonable alternative to obtain the necessary financing (Article 7(2) of the General MAR Delegated Regulation). When examining whether the circumstances described in this written request are exceptional, Article 8(3) of the General MAR Delegated Regulation provides that the company must take into account (among other indicators) whether and the extent to which the PDMR:

(i) is, at the moment of submitting its request, facing a legally enforceable financial commitment or claim;

(ii) has to fulfil or is in a situation entered into before the beginning of the closed period and requiring the payment of a sum to a third party, including a tax liability, and cannot reasonably satisfy a financial commitment or claim by means other than immediate sale of shares.

Given the above requirements, it is likely to be difficult in practice for a PDMR to rely on the exceptional circumstances exemption.

2.4.2 Employee share schemes and options, warrants and bonds

Article 9 of the General MAR Delegated Regulation provides a non-exhaustive list of circumstances in which a company may permit a PDMR to trade on its own account or for the account of a third party during a closed period. This list includes where that PDMR:

- had been awarded or granted financial instruments under an employee scheme, provided that certain conditions set out in Article 9 of the General MAR Delegated Regulation are met;
- had been awarded or granted financial instruments under an employee scheme that takes place in the closed period provided that a pre-planned and organised approach regarding various matters as set out in Article 9 of the General MAR Delegated Regulation is followed;
- exercises options or warrants or conversion of convertible bonds assigned to him or her under an employee scheme when the expiration date of such options, warrants or convertible bonds falls within a closed period, as well as sales of the shares acquired pursuant to such exercise or conversion, provided that certain conditions set out in Article 9 of the General MAR Delegated Regulation are met;
- acquires financial instruments under an employee saving scheme, provided that certain conditions set out in Article 9 of the General MAR Delegated Regulation are met;
- transfers or receives, directly or indirectly, financial instruments, provided that the financial instruments are transferred between two accounts of the PDMR and that such transfer does not result in a change in price of financial instruments; and
- acquires qualification or entitlement of shares of the company and the final date for such acquisition under the company's statute or by-laws falls during the closed period, provided that the PDMR submits evidence to the company of the reasons

for the acquisition not taking place at another time, and the company is satisfied with the provided explanation.

2.5 Restrictions on dealings at other times

Whenever a PDMR (or PCA) deals in the company's securities, he or she must ensure that they are not in possession of inside information. If they are, the PDMR (or PCA) should not conduct the transaction (except on the basis of very clear advice that no offence would be committed) as it may amount to insider dealing under MAR. It is an offence under MAR for anyone in possession of inside information to use that information by dealing in the securities of the company. It is also a criminal offence under the CJA to deal while in possession of inside information. See Chapter 5 for discussion of these offences and when dealing might be legitimate.

3. Share dealing policy

Prior to MAR, the Model Code, in Annex 1 to LR 9, contained various restrictions on dealings in the securities of a premium listed company for the company's directors and other PDMRs. The purpose of the Model Code was to ensure that such individuals did not abuse, and did not place themselves under suspicion of abusing, inside information that they may be thought to have, especially in periods leading up to an announcement of results.

As MAR sets out its own restrictions on share dealings by PDMRs during closed periods (as discussed in section 2 above), and does not mandate the need for a share dealing code which requires pre-clearance to deal (as was the case with the Model Code), the FCA decided to delete the Model Code from LR 9. However, companies may still choose to implement a share dealing code as part of their internal governance structures.

3.1 Adopting a share dealing code

Listed companies may wish to adopt a share dealing code that its directors, other PDMRs and possibly other employees are required to comply with. This could assist the listed company in complying with Listing Principle 1, which requires all listed companies to take reasonable steps to establish and maintain adequate procedures, systems and controls to enable them to comply with their obligations.

As regards the content of any code, there are policy decisions for the listed company to take but areas that a share dealing code could cover include:

- setting out the obligations and restrictions on share dealing under MAR including, in particular, the offence of insider dealing;

- applying the requirements of the code (or at least the prohibition on dealings during a closed period) to certain other employees who are not PDMRs, such as senior managers or those who, because of the nature of their role, are likely to have access to inside information or are involved in preparing the company's financial results;
- imposing clearance requirements in relation to dealing, at least on their directors and other PDMRs, in order to assist in their compliance with MAR and in the prevention of insider dealing. The company may also want to impose dealing restrictions on employees who are not directors or PDMRs (and therefore not subject to Article 19 of MAR) as an additional protection against the risk of insider dealing. See section 3.2 below for further discussion;
- imposing additional closed periods in addition to the 30-day MAR closed periods prior to the annual and half-yearly results;
- requiring PDMRs to ignore the €5,000 *de minimis* threshold contained in MAR and notify all transactions to the company.

The voluntary share dealing code could be a bespoke code, based on the old Model Code (which, as discussed above, used to be set out in Annex 1 to LR 9) or based on the sample code published by the Institute of Chartered Secretaries and Administrators (ICSA).

The code could be part of, or sit alongside, a more general share dealing policy applying to all employees. All employees should in any event be made aware of the insider dealing and market abuse provisions and of the fact that it is an offence to deal in securities while in possession of inside information.

The share dealing policy needs to work alongside the listed company's inside information policy, which will cover the MAR requirements in relation to inside information, including identifying inside information, delaying the announcement of inside information and insider lists. See Chapter 5 for further information.

As a PCA is not an employee, the listed company cannot directly bind a PCA to comply with the terms of its share dealing code or share dealing policy. However, as noted in section 2.1 above, a listed company could require its PDMRs to seek to restrict dealings by their PCAs during closed periods.

3.2 The requirement to obtain clearance to deal

A share dealing code may require PDMRs, and any other employees subject to the code, to seek clearance for any proposed dealings and prohibit dealing unless clearance to deal is given.

In relation to directors and other PDMRs, the type of transaction for which clearance is needed should align with the transactions which are subject to the disclosure and dealing restriction requirements under MAR (as described in sections 1.6.3 and 2.3 above).

One or more nominated directors or the company secretary could be specified as the person who can give clearance to deal. A person should not be able to clear their own dealing and normally the person giving clearance should not be a person whose role reports to the person seeking clearance. The designated person must also be someone who would have sufficient information to determine whether inside information exists in relation to the listed company before giving clearance to deal.

3.2.1 Procedure and timing for clearance

The method of seeking and giving clearance to deal should be stated in the share dealing code.

A listed company will ordinarily want to impose time limits for the clearance procedure. For example, a PDMR or other person subject to the dealing code could be required to apply for clearance one or two days before the intended date of the transaction. This is to give the listed company time to provide clearance. It will also allow time to prepare the necessary notification of the transaction to the FCA and to the market in accordance with Article 19 of MAR (as described in section 1.7 above).

The dealing code will also normally require that, if clearance is granted, the dealing should then take place as soon as possible and in any event within two business days of clearance being obtained. This reduces the risk of inside information arising before the dealing takes place.

The listed company should maintain a record of any dealing request and of any clearance given.

3.2.2 When clearance to deal should not be given

A director or other PDMR (and any other person subject to the dealing code) should not be given clearance to deal:

- during a MAR closed period prior to the announcement of results unless one of the exceptions to the prohibition under Article 19(12) of MAR applies (but, as discussed in section 2.4 above, these are very limited exceptions); or
- at any time (even if one of the exceptions under Article 19(12) of MAR applies) when there exists any matter which constitutes inside information in relation to the listed company (unless there is a legitimate purpose for the dealing as provided for by Article 9 of MAR, for example, dealings in compliance with a prior legal commitment).

In addition, the listed company may decide to impose longer closed periods in its dealing code than those specified in MAR. In particular, an extended closed period may run from the end of the financial year through to the issue of the preliminary results. Outside the MAR closed periods, it is up to the listed company to specify in its dealing code which exceptions apply to the dealing restriction (subject always to the prohibition on dealing while in possession of inside information).

The listed company should issue notifications to its PDMRs (and any other persons subject to the dealing code) in advance of the closed periods reminding them that they are prohibited from dealing during those periods.

3.3 Notification of dealings by PDMRs and PCAs

As discussed in section 1.7 above, PDMRs and PCAs are required to notify the listed company and the FCA of any dealings by no later than three business days after the transaction. However, in order for the listed company to comply with its obligation under Article 19(3) of MAR to announce the information to the market by no later than three business days from the date of the transaction, the listed company may require (or in the case of a PCA, request) that the notification is made as soon as possible and by no later than one or two business days after the date of the transaction.

Also as discussed above, the listed company's share dealing policy may require (or in the case of a PCA, request) that notification is made to the listed company and the FCA of every transaction, regardless of the annual *de minimis* threshold of €5,000 under MAR.

3.4 Dealings by PCAs

The listed company cannot directly impose dealing restrictions on a PCA assuming they are not an employee or director of the company.

The listed company's share dealing code may, however, provide that PDMRs are required to take reasonable steps to prevent dealings by their PCAs on considerations of a short-term nature or during the closed periods prior to results and that they should advise their PCAs of those closed periods.

A PDMR should not advise a PCA of periods during which dealings cannot take place as a result of there being inside information because the PDMR should not disclose the existence of that inside information to the PCA (to do so would amount to tipping off for insider dealing purposes).

3.5 Penalties for breach of the dealing code

A breach of the dealing code which is also a breach of MAR by the relevant individual would create a liability for sanctions against that individual under MAR (see section 4 below).

In addition, the listed company can set out penalties for a breach of any aspect of the company's share dealing code or policy, whether or not they also amount to a breach of MAR, such as the application of its employee disciplinary procedures.

3.6 Procedures for ensuring compliance

It is best practice for a listed company to ask its PDMRs to reconfirm their shareholdings on an annual basis to allow the company to carry out a reconciliation exercise with its own records.

The listed company should consider placing a note or other form of indication against all the shareholdings of its PDMRs and senior executives so that any movements in these shareholdings are notified to the company secretary immediately. Where a PDMR holds shares other than in his or her own name, the PDMR should provide details of the relevant nominee or custodian to the company so that it can receive notifications of any changes in those shareholdings.

The listed company should ensure its directors, other PDMRs and any other employees who are subject to its share dealing code are aware of the clearance procedures and relevant timelines in the dealing code.

The listed company's share dealing policy should be made available or accessible to all employees and a copy of the share dealing code should be provided to all those to whom it applies. The company should also include a provision in the staff handbook or employment contracts about compliance with the share dealing policy and MAR.

4. Breach of dealing notification requirements and restrictions

Failure to comply with the PDMR and PCA notification requirements and the PDMR restrictions on dealings will be a breach of MAR. The sanctions for a breach of MAR are discussed in Chapters 1 and 5 and include a public censure or the imposition of a fine. There is no requirement for fault or intention in relation to the contravention.

In relation to Article 19 of MAR, PDMRs and PCAs are directly responsible for compliance with their obligations and so may be individually censured or fined by the FCA for a breach of those requirements.

A company could be liable to a censure or fine if it failed to comply with the obligation to announce a dealing once notified by the PDMR or PCA. A breach of any of the securities dealing requirements and restrictions in Article 19 of MAR could also be regarded by the FCA as being a result of a failure of the listed company's procedures, systems and controls; if so, the company could also be found liable, and censured or fined, for breach of the Listing Principles, that is:

- the requirement under Listing Principle 1 in LR 7 to put in place adequate procedures, systems and controls to comply with MAR; and
- the requirement in Premium Listing Principle 1 to take reasonable steps to enable its directors to understand their responsibilities and obligations as directors.

PDMRs and PCAs will also need to be aware of the sanctions which can be imposed for the civil offence of market abuse under MAR and the criminal offence of insider dealing under the CJA.

5. Disclosure of interests in voting rights

The provisions relating to vote-holder notifications are set out in DTR 5, which for the most part implements the requirements of the Transparency Directive (TD) in the UK. The FSA (as it then was) adopted a 'copy out' approach when it implemented the TD in 2006 and, in drafting DTR 5, largely followed its text. As a result, the text may not be as clear as might have been wished.

The detailed requirements of DTR 5 were amended on 26 November 2015 to reflect amendments made to the TD by the TD Amending Directive (Directive 2013/50/EU) though in the UK this resulted largely in changes of detail rather than of substance. A directly applicable Commission Delegated Regulation on Major Holdings ((EU) 2015/761) (the Major Shareholding Regulation) provides regulatory technical standards on certain aspects of the regime. The Major Shareholding Regulation is cross-referenced in DTR 5 and contains directly applicable provisions in relation to certain aspects of the regime, including how interests in listed companies held via instruments with a similar economic effect to a right to acquire shares should be calculated for the purposes of the disclosure requirements.

In determining whether a person has a notifiable interest under DTR 5, it is always necessary to consider carefully the text of DTR 5 in the context of the interest concerned. UKLA Guidance Notes *UKLA/TN/541.1* to *UKLA/TN/ 551.2* give guidance on many aspects of DTR 5. ESMA has also published a Q&A on the Transparency Directive (ESMA/2015/1595).

The general principle behind DTR 5 is to identify who is controlling the way in which voting rights in a relevant issuer are exercised and to require this information to be disclosed to the market. As well as identifying which shareholders have voting rights in an issuer, DTR 5 also aims to identify other persons who may, in practice, be able to control the exercise of voting rights.

The regime does not apply only to interests in listed companies, so the term 'issuer' is used in this section rather than 'listed company'.

To establish whether or not there is a notification obligation under DTR 5, it is necessary to consider the following four-stage test:

(1) Is the interest held in a relevant issuer? (See section 5.1.)

(2) If the answer to question (1) is yes, is the interest in the relevant issuer a relevant interest? (See sections 5.2 and 5.3.)

(3) If the answer to question (2) is yes, has the relevant interest in the relevant issuer reached, exceeded or fallen below a relevant threshold level? (See section 5.4.)

(4) If the answer to question (3) is yes, do any of the exemptions apply such that the interest need not be notified? (See section 5.5.)

Each of these four tests is considered in turn below. While of less immediate relevance to a listed company, the application of DTR 5 to investment managers and their holdings is particularly complex. Figure 7.2 (see p. 330) summarises the impact of DTR 5 on investment managers.

5.1 Meaning of 'issuer' for the purposes of DTR 5

Voting interests must relate to shares of an 'issuer' to fall within DTR 5.

The definition of an issuer for these purposes is set out in the Glossary to the FCA Handbook and includes:

(a) companies whose shares are admitted to trading on any EEA-regulated market (including the Main Market of the London Stock Exchange) and whose home member state is the UK (see Chapter 1 for discussion of an issuer's home member state); and

(b) UK public limited companies (within the meaning of section 4(2) of CA 2006) and other body corporates both incorporated in and having a principal place of business in the UK which, in each case, have shares admitted to trading on a prescribed market (i.e. a market which is established under the rules of a UK recognised investment exchange, such as AIM).

DTR 5 applies to all issuers with a premium listing (LR 9.2.6BR) or standard listing (LR 14.3.23R) on the Official List, unless they comply with corresponding requirements imposed by another EEA member state.

DTR 5 can therefore apply to non-UK incorporated companies.

The notification obligation, in terms of threshold and procedure, depends on the classification of the issuer. In broad terms, the notification requirements are stricter for voting rights in UK issuers with shares admitted to an EEA-regulated market than for non-UK issuers. A 'non-UK issuer' is an issuer whose shares are admitted to trading on a regulated market and whose home member state is the UK, but which is not a UK incorporated company.

In the case of depositary receipts admitted to trading on a regulated market, the issuer for DTR 5 purposes means the issuer of the securities represented by the depositary receipt, irrespective of whether those securities are admitted to trading on a regulated market (see FCA Glossary). In other words, it is necessary to look through the depositary which has actually issued the depositary receipt to the issuer of the underlying security. If shares underlying a depositary receipt are admitted to trading on a regulated market, the holder of the depositary receipt will need to comply with the DTR 5 disclosure obligations as if it were the shareholder of the underlying shares represented by the depositary receipt (see section 5.4.2).

Where depositary receipts are admitted to trading on a regulated market but the underlying securities represented by such depositary receipts are not, the FCA has stated that the depositary receipt issuer (i.e. the issuer of the shares underlying the depositary receipt) will not fall within the scope of DTR 5 (see the consultation draft of the UKLA Guidance Note *Scope and application of vote holder and issuer notification rules* (UKLA/TN/541.2)). The FCA has not however, as yet, published the final version of this guidance note and has stated that discussions on the application of DTR 5 to depositary receipt issuers are taking place at an EU level.

5.2 What interests are relevant for DTR 5 purposes?

Under DTR 5, a person's interest will be relevant for disclosure purposes if:
  (a) they, directly or indirectly, hold shares in a relevant issuer to which voting rights are attached (see sections 5.2.1 and 5.3 below);
  (b) they, directly or indirectly, hold any financial instruments (referred to in this chapter as 'qualifying financial instruments') which on maturity give the holder, under a formal agreement, either the unconditional right to acquire or the discretion to acquire existing shares in a relevant issuer to which voting rights are attached (see section 5.2.2 below); and/or
  (c) they, directly or indirectly, hold any financial instruments which (i) are referenced to shares in a relevant issuer and (ii) have a similar economic effect to, but which are not, qualifying financial instruments, whether or not they confer a right to physical settlement (referred to in this chapter as 'financial instruments having similar economic effect' (FISEEs)) (see section 5.2.3 below).

5.2.1 Shares

References in DTR 5 to shares are to shares which are:
- already issued and carry rights to vote which are exercisable in all circumstances at general meetings of the issuer, including shares (such as preference shares) which, following the exercise of an option for their conversion, event of default or otherwise, have become fully enfranchised for voting purposes (DTR 5.1.1R(3)(a)); and
- admitted to trading on a regulated or prescribed market (DTR 5.1.1R(3)(b)).

Amendments made by the TD Amending Directive mean that rights over unissued shares now fall outside the scope of DTR 5.

5.2.2 Qualifying financial instruments

Qualifying financial instruments are instruments which on maturity give the holder, under a formal agreement, either the unconditional right to acquire or the discretion to acquire existing shares to which voting rights are attached.

The right must be to acquire shares which are already in issue. This would include, for example, physically settled call options but not rights in a rights issue or open offer as they relate to entitlements to acquire shares that have not yet been issued. Similarly, convertible bonds would not usually be disclosable, unless they convert into shares that have already been issued.

Provided that they meet the above criteria, the following types of financial instruments are likely to qualify as relevant financial instruments: transferable securities, options (including calls, puts and any combination thereof), futures, swaps, forward rate agreements, contracts for differences (CfDs) and any other derivative contracts relating to existing shares, in each case where physically settled. ESMA is required under the TD Amending Directive to establish and periodically update an indicative list of financial instruments that are subject to notification requirements, taking into account technical developments in financial markets. The indicative list is available on the ESMA website.

DTR 5.3.3G(1) provides that the following should not be considered to be qualifying financial instruments:

- instruments entitling the holder to receive shares depending on the price of the underlying share reaching a certain level at a certain moment in time; and
- instruments that allow the instrument issuer or a third party to give shares or cash to the instrument holder on maturity.

The financial instruments may be held directly or indirectly. The FCA has said that the circumstances outlined in DTR 5.2.1R (see section 5.3 below) are also relevant in determining whether a person is an 'indirect' holder of financial instruments for the purposes of DTR 5.3.1R.

5.2.3 Financial instruments having similar economic effect

Financial instruments having similar economic effect (FISEEs) are instruments that do not give a legal right to acquire shares, but which have a similar effect in practice. An example of a FISEE is a cash-settled CfD, as it is referenced to and gives economic exposure to the underlying shares.

Financial instruments which are subject to external conditionality (i.e. conditions beyond the control of the parties) and give the holder an economic exposure similar to holding a share or an entitlement to acquire a share are now also within the scope of the FISEE notification requirements, following changes made by the TD Amending Directive. A conditional FISEE will therefore need to be disclosed prior to the future uncertain event actually occurring (rather than waiting for the future event to occur, as was previously the case). ESMA's view is that disclosure of conditional FISEEs should be required as the holder may be in a more advantageous position compared to other market participants to gain access to the shares, either directly from the counterparty or indirectly, for example in the market following sale by the counterparty (see ESMA Final Report 2014/1187).

The Major Shareholding Regulation contains provisions, copied out in DTR 5.3, which specify how the holders of FISEEs are required to calculate how many voting rights they have access to (see section 5.4.5 below).

As noted above, ESMA and the FCA have confirmed that only financial instruments relating to already issued shares need to be disclosed, meaning there is no requirement to disclose, for example, rights to subscribe for shares under an open offer or rights issue (as those rights relate to unissued shares). See also section 5.4.6 below.

As financial markets invent new products on a regular basis and the regime is designed to ensure that disclosure is not avoided on the grounds of a technicality, the FCA has deliberately not provided any set list of FISEEs and the indicative list of financial instruments published by ESMA (see section 5.2.2 above) is not exclusive and can be updated in future. Instead, the rules are drafted in a principles-based way to ensure that all financial products capable of having a similar economic effect to qualifying financial instruments are caught. This potentially captures a broad range of products.

5.2.4 Basket or index of shares

In the case of a financial instrument which is referenced to a basket of shares or an index, the Major Shareholding Regulation provides that the financial instrument only needs to be disclosed if:

- the voting rights in a specific issuer (X) included in the basket or index represent 1% or more of the total voting rights in X; or
- the shares of X in the basket or index represent 20% or more of the total value of the securities in the basket or index.

Where disclosure of the financial instrument is required, the voting rights to be disclosed should be calculated on the basis of the weight of the share in the basket or index (DTR 5.3.3B EU).

Where a financial instrument is referenced to a series of baskets of shares or indices, the voting rights held through the individual baskets of shares or indices should not be accumulated for the purpose of calculating the thresholds set out above (DTR 5.3.3B EU).

5.3 Treatment of indirect holders of shares

Under DTR 5.2.1R, a person will also hold a relevant interest (and be treated as an indirect holder of shares for the purpose of the definition of 'shareholder') to the extent that they are entitled to acquire, dispose of, or exercise voting rights in any of the situations described in DTR 5.2.1R(a) to (h). Those situations are outlined below and can result in a person having a notifiable interest even where they are not the registered holder or beneficial owner of the shares.

In each and every case it is necessary to look at the detailed wording of the relevant rule to establish whether or not it applies. The individual holdings must be aggregated but also separately identified in the notification to the issuer (DTR 5.2.3G).

The obligation to notify indirect shareholdings under DTR 5 can rest with both the relevant direct and indirect shareholder if the proportion of voting rights held by each party reaches, exceeds or falls below an applicable threshold (see further section 5.4 below), although it may be possible to make a single common notification (see section 5.6.4 below).

As previously mentioned, the application of DTR 5.2.1R and related provisions of the DTR 5 regime to investment managers is particularly complex. Figure 7.2 (see p. 330) sets out a summary of the impact of the DTR 5 regime on investment managers.

5.3.1 Concert parties (DTR 5.2.1R(a))

Where voting rights are held by a third party with whom a person has concluded an agreement which obliges them to adopt, by concerted exercise of the voting rights they hold, a lasting common policy towards the management of the issuer in question, all parties to the agreement must comply with the disclosure obligation in DTR 5.1.2R. The meaning and scope of the term 'lasting common policy' is not clear. The only public guidance issued on this was in August 2009, in an announcement and letter from the FSA (as it then was) to the Institutional Shareholders Committee (available on the archived version of the FSA website). The FSA confirmed that this provision is unlikely to be triggered by ad hoc discussions between vote-holders on particular corporate issues or corporate events. The guidance arose from concerns that the call for more active, collective shareholder engagement contained in the Walker Report could clash with the rules on market abuse, on the disclosure of major shareholdings or on change of control in financial institutions.

5.3.2 Temporary transfers of voting rights (DTR 5.2.1R(b))

Where voting rights are held by a third party under an agreement with a person that provides for the temporary transfer for consideration of the voting rights in question, then both the person who acquires the voting rights and who is entitled to exercise them under the agreement and the person who is transferring temporarily for consideration the voting rights must comply with the disclosure obligation in DTR 5.1.2R.

5.3.3 Collateral (DTR 5.2.1R(c))

Where shares are lodged as collateral with a person and that person controls the voting rights and declares its intention of exercising them, both the person holding the collateral and the person lodging the collateral under these conditions must comply with the disclosure obligation in DTR 5.1.2R.

5.3.4 Life interests (DTR 5.2.1R(d))

Where voting rights are attached to shares in which a person has a life interest, the person who has a life interest in the shares, if that person is entitled to exercise the voting rights attached to the shares, and the person who is disposing of the voting rights when the life interest is created, must each comply with the disclosure obligation in DTR 5.1.2R.

5.3.5 Controlled undertakings (DTR 5.2.1R(e))

Where voting rights are held or may be exercised by an undertaking controlled by a person, both the controlling person and, if it has a notification duty at individual level, the controlled undertaking must comply with the disclosure obligation in DTR 5.1.2R.

5.3.6 Depositaries (DTR 5.2.1R(f))

Where shares, together with the voting rights attaching to shares, are deposited with a person who is entitled to use such voting rights at their discretion in the absence of specific instructions from the shareholders, the deposit taker of the shares and the depositor of the shares must each comply with the disclosure obligation in DTR 5.1.2R.

5.3.7 Voting rights held by a third party (DTR 5.2.1R(g))

Where the voting rights are held by a third party in their own name on behalf of another person, the person who controls the voting rights must comply with the disclosure obligation in DTR 5.1.2R.

5.3.8 Proxies (DTR 5.2.1R(h))

Where a proxy is entitled to exercise the voting rights at their discretion in the absence of specific instructions from the relevant shareholder(s), the proxy holder and the shareholder who has given their proxy to the proxy holder must each comply with the disclosure obligation in DTR 5.1.2R.

In particular, this means that where the chairperson of a meeting holds discretionary proxies representing, together with their own interests, more than 3% of the voting rights in the issuer (or 5% in the case of a non-UK issuer), they will have a notification obligation. A proxy that confers only minor and residual discretions (e.g. a discretion to vote on an adjournment) will not result in either a proxy holder (or a shareholder as there is no disposal of voting rights) having a notification obligation (DTR 5.8.5G). See section 5.7 below on the procedural requirements in relation to proxies.

Although DTR 5.2.1R(h) refers to proxies, it also applies to a firm undertaking investment management which is able to determine how voting rights attached to shares under its control are exercised (e.g. through instructions given directly or indirectly to a custodian or nominee) (DTR 5.2.2G(4)).

Figure 7.2: Impact of the DTR 5 regime on investment managers

> The FCA has published a UKLA Guidance Note in relation to issues regarding aggregation of holdings for management companies and investment firms (see UKLA Guidance Note *Aggregation of managed holdings (UKLA/TN/547.2)*).
>
> There is also a separate UKLA Guidance Note giving further examples in relation to aggregation for asset managers (UKLA Guidance Note *Asset managers (UKLA/TN/549.2)*).
>
> **1. Voting rights that an investment manager will need to consider**
>
> When considering its notification obligations under the DTR 5 regime, an investment manager will need to consider:
>
> - its own direct holding of shares (as principal) (DTR 5.1.2R);
> - the shares it holds as an indirect shareholder on behalf of clients (DTR 5.2.1R(h)) and as a parent undertaking (DTR 5.2.1R(e), but see exemption from aggregation for parent undertakings discussed below);
> - its own indirect holding of shares (as principal) (see other cases in DTR 5.2.1R);
> - its own holding of financial instruments (as principal) which result in an unconditional right or discretion to acquire shares (DTR 5.3);
> - the financial instruments it holds as an indirect holder which result in an unconditional right or discretion to acquire shares (DTR 5.2.3G);
> - its own holding of FISEEs (as principal) (DTR 5.3); and
> - the FISEEs it holds as an indirect holder.
>
> Indirect shareholders are those who are entitled to acquire, dispose of or exercise voting rights of a third party and who may be able to control the manner in which voting rights are exercised. Apart from the cases identified in DTR 5.2.1R(a) to (h), the FCA does not expect any other significant category of indirect shareholder to be identified. An investment manager able to determine the manner in which voting rights attached to shares under its control are exercised will be an indirect holder of those shares for the purpose of the definition of shareholder. These indirect holdings have to be aggregated, but also separately identified, in a notification to the issuer.
>
> To illustrate how the basic notification obligation in relation to indirect holdings of shares arises in the context of investment management and the interaction between the notification obligations of the underlying client and the investment manager, consider the position of a client who appoints a fund manager to act on a discretionary basis:
>
> - The appointment results in a transfer of voting rights if the fund manager is given discretion to vote the shares in the portfolio. The fund manager may have a notifiable interest if the relevant notification thresholds have been reached or exceeded.
> - The client ceases to have a separate notifiable interest. This is so even if the client has retained power to give the fund manager instructions in respect of its assets. In this case, the client will only have a separate notifiable interest when he or she exercises that power.
> - The fund manager needs to make a notification if there are changes in shareholdings.

2. Notification thresholds for investment managers

Under DTR 5, voting rights attached to shares held by investment managers (on behalf of clients), by scheme operators and investment companies with variable capital (ICVCs) are disclosable at the thresholds of 5%, 10% (but not at the percentages in between 5% and 10%) and at every percentage above 10% (DTR 5.1.5R). This is an exemption from the lower notification thresholds in DTR 5.1.2R.

Previously this exemption was only available for EEA investment managers and US investment managers but the FCA has now extended the exemption so that all investment managers may make vote-holder notifications at the EU minimum notification thresholds, regardless of their jurisdiction. Non-EEA investment managers can rely on this exemption provided they are lawfully managing the relevant investments in their home jurisdiction and would, if they were managing those investments in the UK, require permission under Part 4A of FSMA (DTR 5.1.5R).

3. Aggregating principal holdings and holdings which may be disregarded

If an investment manager has holdings on behalf of a client (disregarded holdings) and holdings as principal (other holdings), the FCA has stated that these should be aggregated.

If the total of disregarded holdings and other holdings is equal to or exceeds 5%, then this aggregate holding should be disclosed. If the aggregate holding is already equal to or above 5% and there is a further acquisition of shares, then the disclosure position depends on the nature and size of the acquisition:

- if disregarded holdings are acquired, no further disclosure is required until the aggregate equals or exceeds 10%; and
- if other holdings are acquired, the aggregate total should be disclosed if the acquisition increases total voting rights by 1% or more.

4. Parent undertakings of investment managers: exemption from aggregation

DTR 5.2.2G(1) clarifies that it is always necessary for a parent undertaking of a controlled undertaking to aggregate its holdings with any holding of its subsidiary investment manager or UCITS management company save where an exemption applies. In other words, the voting rights, which are under the control of an investment manager, will need to be aggregated with those of its parent undertaking when looking at the reporting obligations of the parent undertaking unless an exemption applies.

The exemptions for parent undertakings of UCITS management companies and authorised investment managers in relation to the aggregation of interests are set out in DTR 5.4.1R(1) and DTR 5.4.2R(1). Where the relevant exemption applies, the relevant parent undertaking is not required to aggregate its shares in an issuer with that of the UCITS management company or investment manager, as the case may be.

The DTR 5.4.2R(1) exemption for parent undertakings of investment managers is described in greater detail below. While not covered in detail here, the exemption for parent undertakings of UCITS management companies in DTR 5.4.1R(1) is similar and DTR 5.4.9R to 5.4.11R provide similar exemptions from aggregating holdings for non-EEA state undertakings that meet certain criteria.

The parent undertaking of an investment manager may only rely on the exemption in DTR 5.4.2R(1) if the following criteria are satisfied:

- **Must be parent of an authorised investment manager:** The entity applying for the exemption is a parent undertaking (the 'parent') of an investment manager (who must be authorised under MiFID) authorised to provide portfolio management services (the 'subsidiary') (DTR 5.4.2R(1)(a)).
- **Independence of portfolio management services:** The subsidiary may only exercise the voting rights attached to such shares (i) under instructions given in writing or by electronic means, or (ii) if it ensures that individual portfolio management services are conducted independently of any other services by putting in place appropriate mechanisms (DTR 5.4.2R(1)(b)).
- **Independent voting:** The subsidiary must exercise its voting rights independently from the parent (DTR 5.4.2R(1)(c)).
- **Independence criteria:** The 'independence criteria' in DTR 5.4.3R are met i.e. the parent must be able to confirm its independence based on the following criteria: (i) the parent must not interfere by giving direct or indirect instructions or in any other way interfering in the exercise of the voting rights held by the subsidiary; and (ii) the subsidiary must be free to exercise, independently of the parent, the voting rights attached to the assets it manages.

The exemption in DTR 5.4.2R(1) may only be used by a parent undertaking in relation to shares admitted to trading on a regulated market if it has notified the FCA without delay of (i) a list of its investment management subsidiaries concerned, including the relevant competent authority that supervises them (there is no need to list the names of the issuers), to be updated on an ongoing basis and (ii) confirmation that, in each case, the parent undertaking complies with the independence criteria set out above (DTR 5.4.4R). In practice, this means that if an investment manager only invests in shares traded on a prescribed market (such as AIM) and not shares traded on the Official List, in order to benefit from the aggregation exemption, its parent undertaking would not be required to notify the FCA.

DTR 5.4.2R(2) provides that the exemption in DTR 5.4.2R(1) will not apply if the parent or another subsidiary of the parent has:

- invested in holdings managed by the subsidiary;
- the subsidiary has no discretion to exercise the voting rights attached to such holdings; and
- the subsidiary may only exercise such voting rights under direct or indirect instructions from the parent or another subsidiary of the parent.

In addition, the parent undertaking must, in relation to shares admitted to trading on a regulated market, be able to demonstrate to the FCA, on request, that the requirements of independence outlined in DTR 5.4.6R and set out below have been met:

- the parent must be able to demonstrate that the organisational structures of the parent and the subsidiary concerned are such that voting rights are exercised independently of the parent. At a minimum, there must be written policies and procedures reasonably designed to prevent the distribution of information between the parent and the subsidiary in relation to the exercise of voting rights;
- the persons who decide how the voting rights are exercised must act independently; and
- if the parent is a client of the subsidiary, or has a holding in the assets managed by the subsidiary, there must be a clear written mandate for an arm's-length customer relationship between the parent and the subsidiary.

Investment managers and their parent undertakings will need to consider whether to apply for the exemption and, if so, comply with the requirements set out above. This involves notifying the FCA that the exemption applies. In order to demonstrate independence, firms will need to review investment management agreements as well as compliance procedures within the group.

5.4 Voting rights to be notified and aggregated

5.4.1 Notification thresholds

A person may have a notifiable interest if the percentage of voting rights which it holds directly or indirectly as a shareholder (see below for details of the wide definition given to the term shareholder) and/or through its direct or indirect holding of a qualifying financial instrument and/or FISEE, reaches, exceeds or falls below:

- the thresholds of 3%, 4%, 5%, 6%, 7%, 8%, 9% and 10% and each 1% threshold thereafter in the case of a UK incorporated issuer; or
- the thresholds of 5%, 10%, 15%, 20%, 25%, 30%, 50% and 75% in the case of a non-UK issuer (DTR 5.1.2R(1)).

The notification obligation may be triggered as the result of an acquisition, disposal or events changing the breakdown of voting rights on the basis of information disclosed by the issuer in accordance with DTR 5.6.1R and DTR 5.6.1AR (in each case rounding down the subsequent percentage interest to the nearest whole number (DTR 5.1.1R(6)).

An acquisition or disposal of shares is to be regarded for the purposes of DTR 5 as effective when the relevant transaction is executed unless the transaction provides for the settlement to be subject to conditions which are beyond the control of the parties, in which case the acquisition or disposal is to be regarded as effective on the settlement of the transaction (DTR 5.1.1R(4)). For example, this would be the case where the transaction in question was subject to clearance from a regulator. This should be contrasted with the position of conditional FISEEs which can require disclosure prior to fulfilment of the conditions (see section 5.2.3).

The notification obligation may be triggered in circumstances other than on an acquisition or disposal of relevant shares, voting interests or relevant financial instruments by reason of DTR 5.1.2R(2) and may solely be due to a change in circumstances (e.g. where a percentage holding is increased by reason of a company purchasing or redeeming its own shares or reduced by virtue of conversion of convertible preference shares or enfranchisement of shares that were previously non-voting). The UKLA Guidance Note *Changes in holdings* (UKLA/TN/545.2) provides some useful worked examples to show this (see section 5.6.2).

5.4.2 Meaning of 'shareholder'

A shareholder is a natural person or legal entity who directly or indirectly holds shares in their own name (on their own account or on behalf of another person or legal entity) or holds depositary receipts (in which case, they are deemed to be the holder of the underlying shares represented by the depositary receipts) (see FCA Glossary). Under DTR 5.2.1R, a person is an indirect holder of shares for the purpose of the definition of shareholder to the extent that they are entitled to acquire, dispose of or exercise voting rights in any of the situations described in DTR 5.2.1R(a) to (h) (see section 5.3).

The distinction between being a direct and an indirect holder is important as it is made on the standard notification form.

5.4.3 Aggregation of holdings

Shares and financial instruments

Where a person is a direct or indirect holder of voting rights under DTR 5.1.2R(1) or DTR 5.2.1R and/or holds qualifying financial instruments and/or FISEEs under DTR 5.3.1R(1) the person must, in accordance with DTR 5.7.1R, aggregate their holdings to establish whether a disclosure obligation arises. If the total is greater than or equal to 3% in the case of a UK issuer, or 5% in the case of a non-UK issuer, then a disclosure obligation arises. Disclosure must be made by reference to the following three categories for aggregation of voting rights (DTR 5.7.1R):

- the aggregate of all voting rights which the person holds as a direct or indirect shareholder and as the direct or indirect holder of financial instruments falling within DTR 5.3.1R(1);
- the aggregate of all voting rights held as a direct or indirect shareholder (disregarding for this purpose holdings of financial instruments); and
- the aggregate of all voting rights held as a result of direct and indirect holdings of financial instruments falling within DTR 5.3.1R(1).

The FCA gives examples of how to aggregate in the UKLA Guidance Note *Aggregation of holdings (UKLA/TN/551.2)*. The examples include the following:

- A shareholder has a 1.5% direct or indirect holding of shares and a 1% holding of qualifying financial instruments. In this case there is no requirement to disclose as total holdings are below 3%.
- The shareholder increases its holdings of qualifying financial instruments to 1.5% (a 0.5% increase) but the value of direct or indirect holdings of shares remains unchanged. Here the disclosure obligation is of a 3% holding, as combined holdings greater than or equal to 3% must be disclosed.

Although financial instruments falling in DTR 5.3.1R(1)(a) and (b) (qualifying financial instruments and FISEEs respectively) will be aggregated for the purposes of calculating whether a notifiable interest exists, DTR 5.3.5R requires the notification to include a breakdown by type of financial instruments, and to distinguish between physically settled and cash settled financial instruments. The FCA has confirmed that a breakdown by type means not only the disclosure of the different types of financial instruments held (e.g. qualifying financial instrument or FISEE) but also refers to the different types of instrument held within each of those categories.

Group companies

Under DTR 5, a person is required to aggregate their holdings with those of any undertaking controlled by them (DTR 5.2.1R(e) and DTR 5.2.2G(1)). A person will be considered to control an undertaking where:

- they hold the majority of the voting rights;
- they are a shareholder and can appoint or remove the majority of the Board;
- they have the right to exercise dominant influence over the undertaking; or
- they are a member and control alone, pursuant to an agreement with other shareholders or members, a majority of the voting rights in the undertaking.

See the definition of 'controlled undertaking' in the FCA Glossary and the definition of subsidiary undertaking in CA 2006 for more details.

See section 5.6.4 below for details on the notifications that may be made by groups of companies. The ESMA Q&A on the Transparency Directive also provide guidance on disclosures by group companies and give examples of disclosure on a group basis.

5.4.4 Change in composition of holdings

In the situation where the total holding of voting rights, qualifying financial instruments and/or FISEEs remains the same, but the respective size of these components changes, a notification to the issuer may be required (see DTR 5.7.2G).

For example, if an individual held 3% of the voting rights as a direct or indirect shareholder and 6% by way of a financial instrument and then increased their holding as a direct or indirect shareholder to 6% and decreased their holding by way of a financial instrument to 3%, even though the total holding would be 9%, as previously disclosed, the components of shareholdings and financial instruments would cross notifiable thresholds, so a further notification would be required. The standard form distinguishes between the different interests (see section 5.4.3 above).

5.4.5 Calculation of voting rights

Voting rights must be calculated on the basis of all the shares to which voting rights are attached even if the exercise of such rights is suspended (DTR 5.8.7R). The calculation should be made on the basis of all of the issuer's shares with voting rights attached rather than on a class-by-class basis (see the ESMA Q&A on the Transparency Directive).

At the end of each month during which there is an increase or decrease in its share capital, an issuer must announce (i) the total number of voting rights and capital for each class of its shares; and (ii) the total number of voting rights attaching to its shares which are held in treasury (DTR 5.6.1R). An issuer is also required to make an announcement containing the same information as that required by DTR 5.6.1R if during a month there is a 'relevant increase or decrease' in the total number of voting rights. This announcement should be made as soon as possible and in any event no later than the end of the business day following the day on which the increase or decrease occurs (DTR 5.6.1AR). While it is up to issuers to assess whether the effect on the total voting rights is material, the guidance in the rules provides that a change of 1% or more is likely to be material (DTR 5.6.1BG). These announcements are known as 'TVR announcements'. Vote-holders should use the issuer's most recent TVR announcement to calculate whether a threshold has been crossed (disregarding any voting rights attached to any treasury shares held by the issuer) (DTR 5.8.8R).

The level of interest held through a FISEE must be calculated on a delta-adjusted basis. The delta measure effectively represents the number of shares the derivative writer would need to hold to hedge its exposure under the derivative (i.e. the potential voting rights the holder may be taken to have implied access to).

The Major Shareholding Regulation gives further detail on this calculation and this is replicated in DTR 5.3.3CEU. In summary, the number of voting rights attaching to exclusively cash-settled instruments with a linear symmetric pay-off profile is treated as equal to one. Otherwise, the number of voting rights must be calculated on a delta-adjusted basis, using a 'generally accepted standard pricing model', taking account of: interest rates, dividend payments, time to maturity, volatility and the price of the underlying share. Only long positions should be taken into account for the calculation of voting rights and long positions may not be netted with short positions relating to the same issuer.

Requiring disclosure on a delta-adjusted basis means that holders need to monitor delta changes over time to establish whether they have a disclosure obligation. Holders may need to monitor delta changes at the end of each trading day to determine whether a disclosure is required.

5.4.6 Increase or decrease in total number of shares with voting rights attached

As noted above, any increase or decrease in an issuer's total number of shares with voting rights attached may trigger a disclosure obligation even though the person subject to the disclosure obligation has neither increased nor decreased the level of their shareholding or holding of financial instruments. For example, if there is a change in the total number of shares (the denominator in the calculation) which changes the proportion of voting rights a person holds, this may trigger a disclosure obligation. Take the following scenario:

- Listed company XYZ (UK-incorporated and listed on the Official List) has 2,000 shares with voting rights attached in issue. Person A purchases 120 shares in issuer XYZ. Their holding amounts to 6% of total shares; this exceeds the 3% threshold, so a disclosure obligation is triggered.
- Listed company XYZ issues a further 1,000 shares with voting rights attached bringing the total number of shares in issue to 3,000. The company announces the change in the total number of voting rights. Even though there is no change in the number of shares held by person A, the percentage of voting rights held decreases from 6% to 4%, which triggers a disclosure obligation. This obligation arises in spite of the fact that person A has not changed their aggregate holding.

Where a person has not taken any action and the number of shares, qualifying financial instruments and FISEEs they hold remains the same but their proportionate holding of voting interests in the issuer has increased or decreased by a relevant amount (as illustrated above), the relevant denominator that the person should use is as per the issuer's most recent TVR announcement. Such person does not, therefore, have to make any announcement until the next TVR announcement is made by the issuer, even if the person obtained actual knowledge from source (e.g. knew of the new figure arising from a share placing by the issuer).

As noted in section 5.2.3 above, ESMA has confirmed that only financial instruments relating to already issued shares need to be disclosed. Therefore a conditional right issued under a rights issue such as under a Provisional Allotment Letter will not constitute a FISEE and so will not be subject to DTR 5.

5.4.7 End of day netting-off

Persons subject to the disclosure obligation are not required to make a number of different notifications about voting interests in the same issuer on the same day. In establishing whether a notification is required, a person's net (direct or indirect) holding in a share (and of relevant financial instruments) may be assessed by reference to that person's holding at a point in time up to midnight on the day for which the determination is being made (taking account of any acquisitions or disposals in the course of that day) (DTR 5.8.11R).

5.5 Exemptions to general notification requirements

The general notification requirement does not apply in certain situations – these are outlined below. In each and every case it is necessary to look at the detailed wording of the relevant rule to establish whether or not the exemption applies. Listed companies will wish to understand the exemptions that apply, even those for market makers and credit institutions, to understand why certain vote-holders may not be required to make notifications.

5.5.1 Shares acquired for settlement purposes

The general notification obligation does not apply where the relevant shares have been acquired for the sole purpose of clearing and settlement within a settlement cycle not exceeding the period beginning with the transaction and ending at the close of the third trading day following the day of execution of the transaction (irrespective of whether the transaction is conducted on or off exchange) (DTR 5.1.3R(1)).

5.5.2 Custodians and nominees

The general notification obligation does not apply where custodians (or nominees) hold shares in their custodian (or nominee) capacity, provided they can only exercise the voting rights attached to such shares under instructions given to them in writing or by electronic means (DTR 5.1.3R(2)).

5.5.3 Market makers

The general notification obligation does not apply to the acquisition or disposal of shares held by a market maker acting in that capacity provided that the percentage of shares held is less than 10% and the market maker satisfies the conditions and operating requirements set out in DTR 5.1.4R (DTR 5.1.3R(3)). A market maker for these purposes is defined as 'a person who holds himself out on the financial markets on a continuous basis as being willing to deal on own account by buying and selling financial instruments against his proprietary capital at prices defined by him'. Further detail in relation to the definition can be found in DTR 5.1.4R and UKLA Guidance Note *Voting rights that are disregarded for notification purposes* (UKLA/TN/546.2). For details about how the exemption operates in practice, see UKLA Guidance Note *Market makers* (UKLA/TN/548.2).

5.5.4 Shares held by a credit institution or investment firm (the 'trading book exemption')

The general notification obligation does not apply in respect of voting rights attached to shares which are held by a credit institution or investment firm provided that:

- the shares are held within the trading book of the credit institution or investment firm;
- the voting rights attached to such shares do not exceed 5% of the issuer's total voting rights; and
- the voting rights attached to the shares in the trading book are not exercised or otherwise used to intervene in the management of the issuer (DTR 5.1.3R(4)).

5.5.5 Collateral

The general notification obligation does not apply to voting rights attached to shares held by a collateral taker under a collateral transaction which involves the outright transfer of securities, provided that the collateral taker does not declare any intention to exercise (and does not exercise) the voting rights attaching to such shares (DTR 5.1.3R(5)).

5.5.6 Stabilisation

The general notification obligation does not apply to voting rights attached to shares acquired for stabilisation purposes in accordance with Buybacks and Stabilisation Regulation ((EU) 2016/1052), provided the voting rights are not exercised or otherwise used to intervene in the management of the issuer (DTR 5.1.3R(7)). This exemption was introduced by the TD Amending Directive.

5.5.7 Previous exemptions no longer available

It used to be the case that a stock-lending agreement which provided for the outright transfer of securities and which provided the lender with a right to call for re-delivery of the lender's stock (or its equivalent) was not, as regards the lender, to be taken as involving a disposal of any shares which may be the subject of the stock loan. When implementing the TD Amending Directive, the FCA decided to delete the exemption for stock lending and stock borrowing and voting rights disposed of or acquired under these transactions are now treated in the same way as any other acquisition or disposal.

Also as part of the TD Amending Directive implementation, the former exemption for firms acting in a client serving capacity was deleted. However, some transactions which used to fall under this exemption will fall under the credit institution and investment firm exemption referred to above.

5.6 Procedural requirements for vote holder

A person is required, in the event the percentage of its voting rights passes through a relevant threshold, to notify the issuer and, if the notification relates to shares admitted to trading on a regulated market, the FCA. The issuer must then make the information in the notification public, via an RIS announcement.

5.6.1 Timing of notification by a vote holder

A notification under DTR 5 must be effected by the person who is required to notify the interest so as to be received by the issuer as soon as possible and, in any event, no later than:

- in the case of a UK issuer, two trading days; and
- in the case of a non-UK issuer, four trading days

after the date on which the relevant person: (i) becomes aware, or should have become aware, of the notifiable interest; or (ii) is informed of a change in the total voting rights in the issuer (DTR 5.8.3R).

The FSA (as it then was) has previously informally advised that the term 'effected' used in DTR 5.8.3R means that the issuer must have received the notification by that time.

As described in section 5.4.1 above, an acquisition or disposal of shares is regarded as having taken place when the relevant transaction is executed, unless settlement is subject to conditions beyond the control of the parties, in which case the effective date is settlement (DTR 5.1.1R(4)).

Where the relevant person is party to a transaction or has instructed a transaction to take place, they will be deemed to have learnt of the transaction no later than two trading days following the transaction. If a transaction is conditional on approval by public authorities or future uncertain events outside the control of the parties, the relevant person is deemed to have learnt of the transaction only when the relevant approvals are obtained or the event happens (DTR 5.8.3R and UKLA Guidance Note *Shareholder obligations (UKLA/TN/543.2)*). This should be contrasted with the position of conditional FISEEs which can require disclosure prior to fulfilment of the conditions (see section 5.2.3).

5.6.2 The notification form for notification to the issuer

Notification (in relation to shares admitted to trading on a regulated market only) must be made to the issuer using the standard form provided by the FCA for this purpose (Form TR-1), which is available on the FCA website (DTR 5.8.10R). The notification to the issuer should not include the Annex to Form TR-1 (which is sent to the FCA only). The method of delivery (e.g. e-mail, post or fax) of a notification to the issuer is not prescribed.

For issuers listed on a prescribed market (such as AIM) there is no standard form for the notification although, in practice, Form TR-1 is often used.

In October 2015, ESMA published a new standard form for the notification of major holdings. The FCA introduced a new Form TR-1 on 30 June 2017, which is based on the ESMA standard form with some minor amendments.

5.6.3 Filing of information with the FCA

A person making a notification to an issuer must, if the notification relates to shares admitted to trading on a regulated market in the UK, at the same time electronically file a copy of the notification with the FCA (DTR 5.9.1R(1) and DTR 5.10.1R). This obligation does not, therefore, apply in respect of issuers whose shares are admitted to trading on AIM. The information filed must include the contact details of the person making the notification in the Annex to Form TR-1 (DTR 5.9.1R(2)).

5.6.4 Person who must make the notification and delegation of notification obligation

In order to determine who is responsible for making a notification under DTR 5, it is necessary to look at who is the direct or indirect holder of the shares, qualifying financial instruments or FISEEs, as the case may be.

In relation to indirect shareholdings, the obligation to notify rests with the relevant direct or indirect shareholder or both if the proportion of voting rights held by each party reaches, exceeds or falls below an applicable threshold (DTR 5.8.4R(1)).

When the duty to make a notification under DTR 5 lies with more than one person, a notification may be made by means of a single common notification, but this does not release any of those persons from their responsibilities in relation to the notification (and so each person will take responsibility for the notification) (DTR 5.8.4R(4)).

In the case of companies, an undertaking is not required to make a notification if instead a notification is made by its parent undertaking (DTR 5.8.6R).

A person who is required to make a notification may appoint another person to make the notification on their behalf (DTR 5.2.5R(1)). Similarly, where two or more persons are required to make a notification, such persons may arrange for a single notification to be made (DTR 5.2.5R(2)). However in each case this will not affect the responsibility of the person who is subject to the notification requirement and such person will therefore remain responsible for the announcement, notwithstanding it may be made by another person.

5.6.5 Contents requirements for disclosure of interests in shares

The notification given pursuant to DTR 5.1.2R must include the following information (DTR 5.8.1R):

- the resulting situation in terms of voting rights;
- the chain of controlled undertakings through which voting rights are effectively held (if applicable);
- the date on which the threshold was reached or crossed; and
- the identity of the shareholder (even if that shareholder is not entitled to exercise voting rights under the conditions laid down in DTR 5.2.1R) and of the person entitled to exercise the voting rights on behalf of that shareholder.

5.6.6 Contents requirements for disclosure of interests in financial instruments

A notification given in relation to qualifying financial instruments or FISEEs must include the following information (DTR 5.8.2R(1)):

- the resulting situation in terms of voting rights;
- if applicable, the chain of controlled undertakings through which financial instruments are effectively held;

- the date on which the threshold was reached or crossed;
- for instruments with an exercise period, an indication of the date or time period where shares will or can be acquired, if applicable;
- date of maturity or expiration of the instrument;
- the identity of the holder; and
- the name of the underlying issuer.

If the financial instrument relates to more than one underlying share, a separate notification must be made to each issuer of the underlying shares (DTR 5.8.2R(3)).

5.7 Procedural requirements in relation to proxies

5.7.1 Notification procedure for shareholders giving a proxy

If a shareholder gives its proxy in relation to one shareholder meeting, notification may be made by the shareholder under DTR 5.2.1R(h) by means of a single notification when the proxy is given, provided that it is made clear in the notification what the resulting situation in terms of voting rights will be when the proxy may no longer exercise the voting rights at its discretion (DTR 5.8.4R(2)). This will avoid the need to make a separate DTR 5 announcement upon expiry of the proxy.

5.7.2 Notification procedure for proxy holders

If a proxy holder receives one or several proxies in relation to one shareholder meeting, notification may be made by the proxy holder by means of a single notification on or after the deadline for receiving proxies, provided that it is made clear in the notification what the resulting situation in terms of voting rights will be when the proxy may no longer exercise the voting rights at its discretion (DTR 5.8.4R(3)). The proxy holder does not need to include the names of all of the people who have made them a proxy. They need only provide details of any individual holdings they have received that in themselves amount to a notifiable disposal of voting rights by the relevant shareholder (see UKLA Guidance Note *Shareholder obligations (UKLA/TN/543.2)*). This provision will apply to the chairman of a meeting.

5.7.3 Joint notifications for proxy holders and shareholders giving a proxy

There will be circumstances when both the relevant shareholder and the proxy holder are required to make a notification. However, pursuant to DTR 5.8.5G, provided certain criteria are satisfied, only one notification will need to be made. For example, if a direct holder of shares has a notifiable holding of voting rights and gives a proxy in respect of those rights (such that the proxy holder has discretion as to how the votes are cast) then, for the purposes of DTR 5.1.2R, there has been a disposal of such rights; this gives rise to a notification obligation. In addition, the proxy holder may also have an obligation by virtue of their holdings under DTR 5.2.1R. Separate notifications will not, however, be necessary pursuant to the guidance in DTR 5.8.5G, provided that a single notification (whether made by the direct holder of the shares or the proxy holder) makes it clear what the situation will be when the proxy has expired.

5.8 Procedural requirements for issuers

5.8.1 Total voting rights disclosures

At the end of each calendar month in which an increase or decrease has occurred in the total number of voting rights and capital which it has in issue, an issuer must disclose to the public:

- the total number of voting rights and capital for each class of shares which it has in issue and which are admitted to trading on a regulated or prescribed market (DTR 5.6.1R(1) and DTR 5.6.2G); and
- the total number of voting rights attaching to shares of the issuer which are held by it in treasury (DTR 5.6.1R(2)).

The FCA has said vote holders should rely on the figures in these TVR announcements when working out whether or not they need to make a notification under DTR 5.

In respect of an issuer's initial TVR announcement following an IPO, it would not, on a strict interpretation of DTR 5, need to be made until the end of the month in which admission occurred. However, as vote holders rely on the figures in a TVR announcement to determine their notification obligations under DTR 5, an issuer might wish to make its TVR announcement on admission to clarify the situation for its vote holders. In practice, the approach adopted by issuers on this point varies; some issuers have made an initial TVR announcement on admission, whereas others have decided to wait until the end of the month.

If an issuer undertakes a transaction which results in a material change in the issuer's total voting rights it must make a new TVR announcement as soon as possible and in any event by the end of the business day following the day on which the increase or decrease occurs (DTR 5.6.1AR(1)). It is for issuers to assess whether the effect on the total number of voting rights is material, but a change of 1% or more is likely to be material (DTR 5.6.1BG). This means that following an issue of shares (such as a rights issue or open offer) or a reduction in an issuer's share capital (e.g. following a share buy-back) an issuer will need to immediately consider whether a TVR announcement needs to be made.

The FCA has confirmed that where a TVR announcement is made under DTR 5.6.1AR, the issuer will also have to make a DTR 5.6.1R announcement at the end of the relevant calendar month even where there are no further changes in the total voting rights during that calendar month (see also section 5.4.5 above).

5.8.2 Announcement of receipt of vote holder notification

UK issuers with shares admitted to trading on a regulated market must make public all of the information contained in a notification made to them under DTR 5 as soon as possible and in any event by the end of the trading day following its receipt (DTR 5.8.12R(1)).

For all other issuers (i.e. issuers admitted to trading on prescribed markets such as AIM, and non-UK issuers) the notification must be made as soon as possible and in any event by not later than the end of the third trading day following receipt of the notification (DTR 5.8.12R(2)). However, a non-EEA issuer is exempt from this requirement if: (i) the law of the relevant non-EEA state contains equivalent requirements; or (ii) the issuer complies with requirements of the law of a non-EEA state that the FCA considers as equivalent (DTR 5.8.12R(3)). See section 5.8.5 below for further information on which countries the FCA considers to have equivalent regimes.

AIM companies must also comply with Rule 17 of the AIM Rules for Companies, which requires disclosure of changes to significant shareholders. The Guidance Notes to Rule 17 contain further information to address the interaction between DTR 5 and AIM Rule 17.

Under DTR 1A.3.2R, an issuer must take all reasonable care to ensure that any information it notifies to an RIS is not misleading, false or deceptive and does not omit anything likely to affect the import of the information. Previously there had been some confusion as to the extent to which an issuer was obliged to check the information set out in a notification it had received before forwarding it to the market. DTR 1A.3.2AR clarifies that the duty imposed by DTR 1A.3.2R does not apply to disclosures made by issuers under DTR 5.8.12R.

The Form TR-1, which is used to notify issuers, was mandated by the EU requirements. There is, however, no set format for issuers to submit their notifications to an RIS. The options available to an issuer upon receipt of a DTR5 notification include:

- forwarding the Form TR-1 to an RIS (this should not include the Annex);
- forwarding the information on an electronic version of the Form TR-1 (without the Annex), possibly obtained from their chosen RIS provider; or
- making the announcement in a free-text format.

Provided the relevant RIS service can process a Form TR-1, it will often be easier for an issuer to forward it rather than draft a form of disclosure.

5.8.3 Acquisition or disposal of own shares by an issuer

If an issuer acquires or disposes of its own shares, either itself or through another person acting in their own name but on the issuer's behalf and, as a result, the number of shares held by the issuer in treasury reaches, exceeds or falls below the thresholds of 5% or 10% of the voting rights, the issuer must make public the percentage of voting rights attributable to those shares as soon as possible, and in any event within four trading days following such acquisition or disposal (DTR 5.5.1R).

UKLA Guidance Note *Issuer's obligations (UKLA/TN/542.2)* clarifies that the obligation to notify only applies if the issuer has treasury shares, and that the 5% and 10% thresholds relate to the total number of shares held in treasury and not whether the transaction itself is greater than 5% or 10% of the total voting rights. Where shares are bought back and cancelled, there is no disclosure obligation on the issuer under DTR 5, unless the cancellation has the (indirect) effect of altering the proportion of shares held in treasury such that the proportion reaches, exceeds or falls below the 5% or 10% thresholds.

This notification obligation is separate from the requirement to announce the number of treasury shares that the issuer has as part of the total voting rights announcement (see section 5.8.1 above) and also from the requirement for an issuer with a premium listing to issue an RIS notification following a purchase of own shares in accordance with LR 12.4.6R.

5.8.4 Disclosures in annual report

UK premium listed issuers are required pursuant to LR 9.8.6R(2) to include a statement in their annual financial report in relation to the interests disclosed to them in accordance with DTR 5. The statement must set out:

- all interests disclosed to the issuer as at the end of the financial period under review (i.e. the net position of each significant vote holder); and
- all interests disclosed to the issuer from the end of the financial period under review to a date not more than one month before the date of the AGM notice. Where no interests are disclosed to the issuer pursuant to DTR 5 in this period, the statement must note this.

5.8.5 Equivalence – when compliance with overseas laws is deemed sufficient

There is an exemption to the disclosure requirements of DTR 5 for issuers incorporated in the USA, Japan, Israel and Switzerland. This exemption applies as the laws governing disclosure of major shareholdings in these countries are considered equivalent to the requirements of the TD (see DTR 5.11.4R). However, it should be noted that this exemption applies to the issuer only and vote holders themselves are not exempt and must still notify the issuer of their interests in the same way as they do for other companies subject to DTR 5. The UKLA has published a Guidance Note on third country equivalent obligations (see the UKLA Guidance Note *Third country equivalent obligations (UKLA/TN/544.2)*). The list of third countries which the FCA considers equivalent is available on the UKLA section of the FCA website.

5.9 Enforcement and penalties for breach

The FCA may censure or impose a fine of such amount as it considers appropriate on an issuer or a person (i.e. the holder of the interest) that has contravened any provision of DTR 5 (FSMA ss 91(1B) and 91(3)). If the FCA considers a person who was at the material time a director of the issuer was 'knowingly concerned in the contravention' of DTR 5, it may also impose a penalty on them (FSMA s. 91(2)).

In August 2011 Sir Ken Morrison, former chairman of Wm Morrison Supermarkets plc, was fined £210,000 for breaches of DTR 5.1.2R relating to his failure to notify the company about a series of four separate disposals which reduced his holdings from over 6% to 0.9% between March 2008 and March 2011.

As part of the implementation of the TD Amending Directive, changes were made to FSMA to give the FCA power to apply to court for an order to suspend the voting rights of shares held by a vote holder for a serious breach of DTR 5 (FSMA s. 89NA). In deciding whether the contravention is serious enough to make an order suspending voting rights, the court may take into account (FSMA s. 89NA(4)):

- whether the contravention was deliberate or repeated;
- the time taken for the contravention to be remedied;
- whether the vote holder ignored warnings or requests for compliance from the FCA;
- the size of the holding to which the contravention relates;
- the impact of the contravention on the UK financial system; and
- the effect of the contravention on any company merger or takeover.

A voting rights suspension order under FSMA can only be made in relation to shares that are traded on a regulated market (FSMA s. 89NA(1)). Therefore such orders will not apply to shares in AIM companies.

5.10 Summary of notification obligations

Vote holder obligations

	UK issuer (shares admitted to a regulated or a prescribed market)	Non-UK issuer (shares admitted to a regulated market)
Notification threshold	3% and each whole percentage point above 3% (DTR 5.1.2R)	5%, 10%, 15%, 20%, 25%, 30%, 50% and 75% (DTR 5.1.2R)
Notification made to	Issuer and (if a regulated market issuer) the FCA (DTR 5.9.1R)	Issuer and FCA (DTR 5.9.1R)
Timing for notification	Within two trading days (DTR 5.8.3R)	Within four trading days (DTR 5.8.3R)

Issuer obligations

	UK issuer (shares admitted to a regulated market)	UK issuer (shares admitted to a prescribed market)	Non-UK issuer (shares admitted to a regulated market)
Total voting rights	Notify at the end of each calendar month the total number of voting rights and capital in respect of each class of shares if there was an increase or decrease during the month (DTR 5.6.1R) and as soon as possible and in any event no later than the end of the business day following the day on which there is a material increase or decrease following completion of a transaction (DTR 5.6.1AR)		
Notifications from vote holders	Notify market of notifications received by end of next trading day (DTR 5.8.12R(1))	Notify market of notifications received by end of third trading day (DTR 5.8.12R(2))	
Acquisition or disposal of own shares	Disclose within four trading days any acquisitions or disposals out of treasury of own shares that cross 5% or 10% thresholds (DTR 5.5.1R)		

CHAPTER 8

Market announcements and shareholder communications

OVERVIEW

- A listed company is required to make various announcements under the Listing, Prospectus and Transparency Rules and MAR in order to keep its shareholders and the market well informed.

- The LPDT Rules and MAR protect shareholders and ensure proper disclosure to the markets through prescribing the form and content of information required to be made available and the manner in which it must be communicated and, for premium listed companies, by giving shareholders certain consent or approval rights.

- Listing Rule 9 requires premium listed companies to make announcements to the market about certain matters, for example, on the appointment and removal of directors. DTR 6 contains additional announcement obligations that apply to both standard and premium listed companies.

- DTR 6 also contains various provisions aimed at ensuring shareholders receive adequate information in relation to the exercise of their rights, particularly at company meetings.

- Listing Rule 9 requires premium listed companies to obtain shareholder approval for the adoption of certain employee share schemes and LTIPs.

- A listed company is required to disseminate 'regulated information' to shareholders through RIS announcements.

- Certain information sent to shareholders will be classified as a 'circular'. A circular will need to comply with the requirements of Listing Rule 13 and may need to be approved by the FCA.

- Circulars and other documents sent to shareholders are required to be filed with the National Storage Mechanism.

- DTR 6 and CA 2006 provide for electronic communication with shareholders, potential investors and the public.

- Under section 90A of the FSMA, a listed company can be held liable to investors for any misleading or inaccurate information released through an RIS.

MARKET ANNOUNCEMENTS AND SHAREHOLDER COMMUNICATIONS

- The provisions of Listing Rules 9 and 13, DTR 6 and section 90A of the FSMA should be considered alongside the provisions of Article 17 of MAR on the control and disclosure of inside information and the offence of market abuse under Articles 14 and 15 of MAR which are discussed in more detail in Chapter 5.

1. Matters required to be announced to the market

In addition to the requirement to disclose inside information to the market, discussed in Chapter 5, Listing Rule 9 and DTR 6 contain a number of other provisions aimed at ensuring that the market remains informed about certain corporate changes.

The key announcements a premium listed company is required to make to the market are listed in Figure 8.1.

For premium listed companies, the key provisions that require the disclosure of specific information to shareholders and the market concern:

- the appointment and removal of directors and certain changes in their role or details (LR 9.6.11R to LR 9.6.15G);
- changes to a company's name or accounting reference date (LR 9.6.19R and LR 9.6.20R); and
- passing of resolutions by the company other than resolutions concerning ordinary business passed at an annual general meeting (LR 9.6.18R).

The requirements of Listing Rule 9 and the DTRs in relation to announcements of changes in a premium listed company's share capital are considered in Chapter 10.

In addition, for both standard and premium listed companies, DTR 6 requires certain matters to be disclosed to the market including proposed changes to a company's constitution.

Figure 8.1: Key announcement obligations for premium listed companies under the Listing Rules and Disclosure and Transparency Rules

Key announcement obligations for premium listed companies under the Market Abuse Regulation, Listing Rules and Disclosure and Transparency Rules	
Accounting reference date change	LR 9.6.20R
Circulars, notices, reports, resolutions etc announcement when documents lodged at the NSM	LR 9.6.3R
Dealings in shares etc ■ by major shareholders ■ by PDMRs ■ by the company	DTR 5.8.12R MAR Article 19(1) DTR 5.5.1R

Key announcement obligations for premium listed companies under the Market Abuse Regulation, Listing Rules and Disclosure and Transparency Rules	
Directors Board changes and changes in directors' details	LR 9.6.11R to LR 9.6.15G
Dividends	LR 9.7A.2R
Inside information disclosure of	MAR Article 17(1)
Listing ■ intended cancellation ■ withdrawal of request for cancellation ■ transfer between listing segment/category	LR 5.2.5R and LR 5.2.7R LR 5.3.7G LR 5.4A.4R and LR 5.4A.5R
Lock up arrangements ■ disposal pursuant to an exemption ■ variation	LR 9.6.16R LR 9.6.17R
Name change	LR 9.6.19R
Periodic financial information ■ preliminary annual results ■ annual results ■ half-yearly results	LR 9.7A.1R and DTR 6.3.5R DTR 4.1.3R and DTR 6.3.5R DTR 4.2.2R and DTR 6.3.5R
Proxies ■ details of proxies held by the chairman	DTR 5.8.4(3)R
Purchase of own equity shares ■ Board decision to seek authority to buy back ■ result of meeting ■ notification of purchases	LR 12.4.4R LR 12.4.5R LR 12.4.6R
Purchase of own securities other than equity shares	LR 12.5.1R and LR 12.5.2R
Secondary capital raisings ■ principal terms and results of a rights issue ■ principal terms of open offer or placing	LR 9.5.5R LR 9.5.8BR and LR 9.5.10R
Share capital and voting rights ■ change in structure, redemptions or results of a new issue ■ change in class rights ■ total voting rights	LR 9.6.4R and DTR 6.1.13R DTR 6.1.9R DTR 5.6.1R and DTR 5.6.1AR

Key announcement obligations for premium listed companies under the Market Abuse Regulation, Listing Rules and Disclosure and Transparency Rules	
Shareholder resolutions	LR 9.6.18R
Significant and related party transactions ■ Class 2 ■ Class 1 ■ reverse takeover ■ related party	 LR 10.4.1R and LR 10.4.2R LR 10.5.1R and LR 10.8.4G LR 5.6.3R and LR 10.5.1R LR 11.1.7R and LR 11.1.10R
Treasury shares ■ bonus issue to company ■ purchase of shares into treasury ■ sale, transfer or cancellation	 LR 12.6.3R DTR 5.5.1R LR 12.6.4R and DTR 5.5.1R

1.1 Disclosure of information relating to directors

Listing Rule 9 imposes various obligations on a premium listed company to disclose information relating to its directors.

A listed company must notify an RIS without delay, and by no later than the end of the following business day, after it has made any decision about the appointment of a new director (stating whether the position is executive, non-executive or the chairmanship and the nature of any specific function or responsibility of the position) or the resignation, removal or retirement of a director or any important change in the role, functions or responsibilities of a director (LR 9.6.11R). The notification must state the effective date of the change if it is not with immediate effect. If the effective date is not known or has not yet been determined, the notification must state this fact and the company must notify an RIS of the effective date once decided (LR 9.6.12R).

A premium listed company must also notify an RIS of certain details relating to any new director. This can be done at the same time as the announcement of his appointment and must be done, in any event, within five business days of the decision being taken. The details required to be disclosed are details of: any directorships held in any other publicly quoted company at any time in the previous five years; any unspent convictions for indictable offences; links to companies or partnerships that have gone into liquidation, administration or receivership where the director was, at the time or in the preceding 12 months, an executive director or partner; and details of any public criticisms by any statutory or regulatory body or disqualification from acting as a director or manager (LR 9.6.13R). If there is no information to be disclosed pursuant to this rule, the notification must state that fact (LR 9.6.15G).

A premium listed company must also notify an RIS as soon as possible of any changes in this information in relation to existing directors, including the appointment of the relevant director to the Board of other publicly quoted companies (LR 9.6.14R).

A premium listed company is also subject to the disclosure requirements set out in LR 9.8 requiring certain information to be included in its Annual Financial Report, including details of the directors' interests in shares and of the unexpired term of any director's service contract where the director is being proposed for election or re-election. The CA 2006 and Corporate Governance Code also contain provisions on disclosure of directors' remuneration and directors' service contracts (see Chapter 6 for more information).

1.2 Information about general meetings

A premium listed company is required, as soon as possible after a general meeting has been held, to notify an RIS of all resolutions passed (other than resolutions concerning ordinary business at an AGM) (LR 9.6.18R).

DTR 6 contains detailed requirements about the information to be given to shareholders of a listed company ahead of a meeting. Listing Rule 9 also prescribes certain requirements for proxy forms for premium listed companies. These requirements are discussed in section 2.4 below.

1.3 Changes to a company's name and accounting reference date

When a premium listed company changes its name, it must notify an RIS as soon as possible of the change (stating the date it takes effect), inform the FCA in writing and, if it is a UK incorporated listed company, send the FCA a copy of the revised certificate of incorporation (LR 9.6.19R).

On a change of accounting reference date, a listed company must notify an RIS as soon as possible of the change and the new accounting reference date (LR 9.6.20R).

1.4 Information about changes in share rights

Both premium and standard listed companies must disclose to the public without delay any changes to the rights attaching to any of the various classes of its shares, including rights attaching to its derivative securities, and to the rights attaching to securities other than shares admitted to trading on a regulated market (DTR 6.1.9R and DTR 6.1.10R).

1.5 Information about dividends and issues of new shares

Both premium and standard listed companies must publish notices or send circulars about the payment of dividends and any issue of new shares. Where the notice relates to the issue of new shares it must include information on allotment, subscription, cancellation or conversion of such shares (DTR 6.1.13R).

A premium listed company is subject to an additional requirement to notify an RIS as soon as possible after the Board has approved any decision to pay any dividend or distribution giving details of the exact net amount payable per share, the payment date, the record date (where applicable) and any foreign income dividend election, together with any income tax treated as paid at the lower rate and not repayable (LR 9.7A2R). This requirement is discussed in section 2.2 of Chapter 6.

On an issue of new shares, a premium listed company will also need to comply with the requirements in Listing Rule 9, which are discussed in Chapter 10.

1.6 Announcements about information filed at the NSM

A premium listed company must announce via an RIS when it files a document at the NSM unless the full text of the document is released via an RIS (LR 9.6.3R). The NSM is discussed in more detail in section 4.3.

1.7 Notifications regarding lock-up arrangements

If a premium listed company has disclosed any lock-up arrangements in accordance with the PD Regulation (e.g. in a prospectus), it must notify an RIS as soon as possible if equity shares are disposed of pursuant to an exemption under those lock-up arrangements (LR 9.6.16R).

If any lock-up arrangements which have been disclosed, whether in accordance with the PD Regulation or in any announcement, are subsequently varied, a premium listed company must announce details of those changes via an RIS (LR 9.6.17R).

2. Ensuring shareholders receive adequate information about their rights

DTR 6 contains a number of provisions aimed at ensuring that security holders in premium and standard listed companies receive adequate information, in particular about meetings and how to exercise their rights at them, including how to use a proxy form. The key provisions concern:

- equal treatment of shareholders (DTR 6.1.3R);
- electronic communication (DTR 6.1.8R);

- appointing a financial agent (DTR 6.1.6R); and
- information about meetings and exercise of rights by holders of securities or their proxies (DTR 6.1.4R and DTR 6.1.5R).

For premium listed companies, Listing Rule 9 contains additional requirements in relation to proxy forms (see section 2.4.3 below).

2.1 Equality of treatment

DTR 6.1.3R(1) imposes an obligation on a listed company to ensure equality of treatment for holders of shares who are in the same position. Companies may not, therefore, treat shareholders in the same class differently. This can pose an issue where a listed company wishes to exclude shareholders from certain non-EEA jurisdictions from an offer or from receiving a circular.

The FCA recognises that there may be securities laws issues if certain documents are sent to shareholders in particular jurisdictions. It will generally expect all shareholders within the EEA to be treated equally (a specific dispensation from the FCA will be required if a company does not wish to send circulars to shareholders within the EEA). For shareholders outside the EEA, the FCA has said that listed companies must be able to justify any reason for non-circulation. If there is any doubt, the FCA should be consulted in advance.

2.2 Electronic communications

DTR 6 and CA 2006 are intended to make it easier for listed companies to communicate with their shareholders electronically, while accommodating the rights of shareholders to receive information in hard copy if they so wish. The use of electronic communications by a listed company must be approved by the shareholders of the company in general meeting (DTR 6.1.8R(1)). The requirement to have individual shareholder consent to electronic communications in DTR 6.1.8R(4) is, however, disapplied in the case of UK incorporated listed companies because they are subject to the separate CA 2006 regime for approval of electronic communications.

The use of electronic communications must be available to all security holders irrespective of where they are located (DTR 6.1.8R) but the FCA recognises that electronic communication with shareholders will not be possible in some jurisdictions because of legal restrictions. Where such restrictions exist, previous informal guidance on the rule issued by the then FSA said that it would not regard the principle of equality of shareholder treatment as being breached merely if the company does not offer to communicate by electronic means with such shareholders (see List! Issue No. 14 updated, paragraph 4.5, and p. 34 of the FSA's 2010 Technical Note: *Disclosure and Transparency Rules*). This commentary has not, however, been repeated in the relevant UKLA Guidance Notes and there is therefore no formal guidance on the point.

The provisions of DTR 6 and CA 2006 concerning a listed company's ability to communicate electronically with security holders and proxies are discussed in more detail in section 5.

2.3 Financial agent

A listed company must appoint a registrar or financial institution through which security holders may exercise their financial rights (DTR 6.1.6 R).

2.4 General meetings

2.4.1 Information to be given to shareholders

A listed company must provide shareholders with information on the place, time and agenda of meetings, the total number of shares and voting rights, and the rights of holders to participate in such meetings (DTR 6.1.12R).

A premium listed company will also be required to comply with the requirements of Listing Rule 13, and in particular LR 13.8.8R, when sending a circular to shareholders convening the meeting. The requirements for circulars are discussed in more detail in section 4.2.

As discussed in section 1.2, a premium listed company must also notify an RIS of the outcome of any meeting.

2.4.2 Exercise of rights by holders and proxies

Listed companies must ensure that all the facilities and information are in place to enable holders of securities to exercise their rights. A listed company is also required to ensure that the integrity of such data and information is preserved (DTR 6.1.4R). Securities holders must not be prevented from exercising their rights by proxy if they so choose. The proxy form must be made available either with the notice of the meeting or after the announcement of the meeting is made (DTR 6.1.5R).

2.4.3 Format of proxy forms

A premium listed company must ensure that, in addition to meeting CA 2006 obligations, a proxy form provides for at least three-way voting on all resolutions (other than purely procedural resolutions) and states that if it is returned without a direction as to how the proxy should vote, the proxy will exercise discretion as to how and whether to vote (LR 9.3.6R).

Where resolutions to be proposed include the re-election of six or more retiring directors, the proxy form may give shareholders the opportunity to vote for or against the re-election of the retiring directors as a whole, but must also allow votes to be cast for or against the re-election of each director individually (LR 9.3.7R).

3. Adoption of employee share schemes

A premium listed company must ensure that certain employee share option schemes and LTIPs are approved by an ordinary resolution of shareholders before they are adopted (LR 9.4.1R(2)).

Broadly, this requirement applies to:

- an employee share scheme that involves or may involve the issue of new shares or the transfer of treasury shares (LR 9.4.1R(1)(a)); and
- a long-term incentive plan in which one or more of the directors of the listed company is eligible to participate (LR 9.4.1R(1)(b)).

The requirement to seek shareholder approval does not apply where an LTIP is offered on similar terms to all, or substantially all, of the company's or group's employees (LR 9.4.2R(1)) or to a specific arrangement with one director of the listed company that is designed to facilitate, in unusual circumstances, such director's recruitment or retention (LR 9.4.2R(2)).

In relation to a specific one-off arrangement, the listed company must make the disclosures required by LR 9.4.3R in the first Annual Financial Report published after the date upon which the individual becomes eligible to participate in the arrangements. This must include the name of participant, relevant dates, why the circumstances were unusual, the conditions to be satisfied and the maximum award, as well as the information required by LR 13.8.11R in respect of share schemes and LTIPs for which shareholder approval is required. The FCA says that it expects the exemption for a long-term incentive scheme which is set up to retain/recruit a director to be rarely used in practice (UKLA Guidance Note *Long-term incentive schemes* (*UKLA/TN/208.1*)).

Discounted option arrangements must also first be approved by shareholders under LR 9.4.4R unless they are offered on similar terms to all or substantially all employees (LR 9.4.5R).

4. Making information available to shareholders

Information can be given to shareholders by listed companies in a number of different ways including via an RIS announcement or by sending a circular to shareholders.

4.1 Dissemination of regulated information

4.1.1 Requirement to disclose regulated information

A listed company must disclose 'regulated information' (i.e. information that a listed company is required to disclose under the Listing Rules, the DTRs, the TD and/or MAR) through an RIS (DTR 6.3.3R).

Regulated information includes:

- inside information (see Chapter 5);
- other announcements required to be made to the market (discussed in section 1 above);
- annual report and accounts and half-yearly financial reports (see Chapter 6);
- circulars;
- notice of AGMs and general meetings; and
- proxy forms.

DTR 6.3.5R requires regulated information to be disseminated in unedited full text. On the face of it, this means that a listed company must, for example, disseminate a Class 1 circular in unedited full text via an RIS. The FCA has, however, indicated that, where a listed company uploads a circular onto the NSM in compliance with LR 9.6.1R and then announces this under LR 9.6.3R, it accepts that there is generally no need for the company to communicate the circular in unedited full text via an RIS under DTR 6.3.5R.

This is not the case, however, for annual reports, in respect of which the FCA still requires certain information to be released in unedited full text in compliance with DTR 6.3.5R; only the information required for a half-yearly results announcement needs to be included in full text in the RIS announcement (not the entire annual report). See Chapter 6 for a more detailed description of the publication requirements for financial information under DTR 4.

Disclosure must be synchronised as closely as possible in all jurisdictions where it has financial instruments admitted to trading on a regulated market (DTR 6.3.4R).

A listed company is also required to post and maintain on its website all inside information which it has disclosed publicly for a period of at least 5 years (Article 17(1) of MAR)

DTR 6.2.2R requires a listed company which discloses regulated information also to file that information with the FCA at the same time. DTR 6.2.3G makes it clear that disseminating the information via an RIS will satisfy that obligation.

4.1.2 Making an RIS announcement

The requirement for a listed company to disseminate regulated information in a manner ensuring that it is capable of being disseminated to as wide a public as possible and disclosed as simultaneously as possible in the home member state and in other EEA states (DTR 6.3.4R) is satisfied by a listed company disclosing regulated information to an RIS. The RIS will then disseminate that information to the market.

A number of RISs have been approved by the FCA and DTR 8 contains the regulatory regime for the Primary Information Providers (PIPs) who provide RIS services. A company is free to choose the RIS that it uses for the dissemination of information to the market. A list of RISs can be found on the FCA website. Among others, these include the RNS provided by the London Stock Exchange. An RIS will charge the company for its services.

The information must be communicated to an RIS in a manner which makes it clear it is regulated information and identifies the listed company concerned, the subject matter and the time and date of the communication (DTR 6.3.7R). Headline categories for RIS announcements are in the Appendix of the FCA's Criteria for Regulated Information Services, which can be found on the FCA's website.

Under DTR 6.3.8R, a listed company must be able to tell the FCA (if asked):

- who communicated the information to the RIS;
- the security validation details;
- the time and date on which the regulated information was communicated to the RIS;
- the medium in which it was communicated; and
- details of any embargo placed on it.

Any announcement made using an RIS will automatically be uploaded on to the NSM. A listed company is not required to file its RIS announcements with the NSM.

A Delegated EU Regulation in connection with the Transparency Directive requires ESMA to set up and operate a web portal to be called the European Electronic Access Point (EEAP), which will provide access to all published regulatory information made accessible via each member state's storage service. In the UK all regulated information is held on the National Storage Mechanism (NSM).

To assist in the functionality of the EEAP, issuers are required to have a legal entity identifier (LEI) number. The Regulation also requires each type of regulatory information to be classified into categories (e.g. annual financial and audit reports, inside information, major shareholding notifications, total voting rights). These requirements came into force with effect from 1 January 2017. Following a consultation process, the FCA has published amendments to the Transparency Rules to reflect the Delegated Regulation. The FCA will add new DTRs 6.2.2A and 6.2.2B to the Transparency Rules. These will require an issuer to notify the FCA of its LEI and the relevant classification(s) when it files regulatory information with the FCA pursuant to DTR 6.2.2R. The new rules will come into force on 1 October 2017. However, in its consultation paper, the FCA encouraged issuers to provide LEIs and to classify regulatory information from 1 January 2017.

4.1.3 'Out-of-hours' announcements

The fact that an RIS is not open for business is not, in itself, sufficient grounds for delaying the disclosure of inside information (DTR 1.3.7G). When an RIS is not open for business, issuers may satisfy their obligation to make inside information public as

MARKET ANNOUNCEMENTS AND SHAREHOLDER COMMUNICATIONS **359**

soon as possible under Article 17 of MAR by using the out of hours method set out in DTR 1.3.6G. Under DTR 1.3.6G, if a listed company is required to notify information to an RIS at a time when it is not open for business, it may distribute the information as soon as possible to two national newspapers, two newswires services operating in the UK and an RIS for release as soon as it opens.

4.1.4 Announcement procedures

In addition to the procedures a listed company is required to have in place to comply with Listing Principle 1 and the specific requirements of LR 7.2.2G and LR 7.2.3G, a listed company should have clear procedures for making announcements to the market to ensure:

- the company can monitor whether an announcement obligation has arisen;
- announcements are made in a timely fashion;
- inside information is not inadvertently released to the press; and
- any announcement is true and accurate and released without delay so that it will not give rise to any potential liability under section 90A of the FSMA (see section 6 below).

A checklist for use by premium listed companies when releasing an RIS announcement is set out in Figure 8.2 below.

Figure 8.2: Checklist of key points to consider when making an RIS announcement

Checklist of key points to consider when making an RIS announcement
☑ Is there a deadline by which the announcement must be made?
☑ Does the announcement need to be made as soon as possible? Is the announcement being released in a timely manner and without delay?
☑ Does the announcement have the correct regulatory headline?
☑ Does it make clear the information is regulated information?
☑ Does it clearly identify the issuer, the subject matter and the time and date of communication?
☑ Does the announcement comply with any applicable contents requirements (including the requirements under MAR for announcements of inside information)?
☑ Does the announcement contain the necessary rubric (e.g. stating that documents have been submitted to the NSM or stating if the announcement is not to be released in certain jurisdictions)?
☑ If the announcement refers to the availability of any other information, is the company happy that the information may be brought within section 90A of the FSMA liability regime?

☑ Does the announcement omit anything likely to affect the import of the information in the announcement?
☑ Is the announcement misleading, false or deceptive in any way?
☑ Have the contents been properly verified?
☑ Has the announcement been taken out of code (where relevant), proof read and spell checked?
☑ Has the announcement been released via an RIS?
☑ Has the RIS announcement been put on the company's website if required?
☑ Do any documents need to be lodged with the NSM?
☑ Are there any other filing and/or notification requirements?
☑ Does the announcement need to be released in any other jurisdictions?

4.2 Circulars to shareholders

4.2.1 Meaning of 'circular'

A circular is another way of describing a document that is sent to shareholders to give them certain types of information. A circular is defined in the Listing Rules as:

> any document issued to holders of listed securities including notices of meetings but excluding prospectuses, listing particulars, annual reports and accounts, interim reports, proxy cards and dividend or interest vouchers.

Accordingly, most documents sent to shareholders are circulars, with the exception of certain specific documents. In certain circumstances a listed company will be required by the Listing Rules to send a circular to its shareholders.

For companies with a premium listing, Listing Rule 13 sets out the general content requirements for all circulars, specific requirements for certain types of circulars and the circumstances in which a listed company is required to send a circular to its shareholders.

In some cases, as described below, a circular will need to be approved by the FCA before it can be sent to shareholders.

4.2.2 Content requirements of all circulars

Listing Rule 13.3.1R sets out the general content requirements for all circulars. These requirements include, among others, that:

- the circular provides a clear and adequate explanation of its subject matter (LR 13.3.1R(1));

- if voting or other action is required, the circular contains all information necessary for shareholders to make a properly informed decision (LR 13.3.1R(3));
- if voting is required, the circular contains a recommendation from the Board as to the voting action shareholders should take and indicates whether or not the proposal is, in the Board's opinion, in the best interests of security holders as a whole (LR 13.3.1R(5)); and
- if a person is named in the circular as having advised the company, a statement must be included that the adviser has given and not withdrawn its consent to the inclusion of the reference to the adviser's name (LR 13.3.1R(10)).

The remainder of LR 13 sets outs additional requirements for particular types of circulars, including:

- Class 1 and related party circulars (LR 13.4, 13.5 and 13.6) (discussed in more detail in Chapter 9);
- circulars in connection with a share buy-back (LR 13.7) (discussed in more detail in Chapter 10);
- circulars in connection with meetings (LR 13.8.8R); and
- circulars in connection with amendments to the company's constitution (LR 13.8.10R).

A premium listed company can incorporate information in a circular by reference to relevant information contained in a prospectus, listing particulars or any other published document that has been filed with the FCA (LR 13.1.3R). If a company chooses to incorporate information by reference, it must include a cross-reference list in the circular stating where the information can be found (LR 13.1.6R).

A company may, with the consent of the FCA, omit information required to be included in a circular if disclosure would be contrary to the public interest or seriously detrimental to the listed company, provided that the omission would not be likely to mislead the public with regard to facts and circumstances, knowledge of which is essential for the assessment of the subject matter covered by the circular (LR 13.1.7G). LR 13.1.8R sets out the information the company should include in a request to omit information from a circular.

4.2.3 Approval and publication of circulars

A listed company must not circulate or publish any of the following types of circular unless it has been approved by the FCA (LR 13.2.1R):

- a Class 1 circular;
- a related party circular;
- a circular that proposes a share buy-back or reconstruction or re-financing, in each case where a working capital statement is required by LR 13.7.1R(2) or LR 9.5.12R (as applicable);

- a circular that proposes a cancellation of listing which is required to be sent to shareholders under LR 5.2.5R(1); and
- a circular that proposes a transfer of listing which is required to be sent to shareholders under LR 5.4A.4R(2).

Where a circular requires approval, the procedure detailed in LR 13.2.4R to LR 13.2.9G must be followed. This will include, in certain circumstances, submitting to the FCA a Sponsor's Declaration for the Production of a Circular, a letter setting out any Listing Rule requirements which are not applicable and any other documents that the FCA has requested from the listed company or its sponsor. Two copies of the draft circular, plus this documentation must be submitted to the FCA at least ten clear business days before the date on which it is intended to publish the circular (LR 13.2.5R).

Once a circular has been approved by the FCA (if applicable) the company must file a copy with the NSM and send copies to shareholders as soon as is practicable after it has been approved (LR 13.2.10R).

The FCA has published a Procedural Note on the mechanics and timeline for the review and approval of documents (see the UKLA Guidance Note *Review and approval of documents (UKLA/PN/903.3)*).

4.2.4 Supplementary circulars

Where a company has published a circular pursuant to the requirements under LR 10 or LR 11, in some circumstances, a supplementary circular may be required. This is discussed in Chapter 9.

4.3 National Storage Mechanism

Under the Transparency Directive (TD) all member states are required to appoint a mechanism for the storage of regulated information. In the UK, Morningstar plc provides the National Storage Mechanism (NSM). This is available at www.morningstar.co.uk/uk/nsm.

Listed companies are required to use the NSM to fulfil their obligation under LR 9.6.1R to forward certain documents to the FCA for publication through the Document Viewing Facility (DVF) (the FCA states on its website that references to the DVF should be read as being references to the NSM).

Listed companies are required to register with Morningstar to upload documents. Once a company has registered, it can either use the 'issuer upload facility' to upload the document directly to the NSM or can e-mail the document to Morningstar. These e-mails must contain certain information including the company name, its ISIN, its symbol/ticker code, the document type (e.g. Annual Financial Report, circular) and the headline.

All documents to which the Listing Rules apply must be filed at this NSM (LR 9.6.1R). These include, among others:

- circulars;
- notices;
- reports; and
- resolutions passed by the company (other than resolutions concerning ordinary business at an AGM) (LR 9.6.2R).

Although LR 9.6.1R requires listed companies to send two hard copies of circulars etc to the FCA, this obligation is fulfilled by posting the document on the NSM. The FCA does not require hard copies.

A listed company must announce via an RIS when it files a document at the NSM unless the full text of the document is released via an RIS (LR 9.6.3R). The text of the announcement need only say:

Document on [Title of document]

A copy of the above document has been submitted to the National Storage Mechanism and will shortly be available for inspection at www.morningstar.co.uk/uk/nsm.

The NSM automatically gathers all RIS announcements made by listed companies and stores them in a central repository. Companies do not need to upload their RISs to the NSM.

Filing documents with the NSM does not satisfy any requirement in the LPDT Rules for a listed company to publish information via an RIS, or to publish a prospectus in accordance with the Prospectus Rules. As well as filing a prospectus with the NSM, the company must still publish it in accordance with the Prospectus Rules.

The FCA has further information on using the NSM on its website.

5. Electronic communication

DTR 6 and CA 2006 both contain provisions relating to electronic communications and both must be considered. The process under DTR 6.1.8R for obtaining shareholder consent to electronic communications will only apply in those limited circumstances in which the provisions set out in CA 2006 do not apply.

A summary of the key requirements under CA 2006 are set out in Figure 8.3 (see p. 366).

5.1 DTR 6 and the Companies Act 2006

Under the Listing Rules, where a listed company is required to send documents to shareholders it may use electronic means as described in DTR 6.1.8R to do so (LR 1.4.9G).

To use 'electronic means' a listed company must comply with the following:

- a decision to use such means must be taken in general meeting;
- the use of such means cannot depend on the location/residence of the shareholders, debt holders or their proxies, or those parties referred to in DTR 5.2.1R (that is indirect holders of shares);
- identification arrangements must be in place so that persons entitled to receive such communications are effectively informed;
- shareholders, debt holders or their proxies, or indirect holders of shares, must be contacted in writing to request their consent to the use of such means and, if they do not object within a reasonable period of time, their consent is deemed to have been given to such communication (unless the provisions in CA 2006, Sch. 5 apply);
- they must also be able to request at any time in the future that information be conveyed in writing (unless the provisions in CA 2006, Sch. 5 apply); and
- any apportionment of the costs entailed in the use of such means must be determined in accordance with the principle of equal treatment (DTR 6.1.8R).

The Institute of Chartered Secretaries and Administrators (ICSA) has also published guidance on electronic communications with shareholders in which it states that the UKLA has confirmed that a resolution to amend the articles to insert the relevant provisions on electronic communications will be treated as shareholder approval for the purpose of DTR 6.1.8R(1).

Although the choice to use electronic communications must not depend on the location of the recipient (DTR 6.1.8R(2)), in previous informal guidance it was acknowledged that, in certain jurisdictions, electronic communication with such persons is not lawful (see List! Issue No. 14 updated, paragraph 4.5, as confirmed on p. 34 of the old 2010 Technical Note: *Disclosure and Transparency Rules*). The FSA stated that it:

> 'would not regard the principle of equality of shareholder treatment as being breached merely if the listed company does not offer to communicate by electronic means with such shareholders'.

However, this has not been repeated in the UKLA Guidance Notes, so there is no formal guidance on the point.

The requirement for identification arrangements (DTR 6.1.8R(3)) means that a listed company will need to have proper record-keeping processes in place to keep track of these e-mail addresses. This will need to be considered carefully by the company, as e-mail addresses tend to change more frequently than postal addresses.

As referred to above, the provisions as to shareholder consent (DTR 6.1.8R(4)) do not apply where Schedule 5 of the CA 2006 applies. Instead the process for obtaining consent from such persons will be as provided in CA 2006.

DTR 6.1.8R(4) states that consent to electronic communication will be deemed to be given if no objection is made within 'a reasonable period of time'. Under CA 2006, a shareholder is deemed to consent to electronic communication if he does not object within 28 days. The FSA stated in paragraph 4.3 of List! Issue No. 14 that on this basis it would consider 28 days as satisfying the 'reasonable time' provision for the purposes of DTR 6.1.8R(4). This has not been repeated in the relevant UKLA Guidance Notes, so there is no formal UKLA guidance on the point.

5.2 Interaction with Listing Rule 13

CA 2006 provides that shareholders' agreement must be obtained if they are to be sent a document electronically. Anything sent to a shareholder asking for such agreement falls within the definition of a 'circular' under the Listing Rules and must comply with the general provisions on the contents of all circulars in LR 13.3.1R.

The FSA has previously stated that letters sent to shareholders (in accordance with Sch. 5 of CA 2006) notifying them that an electronic circular is available on the company's website are treated in the same way as other letters sent accompanying company communications such as circulars (see List! Issue No. 17, paragraph 12, as confirmed on p. 34 of the 2010 Technical Note: *Disclosure and Transparency Rules*) and should comply with the following requirements:

- warnings/headers are included which clearly state that the 'purpose of this letter is to introduce the proposals contained in the attached document which should be read before taking a decision' and that 'this letter is not a summary of the proposals and should not be regarded as a substitute for reading the full documentation';
- the only action required in the letter is that shareholders read the full accompanying documentation; and
- there are no statements of benefits or references to the word recommendation in the letter.

This has not been repeated in the relevant UKLA Guidance Notes, so there is no formal guidance on the point.

Figure 8.3: Electronic communications by companies under CA 2006

---

1. CA 2006: general approach

CA 2006 was intended to make it easier for companies to communicate with their shareholders electronically. This was stated by the government to be one of the key cost savings for listed companies arising as a result of CA 2006. In particular, companies are allowed to communicate with a shareholder by means of a website as the default position if the shareholder does not respond to a request for consent to do so.

The approach taken in CA 2006 is to have general provisions about communications by a company, rather than specific provisions by reference to each type of document. These powers give the company power to communicate electronically, even if not expressly provided for in the relevant provision in CA 2006 or in the company's articles (subject to the requirement for general shareholder consent in relation to default website use).

2. General provisions and definitions

The requirements for each form of communication by companies are set out in sections 1143 to 1148, section 1168 and Schedule 5 of CA 2006. The provisions that relate to website and e-mail communications are described in paragraphs 3 and 4 below.

The key general provisions and definitions are as follows:

Definitions: Section 1168 of CA 2006 defines what is meant by a document being sent in 'hard copy form' or in 'electronic form' for the purpose of CA 2006. A document is sent in hard copy form if it is supplied in a paper copy or similar form capable of being read. A document or information is sent or supplied in electronic form if it is sent or supplied by 'electronic means' (e.g. by e-mail or fax) or by any other means while in electronic form (e.g. sending a disk by post). In all cases when a document is sent or supplied in electronic form it must be done in a manner that will enable the recipient to read it (this means being capable of being read by the naked eye, including maps and images) and to retain a copy of it (either an electronic or a hard copy is sufficient).

Authentication of document sent electronically: A company can specify how a document to be received by it in electronic form must be authenticated (CA 2006 s. 1146). If it does not specify, then a statement by the sender as to his identity is sufficient if the company has no reason to doubt it.

Right to hard copy: A shareholder who has received a document electronically always has a right at any time subsequently to ask for a hard copy of it (CA 2006 s. 1145). The company must supply a hard copy within 21 days of a request from a shareholder.

Address includes electronic address: 'Address' for the purposes of the company communication provisions includes any number or address given for the purposes of sending or receiving documents by electronic means (CA 2006 s. 1148(1)).

Joint holders: Subject to any contrary provision in the articles of the company, the agreement of all joint holders must be obtained in relation to the form of communications to be sent, but communications can then just be sent to the first named holder (CA 2006, Sch. 5, para. 16).

Death/bankruptcy: Unless the articles of association provide otherwise, on the death or bankruptcy of a member, the company can continue to supply documentation in the manner in which the documentation had previously been supplied, until such time as an address in the UK is supplied by a person claiming on death or bankruptcy (CA 2006, Sch. 5, para. 17).

3. Website communications by companies

Under Part 4 of Schedule 5 of CA 2006, companies are able to use website communication with shareholders by express agreement and also as the default position if a shareholder fails to respond to a request for his agreement. This concept covers all forms of communications with shareholders under the CA 2006, including notices of meetings and other documentation such as annual reports. There are similar provisions applicable to communications with holders of debt securities. As described in paragraph 5 below, Part 4 of Schedule 5 also applies to the underlying owners of shares traded on a regulated market who have been nominated to receive hard copy information rights under Part 9 of CA 2006, but there is also a separate website default route for those persons.

In order to make use of the ability to communicate with shareholders using a website as the default position, there are a series of steps that a company needs to take. The requirements, which are set out in Part 4 of Schedule 5 of CA 2006, are as follows:

Resolution or provision in articles: There must be a provision in the articles or approval by an ordinary resolution for the use of a website for communications – the power only applies to the extent of that provision. The inclusion of a provision in the articles is preferable to a resolution because it can provide the necessary power in relation to all documents and not just those under CA 2006 and allows other related issues, such as the time for deemed receipt of documents and treatment of joint holders, to be addressed.

Seeking agreement from shareholders: The company must write to shareholders individually asking for their consent to receive communications via the website. Consent can be requested in relation to all or any communications from the company. The notice to shareholders must comply with the requirements set out in paragraph 10 of Schedule 5 of CA 2006 and, in particular, must make clear the consequences of failing to respond. A failure by a shareholder to respond within 28 days can be taken as consent to receive communications in this way. Shareholders can always revoke their deemed consent by notice to the company at any time.

Notification of availability on website: Where consent is given, the communication with the shareholder can be made by the document being made available on a website. The company must still notify the shareholder of the presence of the document on the website and how it can be accessed on the website. This notification must be in hard copy unless the shareholder has expressly consented to e-mail communication and provided an e-mail address (see paragraph 4 below). The cost saving is therefore only in relation to sending long documents, such as the report and accounts, unless a significant number of shareholders elect to receive this notification via e-mail.

Notices of meeting: In relation to notices of meeting, there is a further requirement, set out in section 309 of CA 2006. The notification of availability must state that it concerns a notice of the meeting and specify the place, date and time of the meeting and, for public companies, must state whether the meeting will be an annual general meeting.

Time at which communication given: The notification is deemed to have been given, or the document to have been sent, on the date on which the shareholder is sent the notification of availability or, if later, the date on which the document appears on the website.

Time period for website availability: The document must stay on the website during the period required by a specific provision in CA 2006 relating to that documentation or, in the absence of such a specific provision, for at least 28 days. In the case of notices of meeting, this requirement is set out in section 309(3) of CA 2006 and requires the notice to be available until the conclusion of the meeting.

Annual limit for requests: Each shareholder can be asked at most once every 12 months whether he is prepared to accept communications by means of a website and therefore be subject to the deemed consent provisions if he fails to respond. Shareholders do not have to be asked every 12 months – that is just the minimum time period allowed for a repeat request.

Indefinite consent: Once a shareholder is deemed to have accepted communications via a website then (unless stated otherwise in the request) that consent applies indefinitely and the shareholder does not need to be given an opportunity to opt back in to hard copy – the company must just respond at any time to an express request from a shareholder to do so.

Companies should have agreed protocols with their registrars for managing this process. Details about the requirements and how they should be managed in practice are set out in the ICSA's 2014 *Guidance on electronic communications with shareholders*. For example, ICSA recommends that companies should carry out a mailing seeking consent only at set intervals every few years, as part of another regular mailing. Companies may still want to contact each new member about communication methods when they first are put on the register, but they could just ask new shareholders if they want to positively elect for e-mail or website communication, so that the 12-month period for requesting website acceptance is not triggered at that time (otherwise there will be a different time limit for each new shareholder).

A shareholder may agree to receive documentation or information in electronic form either generally or specifically under Schedule 5 of CA 2006. Consent can therefore be given generally or specifically but there is no requirement that a notice from the company must give those options – a company can say it is all or nothing.

Companies should reserve the right to send documents in hard copy at any time to cover situations in which it decides to send certain documents to all shareholders in hard copy notwithstanding the ability just to give notice of availability on the website (e.g. proxy forms) and to cover other issues, such as technical problems with the website or overseas securities laws restrictions.

4. E-mail communications by companies

Communications by e-mail to shareholders are covered by paragraphs 5 to 7 of Schedule 5 of CA 2006. There is still a requirement for a specific opt-in by individual shareholders, largely because the company needs to obtain their e-mail address in order to send information to them in that way. Companies can write to shareholders at any time to ask whether they would like to opt in to receive all or any communications by e-mail rather than receiving documentation in hard copy and then can only use e-mail if they get a positive response from the shareholder. Shareholders can revoke their consent to receive communications by e-mail at any time.

E-mail addresses change a lot more frequently than house addresses (e.g. as a result of a change in internet provider). Companies will therefore have to have effective methods agreed with their registrars to keep track of shareholder e-mail addresses.

> **5. Persons nominated to receive information rights**
>
> CA 2006 contains a right allowing a shareholder who holds shares which are traded on a regulated market to nominate another person, on behalf of whom he holds the shares to receive all communications sent by the company. That person then has a right to receive those communications in addition to (rather than instead of) the shareholder. This is one of the collection of shareholder rights set out separately in Part 9 of CA 2006 (Exercise of members' rights). The communications provisions in CA 2006 apply to communications sent to the nominated persons because they are communications required by CA 2006. However, they are not treated in the same way as shareholder communications.

6. Issuer liability regime

6.1 Introduction

The original section 90A of the FSMA was introduced in connection with the TD and established a statutory liability regime for misstatements in periodic financial disclosures required under the TD. The liability in this case is of the issuer to an investor in the issuer. The original liability regime under section 90A was controversial for multiple reasons, including that its scope was limited, covering only periodic financial reports and issuers with securities listed on the Official List, and because of the application of the liability regime in favour of buyers of securities, but not holders or sellers.

In April 2010, the Financial Services and Markets Act 2000 (Liability of Issuers) Regulations 2010 (the 'Issuer Liability Regulations') were issued with the effect of substantially expanding the statutory liability regime. The amendments to the section 90A liability regime apply to any information published via an RIS on or after 1 October 2010.

The details of the regime are set out in Schedule 10A of the FSMA.

6.2 Scope of the regime

6.2.1 To which issuers does it apply?

Section 90A of the statutory liability regime, as amended by the Issuer Liability Regulations, applies to all issuers (UK and overseas) that have securities traded on a regulated or unregulated market situated or operating in the UK. It also applies to UK issuers with securities trading on an equivalent securities market outside the UK.

The statutory liability regime therefore applies to all issuers on the London Stock Exchange's main market, AIM, NEX Exchange or the exchange-regulated PSM and UK-incorporated issuers with securities admitted to trading on overseas markets (e.g. in the US).

6.2.2 To what information does it apply?

The liability regime applies to all announcements made via an RIS and all information the availability of which is announced via an RIS (or via another means required or authorised to be used when an RIS is unavailable). This will not only capture disclosure of inside information and regulated information, but also any other information released, or referred to as being available, via an RIS (e.g. takeover offer documents). It does not matter whether the information is required to be published via an RIS. The liability regime applies to all announcements, whether obligatory or voluntary.

The liability regime also covers information disseminated by UK issuers outside the EEA, if local rules require the information to be disclosed or the service provider disseminating the information is equivalent to an RIS (e.g. information made public by UK issuers on the SEC's EDGAR database system in the US would be caught).

6.3 When will an issuer be liable?

Liability may arise if the announcement or information:

- contains an untrue or misleading statement; or
- omits any matter required to be included in it (FSMA Sch. 10A, para. 3(1)).

An issuer will only be liable where a PDMR:

- in the case of a statement, knew that it was untrue or misleading or was reckless as to whether it was untrue or misleading; or
- in the case of omission, knew that it was a dishonest concealment of a material fact (FSMA Sch. 10A, para. 3(2) and (3)).

Liability may also arise if a PDMR dishonestly delayed the publication of information (FSMA Sch. 10A, para. 5). Dishonesty is described as a person who is aware (or who must be taken to have been aware) that his conduct would be regarded by regular users of the market as dishonest (FSMA Sch. 10A, para. 6).

The fact that there must be an element of recklessness or dishonesty may mean that, in practice, it is hard for investors to establish the basis for a claim.

6.4 To whom is the issuer liable?

Statutory liability is owed to persons who:

- acquire, continue to hold or dispose of securities in reliance on the published information at a time when, and in circumstances in which, it was reasonable for them to rely on that information; and
- suffer loss in respect of the securities as a result of the untrue or misleading statement or omission, or as a result of the delay in publishing the information (FSMA s. 90A and Sch. 10A paras. 3(1) and(4) and para. 5).

References to the acquisition and disposal of securities include contracts to acquire or dispose of securities or any interest in them, but exclude depositary receipts, derivative instruments or other financial instruments representing securities (FSMA Sch. 10A, para. 8(3)).

Holders may have difficulty demonstrating that they relied on published information by the issuer when they decided to continue to hold the securities.

6.5 Safe harbour from liability

Section 90A of the FSMA is often referred to as a 'safe harbour', even though its main purpose is to establish a compensation regime for investors. It provides a safe harbour because:

- it excludes liability in respect of information released via an RIS other than in the circumstances provided for and in particular an issuer will not be liable in the event of negligence (dishonesty or recklessness is required); and
- issuers should not be subject to any liability in respect of any loss suffered by an investor in relation to an untrue or misleading statement, or omission in published information or dishonest delay in published information not covered by the section (e.g. voluntary information not disseminated via an RIS would not be caught).

The safe harbour does not extend to (i.e. does not exclude) liability for a civil penalty, liability for a criminal offence or the powers of the Court and the FCA to order restitution (FSMA s. 90A and Sch. 10A, para. 7). Civil liability claims (i) under section 90 of the FSMA for statements in listing particulars and prospectuses, (ii) under section 954 of the Companies Act 2006 for compensation ordered by the Takeover Panel, (iii) when in breach of contract, (iv) under the Misrepresentation Act 1967, or (v) arising by virtue of a voluntary assumption of responsibility will also not be affected by the liability regime in section 90A (FSMA Sch. 10A, para. 7) or its safe harbour.

The provisions also provide a safe harbour to persons other than the issuer (e.g. external consultants and directors) and exclude these persons from liability for losses sustained by investors covered under section 90A, except liability to the issuer itself (FSMA s. 90A and Sch. 10A, para. 7(2)). Again, however, the safe harbour for such a person does not extend to specific types of civil liability claims (e.g. where the person has assumed responsibility for the published information for a particular purpose to a particular person). This exception from the safe harbour aims to maintain the person's liability for negligent misstatement on a Hedley Byrne v Heller basis (i.e. where the person has provided advice to another person for a particular purpose, the adviser is aware that the recipient is relying on that advice for that purpose and the recipient suffers loss as a result of relying on the negligent advice).

6.6 Position of directors

Directors of a listed company are not subject to any liability, other than potentially to the company (in the event of a breach of duty), for any liability arising under section 90A of the FSMA (FSMA Sch. 10A, para. 7(2)). However, a director of a UK listed company will be at risk of a claim under section 463 of the CA 2006 (Liability for false or misleading statements in reports) from the listed company where any statutory liability claim against the company succeeds if it is his actions that have exposed the company to a claim under section 90A of the FSMA. There is also a risk that, in situations where a listed UK company decides to take no action against a director, shareholders of the company may undertake a derivative action under sections 260 to 264 of the CA 2006 to force the company to do so, although such actions are extremely rare and are subject to significant legal hurdles.

6.7 Sanctions for issuing misleading statements

A listed company must take all reasonable care to ensure that any information that it notifies to an RIS is not misleading, false or deceptive and does not omit anything likely to affect the import of such statement, forecast or information (LR 1.3.3R and DTR 1A.3.2R). This is the case irrespective of whether the information being disclosed is inside information.

For example, a listed company may breach LR 1.3.3R and DTR 1A.3.2R by a failure to announce a piece of information but where the failure to make the announcement causes prior statements made by the company to be misleading or inaccurate.

In 2015, the FCA censured the Co-operative Bank plc for breach of the Listing Rules for publishing misleading information in its annual report and accounts. The FCA found that the Co-op Bank's 2012 annual report and accounts included misleading statements about its capital position in breach of the obligation imposed on issuers under LR 1.3.3R to take reasonable care to ensure that any information notified to a regulatory information service or made available through the FCA is not misleading, false or deceptive.

In 2017, the FCA publicly censured Tesco and ordered it to pay compensation to certain shareholders and bondholders following the FCA's finding that it and a subsidiary had committed market abuse in relation to a trading update published in August 2014. The FCA found that the trading update gave a false or misleading impression as to the value of Tesco plc's shares and publicly traded bonds issued by other Tesco group companies. See section 10 of Chapter 5 for more detail.

CHAPTER 9

Significant transactions, reverse takeovers, related party transactions and companies with controlling shareholders

OVERVIEW

- Certain transactions entered into by a premium listed company are subject to the requirements of Listing Rules 10 and 11 if they are a Class 1 or 2 transaction or a related party transaction, while certain transactions entered into by a listed company (premium or standard listed) are subject to the requirements of Listing Rule 5.6 if the transaction is a reverse takeover.

- A listed company should have systems and controls in place to identify transactions that may be subject to these requirements and, when contemplating such a transaction, a premium listed company must consult a sponsor to assist in determining how the rules apply. The larger the transaction relative to the size of the premium listed company, the greater the regulatory requirements and the protection for shareholders, through disclosure or approval rights.

- 'Class transactions' include acquisitions and disposals of shares, businesses or assets by a listed company other than in the ordinary course of business. Class 2 transactions require a premium listed company to make an RIS announcement, whereas Class 1 transactions require a premium listed company to make an RIS announcement, send a circular to shareholders and obtain shareholder approval for the transaction.

- 'Reverse takeovers' include acquisitions of shares, businesses or assets by a listed company where any of the 'class tests' are 100% or more or which involve a fundamental change in its business or in board or overall voting control by shareholders. A premium listed company is required to make an RIS announcement, send a circular to shareholders, obtain shareholder approval for the transaction and publish a prospectus. A listed company's listing may be suspended following a leak or announcement of a reverse takeover until there is sufficient information about the transaction in the public domain (which may not be until publication of the circular or a prospectus). The company may also be required to re-apply for admission to listing on completion of the transaction.

- 'Related party transactions' are transactions with, or the purpose and effect of which is to benefit, a connected party such as a director, substantial shareholder or their associates, other than in the ordinary course of business. Unless an exemption applies, smaller related party transactions require a premium listed company to make an RIS announcement and a sponsor must confirm that it considers the relevant transaction to be fair and reasonable, whereas larger related party transactions require an RIS announcement to be made, a circular to be sent to shareholders and shareholder approval obtained for the transaction.

- If a premium listed company has a controlling shareholder (i.e. a person who exercises or controls 30% or more of the voting rights in the company, either on their own or together with persons acting in concert with him), the Listing Rules impose additional requirements on the company, including a requirement to enter into an agreement with that shareholder and ensure its business is independent of that shareholder.

1. Significant transactions

Certain transactions entered into by a premium listed company are subject to the requirements of Listing Rule 10. The requirements will depend on their classification, namely as a Class 1 or 2 transaction. If the transaction is very large, it may be a reverse takeover. A premium listed company is obliged to obtain the guidance of a sponsor to assess the application of the rules when proposing to enter into a transaction that could amount to a Class 1 transaction or a reverse takeover (LR 8.2.2R).

Classification is determined by reference to the size of the transaction relative to the size of the listed company (LR 10.2.1G), with the classification made by using four ratios known as the 'class tests'. The general principle is that the more substantial the transaction is relative to the size of the listed company, the greater the protection afforded to existing investors, either through disclosure or the requirement to obtain shareholder consent at a general meeting.

In summary terms, the different classifications are as follows:

- *Class 2 transaction* – a mid-size transaction, where any one or more of the ratios produced by the class tests is 5% or more, but each is less than 25%. This requires an announcement through an RIS containing prescribed information relating to the transaction.

- *Class 1 transaction* – a large transaction, where one or more of the ratios produced by the class tests is 25% or more. The agreement to effect the transaction must be conditional upon shareholder approval, an announcement must be made through an RIS containing prescribed information (the same as for a Class 2 transaction) and a shareholder circular containing prescribed information must be sent to shareholders as part of the process of seeking shareholder approval for the transaction.

- *Reverse takeover* – a transaction where one or more of the ratios produced by the class tests is 100% or more or which involves a fundamental change in the business or in a change in board or voting control of the listed company. Where a premium listed company agrees a transaction that is a reverse takeover, it must comply with the requirements for a Class 1 transaction (i.e. the agreement to effect the transaction must be conditional upon shareholder approval, an announcement must be made through an RIS containing the prescribed information, a shareholder circular containing prescribed information must be sent to shareholders as part of the process of seeking shareholder approval for the transaction) and a prospectus must be published. In addition, a reverse takeover may involve a suspension of the company's listing until sufficient information on the transaction is in the public domain (usually on publication of the circular or prospectus) and generally requires the listed company to re-apply for admission to listing on completion of the transaction as if it were a new applicant.

1.1 Types of transaction

Which transactions are caught by the rules? The definition of 'transaction' extends to all agreements and amendments to agreements entered into by a listed company or its subsidiary undertakings (LR 10.1.3R).

However, the definition of 'transaction' does not extend to:

- *agreements, or amendments to agreements, relating to transactions in the ordinary course* – this category would include ordinary course trading arrangements with customers or clients;
- *agreements or amendments to agreements relating to the issue of securities or pure financing* – this category would include placing and underwriting agreements between a listed company and an investment bank relating to the issue of new shares or other securities and facility agreements; or
- *intra-group agreements* – this category would include agreements between a listed company and its wholly owned subsidiary undertakings or between wholly owned subsidiary undertakings.

Guidance is given in the Listing Rules as to the scope of the transactions that are caught by LR 10.1.3R and what is considered to be outside the 'ordinary course'. Listing Rule 10 applies to those transactions outside the ordinary course of a company's business that may change a security holder's economic interest in the company's assets or liabilities (LR 10.1.4G). In considering whether a transaction is or is not in the ordinary course of business, regard should be had to the size and incidence of similar transactions that have been entered into by the listed company (LR 10.1.5G).

In the case of a grant or acquisition of an option, where the exercise of the option is solely at the discretion of the listed company or its subsidiary, the consideration for the option is classified at the time of the grant or acquisition; when the option is actually exercised, the exercise will need to be classified too. In other situations, the transaction is generally classified at the time of the grant or the acquisition as if the option had been exercised. There is then no need to classify the transaction again when the option is exercised.

1.2 Classification tests

1.2.1 Four class tests

The Listing Rules set out four mathematical tests, each test giving a percentage, that are used to determine the size of, and consequently the regulatory requirements that apply to, a transaction by a premium listed company:

- the 'gross assets' test;
- the 'profits' test;
- the 'consideration' test; and
- the 'gross capital' test.

Each of these four tests is set out in Annex 1 to Listing Rule 10 which also contains guidance on how to calculate the tests. There are certain modified requirements for specialist companies which are set out in LR 10.7. The tests are considered in more detail in sections 1.2.2 to 1.2.5 below. Previous informal UKLA guidance confirmed that final class tests should be calculated immediately before announcement of the relevant transaction (see the FSA's old 2010 Technical Note: *Listing rules* (p. 12)). This commentary has not been repeated in the relevant UKLA Guidance Notes so there is no formal UKLA guidance on the point, but this remains the UKLA's expectation in practice.

The FCA's formal guidance on the class tests is set out in its UKLA Guidance Note *Classification tests (UKLA/TN/302.1)*.

1.2.2 'Gross assets' test

The 'gross assets' test is set out in paragraphs 2 and 3 of Annex 1 to Listing Rule 10. It is calculated by dividing the gross assets that are the subject of the transaction by the gross assets of the listed company as follows:

$$\frac{\text{Gross assets which are subject of the transaction}}{\text{Gross assets of the listed company}} \times 100\%$$

For the purposes of the calculation:

- *Definition of gross assets* – 'Gross assets of the listed company' means the total non-current assets plus the total current assets of the listed company.
- *Acquisition or disposal of shares* – Where the transaction involves either an acquisition of an interest in an undertaking that will result in the consolidation of the undertaking's assets in the accounts of the listed company or a disposal of an interest in an undertaking that will result in the undertaking's assets no longer being consolidated in the accounts of the listed company, the 'gross assets the subject of the transaction' means the value of 100% of the undertaking's assets irrespective of the interest acquired or disposed of. For example, if a listed company sells a 75% stake in a subsidiary to a third party and, as a consequence, the subsidiary's assets will no longer be consolidated in the listed company's accounts, then the 'gross assets the subject of the transaction' will be the value of 100% of the subsidiary's assets. Where the transaction involves any other acquisition or disposal of an interest in an undertaking, the 'gross assets the subject of the transaction' means in the case of an acquisition the consideration together with any liabilities assumed, and in the case of a disposal the assets attributed to that interest in the listed company's accounts.
- *Acquisition of a business or assets* – Where the transaction involves an acquisition of assets other than an interest in an undertaking, the 'gross assets the subject of the transaction' means the greater of (i) the consideration to be paid for the assets, and (ii) the book value of the assets that will be included in the listed company's balance sheet.
- *Disposal of a business or assets* – Where the transaction involves a disposal of assets other than an interest in an undertaking, the 'gross assets the subject of the transaction' means the book value of the assets in the listed company's balance sheet.
- *Modifications* – The FCA can modify the definition of 'gross assets the subject of the transaction' to require the inclusion of further amounts if contingent assets or indemnities are involved (LR 10 Annex 1, paragraph 3G), effectively broadening the scope of those transactions that may require shareholder approval.

1.2.3 'Profits' test

The 'profits' test is set out in paragraph 4 of Annex 1 to Listing Rule 10 and is calculated by dividing the profits attributable to the assets the subject of the transaction by the profits of the listed company as follows:

$$\frac{\text{Profits attributable to the assets the subject of the transaction}}{\text{Profits of the listed company}} \times 100\%$$

For the purposes of the calculation:

- *Assets the subject of the transaction* – The assessment of 'assets the subject of the transaction' is the same as in the asset test (described in section 1.2.2 above).
- *Definition of profits* – Paragraph 4R(2) of Annex 1 to Listing Rule 10 sets out the definition of 'profits' for the purposes of the calculating profits test and states that the Profit Before Tax (PBT) figure should be used (i.e. profits after deducting all charges except tax).

    The FCA has issued guidance on the treatment of exceptional items (see the UKLA Guidance Note *Classification tests (UKLA/TN/302.1)* and says that a profit figure adjusted for exceptional items is a modification of the applicable Listing Rule, and so companies should always consult the FCA who will decide on a case-by-case basis, and taking into account the company's specific circumstances. The FCA's decision-making process is informed by an understanding of whether or not the exceptional item in question is a genuine one-off cost, if the item appears in the listed company's accounts as an exceptional item, and the sponsor's view on whether, under the circumstances, the item should be treated as exceptional. The fact that an item is 'exceptional' in an company's accounts does not mean the FCA will agree that it should be adjusted for in the profits test and items that are a recurring feature of a listed company's business are unlikely to be considered as exceptional even if they appear in the accounts as an exceptional item.

    The FCA is frequently asked by sponsors to allow adjustments to the calculation of the 'profits' test; as a result of this, the FCA published a consultation paper (CP 17/4) in February 2017 which proposes changes to the Listing Rules which would allow a premium listed company to make certain adjustments to the profit figure without consultation with the FCA where the 'profits' test produces a ratio of 25% or more and this result is anomalous (see section 1.2.7 below).

- *Acquisition or disposal of shares* – Where the transaction involves the acquisition of an interest in an undertaking which will result in the consolidation of the assets of the undertaking in the listed company's accounts, or a disposal of an interest in an undertaking which will result in the assets of the undertaking no longer being consolidated in the accounts, the term 'profits attributable to the assets the subject of the transaction' means 100% of the profits of the undertaking (irrespective of the level of interest acquired or disposed of by the listed company). In contrast, paragraph 4R(3) in Annex 1 to Listing Rule 10 states that the profits test is not applicable if the acquisition or disposal of the interest will not result in the consolidation (or deconsolidation) of the target. The FSA said in previous informal guidance that the only tests that would be applicable in that situation are the gross assets test and the consideration test (see List! Issue No. 13 and the 2010 Technical Note: *Listing rules*). This commentary has not, however, been repeated in the UKLA Guidance Notes and there is, therefore, no formal guidance on the point.

- *Treatment of losses when applying the profits test* – Paragraph 4AG in Annex 1 to Listing Rule 10 states that the amount of loss is relevant in calculating the impact of a proposed transaction under the profits test. A listed company should include, therefore, the amount of the losses of the listed company or target in the test (by disregarding the negative when applying the test).

1.2.4 'Consideration' test

The 'consideration' test is set out in paragraphs 5 and 6 of Annex 1 to Listing Rule 10 and is calculated by taking the consideration for the transaction as a percentage of the aggregate market value of all of the ordinary shares (excluding treasury shares) of the listed company as follows:

$$\frac{\text{Consideration for the transaction}}{\text{Aggregate market value of the listed company's ordinary shares (excluding treasury shares)}} \times 100\%$$

For the purposes of the calculation:

- *Definition of consideration* – 'Consideration' is the amount paid to the contracting party. The FCA can modify the definition of 'consideration' to require the inclusion of further amounts (e.g. if the purchaser agrees to discharge any liabilities including the repayment of inter-company or third-party debt, actual or contingent, as part of the terms of the transaction).
- *Securities as consideration* – If all or some of the consideration is in the form of traded securities, the consideration attributable to those securities is the aggregate market value of those securities. Where the securities comprising the consideration are of a class that is already listed, the figures used to determine the consideration must be the aggregate value of all of those securities on the last business day before the announcement of the transaction. Where the securities comprising the consideration are of a new class to be listed, the figures used to determine the consideration must be the expected aggregate market value of all of those securities.
- *Deferred consideration* – If deferred consideration is or may be payable or receivable by the listed company at some point in the future, the 'consideration' for the purposes of the calculation is the maximum total payable or receivable under the agreement.
- *Uncapped consideration* – If the total consideration is not subject to any maximum and the other class tests indicate that the transaction is a Class 2 transaction, then the transaction will be treated as a Class 1 transaction. If the total consideration is not subject to any maximum and the percentages on the other class tests all are less than 5%, then the transaction will be treated as a Class 2 transaction.
- *Aggregate market value of the listed company's ordinary shares* – The figure used to determine market capitalisation is the aggregate market value of all the ordinary shares (excluding any treasury shares) of the listed company at the close of business on the last business day before announcement of the transaction.

The UKLA has indicated in its Guidance Note *Classification tests* (UKLA/TN/302.1) that it considers a company's market capitalisation as significant in assessing the size and importance of a particular transaction. The UKLA says that it is generally not minded to waive the market capitalisation test or allow enterprise value to be used as a substitute test. The key reasons for this are:

- the market capitalisation test is the primary indicator of a listed company's size as at the date of the transaction;
- it is the only test which does not use historical financial information;
- if the company was to be sold or become the subject of a takeover offer, the market capitalisation is the starting point for valuation; and
- arguments that market capitalisation is anomalous are inherently flawed as, if the market is valuing companies incorrectly, this would suggest that full information is not in the market.

1.2.5 'Gross capital' test

The 'gross capital' test is set out in paragraph 7 of Annex 1 to Listing Rule 10 and is calculated by dividing the gross capital of the company or business being acquired by the gross capital of the listed company as follows:

$$\frac{\text{Gross capital of the company or business being acquired}}{\text{Gross capital of the listed company}} \times 100\%$$

This test is only applied for an acquisition of a company or a business.

For the purposes of the calculation:

- *Gross capital of a company being acquired* – In the context of an acquisition of a company, 'gross capital' means the aggregate of (i) the consideration (as calculated for the purposes of the 'consideration' test), (ii) any shares (other than treasury shares held by the company) and debt securities not being acquired in the transaction, (iii) all other liabilities (other than current liabilities) of the company including minority interests and deferred taxation, and (iv) any excess of current liabilities over current assets. For the purpose of calculating the value of any shares or debt securities not being acquired in the transaction, the value of the shares should be the aggregate market value of all those shares (or if not available before the announcement, their nominal value) and the value of the debt securities should be taken as the issue amount.
- *Gross capital of a business being acquired* – In the context of an acquisition of a business, 'gross capital' means the aggregate of (i) the consideration (as calculated for the purposes of the 'consideration' test), (ii) all other liabilities (other than current liabilities) of the business including minority interests and deferred taxation, and (iii) any excess of current liabilities over current assets.

- *Gross capital of the listed company* – In this context, 'gross capital' means the aggregate of the market value of the listed company's shares (excluding treasury shares) and the issue amount of its debt securities, all other liabilities (other than current liabilities) of the listed company including minority interests and deferred taxation and any excess of current liabilities over current assets.

1.2.6 Figures to be used and accepted adjustments

Further general guidance is given by the FCA on the figures used to classify assets and profits for the purposes of calculating the class tests in paragraphs 8 and 9 of Annex 1 to Listing Rule 10 and the UKLA Guidance Note *Classification tests (UKLA/TN/302.1)*:

- Figures used should be those shown in the latest published audited consolidated accounts or, if the listed company has or will have published a preliminary statement of later annual results at the time the terms of the transaction are agreed, the figures shown in that preliminary statement. If a balance sheet is available from a later interim statement, gross assets and capital assets should be taken from such balance sheet.
- Figures for the listed company must be adjusted for certain post-balance sheet transactions for the listed company and the target. In relation to both the company and the target, adjustment must be made for post-balance sheet transactions which are Class 2 or larger. These adjustments are only required for transactions that have completed, not those that have been announced but not yet completed. The FCA confirms in the UKLA Guidance Note *Classification tests (UKLA/TN/302.1)* that it would apply this approach in relation to transactions completed during the last financial year for both the listed company and the target. In CP 17/4, the FCA proposes to change this guidance into a Listing Rule.
- Figures on which auditors are unable to report without modification must be disregarded for the purposes of the tests; this is to ensure certainty and integrity of calculations. However, the FCA may modify this rule to permit figures to be taken into account.

1.2.7 Anomalous results

If a calculation under any of the class tests produces an anomalous result or is inappropriate having regard to the activities of the listed company, then the FCA may modify the requirements to substitute an alternative indicator of size, including industry-specific tests (see paragraph 10 of Annex 1 to Listing Rule 10).

At its series of 'sponsors' seminars' in July 2006, the FSA (the predecessor to the FCA) summarised its general approach to the class tests and anomalous results as follows:

- When considering the results of the 'profits' test, it has permitted adjustments to be made to the profits figures used in the calculation of the tests to take account of litigation costs, the costs of running a takeover bid defence, one-off exit costs from a non-core activity and one-off restructuring costs. It has not accepted any adjustment to profits figures used in the calculation to take account of overly aggressive amortisation, ongoing restructuring costs or losses on disposal.

- For those transactions that involve the acquisition or disposal of assets, it accepted that the 'Profits' and 'Gross Capital' tests do not apply and is prepared to consider alternative indicators of size based on numbers of employees, contracts, debt, intellectual property, goodwill etc.
- When looking at alternative indicators of size in general, it accepted that it may be appropriate to consider factors such as numbers of employees and R&D spend.

This commentary has not, however, been repeated in the relevant UKLA Guidance Notes so there is no formal guidance on the point at the moment.

The FCA has, however, in its recently published consultation paper (CP 17/4) proposed changes to the Listing Rules in respect of anomalous results produced by the 'profits' test which would allow premium listed companies:

- to disregard an anomalous 'profits' test result of 25% or more when all of the other class test results are below 5% without having to consult the FCA – this will result in the transaction being treated as unclassified; or
- to make adjustments to the profit figures used in the 'profits' test for certain one-off cost items without having to consult the FCA where the 'profits' test result is 25% or more and is anomalous.

The FCA proposes that adjustments to the profit figures may be made for genuine one-off cost items, including certain costs incurred by the listed company or the target company in connection with an IPO and closure costs that are not part of an ongoing restructuring that will span more than one financial period, without consultation with the FCA. In order to make such adjustments without FCA consultation, the premium listed company would still need to consult a sponsor under LR 8.2.2R and the sponsor would need to conclude that the cost is a genuine one-off.

To disregard the 'profits test', again the premium listed company would need to consult a sponsor under LR 8.2.2R and the sponsor would need to conclude that it is appropriate to disregard the 'profits' test. The FCA notes that there may be some limited situations where it may not be appropriate to disregard the 'profits' test (e.g. if the listed company is acquiring a loss-making entity and the relative size of the entity's losses would have a significant impact on the listed company's medium-term prospects). In those circumstances, a sponsor would need to consult with the FCA.

For all other circumstances where the 'profits' test produces an anomalous result, the company's sponsor should discuss the application of the profits test with the FCA. In the meantime, the listed company and sponsor should continue to consult the FCA early in the process to agree appropriate calculations. The sponsor should prepare detailed reasons if it wishes to argue that the tests are not appropriate and be prepared to suggest alternative tests and indicators of size. In practice, the sponsor will write to the FCA in the early stages of a transaction with its suggestions and illustrative calculations to demonstrate which classification should apply to the transaction. Paragraph 11G in Annex 1 to Listing Rule 10 reiterates that, where a listed company wishes to adjust figures used in calculating the class tests pursuant to paragraph 10G of Annex 1 to Listing Rule 10, it should discuss this with the FCA before the class tests crystallise. In addition, on occasion, the FCA will require additional class tests to be calculated.

1.2.8 Transactions by specialist companies

LR 10.7 sets out alternative class tests that apply to transactions involving property companies and an additional 'reserves' test that applies to listed mineral companies. Scientific research-based companies are required to consult the FCA to determine whether industry specific tests are required instead of or in addition to the class tests.

1.2.9 Indemnities

Without prejudice to the general class tests, the Listing Rules also contain express provisions relating to agreements that are entered into by a listed company that contain 'indemnities' or similar arrangements.

LR 10.2.4R provides that the granting of an indemnity or similar arrangement to a party – other than an agreement with a wholly owned subsidiary – will be deemed to be a Class 1 transaction if under that agreement or arrangement:

- the listed company agrees to discharge the liabilities of the party for costs, expenses, commissions or losses, whether or not on a contingent basis;
- the indemnity or similar arrangement is 'exceptional'; and
- the maximum liability of the listed company is unlimited or equal to or exceeds 25% of the average of the listed company's profits (with losses counted as nil profits) for the last three financial years. The FCA may substitute other indicators of size in the event of an anomalous result (LR 10.2.6G).

To assist a listed company and its sponsor in considering whether or not an indemnity is exceptional, the FCA provides certain guidance as to those indemnities that it does not consider to be exceptional (LR 10.2.5G). For example, the following are not considered exceptional:

- indemnities customarily contained in a share purchase agreement;
- indemnities customarily given to underwriters in an underwriting agreement;
- indemnities given to advisers against any third-party liability arising out of advisory services; and
- any other indemnities specifically permitted to be given to directors or auditors under CA 2006.

The FCA issued for consultation in February 2013 a draft technical note which contained guidance on whether a parent guarantee under section 479C of the CA 2006 (in relation to the outstanding liabilities of a subsidiary so that the subsidiary can be exempt from the requirement for mandatory audit) would fall within the scope of LR 10.2.4R. However, it subsequently said that the issues raised in the feedback warranted further consideration and perhaps additional consultation. The FCA's approach to such guarantees is therefore not clear.

The provisions governing indemnities do not apply to break fees; these are regulated separately as discussed in section 1.2.10 below.

1.2.10 Break fees

Without prejudice to the other class tests, the Listing Rules also contain express provisions relating to agreements that are entered into by a listed company which constitute 'break fee arrangements'. LR 10.2.6AR and 10.2.6BG make it clear that the rule is intended to capture arrangements beyond those that take the form and label of a simple break fee.

For Listing Rule purposes, an arrangement is a break fee arrangement if the purpose of the arrangement is that a compensatory sum will become payable by a listed company to another party (or parties) to a proposed transaction if the transaction fails or is materially impeded and there is no independent substantive commercial rationale for the arrangement (LR 10.2.6AR). In its consultation on the rules regarding break fees in 2012 (see consultation paper CP 12/2), the FCA said that it is the purpose served by the arrangement that is the key factor in determining whether something should be caught as a break fee arrangement (i.e. whether it is 'money for nothing').

LR 10.2.6BG provides guidance on the types of arrangements that will meet the definition of break fee arrangements and those likely to fall outside of the definition.

The following arrangements fall within the definition of break fee arrangement in LR 10.2.6AR:

- 'no shop' and 'go shop' type provisions, requiring payment of a sum to another party if the seller finds an alternative purchaser;
- a requirement to pay another party's wasted costs if a transaction fails; and
- non-refundable deposits.

The above list is not exhaustive and should not be treated as a comprehensive list; it is simply an illustration as to how the rule will operate.

By contrast, payments in the nature of damages (liquidated or unliquidated) for a breach of an obligation with an independent substantive commercial rationale are not break fee arrangements (e.g. breaches of the typical business protection covenants that apply between exchange and completion of a share or asset acquisition agreement, or breaches of co-operation and information access obligations relating to obtaining merger or other clearances).

LR 10.2.7R(1) provides that the granting of a break fee will be deemed to be a Class 1 transaction if the total value of the fee or fees in aggregate exceeds:

- 1% of the value of the listed company calculated by reference to the offer price if the listed company is being acquired; and
- in all other cases, 1% of the market capitalisation of the listed company.

LR 10.2.7R(2) sets out further guidance on the calculation:

- the 1% limit is calculated on the basis of fully diluted equity share capital of the listed company;
- save to the extent VAT is recoverable by the listed company, any VAT that is payable on the break fee should be taken into account when considering the 1% limit; and
- in a securities exchange offer, the value of the listed company is to be fixed by reference to the value of the offer at the time of announcement of the transaction.

LR 10.2.7R(1A) makes it clear that the total value of sums payable pursuant to break fee arrangements for the purposes of LR 10.2.7R(1) is the sum of:

(a) any amounts paid or payable pursuant to break fee arrangements in relation to the same transaction or in relation to the same target assets or business in the previous 12 months (unless any of those arrangements were approved by shareholders); and

(b) the aggregate of the maximum amounts payable pursuant to break fee arrangements in relation to the transaction, save that if the arrangements are such that a particular sum will only become payable in circumstances in which another sum does not, the lower sum may be left out of the calculation of the total value. This means that where a listed company has committed to more than one break fee arrangement as part of a transaction it must aggregate those break fee arrangements unless they are mutually exclusive.

Listed companies which are subject to the City Code may be subject to additional, more onerous restrictions on break fees per Rule 21.2 of the City Code, in the context of a takeover offer for the listed company.

1.2.11 Share issues by major subsidiaries

The dilution of a listed company's interest in a major subsidiary undertaking may be treated as a Class 1 transaction. Under LR 10.2.8R, a share issue by a subsidiary will constitute a Class 1 transaction if:

- a 'major subsidiary undertaking' of the listed company (i.e. a subsidiary undertaking representing 25% or more of the aggregate of the gross assets or profits (after deducting charges except taxation) of the group) issues equity shares for cash, in exchange for other securities or to reduce indebtedness;

- the issue would dilute the listed company's percentage interest in the subsidiary; and
- the economic effect of the dilution is equivalent to a disposal of 25% or more of the aggregate of the gross assets or profits (after deducting charges except taxation) of the group.

LR 10.2.8R does not apply where the major subsidiary undertaking is itself a listed company (LR 10.2.9R).

1.2.12 Aggregation of transactions

Notwithstanding that any one transaction may not, itself, constitute a Class 1 or 2 transaction or a reverse takeover, a listed company also needs to consider the aggregate impact of a current transaction with any connected transactions that it has completed in the preceding 12 months.

Under LR 10.2.10R, transactions completed during the 12 months before the date of the latest transaction must be aggregated with the latest transaction for the purposes of classification if:

- they were entered into by the company with the same person or with persons connected with each other;
- they involve the acquisition or disposal of securities or an interest in one company; or
- together they lead to substantial involvement in a business activity which did not previously form a significant part of the company's principal activities.

In the UKLA Guidance Note *Aggregating transactions* (UKLA/TN/307.1), the FCA confirms that when aggregating transactions, the class tests crystallise at the point at which each transaction is announced. Companies do not have to recalculate the test results for the earlier transactions. They should add together the class test percentages from the earlier transaction with the percentages from the latest transaction. The combined percentage will indicate the aggregated classification of the transactions.

The Guidance Note also gives examples of how the calculations work when aggregating transactions.

Where the aggregation of a current transaction with any connected transactions would result in a requirement for shareholder approval, then approval is only required for the latest transaction.

In the UKLA Guidance Note *Aggregating transactions* (UKLA/TN/307.1), the UKLA also confirms that:

- the aggregation rules in LR 10.2.10R could mean that a transaction is classified as a Class 1 transaction, even though on its own it is relatively small;

- it will typically employ discretion provided to it under LR 10.2.11G to apply the aggregation principles where it has concerns that a company is structuring a transaction in such a way as to avoid shareholder approval under LR 10; and
- a series of smaller transactions must be aggregated for the purposes of classification in accordance with LR 10.2.10R(1)(c).

Separate rules apply to the aggregation of break fees (see section 1.2.10 above).

1.3 Abolition of Class 3 transactions

Prior to 1 October 2012, the Listing Rules had the concept of Class 3 transactions (the smallest of categories, where all the percentage ratios under the class tests were less than 5%); however, this was abolished. It was felt that the Class 3 notification requirements resulted in immaterial information being disclosed, in some cases years after the relevant transaction was entered into (as the then applicable LRs did not provide a minimum threshold or a time limit for transactions subject to Class 3 notification requirements). It was also felt that the Class 3 notification requirements did not afford shareholders and investors protection above the listed company's obligations to disclose inside information under the Market Abuse Regulation.

1.4 Class 2 requirements

The key requirement for a Class 2 transaction is that as soon as possible after the terms of the transaction have been agreed (this does not mean that a legally binding agreement needs to have been signed), the listed company must make a Class 2 announcement through an RIS to the market (LR 10.4.1R(1)).

The Class 2 announcement must include disclosure of the following items (required by LR 10.4.1R(2)):

- details of the transaction including the name of the other party (i.e. a sale of X to Y, an acquisition of X from Y);
- a description of the business carried on by, or using, the net assets the subject of the transaction (i.e. what is the listed company buying or selling?);
- details of the consideration, how it is being satisfied and, where relevant, the terms of any arrangements for deferred consideration (i.e. how much is X being sold or bought for? Is the consideration payable in cash, shares etc? Will all consideration be paid on closing or will some be paid over time? Are there any retention arrangements or earn outs?);
- the value of the gross assets the subject of the transaction and details of the profits attributable to the assets the subject of the transaction;

- the effect of the transaction on the listed company, including any benefits that are expected to accrue as a result of the transaction;
- details of key individuals who are important to the business or company the subject of the transactions; and
- details of any service contracts of proposed directors of the listed company (i.e. will there be any Board changes as a result of the transaction?).

In addition, where the transaction involves a disposal by the listed company, the Class 2 announcement must include:

- the application of the sale proceeds (i.e. will the proceeds be used to repay debt, for acquisitions, to return value to shareholders, for general corporate purposes or for some other purpose?); and
- if securities are to form part of the consideration received by the listed company, a statement whether the listed company intends to sell or retain such securities.

If the transaction involves a takeover of another listed company then the announcement of the offer for the target will, to the extent that the transaction is a Class 2 or Class 1 acquisition, be required to comply with the requirements of LR 10.4.1R as well the requirements of the City Code.

If, following the announcement, either a significant change occurs that affects any matter in the announcement or a significant new matter arises that would have been required to be disclosed in the original announcement, then, under LR 10.4.2R, the listed company must make a supplementary announcement through an RIS.

The supplementary announcement must give details of the significant change or the significant new matter and must confirm that there has been no other significant change affecting any matter contained in the earlier announcement and no other significant new matter has arisen which would have been required to be mentioned had it arisen at the time of the earlier announcement (LR 10.4.2R(2)).

In determining the significance of a change or new matter, 'significant' means significant for the purpose of making an informed assessment of the assets, liabilities, financial position, profits, losses and prospects of the listed company and the rights attaching to shares in the listed company (LR 10.4.2R(3)). 'Significant' also includes any change in the terms of the transaction that affects the percentage ratios and requires the transaction to be reclassified into a higher category (e.g. a Class 1 rather than a Class 2 transaction) (LR 10.4.2R(3)).

It is worth noting that if the transaction involves the publication of a prospectus by the listed company, then the test for a supplementary notification is different from the test for when a supplementary prospectus is required to be prepared and published in accordance with PR 3.4 and section 87G of the FSMA (see section 4.1 of Chapter 4).

1.5 Class 1 requirements

1.5.1 Class 1 requirements and procedure

Any agreement that gives effect to a Class 1 transaction must be conditional on the shareholders of the listed company giving their prior approval for the transaction in general meeting (LR 10.5.1R(2) and (3)).

As soon as possible after the terms of the transaction are agreed (this does not mean that a legally binding agreement needs to have been signed), a listed company must make an announcement through an RIS (LR 10.5.1R(1)). The information required to be included in the announcement is the same as that required by LR 10.4.1R(2) for a Class 2 transaction (see section 1.4 above).

In addition to making an RIS announcement, a listed company is required to send a circular to its shareholders (LR 10.5.1R(2)). The information required to be included in this circular will include the information required by LR 13.4, LR 13.5 and LR 13 Annex 1, as summarised in section 1.5.2 and in Figure 9.1 (see p. 405). Among other things, a Class 1 circular will include a description of the transaction and its terms, a working capital statement, an update on current trading, a statement on significant change and a responsibility statement. It will also contain the notice of meeting at which the resolution to approve the transaction will be put to shareholders.

Where a listed company is contemplating a transaction that could, because of its size or nature, be classified as a Class 1 transaction (or as a reverse takeover), LR 8.2.2R requires it to obtain the guidance of a sponsor to assess the application of Listing Rule 10 (see section 2.1 of Chapter 3). If a listed company is ultimately required to produce a Class 1 circular, LR 8.2.1R(2) requires it to appoint a sponsor. The sponsor will submit the circular to the FCA for approval together with (as required by LR 8.4.13R) a completed Sponsor's Declaration for the Production of a Circular containing a declaration that the sponsor has come to the reasonable opinion, after having made due and careful enquiry, that:

- the listed company has satisfied all requirements of the Listing Rules relevant to the production of the Class 1 circular;
- the transaction will not have an adverse impact on the listed company's ability to comply with the Listing Rules, the disclosure requirements and the Transparency Rules; and
- the directors have a reasonable basis on which to make the working capital statement required to be included in the Class 1 circular (LR 8.4.12R).

For a further description of the roles and responsibilities of a sponsor, please see Chapter 3.

The Class 1 circular cannot be published until it has been approved in final form by the FCA (LR 13.2.1R) and the sponsor has delivered its Sponsor's Declaration for the Production of a Circular (LR 13.2.4R). To obtain approval, a draft of the Class 1 circular (in an advanced form) must be submitted to the FCA for review at least ten clear business days prior to the intended date of publication (LR 13.2.5R) (although, generally a draft will be submitted significantly earlier).

The sponsor will be required to submit the final Sponsor's Declaration for the Production of a Circular prior to or on the day the Class 1 circular is to be approved by the FCA. The sponsor must ensure that all matters known to it which, in its reasonable opinion, should be taken into account by the FCA in considering the transaction have been disclosed with sufficient prominence in the documentation or otherwise in writing to the FCA (LR 8.4.13R(3)).

In practice, the Class 1 circular can be drafted and submitted for FCA approval during the negotiations of the relevant transaction. This enables the Class 1 circular to be posted very shortly after the conditional transaction documentation has been signed.

A number of supporting documents will be required to be prepared, negotiated and agreed in connection with the publication of a Class 1 circular and in connection with the declaration required to be given by the sponsor to the FCA. Figure 9.2 sets out a checklist of the key documents that will need to be agreed by the date of publication of the Class 1 circular and who has primary responsibility for each document (see p. 412).

Once the FCA has approved the Class 1 circular, it can be published and dispatched to shareholders. Since the purpose of the Class 1 circular is to seek shareholder approval for a Class 1 transaction, notice of the meeting at which the vote on the transaction will be taken accompanies the Class 1 circular.

The Listing Rules require the prior approval of a Class 1 transaction by the shareholders of the listed company in general meeting. This means that an ordinary resolution approving the transaction must be passed, requiring a simple majority of the votes cast by the listed company shareholders present at the meeting in person or by proxy. Under LR 9.2.21R, the vote must be decided by a resolution of the holders of the company's premium listed shares. The minimum notice period for a general meeting for a listed company is generally 21 clear days. However, under CA 2006 the company will be able to hold a general meeting on 14 clear days' notice if three conditions are met: first, the general meeting is not an annual general meeting; second, the company must allow shareholders to vote by electronic means at that meeting (which can be satisfied if there is a facility available to all shareholders to appoint a proxy via a website); and third, shareholders must have passed a special resolution at the company's AGM for that year approving the shortening of the notice period to 14 days. Regard should also be given to provision E.2.4 of the Corporate Governance Code which provides that the notice period for general meetings should be at least 14 working days – if this is not followed a premium listed company will need to explain its reasons for not complying with this recommendation its next annual report (LR 9.8.6R).

1.5.2 Contents of a Class 1 circular

A circular for a Class 1 transaction must include the information that is required by Listing Rule 13.3 to be included in all shareholder circulars (see section 4.2 of Chapter 8). Notably, due prominence must be given in the circular to the essential characteristics, benefits and risks of the transaction and the circular must contain all of the information necessary to allow security holders to make a properly informed decision. LR 13.4.1AG makes it clear that this extends to all the material terms of the Class 1 transaction including the consideration.

In addition, a Class 1 circular must comply with the specific content requirements of Listing Rule 13.4 and include:

- the information required to be included in the RIS announcement under LR 10.4.1R(2) (see section 1.4 above for details);
- the information required to be included by Annex 1R to Listing Rule 13;
- the financial information required to be included by Listing Rule 13.5 (if applicable);
- a declaration by the company and its directors in the following form:

    'The [listed company] and the directors of [listed company], whose names appear on page [XX], accept responsibility for the information contained in this document. To the best of the knowledge and belief of [listed company] and the directors (who have taken all reasonable care to ensure that such is the case) the information contained in this document is in accordance with the facts and does not omit anything likely to affect the import of such information.'

- a statement of the effect of the acquisition or disposal on the group's earnings and assets and liabilities; and
- if a statement or report attributed to an expert (e.g. a report prepared by a listed company's reporting accountants) is included in the Class 1 circular, a statement to the effect that the statement or report is included, in the form and context in which it is included, with the expert's consent.

In earlier commentary on the rules, which is not formal guidance, the UKLA said that where the Listing Rules require disclosure within documents to be provided at 'the latest practicable date', this means the latest date before publication that the disclosure can be prepared and that it would normally expect this to be within 48 hours of the publication date (see List! Issue No. 22). This commentary has not, however, been repeated in the relevant UKLA Guidance Notes, so there is no formal guidance on the point.

General disclosure

Figure 9.1 sets out the skeleton contents and structure of a Class 1 circular and summarises the general information required by Annex 1R to Listing Rule 13 (see p. 405). This includes risk factors, details of litigation and any significant change and a working capital statement. The Annex sets out how the information should be presented (e.g. it requires the working capital statement to be in a single statement on the basis that the acquisition or disposal, as the case may be, has taken place).

Financial disclosure

The financial information required to be included in a Class 1 circular by Listing Rule 13.5 will depend on the nature of the transaction and of the target company, business or assets that is or are the subject of the transaction.

When financial information must be included in the Class 1 circular

Broadly speaking, LR 13.5.1R requires that financial information on the target company, business or assets, in the form of a financial information table (LR 13.5.12R), must be included in a Class 1 circular if:

- the listed company is seeking to acquire an interest in a target which will result in a consolidation of the target's assets and liabilities with those of the listed company (LR 13.5.-1G specifies that for the purposes of LR 13.5, references to consolidation include both consolidation and proportionate consolidation); or
- the listed company is seeking to dispose of an interest in a target which will result in the assets and liabilities no longer being consolidated; or
- the target ('A') has itself acquired a target ('B'), and (i) A acquired B within the three-year period which the financial information must cover under LR 13.5.13R or after the date of the last published accounts, and (ii) the acquisition of B, as at the date of its acquisition by A, would have been classified as a Class 1 acquisition for the listed company at the date of acquisition of A by the listed company.

Financial information for a Class 1 acquisition

In the case of a Class 1 transaction that is an acquisition where financial information is required to be included in the circular (as described above), the Class 1 circular must include financial information as follows:

- A financial information table that covers the target and its subsidiary undertakings (if any) (LR 13.5.14R) for a period of three years up to the end of the last financial period for which that target (or its parent) has prepared audited accounts, or a lesser period if the target's business has been in existence for less than three years (LR 13.5.13R(1) and (2)).
- The financial information table must include, for each period covered, a balance sheet and its explanatory notes; an income statement and its explanatory notes; a cash flow statement and its explanatory notes; a statement showing either all changes in equity or changes in equity other than those arising from capital transactions with owners and distributions to owners; the accounting policies; and any additional explanatory notes (LR 13.5.18R).

- If the target has itself made an acquisition or a series of acquisitions during, or subsequent to, the reporting periods covered by the financial information in the circular, the circular must contain additional financial information tables so that the financial information in the circular represents at least 75% of the enlarged target for the relevant three-year reporting period up to the date of the acquisition by the listed company or the last balance sheet date presented by it, whichever of the two is earlier (LR 13.5.17AR).

Financial information for a Class 1 disposal

In the case of a Class 1 disposal, the financial information in the Class 1 circular must include a financial information table for the target that includes (i) the last annual consolidated balance sheet; (ii) the consolidated income statement for the last three years drawn up to at least the level of profit or loss for the period; and (iii) the consolidated balance sheet and consolidated income statement at the issuer's interim balance sheet date if the issuer has issued interim financial statements since the publication of its last annual audited consolidated financial statements (LR 13.5.30B R(1)).

The above information must be extracted without material adjustment from the consolidation schedules that underlie the listed company's audited consolidated accounts or in the case of (iii) above, the interim financial information, and must be accompanied by a statement to this effect (LR 13.5.30BR(2)).

If the information is not extracted from the consolidation schedules, it must be extracted from the listed company's accounting records and, where an allocation is made, the information must be accompanied by an explanation of the basis for the financial information presented and a statement by the directors of the listed company that such allocations provide a reasonable basis for the presentation of the financial information for the target to enable the shareholders to make a fully informed voting decision (LR 13.5.30BR(3)).

If the target has not been owned by the listed company for the entire three-year reporting period, the information required to be included in the Class 1 circular may be extracted from the target's accounting records (LR 13.5.30BR(4)).

Where a change of accounting policies has occurred during the period covered by the financial information table required by LR 13.5.30BR, the financial information must be presented on the basis of both the original and amended accounting policies for the year prior to that in which the new accounting policy is adopted unless the change did not require a restatement of the comparative information. Therefore the financial information table should have four columns (or more where the changes have occurred in more than one year) (LR 13.5.30CR).

Acquisitions and disposals of interests accounted for as investments or using the equity method

When a listed company is acquiring an interest in a target that will be accounted for as an investment, or disposing of an interest in a target that has been accounted for as an investment, and the target's securities that are the subject of the transaction are admitted to an investment exchange enabling intra-day price formation, LR 13.5.3AR requires the Class 1 circular to include:

- the amounts of the dividends or other distributions paid in the last three years;
- the price per security and the imputed value of the entire holding being acquired or disposed of at the close of business on (a) the last business day of each of the six months prior to the issue of the Class 1 circular; (b) on the day prior to the announcement of the transaction; and (c) at the latest practicable time prior to the submission for approval of the Class 1 circular.

When a listed company is acquiring or disposing of an interest in a target that was or will be accounted for using the equity method in the listed company's consolidated annual accounts, LR 13.5.3BR requires the Class 1 circular to include:

- in the case of an acquisition (a) a narrative explanation of the proposed accounting treatment of the target in the listed company's next consolidated accounts; (b) a financial information table for the target; (c) a statement that the target's financial information has been audited and reported on without modification or a statement (required by LR 13.4.2R and LR 13.5.25R) with regard to any modifications; and (d) a reconciliation of the financial information and opinion thereon in accordance with LR 13.5.17R(2)(a) or, where applicable, a statement from the directors in accordance with LR 13.5.17R(2)(b); and
- in the case of a disposal, the line entries relating to the target from its last audited consolidated balance sheet and those from its audited consolidated balance sheet and those from its audited consolidated income statement for the last three years together with the equivalent line entries from its interim consolidated balance sheet and interim consolidated income statement, where the listed company has published subsequent interim financial information.

Requirement for an independent valuation

A listed company that is entering into a Class 1 transaction which falls within LR 13.5.1R (Financial information in a Class 1 circular), LR 13.5.3AR (Interest accounted for as an investment) or LR 13.5.3BR (Interest accounted for using the equity method) (each as described above) but cannot comply with LR 13.5.12R (Inclusion of a financial information table) or, for an investment, LR 13.5.3AR(2) (Inclusion of price per security and the imputed value of the entire holding), must include an appropriate independent valuation of the target in the Class 1 circular (LR 13.5.3CR). The FCA may dispense with the requirement for an independent valuation if it considers that this would not provide useful information for shareholders, in which case the Class 1 circular must include such information as the FCA specifies (LR 13.5.3DG).

Acquisitions of publicly traded companies

If (i) LR 13.5.3BR (Acquisition of an interest in a target that will be accounted for using the equity method) applies, or (ii) the target is admitted to trading on a regulated market, or (iii) the target is a company whose securities are either listed on an investment exchange which is not a regulated market or admitted to a multilateral trading facility (where appropriate standards as regards the production, publication and auditing of financial information are in place) and none of the financial information of the target is subject to a modified report (LR 13.5.27R(1)(b)), the listed company must include in the Class 1 circular either:

- a reconciliation of financial information on the target for all periods covered by the financial information table on the basis of the listed company's accounting policies, accompanied by an accountant's opinion that sets out (i) whether the reconciliation of financial information in the financial information table has been properly compiled on the basis stated; and (ii) whether the adjustments are appropriate for the purpose of presenting the financial information (as adjusted) on a basis consistent in all material respects with the listed company's accounting policies (LR 13.5.27R(2)(a)); or
- a statement by the directors that no material adjustment needs to be made to the target's financial information to achieve consistency with the listed company's accounting policies (LR 13.5.27R(2)(b)).

The FCA will make an assessment of whether the accounting and other standards are appropriate where the target is admitted to an investment exchange or multilateral trading facility, having regard to matters such as the quality of auditing standards compared with International Standards on Auditing and the quality of accounting standards compared with International Financial Reporting Standards (LR 13.5.27AG). The company's sponsor must submit to the FCA an assessment of appropriateness of the standards against the factors set out in LR 13.5.27AG and any other matters that it considers should be noted. The assessment must be submitted before or at the time the listed company submits the draft Class 1 circular (LR 13.5.27BR).

Form, source and prominence of financial information

In addition to the specific contents requirements, Listing Rule 13.5 also includes a number of general provisions regarding the form, source and prominence of financial information to be included in a Class 1 circular.

A listed company must generally present all financial information that is disclosed in a Class 1 circular in a form consistent with the accounting policies adopted in its latest annual consolidated accounts (LR 13.5.4R(1)), save in certain circumstances, such as in relation to pro forma financial information (LR 13.5.4R(2)(b)) or where the financial information is presented in accordance with the accounting policies to be used in the listed company's next financial statements, provided the listed company's last published annual consolidated accounts have been presented on a restated basis consistent with those used in its next accounts on or before the date of the Class 1 circular (LR 13.5.4R(2)(f)) (e.g. in a prospectus published in connection with the Class 1 transaction – see item 20.1 of Annex I of PR Appendix 3). The listed company must also ensure that audited historical financial information is given greater prominence than any forecast, estimated, pro forma or non-statutory financial information (LR 13.5.10R).

Where a Class 1 circular contains a summary of financial information it must also include a statement that investors should read the whole document and not rely solely on the summarised financial information (LR 13.5.11R).

The source of all financial information disclosed must be cited (see LR 13.5.6R; LR 13.5.7G provides guidance on the application of LR 13.5.6R in practice) and, if the financial information has not been extracted directly from audited accounts, the Class 1 circular must set out the basis and the assumptions on which the financial information was prepared and include a statement that the financial information is unaudited or not reported on by an accountant (LR 13.5.8R). A listed company must provide shareholders with all the necessary information to understand the context and relevance of non-statutory figures, including a reconciliation to statutory accounts (LR 13.5.9R).

Accountant's opinion on a Class 1 acquisition

Unless LR 13.5.3AR (Acquisition of an interest in a target that will be accounted for as an investment), LR 13.5.3BR (Acquisition of an interest in a target that will be accounted for using the equity method) or LR 13.5.27R (Acquisition of a publicly traded company) applies, a financial information table must be accompanied by an accountant's opinion (LR 13.5.21R) setting out whether for the purposes of the Class 1 circular the financial information table gives a true and fair view of the financial matters set out within it (LR 13.5.22R). An accountant's opinion must be given by an independent accountant who is qualified to act as an auditor (LR 13.5.23R). If the accountant's opinion is modified or contains an emphasis-of-matter paragraph, details of all material matters must be set out in the Class 1 circular including all reasons for the modifications or emphasis-of-matter paragraph, and a quantification of the effects, if both relevant and practicable (LR 13.5.25R).

Synergy benefits

Where a listed company includes details of estimated synergies or other quantified estimated financial benefits expected to arise from a transaction, it must also include in the Class 1 circular:

- the basis for the belief that those synergies or other quantified estimated financial benefits will arise;
- an analysis and explanation of the constituent elements of the synergies or other quantified estimated financial benefits (including any costs) sufficient to enable the relative importance of those elements to be understood, including an indication of when they will be realised and whether they are expected to be recurring;
- a base figure for any comparison drawn;
- a statement that the synergies or other quantified estimated financial benefits are contingent on the Class 1 transaction and could not be achieved independently; and
- a statement that the estimated synergies or other quantified estimated financial benefits reflect both the beneficial elements and relevant costs (LR 13.5.9AR).

There is no requirement to include an independent expert's report on the synergy statement in the circular.

Pro forma financial information

As described above, a listed company is required to include a statement of the effect of the transaction on the group's earnings and assets and liabilities (LR 13.4.1R(5)). This requirement may be satisfied by the inclusion of pro forma financial information, customarily a pro forma statement of net assets.

If a listed company includes pro forma information, it must (as required by LR 13.5.31G, LR 13.3.3R and Annex I and Annex II of PR Appendix 3), among other things:

- ensure that the pro forma clearly states the purpose for which it has been prepared and the fact that it is for illustrative purposes and may not reflect the company's actual financial position or prospects;
- prepare the pro forma in a manner consistent with the accounting policies adopted in its last or next financial statements;
- ensure that pro forma adjustments are clear, directly attributable to the transaction and factually supportable; and
- include an accountant's report stating that the pro forma has been properly compiled on the basis stated and that basis is consistent with the listed company's accounting policies.

In relation to pro forma financial information, reference should be made to the UKLA Guidance Note *Pro forma financial information (UKLA/TN/633.1)*.

Treatment of profit forecasts and estimates

If a listed company includes a profit forecast or estimate in a Class 1 circular, this must comply with the requirements for a profit forecast or estimate set out in Annex

1 of the PR Appendix 3 (except that a listed company does not need to include a report on the forecast or estimate from an accountant in the Class 1 circular) (LR 13.5.32R(1)). It must also include a statement confirming that the profit forecast or estimate has been properly compiled on the basis of assumptions stated and that the basis of accounting is consistent with the accounting policies of the listed company (LR 13.5.32R(2)). Annex I of the PR Appendix 3 requires, among other things, the profit forecast or estimate to be accompanied by a statement setting out the principal assumptions upon which the company has based its forecast or estimate.

If, prior to the Class 1 transaction, a profit forecast or estimate was published relating to the listed company, a significant part of the listed company's group or the target, and the forecast or estimate relates to financial information including the period of the forecast which has yet to be published at the date of the circular, the listed company must either include that profit forecast or estimate in the Class 1 circular, or include an explanation of why the profit forecast or estimate is no longer valid and why reassessment of the profit forecast or estimate is not necessary to comply with LR 13.3.1R, which sets out the contents requirements for all circulars (LR 13.5.33R).

If a profit forecast or estimate is included in a Class 1 circular, the listed company will have to comply with the requirements in LR 9.2.18R when it publishes its next annual report and so will have to reproduce the profit forecast or estimate, produce the actual figures for the same period and, if the difference is more than 10%, provide an explanation of the difference.

In relation to profit forecasts and estimates, reference should be made to the UKLA Guidance Note *Profit forecasts and estimates* (UKLA/TN/340.1).

Takeover offers

In recognition of the fact that a listed company may not always have sufficient access to information on a target in a takeover situation, in order to enable it to comply with the contents requirements for Class 1 circulars in LR 13.4 (including the requirement to include a working capital statement on the basis that the acquisition has taken place), LR 13.4.3R sets out certain modifications to the general disclosure requirements for Class 1 circulars in connection with a takeover. These modifications to the general disclosure requirements and the general approach of the UKLA to 'limited access' situations are discussed in the UKLA's Guidance Note *Hostile takeovers* (UKLA/TN/305.2).

LR 13.4.3R(1) clarifies that where a Class 1 circular relates to a recommended takeover offer and the listed company has had access to due diligence information on the target at the time of publication of the Class 1 circular, the listed company must prepare and publish its working capital statement on the basis that the acquisition has taken place.

LR 13.4.3R(2) and (3) to (6) provide that where a takeover offer has not been recommended or the listed company has not had access to due diligence information at the time of publication of the Class 1 circular:

- the listed company must prepare and publish its working capital statement on the basis that the acquisition has not taken place;
- other information on the target required to be included in the Class 1 circular by Annex 1 to Listing Rule 13 should be disclosed on the basis of information that has been published or made available by the target and of which the listed company is aware and free to disclose (i.e. the circular should contain publicly available information from the target's website, RIS announcements, published annual reports and accounts etc); and
- if the takeover offer has been recommended, but the listed company has not had access to due diligence information, the Class 1 circular must explain why access has not been given.

Transactions involving property, mineral resources and scientific research-based companies

Special rules also apply where the transaction consists of an acquisition or disposal of property, an acquisition or disposal of mineral resources or an acquisition of a scientific research-based company or related assets by a listed company.

In summary:

- if the transaction relates to the acquisition or disposal of property or the acquisition of a property company that is not listed, the Class 1 circular must include a property valuation report (LR 13.4.4R);
- if a listed company makes significant reference to the value of property in a Class 1 circular, it must include a property valuation report (LR 13.4.5R);
- if the transaction relates to the acquisition or disposal of mineral resources (i.e. ores, aggregates, oil, gas and solid fuels) or rights to mineral resources, the Class 1 circular must include a mineral expert's report and an accompanying glossary of any technical terms used in the report (LR 13.4.6R) (see also LR 13.4.7G for instances where the FCA may modify the requirement for mineral expert's report); and
- if the transaction relates to the acquisition of a 'scientific research-based company' (broadly a company primarily involved in the laboratory research and development of chemical and biological products) or related assets, the Class 1 circular must contain an explanation of the impact of the acquisition on the listed company's business plan, together with details of the listed company's laboratory operations, expertise and experience of technical staff, collaborative R&D agreements and a description of each product the development of which could have a material effect on the prospects of the listed company (LR 13.4.8R and section 1c of Part III of

the ESMA Recommendations for the consistent implementation of the Prospectus Regulation).

Incorporation of information by reference

A Class 1 circular may incorporate information by reference, rather than it being set out in full in the circular, from a prospectus or any other published document filed with the FCA (LR 13.1.3R).

Notwithstanding this, a Class 1 circular must provide a clear and adequate explanation of its subject matter giving due prominence to its essential characteristics, benefits and risks (LR 13.3.1R(1)) and stating why the listed company's shareholders are being asked to vote (LR 13.3.1R(2)); these matters may not be incorporated by reference (LR 13.1.5R).

Where information is incorporated by reference in the circular, the information must be the latest available to the listed company (LR 13.1.4R). The circular must include a cross-reference list to enable shareholders to identify easily specific terms of information incorporated by reference and where it can be obtained (LR 13.1.6R).

1.5.3 Amending the terms of a transaction and supplementary circulars

If a significant change arises after obtaining shareholder approval but before completion of a Class 1 transaction or reverse takeover, the company must, as soon as possible, comply again with the requirements of LR 10.5.1R (i.e. make an announcement through an RIS, publish a further circular and seek its shareholders' consent to the revised transaction) (LR 10.5.2R). The FCA will generally consider an increase in consideration of 10% or more to be a material change of terms (LR 10.5.3G).

If a material change affecting any matter disclosed in the Class 1 circular or a material new matter that would have been required to be disclosed in the circular arises after the publication of the circular but before the date of the general meeting seeking shareholder approval, then the company must notify the FCA and send a supplementary circular to shareholders providing an explanation of the material change or material new matter (LR 10.5.4R). It may become necessary for the listed company to adjourn a convened shareholder meeting if a supplementary circular cannot be sent to shareholders at least seven days prior to the convened shareholder meeting as required by LR 13.1.9R.

When considering the materiality of any change for the purposes of LR 10.5.2R and LR 10.5.4R, the listed company must have regard to LR 13.3.1R(3), which requires a circular to contain all information necessary to allow the security holders to make a properly informed decision.

The FCA notes, in the UKLA Guidance Note *Amendments to the terms of a transaction* (UKLA/TN/304.1), that it is common for resolutions seeking shareholder approval for Class 1 transactions to be subject to non-material amendments to the terms of the transaction, in order to enable directors to make small administrative changes following shareholder approval. The Guidance Note reminds companies that any amendment must be non-material as a material change would probably require fresh shareholder approval or would require a supplementary circular. It is for the UKLA to decide whether any change to the terms of a transaction requires shareholder approval under the Listing Rules, not the company's directors.

The general position is relaxed in takeover offer situations, where the UKLA recognises that in waiving the conditions to the offer, a company could be deemed to be making a material amendment to the terms of the transaction. In these situations, a resolution need not be expressly limited to non-material changes. However, the UKLA will seek confirmation from the company that any material change to the offer price will not be made without prior shareholder approval or by way of a supplementary circular, as applicable.

1.6 Exemption for companies in severe financial difficulty

The FCA recognises that a listed company in severe financial difficulty may find itself with no alternative but to dispose of a substantial part of its business within a short time frame to meet its ongoing working capital requirements or to reduce its liabilities.

Due to time constraints, the listed company may not be able to comply with all of the usual requirements of a Class 1 transaction, described in section 1.5 above, and in particular, may not be able to prepare a circular and convene a general meeting in order to obtain the prior approval of its shareholders (LR 10.8.1G).

Accordingly, the FCA may modify the requirements of Listing Rule 10.5 to prepare a Class 1 circular and to obtain prior shareholder approval for a disposal if the listed company can demonstrate that it is in severe financial difficulty (LR 10.8.1G(2)(a)).

The listed company will need to demonstrate that it could not reasonably have entered into negotiations earlier to enable shareholder approval to be obtained (LR 10.8.2G).

A company seeking to use this exemption should bring the application to the FCA's attention at the earliest available opportunity and at least five clear business days before the terms of the disposal are agreed (LR 10.8.1G(3)).

Once the FCA has granted the waiver, the company will have to announce details about the transaction through an RIS no later than the date the terms of the disposal are agreed (LR 10.8.4G).

1.6.1 Written confirmation to the FCA

The listed company will be required to confirm in writing to the FCA (there is no prescribed form) that:

- negotiation does not allow time for shareholder approval;

- all alternative methods of financing have been exhausted and the only remaining option is to dispose of a substantial part of the business;
- by taking the decision to dispose of part of the business to raise cash, the directors are acting in the best interests of the company and the shareholders as a whole and that unless the disposal is completed receivers, administrators or liquidators are likely to be appointed; and
- where the disposal is to a related party, the disposal to the related party is the only available option in the current circumstances.

The listed company's sponsor will be required to confirm in writing (LR 10.8.3G(2)) to the FCA that, in its opinion and on the basis of information available to it, the listed company is in severe financial difficulty and will not be able to meet its obligations as they fall due unless the disposal takes place in accordance with the proposed timetable.

The persons financing the listed company (i.e. banks providing working capital facilities etc) will be required to confirm in writing (LR 10.8.3G(3)) to the FCA that further finance or facilities will not be made available and that current facilities will be withdrawn unless the disposal is effected immediately.

1.6.2 Announcement of the disposal (LR 10.8.4G)

The listed company will be required to release an announcement via an RIS by no later than the date the terms of the disposal are agreed which should contain:

- all relevant information required to be notified under LR 10.4.1R;
- the name of the acquirer and the expected date of completion of the disposal;
- full disclosure about the continuing group's prospects for at least the current financial year;
- a statement that the directors believe that the disposal is in the best interests of the company and shareholders as a whole, together with a statement that if the disposal is not completed the company will be unable to meet its financial commitments as they fall due and consequently will be unable to continue to trade, resulting in the appointment of receivers, liquidators or administrators;
- a statement incorporating the details of all the confirmations provided to the FCA in LR 10.8.3G (as described above);
- details of any financing arrangements (either current or future) if they are contingent upon the disposal being effected;
- if the disposal is to a related party, a statement that the transaction is fair and reasonable as set out in LR 13.6.1R(5); and
- a statement by the listed company that in its opinion the working capital available to the continuing group is sufficient for the group's present requirements (i.e. for at

least 12 months from the date of the announcement) or, if not, how it proposes to provide any additional working capital that the company thinks it will need.

The announcement should also contain any further information that the listed company and its sponsor consider necessary, including any historical price sensitive information which has already been published in relation to the disposal or any further information required to be disclosed under Articles 17 and 18 of MAR (LR 10.8.5G).

1.6.3 Procedure and FCA approval process

The FCA will wish to examine the written confirmation from the listed company, its sponsor and providers of finance, as required by LR 10.8.3G, and a draft of the RIS announcement before it grants the modification and the announcement is released (LR 10.8.6G(1)).

Accordingly, such documents should be lodged with the FCA in draft form at least five clear business days before the terms of the disposal are agreed and in final form on the day on which approval is sought (LR 10.8.6G(2)).

In relation to the listed company's financial position, Articles 17 and 18 of MAR continue to apply while the company is seeking a modification.

In any event, the directors should consider whether the listed company's financial position is such that they should request a suspension of listing pending publication of an announcement and clarification of the company's financial position (LR 10.8.8G).

1.7 Acquisitions out of administration

In the UKLA Guidance Note *Classification tests (UKLA/TN/302.1)*, the FCA provides guidance to assist companies in determining what financial information to use for the purpose of the class tests in LR 10, and which of the various class tests are relevant, when acquiring a business or assets from liquidators or out of administration.

The FCA has stated that the relevant class tests will depend on what the company is acquiring. If the company is acquiring a business then all tests are relevant, but if it is acquiring assets, the profits test would not be relevant as there is not a relevant profit stream to measure.

The FCA also says in the Guidance Note that when determining what it is acquiring, the company and its advisers may need to consider the type of assets being acquired and whether on a 'look through basis' the company has effectively acquired a business (e.g. if the transaction has been structured as an asset deal for tax or other reasons, despite the intention being for the company to operate the newly acquired entity as a business). The UKLA believes that indications that a company is buying a business for class test purposes might be, for example, an employee transfer and the transfer of contracts and licences; a listed company should look at the commercial reality of the transaction, irrespective of the strict legal form.

As regards financials to be used as a basis for the class test calculations, the FCA states that the company should use the most recent set of accounts available for the target. Where these are significantly out of date, the FCA says that it is happy to discuss alternative sources and the appropriateness of the tests where the results are considered anomalous. However, the FCA reminds advisers that it would often consider the best indicator of the size of the business to be the accounts immediately before the company went into administration. The FCA notes that these accounts are often audited and are considered more reliable than management information. In circumstances where issuers are acquiring businesses or assets out of administration, the FCA suggests that it should be contacted as soon as possible to discuss the issue.

1.8 Joint ventures

LR 10.8.9G deals with how the Listing Rules on significant transactions in LR 10 apply to joint ventures and, in particular the exit provisions. Typically, these give each joint venture partner a combination of rights and obligations either to sell their own holding or to acquire their partner's holding should certain triggering events occur.

Under LR 10.8.9G, if the listed company retains sole discretion over the triggering event, or if the listed company is making a choice to purchase or sell following an event which has been triggered by the joint venture partner, the purchase or sale must be classified when this discretion is exercised or when the choice to purchase or sell is made.

If the listed company does not retain sole discretion over the event which requires it either to purchase the joint venture partner's stake or to sell its own, the obligation to buy or sell must be classified at the time it is agreed as though it had been exercised at that time. If the consideration to be paid is to be determined by reference to the future profitability of the joint venture or an independent valuation at the time of exercise, this consideration will be treated as being uncapped. If this is the case, the initial agreement will be classified in accordance with LR 10 Annex 1 paragraph 5R(3) and (3A) at the time it is entered into. Therefore, if all of the other tests indicate the transaction to be a Class 2 transaction, it will be treated as a Class 1 transaction; if all the other tests indicate the transaction to be a transaction where all the percentage ratios are less than 5% the transaction is to be treated as a Class 2 transaction.

Where the company agrees a joint venture exit arrangement which takes the form of a put or call option and exercise of the option is solely at the discretion of the other party to the arrangement, the transaction should be classified at the time it is agreed as though the option had been exercised at that time.

The FCA states in its UKLA Guidance Note *Classification tests* (UKLA/TN/302.1) that when a premium listed company enters into a joint venture, it should consider whether the terms of the joint venture agreement result in the transaction being classified as a Class 1 transaction under LR 10. The FCA says that it would expect a listed company to classify both sides of the transaction, so that both the disposal of assets into the joint venture and the acquisition of an interest in the joint venture are classified. The FCA says that, as the disposal and acquisition are effectively one transaction, it would not expect the two sets of class tests to be aggregated, but the highest results from the class tests will determine the overall classification of the transaction.

The provisions of Listing Rule 10 and Listing Rule 11 (discussed in section 3 below) must be considered prior to entry into a joint venture by a listed company or its subsidiaries and the exit provisions in the joint venture arrangements may need to allow for the listed company to obtain shareholder approval on an exit.

The FCA recognises that joint venture arrangements can be complex and that classification will depend on the facts of each case (e.g. including the value added by each partner and further funding commitments). As such, the FCA urges issuers and their advisers to contact the UKLA to discuss the correct application of the class tests to their specific transaction.

The FCA recognises that in certain industries, the establishment of a joint venture can be considered as being in the 'ordinary course of business' for a listed company. This may take the transaction outside the scope of Listing Rule 10 (note that the requirement for a transaction to be 'of a revenue nature' (as well as being in the ordinary course of business) was deleted with effect from 1 October 2012). In Consultation Paper CP 06/17, the FSA acknowledged that this may be the case where the joint venture arrangements are close to simple financing arrangements, although the FSA noted that companies would still need to establish that the exemption in LR 10.1.3R(3) should apply having regard to the facts of the particular case. However, the UKLA is less receptive to arguments that any exit arrangements are in the ordinary course of business. It will be harder to prove that the disposal or acquisition of interests in joint ventures is in the ordinary course of business.

Figure 9.1: Skeleton contents of a Class 1 circular

Heading	Disclosure required
Cover	This will include a statement that the document contains important information and that a shareholder should consult his or her financial adviser if in doubt as to the action to be taken (see LR 13.3.1R(4)) and a statement instructing a shareholder to forward the documentation if the shareholder has sold his or her shares (see LR 13.3.1R(6)). In addition, this usually includes statements to draw shareholders' attention to Part I – Letter from the chairman and the recommendation of the directors (see LR 13.3.1R(5)) and to encourage shareholders to read Part II – Risk factors (see LR 13.3.1R(1)).

Heading	Disclosure required
Contents and expected timetable	The contents of the circular and key expected dates in relation to the transaction, including the latest time and date for receipt of proxies, the date of the general meeting and the date on which the transaction is expected to complete.
Part I – Letter from the chairman	This section is usually consistent with the text of the Class 1 announcement (see LR 13.4.1R(1)).
Introduction	A short summary of the transaction that clearly explains why shareholder approval is required, with all the information required to enable shareholders to make a properly informed decision (see LR 13.3.1R(1), (2) and (3)).
Background to and reasons for the transaction	The background to and reasons for the transaction (see LR 10.4.1R(2)(a)). It may include details of any merger benefits and/or cost savings (see LR 10.4.1R(2)(f) and LR 13.3.1R(1)). Any statements on synergies must include the basis for the belief that those synergies will arise (see LR 13.5.9AR).
Information on the target	Information on the business or assets being acquired or sold including a general description of the business or assets and the value of, and gross profits attributable to, the assets (see LR 10.4.1R(2)(b), (d) and (e)).
Principal terms and conditions of the transaction	The key terms of the transaction including the names of the other parties, key details of transaction structure and documentation and the consideration and how it is being satisfied (see LR 10.4.1R(2)(a) and (c) and LR 13.4.1AG), with a cross-reference to the more detailed information in Part III – Principal terms and conditions of transaction.
Financial effects of the transaction	The effects of the transaction on the listed company including any benefits that are likely to accrue to the company as a result of the transaction (see LR 10.4.1R(2)(f)). It must also include a statement of the effect of the transaction on the group's earnings and assets and liabilities (see LR 13.4.1R(5)) – this requirement may be satisfied by the inclusion of some form of earnings enhancement statement and, if included, a cross reference to Part V – Pro forma financial information prepared to show the impact of the transaction on the listed company.
Application of sale proceeds	(On a disposal only), details of what the company will do with the sale proceeds. If shares or other securities form part of the consideration received, whether the securities will be sold or retained (see LR 10.4.1(2)(h) and (i)).

SIGNIFICANT TRANSACTIONS 407

Heading	Disclosure required
Management and employees	A summary of any proposed changes to the Board and management team as a result of the transaction, including details of any key individuals that are important to the business or assets being acquired or sold and details of any proposed directors and the terms of their proposed service contracts (see LR 10.4.1R(2)(g) and (j)).
Current trading, trends and prospects	This should include, for both the listed company and the company or business the subject of the transaction: details of most significant recent trends in trading since the end of the last financial year, together with information on any known trends, uncertainties, demands, commitments or events that are reasonably likely to have a material effect on prospects for at least the current financial year (see Annex 1 to LR 13 and item 12 of Annex I of PR Appendix 3). Where the transaction involves an acquisition, the trend information should be given in a single statement by the listed company on the assumption that the acquisition has taken place. Where the transaction involves a disposal, the information should be given in a single statement by the listed company on the assumption that the disposal has taken place (Annex 1.1 to LR 13, paragraph 1(2))
Shareholder meeting and action to be taken	A summary of the various resolutions to be put to the shareholder meeting, the arrangements for the meeting and details of how a shareholder can vote by proxy (see LR 13.3.1R(4)).
Further information	Where a Class 1 circular contains a summary of financial information, it should include a statement that investors should read the whole document and not rely solely on the summarised financial information (LR 13.5.11R).
Recommendation	A recommendation from the Board as to the voting action that the shareholders should take, indicating whether or not the proposal in the circular is, in the Board's opinion, in the best interests of shareholders as a whole (see LR 13.3.1R(5)).
Part II – Risk factors	The circular is required to include prominent disclosure of the risk factors attached to the listed company and the industry in which they operate (see item 4 of Annex I of PR Appendix 3). Annex 1.1 to LR 13 paragraph 3(4) specifies that only risk factors which: (a) are material risk factors to the proposed transaction; (b) will be material new risk factors to the group as a result of the proposed transaction; or (c) are existing material risk factors to the group which will be impacted by the proposed transaction should be included in the circular.

Heading	Disclosure required
Part III – Principal terms and conditions of transaction	Material terms and conditions of the transaction including the names of the other parties, key details of transaction structure, documentation and the consideration and how it is being satisfied (see LR 10.4.1R(2)(a) and (c) and LR 13.4.1R). Where the transaction involves an issue of listed securities (e.g. as consideration for an acquisition) this section will include details of the proposed date of issue and listing, how the securities rank for dividends and voting compared with the existing listed securities, the treatment of fractions and settlement and trading arrangements (see LR 13.3.1R(9)).
Part IV – Financial information	Includes financial information on the target, namely the company, business or assets that are the subject of the transaction. The information required to be included will depend on the transaction (e.g. an acquisition of a target that will result in the consolidation of the target's assets with those of the listed company or a disposal of an interest in a target that will result in the target's assets no longer being consolidated with the listed company and may or may not require an accountant's report) (see LR 13.5).
Part V – Pro forma financial information	As described above, a listed company is required to include a statement of the effect of the transaction on the group's earnings and assets and liabilities (see LR 13.4.1R(5)). This requirement may be satisfied by the inclusion of pro forma financial information, customarily a pro forma statement of net assets of the continuing or enlarged group. If a listed company includes pro forma information in the circular, the information must include a description of the transaction, the business or the assets involved and the period to which it refers and the company must among other things: ■ ensure that the pro forma clearly states the purpose for which it has been prepared and the fact that it is for illustrative purposes and may not reflect the company's actual financial position or prospects; ■ prepare the pro forma in a manner consistent with the accounting policies adopted in its last or next financial statements; ■ ensure that pro forma adjustments are clear, directly attributable to the transaction and factually supportable; and ■ include an accountant's report stating that the pro forma has been properly compiled on the basis stated and that basis is consistent with the listed company's accounting policies. (See LR 13.3.3R, LR 13.5.31G, item 20.2 of Annex 1 and Annex II of PR Appendix 3.)

Heading	Disclosure required
Part VI – Additional information	Additional information that is required to be included in the circular by the Listing Rules. It typically includes the headings set out below.
Responsibility statement	A declaration from the company and the company directors to the effect that they accept responsibility for the contents of the document and that the information in the document is correct and complete (see LR 13.4.1R(4) for the prescribed wording).
Directors, senior managers and registered office	Names, addresses and functions of the directors and senior managers and details of the listed company's registered office (see Annex 1 to LR 13 and items 5.1.1 and 5.1.4 of Annex I of PR Appendix 3).
Directors' and senior managers' remuneration and service agreements	Details of the service contracts of the directors and senior managers of the listed company (see LR 10.4.1R(2)(g), Annex 1 to LR 13 and item 16.2 of Annex I of PR Appendix 3). If the information relating to terms of service contracts has already been published before the circular is sent (e.g. in a listed company's annual report and accounts) then it does not need to be included in the circular.
Directors' and senior managers' interests	Details of interests in shares and options over shares of directors and senior managers of the listed company (see Annex 1 to LR 13 and item 17.2 of Annex I of PR Appendix 3). If the transaction involves the listed company issuing shares that will be listed, then this statement must be given for the share capital before and after the issue of the new shares for which listing will be sought (Annex 1 to LR 13, paragraph 3(1)).
Major shareholdings	Details of those shareholders that are required to notify their interests in voting rights, whether any such shareholders have different voting rights and whether the listed company is controlled by a party and the measures in place to ensure that such control is not abused, or appropriate negative statements (see Annex 1 to LR 13 and item 18.1 of Annex I of PR Appendix 3). If the transaction involves the listed company issuing shares that will be listed, then this statement must be given for the share capital before and after the issue of the new shares for which listing will be sought (Annex 1 to LR 13, paragraph 3(1)).
Material contracts	A summary, for both the listed company and the company or business which is the subject of the transaction of (a) material contracts entered into in the two years prior to the date of the circular, other than in the ordinary course of business, to which the listed company or any member of its group is a party; and (b) any other contracts, not entered into in the ordinary course of business, which contain any provision under which any member of the group has an obligation or entitlement which is material to the group as at the date of the circular (see Annex 1 to LR 13 and item 22

Heading	Disclosure required
Material contracts	of Annex I of PR Appendix 3). In determining what information should be included in the circular, the listed company should have regard to information that a shareholder would reasonably require to make an informed assessment about how to vote on the transaction described in the circular (Annex 1 to LR 13, paragraph 2). Where the transaction involves an acquisition by a listed company, the information must be given for the listed company, its group and also for the target. Where the transaction involves a disposal by a listed company, the information must be given for the listed company, its group (assuming the disposal had taken place) and also for the target being disposed of (Annex 1 to LR 13, paragraph 1). If there is no information to disclose, it is customary to include a negative statement.
Related party transactions	Details of related party transactions (as defined by IFRS) that the listed company has entered into prior to the date of the circular (see Annex 1 to LR 13 and item 19 of Annex I of PR Appendix 3). If the information required to be disclosed has already been published before the circular is sent (e.g. in a listed company's annual report and accounts) then it does not need to be included in the circular.
Litigation	Information, for both the listed company and the company or business which is the subject of the transaction, on any governmental, legal or arbitration proceedings (including where pending or threatened) during a period covering at least the last 12 months which may have or have had in the recent past, significant effects on the listed company and the group's financial position or profitability (see Annex 1 to LR 13 and item 20.8 of Annex I of PR Appendix 3). Where the transaction involves an acquisition by a listed company, the information must be given for the listed company, its group and also for the target. Where the transaction involves a disposal by a listed company, the information must be given for the listed company, its group (assuming the disposal had taken place) and also for the target being disposed of (see Annex 1 to LR 13, paragraph 1). If there is no information to disclose, a negative statement is required.
Significant change	Details, for both the listed company and the company or business which is the subject of the transaction, of any significant change in the financial or trading position of the group which has occurred since the end of the last financial period for which either audited financial information or interim financial information has been published (see Annex 1 to LR 13 and item 20.9 of Annex I of PR Appendix 3). If relevant, the circular must include a clear explanation of recent developments that constitute a significant change. The FCA will not accept a cross-reference to the current trading and prospects. Where the transaction involves an acquisition

SIGNIFICANT TRANSACTIONS

Heading	Disclosure required
Significant change	by a listed company, the information must be given for the listed company, its group and also for the target. Where the transaction involves a disposal by a listed company, the information must be given for the listed company and its group (assuming the disposal had taken place) and also for the target being disposed of (see Annex 1 to LR 13, paragraph 1). If there is no information to disclose, a negative statement is required.
Working capital	The circular is required to include a statement by the listed company that, in its opinion, the working capital is sufficient for the issuer's present requirements (i.e. for at least the next 12 months from the date of the circular) or, if not, how it proposes to provide the additional working capital needed (see Annex 1 to LR 13 and item 3.1 of Annex III of PR Appendix 3). Where the transaction involves an acquisition by a listed company, the statement should be given by the listed company on the assumption that the acquisition has taken place. Where the transaction involves a disposal by a listed company, the statement should be given by the listed company on the assumption that the disposal has taken place (see Annex 1 to LR 13, paragraph 1(2)).
Consents	A confirmation that where a person is named as having advised the directors of the listed company, such person has given and not withdrawn his or her written consent to the inclusion of references to his or her name in the circular (e.g. financial advisers and accountants) (see LR 13.3.1R(10) and LR 13.4.1R(6)).
Documents available for inspection	The documents that are available for inspection in connection with the publication of the circular (e.g. the listed company's memorandum and articles of association, annual report and accounts and any accountants' reports included in the circular) (see Annex 1 of LR 13 and item 24 of Annex I of PR Appendix 3). See also UKLA Guidance Note *Documents on display (UKLA/TN/623.1)*, which sets out the FCA's view that the sale and purchase agreement should be put on display.
Information incorporated by reference	Where information is incorporated by reference into the circular, rather than being set out in full in the circular, the circular must include a cross-reference list setting out details of the information incorporated by reference and from where it can be obtained (see LR 13.1.3R, but note the requirements of LR 13.1.5R).
Definitions	Defined terms used in the circular. Where it is helpful to assist the shareholders' understanding of the transaction and/or the business or assets being acquired or sold, the company may also choose to include a glossary of technical terms.
Notice of meeting	The notice of the meeting containing a resolution to approve the transaction is generally included in the back of the circular, rather than in a separate document.

Figure 9.2: List of key documents required in connection with the preparation and publication of a Class 1 circular

Key document	Primary responsibility
Announcement	Listed company, listed company's lawyers and the sponsor
Circular	Listed company, listed company's lawyers and the sponsor
Notice of meeting	Listed company and its lawyers
Form of proxy	Listed company and its lawyers
Board minutes	Listed company and its lawyers
Directors' responsibility statements	Listed company's lawyers
Memorandum on directors' responsibilities	Listed company's lawyers
Verification notes	Listed company and its lawyers
Financial adviser's engagement letter	Sponsor and its lawyers
Sponsor's agreement	Sponsor and its lawyers
Sponsor's comfort letters	Sponsor, its lawyers and the providers of the comfort letters
Reporting accountants' engagement letter	Reporting accountants
Working capital report and comfort letter	Reporting accountants
Significant change comfort letter	Reporting accountants
Correct extraction comfort letter	Reporting accountants
Report on pro forma financial information	Reporting accountants
Report on reconciliation of financial information (if applicable)	Reporting accountants
Consent letter for inclusion of reports in the circular	Reporting accountants
Letter to the FCA confirming application of the class tests	Sponsor
Sponsor's declaration on publication of a circular	Sponsor

2. Reverse takeovers

Unlike the rules on significant transactions and related party transactions, which only apply to premium listed companies, the reverse takeover regime applies to premium and standard listed companies (and to issuers with a standard listing of certificates representing equity securities (including global depositary receipts (GDRs)). The rules are set out in LR 5.6.

A reverse takeover is a transaction involving an acquisition of a business, a company or assets where any percentage ratio is 100% or more (using the class tests in LR 10, discussed in section 1.2 above, including LR 10.2.10R on aggregation of transactions) or which, in substance, results in a fundamental change in its business or in a change in board or voting control of the company (LR 5.6.4R). The regime applies whether the transaction is effected by way of a direct acquisition by the listed company or a subsidiary, or by a new holding company of the listed company or otherwise.

The FCA states in LR 5.6.5G that it considers that the following factors are indicators of a fundamental change:

- the extent to which the transaction will change the strategic direction or nature of the business; or
- whether its business will be part of a different industry sector following the completion of the transaction; or
- whether its business will deal with fundamentally different suppliers and end users.

2.1 Application of rules to a premium listed company

If the company has a premium listing, in addition to complying with the requirements in LR 5.6 (discussed below), it must also comply with the Class 1 requirements in LR 10.5 for the reverse takeover transaction (i.e. make an RIS announcement, prepare a Class 1 circular and obtain shareholder approval, as detailed in section 1.5 above) (LR 5.6.3R).

The requirements for a reverse takeover do not apply where the listed company acquires a target in the same category of listing as the company (e.g. when a premium listed company acquires another premium listed company) regardless of size (LR 5.6.2R). This exemption is narrower than that previously available under LR 10.6, which applied as long as the target was listed, irrespective of the listing category. Accordingly, the exemption is not available if a premium listed company is acquiring a standard listed company or vice versa. In the FCA's view, the exemption should not be used as a 'back-door' route for entities to obtain a listing when they would not be eligible for that type of listing.

2.2 Suspension of listing

Generally, when a reverse takeover is announced or leaked, there will be insufficient information in the market about the proposed transaction and the listed company will be unable to assess its financial position with accuracy and inform the market accordingly. This will invariably be the case where the target is a privately held company, business or assets in relation to which there is little publicly available information. In this case the FCA will often consider that suspension of listing will be appropriate. Accordingly, a listed company or, in the case of a premium listed issuer, its sponsor, will need to contact the FCA as early as possible before announcing a reverse takeover that has been agreed or is in contemplation or where details of the transaction have leaked (LR 5.6.6R).

LR 5.6.7G sets out examples of when the FCA will consider that a reverse takeover is in contemplation and sufficiently advanced to trigger a potential suspension requirement. These examples include situations where the company has approached the target's Board; where the company has entered into an exclusivity period with the target; or where the company has been given access to begin due diligence work. The UKLA has indicated that it appreciates that, at times, the situation may not be as clear cut as set out in these examples and there may be situations where there has been a purely speculative leak where a potential suspension would be inappropriate. In 2013, the FSA fined Prudential plc £14 million for a breach of what is now Listing Principle 2, which requires listed companies to deal with the UKLA in an open and co-operative manner. The fine related to a proposed reverse takeover. At the time, there was no separate obligation under the Listing Rules to notify the FSA of a proposed reverse takeover. The FSA concluded that Prudential plc breached the Listing Principle by failing to inform the UKLA of its proposed acquisition of AIA as the company only approached the FSA after the proposal had leaked. The final notice contains some commentary on when the FCA should be notified of a proposed reverse takeover. The FSA said that the company should have informed the UKLA about the transaction when the company's leak strategy changed so that, instead of ending talks in the event of a leak, it agreed it would confirm that discussions were ongoing.

In the UKLA Guidance Note *Reverse takeovers* (UKLA/TN/306.3), the UKLA states that the Listing Rules create a 'rebuttable presumption' that a company will be suspended upon announcement or leak of a reverse takeover. When suspending, the UKLA will rely on the general suspension powers set out in LR 5. LR 5.1.2G(4) (which gives examples of when the FCA may suspend a listing) refers only to a 'proposed transaction'. However, the UKLA considers this to refer to the situation where information has been announced or leaked in relation to transactions under contemplation, as well as those where the terms have been agreed.

The FCA has published a consultation paper (CP 17/4) which proposes changes to the Listing Rules in respect of reverse takeovers. Under the current rules, when a proposed reverse takeover becomes public, the FCA will suspend the issuer's listing if there is insufficient information about the proposed transaction available for the market to properly assess the transaction. The FCA is proposing to remove this 'rebuttable presumption' of suspension in Listing Rule 5, on the basis that it will assume that proper price formation can occur on the basis of the information that listed companies make public as part of their compliance with their existing continuing obligations, including under MAR. However, the 'rebuttable presumption' of suspension will still apply to shell companies. The FCA states in its UKLA Guidance Note *Reverse takeovers* (UKLA/TN/306.3) that it is also aware that competitive auction processes are often difficult to fit into this framework, so it is open to discussing the specifics of each case with companies and their advisers. It also indicates that in making the decision about whether it is appropriate to consider suspension, it would expect companies to apply a similar rationale as they would when considering the announcement requirements under MAR and the FCA notes that it would not, for example, expect a company to request a suspension where the transaction in question is too speculative to trigger an announcement.

2.2.1 When a suspension will not be required

Where the FCA is satisfied that the market has sufficient information about the transaction, it may agree that suspension is not required. The FCA will generally be satisfied that a suspension is not required in the circumstances set out in LR 5.6.10G to LR 5.6.18R (described below).

Target admitted to a regulated market (LR 5.6.10G)

The FCA will generally be satisfied that suspension is not required where the target is admitted to an EU-regulated market and the company announces via an RIS that the target has complied with that market's disclosure requirements.

Target subject to disclosure regime of another market (LR 5.6.12G)

If the target is admitted to a market other than an EU regulated market, the FCA will generally be satisfied that there is sufficient publicly available information in the market about the transaction if the company confirms, in a form acceptable to the FCA, that the requirements of that other market in relation to financial information and inside information are not materially different from the disclosure requirements under MAR (LR 5.6.12G(1)). In addition, the company must announce via an RIS that the target has complied with the disclosure requirements applicable on the market to which it is admitted and that there are no material differences between those disclosure requirements and the disclosure requirements under MAR (LR 5.6.12G(2)).

Where the company is a premium listed company, the confirmation provided for the purposes of LR 5.6.12G(1) must be given by the company's sponsor (LR 5.6.13R).

With regard to the need for a written confirmation and announcement, the FCA (then, the FSA) indicated in its consultation on the rules, CP 12/25, that LR 5.6.12G is not a requirement, but rather a concession from the normal requirement for the suspension of a company's securities. The over-arching policy objective in this area is to ensure that there is sufficient publicly available information to enable a company's securities to continue to trade. The FCA made it clear that if the company itself is not able to confirm that this is the case, it would not be appropriate to grant such concession.

Target not subject to a public disclosure regime (LR 5.6.15G)

Where the target in a reverse takeover is not subject to a disclosure regime, or where the company is unable to give the requisite confirmation about the disclosure regime, the FCA will generally be satisfied that there is sufficient publicly available information in the market about the proposed transaction, such that a suspension is not required, where the listed company makes an RIS announcement containing:

- financial information on the target covering the last three years (information on profit and loss, balance sheet information and cash flow and a description of the key differences between the listed company's accounting policies and the policies used to present the target's financial information will generally be sufficient);
- a description of the target including appropriate key non-financial operating or performance measures appropriate to the target's business operations and the information as required under PR Appendix 3 Annex 1 item 12 (trend information) for the target;
- a declaration that the directors of the listed company consider that the announcement contains sufficient information about the business to be acquired to provide a properly informed basis for assessing its financial position; and
- a statement confirming that the company has made the necessary arrangements with the target vendors to enable it to keep the market informed without delay of any developments concerning the target that would be required to be released were the target part of the issuer (LR 5.6.15G).

Where the company has a premium listing, the sponsor must provide written confirmation to the FCA that, in its opinion, it is reasonable for the company to provide the final two declarations above (LR 5.6.17R).

Where the FCA is satisfied that a suspension is not necessary as a result of this information having been announced, the listed company must disclose inside information on the basis that the target already forms part of the enlarged group. In practice, this means that the company will be required to keep the market informed without delay of any developments concerning the target business that would be required to be released were the enlarged group listed. The company must, therefore, put systems and controls in place to ensure that the target is brought within its existing disclosure processes.

2.3 Cancellation of listing

When the reverse takeover is completed, the FCA will generally seek to cancel the listing of the listed company's securities (LR 5.6.19G) and the company will, if it wishes to remain admitted to listing on the Official List, need to reapply. This will require the preparation and production of a prospectus for the enlarged group in relation to the re-admission of its securities.

On a re-application, the company benefits from a relaxation to the listing requirements set out in LR 6.1.3R(1)(b) and LR 6.1.3R(1)(e) in that it is not required to have audited financial statements for a period ending not more than six months before the prospectus (LR 5.6.21R). However, the financial information on the target will have to comply with those requirements.

2.3.1 When the company's listing will not be cancelled

Notwithstanding the above, in certain circumstances the FCA will generally be satisfied that a cancellation of listing is not required on completion of a reverse takeover.

Company maintaining its listing category (LR 5.6.23G to LR 5.6.26R)

Where a listed company acquires a target's shares or certificates representing equity securities of a target with a different listing category and the company wishes to remain in the same listing category, the FCA will generally be satisfied that a cancellation is not required if:

- the company will continue to be eligible for its existing listing category after completion of the transaction;
- the company (or the sponsor if the company has a premium listing) provides an eligibility letter to the FCA setting out how the company, as enlarged, satisfies the eligibility requirements for its listing category; and
- the company makes an RIS announcement or publishes a circular explaining the background and reasons for the acquisition; any changes to the company's business that have been made or are proposed in connection with the acquisition; the effect of the transaction on the company's Listing Rule obligations; how the company will continue to meet eligibility requirements (if appropriate); and any other matter that the FCA may reasonably require.

Company changing listing category (LR 5.6.27G to LR 5.6.29G)

If a listed company acquires a target in a different listing category and the company wishes to transfer its listing to a different listing category in conjunction with the acquisition, the FCA will generally not cancel the company's listing if the company, as enlarged by the acquisition, complies with the Listing Rule requirements in relation to a transfer to a different listing category (as set out in LR 5.4A). LR 5.4A requires a notification to the FCA, preparation of a circular and shareholder approval in certain circumstances or an RIS announcement, and an application for transfer (see Chapter 2 for more information on transferring between listing categories).

A company wishing to transfer from a premium listing to a standard listing should note LR 5.4A.2G which says that a premium listed investment company cannot transfer to a standard listing, unless (a) it has ceased to be an investment company or (b) it continues to have a premium listing of a class of its equity shares.

Where the company is transferring between listing categories to avoid a cancellation, the FCA will normally waive the requirement for shareholder approval under LR 5.4A.4R for that transfer where the company is obtaining separate shareholder approval for the acquisition (LR 5.6.29G).

3. Related party transactions

Listing Rule 11 sets out safeguards that apply to transactions and arrangements between a premium listed company and a related party or between a premium listed company and a third party the purpose and effect of which is to benefit a related party. The safeguards are designed to protect shareholders of the listed company by preventing a related party of the listed company (or its subsidiaries) taking advantage of its position and also preventing any perception that it may have done so (LR 11.1.2G).

In broad terms, subject to limited exceptions, where any transaction or arrangement (other than a transaction or arrangement in the ordinary course of business) is proposed between a listed company (or any of its subsidiary undertakings) and a related party, or between a listed company and a third party the purpose and effect of which is to benefit a related party, an RIS announcement, a circular and the prior approval of the shareholders in general meeting will generally be required (LR 11.1.7R(1) to (3)). Further, the related party will not be permitted to vote at that meeting (LR 11.1.7R(4)).

The circular to be sent to shareholders in connection with a related party transaction must include a confirmation from the directors that the transaction is 'fair and reasonable' and that the directors have been so advised by a sponsor (LR 13.6.1R(5)).

3.1 Defining 'related party transactions'

3.1.1 Meaning of 'transaction'

Under LR 11.1.5R, a 'related party transaction' is:

- a transaction (other than a transaction in the ordinary course of business) between a listed company and a related party;
- an arrangement (other than an arrangement in the ordinary course of business) pursuant to which a listed company and a related party each invests in, or provides finance to, another undertaking or asset; or

- any other similar transaction or arrangement (other than a transaction in the ordinary course of business) between a listed company and any other person the purpose and effect of which is to benefit a related party.

References to transactions or arrangements by a listed company in LR 11 includes transactions or arrangements by its subsidiary undertakings and is – unless the contrary intention appears – a reference to the entering into of the agreement or arrangement (LR 11.1.3R(1)).

Variations or novations of an existing agreement or arrangement between a listed company and a related party will also constitute 'related party transactions' whether or not the related party was such at the time the original agreement was entered into (LR 11.1.9G).

As is the case for significant transactions, guidance is given in the Listing Rules as to what is in the 'ordinary course of business'. LR 11.1.5AG provides that, in assessing whether or not a transaction is in the 'ordinary course of business', regard should be had to the size and incidence of the transactions and whether or not its terms and conditions are unusual. This reflects the FCA's recognition of the argument that, for example, in certain industries joint ventures may be entered into in the ordinary course of business.

In its UKLA Guidance Note *Ratification circulars (UKLA/TN/204.2)*, the FCA provides some guidance as to whether ratification circulars, in which a resolution is put to shareholders proposing to ratify an action or omission by a director, constitutes a related party transaction. A typical example would be the passing of a resolution to remedy the invalid declaration of a dividend. As this action would have the effect of removing an actual or potential liability of the director, such circular could be viewed as a related party transaction under LR 11.1.5R(3). The FCA says in its Guidance Note that it will not normally be appropriate to treat these as related party transactions, as the potential benefit to the director is very remote. However, where a specific resolution (or part of a resolution) is included in the circular that has the effect of expressly releasing the directors from liability, in the UKLA's view it is hard to conclude that any potential benefit is only ancillary or remote. There may be other cases where a proposed ratification resolution confers a clear benefit on a related party and should be regulated by LR 11. If companies or advisers are concerned that this might be case, they should contact the UKLA at an early stage.

3.1.2 Meaning of 'related party'

LR 11.1.4R specifies four categories of 'related parties':

- any person who is (or was within the 12 months prior to the date of the transaction or arrangement) a substantial shareholder;
- any person who is (or was within the 12 months prior to the date of the transaction or arrangement) a director or shadow director of the listed company (or any company within its group);

- any other person who exercises significant influence over the listed company; and
- any associate of such persons.

A substantial shareholder is defined in LR 11.1.4AR, as a person who is entitled to exercise, or to control the exercise of, 10% or more of the votes able to be cast on all (or substantially all) matters at general meetings of the company (or of any company which is its subsidiary undertaking or parent undertaking or of a fellow subsidiary undertaking of its parent undertaking).

Certain voting rights are disregarded for the purposes of calculating voting rights, such as those exercised independently in the capacity as bare trustee, investment manager or collective investment undertaking (subject to certain restrictions set out in LR 11.1.4AR(1)), those held in relation to the underwriting of securities and those held for a very short period of time (e.g. a bank arranging a block trade of shares in a listed company).

The definition of 'associate' for the purposes of LR 11 where the related party is an individual includes:

- an individual's spouse, civil partner or child;
- trustees of any trust of which the individual or an individual's family member is a beneficiary or discretionary object;
- any company where the individual or any member of the individual's family (taken together) controls 30% or more of the voting rights or is able to appoint or remove directors holding a majority of voting rights at Board meetings on substantially all matters; or
- any partnership, limited partnership or limited liability partnership where the individual or any member of his family (taken together) control a voting interest greater than 30% in the partnership, or at least 30% of the partnership.

Where the related party is a company, its associates will include its subsidiary undertakings, parent undertaking and fellow subsidiary undertakings.

3.1.3 Applying the rules to joint ventures and dual listed company structures

Fifty-fifty joint venture partners used to be expressly included as related parties but the definition of a 'related party' was amended to remove them. However, joint venture partners may still be caught because a party which holds more than 10% of shares in a listed company's subsidiary undertaking will be a related party of the listed company. Where a joint venture company is a subsidiary undertaking of the listed company (i.e. the listed company holds a majority of the voting rights, has the right to appoint a majority of directors or has the right to exercise a dominant influence over the joint venture company), any other partner to the joint venture which holds between 10% and 49% of the joint venture will be a related party of the listed company.

There is an exemption for joint investment arrangements which may exempt an investment in a joint venture. However, it will only be available if the specific requirements of the exemption are met (see section 3.2.4) and will only apply to any investments in the joint venture and not, for example, to any exit arrangements.

The 'insignificant subsidiary undertakings' exemption (discussed in section 3.2.4 below) may also apply.

If the joint venture partner is a related party and there are any circumstances where, for example, the listed company may be required to sell its interest in the joint venture or to buy the other party's interest in the joint venture, those requirements will have to be conditional on the listed company obtaining shareholder approval.

In earlier informal guidance on the rules, the then FSA set out guidance on how the rules might apply to a dual listed company (DLC) structure. It noted that, in determining whether a shareholder should be treated as a substantial shareholder for the purposes of LR 11.1.4R, the percentage holding across the two parent companies of a dual listed company should be aggregated, rather than just taking the individual holdings within each parent (see List! Issue No. 22 and p. 21 of the FSA's old 2010 Technical Note: *Listing Rules*). However, this has not been repeated in the UKLA Guidance Notes so there is no formal guidance on this.

3.1.4 The need for systems and controls to identify related party transactions

In June 2015, the FCA fined Asia Resource Minerals (formerly known as Bumi) £4.65 million for breaches of the Listing Rules, principally for failing, in its systems and controls, to identify related party transactions.

Asia Resource Minerals had a key Indonesian subsidiary in which it held a majority stake. The subsidiary was itself listed on the Indonesian Stock Exchange. Following a review of its internal processes and historic potential related party transactions in 2012, Asia Resource Minerals identified three transactions entered into by the subsidiary that were related party transactions, because they were with companies associated with a non-executive director of Asia Resource Minerals, but which had not been identified as such at the time they were entered into.

Asia Resource Minerals had also failed to aggregate the transactions as required by LR 11.1.11R. Had they done so, the rules for smaller related party transactions would have applied (see section 3.5 below). Asia Resource Minerals was also unable to confirm that all other previously unknown related party transactions had been identified.

The FCA found that Asia Resource Minerals had breached:

- what is now Listing Principle 1 (formerly Listing Principle 2) for failing to adequately implement its related party transaction policy, including providing appropriate training for the subsidiary board and other employees on RPT procedures;

- Listing Rule 11 for failing to comply with the requirements for related party transactions; and
- LR 8.2.3R for failing to consult a sponsor when proposing to enter into the related party transactions.

This case illustrates the FCA's focus on systems and controls around related party transactions, the need to implement, as well as draw up, policies and the need for training at board, subsidiary board and senior management level.

Prior to this, in April 2012, Exillon Energy, a premium-listed Isle of Man company, was also fined £292,950 for breaching the rules on related party transactions in LR 11.

Following its listing in 2009, Exillon continued a practice it had previously adopted of paying its chairman's personal (not business-related) expenses. At the end of the year, there was then a reconciliation process and these payments were deducted from his salary. If the expenses exceeded his unpaid salary, the chairman repaid the excess with interest.

The then FSA concluded that these payments constituted related party transactions. They amounted to a loan from the company to a related party (i.e. the director). When they exceeded, in aggregate, more than 0.25% of Exillon's market value, the company should have complied with the rules for smaller related party transactions.

The FSA also concluded that the company had breached what is now Listing Principle 1 because it had failed to take reasonable steps to establish and maintain procedures, systems and controls to enable it to comply with its related party transaction obligations. It said that the training provided to the operational managers who were responsible for identifying related party transactions was inadequate and, as a result, they failed to identify the payment of the chairman's expenses as related party transactions.

Both of these notices highlight the importance not only of having policies to assist in compliance with the LPDT Rules (and MAR) but also of ensuring that they are properly implemented.

3.2 Transactions that are not subject to the requirements of Listing Rule 11

3.2.1 Application of Listing Rule 11

Listing Rule 11 does not automatically apply to each transaction or arrangement that falls within the definition of 'related party transaction'. It does not apply to small transactions or certain types of related party transactions that do not have unusual features (LR 11.1.6R), as described below.

Where a listed company is contemplating a transaction or arrangement that could be a related party transaction, it is required to obtain the guidance of a sponsor on the potential application of Listing Rule 11 to the transaction or arrangement in question (LR 11.1.6R) (see section 2.1 of Chapter 3).

3.2.2 Small transactions

A 'small transaction' is a transaction or arrangement where each of the percentage ratios used to assess the size of a transaction for the purposes of Listing Rule 10 (see section 1.2 above) is equal to or less than 0.25%. Small transactions are not subject to the requirements of Listing Rule 11 (LR 11.1.6R(1) and paragraph 1 of Annex 1 of Listing Rule 11).

3.2.3 Transactions agreed before a person became a related party

These are transactions whose terms were agreed at a time when no party to the transaction, or person who was to receive the benefit of the transaction, was a related party and which have not been amended, or required the exercise of discretion by the listed company under those terms, since the party or person became a related party (LR 11 Annex 1, paragraph 1A).

3.2.4 Other exempt transactions or arrangements

Paragraphs 2 to 9 of Annex 1 of Listing Rule 11 set out details of other transactions or arrangements that are also exempt from the requirements of Listing Rule 11 provided that they have no unusual features.

There is no official guidance on what 'unusual features' are but, at its series of 'sponsors' seminars' in Summer 2005, the then FSA indicated that 'unusual features' could include a transaction that had been structured to exploit a loophole in the Listing Rules or where the underlying reason for the transaction was pressure from a related party.

The exemptions in Annex 1 of Listing Rule 11 can be summarised as follows:

- *Issue of new securities and sale of treasury shares* – the take up of new securities or treasury shares by a related party under its entitlement in a pre-emptive offering or an issue of new securities made under the exercise of conversion or subscription rights attaching to a listed class of securities (LR 11 Annex 1, paragraph 2).
- *Employee share schemes* – the receipt of any asset (including cash or securities of the listed company) by, or the grant of an option or other right to acquire an asset to, a director of the listed company, its parent undertaking or any subsidiary undertaking (or the provision of a gift or loan to the trustees of an employee benefit trust to finance the same) in accordance with the terms of an employees' share scheme or a long-term incentive scheme (LR 11 Annex 1, paragraph 3).
- *Credit arrangements* – any grant of credit (including lending of money or guaranteeing a loan) (i) to a related party on normal commercial terms, (ii) to a director for an amount and on terms no more favourable than those offered to group employees, or (iii) by the related party on normal commercial terms and on an unsecured basis (LR 11 Annex 1, paragraph 4).

- *Directors' indemnities and loans* – any transaction that consists of (i) granting an indemnity, in terms permitted to be given to a director under CA 2006, to a director of the listed company or its subsidiaries, (ii) maintaining a contract of insurance if the insurance is in accordance with that specifically permitted to be maintained under CA 2006, or (iii) a loan or assistance to a director by a listed company or its subsidiaries in terms permitted to be given to a director under sections 204, 205 or 206 of CA 2006 (LR 11 Annex 1, paragraph 5). The CA 2006 test for the permitted terms of the indemnity or contract of insurance applies even if the listed company is not itself subject to the CA 2006.
- *Underwriting arrangements* – save to the extent that a related party is underwriting securities which it is entitled to take up under an issue, the underwriting by a related party of all or part of an issue of securities by the listed company or its subsidiaries provided the commission to be paid by the listed company or its subsidiaries is (i) no more than usual commercial underwriting consideration and (ii) the same as that to be paid to any other underwriters (LR 11 Annex 1, para. 6).
- *Joint investment arrangements* – an arrangement where a listed company or its subsidiaries and a related party each invests in (or provides finance to) another undertaking or asset provided that: (i) the related party does not invest more than 25% of the amount invested by the listed company or its subsidiaries, and (ii) a sponsor provides a written opinion to the FCA (before the investment is made or the finance provided) stating that the terms and circumstances of the investment or provision of finance by the listed company or subsidiary undertaking are no less favourable than the terms upon which the related party is investing or providing finance (LR 11 Annex 1, para. 8).
- *Insignificant subsidiary undertakings* – transactions where the related party is only a related party through being a substantial shareholder, director or shadow director (or any such person's associate) of an insignificant subsidiary of the listed company. For these purposes, an insignificant subsidiary is a subsidiary which has (or, if there is more than one subsidiary, that have in aggregate) contributed less than 10% of the profits of, and represented less than 10% of the assets of the listed company for each of the three full financial years preceding the date of the transaction for which accounts have been published (and subject to the satisfaction of further conditions set out in LR 11 Annex 1, para. 9, including that the subsidiary undertaking has been in the listed company's group for one full financial year or more).

Where a company is entering into, or amending, a relationship agreement to comply with the Listing Rule requirements in relation to controlling shareholders (see section 4 below), the FCA said in its policy statement on those rules (PS 14/8) that it would not see these as being related party transactions where it is purely intended to address the requirements in LR 6.1.4BR(1) or LR 9.2.2AR(2)(a).

3.2.5 The enhanced oversight regime where a premium listed company has a controlling shareholder

Where a premium listed company has a controlling shareholder, as discussed in section 4 below, it must have an agreement in place with that controlling shareholder which contains binding undertakings (referred to in the rules as 'independence provisions'). In order to ensure a controlling shareholder complies with the requirements, the Listing Rules provide that the company's independent shareholders (i.e. the shareholders in the company other than the controlling shareholder(s)) have 'enhanced oversight' (i.e. they will have the right to vote on all related party transactions between a controlling shareholder and the company regardless of size or whether another exemption is available), if:

- the company fails to put in place a relationship agreement;
- the company has not complied with the independence provisions contained in any such agreement;
- the company becomes aware that the controlling shareholder or any of its associates has not complied with the independence provisions;
- the company becomes aware that the controlling shareholder has failed to procure that another controlling shareholder or its associates complies with the provisions where it has undertaken to do so in the agreement; or
- an independent director does not agree with the Board's assessment of whether these obligations have been complied with (as discussed in section 4 below, the company's annual report must include a statement by the Board regarding compliance with the independence provisions) (LR 11.1.1AR and LR 11.1.1CR).

These protections will stay in place until the next annual report in which the Board gives a clean statement of compliance for the preceding financial year, with no dissent from any of the independent directors (LR 11.1.1ER).

The FCA may waive or modify these requirements (LR 11.1.BG and LR 11.1.1DG). The FCA said in its policy statement on the rules (PS 14/8) that, if a company goes into the enhanced oversight regime, it would expect the company to discuss and agree with the FCA the types of transactions that could continue to be treated as ordinary course, and thus be exempt from the approval requirements, because the intention is not to prohibit ordinary course transactions, but to subject them to increased scrutiny. The obligation to pre-clear such transactions with the UKLA is part of the enhanced oversight measures and is not a simple notification obligation.

3.3 Requirements for a related party transaction

3.3.1 Related party transaction requirements and procedure

Where a listed company is contemplating a transaction that is or may be a related party transaction, LR 8.2.3R requires it to obtain the guidance of a sponsor to assess the application of Listing Rule 11 (see section 2.1 of Chapter 3). This requirement applies even if the transaction turns out to be small and not subject to the requirements of Listing Rule 11.

When a company enters into a related party transaction it must:

- make an RIS announcement containing prescribed detailed of the transaction and the related party;
- send a circular to its shareholders; and
- obtain shareholder approval for the transaction either before it is entered into or before it is completed (LR 11.1.7R).

The company will also need confirmation from a sponsor that the terms of the transaction are fair and reasonable (LR 13.6.1R(5)).

These requirements are modified where the transaction is a 'smaller related party transaction' – see section 3.5 below.

Notification to an RIS

As soon as possible after the terms of the transaction are agreed, a listed company must make an announcement through an RIS (LR 11.1.7R(1)). The information required to be included in the announcement is the same as that required by LR 10.4.1R(2) for a Class 2 transaction (see section 1.4). The announcement must also include the name of the related party and details of the nature and extent of the related party's interest in the transaction or arrangement.

Circular

In addition to making an RIS announcement, a listed company is required to send a circular to its shareholders containing the information required by LR 13.3 and LR 13.6 (summarised in section 3.3.2 and in Figure 9.3 (see p. 432). Among other things, a related party circular will include a description of the transaction and its terms and a statement by the Board that the transaction or arrangement is fair and reasonable as far as the shareholders of the company are concerned and that the directors have been so advised by a sponsor.

The related party circular cannot be published until it has been approved in final form by the FCA (LR 13.2.1R). To obtain approval, a draft of the circular (in an advanced form) must be submitted to the FCA for its review at least ten clear business days prior to the intended date of publication (LR 13.2.5R) (although, generally a draft will be submitted significantly earlier than that).

In practice, the related party circular can be drafted and submitted for FCA approval during the negotiations of the relevant transaction. This enables the related party circular to be posted very shortly after the conditional transaction documentation has been signed.

A number of supporting documents will be required to be prepared, negotiated and agreed in connection with the publication of a related party circular. Figure 9.4 sets out a checklist of the key documents that will need to be agreed by the date of publication of the related party circular and who has primary responsibility for each document (see p. 436).

Once the FCA has approved the related party circular, it can be published and dispatched to shareholders. Since the purpose of the related party circular is to seek shareholder approval for a related party transaction, the notice of the meeting at which a resolution to approve the transaction will be put to shareholders will also be set out in the circular.

3.3.2 Contents of a related party circular

A circular for a related party transaction must include certain information that is required by Listing Rule 13.3 to be incorporated in all shareholder circulars (see section 4.2 of Chapter 8). Among other things, due prominence must be given in the circular to the essential characteristics, benefits and risks of the transaction.

In addition, a related party circular must comply with the specific content requirements of Listing Rule 13.6 (Related party circulars) and include:

- in all cases the information required by item 5.1.1 (issuer name), item 5.1.4 (issuer address), item 18.1 (major shareholders), item 20.9 (significant changes), item 22 (material contracts) (if it is information which shareholders of the company would reasonably require to make a properly informed assessment of how to vote) and item 24 (documents on display) of Annex I of PR Appendix 3 (LR 13.6.1R(1));

- for a transaction or arrangement where the related party is (or was within the 12 months before the transaction or arrangement), a director or shadow director, or an associate of a director or shadow director, of the company (or of any other company which is its subsidiary undertaking or parent undertaking or a fellow subsidiary undertaking) the information required by item 16.2 (service contracts), item 17.2 (directors' interests in shares) and item 19 (related party transactions) of Annex I of PR Appendix 3 (LR 13.6.1R(2));

- full particulars of the transaction or arrangement, including the name of the related party concerned and the nature and extent of the interest of the party in the transaction or arrangement and also a statement that the reason the security holder is being asked to vote on the transaction or arrangement is because it is with a related party (LR 13.6.1R(3));

- for an acquisition or disposal of an asset where any percentage ratio produced by the class tests is 25% or more and for which appropriate financial information is not available, an independent valuation (LR 13.6.1R(4));

- a statement by the Board that the transaction or arrangement is fair and reasonable as far as the security holders of the company are concerned and that the directors have been so advised by a sponsor (LR 13.6.1R(5)). For the purposes of this statement, any director who is, or an associate of whom is, the related party or who is a director of the related party should not take part in the Board's consideration of the matter and the statement should specify that such persons have not taken part in the Board's consideration of the matter (LR 13.6.2R);
- if applicable, a statement that the related party will not vote on the relevant resolution and that the related party has undertaken to take all reasonable steps to ensure that its associates will not vote on the relevant resolution at the meeting (LR 13.6.1R(6));
- if LR 11.1.11R (aggregation of transactions) applies (see section 3.4 below), details of each of the transactions or arrangements being aggregated (LR 13.6.1R(8)); and
- if a statement or report attributed to an expert (e.g. a report prepared by a listed company's reporting accountants) is included in the related party circular, a statement to the effect that the statement or report is included, in the form and context in which it is included, with the expert's consent (LR 13.6.1R(9)).

General and financial disclosure

Figure 9.3 sets out the skeleton contents and structure of a related party circular and describes the general information required by Listing Rule 13.6 (see p. 432).

Pro forma financial information

Under LR 13.6.4G and LR 13.3.3R, if a listed company includes pro forma financial information in a related party circular it must comply with the requirements for pro forma financial information set out in LR 13.3.3R that include, among other things, a requirement to:
- ensure that the pro forma clearly states the purpose for which it has been prepared and the fact that it is for illustrative purposes only and may not reflect the company's actual financial position or prospects;
- prepare the pro forma in a manner consistent with the accounting policies adopted in its last or next financial statements;
- ensure that pro forma adjustments are clear, directly attributable to the transaction and factually supportable; and
- include an accountant's report stating that the pro forma has been properly compiled on the basis stated and that basis is consistent with the listed company's accounting policies.

In relation to pro forma financial information, reference should be made to the UKLA Guidance Note *Pro forma financial information (UKLA/TN/633.1)*.

Incorporation of information by reference

A related party circular may incorporate information by reference, rather than it being set out in full in the circular, from a prospectus or any other published document filed with the FCA (LR 13.1.3R).

Notwithstanding this, a related party circular must provide a clear and adequate explanation of its subject matter giving due prominence to its essential characteristics, benefits and risks (LR 13.3.1R(1)) and state why the listed company's shareholders are being asked to vote (LR 13.3.1R(2)); these matters may not be incorporated by reference (LR 13.1.5R).

Where information is incorporated by reference into the circular, the information must be the latest available to the listed company (LR 13.1.4R) and the circular must include a table setting out details of the information incorporated by reference and from where it can be obtained (LR 13.1.6R).

3.3.3 Shareholder approval

Shareholder approval must be obtained before the transaction or arrangement is entered into or the transaction must be conditional on shareholder approval being obtained, in which case such approval must be obtained prior to completion (LR 11.1.7R(3)).

The Listing Rule requirement for the approval of the shareholders of the listed company in general meeting means that an ordinary resolution approving the related party transaction must be passed, requiring a simple majority of the votes cast by the listed company shareholders present at the meeting in person or by proxy. Under LR 9.2.21R, the vote must be decided by a resolution of the holders of the company's premium listed shares.

The listed company must ensure that the related party does not vote on the relevant resolution and that the related party takes all reasonable steps to ensure that its associates do not vote on the relevant resolution (LR 11.1.7R(4)). It is common for the listed company to seek an undertaking from the related party to comply with its obligations under the Listing Rules.

3.3.4 Material change

If after obtaining shareholder approval but before completion of a related party transaction, there is a material change to the terms of the transaction, the listed company must comply again separately with the requirements of LR 11.1.7R in relation to the transaction (i.e. as described in section 3.3.1 above, make an RIS announcement, send a circular to shareholders and obtain shareholder approval for the transaction) (LR 11.1.7AR). The FCA will generally consider an increase in consideration of 10% or more to be a material change of terms (see LR 11.1.7BG).

If there is a material change affecting any matter disclosed in the circular, or a material new matter that would have been required to be disclosed in the circular, after the publication of the circular but before the date of the general meeting seeking shareholder approval, then the listed company must notify the FCA and send a supplementary circular to shareholders providing an explanation of the material change or material new matter. It may be necessary for the listed company to adjourn a convened shareholder meeting if a supplementary circular cannot be sent to shareholders at least seven days prior to the convened shareholder meeting as required by LR 13.1.9R.

Where a meeting of the listed company has been called to approve a transaction or arrangement and, after the date of the notice, but prior to the meeting, a party to the transaction becomes a related party then, to comply with LR 11.1.7R, the listed company should:

- ensure that the related party concerned does not vote on the relevant resolution and that it takes all reasonable steps to ensure that its associates do not vote on the relevant resolution; and
- send a further circular, for receipt by shareholders at least one clear business day before the deadline for proxies, containing any information required by LR 13.3 and LR 13.6 that was not contained in the original circular with notice of the meeting (LR 11.1.8G).

3.4 Aggregation of transactions

LR 11.1.11R provides for the aggregation of related party transactions. In the event that a listed company enters into transactions or arrangements with the same related party (and any of its associates) in any 12-month period and such transactions or arrangements have not been approved by shareholders, including small related party transactions falling under LR 11 Annex 1, paragraph 1 and smaller related party transaction falling under LR 11.1.10R (see section 3.5), then they must be aggregated (LR 11.1.11R(1)).

If, on aggregation, any of the class test ratios (see section 1.2 above) is 5% or more for the aggregated transactions or arrangements, the listed company must comply with the requirements of LR 11.1.7R in respect of the latest transaction or arrangement (LR 11.1.11R(2)), namely make an RIS announcement, send a circular to shareholders and obtain shareholder approval for the transaction, ensuring that the related party does not vote. Details of any aggregated transactions must be included in the shareholder circular (LR 13.6.1R(8)).

If transactions or arrangements that are small transactions under paragraph 1 of Annex 1 of Listing Rule 11 (see section 3.2.2) are aggregated in accordance with LR 11.1.11R(1) and each of the percentage ratios is less than 5%, but one or more of the percentage ratios exceeds 0.25%, then the listed company must comply with the modified requirements applicable to smaller related party transactions set out in:

- LR 11.1.10R(2)(b), described in section 3.5 below, in respect of the latest small transaction (i.e. obtain confirmation from a sponsor that the transaction is fair and reasonable); and
- LR 11.1.10R(2)(c), that is announce certain details (described in section 3.5 below) in respect of all the aggregated small transactions.

3.5 Modified requirements for smaller related party transactions

LR 11.1.10R provides certain modified requirements for 'smaller related party transactions' defined as those where each percentage ratio produced by the class tests (see section 1.2) is less than 5%, but where one or more of the percentage ratios exceeds 0.25%.

Where a transaction is a smaller related party transaction, the usual requirements for a related party transaction (set out in LR 11.1.7R) do not apply. However, before entering into the transaction or arrangements, the listed company must:

(a) obtain written confirmation from a sponsor that the terms of the proposed transaction or arrangements with the related party are fair and reasonable as far as the shareholders of the listed company are concerned (LR 11.1.10R(2)(b)). The UKLA provides some guidance on the wording of the confirmation by the sponsor in the UKLA Guidance Note *Related party transactions – Modified requirements for smaller related party transactions (UKLA/TN/308.3)*. It says that it is inappropriate and unnecessary to include language which seeks to limit the use of the confirmation or to include disclaimers. Instead, a clean confirmation, tracking the wording used in LR 11.1.10R(2)(b) should be given; and

(b) as soon as possible upon entering into the transaction, make an RIS announcement setting out the identity of the related party, value of the consideration, a brief description of the transaction, the fact it is a smaller related party transaction and all other relevant circumstances (LR 11.1.10R(2)(c)). In the UKLA Guidance Note *Related party transactions – Issuer's undertaking (UKLA/TN/309.2)*, the UKLA stated that it is essential that premium listed companies take reasonable care to ensure that the relevant disclosure is not misleading or confusing and that the transaction is easily identifiable as a related party transaction.

These details of smaller related party transactions were previously included in the company's annual report but, as they are now announced immediately, they no longer need to be included in the annual report.

3.6 Possible future changes to the rules on related party transactions

On 9 June 2017, an EU directive (EU/2017/828) amending the Shareholder Rights Directive came into force which seeks to enhance transparency and encourage long-term shareholder engagement in companies whose shares are traded on an EU regulated market (which includes the main market of the London Stock Exchange).

One of the topics addressed in the amending directive is related party transactions. Certain material transactions between a listed company and a related party will have to be publicly disclosed and/or approved by the independent shareholders of a listed company under the amending directive. A 'related party' for these purposes has the same meaning as that contained in the International Accounting Standards Regulation (Regulation 1606/2002) and so is wider than the definition in Listing Rule 11 (see section 3.1.2 above). The definition of what constitutes a 'material transaction' for these purposes is left to EU Member States to define.

Many of the requirements for related party transactions contained in the amending directive are already reflected in Listing Rule 11 in the UK, although there are some detailed differences. For example, transactions entered into in the ordinary course of business are currently exempt under the provisions in LR 11; however, under the amending directive an ordinary course transaction will also have to be 'concluded on normal market terms' in order to be exempt. Standard listed companies would also have to comply with the requirements if the amending directive is implemented in the UK.

The amending directive must be implemented by EU Member States through national legislation by 10 June 2019. If the UK leaves the EU prior to 10 June 2019, the amending directive will not apply in the UK unless the UK Government implements it into national law prior to the UK's exit from the EU.

Figure 9.3: Skeleton contents of a related party circular

Heading	Disclosure required
Cover	This will include a statement that the document contains important information and that a shareholder should consult his or her financial adviser if in doubt as to the action to be taken (see LR 13.3.1R(4)) and a statement instructing a shareholder to forward the documentation if the shareholder has sold his or her shares (see LR 13.3.1R(6)). In addition, this usually includes statements to draw shareholders' attention to Part I – Letter from the chairman and the recommendation of the directors (see LR 13.3.1R(5)).
Contents and expected timetable	Sets out the contents of the circular and key expected dates in relation to the transaction, including the latest time and date for receipt of proxies, the date of the general meeting and the date on which the transaction is expected to complete.

SIGNIFICANT TRANSACTIONS

Heading	Disclosure required
Part I – Letter from the chairman	This section is usually based on the RIS announcement (see LR 11.1.7R(1)). The letter is typically set out on headed paper or otherwise includes details of the listed company's name and address if not included in Part IV – Additional Information (see the requirements in LR 13.6.1R(1)(a) and (b) and items 5.1.1 and 5.1.4 of Annex I of PR Appendix 3).
Introduction	Sets out a short summary of the transaction and explains why shareholder approval is required, namely that the transaction is with a related party and the nature and extent of the interest of the party in the transaction (see LR 13.3.1R(1), (2) and (3) and LR 13.6.1R(3)). Also includes a statement that the related party will not vote on the relevant resolution and has undertaken to take all reasonable steps to ensure that its associates will not vote on the resolution to approve the transaction (LR 13.6.1R(6)).
Principal terms and conditions of the transaction	Key terms of the transaction including the name of the related party and details of the nature and extent of the interest of the related party in the transaction (LR 13.6.1R(3)), with a cross-reference to the more detailed information in Part II – Principal terms and conditions of transaction.
Shareholder meeting and action to be taken	Summary of the various resolutions to be put to the shareholder meeting, the arrangements for the meeting and details of how a shareholder can vote by proxy (see LR 13.3.1R(4)).
Recommendation	A recommendation from the Board as to the voting action that shareholders should take, indicating whether or not the proposal in the circular is, in the Board's opinion, in the best interests of shareholders as a whole (see LR 13.3.1R(5)). The Board must also include a statement that the transaction or arrangement is fair and reasonable as far as the shareholders are concerned and that the directors have been so advised by a sponsor (LR 13.6.1R(5)). If applicable, the statement should specify that any director who is, or an associate of whom is, the related party or who is a director of the related party have not taken part in the Board's consideration of the matter (LR 13.6.2R).
Part II – Principal terms and conditions of the transaction	Full particulars of the transaction including the name of the related party and of the nature and extent of the interest of the related party in the transaction (LR 13.6.1R(3)). Where the transaction involves an issue of listed securities (e.g. as consideration for an acquisition), this section will include details of the proposed date of issue and listing, how the securities rank for dividends and voting compared with the existing listed securities, the treatment of fractions and settlement and trading arrangements (see LR 13.3.1R(9)).

Heading	Disclosure required
Part III – Pro forma financial information	If a listed company includes pro forma information in the circular, the company must among other things: ■ ensure that the pro forma clearly states the purpose for which it has been prepared and the fact that it is for illustrative purposes and may not reflect the company's actual financial position or prospects; ■ prepare the pro forma in a manner consistent with the accounting policies adopted in its last or next financial statements; ■ ensure that pro forma adjustments are clear, directly attributable to the transaction and factually supportable; and ■ include an accountant's report stating that the pro forma has been properly compiled on the basis stated and that basis is consistent with the listed company's accounting policies. (see LR 13.6.4G, LR 13.3.3R and Annex II of PR Appendix 3).
Part IV – Additional information	This includes all of the additional information that is required to be included in the circular by the Listing Rules and typically includes the headings set out below.
Name and registered office	If not included elsewhere in the circular, the name of the listed company and its registered office (see LR 13.6.1R(1)(a) and (b) and items 5.1.1 and 5.1.4 of Annex I of PR Appendix 3).
Directors' service agreements	For a transaction or arrangement where the related party is (or was within the 12 months before the transaction or arrangement), a director or shadow director, or an associate of the same, of the listed company (or of any other company which is its subsidiary undertaking or parent undertaking or a fellow subsidiary undertaking) a summary of the terms of that director's service contract (see LR 13.6.1R(2)(a) and item 16.2 of Annex I of PR Appendix 3).
Directors' interests	For a transaction or arrangement where the related party is (or was within the 12 months before the transaction or arrangement), a director or shadow director, or an associate of the same, of the listed company (or of any other company which is its subsidiary undertaking or parent undertaking or a fellow subsidiary undertaking) details of that director's interests in shares and options over shares of the listed company (see LR 13.6.1R(2)(b) and item 17.2 of Annex I of PR Appendix 3).

SIGNIFICANT TRANSACTIONS

Heading	Disclosure required
Related party transactions	For a transaction or arrangement where the related party is (or was within the 12 months before the transaction or arrangement), a director or shadow director, or an associate of the same, of the listed company (or of any other company which is its subsidiary undertaking or parent undertaking or a fellow subsidiary undertaking) details of related party transactions (as defined by IFRS) that the listed company has entered into with that director prior to the date of the circular (see LR 13.6.1R(2)(c)) and item 19 of Annex I of PR Appendix 3).
Major shareholdings	Details of those shareholders that are required to notify their interests in voting rights, whether any such shareholders have different voting rights and whether the listed company is controlled by a party and the measures in place to ensure that such control is not abused, or appropriate negative statements (see LR 13.6.1R(1)(c)) and item 18 of Annex I of PR Appendix 3).
Material contracts	If it is information that a shareholder would reasonably require for the purpose of making an informed assessment about how to vote on the transaction described in the circular, a summary of (i) material contracts entered into in the two years prior to the date of the circular, other than in the ordinary course of business, to which the listed company or any member of its group is a party and (ii) any other contracts, not entered into in the ordinary course of business, which contain any provision under which any member of the group has an obligation or entitlement which is material to the group as at the date of the circular (see LR 13.6.1R(1)(e) and item 22 of Annex I of PR Appendix 3).
Significant change	Details of any significant change in the financial or trading position of the group which has occurred since the end of the last financial period for which either audited financial information or interim financial information have been published (see LR 13.6.1R(1)(d) and item 20.9 of Annex I of PR Appendix 3). If relevant, the circular must include a clear explanation of recent developments that constitute a significant change. If there is no information to disclose a negative statement is required.
Consents	A confirmation that where a person is named as having advised the directors of the listed company, such person has given and not withdrawn his or her written consent to the inclusion of references to his or her name in the circular (e.g. financial advisers) (see LR 13.3.1R(10)).
Documents on display	A list of documents that are on display in connection with the publication of the circular (e.g. the listed company's memorandum and articles of association, annual report and accounts and any accountants' reports included in the circular (see LR 13.6.1R(1)(f) and item 24 of Annex I of PR Appendix 3)).

Heading	Disclosure required
Information incorporated by reference	Where information is incorporated by reference into the circular, rather than being set out in full in the circular, the circular must include a table setting out details of the information incorporated by reference from where it can be obtained (see LR 13.1.3R, but note the requirements of LR 13.1.5R).
Definitions	Sets out defined terms used in the circular. Where it is helpful to assist shareholders' understanding of the transaction, the company may also choose to include a glossary of technical terms.
Notice of meeting	The notice of the meeting containing the resolution to approve the related party transaction is generally included in the back of the circular, rather than in a separate document.

Figure 9.4: List of key documents required in connection with the preparation and publication of a related party circular

Key document	Primary responsibility
Announcement	Listed company, listed company's lawyers and the sponsor
Circular	Listed company, listed company's lawyers and the sponsor
Notice of meeting	Listed company and its lawyers
Form of proxy	Listed company and its lawyers
Voting undertakings	Listed company and its lawyers
Board minutes	Listed company and its lawyers
Verification notes	Listed company and its lawyers
Sponsor's engagement letter and/or agreement	Sponsor and its lawyers
Sponsor's comfort letters	Sponsor, its lawyers and the providers of comfort letters
Confirmation that the transaction is fair and reasonable	Sponsor
Reporting accountants' engagement letter	Reporting accountants
Significant change comfort letter	Reporting accountants
Correct extraction comfort letter	Reporting accountants

Report on pro forma financial information, if applicable	Reporting accountants
Consent letter for inclusion of reports in the circular, if applicable	Reporting accountants
Letter to the FCA confirming application of the class tests under Chapter 11, if required by the FCA	Sponsor

4. Companies with controlling shareholders

Additional requirements apply under the Listing Rules to premium listed companies with a controlling shareholder.

4.1 Who is a controlling shareholder?

A controlling shareholder is defined as a person who exercises or controls 30% or more of the voting rights of a premium listed company, either on their own or together with any persons acting in concert with them.

As well as capturing registered holders of shares, the reference in the definition to a person who 'controls' the votes means that it will also capture:

- a person who is the beneficial owner of the shares, and controls how the registered holder exercises its votes; and
- a company or other entity that controls more than 50% of the entity that owns the shares (or otherwise controls that entity), and so is treated as having de facto control over how the votes are cast.

The voting rights of a person who holds the shares as a bare trustee are disregarded and so a bare trustee is not treated as a controlling shareholder. To fall within this category, the trustee must not have any ability to determine how the votes are cast.

A person who exercises, or controls the exercise of, the votes attaching to any shares in the listed company and who is 'acting in concert' with a shareholder who is a controlling shareholder will also be a controlling shareholder in their own right (or where there is no single shareholder with control over 30% or more of the votes but together a group of people who are acting in concert control 30% or more of the votes, then again they will all be controlling shareholders).

All of the restrictions that apply to controlling shareholders therefore apply equally to any person who is acting in concert with the main controlling shareholder if they themselves own or control any shares in the listed company.

The FCA has said that the test of acting in concert is whether persons are acting together to control the exercise of 30% of more of the votes on all or substantially all matters at general meetings of the company. There is no separate definition or guidance in the Listing Rules of who is treated as 'acting in concert' for the purposes of the controlling shareholder definition. However, the FCA has said that, in practice, it thinks it is unlikely that its decision on who is acting in concert would be substantially different from the conclusion of the Takeover Panel (FCA policy statement PS 14/8, paragraph 3.11). The definition of acting in concert in the City Code looks at whether shareholders have an agreement or understanding to co-operate to obtain or consolidate control of a company and also sets out a list of persons who are presumed to be acting in concert with each other unless this is established to the contrary.

4.2 Requirement for a relationship agreement

A premium listed company with a controlling shareholder must put an agreement in place with the controlling shareholder and any other shareholder with whom that controlling shareholder is acting in concert (LR 6.1.4BR(2) and LR 9.2.2AR(2)(a)). The agreement must contain binding undertakings (referred to in the rules as 'independence provisions') that:

- transactions and arrangements with the controlling shareholder (and/or any of its associates) will be conducted at arm's length and on normal commercial terms;
- neither the controlling shareholder nor any of its associates will take any action that would have the effect of preventing the company from complying with its obligations under the Listing Rules; and
- neither the controlling shareholder nor any of its associates will propose or procure the proposal of a shareholder resolution which is intended or appears to be intended to circumvent the proper application of the Listing Rules (LR 6.1.4DR).

Each person who is a controlling shareholder of the company (which, as discussed above, includes persons acting in concert) must enter into a relationship agreement. Alternatively, a controlling shareholder may just be named in the relationship agreement, rather than becoming a party to it, provided that at least one controlling shareholder enters into the agreement and agrees to procure compliance by any non-signing controlling shareholders and their associates with the independence provisions contained in the agreement. The listed company must reasonably consider, in light of its understanding of the relationship between the relevant shareholders, that the signing controlling shareholder can procure compliance with the provisions by the non-signing controlling shareholders and their associates (LR 6.1.4CR and LR 9.2.2BR).

The FCA gave some commentary on the requirements in its policy statement PS 14/8. It says that the requirement that transactions be conducted at arm's length and on normal commercial terms only applies to transactions entered into after the rules came into force (on 16 May 2014) or after the event that results in the company having a controlling shareholder. However, if the listed company still has any discretion in relation to the transaction, then it is treated as occurring at the point that such discretion is exercised.

The FCA also said that the independence provisions are not intended to prevent a shareholder engaging fairly with the company or the legitimate exercise of shareholder powers and gave examples of activities that a shareholder can legitimately undertake without breaching the provisions (e.g. accepting or making a takeover offer).

As discussed in section 3 above, the FCA confirmed that an amendment of an existing relationship agreement or the entry into a new one will not be a related party transaction requiring shareholder approval where it is purely to address the Listing Rule requirements.

When a person becomes a controlling shareholder in a premium listed company, LR 9.2.2CR allows companies a period of six months to put the requisite agreement in place.

4.3 Independent business

As discussed in Chapter 2, a premium listed company must carry on an independent business as its main activity at all times (LR 6.1.4R). The purpose of the relationship agreement is to help to ensure that this is the case. In addition, there is guidance in the Listing Rules (LR 6.1.4AG) which sets out factors that may indicate that a company does not satisfy the requirement to carry on an independent business because of its relationship with its controlling shareholder. This includes where a company cannot demonstrate that it has access to financing other than from a controlling shareholder, where a majority of the revenue generated by the company's business is from business conducted directly or indirectly with the controlling shareholder or where a controlling shareholder appears to be able to influence the operations of the company outside its normal governance structures or via material shareholdings in one or more significant subsidiary undertakings of the company (see Chapter 2).

In its consultation paper CP 17/4, the FCA is proposing to clarify the requirement for an applicant to have an independent business by splitting the existing rule into three separate provisions. The provisions will cover: the need to have an independent business; the company's relationship with any controlling shareholder; and the requirement for a company to control its business. Additional guidance will be incorporated into the rules to explain the operation of each element. The guidance in relation to the independence test and controlling shareholders includes a new test of whether the controlling shareholder 'appears to be able to exercise improper influence' over the company. A new UKLA Guidance Note *The independent business requirements for companies applying for premium listing – Interpretation of LR 6.4, LR 6.5 and LR 6.6 (UKLA/ TN/103.1)* is also proposed to assist in interpreting the independence provisions. The draft Guidance Note (in Appendix 1 to CP 17/4) gives examples of indicators of circumstances where an applicant for listing is not sufficiently independent. These include a controlling shareholder installing staff with familial or other relationships in key roles to gain day-to-day control.

4.4 Statement on compliance with the relationship agreement to be included in the annual report

A premium listed company with a controlling shareholder must confirm each year in its annual report that:

- it has entered into an agreement with its controlling shareholder containing the requisite independence provisions;
- it has complied with the independence provisions throughout the relevant period;
- so far as the listed company is aware, the independence provisions have been complied with by the controlling shareholder and its associates throughout the relevant period; and
- where the controlling shareholder has agreed to procure that another controlling shareholder and its associates will comply with the independence provisions, so far as the listed company is aware that procurement obligation has been complied with.

If the company is unable to confirm compliance with any of these, the annual report must contain a statement that the FCA has been notified and the reasons for the non-compliance (LR 9.8.4R(14)). If any independent director of the company declines to support the compliance statement, it must record that fact (LR 9.8.4AR) and the company will go into the 'enhanced oversight regime', under which all transactions and arrangements between the company and the shareholder will have to be approved by the company's independent shareholders, regardless of size (unless the FCA grants an exemption). The enhanced oversight regime is discussed in more detail in section 3.2.5 above. Non-compliance with the independence provisions could ultimately result in the FCA requiring the company to move from a premium listing to a standard listing.

4.5 Election/re-election of independent directors

Additional requirements apply to the election or re-election of the independent directors of a premium listed company with a controlling shareholder. The term 'independent director' is given the same meaning as it has under the Corporate Governance Code, so that a director whom the Board has decided is independent for Governance Code purposes will also be an independent director for the purposes of the Listing Rules (see Chapter 6 for discussion of independence). If a premium listed company has a controlling shareholder, a resolution to elect or re-elect any independent director must be approved by a majority of the votes cast by:

- the shareholders of the listed company as a whole; and
- the independent shareholders of the listed company (i.e. all shareholders entitled to vote on the resolution excluding any controlling shareholder) (LR 9.2.2ER).

The FCA confirmed in its policy statement PS 14/8 that a single resolution (rather than two separate resolutions) can be used if the company can separately identify the votes of its independent shareholders.

If one of these thresholds is not met, the company may propose a further resolution, to be passed by the shareholders as a whole, following a 90-day period after the original vote (but within 120 days of the original vote) (LR 9.2.2FR). During that period, a director who has already been appointed can remain in office until the second vote (LR 9.2.2DG).

The Listing Rules state that the company's constitution must 'allow' for this procedure for electing independent directors (LR 6.1.4BR(2) and LR 9.2.2AR(2)(b)). The FCA confirmed in its policy statement PS 14/8 that companies are not required to amend their constitutions to comply with these rules, as long as their constitution does not prohibit elections from taking place in accordance with the new rules.

In the event that a person becomes a controlling shareholder in a company that is already listed, the company's constitution must allow for the new procedure for the election of independent directors by the company's next annual general meeting, unless notice of the meeting has already been given or is given within three months of the person becoming a controlling shareholder (LR 9.2.2CR(2)).

4.6 Circulars in relation to election or re-election of independent directors

Premium listed companies with controlling shareholders must include the following information in any circular relating to the election or re-election of an independent director:

- details of any previous or existing relationship, transaction or arrangement between the independent director and the company, any of its directors, a controlling shareholder or any of its associates (or a confirmation that there have been none);
- why the company considers the director will be an effective director;
- how the company has determined that the proposed director is independent; and
- the process followed by the company when selecting the independent director (LR 13.8.17R).

This requirement is wider than a determination made under the Corporate Governance Code's Principle B.1.1 because there is no time limit on relationships that have to be considered and the nature of the relationships that have to be disclosed is broader. The FCA's policy statement PS 14/8 made it clear that the focus is on whether an ostensibly independent director can actually be relied upon to be independent. The FCA stated that, although there is no materiality threshold or time limits, 'less material and more extensive dealings' can be described in more general terms and it expects listed company Boards to take a view on the appropriate extent of disclosure to shareholders, having regard to facilitating an informed voting decision.

4.7 Cancellation of listing

As discussed in Chapter 2, a premium listed company with a controlling shareholder which wants to cancel its premium listing other than following a takeover offer must obtain approval for the cancellation by a shareholder resolution which is approved by: (i) more than 50% of the votes cast by its independent shareholders; and (ii) at least 75% of all the votes cast.

Where the cancellation follows a takeover offer, a bidder who is interested in 50% or less of the shares of the listed company before announcing its firm intention to make its takeover offer, who has obtained acceptances in relation to 75% of the shares, and who states in the offer document that a notice period of not less than 20 business days prior to cancellation will commence either on the bidder obtaining the required 75% or on the first date of the issue of compulsory acquisition notices under section 979 of CA 2006, can then delist without shareholder consent. However, if a bidder is interested in more than 50% of the voting rights of the listed company before announcing its offer, it must obtain acceptances or acquire shares from a majority of the independent shareholders in addition to reaching the 75% acceptance threshold before it is able to delist.

CHAPTER **10**

Further share issues and share buy-backs

OVERVIEW

- A listed company may want to raise cash, for working capital, to reduce debt or to fund an acquisition, by issuing further shares in a rights issue, open offer or placing.

- A 'rights issue' is a pre-emptive issue to existing shareholders of rights to subscribe for further shares, usually at a discount to market value, pro rata to their existing shareholdings. The right to subscribe is given to shareholders by the allotment of nil-paid rights to subscribe for a number of new shares. The nil-paid rights are given to shareholders either by way of a credit to their CREST accounts or by means of the issue of provisional allotment letters (known as PALs). If shareholders do not wish to take up their rights, they can sell all or some of their nil-paid rights.

- An 'open offer' is a pre-emptive offer to existing shareholders to subscribe for further shares pro rata to their existing shareholdings. The right to subscribe cannot be traded and has no value. A shareholder who does not take up his entitlement will receive nothing if his shares are sold elsewhere.

- A 'compensatory open offer' is an offer to existing shareholders to subscribe for further shares pro rata to their existing shareholdings. The right to subscribe cannot be traded and has no value. However, in contrast to a standard open offer, a compensatory open offer allows for a shareholder who does not take up his entitlement to receive the proceeds (less the issue price) if the shares are sold elsewhere.

- A 'placing' is a non-pre-emptive offer to a third party or third parties to subscribe for new shares. The placing may take a number of different forms and may be concluded very quickly, depending on whether shareholder consent is required for the issue of the new shares (e.g. to disapply pre-emption rights). An open offer is often combined with a placing.

- When issuing new shares, in addition to applicable company law, a premium listed company must comply with the requirements of Listing Rules 9 and 13 in relation to further issues of new shares.

- A further issue of shares may also involve an offer of shares to the public and/or an admission of shares to trading on a regulated market requiring the preparation and publication of a prospectus.

- If a listed company has surplus cash that is not required for corporate purposes, it may decide to return value to its shareholders. A common method of doing this is to buy back its own shares.
- In addition to applicable company law, a premium listed company must comply with the requirements of Listing Rule 12 and MAR in relation to a buy-back of shares.

1. Further share issues

There are a number of methods by which a company can raise cash by the issue of shares, either for general purposes (e.g. to increase working capital or to reduce debt) or to fund an acquisition. The main methods are a rights issue, open offer or placing.

Which method a company chooses to use will depend on a number of factors including the number of shares to be issued, whether the company needs shareholder approval to issue the shares and the discount to market price at which the new shares are to be sold. Figure 10.1 below summarises the key considerations of each type of further share issue which are discussed in more detail later in this chapter.

Figure 10.1: Comparison of key considerations for a further share issue by a premium listed company

	Rights issue	Open offer	Placing
Need to disapply pre-emption rights	Yes (unless existing disapplication or within CA 2006 pre-emption rights)	Yes (unless existing disapplication or within CA 2006 pre-emption rights)	No (unless not within existing disapplication)
Period for which offer must be open	10 business days (LR 9.5.6R) (or 14 days if CA 2006 compliant)	10 business days (LR 9.5.7AR)	Can be as short as one day (on an accelerated book built placing)
Need for shareholder approval to be obtained before offer can open	Yes (unless authorised by existing authorities)	No – GM notice period and offer period can run concurrently	No
Maximum discount to market price at which new shares can be issued	No limit	10% unless shareholder approval obtained for greater discount (LR 9.5.10R(1))	5% (Pre-emption Group Statement of Principles); 10% unless shareholder approval obtained for greater discount (LR 9.5.10R(1))

	Rights issue	Open offer	Placing
Maximum size of offering	No limit	15–18% (view previously expressed by the ABI)	5% (or 10%, for a share issue connected to an acquisition/capital investment), with a limit of 7.5% in a rolling three year period (Pre-emption Group Statement of Principles) 10% on a vendor placing (Investment Committee Guidelines)
Prospectus required	Probably, yes (NB proportionate disclosure regime)	Probably, yes	Exemptions likely to be available

1.1 Rights issues, open offers and placings

1.1.1 Key features of a rights issue

The key features of a rights issue are:

- new shares are issued for cash, often at a substantial discount to the market value of the listed company's shares;
- the new shares are first offered to existing shareholders pro rata to their current shareholdings in the company;
- shareholders are sent a provisional allotment letter (PAL) setting out how many new shares they are entitled to subscribe or have nil-paid rights credited to their CREST accounts (depending on whether they hold their shares in 'certificated' or 'uncertificated' form);
- shareholders can either take up and pay for those new shares they are entitled to acquire or, if they do not wish to take up the offer of new shares, they can sell some or all of their nil-paid rights (i.e. sell the right to subscribe for new shares at the rights issue price, which is typically at a discount to the market price); and
- arrangements are made for the sale of shares not taken up by shareholders so that even if a shareholder does nothing ('lazy shareholder'), he may still receive a cash payment if the shares which are provisionally allotted to him are sold in the market for more than their subscription price.

1.1.2 Key features of an open offer

The key features of an open offer are:

- new shares are issued for cash;
- the new shares are offered to existing shareholders pro rata to their current shareholdings in the company;
- shareholders are sent an application form or have an open offer entitlement credited to their CREST accounts;
- shareholders are not able to trade their entitlement to subscribe for shares under the open offer; and
- generally no arrangements are made for the sale of shares not taken up by shareholders and so shareholders who do not apply for shares do not usually receive any cash payment (though it is possible to conduct a 'compensatory open offer', where shareholders who do not take up their shares have those shares sold in the market and receive any premium achieved on the sale).

The key difference between an open offer and a rights issue is that on a rights issue, the right to subscribe for new shares is tradable and a shareholder who does nothing may still receive some money if the shares which were provisionally allotted to him are sold by the company on the market at a premium to the subscription price. On an open offer, a shareholder who does not take up his entitlement generally does not receive any compensation for the dilution of his shareholding unless the open offer is structured as a 'compensatory open offer' (as described above).

1.1.3 Key features of a placing

In its basic form, a placing is simply an issue of shares by a company to a group of institutions or underwriters who are known as placees. It is not done on a pre-emptive basis.

Common forms of placing include:

- *Accelerated bookbuilt cash placing* – Placings were traditionally done on the basis of a placing agreement and placing letters: the company's financial adviser would sign up to a placing agreement with the company, which contained a commitment to procure subscribers for, or itself subscribe for, the shares at a set price. It would then approach potential placees who signed a placing letter containing the terms and conditions of the placing. However, accelerated bookbuilt placings are now commonplace, with the bookbuilding process taking just one day. The bank doing the bookbuild agrees, in the placing agreement, to invite bids for shares from professional investors. Once the bids are in (which may take as little as a few hours), the company and the investment bank fix the issue price and the investment bank confirms to the placees their allocation and the price payable. The terms and conditions of the placing are set out in the announcement released at the start of the

bookbuilding and investors are deemed to give any necessary representations in submitting a bid, so doing away with the need for a placing letter.
- *Bought deal* – A bought deal is effectively a placing where just one investor, usually a large bank, takes a block of shares with a view to trading out of its position at a profit (whereas on a normal placing, a placee would typically keep the shares for his own account). As with a cash placing, a bought deal is likely to involve shares representing less than 5% of the company's issued share capital (or 10%, if the placing is being used to fund an acquisition or capital investment), as this is the amount for which a disapplication of pre-emption rights is typically sought at each AGM (see section 1.2.3). Anything above that is likely to need additional shareholder approval, which may not be forthcoming.
- *Placing with an open offer* – The Pre-emption Group, the Investment Association and the PLSA (see section 1.2.3) may require shares which are to be issued for cash to be offered first to existing shareholders so that shareholders are given the opportunity to prevent their shareholding being diluted. This is referred to as 'clawback'. An open offer is made to shareholders and any shares not taken up by shareholders are sold to the placees.
- *Vendor placing* – This is when a company making an acquisition issues its shares as consideration for the purchase, but the consideration shares are immediately placed with placees for cash, so that the vendor actually receives cash equal to the purchase price. Under LR 9.5.9R, all vendors must have an equal opportunity to participate in a vendor placing. The principal advantages of a vendor placing are that the company is able to use shares rather than cash to fund an acquisition and it does not constitute an issue of shares for cash and so existing shareholders' statutory pre-emption rights under section 561 of CA 2006 do not apply. The Investment Committee Guidelines (see section 1.2.3) require shareholders to be offered claw back when a vendor placing is of more than 10% of the issued share capital or is at a discount of more than 5%. The offer to shareholders is made by way of an open offer and any shares not taken up by shareholders are sold to the placees.
- *Cash box placing* – A cash box placing uses a structure which enables a company to issue up to 10% of its shares on a non-pre-emptive basis. Prior to 2015, a listed company was usually only able to issue shares representing 5% of its current share capital because this was the maximum disapplication of pre-emption rights which the Pre-emption Group's 2008 Statement of Principles permitted a company to seek on an annual basis (see section 1.2.3). On a cash box placing, the issue of shares is structured so that the consideration is not cash: pre-emption rights do not apply on an issue of shares for non-cash consideration. The listed company issues shares to placees; the placees pay the cash for those shares to the investment bank which uses the funds to pay up redeemable preference shares in a newly incorporated company, usually registered in Jersey (the 'cash box company'). The shares in the cash box company (whose only asset is the placing proceeds) are then transferred

to the listed company as consideration for the issue of the placing shares. As the placing shares are issued for non-cash consideration (namely the shares in the cash box company), the pre-emption requirements in CA 2006 should not apply (although a detailed legal analysis is required in each case to confirm if this is the case and that relevant CA 2006 requirements are being complied with). However, the Pre-Emption Group published a revised Statement of Principles in 2015 which provides that companies may seek a disapplication of pre-emption rights in respect of further 5% (meaning a disapplication of 10% in total), provided the extra 5% is used only for an issue of shares in connection with an acquisition or a specified capital investment which is announced at the same time as the non-pre-emptive issue (or which has taken place in the preceding the six months). Companies that have a disapplication in respect of 10% will no longer need to use a cash box structure where the issue is to raise funds for an acquisition or capital investment. The Statement suggests that the use of a cash box structure to raise funds where there is no associated acquisition or capital investment will now be subject to greater scrutiny and could lead to institutional shareholder criticism.

1.2 Authority to allot, pre-emption rights and other share capital considerations

1.2.1 CA 2006 requirements

A listed company wishing to do a further issue of shares (such as a rights issue, open offer or placing) will have to check that its directors have sufficient authority to allot the requisite number of shares and decide whether it will comply with the pre-emption requirements in CA 2006 and, if not, check whether there is already a sufficiently large disapplication of pre-emption rights in place.

It will also need to check that there is no limit on the number of shares it may issue; although the concept of authorised share capital was abolished under CA 2006, the transitional provisions made in relation to CA 2006 coming into force mean that there may still be a limit on the number of shares a company may issue (see Figure 10.2). If there is a limit on the number of shares a company may issue and the capital raising is not within that limit, the limit will need to be removed or increased.

The listed company must also ensure that the proposed issue price is not at a discount to the nominal value of the shares.

If additional shareholder authority is required to address any of these issues, it will need to convene a general meeting to obtain the requisite approval. The circular containing the notice of meeting will have to comply with the requirements of Listing Rule 13, in particular LR 13.8 (see section 1.5 for further information on the documentation required).

A summary of the company law requirements is set out in Figure 10.2.

1.2.2 Listing Rule requirements

In addition to CA 2006 provisions on pre-emption rights, a premium listed company must comply with LR 9.3.11R. This imposes a requirement for pre-emption rights for existing shareholders on an issue of new shares (or a sale of treasury shares) for cash. These rules will not apply if the issue of shares is within the company's general disapplication of pre-emption rights.

Furthermore, on a rights issue or open offer, the company is not required to comply with the pre-emption rights requirements in the Listing Rules in respect of 'fractional entitlements' nor is it required to offer shares pre-emptively where to do so would be in breach of overseas securities laws (LR 9.3.12R(2)).

A company will not issue fractions of shares to shareholders on a rights issue. It will aggregate any fractional entitlements and sell them as whole shares in the market either for the benefit of the shareholders or, where the value is less than £5, for its own benefit (LR 9.5.13R). On a rights issue strictly complying with the pre-emption rights in CA 2006 (a 'Companies Act rights issue') the company will round down shareholders' entitlements to the nearest whole number.

In practice, for a company that is subject to the requirements of CA 2006, the Listing Rule pre-emption provisions are unlikely to have any significant impact.

Figure 10.2: Impact of CA 2006 on a UK incorporated listed company contemplating a further share issue

Authorised share capital	
Relevant provisions	There are no provisions on authorised share capital in CA 2006, but note the transitional provisions in relation to the CA 1985 in the Eighth Commencement Order.
Is there a limit on the number of shares that may be allotted?	Under CA 1985, a company had an authorised share capital (contained in its memorandum); this represented a limit on the number of shares it could allot. If it wished to allot shares in excess of that number, it had to pass an ordinary resolution to increase its authorised share capital. CA 2006 abolished the concept of authorised share capital. However, the statement of a company's authorised share capital in a company's memorandum automatically moved to the company's articles on 1 October 2009. Under the transitional provisions in the Eighth Commencement Order, that statement will act as a limit on the number of shares that the company can allot until it either passes an ordinary resolution to amend the articles to remove the limit or adopts new articles which do not contain it.

Action point	A listed company wishing to issue new shares will need to check whether it still has such a limit and, if it does, whether the issue would breach that limit. If it would, it will have to either remove the limit (by adopting new articles or passing an ordinary resolution) or increase it.
Allotting shares	
Relevant provisions	Sections 549 to 559 of CA 2006 and section 580 of CA 2006.
What authority is required for directors to allot shares?	Authority for the directors to allot shares must be contained in the articles or conferred by an ordinary resolution.
Are there any limits on the authority that may be taken?	The authority cannot be taken for more than five years and must state the maximum number of shares that can be allotted. Listed companies also need to be aware of the Investment Association guidelines on directors' authority to allot which permit directors to take an annual authority to allot shares representing up to one-third of the company's existing share capital plus an additional one-third available for use on rights issues only.
Can the company allot shares at a discount to their nominal value?	A company may not allot shares at a discount to their nominal value.
Action points	The company must check it has sufficient authority to allot before issuing new shares. If it does not have sufficient existing authority, a new authority under section 551 of CA 2006 will be required. If a company wishes to issue shares at a price that is lower than the current nominal value of the company's shares it will first have to sub-divide its shares into shares with a smaller nominal value. This requires an ordinary resolution.
Relevant provisions	Sections 560 to 577 of CA 2006.
What are the pre-emption requirements under CA 2006?	A company issuing shares for cash must first offer them pre-emptively to existing shareholders.
How does a company make a pre-emptive offer under CA 2006?	A company making a pre-emptive offer to shareholders in compliance with the requirements of CA 2006 (i.e. a 'Companies Act rights issue') must keep the offer open for 14 days. The offer may be made electronically or in hard copy. Note that for non-Companies Act rights issues (i.e. where pre-emption rights have been disapplied) the Listing Rules require the offer to be kept open for ten business days.

How does a company make a pre-emptive offer under CA 2006?	The offer must be made on an individual basis to shareholders within the EEA. Outside the EEA, the offer may be made by means of a notice in the London Gazette. The requirement to make the offer on an individual basis to all shareholders within the EEA may require local securities law advice to be sought in the relevant jurisdiction(s).
Action point	Listed companies should be aware of the detailed requirements when doing a Companies Act rights issue, in particular the minimum offer period and the requirement to make the offer to all shareholders in the EEA.
How can a company disapply pre-emption rights under CA 2006?	Pre-emption rights can be disapplied in the company's articles or by special resolution. The disapplication must expire at the same time as the authority to allot to which it relates. Listed companies will also need to be aware of the Pre-emption Group's Statement of Principles on the disapplication of pre-emption rights which permit companies to issue, on a non-pre-emptive basis, shares representing up to 5% of the company's existing share capital in any one year or 10%, provided the extra 5% is used only for an issue of shares in connection with an acquisition or capital investment, with a limit of 7.5% (excluding any shares issued in connection with a specific acquisition/capital investment) in a rolling three-year period.
Action point	A company issuing new shares where the issue does not comply with the pre-emption rights of CA 2006 must check it has a sufficient existing disapplication. If its existing disapplication is not sufficient, it will have to seek a new disapplication under CA 2006, ss 570 and 573.
Convening a general meeting	
Relevant provisions	Sections 307 and 307A of CA 2006.
What is the notice period for convening meetings under CA 2006?	For unlisted companies, only 14 days' notice is required for shareholder meetings (except in the case of a public company's AGM for which 21 days' notice is required), provided there is nothing in the company's articles to the contrary. For listed companies, 21 clear days' notice must be given (for both ordinary and special resolutions) unless the company has passed an annual special resolution permitting it to hold shareholder meetings on 14 clear days' notice and allows all shareholders to vote electronically. This requirement is satisfied if a company allows all shareholders to appoint a proxy electronically via a website. Provision E.2.4 of the UK Corporate Governance Code supplements the statutory notice requirements by stating that companies should send out notices of general meeting (other than AGMs) at least 14 working days in advance of the general meeting, excluding the date of the meeting, such that the Code provides for a longer notice period than the statutory minimum.

What is the notice period for convening meetings under CA 2006?	In April 2015, the ICSA published a Guidance Note on E.2.4 recommending that as a general rule companies should comply with the Code's recommendations unless there is a need for urgency, in which case an explanation in the company's annual report should be provided.
Action point	A listed company will need to establish what the requisite notice period is for any meeting by checking (i) its articles to see if they contain any provision as to the notice required for shareholder meetings and in particular whether there is any distinction between the notice period for ordinary resolutions and special resolutions; and (ii) whether it has passed a special resolution at its AGM permitting it to hold meetings on 14 days' notice for that year and whether it allows all shareholders to appoint proxies electronically via a website.
Relevant provisions	Section 555 of CA 2006.
What does a company have to do once it has issued the new shares?	Under CA 2006, a company must file a statement of capital each time it alters its share capital in any way. The statement of capital will give a snapshot of a company's total issued capital at a particular point in time. The statement of capital will form part of the form to be filed on a return of allotment (Companies House Form SH01) and must set out: the total number of shares of the company; the aggregate nominal value of those shares; for each class of shares, prescribed particulars of the rights attached to the shares; and the amount paid up or unpaid, whether as to nominal value or share premium, on each share.
Action point	As a member of the company may ask for a statement of capital at any time, companies should have a pro forma statement of capital ready at all times.

1.2.3 The Investment Association and Pre-emption Group Guidelines

In addition to the provisions of Listing Rule 9 and CA 2006, the Investment Association, the PLSA and the Pre-emption Group have issued guidelines to address investors' concerns in relation to dilution on a further share issue.

These groups, which represent a range of institutional investors, have two key concerns: first, that existing shareholders should be offered the right to take up a proportionate part of any issue of equity for cash and second, that new investors do not receive shares at a large discount to the market price.

The Investment Association (which was formed as a result of the merger of the ABI's Investment Affairs division with the Investment Management Association in June 2014) has issued Share Capital Management Guidelines which address, among other things, the level of authority to allot shares which its members will accept a listed company seeking on an annual basis. The Share Capital Management Guidelines (which replaced the ABI guidelines published in December 2008) state that Investment Association members will permit, and treat as 'routine', a request for a general authority to allot shares equal to one-third of the company's existing share capital plus an additional authority to allot a further one-third (i.e. two-thirds in total) provided that:

- the additional one-third will only be allotted pursuant to a fully pre-emptive rights issue; and
- the authority to allot is valid for only one year.

As regards a disapplication of pre-emption rights, the Statement of Principles published by the Pre-emption Group in 2015 (which sets out the views of institutional investors) recommends a company's annual disapplication of pre-emption rights does not exceed 5%, or 10% provided the extra 5% is used only for an issue of shares connected to an acquisition or capital investment announced at the same time as the non-pre-emptive issue (or during the six months before). The Pre-Emption Group has published template resolutions and recommends that companies seek the extra 5% disapplication in a second, separate resolution. (Previously, the 2008 Pre-emption Group Statement of Principles provided that a disapplication of pre-emption rights in respect of more than 5% of the company's issued share capital or shares being issued at a discount of more than 5%, would not be likely to be viewed as 'routine' and that existing shareholders should be given the opportunity to acquire new shares *pro rata* to their existing holdings in those circumstances.)

In addition, a company should not allot, on a non-pre-emptive basis, shares representing more than 7.5% of its issued share capital over a three-year rolling period, excluding shares issued in connection with an acquisition or specified capital investment.

Under Investment Committee Guidelines (which have been superseded by the Pre-emption Group's Statement of Principles other than on this issue), if a vendor placing comprises more than 10% of the issued share capital of the company or there is a discount to the market price of more than 5% (or both) then 'claw back' must apply and shareholders must be given the chance to first take the shares pro rata to their holdings (in other words, the company must either carry out a rights issue or there must be an open offer).

Institutional investors prefer rights issues to open offers because shareholders are given an opportunity to sell their rights. There are no formal guidelines on when a rights issue should be used over an open offer, but the Investment Association has previously indicated that a share offering representing above 15–18% of issued capital or where the discount on the issue is above 7.5% should be made by way of rights issue rather than an open offer, unless adequate arrangements are made for the protection of shareholders.

If the company's existing authorities to allot and disapply pre-emption rights are not sufficient to cover the capital raising, the company will need to convene a general meeting to obtain additional authorities.

All these guidelines are available on the IVIS website (www.ivis.co.uk).

1.3 Other relevant Listing Rule and LSE requirements

1.3.1 Rights issues

Listing Rule 9.5 sets out the various provisions that regulate further share issues by a premium listed company.

The key requirement relating to rights issues in the Listing Rules is in LR 9.5.6R, which requires the offer on a rights issue to be open for at least ten business days, beginning on the day which the offer is first open for acceptance. This is a separate requirement to the requirement in CA 2006 that a company making a pre-emptive offer in compliance with the requirements of section 562 of CA 2006 (known as a 'Companies Act rights issue') must keep the offer open for 14 calendar days.

If a general meeting of shareholders is required for the rights issue (because shareholder authority is needed for the issue of new shares), the provisional allotment letters can only be posted after the general meeting, once the necessary approvals have been obtained. The FCA does not allow trading in the nil-paid shares (i.e. the right to take up the new shares) to be conditional. The 'ten business day' offer period will only start running after the general meeting.

The Listing Rules do not prescribe a maximum discount at which shares can be offered in a rights issue, but they do require, where existing shareholders do not take up their rights on a rights issue, the listed company to ensure that such shares are offered for sale or subscription on terms that any premium over the sale or subscription price (net of expenses) is for the account of those shareholders who did not take up their rights. The company may only retain any proceeds of sale or subscription if such proceeds do not exceed £5 (LR 9.5.4R).

If there is a substantial shareholder who constitutes a related party under Listing Rule 11, it will be necessary to check whether the rights issue will involve a related party transaction requiring shareholder approval. There are exemptions (in Annex 1R to Listing Rule 11) for a shareholder taking up shares under its entitlement on a pre-emptive offer and for a shareholder who underwrites an equity offering for normal commercial consideration (except to the extent that it is underwriting its own entitlement to take up shares). Related party transactions are discussed in more detail in Chapter 9.

1.3.2 Open offers

As referred to above, Listing Rule 9.5 sets out the various provisions that regulate further share issues by a premium listed company.

Under LR 9.5.10R(1), the maximum discount at which shares can be offered in an open offer is 10% (unless the shares are issued under a pre-existing general disapplication of pre-emption rights or shareholder approval is obtained), whereas on a rights issue there is no limit.

The timetable for the open offer must be agreed in advance with the recognised investment exchange on which its shares are admitted to trading (LR 9.5.7R).

The open offer must remain open for acceptance for a period of ten business days (LR 9.5.7AR). The first business day is the day on which the offer is first open for acceptance.

As with a rights issue, on a compensatory open offer, a shareholder who does not take up his entitlement will be entitled to receive any premium on the proceeds of the sale of the shares, unless they are less than £5 (LR 9.5.8AR).

Even if a general meeting of shareholders is required to approve the terms, the application forms can be sent with the notice of meeting. Unlike a rights issue there is no need to wait until after the general meeting because there is no provisional allotment and no trading in the rights to take up the shares. Where shareholder approval is required, an open offer will often be faster, and the company will get its money sooner, as the offer period and the notice period can run concurrently.

As with a rights issue, if there is a substantial shareholder who constitutes a related party under Listing Rule 11, you will need to check whether the open offer will involve a related party transaction requiring shareholder approval. The exemptions in Annex 1R to Listing Rule 11 which apply to a rights issue (see section 1.3.1 above) are similarly applicable to an open offer.

1.3.3 Placings

As referred to above, Listing Rule 9.5 sets out the various provisions that regulate further share issues by a premium listed company.

Under LR 9.5.10R(1), the maximum discount at which shares can be offered in a placing is 10%, except with prior shareholder consent (unless the shares are issued under a pre-existing disapplication of pre-emption rights). The discount is calculated by reference to the middle market price of the shares at the time of announcement. Where a placing is entered into during the course of the day, an on-screen intra-day price derived from another market can be used as a reference point (LR 9.5.10R(2A)) but it should discuss the source of the price in advance with the FCA (LR 9.5.10AG).

There are no timing restrictions, provided no shareholder approval is required for the issue of new shares.

1.4 Requirement to publish a prospectus

Unless an exemption applies, a company is required to prepare and obtain FCA approval for a prospectus where it is making an offer of transferable securities to the public (FSMA s. 85(1)) or where it is requesting the admission of transferable securities to trading on a regulated market (FSMA s. 85(2)). The requirements are discussed in detail in Chapter 4.

On a further issue of shares, a listed company will need to consider whether or not it is required to prepare and have approved a prospectus or whether one of the exemptions applies.

1.4.1 Prospectus requirements – rights issues and open offers

Rights issues and open offers of new shares by a listed company will be treated as offers to the public of transferable securities under the Prospectus Rules and the FSMA. The exemptions to the requirement to publish a FCA-approved prospectus for a public offer are unlikely to apply to rights issues or open offers as the minimum denomination of the securities and the minimum amount that can be paid for them is unlikely to be more than €100,000 and the offer is likely to involve large numbers of shareholders (i.e. more than 150 per EEA state), who are not qualified investors (see section 1.5 of Chapter 4).

The admission of transferable securities issued under a rights issue or open offer to the Official List and to trading on the LSE's main market for listed securities is an admission to trading on a regulated market and is therefore a relevant admission to trading for the purpose of the Prospectus Rules and the FSMA. There is an exemption for the admission of shares where the issue represents an increase of less than 10% of the number of shares of the same class already admitted to trading (PR 1.2.3R(1)). However, even if the size of the rights issue or open offer is limited to an increase of less than 10% of the number of shares admitted to trading, a prospectus is still almost certain to be required under the public offer test (see section 1.5 of Chapter 4). Note that the New Prospectus Regulation will replace the Prospectus Directive, following the Commission's review of the prospectus regime in Europe. Under the regulation, the threshold for this exemption will be increased from 10% to 20% and the exemption will apply to all securities rather than just shares. The changes to this exemption came into force at the same time as the New Prospectus Regulation came into force, in July 2017 (see the FCA's Quarterly Consultation Paper CP 17/6).

The PD provides for a proportionate disclosure regime for rights issues, so a company is not required to produce a full prospectus. It is available both on Companies Act-compliant rights issues (where the rights issue is made in compliance with statutory pre-emption rights) and on rights issues where a company has disapplied the statutory pre-emption rights provided that 'near-identical' rights are conferred on shareholders in their place. In order for near-identical rights to have been conferred, certain conditions need to be met, including that the rights must be negotiable and transferable or, if not, the shares which arise from unexercised rights at the end of the offer period must be sold for the benefit of the shareholders who did not take up those entitlements. Arguably a compensatory open offer structure would meet the requirements but an open offer will not.

The level of disclosure required under the regime is quite reduced as compared to the disclosure requirements for a full prospectus. In particular, the company will only be required to include audited historical financial information for the last financial year and it will not be required to include an operating and financial review in the prospectus. The specific disclosure requirements are set out in Annexes XXIII and XXIV of Appendix 3 to the Prospectus Rules.

Where the proportionate disclosure regime is used on a rights issue, a prescribed statement must be included at the start of the prospectus noting that it is addressed to shareholders of the company and that the level of disclosure is proportionate to that type of issue (see PR 2.3.1A). In practice, companies are, however, reluctant to use the proportionate disclosure regime, due to liability concerns and disclosure requirements in other jurisdictions, particularly in the US. The New Prospectus Regulation also provides for an 'alleviated disclosure regime' for rights issues and other secondary issues, although it remains to be seen if it will be widely adopted; the same concerns regarding liability and overseas requirements are likely to be an issue.

1.4.2 Prospectus requirements – placings

A placing of new shares by a listed company will be a public offer of transferable securities under the Prospectus Rules and the FSMA. However, an exemption from the requirement to produce a prospectus will usually apply. The most relevant exemptions for a placing will include the exemptions for offers made to qualified investors and offers addressed to fewer than 150 persons per EEA state (see section 1.5 of Chapter 4).

The admission of the transferable securities issued on a placing to trading on the London Stock Exchange's main market for listed securities is an admission to trading on a regulated market and is, therefore, a relevant admission to trading for the purpose of the Prospectus Rules and the FSMA. The key exemption to the requirement to produce a prospectus for this type of admission is the exemption for the admission of shares representing an increase (in aggregate over 12 months) of less than 10% of the number of shares of the same class already admitted to trading (PR 1.2.3R(1))(see section 1.6 of Chapter 4). As noted above, the New Prospectus Regulation will increase this limit from 10% to 20% with effect from July 2017.

Accordingly, if the new shares are placed with qualified investors and the size of the placing is within the exemption for an increase of less than 10% of the shares (or 20% from July 2017) of the same class already admitted, it is likely that the listed company will be able to avoid the need to prepare a prospectus.

1.4.3 Supplementary prospectuses and withdrawal rights

If a company does prepare a prospectus, it will have to bear in mind its obligations to produce a supplementary prospectus. If at any time after a prospectus is approved and before the final closing of the offer or admission to trading (and where there is both an offer and admission, before the later of the closing of the offer and admission) there arises 'a significant new factor, material mistake or inaccuracy relating to the information included in the prospectus', a supplementary prospectus containing details of the new factor, mistake or inaccuracy must be submitted to the FCA for its approval and then (if approved) published (PR 3.4 and s. 87G of the FSMA).

PR 3.4.4 sets out the circumstances in which a supplementary prospectus must be published by an issuer of equity securities (or equivalent) or depositary receipts which include (but are not limited to):

- publication of new annual audited financial statements;
- publication of any modification to a profit forecast or profit estimate contained in the initial prospectus;
- a change of control of the company;
- if the company's working capital becomes insufficient for its requirements (or, conversely, if a qualified working capital statement was included in the initial prospectus, the company's working capital becomes sufficient for its present purposes); and
- if the prospectus is used to make a public offer into an additional EU member state or to seek admission to trading on an additional EU regulated market, which is not contemplated in it.

This list is not comprehensive but simply prescribes situations where a supplementary prospectus must be published. In situations outside the scope of the list, it is the company's responsibility to determine the significance of an event, taking into account the company and the securities in question, and decide whether publication of a supplementary prospectus is required (see section 4 of Chapter 4 for more information).

A premium listed company must appoint a sponsor when submitting a supplementary prospectus to the FCA (LR 8.2.1R(1)(a)).

An amending advertisement must also be disseminated if any earlier advertisement is rendered inaccurate or misleading by a significant new factor or material mistake or inaccuracy disclosed in, or corrected by, a supplementary prospectus (see PR 3.3.3A).

Where a supplementary prospectus has been published, a person may withdraw their acceptance of an offer of transferable securities to the public before a specified deadline if certain conditions are met. The conditions are set out in section 87Q(5) of the FSMA and are:

- a prospectus which relates to an offer of transferable securities to the public has been published;
- a supplementary prospectus has been published;

- prior to the publication of the supplementary prospectus, the person agreed to buy or subscribe for transferable securities to which the offer relates; and
- the significant new factor, material mistake or inaccuracy which caused the supplementary prospectus to be published arose before delivery of the securities.

The withdrawal rights can be exercised before the end of the second working day after the day on which the supplementary prospectus was published, or such later time as may be specified in the supplementary prospectus (FSMA s. 87Q(6)) (see section 4.6 of Chapter 4).

In relation to a rights issue, there will be no withdrawal rights in relation to nil-paid rights (i.e. the right to subscribe for new shares) because there is no offer by the listed company of the nil-paid rights. They are automatically given to all shareholders without any payment, or any agreement to buy or subscribe, on the date of issue of the nil-paid rights. In relation to fully paid rights (i.e. once the investor has sent payment for the shares) the concern is whether withdrawal rights would apply in the event that a supplementary prospectus is required to be produced prior to the last day for acceptance of the rights issue.

It is thought that an investor's right to withdraw following the publication of a supplementary prospectus will cease when the contract between the offeror and the offeree has been effectively performed but there is no formal guidance on this point. On a rights issue, this would mean that withdrawal rights cease when an investor has paid the subscription price in full and the shares have been unconditionally allotted to him (it does not matter if the share has not yet been issued – allotment will be sufficient). Therefore, if an investor has sent a cheque with his PAL he would have a withdrawal right if that application had not yet been processed and he had not yet been allotted a fully paid share. Similarly, a CREST instruction that has not yet been settled could be withdrawn. However, if a fully paid right had already been allotted there would no longer be a right to withdraw. This means there are very limited circumstances in which a withdrawal right would arise on a rights issue. It is generally accepted that withdrawal rights following a supplementary prospectus are not available.

The Board minutes in relation to the rights issue should reflect the fact that shares will be immediately and unconditionally allotted to applicants on receipt of the application to take up rights together with payment.

If a supplementary prospectus is issued in the final two working days prior to the close of the offer, the timetable for the rights issue would have to be extended on the basis that, if there were outstanding applications to be processed, the investors concerned would be entitled to a two-working-day withdrawal period.

In relation to an open offer, the shares are not normally allotted or issued prior to the end of the offer period because the open offer is normally conditional on shareholder approval being obtained, with the general meeting notice period running concurrently with the offer period; admission does not occur until after the close of the offer.

Withdrawal rights would therefore arise if a supplementary prospectus were issued at any time during the offer period prior to admission. Withdrawal rights will, therefore, be more of a concern on an open offer than they are on a rights issue (where shares are allotted during the course of the offer period). The same timetabling issue would arise as on a rights issue if a supplementary prospectus were to be published less than two working days before the end of the offer period.

1.5 Notification and documentation requirements under the Listing Rules and Transparency Rules

Having considered the requirements of Listing Rule 9 in connection with an issue of new shares and decided whether or not the issue requires the publication of a prospectus, a premium listed company will need to comply with any relevant notification obligations it has under the Listing Rules and the requirements of Listing Rule 13 in relation to any circular to be published.

Both standard and premium listed companies must consider whether a Total Voting Rights (TVR) announcement will be required.

The requirements under MAR for a further share issue, including the obligation to announce inside information as soon as possible, the market soundings regime and the rules on PDMR dealings, are discussed in section 1.6 below.

1.5.1 Requirements for rights issues

A premium listed company must ensure, once it decides to launch a rights issue, that the issue price and principal terms of the issue are notified to an RIS as soon as possible. It must also notify an RIS of the results of the issue and, if any rights not taken up are sold, details of the sale (including date and price per share) (LR 9.5.5R).

If shareholder approval is required to obtain authority to allot new shares or to disapply pre-emption rights over the new shares, a circular will have to be produced.

As well as complying with the general requirements for circulars set out in Listing Rule 13, if a premium listed company is seeking authority to allot shares it will have to include additional information in its circular (under LR 13.8.1R) such as:

- the maximum amount of relevant securities which the directors will have authority to allot and the percentage which that amount represents of the total ordinary share capital in issue; and
- a statement by the directors as to whether they have any present intention of exercising the authority, and if so for what purpose.

If the company is also seeking authority to disapply pre-emption rights, it will have to include in its circular a statement of the maximum amount of equity securities which the disapplication will cover (LR 13.8.2R).

If the fundraising is in connection with a Class 1 acquisition, shareholder approval will also be sought for that and the circular will have to comply with the Listing Rule requirements for Class 1 circulars (see sections 1.5.1 and 1.5.2 in Chapter 9).

If there is a substantial shareholder whose interest may go above 30% or has an existing interest of more than 30% but less than 50% which may increase as a result of the rights issue, the company may need to pass a 'whitewash' resolution to avoid triggering a requirement for the shareholder to make a mandatory bid under Rule 9 of the City Code. This will require dispensation from the Panel and a vote by the independent shareholders so the circular will need to contain a whitewash resolution and the information relating to a whitewash required by the City Code, if relevant.

As indicated above, a prospectus is likely to be required on a rights issue. If that is the case, the circular and prospectus may be (but do not have to be) combined into one document, in which case the combined document will need to comply with both the requirements of the Prospectus Rules and the requirements for circulars set out in Listing Rule 13.

The listed company must lodge copies of the resolutions and circular with the National Storage Mechanism, and notify an RIS that it has done so (LR 9.6.1R, LR 9.6.2R and LR 9.6.3R). Any proposed alteration of the company's capital structure must be notified to an RIS as soon as possible (LR 9.6.4R(1)).

The PAL must comply with the requirements of LR 9.5.15R on temporary documents of title (e.g. they must state the time in which the offer may be accepted and how securities not taken up will be dealt with).

1.5.2 Requirements for open offers

As with a rights issue, a prospectus is likely to be required in connection with the issue of new shares pursuant to an open offer. If shareholder approval is also required to obtain authority to allot the new shares or to disapply pre-emption rights in connection with the new shares, a circular may be required.

Again as with a rights issue, the circular and prospectus may be produced as two separate documents or combined in a single document.

For a premium listed company, in addition to complying with the general requirements for circulars set out in Listing Rule 13 and the additional information required for authorities to allot and disapply pre-emption rights, discussed in section 1.5.1 above, any open offer circular must not contain any statement which implies that the offer gives the same rights as a rights issue unless it is a compensatory open offer (LR 9.5.8R(2)).

Any announcement made in connection with the open offer must state if the offer is subject to shareholder approval (LR 9.5.8R(1)).

Again, the listed company must lodge copies of the resolutions and the circular with the National Storage Mechanism, and notify an RIS that it has done so (LR 9.6.1R, LR 9.6.2R and LR 9.6.3R). Any proposed alteration of the company's capital structure must be notified to an RIS as soon as possible (LR 9.6.4R(1)).

1.5.3 Requirements for placings

As discussed above, a placing may be conducted simply on the back of an announcement with little further documentation required. If shareholder approval is also required to obtain authority to allot the new shares or to disapply pre-emption rights in connection with the new shares, a shareholder meeting may have to be convened and a circular prepared (complying with LR 13.8.1R and LR 13.8.2R particularly in the case of a premium listed company).

Any proposed alteration of a premium listed company's capital structure must be notified to an RIS as soon as possible (LR 9.6.4R(1)).

1.5.4 Total voting rights announcements

Following a rights issue, open offer or placing, the company will have to announce its enlarged share capital in its total voting rights (TVR) announcement. Assuming the increase in the company's share capital is material (likely to be 1% or more) the announcement must be made as soon as possible and, in any event, before the end of the next business day. A TVR announcement will also be required at the end of the month (DTR 5.6.1R and 5.6.1AR). The requirements for a TVR announcement are discussed in more detail in Chapter 7.

1.5.5 Notifications by major shareholders and PDMRs

A further share issue may result in a major shareholder, director or other PDMR having to make a notification in relation to their interests in the listed company's shares.

The PDMRs in a company and persons closely associated with them (their PCAs) are required, under Article 19(1) of MAR, to notify the company and the FCA of any transactions in the company's securities conducted on their own account within three business days of the transaction. The company is then required to announce that information to the market, within the same three business days. The PDMR notification requirements on a further share issue are discussion in section 1.6 below.

For major shareholders, DTR 5 requires interests in listed company qualifying instruments (such as shares) and financial instruments having similar economic effect to be disclosed where the interest reaches, exceeds or falls below certain thresholds (generally 3% or a whole percentage above that level). See Chapter 7 for a detailed discussion of the DTR 5 requirements.

Previously the FCA treated both nil-paid and fully paid rights as financial instruments having similar economic effect to a qualifying instrument and so they were within the scope of DTR 5. Following the introduction of the changes made to implement the Transparency Directive Amending Directive (TDAD) in November 2015, ESMA's Final Report on the TDAD and the FCA's policy statement in connection with its implementation, PS 15/26, make it clear that only financial instruments already in issue are subject to the notification regime. Therefore, DTR 5 does not apply to nil-paid rights on a rights issue nor entitlements to shares on an open offer and so no DTR 5 notification is required in respect of them. Only financial instruments relating to already issued shares are in scope for the disclosure regime.

Once the shares under the rights issue, open offer or placing are issued, shareholders will have to consider whether they have a notification obligation under DTR 5.1.2R (i.e. if a relevant percentage threshold has been crossed). An existing shareholder may have a notification obligation even if they did not take up shares, because the company's total voting rights in issue will have changed and so the percentage of the total voting rights held by that person may have changed.

There is an additional disclosure requirement in respect of short selling. Under the EU Short Selling Regulation (No. 236/2012), which is directly effective in the EEA, including the UK, net short positions of 0.2% or more in the issued share capital of a company, and any changes in that position (in 0.1% increments, up to 0.5%) must be privately notified to the relevant competent authority (the FCA in the UK). Net short positions of 0.5% or more in the issued share capital of a company and any change in that position (in 0.1% increments) must be disclosed to the relevant competent authority, which will make that information public. A 'net short position' is the position that remains after deducting any long position that a person holds in the issued share capital of a company from any short position that a person holds in the issued share capital of that company (including via contracts referenced to the share price).

The FSA had previously considered (see DP 09/01) whether short selling by underwriters should be prohibited but ruled it out on the basis that the disclosure regime and legal and contractual restrictions were adequate.

1.6 The Market Abuse Regulation

A company conducting a secondary share issue will have to consider its obligations under MAR, including the requirements in relation to:

- inside information;
- maintaining insider lists;
- market soundings (i.e. sounding out investors in connection with the proposed transaction prior to its announcement); and
- share dealings by PDMRs and PCAs.

These requirements are discussed further below.

Companies should also be aware of the civil offences of market abuse (set out in Articles 8, 10, 12, 14 and 15 of MAR) which are:

- insider dealing;
- unlawful disclosure of inside information otherwise than in the normal exercise of an employment, profession or duties; and
- market manipulation.

These offences are discussed in more detail in Chapter 5.

A listed company should have policies and procedures in place to ensure compliance with MAR on an ongoing basis (see Chapter 5 for more detail) and its advisers are likely to want to see copies of such policies and procedures at the outset of a transaction to ensure that (i) they are properly compliant with MAR; and (ii) notifications and procedures undertaken as part of the further share issue are carried out in accordance with those policies.

1.6.1 Obligation to announce inside information

A listed company planning to undertake a secondary issue needs to comply with its obligations relating to inside information in Article 17 MAR, including the obligation to announce inside information as soon as possible and the record keeping and notification procedures when legitimately delaying the disclosure of inside information to the market.

The fact that a listed company is planning to undertake a secondary issue is likely to constitute inside information under Article 7 of MAR, which, broadly, provides that information will be inside information if it is:

- of a precise nature;
- non-public;
- relates to qualifying financial instruments; and
- if made public, would be likely to have a significant effect on the price of those financial instruments.

The definition of inside information is discussed in more detail in Chapter 5. As regards whether information is 'precise' when a company is just contemplating a capital raising (where the details have not been finalised), Recital (16) of MAR states that an intermediate step in a protracted process can be inside information by itself if it satisfies the test. Recital (17) then specifically gives as an example the possibility of the placement of financial instruments.

Inside information must be announced as soon as possible (unless a delay is permitted, as discussed below). There are various content requirements for announcements of inside information, as discussed in Chapter 5, including a statement that the information communicated is inside information and the identity of the person making the notification. The announcement must also be made available on the company's website for five years (MAR, Art.17(1)).

A company is only permitted to delay disclosure of inside information, under Article 17(4) of MAR, where the following conditions are met:

- immediate disclosure is likely to prejudice the company's legitimate interests;
- the delay in disclosure is not likely to mislead the public; and
- the company is able to ensure the confidentiality of that information.

A listed company planning to undertake a secondary issue would need to ensure that it satisfies these requirements if it wishes to delay disclosing the capital raising to the market. If it does delay, it must create a record of delay, in accordance with the Inside Information Implementing Regulation recording, among other things:

- the precise time when the inside information first existed;
- who was responsible for the decision to delay; and
- how the conditions for delay were met.

When the company then announces the inside information to the market, it must also notify the FCA privately of the delay.

See Chapter 5 for further information on when a delay is permitted and the requirements that apply when disclosure is delayed.

1.6.2 Maintaining insider lists

Article 18 of MAR requires companies to compile and maintain insider lists of people working for them who have access to inside information. Companies must also ensure that advisers and other persons acting on its behalf maintain an insider list. Advisers may maintain their own separate lists but the company remains responsible for the obligation.

The Insider List Implementing Regulation (2016/347/EU) contains the content requirements for insider lists. The MAR requirements for insider lists are discussed in more detail in Chapter 5.

In the context of a capital raising, both the company and its advisers should create and maintain insider lists until the share issue is announced to the market.

1.6.3 Sounding out investors and the market soundings regime

If a company has concluded it can legitimately delay disclosure of inside information in relation to a proposed further share issue and wants to sound out potential investors, it will have to consider whether it is able to selectively disclose inside information about the proposed share issue to those investors.

Under MAR, the unlawful disclosure of inside information is an offence. As discussed in Chapter 5, a company may selectively disclose inside information to a third party provided the disclosure is in the normal exercise of an employment, profession or duties and the third party owes the company a duty of confidentiality (MAR, Art 17(8)).

Paragraph 1.4.5G of the FCA Market Conduct Sourcebook (FCA MAR) sets out factors that the FCA may consider indicate that disclosure was in the normal exercise of a person's employment, profession or duties. These include where the disclosure is reasonable and for the purpose of facilitating any commercial, financial or investment transaction (including prospective underwriters or placees of securities).

MAR also provides a safe harbour (MAR, Art 11) from the offence of unlawful disclosure where inside information is disclosed pursuant to a 'market sounding', that is the sounding out of investors ahead of a share issue, provided certain procedures are followed.

If the procedural requirements are followed, the disclosure of inside information in the course of a market sounding will be deemed to have been made in the normal exercise of a person's employment, profession or duties and therefore in compliance with MAR.

Under Article 11(1) of MAR, a market sounding is:

> [the] communication of information, prior to the announcement of a transaction, in order to gauge the level of interest of potential investors in a possible transaction and the conditions relating to it such as its potential size or pricing, to one or more potential issuers by ... an issuer.

In order to be a market sounding for the purposes of Article 11(1), the market sounding must:

- involve the communication of information (not necessarily inside information);
- be directed at one or more potential investors;
- be conducted prior to the announcement of a transaction; and
- be intended to gauge the level of interest in a possible transaction.

Sounding out potential investors prior to the launch of a secondary issue (commonly referred to as 'wall-crossing') will therefore usually constitute a market sounding for the purposes of Article 11(1) of MAR.

The persons conducting the soundings, likely to be the company and its advisers, are referred to as 'disclosing market participants' (DMPs).

The procedural requirements relating to market soundings are set out in the Market Sounding Delegated Regulation (2016/960/EU) and Implementing Regulation (2016/959/EU). ESMA takes the view that there is a risk that inside information will be passed during a market sounding even if the DMP has categorised it as not containing inside information. It therefore requires DMPs to keep records of market soundings even where the DMP has concluded that no inside information will be disclosed.

The key requirements for DMPs on a market sounding include:

- establishing procedures, prior to any sounding, for how the sounding will be conducted;
- providing a set of materials, with prescribed contents, to all recipients of a sounding;
- using recorded phone lines when available (provided the recipient of the market sounding (the 'market sounding recipient' (MSR)) consents to their use);
- giving MSRs an estimate of when the information will cease to be inside information;
- informing the MSR when the information has ceased to be inside information; and
- maintaining a record of prescribed information in relation to the market sounding for five years post-sounding.

ESMA has published guidelines for persons receiving market soundings (MSRs) (ESMA/2016/1477), which require them to implement procedures in relation to market soundings and to make their own assessment of whether information they receive is inside information.

Disclosure of inside information as part of a sounding that does not fully comply with the procedural requirements imposed under Article 11 of MAR will not necessarily be unlawful (MAR Recital (35)). However, the CLLS/Law Society Q&A suggest that the obligation under Article 11(3) must be complied with in all cases (i.e. the DMP must always consider in advance whether the sounding will involve disclosure of inside information and make a written record of its conclusions and the reasons therefor).

1.6.4 PDMR dealings

Restrictions on PDMR dealings

Article 19(11) of MAR prohibits a PDMR from conducting any transactions 'on its own account or for the account of a third party' during a closed period (i.e. in the 30 days prior to the announcement of an interim report or year-end report). There are limited exceptions to this rule in Article 19(12), which allow a company to permit a PDMR to deal during a MAR closed period in certain situations, including where the transaction is in relation to a 'qualification or entitlement of shares'. Although there is no definition of this term, the CLLS/ Law Society Q&A consider that it would be broad enough to encompass rights issues under which (subject to exclusions for certain overseas shareholders) all shareholders are allocated nil-paid rights. Provided, therefore, that a PDMR is given permission by the company to deal and the transaction cannot be conducted at a time other than during a MAR closed period (because the opening date and the final date for the entitlement falls during a MAR closed period) in the view of the CLLS/Law Society a PDMR would be permitted to undertake or elect to take up entitlements under a rights issue, provided they have no inside information.

Notifications by PDMRs and their PCAs

Article 19(1) of MAR requires persons discharging managerial responsibility (PDMRs) within a company and persons closely associated with them (PCAs) to disclose to the company transactions conducted on their own account in the company's securities within three business days of the day on which the transaction occurred. The company must then notify the market of such transactions, within the same three business day period.

There is a mandatory form for this notification, set out in the PDMR Transaction Notification Implementing Regulation (2016/523/EU), and the FCA website sets outs the process and form for the notification to the FCA. Article 10 of the MAR General Delegated Regulation (2016/522/EU) provides an extensive but non-exhaustive list of transactions within the scope of this requirement. In general, the scope is very broad and there is no requirement that transactions be conducted by (as opposed to on behalf of) the PDMR in order to be caught. Any change in a PDMR's or PCA's holding is likely to trigger a notification obligation.

When considering the requirements in relation to PDMR dealings, as well as the provisions of MAR, it will be important to check any share dealing code that the company may have as this may impose more stringent requirements.

The MAR requirements in relation to PDMR dealings are discussed in more detail in Chapter 7.

2. Share buy-backs

A listed company may use a share buy-back as a means of returning surplus cash to shareholders, increasing earnings per share or net assets per share or adjusting the overall gearing ratio of its balance sheet.

There are a number of different regimes that a premium listed company has to consider when proposing a share buy-back. The requirements with which it must comply will vary according to the particular features of the share repurchase. For example, it may buy back its shares either on-market (i.e. on a recognised investment exchange) or off-market; it may have an ongoing share buy-back programme or conduct a one-off repurchase or a tender offer (where the company invites shareholders to tender their shares to the company to be repurchased at a maximum or fixed price); and when it buys back the shares it may either hold the shares in treasury or cancel them.

The different regimes that a company with a premium listing must consider are:

- the relevant provisions of CA 2006;

- Chapter 12 of the Listing Rules;
- the Investment Association's views on share repurchases;
- MAR; and
- the requirements of the City Code.

The requirements of these regimes fall into two broad categories: the authorities required to conduct a share repurchase (including limits applicable to the number of shares that may be bought back and to the price that may be paid); and restrictions on when buy-backs can be carried out.

A listed company will also have to ensure that the buy-back does not mean that it no longer meets the free float requirement (i.e. that the percentage of its shares in public hands does not fall below 25%) (LR 9.2.15R). This will also be relevant to a company with a standard listing. Beyond that, however, there are no specific requirements in the Listing Rules for a share buy-back by a standard listed company.

Where a premium listed company has a controlling shareholder (i.e. one holding 30% or more of the voting rights), the Listing Rules impose certain additional requirements, including a requirement that the company enter into a formal agreement with its controlling shareholder(s) containing certain prescribed 'independence provisions' (see Chapter 9 for more information). When conducting a buy-back, a company will have to bear these provisions in mind if the buy-back will affect percentage holdings between members and could result in a shareholder becoming a 'controlling shareholder' for the purposes of the Listing Rules (or trigger a restriction in an existing relationship agreement with a shareholder).

Before seeking to do a share repurchase, a premium listed company must ensure that it will comply with the applicable requirements. Figure 10.3 sets out a short checklist of the relevant requirements (see p. 477). A premium listed company will usually seek an annual authority at its AGM to repurchase its own shares within certain limits; if a proposed buy-back does not fall within that authority, additional shareholder approval must be sought.

2.1 General requirements for a share repurchase

2.1.1 CA 2006 requirements

CA 2006 imposes various requirements on a company proposing to conduct a share buy-back. However, in some areas, the other regimes with which a premium listed company must comply impose more onerous requirements, so compliance with CA 2006 alone will not be sufficient.

The key provisions in CA 2006 for a share buy-back are as follows:

- a company may only purchase its own shares if it is not prohibited or restricted from doing so by its articles of association;

- a company must obtain authority from its shareholders to conduct a share buy-back (the requirements for a repurchase authority are considered in more detail in section 2.2);
- any contract for an off-market purchase must be approved in advance by independent shareholders (i.e. excluding the holder(s) of the shares to be repurchased) or be conditional upon obtaining such shareholder approval (CA 2006 s. 695);
- when a listed company purchases its own shares, payment for the shares must be made on purchase;
- if the company is a public limited company, payment must generally be made out of the distributable profits of the company or out of the proceeds of a fresh issue of shares made for the purpose of the financing of the repurchase; however, any premium payable on the purchase which exceeds the lesser of the premium paid on the issue and the current share premium must be made out of distributable profits. If the shares are to be held in treasury they must be paid for out of distributable profits; and
- repurchased shares must either be cancelled or held in treasury.

2.1.2 Listing Rule requirements for a purchase of equity shares

Listing Rule 12 sets out the requirements in relation to share buy-backs and applies to companies with a premium listing of equity securities. Other provisions in the Listing Rules, including the rules on circulars in Listing Rule 13 and the provisions regarding related party transactions in Listing Rule 11, may also be relevant to a share buy-back.

The Listing Rules distinguish between a purchase of equity shares and a purchase of other securities. The requirements for purchases of securities other than equity shares are considered in section 2.6.

Price payable on a repurchase of equity shares

Unless a tender offer is made to all holders of the class, when a listed company repurchases less than 15% of any class of its equity shares (excluding treasury shares) pursuant to a general authority, it may not pay more than the higher of:

- 5% above the average market price of the shares for the five business days prior to the day the purchase is made; and
- the price stipulated by Article 5(6) of MAR (LR 12.4.1R).

Article 5(6) of MAR refers to technical standards which can be found in the Buyback and Stabilisation Regulation ((EU) 2016/1052). Under that Regulation, the price stipulated is the price which is the higher of the last independent trade and the highest current independent bid on the trading venue where the purchase is carried out. Note that if a company wishes to fall within the MAR safe harbour for buy-backs in MAR Art 5 and the Buyback and Stabilisation Regulation, the price cannot exceed that stipulated in Article 5(6) of MAR (i.e. the company cannot pay any higher price which would otherwise be permitted under the first limb of LR 12.4.1R). The MAR safe harbour is discussed in more detail at section 2.1.3 below.

There is no limit on the price payable on a tender offer under the Listing Rules.

When a repurchase must be made by way of tender offer

LR 12.4.2R provides that if a listed company is purchasing 15% or more of any class of its equity shares, either the purchase must be by way of tender offer to all shareholders of that class (pursuant to a general shareholder authority) or the full terms of the share purchase must be specifically approved by shareholders (LR 12.4.2AR).

A tender offer will also be required if the price the listed company will pay will exceed the higher of:

- 5% above the average market price of the shares for the five business days prior to the day the purchase is made; and
- the price stipulated in Article 5(6) of MAR (that is, as discussed above, the higher of the last independent trade and the highest current independent bid on the trading venue where the purchase is carried out) (LR 12.4.1R).

A tender offer is an offer by a company to purchase all or some of a class of its listed equity securities at a maximum or fixed price. The price may be established by means of a formula.

The tender offer must be:

- communicated to all holders of that class by means of a circular or advertisement in two national papers;
- open to all holders of that class on the same terms for at least seven days; and
- open for acceptance by all holders of that class pro rata to their existing holdings.

Where a series of purchases are made pursuant to a general authority, a tender offer is only required in respect of any purchase that takes the aggregate number of shares purchased to 15% or more. Purchases that have been specifically approved by shareholders are not taken into account when calculating whether the 15% threshold has been reached (LR 12.4.3G).

Repurchase from a related party

If the company is buying equity securities or preference shares from a related party such as a director or significant shareholder (or someone who was in the past 12 months a director or significant shareholder), the rules on related party transactions in Listing Rule 11 will have to be considered. There is an exemption for a repurchase from a related party where it is done as part of a tender offer made to all holders of that class of securities or as part of a general market purchase pursuant to a general authority granted by shareholders without any prior understanding, arrangement or agreement between the listed company and the related party (LR 12.3.1R). If the repurchase does not fall within that exemption or any of the exemptions in Listing Rule 11, shareholder approval may be required. See Chapter 9 for more detail on who is a related party for the purposes of the Listing Rules and on related party transactions generally.

The FCA has confirmed in the UKLA Guidance Note *Share buy-backs with mix and match facilities (UKLA/TN/202.1)* that, where a company effects a share buy-back via a tender offer using an intermediary and the shares bought by the intermediary are automatically cancelled or held as treasury shares by the company, it will look through the intermediary to the company itself. As a consequence, the 'sale' of the buy-back shares by the intermediary to the company would not constitute a related party transaction, even if the intermediary initially acquired over 10% of the company's share capital in its own right. Where there is a mix-and-match facility (i.e. the intermediary offers the shares that it has purchased under the tender offer to certain new and/or existing shareholders before the eventual sale back to the company) the FCA's view is that any shares that the intermediary buys under the tender offer should be treated as treasury shares and the offer to sell those shares should therefore be conducted in accordance with the relevant rules for treasury shares.

Requirement for approval by holders of convertible or exchangeable securities

If a company has listed securities which are convertible into, exchangeable for or which carry a right to subscribe for equity shares of the class proposed to be purchased, then prior to entering into any agreement to repurchase, the company must convene a separate meeting of the holders of those securities and obtain their approval for the proposed purchase by way of a special resolution (LR 12.4.7R). This requirement for a separate meeting does not apply where the terms of issue of the securities permit the purchase (LR 12.4.8R). Any circular convening such a meeting must (as well as complying with Listing Rule 13) include a statement of the effect of the purchase on the conversion expectations of the holders (in terms of attributable assets and earnings) and any adjustments to the rights of the holders (LR 12.4.9R).

Notifications in connection with repurchases of equity shares

Unless it is just seeking a renewal of an existing authority, when a Board decides to seek shareholder approval for authority to purchase its own equity shares, the company must notify an RIS as soon as possible (LR 12.4.4R). The notification must state whether the proposal relates to specific purchases and, if so, the names of the persons from whom the purchases are to be made, or to a general authorisation to make purchases.

The company must also notify an RIS as soon as possible of the outcome of the shareholders' meeting (LR 12.4.5R).

When it repurchases equity shares, the company must notify an RIS as soon as possible and in any event by no later than 7.30am on the business day following the calendar day on which the purchase occurred (LR 12.4.6R). The notification must include:

- the date of the purchase;
- the number of equity shares purchased;
- the highest and lowest price paid;
- how many of the shares purchased will be cancelled and how many held in treasury; and
- where the shares are to be held in treasury: (i) the total number of treasury shares of each class that will be held by the company following the purchase; and (ii) the number of equity shares of each class that the company has in issue less the total number of treasury shares of each class following the purchase.

Transactions similar to a buy-back

Under LR 12.4.10G, where a premium listed company is intending to enter into a transaction that would have a similar effect to a share buy-back, the company should consult the FCA. This is discussed in more detail in the UKLA Guidance Note *Share buybacks – novel/complex approaches and Premium Listing Principle 5 (UKLA/TN/310.1)*.

2.1.3 Market abuse

When conducting a share buy-back, a listed company must bear in mind the requirements and restrictions under MAR.

As well as considering whether information about a proposed buy-back amounts to inside information (see Chapter 5 for further information) a listed company will have to ensure it does not commit market abuse when conducting the buy-back.

The offences of insider dealing and market manipulation

It is an offence to deal, or attempt to deal, on the basis of inside information (MAR, Arts 8 and 14). Under Recital (24) of MAR, there is a presumption, where a person deals while in possession of inside information, that the person has used that information. A listed company could therefore commit the offence of insider dealing if it buys back shares while it is in possession of inside information.

It is also an offence to engage in, or to attempt to engage in, market manipulation (MAR, Arts 12 and 15). This includes entering into a transaction, placing an order or any other behaviour which gives false or misleading signals as to the supply of, demand for or price of financial instruments, or which secures the price at an abnormal or artificial level.

The safe harbour for share buy-backs

Article 5 of MAR contains a safe harbour for share buy-backs which provides a complete exemption from the prohibition on insider dealing and market manipulation for buy-backs, provided they meet certain conditions, which are set out in MAR and the Buyback and Stabilisation Regulation.

The conditions which a company must satisfy in order to rely on the safe harbour relate to:

- the purpose of the buy-back;
- price and volume limitations;
- disclosure requirements; and
- the timing of the buy-back (see section 2.4.1 below).

The volume and price limits and disclosure requirements are substantially similar to those under the previous safe harbour under the Market Abuse Directive (MAD). In the UK, companies did not in practice usually rely on the MAD safe harbour due to the onerous nature of the requirements. MAR also recognises that the safe harbour does not have to be complied with (MAR, Recital (12)) and there is no presumption of market abuse if the safe harbour is not complied with.

Note that the safe harbour is only available for share buy-backs, not for repurchases of other securities.

Buy-back programmes

If a company chooses not to rely on the safe harbour then it will have to consider whether the buy-back might amount to market abuse on a case-by-case basis.

In particular, it must ensure that there is no insider dealing (i.e. it must not deal while in possession of inside information). This means that a company cannot buy back its shares at a time when inside information exists in relation to the company, unless it has a pre-agreed buy-back programme in place.

If there is a pre-agreed buy-back programme in place, a buy-back pursuant to that programme could fall within Article 9(3) of MAR, which provides a safe harbour from the offence of insider dealing where a transaction is carried out pursuant to a pre-existing agreement. In order to fall within this safe harbour, the programme must have been entered into before the inside information existed (Art. 9(3)) and there must not be an illegitimate reason for the trade (Art. 9(6)). See section 2.4.2 below for further discussion on buy-back programmes.

Under MAD, and the Listing Rules in force at the time, companies often used to put in place buy-back programmes. The programmes were entered into prior to the commencement of the 'prohibited period' under the Model Code (during which share buy-backs were not permitted) and either (i) the dates and quantities of securities to be traded during the prohibited period were fixed and disclosed in a notification made in accordance with LR 12.4.4; or (ii) the programme was managed by an independent third party which made the trading decisions independent of, and uninfluenced by, the company. Although there is no equivalent prohibition in MAR on a company buying back shares during a closed period, the practice of entering into share buy-back programmes is expected to continue under MAR (see the CLLS/Law Society Q&A on this, discussed below).

2.1.4 The City Code

Consideration will have to be given to the City Code where it applies to the company (which will include all UK-incorporated companies with listed securities). A buy-back of voting shares by a company will generally result in the remaining shareholders holding an increased percentage of voting rights. Under Rule 37 of the City Code, that increase is treated as an 'acquisition' for the purposes of Rule 9 of the City Code. Broadly speaking, Rule 9 requires a person, or group of persons acting together, to make a mandatory takeover offer (or Rule 9 bid) for the company when they acquire shares which, when aggregated with their existing interests, carry 30% or more of the voting rights of the company, or which increases an existing interest of more than 30% but less than 50% of the voting rights of the company.

The obligation to make a Rule 9 bid will generally only apply where the shareholder in question is, or is acting in concert with, a director, has a representative appointed to the Board or is the investment manager of an investment trust. Where a share buy-back would trigger a requirement for a shareholder to make a Rule 9 bid, the Takeover Panel will generally grant a waiver of the obligation to make an offer provided there is an independent vote of shareholders approving the arrangements (known as a 'Rule 9 whitewash'). The Takeover Panel will need to be consulted at an early stage and the procedure set out in Appendix 1 to the City Code followed.

2.1.5 Investment Association Guidelines

In 2016, the Investment Association published an updated version of its Share Capital Management Guidelines, which apply to companies whose shares are admitted to the premium segment of the Official List of the UK Listing Authority and set out the IA's views on share buy-backs. The Guidelines:

- require a special resolution rather than an ordinary resolution for buy-backs (and clarify that this applies in the case of an off market buy-back too, which now only requires an ordinary resolution under the CA 2006);
- confirm that a buy-back authority of up to 10% of a company's share capital is unlikely to cause concern;
- confirm that its members consider that the price limits on buy-backs in the Listing Rules are appropriate;
- say that companies should disclose in their annual reports the justification for any own purchases made in the previous year, including an explanation of why this method of returning capital to shareholders was decided upon and the impact on earnings per share (EPS), total shareholder return (TSR) and net asset value (NAV) per share;

- no longer require companies to undertake in the document that the authority to purchase its own shares will only be exercised if it would result in an increase in earnings per share and is in the best interests of shareholders. However, the Guidelines say that shareholders expect this and where this is not the case, the benefits should be clearly explained;
- discourage off-market buy-backs unless there is transparency on terms and pricing;
- say that investors remain 'concerned' about unusual transactions and structures that relate to returns of capital which might carry unusual risks for investors and these should be approved by a separate special resolution; and
- contain a statement that, while the limit in CA 2006 which prevented companies from holding more than 10% of their shares in treasury has been removed, their preference is for companies not to hold more than 10% in treasury.

2.2 Buy-backs within a listed company's annual authority

A listed company typically takes a general authority to repurchase shares annually at its AGM. The terms of the resolution are determined by CA 2006, the Listing Rules and guidance from the Investment Association.

2.2.1 Key features of the resolution

The key features of the resolution to approve a buy-back are as follows:

- *Type of resolution* – as referred to above, CA 2006 requires an ordinary resolution to authorise an on-market buy-back or an off-market purchase. However, the Investment Association prefers companies to propose these resolutions as special resolutions and so listed companies will generally pass a special resolution to authorise a share buy-back.
- *Duration* – under CA 2006, the resolution must specify the date on which the authority will expire, which must not be more than five years after the date of the resolution. The Investment Association says that a general authority to purchase shares should be renewed annually.
- *Price* – the resolution must determine the minimum and maximum prices that may be paid (CA 2006 s. 701(3)(b)). This can be done by either specifying a price, or providing a basis or formula for calculating the price (provided this is without reference to any person's discretion or opinion). Under the Listing Rules (as noted in section 2.1.2 above) purchases by a listed company of less than 15% of any class of its equity shares (other than by way of tender offer) pursuant to a general authority granted by shareholders may only be made if the price to be paid is not more than the higher of: 5% above the average market price of the shares for the five business days prior to the day the purchase is made; and the price which is the higher

of the last independent trade and the highest current independent bid on the trading venue where the purchase is carried out (LR 12.4.1R). In the Investment Association's view, these Listing Rule requirements are appropriate.

- *Number of shares to be repurchased* – the resolution must specify the maximum number of shares authorised to be repurchased (CA 2006 s. 701(3)(a)). The Investment Association takes the view that a general authority to purchase up to 10% of the existing issued ordinary share capital is unlikely to cause concern and that the Institutional Voting Information Service (IVIS) will note a general authority to purchase more than 10% (but less than 15%) of the existing issued ordinary share capital. In practice, it is usual for companies to seek a general authority to purchase up to 10% at each annual general meeting.

Figure 10.3: Preliminary list of issues for a UK incorporated listed company wishing to conduct a share buy-back

Issues to be considered by the listed company	Key consequences for the proposed buy-back	Relevant legal requirements
Is there any prohibition or restriction in the company's articles?	If there is, the articles will need to be amended to allow a buy-back of shares	CA 2006 s. 690 Articles
Is the purchase to be on-market or off-market?		CA 2006 s. 693
Does the company have existing shareholder authority and is the buy-back within that authority?	If the buy-back is not within the company's existing authority, shareholder approval will be required by way of an ordinary resolution under CA 2006. The Investment Association prefers a special resolution.	CA 2006 s. 693 Share Capital Management Guidelines
Does the company have sufficient distributable profits for the repurchase?	If not, the shares must be repurchased out of the proceeds of a fresh issue for the purpose (though this cannot be done if a premium is being paid for the repurchase or the shares are to be held in treasury).	CA 2006 s. 692
Is the company buying back more than 15% of a class of equity shares?	A tender offer will be required or the full terms must be approved by shareholders.	LR 12.4.2R

Issues to be considered by the listed company	Key consequences for the proposed buy-back	Relevant legal requirements
Is the price to be paid more than the higher of: ■ 5% above the average market price of the shares for the five business days prior to the day the purchase is made; and ■ the price which is the higher of the last independent trade and the highest current independent bid on the trading venue where the purchase is carried out ?	A tender offer will be required.	LR.12.4.1R
Is the company repurchasing shares from a related party?	If so, shareholder approval may be required under LR 11.	LR 11 LR 12.3.1R
Will the share buy-back result in a shareholder's interest increasing above 30% of the voting rights in the company?	If so, independent shareholder approval may be required to 'whitewash' the share buy-back under Rule 37 of the City Code and the Listing Rule requirements relating to controlling shareholders will apply.	Rule 37 City Code and LR 9
Does the company have any listed securities which are convertible into, exchangeable for, or which carry a right to subscribe for the class of shares proposed to be repurchased?	If so, a separate meeting of the holders of those securities must be convened and their approval obtained for the purchase.	LR 12.4.7R
Are there any other classes of shares in issue whose rights will be deemed to be varied by the buy-back?	A class meeting will be required to approve the variation of class rights.	CA 2006 s. 630
Is the company in possession of inside information?	It will not be able to repurchase shares unless it has a pre-existing buy-back programme in place.	MAR
Is the company in a MAR closed period?	During a closed period, the MAR safe-harbour for buy-backs is not available unless the company is buying back shares pursuant to a pre-existing buy-back programme.	MAR

2.2.2 Contents of the share buy-back circular

LR 13.7 sets out specific requirements for a circular concerning the purchase of own securities by a company.

A circular accompanying a notice of AGM containing a buy-back resolution must comply with these requirements and so must include:

- a statement of the directors' intentions about using the buy-back authority;
- whether the company intends to cancel the shares or hold them in treasury;
- if known, a statement as to how the company intends to acquire the shares and the number of shares it intends to acquire in this way;
- details about the price, or the maximum and minimum price, to be paid; and
- the number of outstanding warrants/options, and the proportion of share capital they represent and will represent if the buy-back authority is fully used.

The circular will also have to comply with the general content requirements for listed company circulars in LR 13.3.

As discussed in section 2.1.5 above, the Investment Association Share Capital Management Guidelines say that shareholders expect that a general authority for a company to purchase its own shares will be exercised only if it is in the best interests of shareholders generally and normally only if it would result in an increase in earnings per share (EPS) or, in the case of property companies and investment trusts, if it would result in an increase in asset value per share for the remaining shareholders. Where this is not expected, the benefits should be clearly explained.

The listed company must lodge copies of the resolution and circular with the National Storage Mechanism, and notify an RIS that it has done so (LR 9.6.1R, LR 9.6.2R and LR 9.6.3R).

2.3 Buy-backs not within a listed company's annual authority

If a share buy-back is not within a listed company's annual resolution authorising the company to make on-market share purchases, it will need to obtain specific authority for the repurchase.

In that case, the company will need to make certain announcements under Listing Rule 12 and send a circular to shareholders to convene a general meeting to obtain the requisite shareholder approval. Any circular to accompany a buy-back resolution must comply with Listing Rule 13.

2.3.1 Notifications to an RIS

A listed company must notify an RIS when the directors decide to seek shareholder approval for the purchase by the company of its own equity shares (LR 12.4.4R(1)). This notice must state whether the authority is: (a) for any specific purchases, in which case it must state the names of the persons from whom they will be made; or (b) a general authority to make such purchases (LR 12.4.4R(2)). If the announcement constitutes inside information in relation to the company, the announcement must also comply with the requirements for announcements of inside information (see Chapter 5). No announcement is needed if the company is simply seeking the renewal of an existing authority (LR 12.4.4R(3)).

The listed company must then notify an RIS of the outcome of the general meeting (LR 12.4.5R).

2.3.2 Contents of the share buy-back circular

In addition to making an RIS announcement, a listed company is required to send a circular relating to the purchase of own shares to its shareholders. The Listing Rules require that all circulars comply with its general contents requirements (LR 13.3) (see section 4.2 of Chapter 8).

As discussed above, LR 13.7 sets out specific requirements for a circular concerning the purchase of own securities by a company.

A share buy-back circular accompanying a resolution seeking shareholder approval must include:

- a statement of the directors' intentions about using the buy-back authority;
- whether the company intends to cancel the shares or hold them in treasury;
- if known, a statement as to how the company intends to acquire and the number of shares to be acquired in that way;
- if purchasing from particular parties, the names of those persons and the material terms on which the shares are to be acquired;
- details about the price, or the maximum and minimum price, to be paid;
- the number of outstanding warrants/options and the proportion of share capital they represent and will represent if the buy-back is fully used (LR 13.7.1R(1)); and
- where LR 12.4.2AR applies (i.e. where the purchase is of 15% or more of a class of shares and is not being done by way of a tender offer), an explanation of the potential impact of the proposed share buy-back, including whether control of the listed company may be concentrated following the proposed transaction.

Additionally, if the exercise of the buy-back authority in full would result in the listed company purchasing 25% or more of its own shares (excluding treasury shares), LR 13.7.1R(2) requires that the following additional information be included in the circular:

- risk factors (item 4 of Annex I of PR Appendix 3);
- trend information (item 12 of Annex I of PR Appendix 3);
- director's interests in shares (item 17.2 of Annex I of PR Appendix 3);

- major interests in shares (item 18.1 of Annex I of PR Appendix 3);
- significant changes (item 20.9 of Annex I of PR Appendix 3);
- working capital (item 3.1 of Annex III of PR Appendix 3); and
- if the listed company is including pro forma financial information in its circular it must comply with Annex II of PR Appendix 3 (LR 13.7.2G).

2.3.3 FCA approval of the share buy-back circular

A share buy-back circular will need to be approved by the FCA if the exercise of the authority in full would result in the listed company purchasing 25% or more of its own shares (LR 13.2.1R).

A share buy-back circular for the purchase of own shares from a related party will also need to be approved by the FCA (as a related party transaction circular) unless:

- it is for a tender offer to all holders of that class of shares on the same terms; or
- it is for a market purchase in accordance with the company's general authority to purchase its own shares pursuant to a shareholders' resolution and is made without any prior understanding with the related party (LR 12.3.1R).

Other share buy-back circulars will not need to be approved by the FCA, but will still have to comply with the other requirements of Listing Rule 13. If the circular needs to be approved, two copies of a draft of the circular (in an advanced form) must be submitted to the FCA for review at least ten clear business days prior to the intended date of publication (LR 13.2.5R) (although generally a draft will be submitted significantly earlier than this) (see section 4.2 of Chapter 8).

Where the company is purchasing 25% or more of its own shares, it will need to appoint a sponsor (LR 8.2.1R(4)). The sponsor is required to submit the completed Sponsor's Declaration for the Production of a Circular prior to or on the day the share buy-back circular is to be approved by the FCA. The sponsor must ensure that all matters known to it which, in its reasonable opinion, should be taken into account by the FCA in considering the transaction have been disclosed with sufficient prominence in the documentation or otherwise in writing to the FCA (LR 8.4.13R(3)).

2.4 Restrictions on when a listed company may conduct a share buy-back

Once the company has the requisite authorities in place, there may be timing constraints on when it is actually able to purchase shares.

Prior to the entry into force of MAR in July 2016, Listing Rule 12 contained a prohibition on buy-backs during the close periods set out in the Model Code for Dealings, which used to be in the Annex to Listing Rule 9. Following the introduction of MAR and the deletion at the same time of the Model Code from the Listing Rules, the Listing Rules no longer contain any restrictions on when share buy-backs may be conducted. Companies must still consider whether there are any restrictions under MAR.

This will depend in part on whether the company is relying on the MAR safe harbour for share buy-backs.

2.4.1 Restrictions on timing of share buy-back when relying on safe harbour

When a company is seeking to rely on the safe harbour for buy-backs in MAR, the Buyback and Stabilisation Regulation provides that the trading must not take place:

- during a MAR closed period (as defined in Article 19(11) of MAR), that is in the 30-day period prior to the company's interim or year-end report (or preliminary results if the company releases a preliminary results announcement); or
- when inside information exists,

unless the buy-back is carried out in accordance with a pre-agreed buy-back programme (Buyback and Stabilisation Regulation, Art. 4).

See section 2.1.3 above for further detail on the MAR safe harbour.

2.4.2 Restrictions on timing of share buy-back when not relying on the safe harbour

If a company chooses not to comply with the safe harbour, it must ensure that there is no insider dealing (i.e. it must not deal while in possession of inside information). This means that a company cannot buy back its shares at a time when inside information exists in relation to the company, unless it has a pre-agreed buy-back programme in place (in which case the safe harbour in Article 9(3) of MAR for transactions carried out pursuant to a pre-existing agreement, may apply, as discussed in section 2.1.3 above).

If a company is not seeking to rely on the MAR safe harbour, there is no automatic prohibition on a company conducting a buy-back during a closed period. This means that, unlike under the previous regime, a premium listed company is, in principle, able to buy back shares at any time at which it is not in possession of inside information (provided there is no market manipulation). The CLLS/Law Society Q&A suggest that a company might think it appropriate not to buy back shares during a MAR closed period unless it does so pursuant to a buy-back programme.

Aside from this consideration, if the company is not in possession of inside information and is not seeking to rely on the safe harbour, there are no restrictions on when a company can conduct a further buy-back, provided there is no market manipulation.

2.4.3 The City Code

During the course of an offer, or before the date of an offer if the Board of a listed company has reason to believe that a bona fide offer might be imminent, the company may not purchase its own shares without the approval of the shareholders at a general meeting (Rule 21.1(b) of the City Code). This restriction does not apply where the purchase is made in pursuance of a contract entered into earlier (but the Panel should be consulted and its consent obtained before proceeding).

2.5 Notifications and filings

2.5.1 Notifications under DTR 5

The company will need to comply with its disclosure obligations under DTR 5 in relation to announcements following share buy-backs and changes to company's voting rights. This will require notification of the percentage of voting rights attributable to any shares it holds as a result of the acquisition or disposal of its own shares where the acquisition or disposal reaches, exceeds or falls below 5% or 10% of the total number of voting rights (DTR 5.5.1R) (see section 5 of Chapter 7).

The UKLA Guidance Note *Issuer's obligations (UKLA/TN/542.2)* clarifies that if shares are bought back and held as treasury shares, there will be a notifiable transaction if, as a result, the percentage of voting rights attached to shares held in treasury (ignoring the fact that the company cannot exercise these voting rights) exceeds or falls below the 5% or 10% thresholds. The 5% and 10% thresholds relate to the total number of treasury shares held and not whether any particular buy-back transaction relates to a purchase of shares with voting rights greater than 5% or 10% of the voting rights.

A buy-back will lead to a change in the total voting rights of company, regardless of whether the repurchased shares are held in treasury or cancelled. The company will therefore have to make a notification at the month end of any change in the total number of voting rights under DTR 5.6.1R.

If the change in voting rights is material, the company will also have to make a notification under DTR 5.6.1AR as soon as possible and in any event by the end of the business day following the day on which the change occurred. For these purposes, a change of 1% is likely to be material in the FCA's view. See Chapter 7 for further discussion of a company's notification obligations under DTR 5.

2.5.2 Notifications under the Listing Rules and MAR

The circular and resolutions will need to be filed with the NSM (LR 9.6.1R and LR 9.6.2R) and an announcement released to the market (LR 9.6.3R). See Chapter 8 for information on the NSM.

As well as notifying when it has decided to seek authority to buy back its own shares and the outcome of the shareholder meeting (as discussed in section 2.3.1 above), a premium listed company must notify an RIS of any purchases actually made by the company by no later than 7.30am on the business day following the day on which such purchase of own shares was made. This announcement must include the details set out in LR 12.4.6R, namely the date of the purchase, the number of shares purchased, the highest and lowest price paid and whether (and how many of) the repurchased shares are to be cancelled or held in treasury. Where the shares are to be held as treasury shares, the company must also announce the total number of each class held by the company, and the number of equity shares of each class that the company has in issue (excluding treasury shares), following the purchase.

Note that this assumes that the Buyback and Stabilisation Regulation conditions are not being complied with. In order to comply with the safe harbour requirements of the Buyback and Stabilisation Regulation the company must, in addition to complying with the Listing Rule 12 disclosure requirements, also comply with Article 2 of the Buyback and Stabilisation Regulation. This requires disclosure to the FCA and the competent authority on each trading venue on which the shares are admitted to trading or are traded of all the transactions related to the buy-back programme, in a detailed form and aggregated form. The aggregated form must indicate the aggregated volume and the weighted average price per day and per trading venue. Such disclosure must be made by no later than the end of the seventh daily market session following the execution of the transaction. The information must be kept on a website for five years from the date of publication.

2.5.3 Filings under CA 2006

A resolution authorising a share buy-back must be filed at Companies House (CA 2006 ss 30, 693A(8) and 701(8)). Following a repurchase, form SH03 will also have to be filed. If stamp duty is payable (i.e. the value of or the consideration for the buy-back exceeds £1,000) the form must be stamped by HMRC to show that stamp duty has been paid before filing. If the repurchased shares are cancelled form SH06, which includes a statement of capital for the company, will also need to be filed at Companies House.

2.5.4 Contract to be kept available for inspection

The contract for purchase must be kept available for inspection at the company's registered office (or its alternative inspection location under CA 2006 s. 1136) for ten years from the date of purchase (CA 2006 s. 702).

2.6 Purchase of own securities other than equity shares

Where a company is buying back listed securities other than equity shares, as well as the timing constraints discussed in section 2.4, it must comply with the less onerous requirements of LR 12.5. It will also have to consider whether the repurchase will be a related party transaction (see section 2.1.2).

Unless the purchases are made in accordance with the terms of issue of the relevant securities, where a listed company intends to purchase its own securities and those securities are convertible into its equity shares with a premium listing it must notify an RIS of its decision to purchase and ensure that no dealings in the relevant securities are carried out until that notification has been made (LR 12.5.1R).

Any purchases, early redemptions or cancellations of a company's own securities where the securities are convertible into equity shares with a premium listing must be notified to an RIS:

- when an aggregate of 10% of the initial amount of the relevant class of securities has been purchased, redeemed or cancelled; and
- for each 5% in aggregate of the initial amount of that class acquired thereafter (LR 12.5.2R).

This notification must be made as soon as possible and, in any event, no later than 7.30am on the business day following the calendar day on which the relevant threshold is reached or exceeded. The notification must state the amount of securities acquired, redeemed or cancelled since the last notification, whether or not the securities are to be cancelled and the number of that class of securities that remain outstanding.

In circumstances where the purchase is not being made pursuant to a tender offer and the purchase causes a relevant threshold in LR 12.5.2R to be reached or exceeded, no further purchases may be made until after notification has been made.

Where, within a period of 12 months, a listed company purchases warrants or options over its own equity shares which, on exercise, convey the entitlement to equity shares representing 15% or more of the company's existing issued shares (excluding treasury shares), the company must send to its shareholders a circular containing the following information:

- a statement of the directors' intentions regarding future purchases of the company's warrants and options;
- the number and terms of the warrants or options acquired and to be acquired and the method of acquisition;
- where warrants or options have been, or are to be, acquired from specific parties, a statement of the names of those parties and all material terms of the acquisition; and
- details of the prices to be paid.

2.7 Treasury shares

2.7.1 Dealing with treasury shares

When a listed company buys back its own shares, it may either cancel them or hold them in treasury (i.e. hold the shares itself). For most purposes, a purchase of a company's own shares to be held in treasury is treated in the same way as a purchase of a company's own shares followed by cancellation. The Listing Rule requirements on share buy-backs apply regardless of whether the shares are to be cancelled or held in treasury. LR 12.6 deals with treasury shares.

When a company holds the shares in treasury, it may sell them out of treasury for cash, transfer them for the purposes of an employee share scheme or cancel them.

A sale of treasury shares is treated in broadly the same way as an issue of new shares. While no authority to allot the shares is required (as they remain in issue when they are in treasury) pre-emption rights apply to the sale by a company of its treasury shares in the same way as they apply to an allotment of new shares. These pre-emption rights may be disapplied by the company's articles or by special resolution (CA 2006 s. 573).

The primary benefit of treasury shares lies in their use when making awards under employee share schemes.

2.7.2 Notifications

In a notification of a share buy-back, a company must specify how many shares are to be cancelled and how many are to be held in treasury. Where shares are to be held in treasury, the notification should also set out the total number of treasury shares of each class held by the company following the purchase; and the number of equity shares of each class that the company has in issue which are not held in treasury (LR 12.4.6R).

Any sale for cash, transfer for the purposes of or pursuant to an employees' share scheme or cancellation of treasury shares that represents over 0.5% of the listed company's share capital must be notified to an RIS as soon as possible and in any event by no later than 7.30am on the business day following the calendar day on which the sale, transfer or cancellation occurred (LR 12.6.4R). The notification must include:

- the date of the sale, transfer or cancellation;
- the number of shares sold, transferred or cancelled;
- the sale or transfer price for each of the highest and lowest prices paid, where relevant; and
- a statement of: (a) the total number of treasury shares of each class held by the company following the sale, transfer or cancellation; and (b) the number of shares of each class that the company has in issue less the total number of treasury shares of each class held by the company following the sale, transfer or cancellation.

If, by virtue of its holding treasury shares, a listed company is allotted shares as part of a capitalisation issue, the company must notify an RIS, as soon as possible and in any event by no later than 7.30am on the business day following the calendar day on which allotment occurred, of the following information:

- the date of the allotment;
- the number of shares allotted;

- a statement as to what number of shares allotted have been cancelled and what number is being held as treasury shares; and
- where shares allotted are being held as treasury shares, a statement of: (a) the total number of treasury shares of each class held by the company following the allotment; and (b) the number of shares of each class that the company has in issue less the total number of treasury shares of each class held by the company following the allotment (LR 12.6.3R).

2.7.3 Market abuse

The market abuse offences set out in MAR should be considered in the context of dealings in treasury shares. Knowledge of a particular sale or other dealings in treasury shares may constitute inside information for market abuse purposes. Equally, any dealings in treasury shares while the company is in possession of any other inside information could constitute insider dealing under MAR.

Companies need to take care that treasury share operations do not support or move the share price or mislead the market as this could also constitute market abuse.

As discussed in section 2.1.3 above, Article 5 of MAR and the BuyBack and Stabilisation Regulation provides a safe harbour from market abuse for the purchase of own shares. However, one of the conditions that must be met to fall within the safe harbour is that the purchase is part of a buy-back programme the sole purpose of which is to reduce the capital of a company (in value or in number of shares) or to meet obligations arising from debt financial instruments exchangeable into equity instruments or employee share option programmes or other allocations of shares to employees of the company or of an associate company (MAR, Art. 5(2)).

If a company is buying shares to be held in treasury, it is unlikely that the safe harbour will be available for listed companies unless the purchase is part of a buy-back programme which is only operated to provide equity to satisfy convertible debt or employee share option programmes (which would be unusual). By holding shares in treasury, the listed company's purpose cannot be to reduce its share capital, given that the shares remain issued while in treasury.

If the company is not relying on the safe harbour, it will have to consider whether the buy-back of shares into treasury could constitute market abuse. See section 2 above for further information. The company will also have to consider MAR when selling shares out of treasury and in particular whether it is in possession of inside information. If it does have inside information, it is unlikely to be able to deal in treasury shares.

Further guidance for UK listed companies

This appendix sets out a number of sources of further guidance and information on the UK Listing Regime and MAR. Please also refer to the Quick Reference Table on pages xxvi–xlvi for a summary of the UKLA Guidance Notes.

Guidance on the UK Listing Regime and related topics

1. FCA

The FCA has published 104 Guidance Notes on the LPDT Rules. They give both procedural and technical guidance on the Rules.

The procedural notes cover:

- eligibility process for new listing applicants;
- securities that are the subject of final terms;
- review and approval of documents;
- public offer prospectus – drafting and approval;
- passporting;
- guidance on UKLA standard comments;
- block listings;
- UKLA decision making and review process;
- sponsor firms – ongoing requirements during reorganisations; and
- additional powers to supervise sponsors.

The technical notes are divided into categories including:

- eligibility for listing;
- governance and conduct;
- transactions;
- working capital;
- profit forecasts and estimates;

- closed-ended investment funds;
- specialist companies;
- periodic financial information;
- regulatory announcements including inside information;
- disclosure of positions held by issuers, investors and management;
- public offers, admission to trading and the marketing of securities;
- prospectus content; and
- sponsors.

The FCA also has a wide range of information on its UKLA page, including information on:

- MAR and notifying delayed disclosure of inside information and transactions by PDMRs;
- UKLA forms;
- checklists;
- submitting a prospectus or circular for review and approval;
- submitting a document to the National Storage Mechanism for publication;
- getting guidance on the LPDT Rules;
- paying a fee;
- requesting a prospectus passport;
- disseminating regulatory information to the market; and
- submitting a shareholder notification.

Copies are available online at: www.fca.org.uk

2. Implementing and delegated regulations under MAR

There are a series of Level 2 regulations under MAR which provide additional detail on some aspects of MAR. The key ones for listed company purposes are:

- inside information Implementing Regulation (Regulation 2016/1055/EU);
- insider lists Implementing Regulation (Regulation 2016/347/EU);
- market manipulation, disclosure thresholds, competent authority for notifications of delays, permission for trading during closed periods and types of notifiable managers' transactions Delegated Regulation (Regulation 2016/522/EU) (the General MAR Regulation);
- PDMR transaction notification Implementing Regulation (Regulation 2016/523/EU);
- buy-back and stabilisation Delegated Regulation (Regulation 2016/1052/EU);

- market soundings Delegated Regulation (Regulation 2016/960/EU); and
- market soundings notification templates Implementing Regulation (Regulation 2016/959/EU).

The Regulations can be found on the www.eur-lex.europa.eu.

3. ESMA

ESMA has published a set of recommendations and a set of Q&As on the operation of the PD and TD:

- recommendations for the consistent implementation of the European Commission's Regulation on Prospectuses No. 809/2004;
- frequently asked questions regarding Prospectuses; and
- frequently asked questions regarding the Transparency Directive.

ESMA has also published various documents in relation to the Market Abuse Regulation, including:

- Guidelines on delaying disclosure of inside information
- Guidelines on persons receiving market soundings
- Q&A on the Market Abuse Regulation

It has also published guidelines and Q&A on the use of Alternative Performance Measures (APMs) in regulated information.

Copies are available online at: www.esma.europa.eu.

4. The Financial Reporting Council (FRC)

4.1 Governance Code and Stewardship Code

The FRC publishes and periodically reviews the UK Corporate Governance Code and the UK Stewardship Code:

- 2016 edition of the UK Corporate Governance Code (for accounting periods beginning on or after 17 June 2016);
- 2014 edition of the UK Corporate Governance Code (for accounting periods beginning on or after 1 October 2014); and
- UK Stewardship Code (September 2012).

Copies available online at: www.frc.org.uk/Our-Work/Codes-Standards/Corporate-governance.aspx

4.2 FRC Guidance for companies

The FRC also publishes other guidance for companies including guidance on:
- risk management, internal control and related financial and business reporting;
- Board effectiveness; and
- audit committees.

Copies available online at: www.frc.org.uk/Our-Work/Codes-Standards/Corporate-governance/UK-Corporate-Governance-Code/Guidance-for-boards-and-board-committees.aspx

5. Institutional shareholder guidelines

Various institutional investor bodies issue guidance to listed companies.

The Investment Association has published various guidelines, which can be found on the Institutional Voting Information Service website.

The guidelines on the IVIS website include:
- Share Capital Management guidelines;
- Shareholders' Pre-Emption Rights and Vendor Placings;
- Pre-Emption Group's 'Disapplying Pre-emption Rights – A Statement of Principles';
- Transaction Guidelines; and
- Companies Act and articles of association guidance.

Copies available online at: www.ivis.co.uk/Guidelines.aspx

The PLSA also publishes Corporate Governance Policy and Voting Guidelines to provide guidance for investors and companies on corporate governance matters.

Copies available online at: www.plsa.co.uk/PolicyandResearch/Corporate-Governance.aspx

6. CLLS/Law Society Q&A on MAR

The City of London Law Society and Law Society Company Law Committees' Joint Working Parties on Market Abuse, Share Plans and Takeovers Code have published a Q&A document on MAR which sets out the Joint Working Parties' explanation of how, in their view, MAR should apply to certain practical situations (but note it is subject to review and amendment in the light of practice on the implementation of MAR and to any relevant future UK or EU guidance published in relation to MAR).

The CLLS/Law Society Q&A are available on www.citysolicitors.org.uk.

7. Standards for investment reporting

The FRC website also contains the 'Standards for Investment Reporting' that provide guidance for reporting accountants in connection with the preparation of circulars and prospectuses:

- Ethical Standards for Reporting Accountants (ESRA) (October 2006);
- Standards for Investment Reporting 1000 – investment reporting standards applicable to all engagements in connection with an investment circular (July 2005);
- Standards for Investment Reporting 2000 (Revised) – investment reporting standards applicable to public reporting engagements on historical financial information (March 2011);
- Standards for Investment Reporting 3000 – investment reporting standards applicable to public reporting engagements on profit forecasts (January 2006);
- Standards for Investment Reporting 4000 – investment reporting standards applicable to public reporting engagements on pro forma financial information (January 2006); and
- Standards for Investment Reporting 5000 – investment reporting standards applicable to public reporting engagements on financial information reconciliations under the Listing Rules (February 2008).

Copies available online at: www.frc.org.uk

About Herbert Smith Freehills LLP

Herbert Smith Freehills is a leading and full-service international legal practice with a 1,200 lawyer network across Europe, the Middle East and Asia.

As one of the world's leading law firms, Herbert Smith Freehills advises many of the most ambitious organisations across all major regions of the globe. Our clients trust us with their most important transactions, disputes and projects because of our ability to cut through complexity and mitigate risk. With nearly 3,000 lawyers in offices spanning Asia, Australia, Europe, Africa and the US, we help clients thrive in the global economy and can deliver the expertise they need, wherever they need it.

Alongside our leading dispute resolution and corporate practices, we offer specialist expertise in finance, real estate, competition and employment, pensions and incentives. We are also acknowledged as leaders in a number of industry sectors, including the energy and natural resources and financial institutions sectors. This breadth of our practice capability, our technical and commercial expertise and the consistently high quality of our broader service are all factors that support our reputation as a leading international firm.

Our London-based corporate practice offers market-leading capability on public and private mergers and acquisitions, listings and equity offerings, corporate restructuring, corporate governance, projects and tax. We advise clients from a wide range of business sectors and are ranked as one of the leading advisers to FTSE-listed companies (source: ARL Corporate Adviser Rankings Guide).

Our equity capital markets team advises UK and international companies seeking or considering a UK listing on the practicalities of the process and applicable legal regulatory requirements. We then provide comprehensive support to listed companies including assisting them with raising capital through rights issues, open offers and including acquisitions, takeovers, disposals and related party transactions. Our dedicated Corporate Governance Advisory Team plays a special role in advising listed company boards and senior executive members on their approach to governance and risk. The team provides insights and proactive advice on the duties, responsibilities and liabilities of directors, the operation of boards and board committees, continuing engagement with investors and all other matters which directors and company secretaries must take into account when considering their management structures and compliance procedures.

For further information please visit www.herbertsmithfreehills.com or contact any contributor to this book or Gulya Gulieva on +44 0 207 466 2892 or gulya.gulieva@hsf.com.

Index

A

Accelerated bookbuilt cash placings 446–447
Accounting reference date
  information of changes to 352
Accounting standards 26, 275
  financial reporting, and 251–254
  three-year track record, and 165
Accountants
  role in IPO advisory team 4
  scope of review 4–5
Admission of shares to listing 69–73
  procedure for application 69–73
    alterations in number of shares to be listed 71
    requirements for block listing 72
    retention of related documents 71
    six-monthly block listing return 72
    submission of 48-hour documents 70
    submission of application day documents 70
Admission to listing 51–81
  additional requirements for standard listing 67–68
  key requirements 60–61
    admission to trading 61
    free transferability of shares 60
    incorporation of issuer 60
    listing of whole class of shares 61
    minimum market capitalisation 61
    publication of prospectus 61
    validity of shares 60
  procedure for application 69–73
  requirements for premium listing 61–67
    companies with controlling shareholder 66–67
    externally managed companies 67
    independent business 63

minimum numbers of shares in public hands 64–65
pre-emption rights 65
shares of non-EEA company 65
sufficient working capital 63–64
three-year financial track record 61–63
voting on matters relevant to premium listing 65–66
warrants 65
Admission to Official List *see* Official List
Admission to trading 68–69
  main market of LSE 68–69
  procedural requirements 69–73
  prospectus, and 142–143
Advertisements
  prospectuses, and 196–198
  rubric 197
Advisory team 3–5
  company's lawyers 3–4
  investment bank 3
  investment bank's lawyers 4
  reporting accountants 4–5
Agents
  delegation of sponsor's functions to 93–95
Aggregation of holdings 310
Alternative Investment Market (AIM) 58
  admission document 58
  flexibility 58
Alternative securities markets 55–59
Announcement obligations 349–353
Annual financial reports 256–266
  additional Listing Rule requirements for premium listed companies 262–267
  Alternative Performance Measures (APMs) 260–261
  audit tender 272–273

audited financial statements 258–259
  auditors 271–272
  auditors' report 272
  checklist of disclosure requirements 266
  corporate governance disclosures 262
  directors' remuneration disclosures 263
  going concern disclosures 263–264
  governance disclosures under LR 9 263
  information to be in same place 266
  long-term incentive plan for director 264–265
  management report 259–260
  publication of unaudited financial information 254–255
  publication requirements 257–258
  responsibility statements 260–261
  rotation of auditors 272–273
  statement of compliance about controlling shareholder rules 265
  strategic report with supplementary information 266
Audit committee 273
Auditors' report 272

B
Block listing 72
  requirements for 72
Board
  responsibility 281
Bonus issues 155
Break fees 384–385
Bought deal 447

C
Cancellation of listing 77–81
company's application for 80
  premium listing 78–79
    general requirements 78
    restructuring or insolvency, and 78
    scheme of arrangement, and 79–80
    takeover offer, and 78–79
  procedure for company to request 77
  standard listing
    requirements 79–80
  timing of company's request 80–81

CESR 32–33
  guidance on FSAP Directives 163
Circulars 360–362
  approval of 361–362
  content requirements 360–361
  meaning 360
  National Storage Mechanism 362–363
  publication 361–362
  shareholders, to 360
  supplementary 362
Class 1 transactions
  accountant's opinion on 396
  financial disclosure 392–396, 397
Comfort package 110–136 see also Sponsors
Committee of European Securities Regulators see CESR
Company secretary 285
Compensation
  disclosure, and 174
  due diligence, and 8–9
  open offers of 446
  remuneration 288
  right to 193
  safe harbour 371
Compliance statement 440
Compliance with UK listing regime 37–50
  company's responsibility 37
  directors' responsibilities 37
Concert parties
  voting rights, and 328
Condensed financial statements 268
Consideration
  meaning 379
Constitution of company
  information of changes to 349
Continuing obligations 12–13, 18–20
Controlled undertakings 329
  voting rights, and 329
Controlling shareholder 437–442
  cancellation of listing 442
  election/re-election of independent directors 440–441
    circulars in relation to 441–442
  independent business 439–440

relationship agreement, requirement for 438–439
statement on compliance with relationship agreement 440
who is 437–438
Corporate governance 15–16, 277–296
  accountability and audit 289–291
  annual report and accounts 291
  application of Code 280–281
  application of Code to smaller listed companies 281
  appointments to Board 284
  audit committee 278–279, 287–288
  Board 281
  Board balance and independence 282–283
  Board committees 286–287
  chairman 282
  chief executive 282
  Code 277–278
  directors' remuneration 289
  directors, re-election 285
  DTR 7 regime 278–280
  enforcement by Financial Reporting Council's Conduct Committee 296–297
  guidance relating to Code 291–296
    audit committees 278–279, 292–293
    Board effectiveness 292
    diversity 293–294
    executive remuneration 294–295
    institutional shareholder voting guidelines 295–296
    internal control 292
    risk management 292
  information 285–286
  key provisions of Code 281–291
  nomination committee 289
  performance evaluation 285–286
  professional development 285–286
  remuneration committee 288–289
  shareholders, relations with 291
  statements 279–280
  Stewardship Code 296
Credit arrangements 423

Criminal offences 39–41
  breach of FSMA section 85 39–40
  fraud 41, 250–251
  inside information *see* Inside information
  insider dealing 40, 250
  market abuse 242–249
  misleading statements and conduct 40, 249–250
Custodians
  nominees, and 338
  proxies *see* Proxies

D

Directors
  disclosure of information relating to 351–352
  liability for false or misleading statements in reports 372
  responsibilities for compliance with LPDT Rules 37
Disclosure
  announcement on reverse takeover 109
  annual financial reports 266
  Class 1 acquisitions 392–396, 397
  going concern 263–264
  information relating to directors 351–352
  inside information 14, 201, 203, 209–211
  prospectus, and 162–163
  share dealings 299–314
  sponsors, and 97
  voting rights 307–314
Disclosure guidance 24, 32
Dividends
  information about 353
Due diligence 8–9
  liability for prospectuses, and 194–195

E

E-mail
  communication, and 364, 366, 368
  control requirements, and 224
  Hannam, Ian 246–248
  National Storage Mechanism 362

Photo-Me International, and 239
sponsors, and 88
Electronic communication 363–369
  Companies Act 2006 364–365, 366–369
  DTR6 364–365
  Listing Rule 13 365
Eligible counterparties 148
Employee share option schemes 152–153, 356
  provision of information to shareholders 356
Enforcement of UK listing regime 37–50
EU Market Abuse Regulation 24
European legislative process for financial services legislation 23

F
FCA Handbook 30–32
  Disclosure guidance 32
  Listing Rules 31
  Prospectus Rules 31–32
  Transparency Rules 32
Financial Conduct Authority (FCA)
  enforcement powers 38–39
  guidance notes 488–489
  key enforcement actions 41–50
  role 35–36
Financial instrument
  definition 205
Financial reporting
  annual financial reports see Annual financial reports
  DTR4 regime 254–255
    reporting calendar 254
  half-yearly financial reports see Half-yearly financial reports
  key rules 253–255
  preliminary statements 255–256
  stakeholder reporting requirements 276
  statements of dividends 256
  third country issuers with premium listing 273–276
    audit and auditor requirements 276
    equivalence of accounting standards with IFRS 275
    equivalence of relevant laws 274–275
Financial Reporting Council (FRC)
  enforcement by Conduct Committee 296–297
  Governance Code 490
  guidance for companies 491
  standards for investment reporting 492
  Stewardship Code 490
Financial services action plan (FSAP) 22–35
  guidance on Directives 32–35
    CESR, issues by 32–33
    ESMA, issued by 32–33
    UKLA, issued by 33–34
  home and host member states 27–28
  home member states for different issues in same group 27
  home member states for EEA issuers 27
  home member states for non-EEA issuers 27
  host member states for issuers 28
  implementation of Directives in UK 28–35
  origins 22
  strategic objectives 22
Financial Services Markets Act 2000
  Part 6 revision 2013 29
Four class tests 376
Fraud 41, 250–251
Further guidance for UK listed companies 488–492
Further share issues 17–18, 444–468
  authority to allot 448–454
  Companies Act requirements 444
  comparison of key considerations 444–445
  impact of Companies Act 2006 449
  Investment Association guidelines 452–454
  Listing Rule requirements 449–452
  Market Abuse Regulation 463–468 see also Market Abuse Regulation
  notification and documentation requirements 460–463

notifications required by major stakeholders and PDMRs 462–463
Pre-emption Group guidelines 452–454
pre-emption rights 448–454
prospectus *see* Prospectus
supplementary prospectuses 458–460
total voting rights announcements 462
withdrawal rights 458–460

G

General meetings
　information about 352
　relations with shareholders 291
Gross Assets test 376–377
Gross capital
　meaning 380–381

H

Half-yearly financial reports 268–271
　condensed financial statements 268–269
　interim management report 269–270
　publication requirements 268
　responsibility statements 270–271
High Growth Segment (HGS) 55–56
　eligibility requirements 55–56

I

IAS Regulation 26
Indemnities 383–384
Information filled at NSM
　announcements about 353
Initial public offering (IPO)
　application process 10–12
　corporate governance, and 7
　eligibility criteria 7
　key steps in process 5–7
　marketing 10–12
　outline timetable 6
　preparing to float 7–8
　pricing 10–12
　reasons for 2
　suitability for listing 7–8
Inside information 14, 199–251
　analysts' briefings 222–223
　analysts' research 223
　breach of MAR 234–251
　breach of obligation to announce inside information 234–235
　checklist for identifying 212–213
　checklist of access controls 224
　contents requirements for announcements 233
　control 14, 224
　decision-making process 201–202
　delaying disclosure 213–217
　　ensuring confidentiality 215
　　entitlement 213–214
　　legitimate interests, meaning 214
　　misleading the public, meaning 214–215
　　monitoring continued ability to delay 216
　　notification to FCA 216–217
　　record-keeping requirements 215
　disclosure 14
　disclosure decision tree 203
　disclosure manual 209–211
　disclosure obligation of listed company 201
　documenting disclosures procedures 209–211
　documenting identification 211
　DTR 2, breach of
　　Entertainment Rights 237–238
　　JJB Sports 239–241
　　Lamprell 241–242
　　Photo-Me International 238–239
　　Wolfson Microelectronics 236–237
　　Woolworths Group 235–236
　enforcement actions for breach of requirement to announce pre-MAR 235–242
　financial instruments 205–206
　holding announcements 215–216
　identifying 207–213
　implementing procedures 208–213
　insider lists 225–229
　　acknowledgement of duties 228–229
　　advisers 228

agents 228
content 225–226
illustrative form 227
notification 228–229
procedures for creating and
    maintaining 226–228
third parties 228
market abuse *see* Market abuse
market rumour and speculation 220–223
market rumours and leaks 221–222
market soundings 220
meaning 202
media enquiries 222
method and content of disclosure
    229–234
  approval process for announcements
    229–231
  illustrative terms of reference for
    disclosure committee 230–231
  misleading statements 231–232
  RIS 233–234
  verification of announcements
    232–233
  websites 233–234
monitoring and gathering information
    207–208
obligations in relation to 200–202
precise, meaning 202–205
public, deemed to be 205
regulatory framework 200
related investments 205–206
selective disclosure 217–220
significant effect on price, meaning
    206–207
Insider dealing 40, 250
Institutional shareholder guidelines
    295–296
Intention to float (ITF) 10
Interim Management Statements 254
Investment bank
  member of advisory team, as 3
  underwriter, as 3
Issuer liability regime 369–372
  directors, position of 372
  information subject to 370
  issuer liable, when 370
  safe harbour from liability 371
  sanctions for issuing misleading
    statements 372
  scope 369–370
  to whom issuer liable 369, 370–371
Issues of new shares
  information about 353

J
Joint sponsors 93
Joint ventures
  related-party transactions 420–421

K
Key listing conditions 18–20

L
Life interests 328–329
Listing
  admission to *see* Admission to listing
  admission to trading *see* admission to
    trading
  block *see* Block trading
  cancellation *see* Cancellation of listing
  restoration *see* Restoration of listing
  suspension *see* Suspension of listing
Listing Principles 12–13
Listing Rules 31
Listing segments
  migration between *see* Migration
    between listing agreements
Lock-up arrangements
  notifications regarding 353
London Stock Exchange (LSE)
  Admission and Disclosure Standards
    36–37
  role 36–37

M
Management report 259–260
Market abuse 242–249
  basic offences 243–244
  decisions relating to 246–249
    Einhorn, David 246

Greenlight Capital 246
Hannam, Ian 246–248
Tesco 248–249
importance of offences for listed companies 245
safe harbours from 245
Market Abuse Directive 24
Market Abuse Regulation 24
  further share issues 463–468
    maintaining insider lists 465
    market sounding regime 465–467
    obligation to announce inside information 464–465
    PDMR dealings 467–468
    sounding out investors 465–467
Market announcements 16, 349–353
  key obligations 349–351
Market disclosure
  accuracy 13–14
Market makers 338
Market rumour *see* Inside information
Mergers
  equivalent document, and 152, 154
Mineral resources 399–400
Misleading statements and conduct 40, 249–250
Model Code 372

N

Name of company
  information of changes to 352
National Storage Mechanism 361
Nominees 338
Non-GAAP measures 315

O

Official List 52–81
  alternative securities markets 55–56 *see also* Alternative securities markets
  categories 53–55
  choice of listing segment 54–55
  listing categories 53–55
  listing segments 52–59
  premium segment 52–53
  standard segment 52–53

Open offer 446
  Listing Rule 9.5 424
  notification 461–462
  prospectus requirements 456–457

P

Part 6 rules 29
PDMR
  defining 300–301
PD Regulation 24–25
Placings 446–448
  accelerated bookbuilt cash 446–447
  bought deal 447
  cash box 447–448
  Listing Rule 9.5 455
  notification 462
  open offer, with 447
  prospectus requirements 457
  vendor 447
Pre-emption rights 444, 447–448
Preliminary statement of annual results 255
Premium Listing Principles 12–13
Professional Securities Market (PSM) 59
  debt securities 59
  tax regime 59
Profits
  definition 378
Profits test 377–379
Property
  transactions involving 399–400
Proposed new guidance notes xlvii
Prospectus 9–10, 137–198
  advertisement regime 196–198
  approval 181–182
    applying for 181–182
    requirement for 181
    validity when approved 185
  format and content
    age of latest audited annual financial information 167
    audit requirements 166–167
    capital resources 169
    complex financial history 165–166
    equivalent documents 171–172
    ESMA guidance 163–164

financial disclosure 164–170
general duty of disclosure 162–163
historical financial information 165–168
illustrative contents 172–181
incorporation by reference 170
interim and other financial information 167
omission of information 171
operating and financial review 168
order of contents 158–159
order of required information 159
pro forma financial information 168
proportionate disclosure regime 172
risk factors 161–162
significant change statement 170
significant financial commitment 165–166
single and tri-partite documents 157–158, 159
specific disclosure requirements 163
statement of capitalisation and indebtedness 169
summary 159–161
three-year track record 165
working capital statement 169
liability regime 191–196
due diligence defence 194–195
minimum requirements of PD 191
responsible persons under Prospectus Rule 5.5 192–193
responsibility statement 192–193
new Regulation 198
offer to public 140–142
definition 140–141
FCA, Commission and ESMA guidance 141–142
free shares 142
pre-emptive offers 142
rights issues 142
schemes of arrangement 142
share schemes 141
passporting within EEA 185–186
preparing 137–198
publication

circulation of hard copies 184
FCA website 184
methods 182–185
national storage mechanism 185
requirement 182–184
timing of 184
publishing 137–198
requirement to prepare and publish 138–156, 455–460
150 persons per member state 149
admission to trading 142–143
bonus issues 155
convertibles 155–156
divisions where equivalent document 152, 154–155
E5 million exemption 145–146
E100,000 minimum consideration and denomination 150
E100,000 total consideration 150
employee share schemes 152–153, 155
exchangeables 155–156
exempt admissions to trading 153–156
exempt offers to public 144–153
exempt transferable securities 144–145
exemptions, scope 143–144
exemptions for public offers 151–153
less than 10% of issued share capital 154
mergers where equivalent document 152, 154–155
Prospectus Rules 138
qualified investors 146–149
retail cascades 150–151
scrip dividends 152
securities already admitted to trading 156
shares issued in substitution 151, 154
takeovers where equivalent document 151–152, 154
transferable securities 139–140
statutory liability regime 193–194
duration of liability 193
position in relation to summary 194
position in relation to supplementary

prospectuses 194
right to compensation 193
supplementary 186–191
  impact on offer 188
  impact on summary 188
  method of publication 189
  obligation to prepare and publish 186–188
  Prospectus Rules, and 188
  timing 189
verification 10
Prospectus Directive 24–25
Prospectus Rules 119
Proxies
  procedural requirements 342–343
    joint notifications 342–343
    notification procedure for proxy holders 342
    notification procedures for shareholders 342–343

Q

Qualified investors
  exemption from prospectus requirements 146–149

R

Regulatory framework 21–50
Related party
  meaning 419–420
Related party transactions 17–18, 418–437
  aggregation 430–431
  checklist of key documents for circular 436–437
  circular 426–427
  contents of circular 427–429
    general and financial disclosure 428
    incorporation of information by reference 429
    pro forma financial information 428
  credit arrangements 423
  definition 418–422
  directors' indemnities and loans 424
  dual listed company structures 420–421
  enhanced oversight regime 425
  exemptions 423–424
  insignificant subsidiary undertakings 424
  joint investment arrangements 424
  joint ventures 420–421
  Listing Rule 11 422
  meaning 374
  need for systems and controls to identify 421–422
  notification to RIS 426
  possible future changes to rules 431–432
  related party, meaning 419–420
  requirements for 425–429
  shareholder approval 429–430
    material change 429–430
  skeleton contents of circular 432–436
  small transactions 423
  smaller, modified requirements 431
  transactions agreed before person became related party 423
  underwriting arrangements 424
Relevant interest
  meaning 327
Remuneration committee 281, 288–289
Responsibility statements
  annual financial reports, and 260–261
Restoration of listing 81
  cancellation, following 81
  suspension, following 81
Retail cascades 150–151
Reverse takeovers 413–418
  application of rules to premium listed company 413
  cancellation of listing 417–418
    company changing listing category 417
    company maintaining listing category 417
    not cancelled, when 417–418
  suspension of listing 414–416
    not required, when 415
    target admitted to regulated market 415
    target not subject to public disclosure regime 416

target subject to disclosure regime of
 another market 415–416
Rights issue 445–448
 key features 445
 Listing Rule 9.5 454
 notification 460–461
 prospectus requirements 456–457
RIS
 disclosure of inside information 233

S
Scheme of arrangement
 cancellation of shares, and 79
Scientific research
 transactions involving 399–400
Securities markets
 choice 56
Share buy-backs 17–18, 468–487
 circular, contents of 479, 480–481
 City Code 475, 482–483
 Companies Act 2006 requirements
  469–470
 contract to be kept available for
  inspection 484
 FCA approval of circular 1 481
 filings 484
 general requirements 469–476
 insider dealing 473
 Investment Association Guidelines
  475–476
 listed company's annual authority
  476–477
  key features of resolution 476–477
  number of shares to be repurchased
   477
 Listing Rule requirements 470–473
  approval by holders of convertible or
   exchangeable securities 472
  notifications 472–473
  price payable on repurchase of equity
   shares 470–471
  repurchase from related party 471–472
  tender offer 471
  timing restrictions 435
  transactions similar to buy-back 473

 Listing Rule restrictions 481–483
 market abuse regime 473
 market manipulation 473
 not within listed company's annual
  authority 479–481
 notifications 483–484
 notifications to RIS 479–480
 preliminary checklist of issues 477–478
 programmes 474–475
 restrictions 481–483
 safe harbour 473–474
 securities other than equity shares
  484–485
 treasury shares 485–487
Share dealings
 adopting code 318–319
 breach of notification requirements and
  restrictions 322
 dealings by PCAs 321
 disclosure by PDMRs and persons closely
  associated 299–314
  annual report, and 312
  collective investment undertakings
   306–307
  compliance 313–314
  content 307–310
  correcting notification 312
  de minimis threshold 303–304
  identifying 300–302
  maintaining list of PDMRs and PCAs
   303
  method for notifying 311
  notifications of obligations 303
  PCAs 301–303
  PDMRs 300–301
  portfolio of assets 306–307
  procedures for making 314
  responsibility for 312
  single transactions and aggregation
   310
  template 308–310
  timing 311–312
  transactions to be disclosed 303
  type of security or investment
   304–305

types of transactions 305–306
notification 14–15
notification of dealings by PDMRs and PCAs 321
penalties for breach of dealing code 321
policy 318–322
procedure and timing for clearance 320
procedures for ensuring compliance 322
prohibition on PDMR dealings during closed periods 314–318
   definition of closed period under MAR 314–315
   employee share schemes and options, warrants and bonds 317–318
   exceptional circumstances 316–317
   exceptions 316
   restrictions on dealings at other times 318
   types of transactions falling within dealing prohibition 315–316
requirement to obtain clearance to deal 319–320
when clearance should not be given 320–321
Share rights
information of changes to 352
Shareholder communications 16
Shareholders
provision of information to 353–355
   announcement procedures 359
   electronic communications 354–355
   equality of treatment 354
   financial agent 355
   general meetings 355
   out of hours announcements 358–359
   regulated information 356–360
   RIS announcement 357–358, 359–360
Shares
further issues *see* further share issues
Significant transactions 17–18, 374–437
accepted adjustments 381
acquisitions out of administration 403–404
aggregation of transactions 386–387
amending terms of transaction 400
anomalous results 381–383
break fees 384–385
Class 1 requirements 389–400
   accountant's opinion 396
   contents of circular 391–400
   financial disclosure 392
   form of financial information 395–396
   general disclosure 391–392
   incorporation of information by reference 400
   key documents 412
   procedure 389–390
   prominence of financial information 395–396
   pro forma financial information 397
   property, mineral resources and scientific research-based companies 399–400
   source of financial information 395–396
   synergy benefits 396–397
   takeover offers 398–399
   treatment of profit forecasts and estimates 397–398
Class 2 requirements 387–388
Class 3 transactions, abolition 387
classification tests 376–387
classifications 374–375
consideration test 379–380
exemptions for companies in severe financial difficulty 401–403
   announcement of disposal 402–403
   FCA approval process 403
   procedure 403
   written confirmation to FCA 401–402
figures to be used 381
four class tests 376
gross assets test 376–377
gross capital test 380–381
indemnities 383–384
joint ventures 404–405
profits test 377–379
reverse takeover 375
share issues by major subsidiaries 385–386

skeleton contents of Class 1 circular 405–411
transactions by specialist companies 383
types 375–376
Sponsors 82–136
  agents 93–95
  appointment and consultation 91–95
    apparent breach of Listing Rules 93
    corporate transactions by premium listed companies 92–93
    illustrative form of appointment letter 94
    notifications 93
    premium listing of shares 91
    transfer of listing category 92
  comfort package 110–136
    admission detrimental to investors' interests 116
    application for admission of further shares by listed company 125–128
    application for admission of shares by new applicant 123–125
    application for transfer of listing category 132–136
    compliance with Listing Rules and Prospectus Rules 119
    continuing obligations 119–136
    directors' responsibilities 115–116
    financial reporting procedures 119–136
    historical financial information 118
    impact of transaction on ability to comply with continuing obligations 120
    Listing Rule 8 comfort letters 111
    pro forma financial information 118
    procedures to enable compliance with LPDT Rules 119–120
    production of circular by listed company 128–132
    reporting accountants, from 112–113
    significant change 118
    sponsor's agreement 111–115
    working capital 117–118
  competence 84–85
  experience and expertise 84–85
  criteria and process for approval 83–84
  disclosure announcement on reverse takeover 109
  emails 88
  general duties and obligations 95–100
    assurance responsibilities have been met 96
    disclosure of non-compliance 97
    guidance on understanding and meeting 96–97
    identifying and managing conflicts 97–99
    principles 95–97
  joint 93
  maintenance of records 99–100
  record keeping 87–88
    emails 88–89
    material judgments 88
    records of meetings/calls 88
    use of control schedules 88
  regulatory framework 83–91
    Listing Rule 8 83
    section 88 FSMA 83
  responsibilities 82–136
  role 82–136
  supervision and censure 89–91
    disciplinary sanctions 90–91
    enforcement actions 90–91
    notification 89–90
  systems and controls 86–87
    criteria 86–87
  transaction-specific duties and obligations 100–110
    application for admission of further shares 104–105
    application for admission of new applicant 101–103
    application for transfer of listing category 107–109
    publication of circular by listed company 105–106
Stakeholder reporting requirements 276
Supplementary prospectus *see* Prospectus
Suspension of listing 76, 77

company's application for 80
procedure for company to request 77
timing of company's request 80–81
Syndicate
   underwriters 3

T

Takeover offers
   Class 1 circulars, and 398–399
Takeovers
   Prospectus Rules, and 151–152, 154
   Reverse see Reverse takeovers
Trading
   admission to see Admission to trading
Transaction
   meaning 404–405
Transfer between listing agreements 73–76
   additional requirements if migrating
      from premium to standard 74–75
   additional requirements if migrating
      from standard to premium 75
   company's application 75–76
   notification 74
Transparency Directive 26
   amendments to 26
Transparency Rules 32
Treasury shares 471–472

U

UK Listing Authority (UKLA)
   guidance on FSAP Directives 33–35
   role 35–36
UKLA Guidance Notes xxvi

V

Vendor placing 447
Voting rights 323–345
   aggregation of holdings 334–335
      financial instruments 334–335
      group companies 335
      shares 334–335
   calculation 335–336
   change in composition of holdings 335
   disclosure of interests in 307–314
   disclosures in annual report 345

end of day netting-off 337
enforcement 346
equivalence – when compliance with
   overseas laws deemed sufficient
   345
exemptions to general notification
   requirements 337–339
   collateral 338–339
   custodians 338
   market makers 338
   nominees 338
   previous exemptions no longer
      available 339
   shares acquired for settlement
      purposes 338
   shares held by credit institution or
      investment firm 338
   stabilisation 339
impact of DTR 5 regime on investment
   managers 330–333
increase or decrease in total number of
   shares 336–337
indirect holders of shares 327–333
   collateral 328
   concert parties 328
   controlled undertakings 329
   depositaries 329
   life interests 328–329
   proxies 329
   temporary transfers of voting rights
      328
   voting rights held by third party 329
issuer, meaning 324–325
notification thresholds 333
penalties for breach 346
procedural requirements for vote holder
   339–342
   acquisition or disposal of own shares
      by issuer 344–345
   announcement of receipt of
      voteholder notification 344
   contents requirements for disclosure of
      interests 341–342
   delegation of notification obligation
      341

filing of information with competition authority 340
notification form 340
timing of notification 339–340
total voting rights disclosures 343
procedural requirements for issuers 343–345
proxies, procedural requirements for *see* Proxies
relevant interest, meaning 325–327
  basket or index of shares 327
  financial instruments having similar economic effect 326–327
  qualifying financial instruments 325–326
  shares 325
shareholder, meaning 334
summary of notification obligations 347

W

Websites
  disclosure of inside information 233
  reports on 330